STANDARD
LESSON COMMENTARY
1995-96

International Sunday School Lessons

published by

STANDARD PUBLISHING

Eugene H. Wigginton, *Publisher*

Richard C. McKinley, *Director of Curriculum Development*

James I. Fehl, *Editor*   Hela M. Campbell, *Office Editor*

Forty-third Annual Volume

In This Volume

Cover design by Listenberger Design Associates

Lessons based on International Sunday School Lessons © 1992 by the Lesson Committee.

Index of Printed Texts, 1995-96

The printed texts for 1995-96 are arranged here in the order in which they appear in the Bible.
Opposite each reference is the number of the page on which it appears in this volume.

Cumulative Index

A cumulative index for the Scripture passages used in the STANDARD LESSON COMMENTARY
for the years September, 1992—August, 1996, is set forth below.

V

VI

With Benefits to All

by Ronald G. Davis

A BIBLE SCHOOL TEACHER tries to get learners to attend to the truths of God's Word, understand them, and apply them to everyday life. Perhaps the most significant activity the teacher can hope the learner will engage in is thinking. To elicit that thinking in a classroom setting a teacher must plan a variety of approaches. For many adults, listening spurs significant thought. For others, talking is necessary. And for others, writing, drawing, manipulating, acting, or producing tangible products is the key.

The "Learning by Doing" page in each of the lessons in this manual is designed to stir the teacher to thought, thought about how best to prompt thinking in learners. Various learning activities are suggested in these pages. Because different learners have different learning styles, variety in classroom procedures increases overall group learning and retention. That increase is the primary reason to employ learning activities. However, additional benefits come to both the learners and the teacher. Consider the following:

Learner Benefits

Group socialization grows. In activities such as small group discussions and game-like procedures, which introduce friendly competition, students learn much about one another. The sense of oneness and interdependence that arises is important to biblical instruction. Christian adults should enjoy each other, fellowshiping both in the classroom and in life.

Insights are shared. The teacher of adults is dealing with mature learners, many of whom have lifetime insights into biblical truth. Though one cannot assume learners have diligently studied for a given Sunday's lesson, the teacher must assume that most of his or her learners know biblical principles. Such assumption leads the teacher to choose study techniques that will plumb the wisdom of *all* present.

The learner's own responsibility for growth is highlighted when he or she is expected to participate actively. As long as learners depend on the teacher to "feed them," they are relishing their own infancy in Christ. Both teacher and student alike should desire the spiritual maturity to which all Christians are called. Learning activities call on all to participate actively in the process, and challenge all to maturity and responsibility.

A sense of self worth and importance comes from contributing. In 1 Corinthians 12:14-26 the church is described as a body, with each body part contributing what it—and only it—can. Your class members may have talents in music, arts and crafts, drama, debate, writing, and others. The learning activities suggested in these lessons will provide opportunities for the learners' talents to be employed. It may be that you need a crafts enthusiast to prepare ribbon badges for members to wear through a unit of study, or two actors to act out a biblical or contemporary life scene. Your class members who possess these talents may delight in these activities. Many such opportunities to match your learners' talents with learning activities are found in the "Learning by Doing" pages.

Teachers, Too!

The preceding benefits are characterized as "Learner Benefits," but each contributes an obvious blessing to the teacher as well. Yet, there are specific benefits that come to the teacher.

First, consider the greater understanding you gain of your learners. Their interests, abilities, and knowledge are revealed in an activity as simple as projecting a transparency word-find puzzle for group "play." Such information facilitates your planning task. You begin to see the changes individuals and your group as a whole need to make. The objectives you state for the learning sessions can become more precise; thus, it is easier to focus the studies of your unit. Such specific objectives are the basis of sound lesson planning. In learning activities your adults' offhand comments as well as their planned demonstrations give you the information and understanding you need to plan interesting, effective sessions.

Second, the use of learning activities relieves the teacher of being the authority on things Scriptural. (Of course, the teacher must be well prepared so as to give guidance when it is needed; but as the class members assume more of the burden of study, the teacher will be relieved of the responsibility of being the sole dispenser of biblical truth in the classroom.)

No one can learn for another; no teacher can learn for his or her students. The teacher can only help the students learn, and learning activities involving the students' active participation are effective in helping students do that.

Autumn Quarter, 1995

The Story of Christian Beginnings (Acts)

Special Features

Lessons

Unit 1: Beginnings in Jerusalem

Unit 2: Witnessing in Judea and Samaria

Unit 3: Spreading the Gospel Into All the World

About these lessons

This study reviews the exciting story of the birth of the church on Pentecost and its rapid growth in the months and years following. Lessons focus on key events and persons in the life of the early church and in the spread of the gospel to lands beyond Palestine.

Sep 3
Sep 10
Sep 17
Sep 24
Oct 1
Oct 8
Oct 15
Oct 22
Oct 29
Nov 5
Nov 12
Nov 19
Nov 26

A Wonderful Thought

SURELY ONE OF THE MOST WONDERFUL thoughts we can entertain is that God, the Creator of all things, loves mankind. Not just some of us, but *all* of us. The Bible tells us so.

The Bible does more than say God loves us, however. It shows what He has done to prove His love for us.

The studies in the 1995-96 Sunday school year (which are highlighted by the color panel in the lesson cycle chart below) speak eloquently of God's love for us. Some of our studies take us back to when God was preparing Israel to be the people through whom eventually He would bless the whole world. His love, not only for Israel but for all peoples, and His desire for fellowship with us, are emphasized in the Winter and Summer Quarters.

The incarnation and death of God's Son, by which atonement was made for the sins of mankind, were the crowning demonstration of divine love. While He was among us, Jesus taught. His teachings and the noble life they inspire also reveal the Father's love. We'll see this in the Spring and Summer Quarters.

When Jesus' redemptive work was completed, it was time to announce the gospel of God's love. The exciting story of the proclamation of the gospel on Pentecost, and the resulting birth and rapid growth of the church, will be the focus of the lessons in the Autumn Quarter.

International Sunday School Lesson Cycle
September, 1992—August, 1998

YEAR	AUTUMN QUARTER (Sept., Oct., Nov.)	WINTER QUARTER (Dec., Jan., Feb.)	SPRING QUARTER (Mar., Apr., May)	SUMMER QUARTER (June, July, Aug.)
1992-1993	Old Testament Personalities (Old Testament Survey)	Good News for All (New Testament Survey)	Believing in Christ (John)	Following God's Purpose (Ephesians, Philippians, Colossians, Philemon)
1993-1994	The Story of Beginnings (Genesis)	The Story of Jesus (Luke)	Good News for God's People (Romans) Set Free by God's Grace (Galatians)	God Redeems a People (Exodus, Leviticus, Numbers, Deuteronomy)
1994-1995	From the Conquest to the Kingdom (Joshua, Judges, 1 and 2 Samuel, 1 Kings)	Jesus the Fulfillment (Matthew)	Christians Living in Community (1 and 2 Corinthians)	A Nation Turns From God (1 and 2 Kings, Amos, Hosea, Micah, Isaiah)
1995-1996	The Story of Christian Beginnings (Acts)	God's Promise of Deliverance (Isaiah) God's Love for All People (Jonah, Ruth)	Teachings of Jesus (Matthew, Luke, John)	A Practical Religion (James) God Is With Us (Psalms)
1996-1997	God's People Face Judgment (2 Kings, Jeremiah, Lamentations, Ezekiel, Habakkuk)	New Testament Personalities	Hope for the Future (1 and 2 Thessalonians, Revelation)	Guidance for Ministry (1 and 2 Timothy, Titus) A Call to Faithfulness (Hebrews)
1997-1998	God Leads a People Home (Major Prophets, Minor Prophets, Nehemiah)	God's People in a Troubled World (1 and 2 Peter, 1, 2, 3 John, Jude)	The Gospel of Action (Mark)	Wisdom for Living (Job, Proverbs, Ecclesiastes)

Thinking of Beginnings

by Orrin Root

OMMY, WHERE DID I COME FROM?" Mommy finds it hard to answer the childish question, and so does Daddy. Consequently the silly story of the stork is handed down from generation to generation, even in places where never a stork is seen.

Though hard for parents to answer, the question is important. The child comes from Daddy and Mommy. To a large extent, what they are determines what the child is. Soon people begin to notice that he or she has Daddy's eyes or Mommy's nose. More important things are inherited too, such as high intelligence and native musical talent.

Of course, care and training also have a part in shaping the child. Scholars argue endlessly about the relative importance of heredity and environment. But in normal circumstances parents provide the environment as well as the heredity, so their influence is doubled.

Beginning of the Church

Where did the church come from? It came from God. It is composed of people born of God (John 1:12, 13). Such people are only human, of course. They have human faults and follies and failures, and these are reflected in the church. But people born of God show also a likeness to the Father. They show something of His strength and truth and justice, coupled with something of His mercy and compassion and love. These too are reflected in the church.

How can we know what the church ought to be and do? One way is to consider its beginning and early growth. The apostles were with it then, Jesus had given them three years of intensive training when He was with them on earth. For their postgraduate training He had given them the Holy Spirit in an extraordinary way. They were baptized, submerged, overwhelmed in the Spirit (Acts 1:5). They were under His influence so completely that they could not make a mistake in their teaching. The Spirit guided them into all truth (John 16:13).

How could anyone know the apostles were guided by the Holy Spirit and were not just promoting their own ideas? How can we know it now? The Spirit made His presence known by doing things no man can do. By the gate of the temple lay a beggar, a middle-aged man, a cripple who had never walked. To him Peter said, "In the name of Jesus Christ of Nazareth rise up

and walk." The man rose to his feet and went into the temple, "walking, and leaping, and praising God" (Acts 3:1-10). Most of the miracles are not described so fully, but there must have been hundreds of them. Who could deny that God was with those apostles?

Guided by the Holy Spirit, Luke recorded how the church began and grew. From his record we take our Sunday school lessons this quarter. It will not be hard to find suggestions for Christian living and church growth today.

The thirteen lessons are divided into three units. Here is a preview.

Unit 1. September
Beginnings in Jerusalem

Lesson 1. About forty days after Jesus rose from the dead, He instructed His apostles to wait for the Holy Spirit to bring them power from on high. Then they were to testify for Jesus in widening circles till they reached the uttermost part of the earth. Having said this, Jesus rose from the earth and vanished in a cloud.

Lesson 2. On the Day of Pentecost the Holy Spirit came. Upheld by His power, the apostles faced a huge crowd and declared, "God hath made that same Jesus, whom ye have crucified, both Lord and Christ." The message carried conviction, and about three thousand persons were baptized in the name of Jesus Christ for the remission of sins.

Lesson 3. The church gained more attention when Peter and John brought healing to a lame man, but this brought no joy to the rulers who had managed the death of Jesus. They arrested Peter and John, but to the ruling council the apostles declared that Jesus is the only Savior.

Lesson 4. The apostles' teaching and miracles of healing continued till the whole group of apostles were arrested and ordered not to teach about Jesus. But the apostles answered, "We ought to obey God rather than men."

Unit 2. October
Witnessing in Judea and Samaria

Lesson 5. The Christians spent all their time listening to the apostles' teaching. Some soon ran out of money, but the others took care of them. Seven good men were chosen to manage the care of the poor.

Lesson 6. A young Pharisee by the name of Saul took the lead in opposing the church. He searched Jerusalem for Christians and put them in jail, but many escaped by fleeing to other towns of Judea and Samaria. They took the gospel wherever they went. The apostle Philip converted many Samaritans, and then won a traveler from Ethiopia.

Lesson 7. Saul was vigorously extending his persecution of Christians, but Jesus stopped him on the road to Damascus. The leading persecutor became a leading evangelist.

Lesson 8. For some time the gospel was preached only to Jews, but God's plan was wider. The gospel was meant for all nations, and God used some unusual methods to help the Jewish Christians learn that.

Lesson 9. Christians fleeing from persecution took the gospel to Gentiles as well as Jews in Antioch. A great church grew up in that Gentile city. Grateful for the gospel, it sent financial aid to the Christians in Judea.

Unit 3. November
Spreading the Gospel Into All the World

Lesson 10. The church at Antioch had many prophets and teachers. The Holy Spirit called two of them to work elsewhere. Saul and Barnabas carried the gospel through Cyprus and Asia Minor. Saul now was called Paul, and this trip is known as Paul's first missionary journey.

Lesson 11. Lesson 8 told how God convinced Jewish Christians that Gentiles could be Christians too. That was not questioned again, but at Antioch some Jewish Christians taught that Gentiles who become Christians must become Jews also. After some earnest discussion, that error was repudiated.

Lesson 12. Paul set out on his second missionary journey, taking Silas with him. A vision from God led the evangelists to take the gospel into Macedonia. The lesson centers on their work in Philippi, where they were beaten and jailed. However, an earthquake opened the jail, the jailer became a Christian, and Paul and Silas were released with apologies.

Lesson 13. A sample from Paul's third missionary journey completes our series. Fakers failed to match God's miracles, and former fakers used their books of magic for a public bonfire. A simple statement of Scripture summarizes our series: "So mightily grew the word of God and prevailed."

These lessons bring us thirteen highlights from a magnificent book. Still the thirteen printed texts total only 198 verses of Scripture. This is less than one-fifth of the 1007 verses in the book of Acts. We trust the highlights will be so exciting that every student will eagerly read the other four-fifths of Acts as the studies proceed.

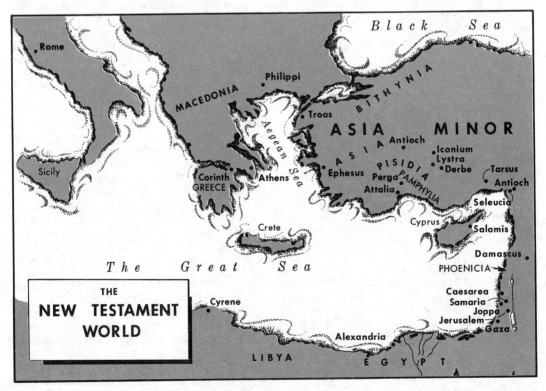

THE
NEW TESTAMENT WORLD

A Gospel for All Time

by Alan G. Ahlgrim

JESUS WAS NEVER BORING. What He said and did jolted people to attention. The same was true of the apostles, who led in establishing the church in the first century. Whenever the gospel was shared and put into practice as Christ intended, the impact was great. The same can and should be true today; unfortunately, in the experience of too many people the church is dull, not dynamic.

A letter in the "Dear Abby" column illustrates the point. The letter was in response to another article involving a churchgoing woman whose minister asked her (loudly) every Sunday morning, "Where is your husband today?"

The letter writer related that her mother-in-law was also a churchgoing woman, but that her father-in-law seldom accompanied her. One day the minister visited their home, and her father-in-law couldn't hide fast enough. Sure enough, the minister cornered him and asked him why he never came to church.

Her father-in-law replied, "Because the seats are too hard and you talk too long!"

The minister never mentioned her father-in-law's absence after that!

For many people these days the thought of being involved in the church is just about as exciting as watching paint dry. In their thinking, the words *church* and *boring* are synonymous. And, tragically, they may also feel that the church has always been as they perceive it to be today. Nothing could be farther from the truth.

That's Exciting!

Recently I was impressed once again by the excitement created by the gospel in the early days of the church. Not long after Jesus had been raised from the dead, the apostles began to preach boldly that Jesus was the long-awaited Messiah. Thousands in Jerusalem believed and were baptized. From that beginning on Pentecost, the church continued to enjoy phenomenal numerical growth. Because the apostles had been specially empowered by the Holy Spirit, people in and around Jerusalem brought their sick to them for healing. Teaching was intense. Christ was magnified. Growth was constant. Opposition was unrelenting. Great faith was evident. It was exciting to be a part of the First Church of Jerusalem!

I wonder, could the church stir up so much excitement, support, opposition, in our time?

Power in Expectations!

On one occasion, the famous nineteenth-century preacher Charles Spurgeon was talking to a young preacher, "feeling him out." Spurgeon said to the young man, "You really don't expect much to happen in your pastorate, do you?"

The man replied, "Well, no. . ."

Spurgeon almost exploded, "Then you won't see much happen, either!"

Spurgeon was right on target. It is said that life is often a self-fulfilling prophecy. The meaning is that while we don't always get what we want in life, in the long run we do get just about what we expect."

Many in the church today consider the gospel merely to be a historic record rather than a personal resource. They read the Bible for information rather than inspiration. They attend classes or services as a routine expecting simply to hear about God rather than to encounter God.

What the church needs is a revival of expectation. We are serving almighty God, who dramatically interrupted the routines of the citizens of Jerusalem on the Day of Pentecost two thousand years ago. He is perfectly capable of interrupting our routines as well. Whenever people come together with that sort of expectancy, worship and fellowship become electric.

What sort of expectations do you have of the gospel? The present time is replete with extraordinary opportunities for the gospel. Spiritual darkness abounds, and the challenge for the Christian messenger is great. But the power of the gospel dispels that darkness, and the gospel's Author promises to be with His servants to meet the challenges involved in confronting the spiritual darkness of this world.

The early church enjoyed great growth, not despite the difficulty and hostility of their culture, but because of it.

Could the same happen today? If the church vigorously undertook the mission given it by the Master, could we not expect Him to bless our efforts to save the lost and thus bring glory and honor to His name?

The Challenge to Change

Clinton T. Duffy was for many years the warden of San Quentin prison and an outspoken advocate of convicts. He was a tough man, but a fair man. He was a man who believed in others.

Someone once challenged Warden Duffy, questioning his attitude toward criminals. His critic said, "Warden, you should know that leopards don't change their spots!"

Duffy snapped back, "You should know that I don't work with leopards. I work with men, and men change every day!"

The gospel is all about change. That is the meaning of repentance. It is a change of heart, of mind, of the direction of one's life. That was the theme of the apostles and evangelists in the early church, as the message of forgiveness and redemption through Jesus Christ was first heralded to a sin-burdened society.

One observer of contemporary church life suggests that the appeal of modern evangelism is not so much for repentance, a true change of heart, as it is for enlistment. The task of the church, however, has not changed. We are to extend to lost sinners the challenge of the high calling and standard of Christ. We are to do so with the certain knowledge that sinners *can* change, and that when they do they will find a warm welcome with the Lord.

The challenge to change is not reserved only for those who are outside of Christ. The Lord's people must always be willing and ready to accept change, and to change, in order to advance the cause of Christ.

A few years ago a woman asked how the old, urban church she attended, which was dying, could be enlivened. She said, "Everybody in the congregation is old, and the community is young. The church members are from well-to-do families, and the surrounding community is poor." The preceding summer approximately sixty children from the community attended VBS, but she lamented that on the Sunday after VBS the church offered no programming for the children. In fact, she said that when some of them returned to the churchyard and asked if they could come in, the chairman of the board went out and locked the gate!

If the church of the twenty-first century is to be Christ's church, and if it is to grow like the church of the first century, there must be a spirit of openness and acceptance among the church's leaders and members alike. We see this illustrated in the book of Acts. The people were challenged to set aside their prejudices and self-interests. They were called to stretch their faith and to grow in love regardless of the changes that were involved.

No wonder the number of Christians grew, nay, multiplied in the church's early days! The gospel was changing lives. People were living in a different and dynamic way because of the message of God's love and grace in Jesus Christ.

Personal Commitment

The gospel made its impact on the world of the first century because of persons such as Peter and Stephen and Paul and Silas. Men on a mission. Men totally committed to Jesus Christ.

The world watched with wonder at the sacrifice these and many others made for Christ and for others. It still does. That is why a tiny Albanian woman known as "Mother Theresa" has had such an impact in our time. She is admired by peasants and honored by presidents. Everyone is impressed with her humble spirit, exemplified by her expression, "I'm just a pencil in the hand of God."

The success of the gospel in any age depends on such commitment by the followers of Christ. Are there others today who are serving Him quietly and faithfully, sharing the blessings of the gospel with the downtrodden and despairing? Surely. And just as most faithful servants of the past were never mentioned in the Bible, most today will never win the acclaim of men. That doesn't mean, however, that they are not witnessing boldly and effectively for Christ. By the fruits of their labors, namely the souls who have been rescued from the stranglehold of sin by the grace of God through Christ Jesus, these servants are proving that the gospel of Christ is God's power unto salvation in our time.

Answers to Quarterly Quiz on page 8

Lesson 1—1. forty. 2. Jerusalem. 3. power. **Lesson 2**—1. the sound of a mighty wind, fire-like tongues, the recipients' ability to speak in other languages. 2. David. 3. repent and be baptized in the name of Jesus Christ. **Lesson 3**—1. Peter and John. 2. from his mother's womb. 3. rise up and walk. **Lesson 4**—1. the angel of the Lord. 2. God, men. **Lesson 5**—1. seven. 2. Stephen. **Lesson 6**—1. the Samaritans. 2. the angel of the Lord. 3. the Ethiopian eunuch. **Lesson 7**—1. Damascus. 2. Ananias. **Lesson 8**—1. Cornelius. 2. respecter, persons. **Lesson 9**—1. Barnabas. 2. Barnabas and Saul. **Lesson 10**—1. Cyprus. 2. Lystra and Derbe. **Lesson 11**—1. that Gentiles could not be saved unless they became Jews and kept the law (see also verse 24). 2. Jerusalem, apostles, elders. **Lesson 12**—1. Macedonia. 2. Lydia. 3. killing himself. **Lesson 13**—1. Sceva. 2. burned.

Share the Good News

by Floyd Strater

THE WORD *gospel* appears in slightly less than one hundred verses of the New Testament in the *King James Version* of the Bible. The word *gospel* comes from an Anglo-Saxon word, which meant "good tidings." The word in the original texts (Greek) in the New Testament means "good news."

There is no mistaking what the writers of the New Testament meant when they referred to the "good news." It is the good news of what God has done for mankind through His Son, Jesus Christ.

Our study for this quarter is taken from the book of Acts, a book full of good news. Let us consider some of its applications to our time.

There Is Hope. All around us are crime and corruption, which lead to the disquiet of our hearts. I live in the Los Angeles area, where shootings occur every day. At the time of this writing, our community is in shock over the shooting deaths of two Japanese students. This senseless act of violence is typical of what is happening in so many urban areas in our country.

On Pentecost Peter urged his hearers, "Save yourselves from this corrupt generation" (Acts 2:40, *New International Version*). The way of escape is still open. By answering the call of Christ, a person can live above the spiritual darkness that threatens to engulf us. We have the good news. Let's share it.

One Source of Salvation. Religions abound in our pluralistic society. Magnificent temples are being built by some of them, and the adherents of these religions are increasing.

There need be no confusion among the followers of Christ, however. The apostle Peter stated unequivocally, "Salvation is found in no one else, for there is no other name under heaven given to men by which we must be saved (Acts 4:12, *New International Version*). When we look around in our religiously divided world, we are confronted by conflicting claims. Don't be misled. Jesus is the only Lord and Savior.

God Has Heroes. The lame man, who had sat daily at the temple gate asking alms, was leaping and praising God. At Peter's command in the name of Christ, the invalid had been miraculously healed. Crowds gathered, and the popularity of Peter and John soared. Envious and angry, the rulers of the temple seized the two apostles and put them in jail, charging the two men not to teach anymore in the name of Jesus. Their lives were on the line. Fearlessly "Peter and John answered and said unto them, "Whether it be right in the sight of God to hearken unto you more than unto God, judge ye. For we cannot but speak the things which we have seen and heard" (Acts 4:19, 20).

With the failure of a few prominent church leaders today, society casts doubt on the sincerity of all who labor in the name of Christ. In truth, many giants of the faith have given of themselves unselfishly throughout their lives. In almost every church humble servants labor unnoticed behind the scenes.

There were many heroes in the church in its early days. Heroism, both the seen and unseen kind, has characterized the church from that time to the present.

God Is No Respecter of Persons. By God's direction Peter went to the home of Cornelius, a Gentile, and shared the gospel with him. Until that time the good news had been given to Jews only. Peter's experience led him to conclude, "Of a truth I perceive that God is no respecter of persons" (Acts 10:34).

Many persons today struggle with low self-esteem. They want to be a success and to be accepted by others. Disappointment and frustration dog them. With God the pressure is off. We are all precious in His sight. That's one of the great things about the good news of Christ.

Dynamic Churches. One theme that runs through the book of Acts is that the church continued to grow stronger in faith, even while there was a daily increase in the number of those being won to Christ. Many congregations today are geared for maintenance. They seem to fear that numerical growth worthy of note will be experienced by the church only at the expense of solid commitment to Christ. That sentiment finds no support in the record in the book of Acts. To the contrary, great spiritual and numerical growth can occur at the same time. That's what happened in the church's early days, and it will happen today when Christians regularly share the good news.

Good News. To the Judean shepherds the angel declared, "Behold, I bring you good tidings of great joy, which shall be to all people" (Luke 2:10). Thus began the ministry of Jesus to the world. That ministry was continued by the apostles and others as recorded in the book of Acts. Let us be faithful servants and share the good news with the unsaved in our generation.

Quarterly Quiz

The questions on this page may be used in several ways: as a pretest at the beginning of the quarter; as a review at the end of the quarter; or as a review after each lesson. The questions are based on the Scripture text of each lesson (King James Version). **The answers are on page 6.**

Lesson 1

1. How many days was Jesus seen by His apostles following His resurrection? *Acts 1:3*
2. Where were the apostles to wait until they received what God had promised? *Acts 1:4*
3. What would the apostles receive when the Holy Spirit came upon them? *Acts 1:8*

Lesson 2

1. What phenomena accompanied the coming of the Holy Spirit on Pentecost? *Acts 2:1-4*
2. What Old Testament person did Peter say spoke of Christ's resurrection? *Acts 2:25-31*
3. What did Peter tell his audience on Pentecost to do for the remission of sins? *Acts 2:38*

Lesson 3

1. What two apostles met a lame man asking alms at a gate of the temple? *Acts 3:1*
2. How long had the man been lame? *Acts 3:2*
3. The apostle instructed the lame man in the name of Jesus Christ to do what? *Acts 3:6*

Lesson 4

1. Jailed for preaching the gospel, the apostles were released at night by whom? *Acts 5:19*
2. Peter told the council that he and the other apostles were required to obey _____ rather than _____. *Acts 5:29*

Lesson 5

1. How many men were chosen to replace the apostles as overseers of the benevolent ministry of the church in Jerusalem? *Acts 6:3*
2. Which of these overseers later was falsely charged before the Jewish council? *Acts 6:9-13*

Lesson 6

1. After the Christians fled Jerusalem because of persecution, Philip had a successful preaching ministry among what people? *Acts 8:5, 6*
2. Who told Philip to go south to the road that went from Jerusalem to Gaza? *Acts 8:26*
3. Whom did Philip meet there? *Acts 8:27*

Lesson 7

1. Saul journeyed to (Antioch, Damascus, Caesarea) to find Christians, whether men or women, and bring them bound to Jerusalem. *Acts 9:2*

2. The Lord appeared to _____ in a vision and instructed him to go to Saul so that Saul might receive his sight. *Acts 9:17*

Lesson 8

1. What Gentile was instructed by an angel to send for Simon Peter so Peter could speak God's message to him? *Acts 10:30-32*
2. Having been directed by the Holy Spirit to the Gentile's home, Peter perceived that God is no _____ of _____. *Acts 10:34*

Lesson 9

1. When the church in Jerusalem heard that the gospel was being preached to Grecians as well as Jews in Antioch, they sent whom to check it out? *Acts 11:22*
2. What two men took the Antioch church's gift to the famine-stricken Christians in Judea? *Acts 11:30*

Lesson 10

1. On their first missionary trip, Barnabas and Saul went first to what island? *Acts 13:4*
2. On that same trip, the two men preached in and around what two cities of Lycaonia after fleeing Iconium? *Acts 14:6*

Lesson 11

1. Certain men came from Judea to Antioch and began to teach the Christians there what false doctrine? *Acts 15:1*
2. The church at Antioch sent Paul, Barnabas, and others to _____ to discuss this matter with the _____ and _____. *Acts 15:2*

Lesson 12

1. A man of what country appeared in a vision to Paul in the night? *Acts 16:9*
2. At Philippi, a woman named _____, who sold purple, was led to Christ by Paul. *Acts 16:14*
3. Paul's cry to the Philippian jailer in the night kept the man from what? *Acts 16:27, 28*

Lesson 13

1. In Ephesus the seven sons of a Jewish priest named _____ tried to cast out a demon by calling on the name of Jesus. *Acts 19:14*
2. The Ephesian sorcerers who became Christians _____ their books of sorcery. *Acts 19:19*

The Promise of the Spirit's Power

September 3
Lesson 1

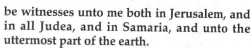

DEVOTIONAL READING: Acts 1:21-26.

LESSON SCRIPTURE: Acts 1.

PRINTED TEXT: Acts 1:1-14.

Acts 1:1-14

1 The former treatise have I made, O Theophilus, of all that Jesus began both to do and teach,

2 Until the day in which he was taken up, after that he through the Holy Ghost had given commandments unto the apostles whom he had chosen:

3 To whom also he showed himself alive after his passion by many infallible proofs, being seen of them forty days, and speaking of the things pertaining to the kingdom of God:

4 And, being assembled together with them, commanded them that they should not depart from Jerusalem, but wait for the promise of the Father, which, saith he, ye have heard of me.

5 For John truly baptized with water; but ye shall be baptized with the Holy Ghost not many days hence.

6 When they therefore were come together, they asked of him, saying, Lord, wilt thou at this time restore again the kingdom to Israel?

7 And he said unto them, It is not for you to know the times or the seasons, which the Father hath put in his own power.

8 But ye shall receive power, after that the Holy Ghost is come upon you: and ye shall be witnesses unto me both in Jerusalem, and in all Judea, and in Samaria, and unto the uttermost part of the earth.

9 And when he had spoken these things, while they beheld, he was taken up; and a cloud received him out of their sight.

10 And while they looked steadfastly toward heaven as he went up, behold, two men stood by them in white apparel;

11 Which also said, Ye men of Galilee, why stand ye gazing up into heaven? this same Jesus, which is taken up from you into heaven, shall so come in like manner as ye have seen him go into heaven.

12 Then returned they unto Jerusalem from the mount called Olivet, which is from Jerusalem a sabbath day's journey.

13 And when they were come in, they went up into an upper room, where abode both Peter, and James, and John, and Andrew, Philip, and Thomas, Bartholomew, and Matthew, James the son of Alpheus, and Simon Zelotes, and Judas the brother of James.

14 These all continued with one accord in prayer and supplication, with the women, and Mary the mother of Jesus, and with his brethren.

GOLDEN TEXT: Ye shall receive power, after that the Holy Ghost is come upon you: and ye shall be witnesses unto me both in Jerusalem, and in all Judea, and in Samaria, and unto the uttermost part of the earth.—Acts 1:8.

The Story of Christian Beginnings (Acts)
Unit 1: Beginnings in Jerusalem (Lessons 1-4)

Lesson Aims

After studying this lesson a student should be able to:

1. Describe Jesus' ascension and tell what the apostles did between that ascension and the beginning of their public preaching.

2. Appreciate the value of a pause for prayer.

3. Have time for personal prayer, and follow prayer with eager service for the Lord.

Lesson Outline

INTRODUCTION
    A. Pause for Prayer
    B. Lesson Background
 I. TIME OF WAITING (Acts 1:1-5)
    A. Former Treatise (vv. 1, 2)
    B. Proof of Resurrection (v. 3)
    C. Command to Wait (v. 4)
    D. Promise of Power (v. 5)
 II. TIME OF PARTING (Acts 1:6-11)
    A. The Father's Secret (vv. 6, 7)
    B. The Apostles' Task (v. 8)
      The Kudzu Effect
    C. The Parting (v. 9)
    D. The Promise of Return (vv. 10, 11)
      Hope-Producing Promise
III. TIME OF PRAYING (Acts 1:12-14)
    A. The Place (v. 12)
    B. The People (v. 13)
    C. The Praying (v. 14)
CONCLUSION
    A. Needs
    B. Prayer
    C. Thought to Remember

Visual 1 of the visuals packet (see page 13) is a chart of the resurrection appearances of Christ. Visual 14 is a poster for the quarter.

Introduction

Dawn crept over the rippling waters of Galilee and pushed the darkness from the streets of Bethsaida. People came early to Simon Peter's house, asking for Jesus. But Jesus was not there. He had risen "a great while before day" and gone out to find a solitary place for prayer (Mark 1:35).

A. Pause for Prayer

Crowds of people pressed upon Jesus so urgently that He could scarcely find time to eat (Mark 6:31). Yet Jesus knew the value of a pause for prayer. Thronging multitudes were eager to hear and to be healed, but still He managed to slip away and pray alone (Luke 5:15, 16). One time He spent the whole night in prayer (Luke 6:12). And Jesus taught that "men ought always to pray" (Luke 18:1).

B. Lesson Background

This week we begin a series of studies from the book of Acts. That book finds its background in the book of Luke, an earlier work of the same author. That background is enhanced by similar records written by Matthew, Mark, and John.

After more than three years of teaching, Jesus gave His life at Calvary to redeem lost sinners. On the third day He rose triumphant over death. For a while He taught again, and sent His disciples to take His message of salvation to all the world. Then He rose to Heaven and took His place at God's right hand.

The book of Acts begins where the book of Luke ends, adding some details of the last minutes before Jesus rose visibly to the sky; and there we begin our study.

I. Time of Waiting
(Acts 1:1-5)

The disciples of Jesus were to testify for Him "in Jerusalem, and in all Judea, and in Samaria, and unto the uttermost part of the earth" (Acts 1:8). What a tremendous task! But they were not to plunge into preaching instantly when the Master said good-bye. They were to wait for "power from on high" (Luke 24:49).

A. Former Treatise (vv. 1, 2)

1. The former treatise have I made, O Theophilus, of all that Jesus began both to do and teach.

The former treatise is the book of Luke, which records much of what Jesus did and taught. It too is addressed to *Theophilus,* of whom we really know nothing more.

2. Until the day in which he was taken up, after that he through the Holy Ghost had given commandments unto the apostles whom he had chosen.

The former treatise ends with *the day* in which Jesus *was taken up* to Heaven, adding merely that the apostles afterward "were continually in the temple, praising and blessing God" (Luke 24:50-53). Verse 8 of our text records the

How to Say It

ALPHEUS. Al-*fee*-us.
BARTHOLOMEW. Bar-*thol*-o-mew.
BETHSAIDA. Beth-*say*-uh-duh.
ISCARIOT. Iss-*care*-e-ut.
MATTHIAS. Muh-*thigh*-us (*th* as in *thin*).
THEOPHILUS. Thee-*ahf*-ih-luss (*th* as in *thin*).
ZELOTES. Zee-*low*-teez.

outstanding commandment that He *had given* not long before He rose to Heaven. *Through the Holy Ghost* seems to mean that Jesus gave this commandment with the guidance of the Holy Spirit who had come to Him at His baptism (Luke 3:21, 22) and had given Him power and guidance all through the years of His ministry. The commandment in verse 8 was given several times in different words (Matthew 28:18-20; Mark 16:15, 16). Jesus did give other commands before He ascended. We see one in verse 4 of our text. But over them all towers the great command to carry the gospel to the whole world.

B. Proof of Resurrection (v. 3)

3. To whom also he showed himself alive after his passion by many infallible proofs, being seen of them forty days, and speaking of the things pertaining to the kingdom of God.

Jesus' *passion* means His suffering and death. He died and was buried, but afterward *showed himself alive . . . by many infallible proofs*. Read about some of them in Luke 24:36-43 and John 20:19-29. Notice the list of witnesses in 1 Corinthians 15:3-8. There can be no doubt that Jesus actually died and returned to life. The apostles saw Him at various times during *forty days* after His resurrection—perhaps many more times than are recorded. He taught them about *the kingdom of God*, saying much that is not included in the record.

C. Command to Wait (v. 4)

4. And, being assembled together with them, commanded them that they should not depart from Jerusalem, but wait for the promise of the Father, which, saith he, ye have heard of me.

Jesus met His disciples in Jerusalem in the evening following His resurrection (John 20:19). During the following forty days He was with them sometimes in Galilee (John 21; Matthew 28:16-20). But near the time of His ascension He was with them in Jerusalem again, and He told them to stay there. That did not contradict the order to go to all the world; it merely postponed their going. They were to wait for a specific

thing before starting out. *Wait for the promise* means wait for what was promised, wait for the promise to be fulfilled. It was a promise made by *the Father,* but the disciples had heard it from Jesus. The next verse tells what was promised.

D. Promise of Power (v. 5)

5. For John truly baptized with water; but ye shall be baptized with the Holy Ghost not many days hence.

More than three years earlier, John the Baptist had startled Israel with his fervent call to repent and be baptized. Many people were wondering if John was the long-expected Christ, but John said the Christ would be far greater than he. He added, "He shall baptize you with the Holy Ghost and with fire" (Luke 3:15, 16). John went on to explain the baptism in fire. The Christ will judge the people of earth, separating wheat from chaff, and "the chaff he will burn with fire unquenchable" (Luke 3:17). John gave no explanation of the baptism with the Holy Spirit, but now Jesus mentioned it as the thing promised by the Father to the apostles. In a few days they would be baptized with the Holy Ghost. Acts 2:1-4 describes that baptism. The apostles were submerged, overwhelmed by the Holy Spirit. They were under His influence so completely that He used their voices to speak in languages unknown to them, but known to some of the hearers (Acts 2:5-11).

Verse 8 of our text adds that the apostles would receive power along with their baptism with the Spirit. In the second chapter of Acts it is apparent that they received power to speak in unknown languages. They also received power to do miracles of healing (Acts 3:1-8). They received power to endure persecution and resist the orders of ungodly rulers (Acts 4:18-20). Furthermore, the Holy Spirit guided them into all truth (John 16:12, 13). He gave them power to understand the kingdom of Christ, a kingdom not of this world (John 18:36). He gave them power to teach God's word without any error, and that is our assurance that we can trust the Bible that was written by them and other men likewise guided by the Holy Spirit.

II. Time of Parting
(Acts 1:6-11)

A. The Father's Secret (vv. 6, 7)

6. When they therefore were come together, they asked of him, saying, Lord, wilt thou at this time restore again the kingdom to Israel?

It seems quite evident that the apostles did not yet understand the nature of God's kingdom,

---

VISUALS FOR THESE LESSONS

The *Adult Visuals/Learning Resources* packet contains classroom-size visuals designed for use with the lessons in the Autumn Quarter. The packet is available from your supplier. Order No. 192.

---

a kingdom not of this world, a kingdom of love instead of force, a kingdom ruling only those who choose to be ruled by it. They were thinking of Israel triumphant, supreme among the nations of the world, as it had been in the time of Solomon. They were asking if the time had come to restore Israel to that ancient glory.

7. And he said unto them, It is not for you to know the times or the seasons, which the Father hath put in his own power.

Jesus did not give a lecture on the true nature of the kingdom. In time the Holy Spirit would guide the apostles to that truth, and they would come to understand that the kingdom would win, not by killing people, but by making friends out of enemies. They would come to understand that the kingdom is vastly larger than Israel, drawing its citizens from all the nations of the world. For the time being, Jesus was content to deal with the question that was asked: was it then time for the kingdom to take charge and be triumphant? That was not for the apostles to know. The time of triumph was God's secret, and it still is (Matthew 24:36).

B. The Apostles' Task (v. 8)

8. But ye shall receive power, after that the Holy Ghost is come upon you: and ye shall be witnesses unto me both in Jerusalem, and in all Judea, and in Samaria, and unto the uttermost part of the earth.

The *power* that would come with the Holy Spirit has been discussed briefly in the comments on verse 5. With that power the apostles had a job to do. Jesus spoke these words in or near *Jerusalem. Judea* was the area around that city; *Samaria* was just north of Judea. But these places were only a tiny beginning. The testimony about Jesus was to explode into all the world. In the lifetime of those apostles it spread rapidly on the east and north sides of the Mediterranean Sea, as we shall see as we continue our studies in Acts. We have no similar book to tell us how swiftly and far the gospel went in Egypt and Mesopotamia and India in those early years. Today there is urgent need for followers of Jesus to take the gospel back to the land of its beginning, and to the wide areas where Communism has suppressed it for decades, and to the teeming millions of India and China and the isles of the sea—to the *uttermost part of the earth.*

THE KUDZU EFFECT

"Kudzu." It's almost like saying, "the plague." Kudzu is a fast-growing vine—up to a foot a day!—with bright green leaves and grape-scented purple blossoms. In the 1930s, it was widely planted in the southern part of the United States. Its deep network of thick roots tenaciously holds the soil, so it seemed a perfect means of stopping soil erosion. But the plant became a relentless monster, covering millions of acres across the South and killing all other vegetation in its path.

Belatedly, beneficial uses for this once-maligned plant are being found. Its roots are rich in starch and B vitamins, and its leaves and vines are a potential source of ethanol for fuel.

Christianity must have seemed like kudzu to the people in the first century. Its Founder had commissioned His followers to start where they were (Jerusalem) and cover the world with the Christian message. To its enemies, Christianity must have seemed like a force that would destroy everything the Jewish world stood for and also consume the whole pagan world in the process. Try as they might, they could not stamp it out.

Christ's Great Commission is still in effect. If we will enthusiastically heed His charge to us to cover the world with the gospel, the world may finally come to appreciate its marvelous benefits!

—C. R. B.

C. The Parting (v. 9)

9. And when he had spoken these things, while they beheld, he was taken up; and a cloud received him out of their sight.

Luke's earlier book records that Jesus had led the apostles out to the Mount of Olives east of Jerusalem. From that spot the visible body of Jesus *was taken up* into thin air till it vanished in *a cloud.* Luke 24:50, 51 records that Jesus was blessing the apostles as He left them; Mark 16:19 adds that "he was received up into heaven, and sat on the right hand of God."

D. The Promise of Return (vv. 10, 11)

10. And while they looked steadfastly toward heaven as he went up, behold, two men stood by them in white apparel.

No doubt these were angels, who took the form of men to communicate with the apostles. Their white apparel symbolized their perfect holiness.

11. Which also said, Ye men of Galilee, why stand ye gazing up into heaven? this same Jesus, which is taken up from you into heaven, shall so come in like manner as ye have seen him go into heaven.

Jesus will come back as He went, in a visible body. "Every eye shall see him" (Revelation 1:7). He vanished in a cloud; He will come back in clouds, but "with power and great glory" (Matthew 24:30, 31). It was useless for the apostles to stand gazing at the sky. Jesus was not coming back that day. They had a job to do before His return.

HOPE-PRODUCING PROMISE

World War II began for the United States on December 7, 1941, when the Imperial Japanese armed forces bombed Pearl Harbor. Within hours of that bombing, the Japanese attacked Hong Kong, Malay, and the Philippines. Many feared that the flag of the rising sun would soon fly over every nation on the western side of what we now call the Pacific Rim.

The Philippine islands quickly fell prey to the Japanese onslaught. General Douglas MacArthur, commander of United States Armed Forces in the Far East, was forced to retreat with his overpowered troops. When he was ordered to withdraw from Philippine soil, General MacArthur made a promise that was to become famous. He vowed, "I shall return." And so he did. As the Japanese were later driven out of the Philippines, General MacArthur returned as conquering hero.

During the week before His crucifixion, Jesus spoke of His triumphant return to earth (Matthew 24). When He stepped off the soil of the Judean hillside and ascended into Heaven, this hope-producing promise was given again, this time by two angels standing by. The enemy, Satan, was strong and controlled the hearts of many in the land. But the apostles took courage in Jesus' promise and, against all odds, began a resistance movement against the forces of evil that continues to this day. The hopeful heart of every Christian is still empowered by Jesus' words: "I shall return!"
　　　　　　　　　　　　　　　　—C. R. B.

visual 1

III. Time of Praying
(Acts 1:12-14)

Prompted by angels, the apostles stopped gazing at that cloud into which their Master had soared. They had a big job to do, but they were not to plunge into it that day or the next. First they must wait for "power from on high" (Luke 24:49).

A. The Place (v. 12)

12. Then returned they unto Jerusalem from the mount called Olivet, which is from Jerusalem a sabbath day's journey.

The apostles must have been filled with awe as they walked down the western slope of the Mount of Olives, across the bridge over the Kidron valley, and into the gate of Jerusalem. That was where Jesus had told them to wait (Luke 24:49), and probably not one of them set a foot outside the city wall before the Spirit came with the promised power.

B. The People (v. 13)

13. And when they were come in, they went up into an upper room, where abode both Peter, and James, and John, and Andrew, Philip, and Thomas, Bartholomew, and Matthew, James the son of Alpheus, and Simon Zelotes, and Judas the brother of James.

Here Luke lists the eleven apostles who remained. Judas Iscariot had committed suicide after betraying Jesus (Matthew 27:3-5). Apparently the eleven were all lodging together in *an upper room* in Jerusalem. It seems, however, that this upper room was only for sleeping and perhaps for eating. Luke ends his earlier book with the statement that the apostles "were continually in the temple, praising and blessing God." That seems to indicate that most of their waking hours were spent there. Other followers of Jesus could gather with them in the spacious court of the temple (Acts 1:15).

C. The Praying (v. 14)

14. These all continued with one accord in prayer and supplication, with the women, and Mary the mother of Jesus, and with his brethren.

In his earlier book Luke records that Jesus was followed in Galilee by many women whom He had rescued from demons and diseases. They showed their gratitude by helping to support Him (Luke 8:1-3). Some of them followed Him to Jerusalem, where they saw Him die on the cross and watched as His body was laid in the tomb. They were the first of Jesus' followers to find His tomb empty on the first day of the week, and to hear angels say He had risen from the dead (Luke 23:49, 55; 24:1-10). No doubt some of them were *the women* who gathered with the apostles after Jesus returned to Heaven. Jesus' mother was there too. Jesus had committed her to the care of His beloved disciple John (John 19:25-27). *His brethren* also were with the group. About six months before He died, they still did not believe in Him (John 7:5). Apparently His resurrection convinced them.

Probably all these men and women met with the apostles in the temple (Luke 24:53) rather than in the upper room. The big outer court of the temple had room for all of them, plus any other believers who wanted to be with them (Acts 1:15).

Prayer was not the only activity of the group in the days of waiting. One item of business was the choice of Matthias to take the place of Judas Iscariot, so the number of apostles again was twelve (Acts 1:15-26). Still Luke writes, *These all continued with one accord in prayer.* Thanksgiving must have had a large place in their praying. After the terrible tragedy of Jesus' death, their hearts were overflowing with gratitude because He was alive, because He had all power (Matthew 28:18), because the movement to which they had given their lives would go on and grow. Still there was reason for concern. The rulers who had contrived the death of Jesus were still ruling, and they would be no less hostile to Jesus' followers. There must have been earnest prayer for courage, for determination, for wisdom, for the promised guidance and power of the Holy Spirit.

Conclusion

How busy we are! We have to work forty hours a week. The round of home duties is endless; the tasks are not done till it is time to begin them again. Children have duties too, and parents have to take them to music lessons and sports events, to school and to parties. We can hardly stop for a deep breath. But our work does not fill all our needs.

A. Needs

We need to eat, and we find time to do it. Is spiritual nourishment less necessary than physical? We take time off to have a tooth pulled or an appendix removed. Is the health of our spirits less important than the health of our bodies?

We need vacations. When God was making laws for a nation, He established three vacations every year; and He decreed how they should be spent. All Israel must go to an appointed place for fun and fellowship and worship: the Passover

feast in spring, the Day of Pentecost in summer, the feast of Tabernacles in autumn. Do you choose a vacation time in which you can attend a Christian convention, conference, or camp?

When God was making laws for a nation, He required a weekly day of rest (Exodus 20:8-11). Part of it was used for worshiping together. Now most of us work five days a week and have two days off. But do we rest? And how many of us worship? Are we neglecting some of our most urgent needs?

Jesus' people had endured the terrible grief of His death and the tremendous joy of His resurrection. They had lived through forty days of excitement in which they met with Jesus again and again in places widely separated. So Jesus told them to take some days off before plunging into the work that would keep them busy for the rest of their lives. Wisely through those days they "continued with one accord in prayer."

Prayer, worship, Scripture study, communion with God—certainly these are some of our most urgent needs. Then let us take time for these—but let us never imagine that they take the place of work, either the work by which we earn a living or the Christian work by which we build God's kingdom. Our time off is to prepare us for our time on.

B. Prayer

You have created us, O God, and we are sure You know our needs better than we do. Thank You for setting before us what we need of work and rest and worship. May we use all of these well and wisely to extend Your kingdom and glorify Your name. In Jesus' name, amen.

C. Thought to Remember

Our time off is to prepare us for our time on.

Home Daily Bible Readings

Monday, Aug. 28—The Spirit's Prediction (Acts 1:15-20)

Tuesday, Aug. 29—God Works Through the Spirit (Zechariah 4:1-6)

Wednesday, Aug. 30—Empowered by the Spirit (Matthew 12:22-28)

Thursday, Aug. 31—The Holy Spirit's Work (John 16:1-15)

Friday, Sept. 1—Life in the Spirit (Romans 8:11-17, 26, 27)

Saturday, Sept. 2—The Spirit Gives Life (2 Corinthians 3:1-6)

Sunday, Sept. 3—God's Affirmation (1 John 4:13-18)

Learning by Doing

This page contains an alternate lesson plan emphasizing learning activities. Classes desiring such student involvement will find these suggestions helpful.

Learning Goals

As students participate in today's class session, they should:

1. List what Acts 1:1-14 tells about the Holy Spirit.

2. Evaluate and list the apostles' emotions as they experienced the events recorded here.

3. Pray for each other about the issues raised by this lesson.

Into the Lesson

Before class write each of the letters of the word *wait* on a different sheet of construction paper. Begin today's session by giving the four sheets to four class members, one sheet to each. Ask the four members to stand before the class and to display the letters. Then ask them to arrange themselves so that they spell a word. When they have formed the word *wait,* thank them and mount the letters on a bulletin board or the wall.

Ask the class members to turn to a partner and discuss, "The most difficult wait I ever endured." After three minutes, ask volunteers to share with the whole class.

Ask, "What makes waiting difficult? Has waiting become easier or more difficult for you as you have become older?

Tell the class that this week's study focuses on the apostles in the weeks after Christ's resurrection and on His order for them to wait.

Into the Word

Since today's session begins a thirteen-week survey of the book of Acts, spend a few moments giving a brief introduction to this book of history. Write on the chalkboard the following headings (shown in italics). Omit the answers shown here in parentheses.

Author: (Luke)

Facts about the author: (A physician. The author of the Gospel that bears his name. Traveled with Paul.)

Date: (Probably around A.D. 62 or 63.)

Purpose: (To inform Theophilus about the Christian faith. To demonstrate what a person must do to become a Christian. A selective history of the early church.)

Point to each of the headings and ask class members to provide the missing information. Supply the facts that they don't know.

Next, divide the class into groups of three to five students each. Then have a volunteer read today's text, Acts 1:1-14, aloud to the class. Half of the groups should listen for and then list everything this passage tells about the Holy Spirit. The other half of the groups should list what they believe the apostle Peter might have been thinking at the time of the events that are recorded in this passage.

(Tell the class that the first four lessons of this quarter all feature the work of the Holy Spirit in the establishment and early ministry of the church. Peter was involved in the incidents recorded in the texts of these lessons. In some of them he will be featured prominently. Thinking about the Holy Spirit and/or Peter in these four lessons will be a good way to tie them together.)

After about six or eight minutes, allow the groups to share what they have written.

Next, lead the class in discussing the following questions:

What was the role of the Holy Spirit in Christ's relationship with the apostles after His resurrection?

What place would the Holy Spirit have in the apostles' future ministries?

How do you think the apostles felt by the command of Jesus to wait in Jerusalem (v. 4)? Frustrated? Comforted? Other?

What emotions do you think the apostles may have experienced at the time of Jesus' ascension (vv. 9-11)?

How do you evaluate the action of the group as recorded in verses 12-14?

Into Life

Give each class member a sheet of paper with these topics written on it:

• A way I find comfort in Christ's presence.

• A command of Christ that I'm having trouble understanding or obeying.

• A way I've discovered peace in the fellowship of other believers.

• Something I've learned by waiting for God to work in my life.

Ask the class members to return to the groups in which they did their Bible study. Each person should choose one of these topics and respond to it in his or her group. Conclude the session by having class members pray for each other in their groups.

Let's Talk It Over

The questions on this page are designed to encourage review of the lesson Scriptures and to promote discussion of the lesson by the class. The answers provided are only discussion starters. Let your class talk it over from there.

1. Some persons complain that they are "too busy to pray." Perhaps, instead, they are actually "too busy *not* to pray." Comment.

The excuse, "I'm too busy," is possibly the most common reason people give for refusing to accept some task in the church or for failing to perform some spiritual duty. Jesus was an extremely busy person, but He made time for what was most important, and that included prayer. His prayer life was clearly a key to His being able to accomplish so much during His earthly ministry. When we are too busy for prayer, Bible study, Christian service, etc., we need to ask ourselves, "Busy with *what?*" Any worthwhile activity that commands our time could be done better if we lifted it in prayer to our heavenly Father and sought the strength and guidance He willingly offers.

2. While they awaited the coming of the Holy Spirit upon them, the apostles must have pondered the "many infallible proofs" of Jesus' resurrection (Acts 1:3). How is it profitable for us to take time to examine the evidences for Jesus' resurrection?

Books such as Josh McDowell's *Evidence That Demands a Verdict* demonstrate just how solid the evidence is for Jesus' bodily resurrection. Our faith is strengthened when we see how well the Gospel records establish this greatest of all miracles. We can test the alternate explanations offered by unbelievers and discover for ourselves their failure to account for all the facts. To examine all the testimony of the eyewitnesses in careful detail gives us a special feel for the excitement that spread throughout the band of disciples as they realized that Jesus truly had risen from the dead.

3. Acts 1:8 records Jesus' plan for the spread of the gospel, and the plan was carried out as He designed it. The remainder of the book of Acts demonstrates this. What are some aspects of this plan that are important for our time?

The gospel was first proclaimed in a city, the city of Jerusalem, and from there it spread into the surrounding regions. Later, Paul followed this same plan, centering his evangelistic efforts in major cities, such as Corinth, Philippi, and Ephesus, and then witnessing the spread of the

gospel into surrounding areas (see Acts 19:8-10). It is obvious that in our own time major cities must still be prominent centers of evangelistic activity. Another aspect of Jesus' plan was its worldwide vision, its ultimate focus on "the uttermost part of the earth." We today must not become nearsighted, focusing all our prayer and energies into our own church and community; we must embrace that same worldwide vision.

4. The remarks of the two angels standing by at Jesus' ascension implied that it was useless for the apostles to gaze into the sky as though expecting Jesus' return that day. Much work needed to be done before His return. How may the angels' remarks be applied to us?

How do we anticipate Christ's return? Do we lie awake at night listening for the sound of a trumpet? Should we quit our jobs, sell our possessions, and gather with other Christians to do nothing but wait? These are very practical questions. We are to expect the coming again of Jesus Christ, but we have to know what is involved in such expectation. The answer is that we wait by working. As part of His discussion regarding His coming again, Jesus described two kinds of servants awaiting their master's return (Matthew 24:45-51). One was careless and idle and therefore tragically unprepared for his master's arrival. The other was diligently working at the task his master had given him, and therefore he was ready for his master's reward. We make our waiting fruitful when we also are diligently at work, doing what Jesus has commanded all of us to do.

5. Many churches place in their bulletins the slogan, "Enter to worship; depart to serve." How can the church's gatherings on the Lord's Day better prepare believers for service?

One obvious answer is for teachers and preachers to present lessons and sermons that call for specific actions on the part of the hearers. Worshipers need regular challenges to witness to at least one person during the following week, to assist one needy family, to write a letter to a missionary giving encouragement, and similar actions. The Sunday bulletin can also be used to list specific tasks that members may undertake following the hour of worship.

The Holy Spirit Comes in Power

DEVOTIONAL READING: Acts 2:16-24.

LESSON SCRIPTURE: Acts 2.

PRINTED TEXT: Acts 2:1-4, 14a, 29-33, 37-39, 44, 45.

Acts 2:1-4, 14a, 29-33, 37-39, 44, 45

1 And when the day of Pentecost was fully come, they were all with one accord in one place.

2 And suddenly there came a sound from heaven as of a rushing mighty wind, and it filled all the house where they were sitting.

3 And there appeared unto them cloven tongues like as of fire, and it sat upon each of them.

4 And they were all filled with the Holy Ghost, and began to speak with other tongues, as the Spirit gave them utterance.

. . . .

14a But Peter, standing up with the eleven, lifted up his voice, and said unto them.

. . . .

29 Men and brethren, let me freely speak unto you of the patriarch David, that he is both dead and buried, and his sepulchre is with us unto this day.

30 Therefore being a prophet, and knowing that God had sworn with an oath to him, that of the fruit of his loins, according to the flesh, he would raise up Christ to sit on his throne;

31 He, seeing this before, spake of the resurrection of Christ, that his soul was not left in hell, neither his flesh did see corruption.

32 This Jesus hath God raised up, whereof we all are witnesses.

33 Therefore being by the right hand of God exalted, and having received of the Father the promise of the Holy Ghost, he hath shed forth this, which ye now see and hear.

. . . .

37 Now when they heard this, they were pricked in their heart, and said unto Peter and to the rest of the apostles, Men and brethren, what shall we do?

38 Then Peter said unto them, Repent, and be baptized every one of you in the name of Jesus Christ for the remission of sins, and ye shall receive the gift of the Holy Ghost.

39 For the promise is unto you, and to your children, and to all that are afar off, even as many as the Lord our God shall call.

. . . .

44 And all that believed were together, and had all things common;

45 And sold their possessions and goods, and parted them to all men, as every man had need.

GOLDEN TEXT: Then Peter said unto them, Repent, and be baptized every one of you in the name of Jesus Christ for the remission of sins, and ye shall receive the gift of the the Holy Ghost.—Acts 2:38.

The Story of Christian Beginnings (Acts)
Unit 1: Beginnings in Jerusalem (Lessons 1-4)

Lesson Aims

After this lesson a student should be able to:

1. Be diligent in learning the apostles' teaching from the Holy Bible.

2. Consider the abilities God has given him or her, and use them vigorously in God's service.

Lesson Outline

INTRODUCTION

    A. About Spirits

    B. Lesson Background

I. COMING OF THE SPIRIT (Acts 2:1-4)

    A. The Sound of His Coming (vv. 1, 2)

    B. The Sign of His Coming (v. 3)

    C. The Result of His Coming (v. 4)

II. MESSAGE OF THE SPIRIT (Acts 2:14a, 29-33)

    A. Prophecy of David (vv. 14a, 29-31)

    B. Prophecy Fulfilled (vv. 32, 33)

III. RESULT OF THE MESSAGE (Acts 2:37-39, 44, 45)

    A. Question and Answer (vv. 37-39)

       Acting on the Evidence

    B. New Way of Life (vv. 44, 45)

CONCLUSION

    A. The Spirit and Power

    B. The Changing, Changeless Church

    C. Prayer

    D. Thought to Remember

Visual 2 of the visuals packet reveals the scope of God's promise in the gospel. The visual is shown on page 21.

Introduction

Who has seen the wind?
  Neither you nor I,
But when the trees bow down their tops
  The wind is passing by.

The wind is invisible, but that does not mean it is not real and powerful. We see results of it. We also hear the sound of it and feel its breath on our faces. If the wind is strong, its force is felt on the whole body.

The Greek language uses the same word to mean either wind or spirit. This reminds us that a spirit is somewhat like a wind. We do not see him, but sometimes we plainly see the results of what he does.

A. About Spirits

We know very little about spirits. Being neither visible nor tangible, they elude scientific investigation. But we can learn a little about them from the Bible.

Angels are spirits (Hebrews 1:14). Usually unseen, they take visible forms when it suits their purpose. In the lesson text for last week we read of two of them who appeared as men (Acts 1:10, 11). The New Testament does not tell us that bad spirits take visible forms, but sometimes they take possession of living human beings. For example, a demon robbed one man of sight and speech (Matthew 12:22). Of course the Holy Spirit, the Spirit of God, does nothing but good. He is the Spirit who has a major part in this lesson study.

B. Lesson Background

Last week we read that Jesus rose from the dead, taught His disciples at different times and places during forty days, and then rose from the Mount of Olives to Heaven. He told His disciples to go into all the world and preach the gospel to every creature. But He told them to wait in the city of Jerusalem till the Holy Spirit would come to them with power from on high. In our text today we shall read of the coming of the Spirit.

I. Coming of the Spirit (Acts 2:1-4)

The Holy Spirit was coming. Jesus had promised it. He had told the apostles to wait for it (Acts 1:4, 5). Waiting and praying, they must have thought often of Jesus' promises. The Spirit would be their comforter, their encourager. He would teach them all things; He would remind them of what Jesus had said (John 14:26). He would guide them into all truth; He would glorify Jesus (John 16:13, 14). So for ten days they waited. Then the Spirit came.

A. The Sound of His Coming (vv. 1, 2)

1. And when the day of Pentecost was fully come, they were all with one accord in one place.

The word *Pentecost* means *fiftieth.* That was the Greek name given to the Jewish festival that came on the fiftieth day after the Sabbath of the Passover celebration (Leviticus 23:15, 16). The Old Testament calls it the feast of weeks (Exodus 34:22) because it came seven weeks after the Passover.

They seems to mean the apostles, for they are mentioned at the end of chapter 1. The *place* where they were is not named here. From other Scriptures we learn that the apostles "abode" in an upper room in Jerusalem (Acts 1:13), but "were continually in the temple" (Luke 24:53). This seems to mean they slept in the upper room, but spent much of their waking time in the temple, where the big courtyard provided room for other believers to gather with the apostles and join in their prayers (Acts 1:14, 15). Probably the *place* mentioned in our text was in the temple. A big crowd promptly gathered there (v. 6).

2. And suddenly there came a sound from heaven as of a rushing mighty wind, and it filled all the house where they were sitting.

This does not indicate that any wind was felt or that anything was blown away; there was only *a sound* like that of a swift and powerful wind. It came from the sky above, and *it filled all the house where they were sitting.* This *house* may have been one of the porches of the temple, open on the side toward the wide court of the temple where a crowd could gather.

B. The Sign of His Coming (v. 3)

3. And there appeared unto them cloven tongues like as of fire, and it sat upon each of them.

As there was a sound of wind without any wind (v. 2), so also there was the appearance of fire without any fire. No fuel was being burned; the apostles were not scorched when something that looked like fire *sat upon each of them.* Instead of *cloven tongues* the *American Standard Version* has "tongues parting asunder." The *New International Version* reads, "They saw what seemed to be tongues of fire that separated and came to rest on each of them." Perhaps we should visualize something that looked like a big flame dividing into twelve flames that rested on the apostles. How big were those flame-like tongues? We are not told; but surely they were big enough to be seen by everyone in the crowd that gathered, and big enough to point out the apostles as the center of this amazing event.

C. The Result of His Coming (v. 4)

4. And they were all filled with the Holy Ghost, and began to speak with other tongues, as the Spirit gave them utterance.

In our time the word *ghost* has come to be used of imaginary phantoms supposed to float about in graveyards and haunt old houses. Most English versions therefore speak of the *Holy Spirit* rather than the *Holy Ghost.* Even the *King James Version* usually translates the word *pneuma* as *spirit;* but when the word *holy* is with it, that version translates *the Holy Ghost.*

How to Say It

ANANIAS. An-uh-*nye*-us.
SAPPHIRA. Suh-*fye*-ruh.
SHEOL. *She*-ol.

When the sound like wind was heard and the tongues like fire were seen, the unseen Holy Spirit filled the apostles. As Jesus had put it in His promise (Acts 1:5), they were baptized in the Holy Spirit. They were submerged, covered. So completely were they under the Spirit's influence that He *gave them utterance*, gave them speech, in *other tongues,* in different languages that were unknown to them. Verses 5-13 tell more about this phenomenon. Though these languages were unknown to the speakers, each language was known to some of the hearers. Hearing the wind-like sound that filled the house where the apostles were, people came quickly to see what was going on. These people included Jews from many nations. They had come to Jerusalem for the feast of Pentecost. Now men of many nations were hearing the languages of their homelands, and they were amazed. They recognized the speakers as men of Galilee, a province not noted for breadth of culture. But here some Galileans were speaking the languages of Parthia and Media and Elam, of Egypt and Crete and Arabia. That was astounding. True, some jokers scoffed that the speakers must be drunk. But those who understood knew they were hearing about "the wonderful works of God." We are not told what works were described; but it is easy to suppose the apostles were reporting some of the marvelous miracles of Jesus, some of His matchless teaching, the facts of His wonderful resurrection.

II. Message of the Spirit (Acts 2:14a, 29-33)

Whatever the apostles were saying in different languages, it was part of the Spirit's message. It served to get the attention of the people, and to turn their thoughts to God. Now came the time for the heart of the message; and it glorified Jesus, as Jesus had said the Holy Spirit would do (John 16:14).

A. Prophecy of David (vv. 14a, 29-31)

14a. But Peter, standing up with the eleven, lifted up his voice, and said unto them.

Had the twelve apostles scattered among the people, speaking to different national groups? We are not told; but if they had been scattered they now came together. Eleven of them stopped talking, and Peter spoke as the Spirit guided him.

Peter stated that the apostles were not drunk, but that God was fulfilling the prophecy of Joel 2:28, 29, which promised that He would pour out His Spirit on His servants, causing them to prophesy (Acts 2:14-18). Then Peter announced that God had raised Jesus from the dead (Acts 2:22-24). He quoted David's words from Psalm 16:10: "You will not abandon me to the grave, nor will you let your Holy One see decay" (see Acts 2:25-27, *New International Version*). The *King James Version* has "hell" instead of "the grave," but the Greek has *hades* and the Hebrew of the psalm has *sheol*. Both these terms mean the place of the dead, and sometimes mean the grave, rather than Hell. The quotation from the psalm provides the basis for Peter's words in verse 29.

29. Men and brethren, let me freely speak unto you of the patriarch David, that he is both dead and buried, and his sepulchre is with us unto this day.

It is plain that the words quoted from the psalm do not refer to David himself. God did leave David in the grave, and his body did decay. His tomb was still there for all to see. What David wrote in the psalm referred to someone else, not to David.

30. Therefore being a prophet, and knowing that God had sworn with an oath to him, that of the fruit of his loins, according to the flesh, he would raise up Christ to sit on his throne.

David was a prophet, inspired to speak God's message, not his own. He knew God had promised that one of David's descendants would be the Christ, the Messiah, the Redeemer and King of God's people.

31. He, seeing this before, spake of the resurrection of Christ, that his soul was not left in hell, neither his flesh did see corruption.

As a prophet, David wrote of the Christ who was to come centuries later. He wrote that God would not leave the Christ in the grave, and that the Christ's body would not decay.

B. Prophecy Fulfilled (vv. 32, 33)

32. This Jesus hath God raised up, whereof we all are witnesses.

Now Peter turned from the prophecy to its fulfillment. As a matter of fact, God did raise Jesus from the dead. He was not left in the grave; His body did not decay. The twelve apostles could testify positively that Jesus was alive after His death—and who would call them liars as they stood there with those spectacular flames upon them?

33. Therefore being by the right hand of God exalted, and having received of the Father the promise of the Holy Ghost, he hath shed forth this, which ye now see and hear.

Besides being raised from the dead, Jesus had been received into Heaven and given a place at God's right hand. Furthermore, Jesus had *received of the Father the promise of the Holy Ghost*, and had passed that promise on to His disciples (Acts 1:4, 5). To fulfill that promise, Jesus had sent the Holy Spirit with a sound like that of wind and with flames that looked like fire. Verses 34 and 35 add David's prophecy that the Christ would be thus exalted: "The Lord said unto my Lord, Sit thou on my right hand, until I make thy foes thy footstool" (see Psalm 110:1). David's prophecies of the Christ were fulfilled in Jesus, and this makes it plain that Jesus is the Christ. So Peter's sermon soared to its climax: "Let all the house of Israel therefore know assuredly, that God hath made him both Lord and Christ, this Jesus whom ye crucified" (v. 36, *American Standard Version*).

III. Result of the Message
(Acts 2:37-39, 44, 45)

It was clear that something supernatural was happening. The sound like wind, the tongues like fire, the many languages—none of these could be explained in ordinary ways. Then with clear reasoning Peter showed that Jesus was the Christ foretold by David. The people were convinced.

A. Question and Answer (vv. 37-39)

37. Now when they heard this, they were pricked in their heart, and said unto Peter and to the rest of the apostles, Men and brethren, what shall we do?

Have you ever been pricked in your heart by realizing that you have done a monstrous wrong? If you have, you know something of how the people felt on that Day of Pentecost. All their lives they had been hoping and praying for the Messiah to come. Now He had come, and they had killed Him (v. 36). God had raised Him from the dead. He was living and ruling from Heaven. His kingdom would go on; but what would become of His killers? Was there any possible way to escape the destruction they deserved? In desperation they cried, *What shall we do?*

38. Then Peter said unto them, Repent, and be baptized every one of you in the name of Jesus Christ for the remission of sins, and ye shall receive the gift of the Holy Ghost.

Peter answered with two commands and a promise. The first command was to *Repent*.

Renounce your rejection of the Christ, grieve over His murder, vow to follow Him faithfully for the rest of your life. The second command was *be baptized*. Wash away your sin (Acts 22:16). Separate yourself from sin: die to it. Be buried in baptism and rise to a new life (Romans 6:1-4). Do this *in the name of Jesus Christ* to secure *the remission of sins*. Then came the promise: *Ye shall receive the gift of the Holy Ghost*. The Holy Spirit, the Spirit of God, who has produced all the wonders of Pentecost—He will be given to you; He will live in you; He will give you power for what you have to do as followers of the Messiah. Some students take a different view of this promise. They think the promised gift is not the Spirit himself, but the forgiveness and salvation the Spirit gives. We need not debate the exact meaning of the promise, for as a matter of fact the Spirit does live in every faithful follower of Christ (1 Corinthians 6:19, 20). He does give power for Christian service. This does not mean He gives all Christians the same power He gave to the apostles. Not all speak in "other tongues." Not all do miracles of healing. Not all are inspired to speak God's truth without error. The Spirit gives different abilities to different people (1 Corinthians 12). Each Christian should recognize his or her ability, and use it well (Romans 12:6-8).

39. For the promise is unto you, and to your children, and to all that are afar off, even as many as the Lord our God shall call.

Sinners are not all beyond redemption. Even murderers of the Christ can be saved in the way just outlined. Such a promise is extended to sinners everywhere: those in Jerusalem at Pentecost, their *children* of all generations to come, and *all that are afar off*. The promise is for all who will accept it. At that time, Peter may have thought that last phrase meant all the faraway Jews; but the Spirit who inspired Peter knew it meant people of all nations, even such depraved heathen as are described in Romans 1:28-32. Acts 10 records how Peter afterward learned to understand as the Spirit did.

What we have been reading is only a summary of Peter's sermon at Pentecost. He had much more to say (v. 40). Many hearers were persuaded. On that day three thousand of them accepted his word and were baptized (v. 41).

ACTING ON THE EVIDENCE

A real-estate partnership in which Allen Fehr was involved was audited by the Internal Revenue Service in 1985. The IRS ruled that Mr. Fehr owed $17,632 in taxes for four years, so he sent in a check for that amount. His canceled check came back with his next bank statement.

visual 2

"The promise is unto you, and to your children, and to all that are afar off, even as many as the Lord our God shall call."

But in the next six months, Fehr received four increasingly threatening, computer-generated letters demanding that he pay his taxes and adding penalties to the bill. Each time he phoned the IRS and explained the facts.

Over a period of two years' time, more than twenty-five letters and phone calls were exchanged between Fehr and the IRS. Even copies of the canceled check did not change the IRS's position! Finally, when the IRS threatened to seize all of his property, Fehr decided to tell a newspaper columnist who printed his sad story of governmental intransigence. Soon a human being at the IRS sent an apology and a check! It seems that Fehr had overpaid his taxes by nearly one thousand dollars!

Not everyone is as immune to the reasonable presentation of facts as some government agencies and their computers. When the first gospel sermon was preached, at least three thousand persons believed the evidence of Jesus' death and resurrection and acknowledged the implication of those facts for their personal salvation. The facts are still the same for us, as well. The sensible person will respond to them in the same way as those first Christians did.

—C. R. B.

B. New Way of Life (vv. 44, 45)

44. And all that believed were together, and had all things common.

Visitors in Jerusalem for the feast of Pentecost included people from all over Palestine and from many foreign countries as well. As we noted, three thousand of them accepted Jesus and were baptized (v. 41). Most of these did not go back to faraway homes, but stayed in Jerusalem to be taught by the apostles (v. 42). Naturally some of them were soon out of money, but others were willing to share. No one thought that what he had was his own; it was the common property of the group (Acts 4:32).

45. And sold their possessions and goods, and parted them to all men, as every man had need.

With unlimited generosity, people even sold their property and shared the proceeds. They turned the money over to the apostles to be distributed to the needy (Acts 4:34, 35). No one had to go out and get a job instead of staying in school and being taught by the inspired apostles. The wisdom of this intensive schooling became apparent when persecution drove the disciples out of Jerusalem. Then they were so well trained that they could be preachers of the gospel wherever they went (Acts 8:1, 4).

The believers had all things common (v. 44), but this was not communism in the modern sense of the term. The funds were given voluntarily: no one was required to give (Acts 5:4). Ananias and Sapphira were punished, not for keeping part of their money, but for lying about it (Acts 5:1-11). Not all of the property owners sold their property. A woman named Mary kept her house in Jerusalem and shared the house instead of the money (Acts 12:12). With this happy sharing and intensive teaching, the church continued to grow day by day (Acts 2:47).

Conclusion

What a tremendous lesson this is! How many conclusions might be drawn from it! Let's think a little about the Holy Spirit's coming in power.

A. The Spirit and Power

Himself unseen, the Spirit came with a roaring sound and a spectacular sight. To the apostles He gave amazing powers: power to talk in languages that they had not learned, power to heal the sick by miracles, power to teach God's word with never an error.

However, the Spirit did not give them power to get rich and live in luxury. Nor did He give them power to escape suffering and persecution. Soon the apostles were imprisoned and beaten (Acts 5:17-42). Soon James was killed (Acts 12:1, 2). Old tradition says all the apostles except John died for their faith.

A few disciples besides the apostles received miraculous powers (Acts 8:5-8), but more did not. Most of us today have powers that are not miraculous. Nearly all of us have power to learn. Are we studying God's Word enough to make use of that power? Some of us have power to teach. Are we teaching, or are we turning away because it is too much work? Some of us have executive ability. Are we leading or loafing in the church? Some of us have a fine ability to be helpful to others. Are we using or wasting it? Most of us have power to give of our means. Are we giving liberally? See Romans 12:6-8. And if our faithful service brings persecution, do not all of us share the apostles' power to endure it?

B. The Changing, Changeless Church

Pentecost is often called the birthday of the church. The newborn church was a robust infant, but an infant does not live like a ten-year-old, and a ten-year-old does not live like an adult. Some features of the young church soon changed, but some things never change.

Members of the first church abandoned jobs and businesses to listen daily to the apostles' teaching. That practice was not continued in other congregations, but no church will prosper and grow unless it gives attention to teaching.

Members of the first church "were together, and had all things common" (Acts 2:44). That was not a general practice among other churches at that time; but in all times and everywhere, Christians do share with brethren in need.

People came into the fellowship of the first church by being convinced that Jesus is the Christ, by turning away from their sins to obey Him, by being baptized in His name for the forgiveness of sins. In the fellowship of the church they continued steadfastly in Christian worship and life (Acts 2:42). These are some of the things that never change.

C. Prayer

How gracious You are, our heavenly Father! For all of us sinners You have provided a way of salvation, and You have given us the Holy Spirit and the power to walk in that way. Continue to give us strength and courage, Father, we pray, that we may be faithful forever. In Jesus' name we pray. Amen.

D. Thought to Remember

The Holy Spirit provides power, but it is useless unless we use it.

Home Daily Bible Readings

Monday, Sept. 4—Baptized With the Spirit (Matthew 3:7-12)
Tuesday, Sept. 5—Empowered by the Spirit (Luke 1:8-17)
Wednesday, Sept. 6—Speaking With Boldness (Acts 4:27-31)
Thursday, Sept. 7—Direct Communication (Acts 13:6-12)
Friday, Sept. 8—Holy Spirit and Joy (Acts 13:47-52)
Saturday, Sept. 9—Insight From the Spirit (Luke 2:22-32)
Sunday, Sept. 10—The Spirit as Teacher (1 Corinthians 2:10-16)

Learning by Doing

This page contains an alternate lesson plan emphasizing learning activities. Classes desiring such student involvement will find these suggestions helpful.

Learning Goals

As students participate in today's class session, they should:

1. List the special actions of the Holy Spirit that made possible the establishment of the church.

2. Outline Peter's sermon on the Day of Pentecost.

3. Describe how Peter's hearers became Christians and how these first Christians functioned as a church in Jerusalem.

4. Choose which of the categories of persons mentioned in Acts 2 they are most like, and decide what implications this has for their lives this week.

Into the Lesson

Before class prepare enough slips of paper to provide one slip for everyone who will attend your class. On one-third of the slips write, "A sermon that pointed me in a new direction." On another third of the slips write, "The day I became a Christian." On the final third write, "A time when I shared the gospel."

Give a slip to each member as he or she enters the classroom. To begin the session, instruct the members to stand and either (a) find another person whose slip has the same phrases as his own or (b) trade slips with another class member and then find someone whose slip matches his new one.

Once everyone has a partner, the couples should spend three minutes talking with each other about the topic on their slips. Then ask volunteers to share briefly their responses with the whole class.

Tell the class that the necessity of preaching and conversion are two of the major topics dealt with in our lesson text.

Into the Word

Allow class members to examine the entire second chapter of Acts in this session. Accomplish this by dividing the chapter into four sections:

1. What the Holy Spirit did (vv. 1-13)

2. What Peter claimed (vv. 14-36)

3. How the people responded (vv. 37-41)

4. What the first church was like (vv. 42-47)

Write these four headings on the chalkboard before class. Have the verses that correspond to each heading read aloud to the class by four class members. Then tell your students that they may choose a learning activity to help them explore one of the paragraphs further. Describe each of these options to your class:

1. Write a newspaper account describing the events recorded in verses 1-13.

2. Make a simple outline of Peter's sermon recorded in verses 14-36.

3. Imagine that you were in the audience when Peter preached his sermon. Then write a diary entry in which you explain your response to his message. Especially consider verses 37-41 as you write.

4. Make a comparison chart. For each of the first church's activities described in verses 42-47, list a comparable activity that you see happening in the church today.

If you have at least twelve class members, have them divide into four groups so that each of the four activities is undertaken. Allot about ten minutes for these activities. Then let each group share with the whole class so all will have an overview of Acts 2.

Into Life

Suggest to the class that three categories of people can be identified in this chapter:

• Messengers with a mission.

• Hearers who needed to repent.

• Believers who were helped by their fellowship with one another.

Ask, "Who from Acts 2 falls into each category?"

Then have your students return to the same groups in which they did their Bible study. Suggest to them that in their groups they tell each other in which category they believe they belong, and why.

Read the following three questions aloud as your students listen with their eyes closed and heads bowed:

1. Do you have a mission to share the gospel with someone? Whom could you tell this week?

2. Does any obstacle stand in the way of your salvation? Do you need to take any of the steps Peter commanded in Acts 2?

3. What place have you taken in the local fellowship of believers? Are you doing your part to make your congregation effective in the service of Christ?

Let's Talk It Over

The questions on this page are designed to encourage review of the lesson Scriptures and to promote discussion of the lesson by the class. The answers provided are only discussion starters. Let your class talk it over from there.

1. Scoffers were present on the Day of Pentecost. Today also there are those who scoff at the Christian faith. How should a Christian respond to them?

It is noteworthy that Peter calmly and briefly dismissed the scoffers' suggestion that he and the other apostles were drunk (see Acts 2:14, 15). Obviously he was not intimidated or distracted by the scoffers. Likewise, a Christian today can remain calm in the face of senseless comments that scoffers may make. Certainly there is no need for a Christian to feel intimidated, for while the foes of Christianity enjoy giving the impression that they are too learned and intelligent to believe the Bible, God has plainly declared such persons to be fools (see Psalm 14:1). Like Peter, a Christian today should not allow scoffers to distract him or her from fulfilling the important task of proclaiming the gospel to those who hunger for it.

2. Peter was throwing down a challenge to unbelievers of his time and subsequent times when he declared, "This Jesus hath God raised up, whereof we all are witnesses" (Acts 2:32). How is this so?

In a sense Peter could have been saying, "The burden of proof is on you. Prove, if you think you can, that we are mistaken in saying that Jesus has been raised from the dead." There was much that verified the apostles' claim: the absence of Jesus' body from the tomb, the many eyewitness reports of His resurrection appearances, the amazing transformation of the frightened apostles into bold spokesmen for the gospel, and the miraculous display of the Holy Spirit's power in and through the apostles on Pentecost. Unbelievers have endeavored in vain to offer naturalistic explanations for these facts. The apostles' claim remains unshaken.

3. Confronted with their sin of having killed the Messiah whom God had sent, the convicted hearers on Pentecost cried out, "What shall we do?" How can we lead non-Christians to voice that same question?

Like Peter, our aim should be to lead people to see that Jesus is the Christ and the one whom God sent to save us from our sins. To great numbers of people Jesus is nothing more than a no-

table teacher, who founded one of the major religions of the world many centuries ago. We must demonstrate that Jesus is the unique Son of God, that He suffered and died on the cross to atone for the sins of mankind, and that His resurrection from the dead is a historical reality. In this way we can point out that Jesus Christ is inescapable. Every human being must either accept the atonement for sin that He provided on the cross or reject it and face the terrible consequences. When confronted with these realities many will be ready to ask, "What shall I do?"

4. How can we tell if a specific talent we possess is an innate ability or a gift of the Holy Spirit? Does it really matter?

A person may have possessed an excellent talent for singing or teaching or leadership long before he or she became a Christian. To speak of such talent as a gift of the Holy Spirit following one's coming to Christ would therefore seem erroneous. And yet, when one consciously dedicates such a well-developed talent to God, the Holy Spirit can surely give it a new level of beauty and power. Sometimes new Christians discover personal abilities for use in the church, without a previous awareness that they had such abilities. Again, it may be that the abilities were there all along, but the Holy Spirit has enabled the believers to recognize them, and He helps the believers to develop them and employ them effectively in Christian work.

5. The lesson writer points out that not all of the practices of the church in Jerusalem were adopted by congregations elsewhere. Changes were made. What principle should guide a congregation in changing any of its practices?

Obviously we are not free to change the doctrines or practices that the New Testament clearly sets forth for the church to follow. Where changes may be needed is in connection with man-made customs and methods used in evangelism, teaching, worship, etc. Some church customs may no longer serve the purpose for which they originally came into existence. Changes need not be made merely for the sake of change; but if a church perceives that a certain tradition or method has passed beyond usefulness, that church would do well to change it.

Healing and Preaching

DEVOTIONAL READING: Acts 3:18-26.

LESSON SCRIPTURE: Acts 3:1—4:31.

PRINTED TEXT: Acts 3:1-8; 4:5-12.

Acts 3:1-8

1 Now Peter and John went up together into the temple at the hour of prayer, being the ninth hour.

2 And a certain man lame from his mother's womb was carried, whom they laid daily at the gate of the temple which is called Beautiful, to ask alms of them that entered into the temple;

3 Who, seeing Peter and John about to go into the temple, asked an alms.

4 And Peter, fastening his eyes upon him with John, said, Look on us.

5 And he gave heed unto them, expecting to receive something of them.

6 Then Peter said, Silver and gold have I none; but such as I have give I thee: In the name of Jesus Christ of Nazareth rise up and walk.

7 And he took him by the right hand, and lifted him up: and immediately his feet and ankle bones received strength.

8 And he leaping up stood, and walked, and entered with them into the temple, walking, and leaping, and praising God.

Acts 4:5-12

5 And it came to pass on the morrow, that their rulers, and elders, and scribes,

6 And Annas the high priest, and Caiaphas, and John, and Alexander, and as many as were of the kindred of the high priest, were gathered together at Jerusalem.

7 And when they had set them in the midst, they asked, By what power, or by what name, have ye done this?

8 Then Peter, filled with the Holy Ghost, said unto them, Ye rulers of the people, and elders of Israel,

9 If we this day be examined of the good deed done to the impotent man, by what means he is made whole;

10 Be it known unto you all, and to all the people of Israel, that by the name of Jesus Christ of Nazareth, whom ye crucified, whom God raised from the dead, even by him doth this man stand here before you whole.

11 This is the stone which was set at nought of you builders, which is become the head of the corner.

12 Neither is there salvation in any other: for there is none other name under heaven given among men, whereby we must be saved.

GOLDEN TEXT: Peter said, Silver and gold have I none; but such as I have give I thee: In the name of Jesus Christ of Nazareth rise up and walk.—Acts 3:6.

> ### The Story of Christian Beginnings
> ### (Acts)
> #### Unit 1. Beginnings in Jerusalem
> #### (Lessons 1-4)

Lesson Aims

After participating in this lesson one should be able to:

1. Remember and retell the story told in our text and adjacent verses.

2. Critically and fairly examine both one's own opinions and the opinions of others.

3. Hold the truth with firmness and tell it with courage.

4. Be strong but courteous in discussion with those who disagree with him or her.

Lesson Outline

INTRODUCTION
    A. The Popular Jesus
    B. Lesson Background
 I. MIRACLE (Acts 3:1-8)
    A. Man in Need (vv. 1-3)
    B. Meeting a Need (vv. 4-7)
      More Than Expected
    C. Joy and Praise (v. 8)
 II. TROUBLE (Acts 4:5-7)
    A. Hostile Rulers (vv. 5, 6)
    B. Hostile Question (v. 7)
III. INSPIRED ANSWER (Acts 4:8-12)
    A. Inspired Preacher (v. 8)
    B. Good Deed (v. 9)
    C. Good Doer (vv. 10-12)
CONCLUSION
    A. Negative
    B. Positive
    C. Prayer
    D. Thought to Remember

The relative importance of material wealth and the power of Jesus is illustrated by visual 3 of the visuals packet. See page 29.

Introduction

It's pleasant to be popular—but it's dangerous. Jesus said, "Woe unto you, when all men shall speak well of you! for so did their fathers to the false prophets" (Luke 6:26).

False prophets in ancient times abandoned the truth to say what people liked to hear, and disaster came to prophets and people together. In our time, a popular entertainer may value ap-plause more than decency. A popular congressman may think bringing federal funds to his district is better than balancing the budget. A popular preacher may put the offering ahead of the truth. But William Cullen Bryant, a poet, put it well:

> Truth, crushed to earth, shall rise again;
> The eternal years of God are hers;
> But Error, wounded, writhes in pain,
> And dies among his worshippers.

A. The Popular Jesus

Surely Jesus was the most popular teacher in Israel. People flocked to Him from all over the country (Matthew 4:25). His miraculous healing was a magnet that drew them (Matthew 4:24), as was His teaching (Luke 5:1, 15).

But Jesus was not popular with "all men." The elite of Israel opposed Him strongly: the highly educated men, the priests, the ruling class, the accredited teachers. Finding no other way to counter Jesus' popularity, the rulers killed Him.

B. Lesson Background

Jesus warned His disciples, "The servant is not greater than his lord. If they have persecuted me, they will also persecute you" (John 15:20). After Jesus went back to Heaven, His followers found that they had inherited both His popularity and His opposition. Their miracles, their good way of life, and their teaching won the favor of the people in Jerusalem, and the young church grew rapidly (Acts 2:43-47). But Jesus' followers gained no favor with the rulers, as we see in our text.

I. Miracle
(Acts 3:1-8)

"Many wonders and signs were done by the apostles" (Acts 2:43). This is repeated with emphasis in Acts 5:12-16. Luke does not pause to discuss many of these miracles, but a sample is recorded clearly in our text.

A. Man in Need (vv. 1-3)

1. Now Peter and John went up together into the temple at the hour of prayer, being the ninth hour.

The ninth hour was midafternoon. We would say at three o'clock. This was one of the daily times of public prayer in Jerusalem. Apparently *Peter and John* were going to attend the prayer meeting. It seems that they and other disciples spent much of their time in Solomon's porch (v. 11; Acts 5:12). This was a roofed colonnade at the east side of the big outer court, the temple court that was open to all the people, Jews and heathen alike. The prayer meeting was held in a smaller court inside the big one. This inner court was on a higher level and surrounded by a wall with signs warning Gentiles that they would be killed if they entered.

2. And a certain man lame from his mother's womb was carried, whom they laid daily at the gate of the temple which is called Beautiful, to ask alms of them that entered into the temple.

This unfortunate man had been crippled from birth. He was now more than forty years old (Acts 4:22). He was so crippled that he could not work for a living. He could not even walk, but family members or friends *carried* him each day and *laid* him at *the gate . . . which is called Beautiful.* It was a good place for a beggar, for many worshiping people are generous people. The gate was a huge one. Its doors, made of brass and richly decorated, towered seventy-five feet above the crippled man. If Peter and John were coming from Solomon's porch, they came naturally to this gate, for it was on the east side of the inner court.

3. Who, seeing Peter and John about to go into the temple, asked an alms.

There is nothing here to indicate that the beggar knew *Peter and John.* He asked them for a donation just as he asked anyone else who passed him to *go into the temple.*

B. Meeting a Need (vv. 4-7)

4. And Peter, fastening his eyes upon him with John, said, Look on us.

Probably most persons who responded to the beggar's plea just dropped small coins without stopping. But this pair stopped, not only looking at the man, but also asking him to look at them.

5. And he gave heed unto them, expecting to receive something of them.

We can imagine that the man looked up very eagerly. If these two wanted to call special attention to their giving, probably the gift would be a big one. And indeed it was, though the man as yet had no inkling of the nature of it.

6. Then Peter said, Silver and gold have I none; but such as I have give I thee: In the name of Jesus Christ of Nazareth rise up and walk.

Perhaps the beggar's heart sank at Peter's first words. He could expect no more than a copper coin if the giver had no *silver and gold.* But how his heart must have leaped as Peter finished! We can only guess how much this man knew about Jesus, but surely he had heard much. Only months earlier, Jesus had received a tumultuous welcome in Jerusalem (Luke 19:28-40). He had come into the temple and "had looked round about upon all things" (Mark 11:11). The next

---

How to Say It

ANNAS. *An*-nus.
CAIAPHAS. *Kay*-uh-fus or *Kye*-uh-fus.
PHARISEES. *Fair*-ih-seez.
SADDUCEES. *Sad*-you-seez.
SANHEDRIN. *San*-huh-drun or San-*heed*-run.

---

day He had driven the crooked merchants from the temple court (Mark 11:15-17). The crippled man at the Beautiful gate must have seen some of the excitement. He must have heard more from passers-by at the gate and from those who carried him to and from his begging place. Among other things, he must have heard of marvelous miracles. Now *in the name of Jesus Christ of Nazareth* he was called to *rise up and walk.* Hope must have surged within him at the word.

7. And he took him by the right hand, and lifted him up: and immediately his feet and ankle bones received strength.

Peter helped with his hand as well as his voice. The lame man made an effort, and suddenly his useless feet were as useful as anyone's.

MORE THAN EXPECTED

Insurance fraud hurts us all. Some people have taken to staging traffic collisions and then filing claim for imaginary—although very expensive—injuries. But it doesn't always work as planned.

Recently, the driver of a car on the freeway swerved in front of a semitrailer truck. Since trucking companies insure their vehicles and because large trucks cannot stop quickly, it seemed like a perfect insurance fraud setup. But it backfired. Instead of merely bumping the car from behind, the truck jackknifed and overturned on top of the car, crushing it. One of the car's occupants was killed. The driver of the car and the two surviving passengers were arrested on suspicion of insurance fraud and faced the prospect of being charged with murder as well. All three got more—and worse!—than they expected.

The lame man at the temple gate wished only for a gift of a few coins, perhaps enough to help his family pay for his care. But because those whom he asked for help were God's servants, he received far more—and far better!—than what he had sought!

When with pure hearts we seek blessing from God, we shall not be disappointed. Perhaps what we receive will be different from what we expected. It may be far better than what we sought.

—C. R. B.

C. Joy and Praise (v. 8)

8. And he leaping up stood, and walked, and entered with them into the temple, walking, and leaping, and praising God.

The man did not need time to learn to walk. He was perfectly capable of *walking, and leaping* as well. He had to go up a flight of stairs to the inner court of the temple, but stairs were no obstacle to his nimble feet. He was also *praising God*, and certainly not in whispers. Imagine the amazement of people gathering for the prayer meeting. Day by day they had seen this man at the gate, helpless and hopeless—but look at him now! (vv. 9, 10).

This man had been laid at the temple gate daily (v. 2). Peter and John and other apostles must have passed him again and again. He may have been there when Jesus had come into the temple and looked around (Mark 11:11). After that, Jesus had taught daily in the temple (Luke 19:47). Naturally we wonder why this lame man had not been healed before.

We can only answer that Peter and John were directed by the Holy Spirit. It was the Spirit, not the apostles, who chose the time for the miracle. No doubt He chose a time when the miracle would most accomplish its purpose.

This reminds us again of the purpose of miracles. They did help needy people, but they were not done for that purpose alone. If they had been, God could have healed from Heaven without any help from Peter and John.

The miracle had two other purposes. First, it caught the attention of many people. Second, it showed that God's power was with the apostles, and this encouraged people to believe that the apostles spoke God's truth.

Don't we still need to attract attention to the gospel of Christ? Don't we still need to convince people that the gospel is really God's message? Of course we do. Then why aren't miracles as common now as they were in the days when the church was just beginning? Perhaps for the same reason that teenagers and adults don't receive the same care that little babies do. The miracles were a special help for a newborn church while it was just getting started.

II. Trouble
(Acts 4:5-7)

Prayer meeting in the inner court may have been a bit unsettled that day. When it ended, the healed man clung to Peter and John as they went back to Solomon's porch. People from the prayer meeting went along. Others saw the excitement and came running. To the gathering crowd Peter explained that he and John had not done this miracle. It was the work of God, who did it to glorify Jesus, His Son whom men had crucified but God had raised from the dead. Peter declared that Jesus is the Christ foretold by the prophets. He urged the people to repent, to have their sins blotted out, to become followers of the crucified and risen Messiah (Acts 3:11-26). But before the sermon was finished, there was trouble.

The priests in charge of the temple were angry and grieved because Peter was lauding Jesus. They were doubly grieved because he was proclaiming the resurrection of the dead. The priests were Sadducees (Acts 5:17), and Sadducees did not believe in any resurrection (Acts 23:8). So they came and brought with them the chief of the temple police and put the apostles in jail (Acts 4:1-3).

A. Hostile Rulers (vv. 5, 6)

5, 6. And it came to pass on the morrow, that their rulers, and elders, and scribes, and Annas the high priest, and Caiaphas, and John, and Alexander, and as many as were of the kindred of the high priest, were gathered together at Jerusalem.

The day was near its end when Peter and John were arrested, so the two were jailed for the night (Acts 4:3). The next day the men in authority were assembled to deal with the prisoners. These verses seem to describe the Sanhedrin, sometimes called the council, which was both legislature and supreme court. It included not only the chief priests, but also *elders* and *scribes*. Probably some of these were Pharisees instead of Sadducees. They believed in resurrection, but not the resurrection of Jesus. They had opposed Jesus throughout His ministry. They envied His popularity; they were angry because He did not respect all their traditions; they were annoyed because He exposed their hypocrisy. The priests must have been angry because Jesus twice had cleansed the temple court of the crooked livestock market allowed by the priests (John 2:13-16; Luke 19:45, 46). Pharisees and Sadducees had their differences and disputes, but they had cooperated to condemn Jesus and persuade the Roman governor to have Him crucified. Now they would cooperate to compel Jesus' followers to stop talking about Him.

B. Hostile Question (v. 7)

7. And when they had set them in the midst, they asked, By what power, or by what name, have ye done this?

The Sanhedrin had about seventy members. They were seated in a semicircle, and probably dressed in elaborate robes. It was an assembly well designed to intimidate a pair of fishermen from Galilee, who now were placed *in the midst,* with hostile eyes on three sides of them. These seventy men were the rulers. Power among the Jews belonged to them, and they certainly had not authorized these Galilean visitors to lecture in the temple. Then *by what power, or in what name,* had these impudent fishermen done what they had done?

III. Inspired Answer
(Acts 4:8-12)

The assembly of rulers was impressive, but Peter and John were not intimidated. Their power came from a higher authority, and they knew it.

A. Inspired Preacher (v. 8)

8. Then Peter, filled with the Holy Ghost, said unto them, Ye rulers of the people, and elders of Israel.

Jesus had given His apostles instructions and a promise for times like this. When they were called into court for obeying Him, they were not to sit up all night to plan their defense. The words would be given to them. Jesus said, "It is not ye that speak, but the Spirit of your Father which speaketh in you" (Matthew 10:17-20). Now Peter was *filled with the Holy Ghost,* and he spoke the words that the Spirit gave him. Courteously he acknowledged that the hostile men before him were in fact *rulers* and *elders* of his people, the Jews.

B. Good Deed (v. 9)

9. If we this day be examined of the good deed done to the impotent man, by what means he is made whole.

These words exposed the awkward position of the rulers. They had arrested two men, kept them in jail overnight, and brought them into court to be questioned, not for some crime done or alleged, but for a deed that was unquestionably good, the healing of a helpless man. The seventy must have been squirming uncomfortably as Peter continued.

C. Good Doer (vv. 10-12)

10. Be it known unto you all, and to all the people of Israel, that by the name of Jesus Christ of Nazareth, whom ye crucified, whom God raised from the dead, even by him doth this man stand here before you whole.

Peter was very glad to answer the question of verse 7. He wanted not only those judges, but also everyone in Israel, to know that *Jesus*

Christ of Nazareth had supplied the power for the healing done in His name. Peter added a reminder that those very judges had condemned Jesus to death and had persuaded the Roman governor to order Him crucified. God had reversed their decision and had brought Jesus back from the dead. If the rulers were squirming before, this certainly did not make them any more comfortable.

11. This is the stone which was set at nought of you builders, which is become the head of the corner.

Psalm 118 sings praises to God for His gracious help. Among other things, it sings of a stone that was rejected by builders, but nevertheless became the chief cornerstone of a structure. The psalm adds, "This is the Lord's doing; it is marvelous in our eyes" (vv. 22, 23). Directed by the Holy Spirit, Peter said that stone is Jesus. The judges in the council were the builders that rejected Jesus. Nevertheless, Jesus is the chief cornerstone of a magnificent structure, His church (Ephesians 2:19-22). "This is the Lord's doing; it is marvelous in our eyes."

12. Neither is there salvation in any other: for there is none other name under heaven given among men, whereby we must be saved.

So the Holy Spirit and Peter brought the speech to its end. Jesus not only is the power that gave healing to this helpless man; He is also the only hope of salvation for all mankind, including the judges who condemned Him.

The rulers must have known from the beginning that they had no case against Peter and John. They hoped to frighten those Galilean fishermen into silence. But their effort had backfired. The fishermen were unabashed; the rulers were frustrated and probably furious. But what could they do? To add to their discomfort, the healed man also had been brought into court. There he stood, a living refutation of anything that might be said against Jesus (v. 14). Those judges themselves knew him well. Often they had seen him lying helpless in his begging place. There was no way to deny that a notable miracle had been done (v. 16). The rulers could only go on with their effort to scare the apostles.

Silver and gold have I none; but such as I have give I thee: In the name of Jesus Christ of Nazareth rise up and walk. —Acts 3:6

The Name of JESUS

visual 3

With threats they "commanded them not to speak at all nor teach in the name of Jesus" (vv. 15-18). Peter and John may have been scared, but they were not silenced. Firmly they replied, "Judge for yourselves whether it is right in God's sight to obey you rather than God. For we cannot help speaking about what we have seen and heard" (vv. 19, 20, *New International Version*).

When Peter and John were released from custody, they and other disciples joined in prayer—not for freedom from trouble, but for courage to go on with their work and for continuing miracles to show that God was with them (Acts 4:21-31). Their prayer was answered: they did go on with their work, the miracles did continue—and more trouble came, as we shall see next week.

Conclusion

Two messages for us leap from the pages of this lesson: one on the negative side, and one on the positive.

A. Negative

On the negative side, we must not fall into the sin of the rulers. They clung tenaciously to their mistaken opinion even when it drove them to murder. Jesus was not one of them; He did not respect all their traditions. Therefore they reasoned that He could not be the Christ, the Son of God. This seemed so obvious that they shut their eyes to the evidence and plunged into battle against Him. Unable to win with reason or argument, they used their political power to kill Him. Then they tried to stop His followers from speaking about Him.

Of course you and I are not in a position to commit legal murder if someone disagrees with us, and of course we are not so unreasonably set in our opinions anyway. But don't you know someone who is? A man stoutly declares that the kind of car he drives is the best kind there is, and he is not even listening when you extol the virtues of your car. A lady is likewise devoted to one brand of shoes, or tea, or laundry detergent. She will not even consider any other brand. A teacher presents his theory of evolution as if it were a group of well-known facts. If you raise a question, he brands you as ignorant. A preacher says his understanding of the millennium is the one and only correct one. Your opinion is silly, he says. A campaign orator tells outrageous lies about his opponent. If you raise an objection, he shouts you down.

Even with the Holy Spirit in our hearts and the Holy Bible in our hands, most of us Christians know we are not so fully inspired as Peter was. We can be wrong, but we can learn. It is helpful to be as critical of our own opinions as we are of an opponent's opinions. It helps if we keep our minds open and try to understand the positions of those who disagree with us. It helps if we look for points of agreement as well as points of disagreement. We can learn, if we are willing to learn.

B. Positive

On the positive side, when our position is clearly the one taught by God's Word, we need to hold it as firmly as Peter and John held theirs. We must cling to truth and right, regardless of the consequences. We must speak out for the Lord, though it brings upon us the scorn of scholars, the threats of foes, and the pity of friends. So let us join the apostles in prayer for courage rather than comfort.

At the same time, let us note that the apostles spoke courteously, even to those who were not courteous. Likewise Jesus spoke with courtesy to Pilate, the governor who pronounced Him innocent and ordered Him to be crucified. Let us follow in the footsteps of our Lord so that we, "speaking the truth in love, may grow up into him in all things, which is the head, even Christ" (Ephesians 4:15).

C. Prayer

Heavenly Father, how good it is to have in our hands the Holy Bible, Your inspired Word! How good it is to see the noble example of our Savior and His saints of ancient times! By Your grace may we find the truth You want us to know. Then may we hold it firmly and proclaim it boldly, for Jesus' sake. In His name, amen.

D. Thought to Remember

Be sure you're right; then go ahead.

Home Daily Bible Readings

Monday, Sept. 11—Commissioned to Heal and Preach (Matthew 10:1-10)
Tuesday, Sept. 12—A Crippled Hand Made Well (Mark 3:1-6)
Wednesday, Sept. 13—Sent Forth (Mark 16:9-16)
Thursday, Sept. 14—Gifts From the Spirit (1 Corinthians 12:1-11)
Friday, Sept. 15—Wondrous Healing (Acts 5:12-16)
Saturday, Sept. 16—Healing Explained (Acts 3:9-16)
Sunday, Sept. 17—Fearless Preaching (Acts 4:13-20)

Learning by Doing

This page contains an alternate lesson plan emphasizing learning activities. Classes desiring such student involvement will find these suggestions helpful.

Learning Goals

As students participate in today's class session, they should:

1. List the feelings and thoughts of the main characters found in the account recorded in Acts 3 and 4.

2. Compare the hostility of the Jerusalem council toward the apostles Peter and John with antagonism Christians may encounter today when sharing the gospel.

3. Decide at least one specific way to respond to this antagonism when they encounter it.

Into the Lesson

Before the class session begins, write each of the following phrases on slips of paper, one phrase per slip:

1. Places in the *world* that are *hostile* to the gospel of Christ.

2. Places in our *country* that are *hostile* to the gospel of Christ.

3. Places in our *community* that are *hostile* to the gospel of Christ.

A. Places in the *world* that are *friendly* to the gospel of Christ.

B. Places in our *country* that are *friendly* to the gospel of Christ.

C. Places in our *community* that are *friendly* to the gospel of Christ.

Begin today's session by dividing your class into groups of between five and seven students each. Give each of the groups a different slip of paper, using the phrases from numbers 1-3 above. If possible, provide each group with a large sheet of paper and a felt-tip marker. Each group is to jot down ideas in response to its assigned phrase. The "places" need not necessarily be specific geographical names; they could be labels for situations, such as "any class taught by my university English professor."

After allotting five minutes to complete the assignment, ask the groups to display their lists. Read a few items from each one.

Then repeat the process, this time assigning the groups the phrases lettered A-C. After five more minutes, read a few of the items from each group's list.

Tell the class that from the church's earliest days there were those who were hostile to the gospel. Nevertheless, amid that hostility, the gospel flourished. Today's study can provide some clues as to how we can spread the gospel today, even in the face of those who are antagonistic toward the claims of Christ.

Into the Word

Use the same groups for Bible study that were formed for the introductory activity. Each of the groups should assume the identity of one of the main characters in the biblical event we are studying today: Peter, John, the lame man, the Jewish authorities, and the citizens of Jerusalem. Each group is to try to determine the thoughts and feelings of its assigned character when the events in today's Scripture text occurred.

Tell your class members to listen carefully as volunteers read aloud the following five paragraphs of Scripture: Acts 3:1-10, 11-16; 4:1-7, 8-12, 13-22. Then ask each group to answer this question: "What did our character think and feel when the events recorded in these paragraphs occurred?"

You may want to make a chart on your chalkboard. Down the left side of the board, list all the characters or groups named above. Across the top write each of the Scripture references. Allot six or eight minutes for the groups to discuss the question. Then complete your chart as a spokesman from each group reports to the whole class.

Into Life

Discuss the following questions:

1. What can we do that will draw attention to the message of Jesus?

2. What can we learn from Peter and John regarding—
   a. the content of our message to a lost world?
   b. the best way to present the message?
   c. how to react when the message is resisted?

Challenge class members to think of the situation in their lives when sharing the gospel is most difficult. Can they find any clues in the example of Peter and John to help them to know how they should react?

If you have time, allow class members to share their personal reaction with others in their small groups. Then they can pray for each other in their groups before the class is dismissed.

Let's Talk It Over

The questions on this page are designed to encourage review of the lesson Scriptures and to promote discussion of the lesson by the class. The answers provided are only discussion starters. Let your class talk it over from there.

1. Like Peter, the church today has something better than silver and gold to give people in need. Why is this important to stress?

Our society clings to the idea that any problem can be solved if enough money is spent on it. However, crime, illicit drug usage, teenage pregnancy, and homelessness are among our society's problems that seem unaffected by great sums of money poured into programs to combat them. It is clear that until people themselves are changed, no amount of money is likely to resolve these social problems. The church holds the key to such change. It is found in the gospel with its promise of "a new creation" (2 Corinthians 5:17, *New International Version*). Of course the church should be generous in aiding with money those who suffer from homelessness, hunger, and illness; but we should never fail to share the transforming gospel of Christ.

2. The first question directed to Peter and John by the members of the council—"By what power, or by what name, have ye done this?"—exhibits their extreme prejudice. How do critics of the church today demonstrate a similar prejudice?

The authorities began with this question instead of making a public acknowledgment of the beneficent miracle the apostles had performed. Among themselves they admitted that these apostles had performed a great miracle (Acts 4:16), but there is no record of their crediting Peter and John with being God's instruments of healing. So today the church's critics frequently seem inclined to regard Christians as meddlers and troublemakers, while virtually ignoring the vast amount of good that is done by believers who feed the hungry, minister to the sick, teach the illiterate, and comfort the brokenhearted. The fact that this is done in the name of Jesus Christ, as Peter's miracle was, seems to make it less acceptable in the world's eyes.

3. In today's atmosphere of tolerance for religious diversity, it may seem unbecoming of Christians to insist that Jesus Christ is the exclusive way to salvation and eternal life. How shall we respond to this?

If it be unbecoming for us to insist that Jesus Christ is the only Savior and Lord, it is nevertheless the only way we can be true to the New Testament. We remember that Jesus himself said, "I am the way, the truth, and the life: no man cometh unto the Father, but by me" (John 14:6). Peter's declaration in Acts 4:12 echoes Jesus' statement. We know that we cannot compel others to conform to our faith, and so we respect their right to believe as they have been taught. But we would betray Jesus Christ if we regarded any other religious leader as being on the same level as He.

4. Regarding spiritual matters, the lesson writer observes that "it is helpful to be as critical of our own opinions as we are of an opponent's opinions." What is involved in accomplishing this?

The first step one must take is to make a distinction between one's opinions and biblical teachings. When people confuse their opinions with biblical truths, they can be subject to Jesus' charge against the scribes and Pharisees, who were "teaching for doctrines the commandments of men" (Matthew 15:9). Second, each must recognize that his or her opinions are not on a higher level of importance than the opinions of others. Each of us may have prejudices or "blind spots" that influence the opinions we hold, thus rendering them fallible. Third, we need to "loosen up" regarding matters of opinion and recognize the other person's right to an opinion that differs from our own. If we can do this, we will avoid stirring up unnecessary conflict.

5. Why is it important for us who are Christians to be courteous and gracious toward persons with whom we disagree?

If we employ rudeness or ridicule, we might win an argument with another individual over some point of doctrine or opinion, but in so doing we might also drive the other person farther away from the truth and from us. It is a hollow victory to "win the battle, but lose the war." Christians more than any other people should be able to contend for the truth in a courteous manner. We should be known for gracious words and a generous spirit, even when others are abusive toward us in their speech. Jesus was characterized by such restraint in the face of abuse (1 Peter 2:23), and so should we be.

Obedient to the Spirit

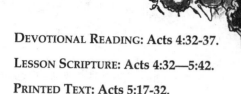

DEVOTIONAL READING: Acts 4:32-37.

LESSON SCRIPTURE: Acts 4:32—5:42.

PRINTED TEXT: Acts 5:17-32.

Acts 5:17-32

17 Then the high priest rose up, and all they that were with him, (which is the sect of the Sadducees,) and were filled with indignation,

18 And laid their hands on the apostles, and put them in the common prison.

19 But the angel of the Lord by night opened the prison doors, and brought them forth, and said,

20 Go, stand and speak in the temple to the people all the words of this life.

21 And when they heard that, they entered into the temple early in the morning, and taught. But the high priest came, and they that were with him, and called the council together, and all the senate of the children of Israel, and sent to the prison to have them brought.

22 But when the officers came, and found them not in the prison, they returned, and told,

23 Saying, The prison truly found we shut with all safety, and the keepers standing without before the doors: but when we had opened, we found no man within.

24 Now when the high priest and the captain of the temple and the chief priests heard these things, they doubted of them whereunto this would grow.

25 Then came one and told them, saying, Behold, the men whom ye put in prison are standing in the temple, and teaching the people.

26 Then went the captain with the officers, and brought them without violence: for they feared the people, lest they should have been stoned.

27 And when they had brought them, they set them before the council: and the high priest asked them,

28 Saying, Did not we straitly command you that ye should not teach in this name? and, behold, ye have filled Jerusalem with your doctrine, and intend to bring this man's blood upon us.

29 Then Peter and the other apostles answered and said, We ought to obey God rather than men.

30 The God of our fathers raised up Jesus, whom ye slew and hanged on a tree.

31 Him hath God exalted with his right hand to be a Prince and a Saviour, for to give repentance to Israel, and forgiveness of sins.

32 And we are his witnesses of these things; and so is also the Holy Ghost, whom God hath given to them that obey him.

GOLDEN TEXT: Peter and the other apostles answered and said,
We ought to obey God rather than men.—Acts 5:29.

Lesson Aims

After this lesson a student should be able to:
1. Repeat the story told in the lesson text.
2. Resolve to obey God rather than men.
3. Try harder to win others to Christ.

Lesson Outline

INTRODUCTION
  A. Easy Decisions
  B. Lesson Background
I. IN AND OUT OF JAIL (Acts 5:17-21a)
  A. In Jail (vv. 17, 18)
    A Jealous Heart
  B. Out of Jail (vv. 19-21a)
II. IN CUSTODY AGAIN (Acts 5:21b-26)
  A. Court in Session (v. 21b)
  B. Prisoners Missing (vv. 22-24)
  C. Prisoners Recaptured (vv. 25, 26)
III. COURT IN ACTION (Acts 5:27-32)
  A. Accusation (vv. 27, 28)
  B. Defense (v. 29)
    A Higher Power
  C. Explanation (vv. 30-32)
CONCLUSION
  A. Questions
  B. Prayer
  C. Thought to Remember

Visual 4 of the visuals packet highlights a principle Christians must follow when facing moral or ethical choices. See page 35.

Introduction

Sometimes the Christian way is perplexing. For example, when John the Baptist was explaining the meaning of repentance, he said, "He that hath two coats, let him impart to him that hath none" (Luke 3:10, 11). So I am a bit disturbed when I look in my closet and see two coats. Does that mean my repentance is not real? My bank account is disturbing too. Jesus said, "Lay not up for yourselves treasures upon earth" (Matthew 6:19). Should I close that bank account and give the money to the poor? But on the other hand, Paul recognized the principle that "children ought not to lay up for the parents, but the parents for the children" (2

Corinthians 12:14). Isn't it reasonable and right to put aside a part of my earnings so my children will not have to pay my rent when I have to live in a nursing home?

A. Easy Decisions

On the other hand, some decisions are easy even if they are costly. If the neighbors have to flee their burning home in a snowstorm, we take them in even if our house is full already. If we have a chance to make a million by defrauding our friends, or even by defrauding our enemies, we turn it down. Fraud has no place in the Christian life.

Likewise easy was the apostles' decision. Jesus told them to tell His gospel to the world; the rulers of Jerusalem told them to shut up. The apostles said, "We ought to obey God rather than men" (Acts 5:29). It was the only choice possible for Christians, even if they were flogged for it (Acts 5:40).

B. Lesson Background

Last week we read that Peter and John were arrested and ordered not to talk about Jesus anymore. When they were released, other disciples joined them in prayer. They did not pray that none of them would be arrested. They prayed for boldness to keep on spreading Jesus' message, and they prayed for continuing miracles to show God's presence and power (Acts 4:29, 30). Both prayers were answered. "They spake the word of God with boldness" (Acts 4:31), and miracles were multiplied (Acts 5:12-16). "And believers were the more added to the Lord, multitudes both of men and women" (Acts 5:14). This did not please the rulers who had ordered the apostles to stop their preaching.

I. In and Out of Jail (Acts 5:17-21a)

The apostles made no secret of their disobedience to the rulers. Their meeting place was Solomon's porch, a huge roofed colonnade in the big outer court of the temple. They also took their ministry of healing out into the streets of Jerusalem, and people from other cities came flocking to be healed. No one, ruler or commoner, could fail to see what was going on (Acts 5:12-16).

A. In Jail (vv. 17, 18)

17. Then the high priest rose up, and all they that were with him, (which is the sect of the Sadducees,) and were filled with indignation.

The high priest was the highest official among the Jews. *They that were with him* were

visual 4

other leaders among the priests. These belonged to *the sect of the Sadducees*. Though they conducted the ceremonies of worship, they were more political and less religious than the Pharisees, who were proud of their devotion to the Scriptures and to the traditions of their sect.

These leaders were not used to having their orders ignored. The apostles were ignoring their order very obviously, and the priests *were filled with indignation*. Their indignation was fueled also by their jealousy. The Greek word may have either meaning, and many versions translate it this way.

18. And laid their hands on the apostles, and put them in the common prison.

Peter and John had been arrested before, but now it seems that all twelve of *the apostles* were seized. They were put *in the common prison* like common criminals, to be held till the ruling council, the Sanhedrin, could deal with them.

A JEALOUS HEART

Few sins are more common than jealousy, and Christians must constantly guard against it. One may be jealous of another's singing voice, exceptional teaching or speaking ability, or simply the winsomeness of a godly personality. We all know that jealousy is not an attitude of a godly heart.

The Sadducees were among the spiritual leaders of Israel, but they were jealous of the apostles. The apostles were honest and sincere men doing God's will by bringing people to Christ.

Jealousy should have no place in those who are committed to the service of God. It only disrupts the work. May our concern be that God alone will receive glory and praise for the talents He has given to each of us.   —C. R. B.

B. Out of Jail (vv. 19-21a)

19, 20. But the angel of the Lord by night opened the prison doors, and brought them forth, and said, Go, stand and speak in the temple to the people all the words of this life.

The supreme rulers of the Jews put these men in prison, but the supreme Ruler of Heaven and earth sent His messenger to release them. Obviously the guards were helpless; possibly they were blinded so they could see nothing, or possibly they were sleeping on duty. It seems that they did not know the prisoners were gone. Had they known, surely they would have reported it. It seems that the guards were totally ignored as the angel led a dozen men out of the prison and sent them to go on with their work of preaching the gospel *in the temple,* under the very noses of the hostile authorities.

21a. And when they heard that, they entered into the temple early in the morning, and taught.

Again the record does not pause to deal with details. What time of night was it when the apostles were released? Did they have time to eat and sleep before they went back to their teaching? We can only wonder about such questions. But *early in the morning,* as soon as anyone would be there to hear, the apostles went back into the temple and kept on teaching God's message to all who would listen.

II. In Custody Again
(Acts 5:21b-26)

Of course the amazing escape could not long be hidden, and of course the apostles could not hope to teach very long without another interruption. Perhaps that was why they started early in the morning. In the meantime, the high priest and his associates were going about their business, never suspecting that their prisoners were no longer in jail.

A. Court in Session (v. 21b)

21b. But the high priest came, and they that were with him, and called the council together, and all the senate of the children of Israel, and sent to the prison to have them brought.

The high priest and his associates lost no time in pressing their case. Messengers were sent to summon the members of the Sanhedrin, the ruling council of Israel. Probably the call went out on the same day when the apostles were arrested, but it was not until the following day when the council assembled. This was a full meeting: *all the senate* means all the elders. The high priest thought the apostles were a serious threat, and he meant to deal with them with all the power of his government. So the whole council assembled, and probably the high priest explained the reason for the meeting. Then the bailiffs were sent to bring the prisoners before the court.

B. Prisoners Missing (vv. 22-24)

22, 23. But when the officers came, and found them not in the prison, they returned, and told, saying, The prison truly found we shut with all safety, and the keepers standing without before the doors: but when we had opened, we found no man within.

What a shock! A bit of routine duty turned into an amazing puzzle. At the prison everything seemed to be in perfect order. The doors were properly shut and locked. The guards on duty were alert. But the jail was empty!

24. Now when the high priest and the captain of the temple and the chief priests heard these things, they doubted of them whereunto this would grow.

Everyone was flabbergasted. There may have been a lot of sound and fury: questioning of the bailiffs who had found the jail empty, questioning of the guards who had been on duty at the prison, shouted charges and fearful denials. The priests must have been furious; the guards must have been frightened. But no one could explain what had happened. There had been an impossible escape, and priests and police were afraid that was only a beginning. What would this affair grow into? They could not guess.

C. Prisoners Recaptured (vv. 25, 26)

25. Then came one and told them, saying, Behold, the men whom ye put in prison are standing in the temple, and teaching the people.

Someone brought news to the agitated gathering. Perhaps it was one of the policemen on duty in the temple. Was it good news or bad? The prisoners had not gone beyond reach of the police—but possibly the priests would have been happier if the escapees had gone to Egypt or Rome. They were right there in the temple, and right back at the work of telling about Jesus. As the priests saw it, that was bad!

26. Then went the captain with the officers, and brought them without violence: for they feared the people, lest they should have been stoned.

How to Say It

SANHEDRIN. *San*-huh-drun or San-*heed*-run.
ARCHEGOS (Greek). are-kay-*goss*.
ARCHE (Greek). are-*kay*.
AGO (Greek). *ah*-go.
SADDUCEES. *Sad*-you-seez.
PHARISEES. *Fair*-ih-seez.
GAMALIEL. Guh-*may*-lih-ul.

The captain probably was chief of the temple police. He took a group of officers and went to arrest the apostles again. Those prisoners had caused so much trouble that the police might have been inclined to treat them roughly, but *they feared the people*. The apostles were teaching a crowd of people, and the many helpful miracles made the people favor the speakers (Acts 5:13). These were excitable people, and riots were easily started. The crowd might get rough with the police if the police would get rough with the apostles. So the police approached with respect, and the apostles let themselves be arrested.

III. Court in Action
(Acts 5:27-32)

At last the seventy assembled judges had the prisoners before them. Nothing was said about the mysterious escape from jail the previous night—or if something was said, it is not recorded. Perhaps the judges preferred not to say or hear anything about it. They proceeded promptly with the case at hand.

A. Accusation (vv. 27, 28)

27. And when they had brought them, they set them before the council: and the high priest asked them.

This court did not proceed as a modern one does, with an unbiased presiding judge who listens while two lawyers develop the case, one for the prosecution and one for the defense. The duty of all the seventy judges was to examine witnesses and develop the case both against and for the defendants. But in this case, the judges themselves were accusers and prosecutors. The high priest made their accusation.

28. Saying, Did not we straitly command you that ye should not teach in this name? and, behold, ye have filled Jerusalem with your doctrine, and intend to bring this man's blood upon us.

The high priest really brought two accusations against the apostles. The two were related, but not the same.

First, the high priest said the apostles had disobeyed the plain command of the council. Two leaders among them, Peter and John, had been commanded "not to speak at all nor teach in the name of Jesus" (Acts 4:18). The command had been given *straitly*: that is, strictly, plainly, strongly. In fact, it had been accompanied by threats, though the threats are not described in the record (Acts 4:17, 21). In spite of a plain order and forceful warning, the apostles had *filled Jerusalem* with their forbidden teaching.

They had openly defied the command of the ruling council, right in the court of the temple, and all Jerusalem knew about it.

Second, the high priest said that the apostles intended to bring Jesus' blood upon the members of that council: that is, they meant to show that those judges were guilty of killing Jesus. The high priest ignored the fact that he and his helpers had cried, "His blood be on us, and on our children" (Matthew 27:25). But now, with the apostles on trial before them, the high priest and all the council wanted to deny that they were responsible for Jesus' death.

B. Defense (v. 29)

29. Then Peter and the other apostles answered and said, We ought to obey God rather than men.

The apostles did not deny that the charges were true. They had indeed disobeyed the command of the ruling council, and they had indeed shown that the members of that council were guilty in the death of Jesus. Their defense was simple. They were obeying the order of a higher authority. The Lord God Almighty had told them what to say, and no court on earth had a right to countermand His order.

A HIGHER POWER

The Twelve-Step program of Alcoholics Anonymous has helped a multitude of people overcome their addiction to alcohol. The first three "steps" state: "We admitted we were powerless over alcohol—that our lives had become unmanageable. [We] came to believe that a Power greater than ourselves could restore us to sanity. [We] made a decision to turn our will and our lives over to the care of God as we understood Him."

An illegitimate power—alcohol or any other drug, undisciplined carnal desire, or another person—can cause us untold suffering. In fact, anything or anyone who comes between us and God will lead us into disaster.

In the early days of the church the apostles had to choose whether or not they would submit to the religious authorities, whose demands conflicted with what God commanded of them. Yielding to the power of the authorities could have guaranteed the apostles' physical safety, but it would have jeopardized their spiritual well-being, since it would have caused them to violate God's will.

Their decision to obey God reflected their obedience to a higher power. It also attested to their personal integrity, for God's command coincided with their own experience in seeing the risen Christ.   —C. R. B.

C. Explanation (vv. 30-32)

30. The God of our fathers raised up Jesus, whom ye slew and hanged on a tree.

These were plain facts that the apostles had been declaring, and now they declared them again. *The God of our Fathers,* Jehovah, the one real and living God, the Almighty—He had raised Jesus from the dead. The apostles knew this beyond the shadow of a doubt, and they announced it at every opportunity. And before God raised up Jesus, these members of the council killed Him. True, Roman soldiers drove the nails and raised the cross, and they did it at the order of the Roman governor, Pilate. But Pilate gave the order because these rulers insisted.

31. Him hath God exalted with his right hand to be a Prince and a Saviour, for to give repentance to Israel, and forgiveness of sins.

God not only raised Jesus from the dead, but also *exalted* Him. *With his right hand* means by His own authority and power. The *New International Version* reads "to his own right hand," meaning that God exalted Jesus by giving Him a place of honor at God's right hand, as stated in Mark 16:19. Either of these translations expresses a truth, and the Greek text can have either meaning.

The English word *prince* comes from Latin and originally meant one who takes the first part. The Greek word is *archegos,* which originally meant a first leader or chief leader (from *arche,* first, and *ago,* to lead). Such is the place God had given to Jesus, though men crucified Him. As Paul puts it, "Wherefore God also hath highly exalted him, and given him a name which is above every name: that at the name of Jesus every knee should bow, of things in heaven, and things in earth, and things under the earth; and that every tongue should confess that Jesus Christ is Lord, to the glory of God the Father" (Philippians 2:9-11). See also Ephesians 1:20-22.

God exalted Jesus not only to be a chief leader, but also to be a *Saviour.* Part of what that means is seen in the phrases that follow. *To give repentance to Israel* means to give Israel an opportunity and a reason to repent, to give an urging to turn away from wrongdoing and become obedient to the chief leader, Jesus. To those who grasp that opportunity, those who do repent and obey Jesus, He gives *forgiveness of sins.* Compare Peter's inspired call in Acts 2:38. Thus sinners are saved from sin and death; thus they become children of God.

32. And we are his witnesses of these things; and so is also the Holy Ghost, whom God hath given to them that obey him.

How can doomed sinners know that Jesus is ready to give them repentance and forgiveness? He has sent *his witnesses* to tell them; He has sent the very apostles that the angry rulers were trying to silence. Another witness is *the Holy Ghost.* Not only was He guiding the apostles in all they said; He was also showing His presence by giving the power to work countless miracles (Acts 5:12-16).

Thus the prisoners not only confessed their disobedience to the supreme court, but also repeated it. Again they spoke of Jesus; again they accused those rulers of killing Him. Now in addition they accused them of trying to silence Jesus' witnesses, and in so doing to silence the Holy Spirit himself.

We can imagine the fury of the rulers. The next verse says, "They were cut to the heart, and took counsel to slay them." The killers of Jesus proposed to kill His witnesses. That would silence them!

In that heated moment, one cooler head prevailed. Wise old Gamaliel had the prisoners removed while he reasoned with his colleagues. There had been other troublesome movements, he said. He mentioned two of them specifically. In each case the leader had died, and the movement had faded away. So Jesus' movement would fade, said Gamaliel, if it was not of God. If it was of God, he warned, these judges would find themselves fighting against God, and they could not win (vv. 33-39).

This calm reasoning prevailed—to a degree. The rulers gave up their plan to kill the apostles, but they gave them a beating and repeated the command "that they should not speak in the name of Jesus." So the prisoners were released, "and daily in the temple, and in every house, they ceased not to teach and preach Jesus Christ" (vv. 40-42).

Conclusion

"We ought to obey God rather than men." Hardly anyone will dispute that, except one foolish enough to say in his heart, "There is no God" (Psalm 14:1). This general agreement gives rise to a number of questions.

A. Questions

1. If men order us to disobey God, of course we obey God as the apostles did. But in most circumstances, God tells us to obey the laws of men (1 Peter 2:13-15). Then why are our jails filled to overflowing?

2. God says we ought to renounce stealing and work to earn a living and to share with the needy (Ephesians 4:28). Then why do we have shoplifters in stores, bankers defrauding depositors, and graft in government?

3. God says one should earn his own living (2 Thessalonians 3:10-12). Then why is there a growing craze for something for nothing? Why is gambling legalized in more and more places? Why do states themselves have lotteries? Why do even churches conduct gambling games?

4. God says fathers should bring up children in the nurture and admonition of the Lord, but without provoking them to wrath (Ephesians 6:4). Then why do we need officers and courts to deal with parents who abuse their children?

5. God says husband and wife are one flesh (Genesis 2:24). He says He hates divorce (Malachi 2:16). Then why are the divorce courts so busy?

Wise men can multiply answers to any of these questions, but there is one answer that fits them all: Many people are not obeying God.

What can be done about it? Stricter laws? Stiffer penalties? More police? These may be needed; but with or without them, it is very hard to get heathen to act like Christians. For more obedience to God, His people today can do nothing better than what the apostles did long ago: "They ceased not to teach and preach Jesus Christ" (Acts 5:42), and "the number of the disciples was multiplied" (Acts 6:1).

B. Prayer

Heavenly Father, how good it is that You have provided a plain way of repentance and forgiveness! May we not only enjoy these ourselves, but also bring many others to enjoy them with us. In Jesus' name, amen.

C. Thought to Remember

"We ought to obey God rather than men."

Home Daily Bible Readings

Learning by Doing

This page contains an alternate lesson plan emphasizing learning activities. Classes desiring such student involvement will find these suggestions helpful.

Learning Goals

Students in today's class session should:

1. List the main events recorded in Acts 5:17-32 and decide the motivation behind the actions of the main characters.

2. Identify one area in their lives in which they find it difficult to "obey God rather than men," and ask God to help them be obedient this week.

Into the Lesson

Ask your students to turn to their neighbors and speak for ninety seconds about one of these topics (write them on your chalkboard before members arrive):

1. A time when I visited a jail

2. A time when someone in authority punished me

3. A time when I took an unpopular stand.

After three minutes, everyone will have had an opportunity to share. Allow three volunteers to share their comments with the whole class, one for each topic.

State that today's lesson will show that the apostles taught about Jesus in spite of the command of the authorities to stop doing it. The apostles were punished by being put in jail. Even though their behavior was unpopular with some, the apostles continued it. As your students examine today's Scripture, they should decide why the apostles behaved as they did.

Into the Word

To set the stage for today's lesson, remind class members of the events in last week's lesson. Summarize the events recorded in Acts 4:32-36 and 5:1-11. Have a volunteer read Acts 5:12-16 aloud to the class. Then lead one of the following Bible-study activities:

Finish the story. Tell your students that you will continue reading from Acts 5, stopping at key points in the story. After each stop, your students should discuss how the story could continue from there, based on the happenings to that point.

Divide the class into groups of five to seven students each. After each stop, let the students discuss in their groups for three or four minutes. Then lead the whole class in discussion. As you do so, focus on the motivations of the main characters in the story.

Stop after these verses: 18, 20, 21, 23, 25, 28, 32.

Correct the order. Give each student a copy of the following list of statements and quotations. Working individually, the students are to arrange the items in chronological order. Have each student compare his or her list with another student's before you announce the correct order. (The numbers are included here for your reference.)

(4) "Go to the temple and preach the gospel."

(7) "The jail was locked, but no one was inside!"

(5) The apostles preached the gospel in the temple early in the morning.

(3) During the night an angel opened the doors of the jail and freed the apostles.

(11) "God raised Jesus from the dead, and wants to give forgiveness to Israel."

(2) The council put the apostles in jail.

(10) "We must obey God, not men."

(6) The officers went to the jail, but the apostles were not there.

(1) The high priest and his colleagues were extremely angry with the apostles.

(9) "We told you not to teach about Jesus."

(8) "The men you put in jail are teaching the people in the temple!"

After either activity, have a student read aloud the following verses: Acts 4:1-3, 7, 10, 13, 18-21; 5:12, 17-20, 27-29. Lead the class in discussing these questions: Why did the apostles behave as they did? What word would you choose to describe the apostles' behavior?

Into Life

Give each student a copy of the following reflection questions.

1. If an angel were to appear to you tonight with a directive from God, what would you guess the angel might tell you to do?

2. In what area of your life do you have difficulty obeying God rather than men? In matters having to do with finances? Use of time? Sources of entertainment? Business or work ethics? Controversial social issues? Something else?

Ask students to write down answers to each question for their personal reference only. If volunteers wish to share what they have written, let them do so. Then close the class session with a time of prayer.

Let's Talk It Over

The questions on this page are designed to encourage review of the lesson Scriptures and to promote discussion of the lesson by the class. The answers provided are only discussion starters. Let your class talk it over from there.

1. As the lesson writer shows in his comments of introduction for this lesson, there are times when we who are Christians must choose between seemingly conflicting principles of Scripture as we fulfill our obedience to God. How are we to handle such situations?

Sometimes our obligations to the church and to our family come into conflict. Then there are those occasional situations when our duty to tell the truth may seem to conflict with our responsibility to be forbearing and compassionate toward others' weaknesses. Biblical principles are not really contradictory, but we may have to choose between two or more of them. We must aim to choose that principle that will bring the richest benefit to the people with whom we are dealing. These situations are ones in which prayer for wisdom is particularly appropriate (see James 1:5).

2. The members of the Sanhedrin were surely thrown into confusion and embarrassment when they discovered that the imprisoned apostles had been freed and were back in the temple preaching and teaching about Jesus. How is this account indicative of what often happens to those who actively oppose the gospel?

How often men and governments have sought to destroy the gospel or at least hinder its spread, only to see their efforts end in pathetic failure! We think of Herod the Great's insane attempt to kill the child he regarded as a rival to the title, "King of the Jews." Soon afterward, however, Herod came to a pitiful end, while the child became a greater king than Herod could have imagined. Equally futile were the attempts of some of the Roman emperors to eradicate the Christian faith. In our time we have witnessed an almost incredible turnabout in the former Soviet Union. A nation in which biblical truth was sternly suppressed is now welcoming Bibles. Once again the gospel's foes have been thwarted.

3. After declaring their intentions "to obey God rather than men" (Acts 5:29), the apostles were beaten and warned again to halt their teaching "in the name of Jesus" (v. 40). Despite the warning, however, they taught and preached Jesus Christ "daily in the temple" (v. 42). How can we imitate their persistence?

What a tremendous surge in the growth of the kingdom of God would result if Christians everywhere were to say, "I am going to tell other people about Jesus Christ, and I am not going to let anyone or anything intimidate me." And this is surely possible. We are all capable of persistence, and many demonstrate that capability in various ways. One may say, "I am determined that I'm going to own a better car," or, "I will learn to use a computer or know the reason why." If we can persist in such mundane matters, surely we can focus this capacity for persistence on the loftiest objective of all: the winning of others to Jesus Christ.

4. Some political candidates speak out for "law and order" as though that were the most pressing issue of our time. How do you feel about that?

First Timothy 2:1-4 urges us to pray for governmental authorities and suggests that the general peace and quietness these rulers can promote will provide an atmosphere conducive to effective evangelism. It is easy to see how a society overrun by crime and violence would be one in which evangelistic work would be extremely difficult. So "law and order" is a Christian concern. At the same time we recognize that tougher laws and penalties, better equipped police forces, and larger prisons are inadequate solutions to the problem of lawlessness. People need to be changed, radically changed, and "grace and discipleship" are best suited to do that.

5. Paul tells Christians to rejoice in all situations in life (Philippians 4:4). James echoes this by calling on Christians to rejoice even in the face of trials (James 1:2). How can such things as open persecutions be a source of joy for a Christian?

We can rejoice over having this kind of opportunity to demonstrate our faith, for such testing develops perseverance. The apostles, when flogged by the council, departed rejoicing that they were counted worthy to suffer shame for Christ (Acts 5:41). We too can count it a blessing to be able to know the fellowship of sharing in Christ's sufferings (see Philippians 3:10).

Chosen to Serve

DEVOTIONAL READING: Acts 7:54—8:3.

LESSON SCRIPTURE: Acts 6:1—8:3.

PRINTED TEXT: Acts 6:1-14.

Acts 6:1-14

1 And in those days, when the number of the disciples was multiplied, there arose a murmuring of the Grecians against the Hebrews, because their widows were neglected in the daily ministration.

2 Then the twelve called the multitude of the disciples unto them, and said, It is not reason that we should leave the word of God, and serve tables.

3 Wherefore, brethren, look ye out among you seven men of honest report, full of the Holy Ghost and wisdom, whom we may appoint over this business.

4 But we will give ourselves continually to prayer, and to the ministry of the word.

5 And the saying pleased the whole multitude: and they chose Stephen, a man full of faith and of the Holy Ghost, and Philip, and Prochorus, and Nicanor, and Timon, and Parmenas, and Nicolas a proselyte of Antioch;

6 Whom they set before the apostles: and when they had prayed, they laid their hands on them.

7 And the word of God increased; and the number of the disciples multiplied in Jerusalem greatly; and a great company of the priests were obedient to the faith.

8 And Stephen, full of faith and power, did great wonders and miracles among the people.

9 Then there arose certain of the synagogue, which is called the synagogue of the Libertines, and Cyrenians, and Alexandrians, and of them of Cilicia and of Asia, disputing with Stephen.

10 And they were not able to resist the wisdom and the spirit by which he spake.

11 Then they suborned men, which said, We have heard him speak blasphemous words against Moses, and against God.

12 And they stirred up the people, and the elders, and the scribes, and came upon him, and caught him, and brought him to the council,

13 And set up false witnesses, which said, This man ceaseth not to speak blasphemous words against this holy place, and the law:

14 For we have heard him say, that this Jesus of Nazareth shall destroy this place, and shall change the customs which Moses delivered us.

GOLDEN TEXT: They set [the seven] before the apostles: and when they had prayed, they laid their hands on them.—Acts 6:6.

The Story of Christian Beginnings
(Acts)
Unit 2: Witnessing in Judea and Samaria
(Lessons 5-9)

Lesson Aims

After this lesson students should be able to:
1. Retell the two stories in our text.
2. Consider their own service for Christ.
3. Do better.

Lesson Outline

INTRODUCTION
    A. Little Pains and Big Pains
    B. Lesson Background
  I. A PROBLEM SOLVED (Acts 6:1-7)
    A. Problem (v. 1)
    B. Solution (vv. 2-4)
    Food Fights
    C. The Chosen Men (vv. 5, 6)
    D. Continuing Progress (v. 7)
  II. ANOTHER CONFLICT (Acts 6:8-10)
    A. New Miracle Worker (v. 8)
    B. New Opponents (v. 9)
    C. Defeated Opponents (v. 10)
 III. UNFAIR OPPOSITION (Acts 6:11-14)
    A. False Accusation (v. 11)
    B. False Arrest (v. 12)
    C. False Testimony (vv. 13, 14)
    So Many Ways to Lie
CONCLUSION
    A. Hurts Little and Big
    B. Are You Ready?
    C. Prayer
    D. Thought to Remember

Visual 5 of the visuals packet lists qualities needed by any who would hold a position of responsibility in the church. See page 46.

Introduction

Susanne had a little pain in her side. It hampered her swing, and her drive fell short. A friend joked that she was getting old, and Susanne joked right back.

The pain grew worse. At the ninth hole Susanne apologized and dropped out. A friend advised her to see a doctor, but she only laughed. "Nah. It'll go away."

The pain did go away, but it came back now and then. It never bothered Susanne at work, and not often at home. She gave up golf.

Susanne never liked housework. When the pain interfered with that, she got a girl to do it for her. But the little pain grew bigger and came more frequently.

At last Susanne did go to her doctor. She had to take time off for a series of tests. The doctor looked grim as he gave his report: "You have a tumor—a big one. I wish you had come to us a year ago."

A. Little Pains and Big Pains

Almost any church has a little pain now and then. It's a trivial thing—a complaint from one crank, grumbling in one Sunday school class, one teacher with some shady notions. We like to ignore it, hoping it will go away. Sometimes it does, but sometimes it comes back bigger than it was before. Sometimes we ignore a little pain till it becomes a big pain, and big trouble.

B. Lesson Background

The background of this lesson is seen in the lessons before it.

Lesson 1. Alive from the dead, Jesus told His disciples to take His message of salvation to the whole world—but first to wait for the Holy Spirit to come with power from on high. Then the Lord ascended to Heaven.

Lesson 2. Empowered by the Holy Spirit, the apostles in Jerusalem began to sound Jesus' call to repentance and salvation. Three thousand people responded in a day, and others responded in the days that followed. Sharing their funds so all could live, the new disciples met daily to be taught by the apostles.

Lesson 3. Drawn by miracles, throngs of people listened as the apostles proclaimed Jesus' message of salvation. Angry priests had Peter and John arrested. The ruling council ordered them not to teach about Jesus—but the two and the other apostles kept on teaching.

Lesson 4. All the apostles were arrested, whipped, and commanded to stop teaching about Jesus. But the apostles had orders from a higher authority (see Acts 5:42). So the church continued to grow, not by twos and threes, but by multitudes (Acts 5:14). Rapid growth brought a problem within as well as opposition from without.

I. A Problem Solved
(Acts 6:1-7)

Problems arise in any new enterprise and in any church that is growing rapidly. Blessed is the church that does not ignore them till they grow big, but deals with them promptly and wisely, with goodwill and good sense.

A. Problem (v. 1)

1. And in those days, when the number of the disciples was multiplied, there arose a murmuring of the Grecians against the Hebrews, because their widows were neglected in the daily ministration.

Those days is a general term meaning the time of the events recorded in the previous chapters of Acts. In that time the apostles were vigorously telling about Jesus, and the rulers of Jerusalem were vigorously objecting, as we have seen in lessons 3 and 4. In spite of the opposition, *the number of the disciples was multiplied,* or "was increasing," as the *New International Version* has it. About a hundred and twenty disciples gathered before the Day of Pentecost (Acts 1:15). On that great day three thousand more were added (2:41). Thereafter there were daily additions (2:47). Acts 4:4 records that the number of men became about five thousand. We can only guess at the number of women, but Acts 5:14 adds that "multitudes both of men and women" came into the fellowship. This rapid growth not only disturbed the opponents, but also brought difficulties in the church itself.

The Grecians and *the Hebrews* mentioned here were all Jewish people. The Hebrews were natives of Palestine, the Jewish homeland. The Grecians were Jews who had been born in other lands or had lived there a long time.

Many such Grecian Jews came to Jerusalem for the feast of Pentecost, and many of them were among the three thousand who accepted Christ that day. Instead of returning to their homes abroad, they stayed in Jerusalem to learn more about the Christian way. New disciples who lived in Palestine also left their jobs to listen to the apostles' teaching daily (Acts 2:46, 47). Grecians and Hebrews alike pooled their resources so all could eat (Acts 2:44, 45). The apostles received contributions and provided for the needs of all (Acts 4:34, 35). This task became more difficult as the number of disciples increased by thousands. In time the Jews from abroad began to complain that widows among them were not getting their fair share. Widows were especially likely to be overlooked because they had no husbands to look out for them, and women traditionally stayed out of the limelight. *The daily ministration* is literally *the daily service.*

B. Solution (vv. 2-4)

2. Then the twelve called the multitude of the disciples unto them, and said, It is not reason that we should leave the word of God, and serve tables.

How to Say It

CILICIA. Sih-*lish*-i-uh.
CYRENIANS. Sye-*ree*-ni-unz.
NICANOR. Ny-*cay*-nor.
NICOLAS. *Nick*-o-lus.
PARMENAS. *Par*-me-nus.
PROCHORUS. *Prock*-o-rus.
TIMON. *Ty*-mon.

The apostles were the ones making the daily distribution, so they were the ones being criticized by the complainers. Instead of reacting with anger, the apostles moved to solve the problem; and instead of imposing a solution by their own authority, they involved *the multitude of the disciples,* including the complainers, in the process.

The twelve apostles were specially chosen and taught by Jesus, and specially empowered by the Holy Spirit, for the purpose of teaching *the word of God.* It was not reasonable or right for them to get so tied up in the distribution of food or funds that they could not give most of their time to the work for which they had been called and prepared.

3. Wherefore, brethren, look ye out among you seven men of honest report, full of the Holy Ghost and wisdom, whom we may appoint over this business.

The apostles proposed to have *seven men* take over the *business* of distributing funds or food. Why did they choose seven? Probably because the apostles, guided by the Holy Spirit, judged that seven were needed to do the job well. The seven were to be chosen by the entire congregation rather than by the apostles, but the apostles described the kind of men who should be chosen. They should be *men of honest report,* men known to be of the kind described. They should be *full of the Holy Ghost.* All Christians receive the gift of the Holy Ghost (Acts 2:38). Those who are full of Him are those who give themselves completely to His leading. The congregation should choose men who were *full of wisdom,* men wise enough to recognize the Spirit's leading, men wise enough to resist selfish people who wanted more than their share, men wise enough to find and help the modest needy who made no demands.

4. But we will give ourselves continually to prayer, and to the ministry of the word.

With seven other good men to see that everyone was properly fed, clothed, and sheltered, the apostles could give their full time to preaching and praying.

FOOD FIGHTS

An unusual type of "food fight" was reported in the *Journal of the American Medical Association* a while back. Two brothers engaged in a contest—with chili peppers as their weapons! The winner ate twenty-five of them in twelve minutes. In truth, however, he was the loser, because the capsaicin—the "hot" ingredient in the peppers—burned through the wall of his intestine! Surgery was required to repair the damage.

Different still was the food fight that occurred between the Grecian and Palestinian Jews in the early church. The Grecians complained that their widows were not being treated as well as the widows of the Hebrews in the daily distribution of food. The apostles realized that the church would only lose in this situation, so they immediately proceeded to rectify it.

In the church, we should have no concern for winning some battle over anything that would set one Christian above another. We are children in the same "family," and our Father wants no fights among us. —C. R. B.

C. The Chosen Men (vv. 5, 6)

5. And the saying pleased the whole multitude: and they chose Stephen, a man full of faith and of the Holy Ghost, and Philip, and Prochorus, and Nicanor, and Timon, and Parmenas, and Nicolas a proselyte of Antioch.

The proposal was so obviously sensible that it *pleased the whole multitude*. It was no small task to choose seven men in a congregation numbering thousands. We are not told how the choice was made; but with the guidance of the Holy Spirit and the goodwill of the people, it was made.

6. Whom they set before the apostles: and when they had prayed, they laid their hands on them.

The ordination ceremony was simple. The apostles *prayed*, doubtless asking God's blessing and help for the seven in the huge task they were undertaking. Then the apostles *laid their hands on them*. It seems probable that this gave the seven something of the divine inspiration and miraculous power that the apostles had. It is recorded that Stephen soon afterward did miracles (v. 8), and so did Philip (Acts 8:6). Those two quickly became notable preachers. We have no record of what the other five did.

D. Continuing Progress (v. 7)

7. And the word of God increased; and the number of the disciples multiplied in Jerusalem greatly; and a great company of the priests were obedient to the faith.

The complaint of the Grecians was answered quickly and in a satisfactory way. Thus dissention in the church was nipped in the bud, and progress continued as before. *The word of God increased* in influence: the gospel was preached to more and more people, and more and more of them responded to it. *Multiplied . . . greatly* does not necessarily mean multiplied by three or four or five; but the number of disciples "increased rapidly," as the *New International Version* has it.

A striking development is recorded in the last statement of verse 7: *A great company of the priests were obedient to the faith*. The priests had been leaders of the opposition (see Acts 4:1-3; 5:17, 18). Now a large number of converts came from the very heart of the opposition. The priests were in a position to know how unfounded the opposition was. Among themselves they had to admit that Peter and John had done a notable miracle (Acts 4:15, 16). They must have known of other notable miracles (Acts 5:12-16). The time came when many of them could no longer go along with the savage effort to silence the truth, and so they took their place with the persecuted ones who told the truth.

II. Another Conflict
(Acts 6:8-10)

As the church in Jerusalem grew, members of the church were growing in usefulness and service, as every Christian ought to do. Seven men were chosen for a special kind of service, and apparently they did it well. Soon some of them were serving in another way. The last part of our text tells about Stephen.

A. New Miracle Worker (v. 8)

8. And Stephen, full of faith and power, did great wonders and miracles among the people.

In verse 5 Stephen is described as "full of faith and of the Holy Ghost"; now he is described as *full of faith and power*. It seems that the Holy Spirit had given him power to do *great wonders and miracles*. We suppose these were miracles of healing such as the apostles had been doing (Acts 3:1-8; 5:12-16).

B. New Opponents (v. 9)

9. Then there arose certain of the synagogue, which is called the synagogue of the Libertines, and Cyrenians, and Alexandrians, and of them of Cilicia and of Asia, disputing with Stephen.

In the first century B.C. the Roman general Pompey took some Jewish prisoners and deported them to Rome where they were sold into slavery. Subsequently they were freed, and some of them returned to Palestine. The *Libertines* are thought to have been chiefly descendants of these people. Some think this verse describes just one synagogue, which also included *Cyrenians, and Alexandrians,* and people *of Cilicia and of Asia.* Other students think each of these national groups may have had a separate synagogue. Be that as it may, some of these people began *disputing with Stephen.* Apparently Stephen was spreading the message of Jesus. Apparently too the opponents accepted the official position of the priests and Pharisees—they thought Jesus was a dead rebel. So they arose to argue with Stephen. We are not told where the disputing occurred.

C. Defeated Opponents (v. 10)

10. And they were not able to resist the wisdom and the spirit by which he spake.

Stephen had been well taught by the apostles. He knew the facts of Jesus' life and death and resurrection. He knew the Old Testament prophecies that were fulfilled in those events. He knew the miracles showed the presence and power of God. *The spirit by which he spake* was the Holy Spirit, who guided his use of facts and arguments. Those who tried to debate with him were defeated at every point.

III. Unfair Opposition (Acts 6:11-14)

Unable to stand against the truth, Stephen's opponents launched a campaign against the man who told the truth. It was a campaign of falsehood after falsehood, but with enough semblance of truth to make it more dangerous than outright lying.

A. False Accusation (v. 11)

11. Then they suborned men, which said, We have heard him speak blasphemous words against Moses, and against God.

Somehow, perhaps with bribes, the defeated debaters persuaded some men to bring this false accusation. *Blasphemous words* are slanderous words, insulting words. No examples are given in the text, but we recall that Jesus had quoted Moses' law and then had added something different: "Ye have heard that it was said by them of old time, Thou shalt not kill; and whosoever shall kill shall be in danger of the judgment: but I say unto you, That whosoever is angry with his brother without a cause shall be in danger of the judgment" (Matthew 5:21, 22). See other examples in the verses that follow in that chapter of Matthew. Stephen may have quoted such say-

ings, and the accusers may have said they were an insulting denial of Moses' law; and of course Moses' law was God's law, so the same words could be twisted to appear as an insult to God.

B. False Arrest (v. 12)

12. And they stirred up the people, and the elders, and the scribes, and came upon him, and caught him, and brought him to the council.

Before this time, action against the apostles had been started by priests and other Sadducees. The action against Stephen was more like a grassroots movement started by common people and their teachers. But Stephen was taken to the same *council* that had tried to silence the apostles, a council composed of both Sadducees and Pharisees.

C. False Testimony (vv. 13, 14)

13. And set up false witnesses, which said, This man ceaseth not to speak blasphemous words against this holy place, and the law.

The earlier accusation was that Stephen had spoken against Moses and God. Now in the courtroom the witnesses added that he had spoken against *this holy place,* that is, the temple, or perhaps the city of Jerusalem. This charge is made more specific in the next verse.

14. For we have heard him say, that this Jesus of Nazareth shall destroy this place, and shall change the customs which Moses delivered us.

Jesus once had said, "Destroy this temple, and in three days I will raise it up." He said that of His body, not the stone temple (John 2:19-21). But the saying was twisted to be used against Him at His trial (Matthew 26:60, 61). At another time Jesus had plainly predicted the destruction

Home Daily Bible Readings

Monday, Sept. 25—Willing to Serve (Psalm 40:4-10)

Tuesday, Sept. 26—Ready to Serve (Isaiah 6:1-8)

Wednesday, Sept. 27—Joy in Service (Psalm 126)

Thursday, Sept. 28—Shared Benefits (John 4:31-38)

Friday, Sept. 29—Christ's Example (Matthew 20:20-28)

Saturday, Sept. 30—Serving Through Hardships (1 Thessalonians 2:1-9)

Sunday, Oct. 1—God's Reward (Ephesians 6:1-8)

of the whole temple (Matthew 24:1, 2). At yet another time He had mourned over the coming fall of Jerusalem (Luke 19:41-44). Stephen may have mentioned some of these things, and the witnesses at his trial may have twisted them into a declaration that Jesus would destroy the holy place. Their purpose was to make it appear that Stephen was intent on destroying the whole Jewish system, temple and customs and all.

Chapter 7 of Acts records the outcome. When Stephen had a chance to speak for himself, he briefly surveyed the long history of Israel. He reminded the rulers that their forefathers had resisted the will of God again and again through all that long history. Then he declared that the present rulers also were resisting God's will, for they had killed the Christ.

The rulers reacted with fury, but Stephen looked up to the supreme Ruler. Raising his eyes, he called out, "Behold, I see the heavens opened, and the Son of man standing on the right hand of God."

That was the last straw. The persecutors dragged Stephen out of town and stoned him to death. So Stephen became the first Christian martyr—but the church went on and on.

SO MANY WAYS TO LIE

Identical twin brothers played on a high school basketball team. Before one game the coach mistakenly listed only one of them in the official scorebook. He was injured in the first half. At halftime, the coach told his brother to put on the injured player's jersey and not check in with the officials. This made him a false witness, since telling the truth about the coach's oversight would have drawn a technical foul.

The ruse worked. After the game, however, the coach's conscience bothered him. He turned himself in to the officials, and he and one of the twins were given a one-game suspension.

The difference between this coach and those who opposed Stephen and the gospel is that the latter seem to have had no conscience. They knowingly brought false witnesses to the council to testify against Stephen. But this wasn't just a game with a technical foul or even a suspension at stake; it was to become a matter of life and death for Stephen.

Lying seems so prevalent in modern society that many are inclined to take it for granted. Misleading advertising, insurance fraud, and cutting corners on quality are just a few examples of lying that have gained tacit acceptance in our society. Christians are called to live by a higher standard of truth.   —C. R. B.

Conclusion

Jesus said, "I will build my church; and the gates of hell shall not prevail against it" (Matthew 16:18). We can depend on that. The Sadducees and the Pharisees could not kill it when it was small; Satan and all his hosts cannot kill it when it is big.

But the deathless church can be hurt. We want to be among those who heal, not those who hurt. Again we have a lesson with two messages for us. Let's call them A and B.

A. Hurts Little and Big

A little wound can be cleansed with peroxide and protected by a Band-Aid till it heals, but a little wound untreated can develop gangrene and require an amputation.

Shall not every little hurt in the church be treated and healed with tender loving care? If it is not, before long there will be some big hurts to deal with.

B. Are You Ready?

If ardent personal evangelists like Stephen were being stoned today, how many of us would be ardent enough to earn that fate?

It is easy to see that popular media, popular entertainment, and popular tastes are becoming more un-Christian and more obscene. Protests, petitions, and boycotts have some effect, but not enough. It is hard to get non-Christians to act like Christians. The original Christians devoted themselves to making more Christians. Three thousand grew swiftly to five thousand, and then multitudes were added (Acts 2:41; 4:4; 5:14). Can we duplicate that effort and that result? Are you ready to do your part?

C. Prayer

Father, we confess that we have not matched the earnestness of the first Christians. We pray that You will so guide our choices and our actions that we shall be better teachers of truth and winners of souls. In Jesus' name, amen.

D. Thought to Remember

You can do better.

visual 5

Learning by Doing

This page contains an alternate lesson plan emphasizing learning activities. Classes desiring such student involvement will find these suggestions helpful.

Learning Goals

As students participate in today's class session, they should:

1. List principles for dealing with "little" and "big" problems a congregation may face.

2. Commit themselves to becoming a part of the solution if a problem ever arises in your congregation.

Into the Lesson

Write the heading "Church Problems" on your chalkboard. Begin today's session by asking the class to brainstorm a list of problems a congregation could face. List their suggestions under the heading on the chalkboard.

As you read the list, have the class help you to decide whether each problem is a "little" problem or a "big" one. Put an "L" beside the "little" problems, and a "B" beside the "big" ones.

Tell the class that the lesson text reveals how the church in its early days dealt with a "little" problem and then a "big" one. The class will discover principles for dealing with each kind in this week's discussion.

Into the Word

Give a brief review of the first four lessons of this quarter. Use the thoughts presented in the Lesson Background section, which is included in the introduction to this lesson.

Using the following questions, lead class members to explore the lesson text. You may find it helpful to write on the chalkboard the italicized words from each question as you ask it.

1. Who were the *Grecians?* How were they different from the Hebrews?

2. Who were the *twelve?*

3. What was the *daily ministration?* Why didn't the twelve take care of it themselves?

4. What were the *qualifications* for the seven men who would perform the daily distribution? What principle may be seen in this regarding the selection of persons for responsible positions of service in the church?

5. It has been noted that the *seven men* who were chosen, had Greek names. What may this suggest? If the seven were Grecian Jews, what principle for problem-solving does this suggest?

6. How do we know that the problem concerning the daily distribution was resolved? What was the *result* for the church?

7. Why was *Stephen* opposed? Who opposed him?

8. What *methods* did Stephen's opponents use to undermine him?

9. *What happened* to Stephen?

If class members do not remember what happened to Stephen, share the summary of Acts 7 included in the comments under verse 14.

Into Life

We have seen that early on in its existence the church faced two problems: a "little" problem and a "big" problem. Ask someone to identify each. Then divide the class in half. Ask one half to write a brief list of principles for solving "little" church problems. The other half should make a list of principles for solving "big" church problems. If your class numbers more than sixteen, divide each half into smaller groups.

The "little" problem group may suggest principles such as the following:

1. Deal with the problem promptly.

2. Leaders should not try to do every task in the church, but should enlist the help of responsible persons and delegate authority to them.

3. Even leaders who minister to "physical" needs of people should be spiritual people.

4. No job is unimportant. We should ask God to bless and guide every ministry.

The "big" problem group may suggest principles such as the following:

1. The gospel is often a threat to those who won't accept it.

2. Don't expect integrity from the gospel's opponents.

3. Don't compromise God's message or your principles in the face of opposition.

4. God can use even hardship or persecution to accomplish His purposes.

Discuss these questions with your class:

Which does a congregation typically experience more, "little" problems or "big" problems" Which are a bigger threat to the life and health of the church? Why?

Ask, "How can Christians prepare themselves to be a part of the solution to either kind of problem?" As students give suggestions, list them on your chalkboard. After a few minutes, challenge class members to choose one of the ideas and decide how he or she can act on it during this week.

Let's Talk It Over

*The questions on this page are designed to encourage review of the lesson
Scriptures and to promote discussion of the lesson by the class. The answers
provided are only discussion starters. Let your class talk it over from there.*

1. Why is it helpful for church leaders to consider problems in the church as opportunities?

When problems arise, the human response is either to ignore them or to fret over them. If we view them instead as opportunities, we will more likely deal with them promptly and relish the challenges they pose rather than dread the damage they may do. Church leaders should train themselves to face a problem with the question, "How can we handle this to make the church stronger and to build a firmer faith in the people involved?" Acts 6:1-7 shows how a potentially divisive problem in the church at Jerusalem was turned into an occasion for developing new leadership and initiating a fresh advance in evangelistic success. That can also happen in our church.

2. The apostles needed to concentrate on their ministry in the word, and the spiritual leaders of the church today need to do likewise. How can this be arranged?

This question offers a specific example of the suggestion in the previous question. The problem many churches face is, "How can our spiritual leaders be freed from office work, building maintenance, financial concerns, etc., so they can focus more on evangelism, teaching, and shepherding of members?" Such a problem is easily seen as an opportunity. If other members can be enlisted to contribute an hour or two per week to deal with these kinds of church business, the work will get done, and those involved in service are likely to become more enthusiastic about the church and its ministries. In time, they may even develop an interest in becoming leaders themselves.

3. Acts 6:3 gives the qualifications for the seven men who would direct the distribution of food. How appropriate are these qualifications as a guideline for selecting members to serve on committees and to perform various services in the church today?

In selecting elders or deacons for the church, we examine them carefully in the light of 1 Timothy 3:1-13 and Titus 1:6-9. Thought should also be given to the qualifications of those who perform other types of ministries in the church.

Anyone who helps plan worship services, or develops evangelistic or educational programs, or contacts people in need of benevolent assistance should certainly be a Christian who will represent Christ and the church well. Acts 6:3, according to the *New International Version*, contains two qualifications: "men . . . known to be full of the Spirit and wisdom." Whether men or women, those who hold responsibility in the church today should be characterized by the fruit of the Spirit (Galatians 5:22, 23) and should exhibit the kind of wisdom described in James 3:17, 18.

4. Acts 6:6 mentions prayer as an important feature in setting people aside for service in the church. What prayers should be offered for our fellow Christians at such times?

In line with the previous question, prayers should be offered that each person would receive strength and guidance through the Holy Spirit and that each would grow in spiritual wisdom. Specific requests should be made for such matters as the discipline to do the job well, the patience to work with people who are slow to cooperate, and the graciousness to handle criticism well. From a negative standpoint it would be appropriate to pray that our fellow Christians will resist the temptation to misuse their authority (see 3 John 9, 10).

5. How is it significant that "a great company of the priests were obedient to the faith"?

This reference in Acts 6:7 is a powerful confirmation of the truth of the gospel. Like Saul of Tarsus, some of these priests had once thought that they "ought to do many things contrary to the name of Jesus of Nazareth" (Acts 26:9), and now they embraced the faith they once tried to destroy. These priests surely were in a position to know the falseness of the rumor circulated from within their ranks that Jesus' body had been stolen from the tomb by His disciples (see Matthew 28:11-15). The fact that they became Christians shows the absurdity of that claim. They now recognized as well that the miracles the apostles were performing—miracles that had earlier mystified them (Acts 4:16)—testified to the divine authority of the apostles' message concerning Jesus Christ.

Philip: Witness to Outcasts

DEVOTIONAL READING: Acts 8:9-24.

LESSON SCRIPTURE: Acts 8:4-40.

PRINTED TEXT: Acts 8:5, 6, 26-38.

Oct 8

Acts 8:5, 6, 26-38

5 Then Philip went down to the city of Samaria, and preached Christ unto them.

6 And the people with one accord gave heed unto those things which Philip spake, hearing and seeing the miracles which he did.

. . . .

26 And the angel of the Lord spake unto Philip, saying, Arise, and go toward the south, unto the way that goeth down from Jerusalem unto Gaza, which is desert.

27 And he arose and went: and, behold, a man of Ethiopia, a eunuch of great authority under Candace queen of the Ethiopians, who had the charge of all her treasure, and had come to Jerusalem for to worship,

28 Was returning, and sitting in his chariot read Isaiah the prophet.

29 Then the Spirit said unto Philip, Go near, and join thyself to this chariot.

30 And Philip ran thither to him, and heard him read the prophet Isaiah, and said, Understandest thou what thou readest?

31 And he said, How can I, except some man should guide me? And he desired Philip that he would come up and sit with him.

32 The place of the Scripture which he read was this, He was led as a sheep to the slaughter; and like a lamb dumb before his shearer, so opened he not his mouth:

33 In his humiliation his judgment was taken away: and who shall declare his generation? for his life is taken from the earth.

34 And the eunuch answered Philip, and said, I pray thee, of whom speaketh the prophet this? of himself, or of some other man?

35 Then Philip opened his mouth, and began at the same Scripture, and preached unto him Jesus.

36 And as they went on their way, they came unto a certain water: and the eunuch said, See, here is water; what doth hinder me to be baptized?

37 And Philip said, If thou believest with all thine heart, thou mayest. And he answered and said, I believe that Jesus Christ is the Son of God.

38 And he commanded the chariot to stand still: and they went down both into the water, both Philip and the eunuch; and he baptized him.

GOLDEN TEXT: Philip opened his mouth, and began at the same Scripture, and preached unto him Jesus.—Acts 8:35.

> **The Story of Christian Beginnings**
> **(Acts)**
> Unit 2: Witnessing in Judea and Samaria
> (Lessons 5-9)

Lesson Aims

After studying this lesson students should be able to:

1. Recount the story of Philip's work in Samaria and on the road to Gaza.

2. Tell how the effort to destroy the church helped it to spread.

3. Examine their own growth in Christian living—and perhaps accelerate it.

Lesson Outline

INTRODUCTION
  A. Benefits of Disaster
  B. Lesson Background
I. THE GOSPEL IN SAMARIA (Acts 8:5, 6)
  A. The Preaching (v. 5)
  B. The Result (v. 6)
    Good News for Everyone
II. THE GOSPEL ON THE HIGHWAY (Acts 8:26-35)
  A. New Field (v. 26)
  B. New Prospect (vv. 27, 28)
  C. New Opportunity (vv. 29-31)
  D. Scripture Reading (vv. 32, 33)
  E. Explanation (vv. 34, 35)
III. EAGER CONVERT (Acts 8:36-38)
  A. Inquiry (v. 36)
  B. Confession (v. 37)
  C. Baptism (v. 38)
    A Natural Response
CONCLUSION
  A. A Growing Christian
  B. A Progressing Church
  C. Pupils Become Teachers
  D. Prayer
  E. Thought to Remember

A Christian's duty to tell others of Jesus is the theme of visual 6 of the visuals packet. The visual is shown on page 53.

Introduction

About the year 1890, my grandfather bought a farm from a western homesteader. The house was a rickety frame structure that threatened to fall apart from its own weight; but it sheltered Grandpa for the rest of his life, and later became my birthplace.

The old house didn't last long after that. The cellar caved in, the building tilted at a terrifying angle, and some joints pulled apart.

My parents were devastated. They were a young couple with two babies, barely making a living on a small farm—and now they had no place to live.

But God was gracious, a moneylender was reckless, and my parents were no strangers to hard work. The house they built was bigger and far better than the old one had ever been.

A. Benefits of Disaster

How many times disaster has proved to be beneficial! The empire trembled when much of Rome was destroyed by fire in A.D. 64. But the new Rome that rose from the ruins was a much finer city. Likewise the new Chicago that followed the famous fire of 1871 was bigger and better—and more fireproof. So was the new San Francisco that rose after the terrible earthquake in 1906.

In Jerusalem, persecution shattered the new church soon after it began. But fragments of the shattered church landed in other towns of Judea and Samaria, and soon there were many churches. The gospel of Christ was starting its journey "to the uttermost part of the earth."

B. Lesson Background

In earlier lessons we have seen that priests had the apostles of Jesus arrested and taken to the ruling council, where they were whipped and ordered not to talk about Jesus anymore. Then some of the common people dragged Stephen to the same council, and he was stoned to death.

At that point we were introduced to an ardent young Pharisee named Saul. Later he became known as Paul the apostle. He watched and approved as Stephen was stoned. Then he took the lead in persecuting the followers of Jesus. Probably the ruling priests assigned a squad of police to help him as he invaded every house where disciples were thought to be. Angrily he arrested the Christians and put them in jail (Acts 7:57—8:3).

It was no small task that Saul undertook. There were many thousands of Christians. Most of them left Jerusalem before he could catch them. They went to other towns of Judea and Samaria (Acts 8:1). Some of them went to more distant places as we shall see in later lessons.

The disciples of Jesus were on fire with the good news of salvation. They took it wherever they went (Acts 8:4). So churches sprang up in many towns of Judea and Samaria. The first part of our text gives one example.

I. The Gospel in Samaria
(Acts 8:5, 6)

It is surprising to see that the scattered Christians went to Samaria as well as Judea. For centuries there had been more hard feeling than friendship between Jews and Samaritans. Jews regarded Samaritans as half-breed Jews, and Samaritans responded with indignation. But probably the fugitives were safer in Samaria than in Judea, which was closer to the vengeful enemies in Jerusalem. Of course Samaritans were not all alike. Jesus found a cordial welcome in one town (John 4:1-43). Another town refused to let Him stay overnight (Luke 9:51-53). Probably the scattered disciples likewise were more welcome in some towns than in others, but they "went every where preaching the word" (Acts 8:4).

A. The Preaching (v. 5)

5. Then Philip went down to the city of Samaria, and preached Christ unto them.

Last week the central figure in our lesson was Stephen; this week it is *Philip*. Like Stephen, Philip was one of the seven men chosen to manage the distribution of funds or food to the needy in the church (Acts 6:1-6). Like Stephen, Philip became a good preacher of the gospel. But Philip was one of those who escaped from Jerusalem and took the message elsewhere.

The Greek word here for *preached* means to announce or proclaim. It is the word used of a royal herald who proclaims the message of a king. In the New Testament it is the word used of a preacher who proclaims the gospel, the message of the King of kings. As Peter had done on Pentecost, Philip announced that Jesus is the Christ promised by ancient Scriptures, and that people should believe in Him, repent of their sins, and be baptized in Jesus' name.

B. The Result (v. 6)

6. And the people with one accord gave heed unto those things which Philip spake, hearing and seeing the miracles which he did.

Like Stephen, Philip had been given power to do miracles. Verse 7 describes some of them. These miracles quickly convinced the Samaritans that Philip was a true herald of Heaven, proclaiming God's own message. Consequently many of them believed Philip and were baptized (v. 12). "There was great joy in that city" (v. 8), both because of the healings and because of the promise of salvation.

The twelve apostles had stayed in Jerusalem when the other disciples of Jesus had fled (Acts 8:1). Now two of them came to help in Samaria.

With prayer they laid their hands on some of the new converts (vv. 14-17). It seems that this imparted to those converts the same inspiration and miraculous power that Philip had received. These then could take the place of Philip. Philip was free to move on to another field.

GOOD NEWS FOR EVERYONE

There are probably more "Good Samaritan" hospitals in the world today than there are Samaritans. Only about five hundred Samaritans are known to exist. From biblical times to the present, these people have been considered outcasts. Their low social ranking is seen in the fact that Jesus' story about one "good Samaritan" put him in a role contradictory to what people normally thought of Samaritans.

In Jesus' day, Samaritans were so despised that many Jews would not walk through Samaria on the way from Judea to Galilee and vice versa.

It is remarkable, therefore, that Philip took the initiative to preach Christ to the Samaritans. The reason he did so is found in the description of this godly man (Acts 6:3-6). He was a man filled with the Spirit of God.

Christians who allow themselves to be led by God's Spirit will look down on no one, but will see all persons as worthy of receiving the gospel of God's love.   —C. R. B.

II. The Gospel on the Highway
(Acts 8:26-35)

You or I, or even Philip, might think it was unwise for an able evangelist to leave a field where people were responding to the gospel. But Philip had his orders from One wiser than any of us. It was time for him to move on.

A. New Field (v. 26)

26. And the angel of the Lord spake unto Philip, saying, Arise, and go toward the south, unto the way that goeth down from Jerusalem unto Gaza, which is desert.

Desert does not mean sandy waste like the Sahara; it means deserted, uninhabited. The road to Gaza led through range land, the kind of country where Abraham and Isaac pastured their flocks. But what can an evangelist do in empty country like that?

How to Say It

CANDACE. *Can*-duh-see.
THEOPHILUS. Thee-*ahf*-ih-luss.

B. New Prospect (vv. 27, 28)

27. And he arose and went: and, behold, a man of Ethiopia, a eunuch of great authority under Candace queen of the Ethiopians, who had the charge of all her treasure, and had come to Jerusalem for to worship.

Knowing where the order came from, Philip obeyed promptly: *he arose and went.* The historian then describes the man whom the Lord was sending Philip to meet: *a man of Ethiopia.*

This Ethiopia was not the same as the country we now call by that name. Its boundaries are not described exactly, but it included the upper Nile Valley south of Egypt. Some students conclude that its population included Africans from the south, Egyptians from the north, and Arabians from the east. We have no description of *Candace,* the *queen.*

This verse tells us several things about the man Philip was to meet:

1. He was *a eunuch,* as were many attendants in royal courts. They were thought to be more docile, more loyal, more dependable than normal men; and they were not likely to become involved in scandalous behavior with ladies of the court.

2. The man held a position of trust and great *authority:* he was the queen's treasurer.

3. He *had come to Jerusalem for to worship.* This indicates that he was Jewish, for Jerusalem was the Jews' central place of worship. Was he a native Ethiopian of African, Egyptian, or Arabian descent, who had been converted to the Jewish religion? Was he a native of Ethiopia born of Jewish ancestors who had moved to Ethiopia generations earlier? Was he a slave, a descendant of Jews who had been captured and enslaved long before? Was he a native of Palestine who had gone to Ethiopia and risen to a high position as Joseph had done in Egypt and Daniel had done in Babylon? For these questions we have no answers.

28. Was returning, and sitting in his chariot read Isaiah the prophet.

It is clear that the man was starting to go back home to Ethiopia, but questions arise instantly. Was he traveling alone? Wouldn't a high official of Ethiopia have at least a servant to drive the chariot and take care of the horses when they stopped for the night? It seems quite probable that such an official would travel with armed and mounted guards. But if the man had any companions, they are not mentioned in the record. Possibly the official thought it was safer to travel alone and incognito.

People who remember the horse-and-buggy days know it is possible to read while driving a slow-moving horse, and horses do not move very rapidly when they have to keep going all day. But wouldn't it be helpful to have someone else do the driving? For our study, the important thing is what the man was doing as he traveled. He was reading *Isaiah the prophet.*

C. New Opportunity (vv. 29-31)

29. Then the Spirit said unto Philip, Go near, and join thyself to this chariot.

Now we know why Philip was sent to this desert place. This chariot carried the man whom God was sending His preacher to meet.

30. And Philip ran thither to him, and heard him read the prophet Isaiah, and said, Understandest thou what thou readest?

The Ethiopian was reading aloud, and Philip recognized the words of Isaiah. His question was well designed to open the way for his preaching. No one in Israel—no one in the world—understood those words of Isaiah till he saw how they were fulfilled in Jesus.

31. And he said, How can I, except some man should guide me? And he desired Philip that he would come up and sit with him.

The man was wise enough to realize that he did not understand the prophecy, and wise enough to rejoice in the prospect of finding some help with it. He invited Philip to join him in the chariot.

D. Scripture Reading (vv. 32, 33)

32, 33. The place of the Scripture which he read was this, He was led as a sheep to the slaughter; and like a lamb dumb before his shearer, so opened he not his mouth: in his humiliation his judgment was taken away: and who shall declare his generation? for his life is taken from the earth.

This is a part of what we call Isaiah 53:7, 8. That chapter sings tenderly of God's servant persecuted and killed, though innocent, yet destined to share with the great. "Surely he hath borne our griefs, and carried our sorrows." What we see in Acts is a free quotation from the Greek version of Isaiah that was commonly used in New Testament times. It is not exactly like the passage as we see it in our version of Isaiah, but any version of the prophecy is fulfilled in Jesus.

E. Explanation (vv. 34, 35)

34. And the eunuch answered Philip, and said, I pray thee, of whom speaketh the prophet this? of himself, or of some other man?

The man of Ethiopia asked a question that puzzled all the scholars of Israel. Obviously the prophet was singing of someone—but whom? Was the song about Isaiah *himself?* He was despised and rejected and persecuted, perhaps killed; but how could it be said that we are healed by Isaiah's stripes? (Isaiah 53:5). How could it be said that Isaiah would justify many? (Isaiah 53:11)? If Isaiah was singing of *some other man,* the same questions remain unanswered. Some students suggested that Isaiah might be singing about the nation of Israel. That nation would indeed suffer much, but what Israelite would believe that his nation might ever die? (Isaiah 53:8).

35. Then Philip opened his mouth, and began at the same Scripture, and preached unto him Jesus.

Jesus! In all history, no one else fits the description written by Isaiah. Innocent as any sheep, Jesus was led to the slaughter, never opening His mouth to scream a protest. He was humiliated in every possible way, and just judgment was taken away from Him. "Generation" (v. 33) is a word with various meanings. Some students take it to mean descendants here. Who can say anything about Jesus' descendants, since He died without any children? Yet there are millions of His spiritual descendants, people who have been born again through Him, and have become God's children. In them "he shall see his seed" (Isaiah 53:10).

Philip may have led his hearer through that fifty-third chapter of Isaiah step by step. He may have emphasized especially "with his stripes we are healed" and other statements of redemption. He may have cited other prophecies too, such as those of David that Peter had used on Pentecost (Acts 2:25-36). As Peter had done, Philip made a convincing case: Jesus is the Christ foretold by the prophets of God.

III. Eager Convert
(Acts 8:36-38)

We have no way of knowing how long Philip continued to preach Jesus. He may have gone on for hours. Certainly many hours could be used in discussing Old Testament prophecies and the wonderful way Jesus fulfilled them. No doubt the Ethiopian felt his conviction growing stronger with every passing mile.

A. Inquiry (v. 36)

36. And as they went on their way, they came unto a certain water: and the eunuch said, See, here is water; what doth hinder me to be baptized?

Obviously Philip's preaching of Jesus had included information about baptism. We are not told what Philip had said about it; but we are sure it did not contradict what Peter had said as recorded in Acts 2:38. He may have said much more than is written there. Luke was writing this record thirty years after the church began. He addressed it to Theophilus, who already had been instructed in the Christian way (Acts 1:1; Luke 1:3, 4). Christian teaching about baptism was well known to Theophilus and others like him. There was no need for Luke to repeat it.

B. Confession (v. 37)

37. And Philip said, If thou believest with all thine heart, thou mayest. And he answered and said, I believe that Jesus Christ is the Son of God.

This verse is not found in the oldest known manuscripts of Acts, and so it is left out of many English versions. It seems probable that Luke did not write it; but of course Philip did not baptize this man without being assured that he believed in Jesus Christ. Whoever wrote the verse, undoubtedly it shows one form of confession that was used among early Christians. Perhaps it originated as a footnote to inform readers and later someone who was copying the book wrote it into the text.

C. Baptism (v. 38)

38. And he commanded the chariot to stand still: and they went down both into the water, both Philip and the eunuch; and he baptized him.

Here we see an indication that the Ethiopian traveler had someone else driving the horses. One does not give a command to a chariot itself. It seems probable that the driver held the horses while Philip and the Ethiopian left the chariot. No doubt the two took off their outer robes, at least. Luke does not include details, but gives the essential facts. The two men waded into the water, and Philip baptized the man of Ethiopia.

"When they were come up out of the water, the Spirit of the Lord caught away Philip." Apparently the preacher simply vanished. "The eunuch saw him no more." The traveler must

Tell of Jesus

To many

Or to one

visual 6

have been greatly puzzled, but "he went on his way rejoicing." He had good reasons for joy. He now understood that puzzling prophecy. Much more than that, he was forgiven, cleansed, redeemed. He was a new man, born again as a child of God.

A NATURAL RESPONSE

During the Gulf War of 1991, many American soldiers found that being in the desert so far from home stimulated them to do some serious thinking. One GI said, "[When I get home] every day when I walk in the door, I'm going to kiss my wife and tell her I love her." He also said that when his daughter asked to go with him on an errand, he would no longer refuse her.

As the troops waited for the war to begin, chaplains reported that soldiers were reading their Bibles more and going to church services more often. Of course, skeptics say this is just the natural response to the threat of imminent battle. The old saying is that "there are no atheists in foxholes," but after the loneliness and danger of the battle are past, most people go back to their old ways.

The Ethiopian treasurer, traveling on the deserted road to Gaza, also turned to the Scriptures, and in his case it made a lasting difference. Exhibiting sincere interest in the Word of God, he accepted the help of Philip, whom God had sent to him. Philip's preaching led the Ethiopian to faith in Christ. The man's response was the natural one for an honest seeker: he heard the gospel message, understood what God had commanded him to do, and then eagerly obeyed. We do well to follow the Ethiopian's example whenever we come to a new understanding of what God expects of us.   —C. R. B.

Conclusion

The church is not designed to stand still. Every Christian can be a growing Christian. Jesus Christ is the same yesterday, today, and forever (Hebrews 13:8). The principles of righteousness are eternal. But God's people on earth are on the move—or ought to be.

A. A Growing Christian

Philip was chosen for a specific job, the care of the poor (Acts 6:1-6). But now we see him as a great preacher of the gospel, successful with many in the city, successful with one in the desert. After that he preached his way up the coast "till he came to Caesarea" (Acts 8:40). Thirty years later he must have been aging; but still he was known as "the evangelist," the teller of good news (Acts 21:8). He kept on keeping on.

B. A Progressing Church

Did Philip abandon the job he was chosen and ordained to do? No, that specific job ceased to exist. The church passed into a new phase, and the work the seven had done was no longer possible. They did their job well when the multiplying thousands of Christians were in Jerusalem; but when those thousands scattered, no seven men could care for all the poor. If only a dozen Christians were in a village, all of them knew one another's needs. If three hundred settled in a town, perhaps they had their own committee. Quickly the church adapted to the new situation, and it was starting on its way to the uttermost part of the earth.

C. Pupils Become Teachers

In Jerusalem the church members had listened to the apostles' teaching. When they scattered, all of them became teachers. They "went every where preaching the word" (Acts 8:4). Hebrews 5:12 criticizes Christians who ought to be teachers, but still need to be taught the basics. Are we too easily content to keep receiving teaching without ever giving it to others?

D. Prayer

Truly, our Father, You have set before us the standard of excellence: "the measure of the stature of the fulness of Christ" (Ephesians 4:13). Strengthen us and help us as we push on toward that standard. In Jesus' name, amen.

E. Thought to Remember

Not enjoyment, and not sorrow,
Is our destined end or way;
But to act that each tomorrow
Finds us farther than today.

Home Daily Bible Readings

Monday, Oct. 2—A Leper Cleansed (Matthew 8:1-4)
Tuesday, Oct. 3—Harlots Accepted (Matthew 21:28-32)
Wednesday, Oct. 4—Tax Collectors Justified (Luke 7:24-30)
Thursday, Oct. 5—A Sinner Forgiven (Luke 7:36-50)
Friday, Oct. 6—Paradise Promised (Luke 23:32-43)
Saturday, Oct. 7—Outcasts Brought In (Isaiah 6:1-3, 10-12)
Sunday, Oct. 8—Faith Generated in One Cast Out (John 9:24-38)

Learning by Doing

This page contains an alternate lesson plan emphasizing learning activities. Classes desiring such student involvement will find these suggestions helpful.

Learning Goals

As students participate in today's class session, they should:

1. Discover principles for effective evangelism from the example of Philip in Acts 8.

2. Choose one principle to put into practice in their own lives.

3. Identify one person from their circle of influence who they think may be receptive to the gospel as the Ethiopian was.

Into the Lesson

Before class write the following open-ended sentences on poster boards, one sentence per board. Display the posters in your classroom before your students arrive. (Or simply write one or two of the statements on your chalkboard.)

"The last time I tried to share the gospel with a non-Christian—"

"My first thought when I hear a sermon about evangelism is usually—"

"The first time someone tried to talk with me about becoming a Christian—"

"The biggest barrier to spreading the gospel today is—"

Use these sentences in one of the following two ways:

1. Give each student a slip of paper. Have each choose one of the incomplete sentences and write the statement and a completion for it on his or her slip. Students are not to sign their names to the slips. Collect the slips and read them to the class.

2. Have each student find a partner. Then each is to complete one of the statements and share it with his or her partner. After ninety seconds, ask volunteers to share their answers with the whole class.

If any of your students have had positive experiences sharing the gospel with a non-Christian, ask them to relate those experiences now. Then ask, "What makes us hesitant sometimes to share the message of Christ with a friend?"

Tell the class that today's Bible study will examine the experience of a successful evangelist. Perhaps this study will help us in our sharing of the gospel.

Into the Word

Distribute a handout on which you have written the following sentences.

He was open to God's leading.

He obeyed when he understood what God required.

He was eager to share the gospel.

He searched the Scriptures diligently.

He relied on God's Word, not his own experiences, to lead the seeker to Christ.

He hungered to know the truth.

He understood the place of Christ in prophecy.

He combined faith with action.

He permitted no social barriers to hinder his preaching to the lost.

His faith in Christ caused him to rejoice.

Arrange your class members in groups of about five. Tell them to examine this list of statements and decide whether each sentence describes the apostle Philip or the Ethiopian official in this week's text. Give them about five minutes, and then ask for their answers. (The first sentence describes Philip. Then the sentences alternate describing the Ethiopian and Philip. Members may feel that some of the sentences describe both of the men.) As you read each sentence aloud, come to agreement on each. Students should then mark "P" or "E" beside each sentence on their handouts.

Next have your class members look at the "P" sentences and in their groups discuss these questions regarding the sentences: "How did Philip demonstrate this principle? Why is this an important principle for serving as a successful evangelist?" The students may discuss any or all of the sentences in their groups. After another five minutes, consider each principle and discuss it with the whole class.

Into Life

Ask class members to decide which of the principles for evangelists seems most important to them. If you have time, members may discuss this in their groups before volunteers share with the whole group.

Ask them if they know anyone who they think may be receptive to the gospel. We are to share the gospel with the whole world, but some in our world would be more easily won than others.

Have the students remain in their groups and close this session by praying that they will seize their opportunities to be evangelists during the coming week.

Let's Talk It Over

The questions on this page are designed to encourage review of the lesson Scriptures and to promote discussion of the lesson by the class. The answers provided are only discussion starters. Let your class talk it over from there.

1. The lesson writer points out that the Greek word for "preached" in Acts 8:5 is "used of a royal herald who proclaims the message of a king." What does this suggest regarding our proclamation of the gospel?

It is not likely that any herald of ancient times would have announced his king's message in a timid and hesitant manner. Instead, he would have spoken clearly and confidently. The application to our modern-day proclamation is obvious. Also, since he represented the king, the herald would have been careful to present only the king's message. He surely would not have mixed his opinions with the king's proclamation. We have legitimate opinions about spiritual matters, and it is not wrong for us to express these to other people, but we must always be clear in distinguishing God's truths from our speculations.

2. The Ethiopian was reading the Scriptures. What is the potential for a spiritual breakthrough when a person is willing to read the Scriptures?

Paul told the Thessalonians, "When ye received the word of God which ye heard of us, ye received it not as the word of men, but, as it is in truth, the word of God, which effectually worketh also in you that believe" (1 Thessalonians 2:13). This is what can happen when one exposes one's mind and heart to the Word of God. The Scriptures can bring conviction of sin and faith in the saving Christ to the unsaved person who gives attention to these inspired writings. The Christian who needs wisdom to resolve a problem or strength to resist a temptation will find in the Scriptures the help needed to achieve a mighty victory to the glory of God.

3. Why is Philip's question to the Ethiopian, "Do you understand what you are reading?" (Acts 8:30, *New International Version*), an appropriate one to ask a Bible reader?

We believe that the Bible is a book the average human being can understand, but that does not mean a person cannot profit from guidance supplied by mature and experienced students of God's Word. Some beginning students may not understand the difference between the Old and New Testaments, and so they require instruction regarding the purpose of each. Others may have difficulty comprehending the divine character and mission of Jesus Christ, but with assistance they can be led to the key passages that spell that out. Such guidance offered in a spirit of loving concern may evoke from a modern-day Bible student the same kind of response given by the Ethiopian: "How can I, except some man should guide me?" (Acts 8:31).

4. Philip "began at the same Scripture, and preached unto him Jesus." Would it be possible to begin at almost any Scripture and lead into a presentation of Jesus Christ? Give examples.

The person and work of Jesus Christ are so much the focus of the Bible that one could easily make a transition from countless Scripture passages to a gospel presentation. For example, from Psalm 23, with its description of the Lord as shepherd, one could lead into a consideration of Jesus as the Good Shepherd who has given His life for the sheep (John 10:11). Any passage that speaks of sin provides an occasion for one to describe the Savior from sin. Any that refer to God's love and mercy provide an obvious connection with Jesus as the embodiment of those qualities. Any that make mention of death open the door to a discussion of Jesus as the victor over death and the grave.

5. Why is it vital for Christians who have received the gospel to find ways of passing that message on to others?

The first reason is quite obvious. If we who have received the good news of salvation in Jesus Christ do not share it with those who are still bound by sin, they will never know the redemption He offers.

A second reason is that in sharing the teaching we have received, we maintain our own spiritual vitality. Those who are actively involved in sharing the gospel with others are apt to be more attentive to what is said in lessons and sermons, for they will be seeking greater understanding of biblical truth and ways to impart it to others. Personal spiritual growth is the natural result of this. Spiritual stagnation, however, is a very real danger for a Christian who is ever learning but who never takes the time to share with others what is learned.

Saul Becomes a Disciple

DEVOTIONAL READING: Matthew 4:17-22.

LESSON SCRIPTURE: Acts 9:1-31.

PRINTED TEXT: Acts 9:1-6, 10-20.

Acts 9:1-6, 10-20

1 And Saul, yet breathing out threatenings and slaughter against the disciples of the Lord, went unto the high priest,

2 And desired of him letters to Damascus to the synagogues, that if he found any of this way, whether they were men or women, he might bring them bound unto Jerusalem.

3 And as he journeyed, he came near Damascus: and suddenly there shined round about him a light from heaven:

4 And he fell to the earth, and heard a voice saying unto him, Saul, Saul, why persecutest thou me?

5 And he said, Who art thou, Lord? And the Lord said, I am Jesus whom thou persecutest: it is hard for thee to kick against the pricks.

6 And he trembling and astonished said, Lord, what wilt thou have me to do? And the Lord said unto him, Arise, and go into the city, and it shall be told thee what thou must do.

. . . .

10 And there was a certain disciple at Damascus, named Ananias; and to him said the Lord in a vision, Ananias. And he said, Behold, I am here, Lord.

11 And the Lord said unto him, Arise, and go into the street which is called Straight, and inquire in the house of Judas for one called Saul, of Tarsus: for, behold, he prayeth,

12 And hath seen in a vision a man named Ananias coming in, and putting his hand on him, that he might receive his sight.

13 Then Ananias answered, Lord, I have heard by many of this man, how much evil he hath done to thy saints at Jerusalem:

14 And here he hath authority from the chief priests to bind all that call on thy name.

15 But the Lord said unto him, Go thy way: for he is a chosen vessel unto me, to bear my name before the Gentiles, and kings, and the children of Israel:

16 For I will show him how great things he must suffer for my name's sake.

17 And Ananias went his way, and entered into the house; and putting his hands on him said, Brother Saul, the Lord, even Jesus, that appeared unto thee in the way as thou camest, hath sent me, that thou mightest receive thy sight, and be filled with the Holy Ghost.

18 And immediately there fell from his eyes as it had been scales: and he received sight forthwith, and arose, and was baptized.

19 And when he had received meat, he was strengthened. Then was Saul certain days with the disciples which were at Damascus.

20 And straightway he preached Christ in the synagogues, that he is the Son of God.

GOLDEN TEXT: He [Saul] is a chosen vessel unto me, to bear my name before the Gentiles, and kings, and the children of Israel.—Acts 9:15.

The Story of Christian Beginnings
(Acts)
Unit 2: Witnessing in Judea and Samaria
(Lessons 5-9)

Lesson Aims

After completing this lesson a student should be able to:

1. Retell the story of Saul's encounter with Jesus on the road to Damascus, and his experience in Damascus.

2. Consider his or her own faith and life to see what changes would be for the better.

3. Make a change.

Lesson Outline

INTRODUCTION
   A. Transforming Power
   B. Lesson Background
I. HALT! (Acts 9:1-6)
   A. Furious Persecution (vv. 1, 2)
   B. Sudden Stop (vv. 3-6)
     Light From Heaven
II. THE LORD'S MESSENGER (Acts 9:10-16)
   A. Order (vv. 10-12)
   B. Protest (vv. 13, 14)
   C. Order Repeated (vv. 15, 16)
     Not Such a Monster, After All
III. SAUL TRANSFORMED (Acts 9:17-20)
   A. The Lord's Message (vv. 17, 18a)
   B. The Lord's New Man (vv. 18b-20)
CONCLUSION
   A. From Sinners to Saints
   B. From Ignorant to Informed
   C. From Indolent to Energetic
   D. Prayer
   E. Thought to Remember

A street "called Straight" in Damascus is the subject of a photo, which is visual 7 of the visuals packet. The visual is shown on page 60.

Introduction

Most of us have heard of John Newton. Early in life he was engaged in the slave trade, transporting people to lives of bondage. Somehow the gospel of Jesus reached him. Touched and transformed, John Newton became a Christian minister, calling slaves of sin to be transported to lives of freedom in Christ. He was the man who gave us the words to our beloved hymn "Amazing Grace."

A. Transforming Power

The power of almighty God is no less amazing than His grace. He transforms sinners into saints, millions of them. Besides, He sometimes transforms those who already are devoted to Him. Moses was a shepherd for forty years, but God made him the leader of a nation. David was a shepherd too, but God made him king. Amos was a southern farmer, but God sent him north to prophesy to the people of Israel. And then there was Saul.

B. Lesson Background

Saul was born in Tarsus of Cilicia, but we meet him first in Jerusalem. There he was a student under Gamaliel, a famous teacher of the Jews (Acts 22:3).

Gamaliel advised restraint in dealing with the Christians who filled Jerusalem with their teaching (Acts 5:33-39), but Saul would have none of that. It seemed to him that these Christians were bent on destroying the ancient religion of Israel, and he could see nothing to do about it but to destroy the Christians. He stood by with approval when Stephen was stoned to death, and then he took the lead in hunting down other Christians and jailing them (Acts 8:1-3). But God almighty had other plans for Saul.

I. Halt!
(Acts 9:1-6)

Saul's campaign failed to accomplish its purpose. Instead of giving up their faith, the Christians gave up their homes. They scattered into the many towns and villages of Judea and Samaria. They took their faith with them, and they told about it wherever they went (Acts 8:1-4). Churches sprang up all over those areas, and soon in regions far beyond them. Now Saul could see nothing to do but to follow the Christians wherever they went, to hunt them down and lock them up.

A. Furious Persecution (vv. 1, 2)

1, 2. And Saul, yet breathing out threatenings and slaughter against the disciples of the Lord, went unto the high priest, and desired of him letters to Damascus to the synagogues, that if he found any of this way, whether they were men or women, he might bring them bound unto Jerusalem.

Damascus was about a hundred and forty miles from Jerusalem, far outside the area ruled by the Jews. At this time it was subject to Aretas, king of Arabia (2 Corinthians 11:32). Apparently the Jewish rulers in Jerusalem had a treaty allowing them to discipline Jews in Damascus. No doubt Saul learned that a strong church was growing stronger there. Still furiously continuing his persecution, he asked the high priest for papers authorizing him to arrest any Christians found in Damascus and take them to Jerusalem. He must have taken along a squad of police as he set out for that foreign city.

B. Sudden Stop (vv. 3-6)

3. And as he journeyed, he came near Damascus: and suddenly there shined round about him a light from heaven.

The journey was near its end when it was interrupted suddenly. It was about noon, but the light from heaven was brighter than the sunlight (Acts 22:6; 26:13).

4. And he fell to the earth, and heard a voice saying unto him, Saul, Saul, why persecutest thou me?

In fear and reverence, Saul fell prostrate on *the earth,* and so did those who were traveling with him (Acts 26:14). Then *a voice* called *Saul* by name. That must have been as terrifying as the light, especially when the voice accused, *Why persecutest thou me?* The men traveling with Saul heard the voice (v. 7), but saw no one and did not understand the words that were spoken (Acts 22:9).

5. And he said, Who art thou, Lord? And the Lord said, I am Jesus whom thou persecutest: it is hard for thee to kick against the pricks.

Whoever was speaking in that unearthly light was entitled to be called *Lord.* Saul was sure of that, but he did not know who it was. Fearfully he asked, *Who art thou?*

I am Jesus! What a shock! Till that moment Saul had felt sure Jesus was a dead impostor. He had thought he was persecuting disciples of that dead man, liars who were also traitors to country and faith and God. Now suddenly Saul's whole frame of mind collapsed. Those disciples were not liars and traitors after all. They were right! Jesus was alive just as they said—alive and ruling in Heaven! Saul himself was the liar, the traitor to country and faith and God! What shame, what grief, what terror must have crushed the man as he cringed on the ground under that blinding light!

It is hard for thee to kick against the pricks. This pictures Saul as a stubborn ox. The ox is pricked by a sharp goad to make him move; but instead of moving, he rebelliously kicks at the goad—and that hurts him the more. Perhaps it means that Paul had been having a hard struggle within himself. He was a good man at heart. What he was doing was painful to him. He was putting many people in jail, but it hurt him.

How to Say It

ANANIAS. An-uh-*nye*-us.
ARETAS. *Air*-ih-tas.
CILICIA. Sih-*lish*-i-uh.
GAMALIEL. Guh-*may*-lih-ul.

That was the prick of conscience urging him to move away from his furious persecution; but instead of moving, he kicked at the prick. He went on more furiously with his persecution because he thought it was his duty—and the more he did it, the more it hurt him.

6. And he trembling and astonished said, Lord, what wilt thou have me to do? And the Lord said unto him, Arise, and go into the city, and it shall be told thee what thou must do.

Saul did not kick against this new goad that urged him away from his persecution. Now he was broken, shamed, humiliated, terrified. He was ready to do whatever Jesus said. It is notable that Jesus did not tell him what to do to be forgiven and saved from his sin. Last week we read that an angel sent Philip to the Gaza road, and the Holy Spirit told him to join a passing chariot. Now we read that Jesus himself stopped Saul's persecution. But neither angel nor Spirit nor Jesus explained the way of salvation. That work has been given to Christians, and no one is going to do it for us. So now Jesus sent Saul on to Damascus. There a human messenger would tell him what to do.

LIGHT FROM HEAVEN

"Shooting stars" are small particles of matter in the solar system that streak into earth's atmosphere and, in a brief burst of light, are vaporized. Sometimes, however, a much larger mass of matter bursts into our thin envelope of air. On these occasions, the meteorite burns with a brilliant light and strikes the ground with tremendous force.

Several thousand years ago a meteorite traveling at forty-three thousand miles per hour hit the earth near what is now Flagstaff, Arizona. We can still see the result: a crater nearly six hundred feet deep and more than three-fourths of a mile across—an amazing effect for such a brief, bright event!

Saul of Tarsus was bent on destroying the church. He was a zealous defender of the law and saw the church as a threat to Judaism. The light from heaven and the accompanying message that came to Saul comprised only one brief event in human history. But the enormous change that took place in Saul's life as a result was a force to be recognized. Saul's zeal for the law was changed into zeal for Christ, and the world bears the marks of that change.

Will what we do for Christ give evidence that we have seen that "light from heaven"?

—C. R. B.

II. The Lord's Messenger
(Acts 9:10-16)

Saul was blinded by that terrific light, but his companions could see, so they led him on to Damascus. For three days Saul remained in utter darkness, eating nothing, drinking nothing, waiting to be told what to do (vv. 8, 9). And he was praying (v. 11).

A. Order (vv. 10-12)

10. And there was a certain disciple at Damascus, named Ananias; and to him said the Lord in a vision, Ananias. And he said, Behold, I am here, Lord.

It seems that *Ananias* was a Jew of Damascus who had been won to Christ. He had heard of Saul's persecution in Jerusalem (v. 13). Now *in a vision* he heard the Lord speak to him. He may have been surprised and startled, but apparently he was not so frightened as Saul had been. He responded promptly and waited to hear more.

11. And the Lord said unto him, Arise, and go into the street which is called Straight, and inquire in the house of Judas for one called Saul, of Tarsus: for, behold, he prayeth.

Saul was praying. No doubt he was praying, among other things, for someone to come and tell him what to do, as Jesus had promised (v. 6). Ananias was to be God's answer to that prayer.

12. And hath seen in a vision a man named Ananias coming in, and putting his hand on him, that he might receive his sight.

Blind Saul was being prepared to receive God's messenger. Already he had seen *a vision* of *a man named Ananias* coming to restore his sight with a touch. When the vision would become reality, Saul would have no doubt that Ananias was really God's messenger.

B. Protest (vv. 13, 14)

13. Then Ananias answered, Lord, I have heard by many of this man, how much evil he hath done to thy saints at Jerusalem.

Christians coming from Jerusalem naturally had told why they came, and Ananias had *heard by many* of Saul's furious campaign.

14. And here he hath authority from the chief priests to bind all that call on thy name.

Apparently Christians were still coming from Jerusalem to Damascus. News of Saul's coming and his purpose had gotten there before he did. Should Ananias go looking for the man who was looking for him with the intention of taking him to Jerusalem to be punished?

C. Order Repeated (vv. 15, 16)

15. But the Lord said unto him, Go thy way: for he is a chosen vessel unto me, to bear my name before the Gentiles, and kings, and the children of Israel.

Incredible as it seemed, Jesus' worst persecutor was to become His best preacher. Fervent Jew though he was, Saul was to be a special messenger to *the Gentiles*. He was to stand before *kings*. He was to speak also to his own people, *the children of Israel*. Everywhere he was to take Jesus' *name*. He was to proclaim Jesus, the Christ, the Son of God. He was to sound Jesus' call and His promise of salvation. This assurance must have quieted Ananias's fear, but still we wonder if his voice trembled a little as he walked up to Judas's house and asked for Saul.

16. For I will show him how great things he must suffer for my name's sake.

The persecutor would become the persecuted. Saul had done great things against the Christians; he would be a Christian, and *great things* would be done against him.

NOT SUCH A MONSTER, AFTER ALL

Boris Karloff portrayed "Frankenstein" as a horrific monster in the famous 1931 film. Through the years since then, a whole series of Frankenstein movies have followed, using the same monstrous motif for the title character.

In 1993, however, a made-for-television movie portrayed Frankenstein as a far more human being—a person with normal human longings for acceptance and companionship. Ironically, this more accurately depicts the character as Mary Shelley, his creator, portrayed him in her 1818 novel. It turns out that Frankenstein is not such a monster, after all.

Saul of Tarsus was "breathing threats and murder" against the church (Acts 9:1, *New American Standard Bible*). When Ananias first heard that Saul was coming to Damascus, he

A street called Straight

visual 7

must have trembled to think of the pain and suffering the church might soon endure at the hands of this monster. So it must have been a great surprise—and one hard to believe—when the Lord revealed that the world would soon see a different, converted Saul. When the sin was washed from Saul's heart, he would be seen as not such a monster, after all!

As difficult as it may be to believe that some hardened sinners can change, we should never doubt the life-changing power of God. —C. R. B.

III. Saul Transformed
(Acts 9:17-20)

Can you imagine how Saul felt? For three long days he could not tell day from night. He was blind. For three long days he had nothing to eat, and not even a drink of water. For three long days he prayed. We know of only one communication he received in those days: a vision of "a man named Ananias." But the three days ended.

A. The Lord's Message (vv. 17, 18a)

17. And Ananias went his way, and entered into the house; and putting his hands on him said, Brother Saul, the Lord, even Jesus, that appeared unto thee in the way as thou camest, hath sent me, that thou mightest receive thy sight, and be filled with the Holy Ghost.

Besides what is recorded here in the verse before us, the Lord's message to Saul included the plain command, "Receive thy sight" (Acts 22:13). It also included this: "And now why tarriest thou? arise, and be baptized, and wash away thy sins, calling on the name of the Lord" (22:16). But the main purpose of verse 17 in our text is to show that Ananias came exactly as Saul in the vision had seen him coming (v. 12). By that Saul was sure that Ananias was really the Lord's messenger.

18a. And immediately there fell from his eyes as it had been scales: and he received sight forthwith.

Ananias's word and touch were effective: instantly Saul could see. It was as if *scales* had been covering his eyes, and now were gone.

B. The Lord's New Man (vv. 18b-20)

18b. And arose, and was baptized.

Saul did this in response to Ananias's plain urging (Acts 22:16). It was not necessary for Ananias to explain the meaning of baptism. Saul must have known what the apostles had been teaching in Jerusalem. But Ananias did mention the feature most reassuring to Saul at the moment: this was the way to get rid of his sins. His sins must have been a heavy burden on his

mind and soul through all those days since Jesus had appeared to him on the way.

19. And when he had received meat, he was strengthened. Then was Saul certain days with the disciples which were at Damascus.

Instead of going back to Jerusalem or going home to Tarsus, Saul stayed for a time with *the disciples which were at Damascus*.

20. And straightway he preached Christ in the synagogues, that he is the Son of God.

Saul was not one to be quiet about his new conviction. Promptly he began to reason with the Jews *in the synagogues*, teaching the same doctrine that had brought death to Stephen in Jerusalem, the same truth for which the disciples had been driven from Jerusalem and had scattered at least as far as Damascus, the same teaching that Saul had been trying to stop.

It may have been soon after this that Saul went away to Arabia for a time. (Galatians 1:15-17). We do not know how long he stayed in Arabia or what he did there; but we can imagine that he spent long days restudying the Scriptures of the Old Testament and seeing how perfectly Jesus fulfilled the prophecies of the Christ. Jesus had called Saul to be a minister and a witness; Jesus would send him to testify far and near (Acts 26:16-18). He was Christ's apostle, for the word apostle means one who is sent. Saul was an apostle as surely and as fully as were the other twelve apostles (2 Corinthians 11:5). He was filled with the Holy Spirit (Acts 9:17), guided and inspired as the other apostles were.

From Arabia Saul went back to Damascus and resumed his teaching in the synagogues. Unbelieving Jews tried to argue with him, but they were defeated (Acts 9:22) just as those in Jerusalem had lost their debates with Stephen (Acts 6:9, 10). Soon Saul began to learn how he must suffer for the Lord's name (Acts 9:16). Unbelievers plotted to kill him, but disciples helped him to escape (Acts 9:22-25).

Conclusion

You Don't Have to Stay the Way You Are. That is the intriguing title of a book that appeared some years ago. If you are not what you would like to be, or if you are not what you ought to be, you can change. It's true. People are changing all the time.

A. From Sinners to Saints

One of the most momentous changes in the world transforms a sinner to a saint. In the language of the New Testament, every Christian is a saint. The name means a person is set apart, dedicated. Even when one fails to live up to one's dedication, he or she is still dedicated, still a saint.

In a former lesson we read that three thousand persons became saints in a single day, the Day of Pentecost. That is unusual, but the same kind of change is going on day by day.

Most of us who read this book have made the change from sinner to saint. Now we are the people who help others make it. Are you doing that? You don't know how? Read the second chapter of Acts to see how Peter appealed to people who believed the Bible. Read Acts 17:16-31 to see how Paul appealed to people who did not believe the Bible. Put their messages in your own words and adapt them to the sinners you know. If you're not very good at that, you can increase your offerings for the support of people who are expert.

B. From Ignorant to Informed

Some people sin without knowing it. Saul is a prime example. After he learned the truth, he said he had been "a blasphemer, and a persecutor, and injurious," but he had done it "ignorantly" (1 Timothy 1:13). When he tried to stop the preaching of the gospel, he thought he was defending God's truth against a lie. When he learned the truth, he found that he had been defending a lie against God's truth. Then he called himself the chief of sinners (1 Timothy 1:15).

The Lord took an unusual way to inform Saul of the facts. He came in a blinding light to prove that He had risen from the dead. Most people learn the facts in other ways, or not at all. Now the facts of Jesus' life and death and resurrection, verified by competent witnesses, are set down in black and white for all to read. Those who do not read the record need someone like you or me to tell them—and your duty and mine is to meet their need. Whom have you told in the past week, or the past year?

Sometimes a careless unbeliever says, "When Jesus comes to me as He came to Saul, then I'll believe." Thoughtless, thoughtless! Do you really want Jesus to call you as He called Saul? Do you want to spend the rest of your life in earnest, ardent preaching of the gospel to nations and kings and the children of Israel? Do you want to endure prison and beating, cold and hunger, shipwreck and peril? (2 Corinthians 11:24-28). Jesus came to call Saul to all that—to make him a minister and a witness, an apostle to the world in spite of terrible persecution (Acts 26:16-18).

That meeting with Jesus on the road to Damascus did not take away Saul's sin and make him a saint. It made him a convicted sinner, a remorseful, penitent sinner, a frightened, blinded, grieving sinner, fasting and praying—but still a sinner. It remained for him to wash away his sin in baptism, even as you and I have done, or can do (Acts 22:16).

C. From Indolent to Energetic

The Lord rebuked the church at Ephesus because it had left its first love. Once it had labored earnestly for the Lord, labored vigorously and long, and had loved it. Now it was content to drift, content with its accomplishments, content with its reputation, content with its past. To that church Jesus called, "Remember therefore from whence thou art fallen, and repent, and do the first works" (Revelation 2:1-7).

Seldom has any church matched the zeal and fervor of the first church in Jerusalem. Despite the frowns of religious leaders, it became a shining light that beckoned sinners to repent and live. Despite the fury of the government, it became a training school that made its members preachers of the gospel. When persecution drove those members from Jerusalem, they "went every where preaching the word."

Is that first love still alive in your congregation? Is it still alive in your heart? If not, hear the call of the Master: "Repent, and do the first works"!

D. Prayer

How unfailing is Your love, our Father! For us You gave Your only Son. Stir our hearts anew, we pray, awaken our love, arouse our energy until we do Your work as well as it was done by Your saints of old. In Jesus' name, amen.

E. Thought to Remember

"Be zealous therefore" (Revelation 3:19).

Home Daily Bible Readings

Monday, Oct. 9—How Paul Became a Disciple (Galatians 1:11-19)

Tuesday, Oct. 10—Called to Preach to Gentiles (Acts 22:12-21)

Wednesday, Oct. 11—Benefited From Roman Citizenship (Acts 22:22-29)

Thursday, Oct. 12—Plot Against Paul's Life (Acts 23:6-15)

Friday, Oct. 13—Paul Preaching in Rome (Acts 28:23-31)

Saturday, Oct. 14—Paul's Care for the Church (1 Thessalonians 3)

Sunday, Oct. 15—Saul on the Damascus Road (Acts 9:1-9)

Learning by Doing

This page contains an alternate lesson plan emphasizing learning activities. Classes desiring such student involvement will find these suggestions helpful.

Learning Goals

As students participate in today's class session, they should:

1. Compare the account of the conversion of the Ethiopian official (Acts 8) with the account of Saul's conversion.

2. Describe how Saul's life was dramatically changed by his encounter with Christ.

3. Recognize the role of a human messenger in the process of a person's conversion to Christ.

Into the Lesson

Write this heading on your chalkboard: "Barriers to the Gospel Today." Ask your class members to identify as many barriers as they can in about ninety seconds. List them on the chalkboard as they mention them.

Then have the students look at the list you have formed and see if they can suggest a person's name to be put beside each barrier. For example, if someone suggests as a barrier, "Anti-Christian bias in the media," write the name of a media person who demonstrates that bias.

Tell the class that today's lesson focuses on a leader of the opposition to Christianity in the first century and shows the surprising way that the Lord dealt with him.

Into the Word

Begin with a brief lecture to establish the background of the life of Saul. Perhaps you could recruit a member of your class several days ahead of time to present this. The lecture should answer the following questions: Who was Saul? Where was he born? How was he educated? What was his religion? What was he famous for? Where is Damascus? Why was Saul interested in going there? (Write these questions as an outline on your chalkboard.)

Then lead your class members to compare the main characters of today's lesson text with those of last week's study. To help them do this give each student a sheet with the following charts and questions.

The first chart has two vertical columns side by side with the headings "Ethiopian Official" and "Saul." To the left of the columns write these questions:

1. What was his background?
2. What was his knowledge of the Scripture?

3. How open was he to the gospel?
4. How did God get his attention?
5. What was the role of a teacher in his conversion?
6. What did he do in response to the teacher's instruction?
7. How did he demonstrate his new relationship with Christ?

Beside two more vertical columns with the headings "Philip" and "Ananias," write these questions:

1. How did God call him to evangelize?
2. How did he respond to the call?
3. Why do you suppose God called him and not someone else?

If you do this activity as a whole class, use each of the questions as a discussion starter. Have your students write answers on their worksheets as the class talks. If you prefer, this study can be done in small groups. Half of the groups can compare the Ethiopian and Saul while the rest of the class compares Philip and Ananias. After allotting ten minutes, each half should report to the other.

Option. Instead of the activity just described, or in addition to it, have class members compare the three accounts of Saul's conversion (Acts 9:1-18; 22:1-16; 26:9-18). Students should work in groups and list in order on poster paper the events from each account. (Divide the groups in thirds and have each third examine a different account.)

Have the groups display the lists; then make a composite list that tells the whole story of Saul's conversion.

Into Life

Write the following principles on your chalkboard. Lead your class in discussing them in light of today's text.

•God depends on His people to take the message of salvation to those who are lost in sin.

•Faith in Christ has the potential to change a life completely.

•No one is too great a sinner to be forgiven by God.

Discuss with the class:

•How does this passage demonstrate each principle?

•Which principle most challenges you as you consider your walk with Christ?

Let's Talk It Over

The questions on this page are designed to encourage review of the lesson Scriptures and to promote discussion of the lesson by the class. The answers provided are only discussion starters. Let your class talk it over from there.

1. When Jesus told Saul that it was hard for him "to kick against the goads" (Acts 26:14, *New American Standard Bible*), it seems that He was referring to a struggle taking place within Saul. Give examples of how one today may experience inner struggles by ignoring the urgings of his or her conscience.

Perhaps we need to apologize to another person for a harsh word we spoke or for an uncharitable deed we did to that person. We kick against the goads if we ignore the urging of our conscience to resolve the matter, and when we go out of our way to avoid that person. Perhaps we deceived someone about a particular matter. If we refuse to correct the situation, we may be kicking against the goads. Sometimes people violate their conscience by engaging in such sins as stealing or sexual misbehavior. Like David, they may feel the burden of an offended conscience, (see Psalm 32:3, 4), but unlike David, they may fail to confess and forsake the sin, and they thereby intensify their inner suffering (Psalm 32:5, 6).

2. Saul asked, "Lord, what wilt thou have me to do?" How is this an appropriate question for a believer to ask on a regular basis?

We human beings are prone to depend on our own judgment and resources until we fall into circumstances that seem beyond us. Then we desperately call on God to bail us out. How much better for us if we could learn to exercise conscious dependence on God regarding every decision and every task to be performed. Obviously this does not mean that we must slavishly bring before God such matters as whether to eat cereal or pancakes for breakfast or whether to wear a blue or grey suit or dress. It is appropriate, however, at the beginning of each day to express a general sense of dependence on God by incorporating in our prayers the attitude voiced by Saul in his question. And it is helpful to repeat this at regular intervals throughout the day.

3. Jesus told Saul that in Damascus he would be told what he must do. The blinded Saul probably spent much time praying for someone to come with that word of instruction. Ananias was the answer to that prayer. Why would it be helpful for us to think of ourselves as potential

"Ananiases"—God's answers to people's prayers?

We may have neighbors, fellow workers, or other acquaintances who are hurting enough that they are crying out to God for help. They may need to hear God's message of salvation, or they may be Christians who are desperate for a listening ear or a word of counsel. It should be an exciting thought for us to realize that we can be answers to such people's prayers. If we develop the habit of asking, "Lord, what wilt thou have me to do?" (see the previous question), that may enable us to cultivate an alertness to the needs of others around us. And it will produce a sensitiveness to God's guidance, so that we indeed may be the answer to the prayer of someone in need.

4. How may it be beneficial for us to think of one another as "saints"?

In the New Testament, all believers are referred to as "saints" (see Romans 1:7; 1 Corinthians 1:2; Philippians 1:1). That term does not mean that Christians have achieved absolute holiness or perfect piety. It signifies that God has called us and set us apart to lives of holiness. If we regularly think of ourselves and our fellow Christians as saints, we may be reminded of our obligation to cultivate holiness in every thought, word, and deed.

5. How can a Christian or a church rekindle zeal for serving Christ?

The first step is to acknowledge one's lack of zeal. We may blame this on the preacher for the quality of his sermons or the church's leaders for their inability to develop appealing programs. But these cannot be used as excuses for our lack of zeal, which we are personally responsible for maintaining (Romans 12:11). The second step is to repent (Revelation 3:19). Keep in mind that repentance is more than sorrow for a sinful condition, it is the turning away from that condition. The third step is the actual cultivation of zeal. Regular meditation on the blessings and promises of the gospel should stir up zeal within us. Our zeal for serving Christ will be stimulated if we frequently recall the change Christ has made in our lives. Persistent prayer for genuine spiritual fervor is another key.

Gentiles Receive the Spirit

October 22
Lesson 8

DEVOTIONAL READING: Acts 10:9-23.

LESSON SCRIPTURE: Acts 10:1—11:18.

PRINTED TEXT: Acts 10:30-39a, 44-48.

Acts 10:30-39a, 44-48

30 And Cornelius said, Four days ago I was fasting until this hour; and at the ninth hour I prayed in my house, and, behold, a man stood before me in bright clothing,

31 And said, Cornelius, thy prayer is heard, and thine alms are had in remembrance in the sight of God.

32 Send therefore to Joppa, and call hither Simon, whose surname is Peter; he is lodged in the house of one Simon a tanner by the sea side: who, when he cometh, shall speak unto thee.

33 Immediately therefore I sent to thee; and thou hast well done that thou art come. Now therefore are we all here present before God, to hear all things that are commanded thee of God.

34 Then Peter opened his mouth, and said, Of a truth I perceive that God is no respecter of persons:

35 But in every nation he that feareth him, and worketh righteousness, is accepted with him.

36 The word which God sent unto the children of Israel, preaching peace by Jesus Christ: (he is Lord of all:)

37 That word, I say, ye know, which was published throughout all Judea, and began from Galilee, after the baptism which John preached;

38 How God anointed Jesus of Nazareth with the Holy Ghost and with power: who went about doing good, and healing all that were oppressed of the devil; for God was with him.

39a And we are witnesses of all things which he did both in the land of the Jews, and in Jerusalem.

. . . .

44 While Peter yet spake these words, the Holy Ghost fell on all them which heard the word.

45 And they of the circumcision which believed were astonished, as many as came with Peter, because that on the Gentiles also was poured out the gift of the Holy Ghost.

46 For they heard them speak with tongues, and magnify God. Then answered Peter,

47 Can any man forbid water, that these should not be baptized, which have received the Holy Ghost as well as we?

48 And he commanded them to be baptized in the name of the Lord. Then prayed they him to tarry certain days.

Oct
22

GOLDEN TEXT: God is no respecter of persons: but in every nation he that feareth him, and worketh righteousness, is accepted with him.—Acts 10:34, 35.

The Story of Christian Beginnings (Acts)

Unit 2: Witnessing in Judea and Samaria
(Lessons 5-9)

Lesson Aims

After the completion of this lesson students should be able to:

1. Recall the story told in our text and explain what it means to the church and the world.

2. Give thanks because the way of salvation is open to them.

3. Try to bring someone else into that way.

Lesson Outline

INTRODUCTION

    A. The Jewish Church

    B. Lesson Background

  I. A READY AUDIENCE (Acts 10:30-33)

    A. Angel's Message (vv. 30-32)

    B. Message Obeyed (v. 33)

       Important Information

 II. A PLAIN MESSAGE (Acts 10:34-39)

    A. Impartial God (vv. 34, 35)

    B. Jesus the Savior (vv. 36-38)

       The God Who Cares for All

    C. Reliable Witnesses (v. 39)

III. A HAPPY ENDING (Acts 10:44-48)

    A. Surprise! (vv. 44-46a)

    B. Question (vv. 46b, 47)

    C. Baptism (v. 48)

CONCLUSION

    A. Purpose of the Tongues

    B. Purpose of the Record

    C. Prayer

    D. Thought to Remember

That persons of any race or nation are welcomed by God is the theme of visual 8 of the visuals packet. The visual is shown on page 69.

Introduction

No one of another race is to go inside the barrier around the temple and enclosure. Anyone who is caught will be responsible for his own death, which will follow.

Those words were carved in stone, and stones inscribed with them were built into the wall that separated the sacred inner court of the temple in Jerusalem from the big outer court that anyone might enter. That wall and that warning were fitting symbols of the agelong separation of the Jews from all the other people of the world. From the time of Abraham, he and his descendants knew they were a people apart, a people God had chosen for His own.

A. The Jewish Church

When the church of Jesus began in Jerusalem, all its members were Jews. It seems that none of them even dreamed that Gentiles ever would be included. Jesus was Israel's Messiah; His blessings were for Israel. So they thought.

Jesus had told His apostles to go to all the world and preach to every creature (Mark 16:15). Apparently they thought that meant every Jewish creature, for Jews then were scattered through all the known world. Saul was specifically sent to Gentiles (Acts 26:16-18), but the brethren in Jerusalem did not know that yet.

The Holy Spirit had come to guide the apostles into all truth (John 16:13). He inspired their preaching, and it was wonderfully effective. But Jesus wanted people of all nations in His church. That was truth too, but it seems that Jewish minds were so firmly closed to it that the Spirit had to use extraordinary methods to teach it to them. In unusual ways two messages came, one to a Gentile and one to a Jew.

B. Lesson Background

Cornelius was not a Jew, but neither was he a heathen. He was a Roman, an officer in the foreign army that occupied the Jews' country. But Cornelius believed in the real God, as the Jews did; and he lived in godly ways. He prayed much, and he was generous in sharing his wealth (Acts 10:1, 2). This officer was stationed in the seacoast city of Caesarea, the headquarters of the Roman governor of Judea and Samaria.

To Cornelius came a heavenly angel, but not to explain the way of salvation. The angel told Cornelius to send for Simon Peter, who then was staying at Joppa, more than thirty miles down the coast. Peter would tell Cornelius what he ought to do. Cornelius promptly sent three men to ask Peter to come (vv. 3-8).

About noon the next day, a vision came to Peter in Joppa. He was praying alone when he saw a big sheet let down from Heaven with all kinds of animals in it. A voice invited hungry Peter to kill an animal and eat.

Peter objected. Such meat would not be kosher. It would be common, ordinary. In Jewish terminology, it would be unclean.

The voice spoke again: "What God hath cleansed, that call not thou common" (vv. 9-16).

While Peter was wondering what the vision meant, the messengers arrived from Cornelius.

Plainly the Holy Spirit told Peter to go with them. Then Peter began to see what the vision meant. He should not call those messengers unclean, Gentiles though they were. He invited the men to stay for the night, and the next day he started to Caesarea with them. Knowing full well that strict Jews at Jerusalem would criticize him for that, Peter asked some Jewish Christians to go along and be witnesses of what was going to happen (vv. 17-23).

In Caesarea, Cornelius was ready for them. He had called together his relatives and friends to hear whatever message Peter would bring. Violating the traditional law of the rabbis, Peter went into that Gentile house and asked why Cornelius had sent for him (Acts 10:24-29).

I. A Ready Audience
(Acts 10:30-33)

What excited expectancy must have filled that house! Cornelius had sent an urgent call for those people. A Jew was coming to tell the Roman what he ought to do. Surely it would be a message from God, for a shining angel had told the Roman to send for that Jew. So there must have been a breathless hush while Cornelius explained why he had sent for Peter.

A. Angel's Message (vv. 30-32)

30. And Cornelius said, Four days ago I was fasting until this hour; and at the ninth hour I prayed in my house, and, behold, a man stood before me in bright clothing.

In answer to Peter's question in verse 29, Cornelius explained exactly why he had sent for Peter. Counting days in the way then customary, he told what had happened *four days ago.* On the first two of those days his messengers had traveled to Joppa; on the third and fourth days they had returned with Peter and other Jewish Christians. On the first of those four days Cornelius had prayed at the customary Jewish hour of prayer, the ninth hour, midafternoon. The oldest manuscripts of Acts do not mention *fasting* here, so it is left out of some English versions. Cornelius may have been fasting, but we cannot be sure. As he was praying an angel appeared (Acts 10:3), whom Cornelius described as *a man . . . in bright clothing.*

31. And said, Cornelius, thy prayer is heard, and thine alms are had in remembrance in the sight of God.

First, the angel assured Cornelius that God had both heard his prayer and taken note of his generous giving. Prayers are more likely to be answered when the one who prays is a sincere worshiper and an unselfish giver.

How to Say It

CAESAREA. Sess-uh-*ree*-uh.
CORNELIUS. Kor-*nee*-lih-us or Kor-*neel*-yus.

---

32. Send therefore to Joppa, and call hither Simon, whose surname is Peter; he is lodged in the house of one Simon a tanner by the sea side: who, when he cometh, shall speak unto thee.

The angel was specific. Simon Peter would have a message for Cornelius, and the angel told exactly where Simon Peter was to be found. Why didn't the angel tell Cornelius to go to Peter instead of inviting Peter to come to him? For one thing, God surely knew Cornelius would bring a houseful of relatives and friends to hear the gospel with him. For another thing, God was bringing about a change in Peter as well as a change in Cornelius. He was breaking down Peter's lifelong aversion to people who were not Jews, and bringing Peter into a Gentile's house was part of the process.

B. Message Obeyed (v. 33)

33. Immediately therefore I sent to thee; and thou hast well done that thou art come. Now therefore are we all here present before God, to hear all things that are commanded thee of God.

Cornelius obeyed the angel *immediately.* Though it was midafternoon when the angel came, Cornelius called his men and started them on their way that very day. That shows how eager he was to get whatever message Peter would bring. Since a heavenly angel ordered the invitation, Cornelius was sure Peter had done right in coming, even though it was contrary to the traditional rules of his people (Acts 10:28).

Now Peter was there, and many Gentiles were there to hear him. They realized that they were *present before God;* before them was the man whom God's angel had told them to call; they were sure they would hear from him what God had commanded him to say. Was ever an audience more ready for a sermon?

IMPORTANT INFORMATION

The "information superhighway" is the latest place one may go to find information. With a computer, a modem, and the appropriate software, one can gain access to many sources that provide an amazing variety of information.

Some major city newspapers now have such an information service. You can get up-to-the-minute "hard" news, plus what is happening in sports, entertainment, or the stock market. You can even "talk" to other readers to compare your response to the news with theirs.

Cornelius was a devout God-fearing, generous man. God had important information for Cornelius—the saving gospel of Christ—so He commanded Cornelius to send for Simon Peter, who would deliver the message to him.

Peter was an eyewitness of the ministry, death, and resurrection of Christ. He would give Cornelius all the information necessary to establish faith in Christ and lead to salvation.

God saw fit to have the testimony of Peter and other eyewitnesses recorded for us in His Word, so that we too may learn of salvation and how we may share in it. That's better than even the *latest* in modern technology can do!   —C. R. B.

II. A Plain Message
(Acts 10:34-39)

Peter too could see that God had arranged this meeting. God's angel had told Cornelius to send for him; God's Spirit had told Peter to come (Acts 10:19, 20). Now he had come, and he had no message except the gospel of Jesus. It was plain that God wanted him to give that message to these Gentiles.

A. Impartial God (vv. 34, 35)

34. Then Peter opened his mouth, and said, Of a truth I perceive that God is no respecter of persons.

God is no respecter of persons; that is, God does not favor any person because that person is a member of a particular group, or holds a high position among men, or is rich, or is powerful. From the Old Testament Peter knew that God does not favor any person for such reasons, and men should not (2 Samuel 14:14; 2 Chronicles 19:7; Deuteronomy 1:17; 16:19). Now he realized, perhaps for the first time, that it applied to all mankind. God does not give special favor to anyone just because one is a Jew.

35. But in every nation he that feareth him, and worketh righteousness, is accepted with him.

God does not respect persons; but He does respect faith and righteousness. Cornelius was a Roman, outside the chosen nation; but He won God's attention by sincere worship and goodness.

B. Jesus the Savior (vv. 36-38)

36. The word which God sent unto the children of Israel, preaching peace by Jesus Christ: (he is Lord of all).

God now was using Peter to send a message to Cornelius and other Romans, and it was the same message that *God sent unto the children of Israel* by Peter and others. It was a message of *peace by Jesus Christ.* Jesus is the Christ, the Messiah, the one whom God has chosen to be prophet and priest and king. Those who believe in Him and obey Him are forgiven, cleansed, purified. Therefore they are at peace with God. They are God's children, and brothers and sisters of one another. Therefore they are at peace among themselves. Jesus the Savior is also the Lord—the commander, the ruler, the owner—and *he is Lord of all.* Now Peter was learning that *all* means Gentiles as well as Jews.

THE GOD WHO CARES FOR ALL

"Flu" and the common cold are no respecters of persons. We all come down with these afflictions in spite of our best efforts to avoid them.

In the days before antibiotics, every family, it seems, had a favorite remedy for these ailments. For example, some treated sore throats by blowing sulphur through a straw against the back of the throat or by rubbing kerosene on the neck. It was thought you could keep germs away by hanging around your neck a bag containing fried onions or asafetida—a foul-smelling gum resin from Oriental plants.

Sin is the common ailment of the human spirit, but fortunately for us all, God loves the people of all races and nationalities alike. His remedy for the disease that destroys our souls is the same for all: fear God, do what is right, and trust in Christ and obey Him.   —C. R. B.

37. That word, I say, ye know, which was published throughout all Judea, and began from Galilee, after the baptism which John preached.

Cornelius was an officer in the Roman army. He and others like him were in Palestine to keep the peace, to prevent any rebellion against Rome. They were alert to every movement among the Jews. They knew that the crowds had flocked to John the Baptist. Some of them had been in those crowds, listening to see if John was stirring up insurrection. After John was put in prison, Jesus came to Galilee with His teaching. Crowds then flocked to Him. Again the Romans listened, but heard no call to rebellion. The Romans knew that Jesus had been crucified; and they knew the teaching of His resurrection had filled Jerusalem and had spread *throughout all Judea.* Because they were watching for any sign of rebellious uprising, the Romans were aware of the facts and the teachings of this religious movement; but until this time, both Romans and Jews had thought that movement was strictly a Jewish matter. Now both were beginning to see that it included Romans as well.

38. How God anointed Jesus of Nazareth with the Holy Ghost and with power: who went about doing good, and healing all that were oppressed of the devil; for God was with him.

Cornelius and his friends knew the basic facts of Jesus' ministry; but Peter now gave a brief summary of them, emphasizing God's part in what was done. *God anointed Jesus of Nazareth with the Holy Ghost.* Luke 3:21, 22 records that the Holy Spirit came to Jesus in a visible form. With Him came *power* by which Jesus *went about doing good.* Jesus encountered many who were *oppressed of the devil.* Whether the oppression was in the form of demons or sickness or crippling deformity, Jesus released those who were oppressed. Why was He able to do such marvelous miracles? *God was with him.*

C. Reliable Witnesses (v. 39)

39. And we are witnesses of all things which he did both in the land of the Jews, and in Jerusalem.

Peter and the other apostles were with Jesus through His three-year ministry. They could testify positively about what He did and said all over the Jewish country and in Jerusalem.

Verses 39-43 record that Peter went on to mention other facts of tremendous importance:

1. Jews and Romans crucified Jesus.

2. God raised Him from the dead and showed Him to the apostles so they could testify positively that He was alive after He died.

3. Jesus told the apostles to testify that God had named Jesus to be the judge of the living and the dead.

4. All the prophets also testify to Jesus, that all who believe in Him will have their sins forgiven.

III. A Happy Ending
(Acts 10:44-48)

Peter had been speaking of the work of God: God anointed Jesus with the Holy Spirit and power; Jesus could do miracles because God was with Him; God raised Jesus from the dead. Now God acted again, acted in a way that surprised both Romans and Jews.

A. Surprise! (vv. 44-46a)

44. While Peter yet spake these words, the Holy Ghost fell on all them which heard the word.

Peter might have said much more if he had not been interrupted; but he was interrupted, and the interruption certainly was from God.

visual 8

45. And they of the circumcision which believed were astonished, as many as came with Peter, because that on the Gentiles also was poured out the gift of the Holy Ghost.

They of the circumcision which believed were the Jewish Christians who had come from Joppa with Peter (Acts 10:23). There were six of them (Acts 11:12). The six must have found themselves in a turmoil as Peter's speech went on. No doubt Peter had told them of his vision in Joppa. No doubt he had said the Holy Spirit told him to go with Cornelius's messengers. The six could not quarrel with that, so they had come along. They had gone with Peter into a Gentile home, but they may have wondered if that was the right thing to do. They must have wondered even more as Peter was speaking. Peter said whoever believed in Jesus would be forgiven (Acts 10:43). Was it possible that he was going to tell them to repent and be baptized—those foreigners, even those in the army of the enemy? Then came the Holy Spirit.

46a. For they heard them speak with tongues, and magnify God.

This was how the Jewish Christians knew the Holy Spirit had come to the Gentiles. *They heard them speak with tongues,* as the apostles had done when the Holy Spirit had come to them on the Day of Pentecost (Acts 2:4). Nothing is said here of a sound like wind or tongues like fire such as appeared on Pentecost. Whether these were present or not, the tongues were clear evidence of the Spirit's presence.

B. Question (vv. 46b, 47)

46b, 47. Then answered Peter, Can any man forbid water, that these should not be baptized, which have received the Holy Ghost as well as we?

Peter's vision had taught him not to call anything unclean when God had cleansed it (Acts 10:15). The Holy Spirit had told Peter to go with Cornelius's men (Acts 10:19, 20). He had learned that a shining angel had told Cornelius to send for him. Now the Holy Spirit had come to a group of Gentiles. At last Peter was fully convinced. The Lord wanted those Gentiles to be saved and accepted in His church. Peter saw no way to escape that conclusion, so he put the question to the Jewish Christians who had come from Joppa with him. Could any of them see a reason why these Romans should not be baptized? No objection was made. All of the Christians were convinced along with Peter.

C. Baptism (v. 48)

48. And he commanded them to be baptized in the name of the Lord. Then prayed they him to tarry certain days.

So the first Gentiles accepted the Savior and came into the fellowship of the church. They asked Peter to stay with them for some days, and no doubt he did stay to teach them more about the way of the Lord.

Conclusion

The obvious conclusion is the one Peter reached. God wants both Jews and Gentiles in His church. Jesus meant what He said when He told His disciples to make disciples of all nations (Matthew 28:19, 20). The gospel is for every human creature in the world (Mark 16:15).

This now is so well known that we can hardly realize what a difficult conclusion it was for the Jews. It was hard for Peter, and he had some explaining to do when he went back to Jerusalem. When he explained, however, all the Jewish Christians came to the same conclusion, and they were gracious enough to praise God because Gentiles also could be saved (Acts 11:1-18).

Some other conclusions have been drawn from this text, and not all of them are as plain and inescapable as that one.

A. Purpose of the Tongues

Since Cornelius and his friends were the first Gentiles to become Christians, some students have concluded that Jews and Gentiles become Christians in different ways. Jews are called to repent and be baptized, they say (Acts 2:38), but Gentiles must wait for the gift of tongues or some other startling experience to show that the Holy Spirit has come to call them.

We do not find that conclusion verified as we read on through the book of Acts. We read that people became Christians in many places, but we do not read that Jews and Gentiles did it in different ways. All of them believed in Jesus; all of them turned away from wrongdoing to follow Him; all of them were baptized.

Why was the gift of tongues given to Cornelius and his friends? It was not to convince them that Jesus is the Christ, the Savior, the

Lord. That was done by the message Peter brought. The gift of tongues was given to do what it did do: It convinced Peter and the other Jews that God wanted to save Gentiles and accept them in His church.

B. Purpose of the Record

Some students are puzzled because Peter did not tell the Gentiles to repent and they did not say they believed in Christ. This reminds us again that Luke wrote this story briefly, not taking time to record all the details of each event.

Luke records that the Romans spoke with tongues and magnified God (v. 46). In magnifying God they may have clearly declared their belief in His Son. Perhaps they also declared their determination to turn away from wrong and follow Jesus. We can be sure Peter did not have these people baptized without some assurance that they believed in Jesus and wanted to follow Him. We do not need to know exactly how that assurance was given.

This tenth chapter of Acts was not written to teach how one becomes a Christian. It was written to record how the Jews learned that God wants Gentiles in His church—and it does that very well.

C. Prayer

How grateful we are that salvation is not offered to one nation only! What a blessing it is to be included among the saved! We ask for wisdom and strength both to live as saved people ought to live and to share the good news of salvation with others.

D. Thought to Remember

"Whosoever will, let him take the water of life freely" (Revelation 22:17).

Home Daily Bible Readings

Monday, Oct. 16—Nations Blessed Through Abraham (Genesis 22:15-19)
Tuesday, Oct. 17—All Families to Worship God (Psalm 22:27-31)
Wednesday, Oct. 18—Israel a Light to the Nations (Isaiah 49:1-7)
Thursday, Oct. 19—All Peoples to Serve God (Daniel 7:13-18)
Friday, Oct. 20—Gentiles, Fellow Heirs (Ephesians 3:1-6)
Saturday, Oct. 21—Gentiles Welcomed (Romans 15:7-21)
Sunday, Oct. 22—All Are Invited (Revelation 22:12-21)

Learning by Doing

This page contains an alternate lesson plan emphasizing learning activities. Classes desiring such student involvement will find these suggestions helpful.

Learning Goals

As a result of participating in today's class session, the students should:

1. Be able to summarize the account of the conversion of Cornelius recorded in Acts 10.

2. Compare the barriers that separated Peter and Cornelius with attitudes and circumstances that Christians today allow to keep them from sharing the gospel with those who need it.

3. Ask God to help them overcome at least one of these barriers.

Into the Lesson

Write the following phrases on eight slips of paper, one phrase per slip. Distribute the slips among your class members at the beginning of the session:

A member of a cult   *A child abuser*
A homeless person   *A drug dealer*
A victim of AIDS   *An unwed mother*
A homosexual   *A gang member*

Have your class members divide themselves into groups, so that each group has only one member with one of the slips of paper. (Each group should have at least three members. Therefore, if your class is small, use an appropriate number of the phrases.)

Write the following questions on your chalkboard, or display them on a poster that you have prepared before class:

Why do I need the gospel?
Why is it difficult for me to share the gospel?

To begin your discussion, each person with one of the slips of paper is to assume the role of the person described on the slip and to tell the others in the group why he or she needs the gospel message (the first question above).

Then the rest of the group members are to discuss why it is difficult for them to share the gospel with the person described on the slip of paper (the second question).

After about six or seven minutes, let each group tell the whole class what they discussed and how they felt.

Ask the class, "How much does another person's social standing, economic status, or moral behavior affect our willingness to share the gospel with that person?"

Tell the class that today's lesson will consider why the Jewish Christians did not at first share the gospel with the Gentiles and what steps God took to lead them to see that the gospel is for all people.

Into the Word

Before considering today's printed text, review the background for it recorded in Acts 10:1-29. Summarize the background according to the following divisions. Write each of the headings on your chalkboard as you talk:

A message (vv. 1-8)
A vision (vv. 9-20)
A welcome (vv. 21-23a)
A journey (vv. 23b-29)

After this summary, read verses 30-33 aloud. Then ask a volunteer to read verses 34-43 aloud while class members listen for the main message of Peter's sermon.

After the verses are read, ask class members to pair off. Have each pair form a sentence that summarizes the sermon. After three minutes, let members share these. Write several of them on the chalkboard.

Next read verses 44-48 aloud. Ask class members to listen to discover what God did and what Peter did.

Into Life

Discuss with your class:

1. Why did God take such dramatic steps to bring Peter and Cornelius together?

2. Why was the gift of tongues given to Cornelius and his relatives and friends? (See comments in the Conclusion of the lesson under the heading, "A. Purpose of the Tongues.")

Ask class members what barriers stood in the way of Peter's sharing the gospel with Cornelius. Write these on the chalkboard. Then ask your students to mention barriers that may keep Christians from sharing the gospel with non-Christians today. Write these also on the chalkboard. Now ask class members which of the listed barriers are the biggest problems facing your community or your congregation. Put stars beside these.

Discuss specific ways class members can overcome these barriers. Close with prayer for God to use your class members to overcome all the barriers that would hinder their taking the gospel to those who are lost.

Let's Talk It Over

The questions on this page are designed to encourage review of the lesson Scriptures and to promote discussion of the lesson by the class. The answers provided are only discussion starters. Let your class talk it over from there.

1. "Now therefore are we all here present before God, to hear all things that are commanded thee of God" (Acts 10:33b). How is this statement of Cornelius an appropriate sentiment for us as we congregate for worship on the Lord's Day?

It is appropriate because it reminds us that when we assemble for worship we are coming as a body into the very presence of God. As we do so, all mental distractions and all unkind or judgmental thoughts toward other persons should be set aside and replaced by a spirit of humility and reverence before God. It is appropriate also because it reminds us that one of the reasons for our assembling is to receive instruction from God's Word. We are so accustomed to being entertained that we may find ourselves judging the elements of the worship service, such as the sermon and the special music, on the basis of their entertainment value. But God may want us to hear messages such as a call to repentance or an exhortation to share our faith with others—messages that may not be entertaining.

2. Peter was led to understand that "God is no respecter of persons." What implication does this fact have for us? Why may some have difficulty accepting it?

Obviously, if our Heavenly Father does not favor anyone because of outward circumstances, neither should any human being. A person may accept this concept easily in principle, but have difficulty applying it to specific circumstances. Perhaps one has grown up with a negative stereotype regarding persons of different races, or nationalities, or economic classes. Or perhaps one had an unpleasant experience involving a person of one of the groups mentioned above and transferred his or her feelings for that person to the whole group. In such ways we may be tempted to view persons who differ from us as being less deserving of God's interest and love. It is often pointed out that those who are saved will share Heaven's glories with people who differ from them in many ways (as Revelation 7:9, 10 demonstrates). May we who are Christians strive very hard to develop and promote an attitude of respect and acceptance and love for all persons.

3. What are the consequences of practicing respect of persons within the Christian community?

Showing respect to persons fosters division, pride, and resentment. An infectious, malignant spirit begins to pervade the fellowship. The ultimate consequence is a church that belongs to a certain kind of people rather than to Jesus Christ.

4. Peter noted, almost in passing, that Cornelius and other Roman army officers knew of Jesus' career (Acts 10:37-42.). How is this a mark of the authenticity of the gospel?

The Gospels record that Jesus spoke to great crowds of people, and Roman military officials surely would have taken notice of anyone who enjoyed such influence. The Gospels describe many of Jesus' miracles, including one done at the request of a Roman centurion (Matthew 8:5-13). One can easily imagine Roman military officials discussing such miracles and pondering what their effect might be on the people. The Gospels record also the Roman soldiers' involvement with the crucifixion of Jesus and the effect it and its accompanying phenomena had on the centurion and his men (Matthew 27:54). So here in the account of Peter's meeting with Cornelius is an example of the harmonious nature of the New Testament narrative, underscoring the truth of what is written.

5. Jesus "went about doing good" (Acts 10:38). Why is this an appropriate description of Jesus' ministry and an example for us?

Today, a person who attempts in a naive and impractical way to improve the conditions under which other people live is derisively called a "do-gooder." Such an individual is regarded as meddling in other people's business and trying to impress his or her life-style or values on them. In no way is the term applicable to Jesus. He brought genuine good to people by healing their sicknesses, by teaching them divine truth, and by encouraging them to trust in the heavenly Father. And by His atoning death, He made possible for all the ultimate good—eternal life. It should be our aim to imitate our Savior by touching people's lives for their lasting good as we go about our daily activities.

The Church at Antioch

October 29
Lesson 9

DEVOTIONAL READING: Acts 12:1-11.

LESSON SCRIPTURE: Acts 11:19-30; 12:24, 25.

PRINTED TEXT: Acts 11:19-30; 12:24, 25.

Acts 11:19-30

19 Now they which were scattered abroad upon the persecution that arose about Stephen traveled as far as Phoenicia, and Cyprus, and Antioch, preaching the word to none but unto the Jews only.

20 And some of them were men of Cyprus and Cyrene, which, when they were come to Antioch, spake unto the Grecians, preaching the Lord Jesus.

21 And the hand of the Lord was with them: and a great number believed, and turned unto the Lord.

22 Then tidings of these things came unto the ears of the church which was in Jerusalem: and they sent forth Barnabas, that he should go as far as Antioch.

23 Who, when he came, and had seen the grace of God, was glad, and exhorted them all, that with purpose of heart they would cleave unto the Lord.

24 For he was a good man, and full of the Holy Ghost and of faith: and much people was added unto the Lord.

25 Then departed Barnabas to Tarsus, for to seek Saul:

26 And when he had found him, he brought him unto Antioch. And it came to pass, that a whole year they assembled themselves with the church, and taught much people. And the disciples were called Christians first in Antioch.

27 And in these days came prophets from Jerusalem unto Antioch.

28 And there stood up one of them named Agabus, and signified by the Spirit that there should be great dearth throughout all the world: which came to pass in the days of Claudius Caesar.

29 Then the disciples, every man according to his ability, determined to send relief unto the brethren which dwelt in Judea:

30 Which also they did, and sent it to the elders by the hands of Barnabas and Saul.

Acts 12:24, 25

24 But the word of God grew and multiplied.

25 And Barnabas and Saul returned from Jerusalem, when they had fulfilled their ministry, and took with them John, whose surname was Mark.

Oct
29

GOLDEN TEXT: [Barnabas] exhorted them all, that with purpose of heart they would cleave unto the Lord.—Acts 11:23.

The Story of Christian Beginnings (Acts)

Unit 2: Witnessing in Judea and Samaria (Lessons 5-9)

Lesson Aims

After this lesson students should be able to:
1. Recall what is told in our text about the church in Antioch.
2. Think about their own recent help given to others.
3. Be more helpful.

Lesson Outline

INTRODUCTION
  A. Problems of a Growing Church
  B. Lesson Background
 I. THE GOSPEL IN ANTIOCH (Acts 11:19-21)
  A. Preaching to Jews (v. 19)
  B. Preaching to Gentiles (v. 20)
  C. Success (v. 21)
    Breaking the Bonds of Culture
 II. HELP FROM JERUSALEM (Acts 11:22-26)
  A. Barnabas (vv. 22-24)
  B. Saul (vv. 25, 26a)
  C. Progress (v. 26b)
    What's in a Name?
III. HELP TO JERUSALEM (Acts 11:27-30; 12:24, 25)
  A. Forecast and Famine (vv. 27, 28)
  B. Help Sent (vv. 29, 30)
  C. Back to Antioch (12: 24, 25)
CONCLUSION
  A. Growing
  B. Teaching
  C. Caring
  D. Prayer
  E. Thought to Remember

Visual 9 of the visuals packet emphasizes the type of commitment Christians should have to Christ. The visual is shown on page 77.

Introduction

Problems come with growth. A baby soon outgrows the rattle and other toys of infancy, and has to have more costly things. A boy outgrows his jeans at an alarming rate, and needs new ones. Parents have to make sure he does not outgrow his habit of willing obedience along with his jeans.

Parents must also make sure the child grows into new things as well as out of old ones: new tasks, new responsibilities, new strength of character. A growing child learns to pick up his clothes and keep his room neat, to wash dishes or rake leaves, to be kind to little sister, to put homework before TV.

A. Problems of a Growing Church

The church in Jerusalem was growing, not by ones and twos, but by thousands (Acts 2:41, 47; 4:4; 6:7). Problems came with growth. Some members were penniless; but the others took care of them, even selling houses and lands for that purpose (Acts 4:32-37). Persecution soon arose; but the disciples clung nobly to their faith, even when they were jailed and beaten (Acts 5:17-42). They were driven from their homes; but they took the gospel with them and started churches all over Judea and Samaria (Acts 8:1, 4). Two weeks ago we saw that they went beyond these areas to Damascus (Acts 9:1, 2), and probably the Ethiopian of lesson 6 carried the good news beyond Egypt to the upper valley of the Nile.

All these actions seem to have come as naturally as a child's growth in stature, but the Father in Heaven had to use some extraordinary methods to persuade the growing church to accept the responsibility of taking the gospel to the Gentiles as well as to the Jews (Acts 10). That too was done, and the way was opened for bearers of the good news to go to the uttermost part of the earth.

B. Lesson Background

In previous lessons we have seen three great forward movements for the strength of the church and the glory of God:

1. The church in Jerusalem grew in spite of persecution, and spread swiftly to places farther and farther away.

2. One of the most furious persecutors of the church became one of its most fervent preachers. Saul then was furiously persecuted. Fleeing from Damascus to save his life, he went back to Jerusalem; fleeing from there, he went to his native land, to Tarsus (Acts 9:1-30).

3. By special revelations from God, Peter was convinced that the Lord wanted His gospel taken to Gentiles as well as Jews (Acts 10). The church accepted that conviction and assumed the new responsibility (Acts 11:1-18).

During the study of this week's lesson we see these three movements coming together. The church continued to spread farther and farther from Jerusalem. More and more Gentiles accepted the gospel and came into the fellowship of the church. Saul left Tarsus and came into the mainstream of the story.

I. The Gospel in Antioch
(Acts 11:19-21)

Luke's record moves swiftly over great events, seldom pausing to note the passing of time. Uncertainly we estimate that this lesson begins about eight years after that great Day of Pentecost when three thousand people accepted the call of Christ (Acts 2:41). Events recorded in the few verses of our text then took perhaps about six more years.

A. Preaching to Jews (v. 19)

19. Now they which were scattered abroad upon the persecution that arose about Stephen traveled as far as Phoenicia, and Cyprus, and Antioch, preaching the word to none but unto the Jews only.

Stephen was the first of Jesus' disciples to be killed for his faith (Acts 6:8—7:60). His death was followed by the furious persecution that drove most of the Christians out of Jerusalem (Acts 8:1). Now we see them moving northward. *Phoenicia* was an area on the east coast of the Mediterranean and north of the Jews' country. *Cyprus* was the big island that still wears that name. *Antioch* was an important city near the coast and farther north than Phoenicia. It was about three hundred miles from Jerusalem. Disciples of Jesus did not reach all of these places at the same time, of course. Probably the progress recorded in this verse took several years, and during those years Peter took the gospel to Cornelius and other Gentiles in Caesarea, as we saw in last week's lesson. Following the custom established when they were first driven from Jerusalem, these scattered disciples "went every where preaching the word" (Acts 8:4). But they preached it only to Jews.

B. Preaching to Gentiles (v. 20)

20. And some of them were men of Cyprus and Cyrene, which, when they were come to Antioch, spake unto the Grecians, preaching the Lord Jesus.

Cyrene was located on the south side of the Mediterranean, west of the land of Egypt. Jews from there had been among the many thousands in Jerusalem on the Day of Pentecost. After becoming followers of Jesus, they had stayed in Jerusalem to be taught by the apostles. Now they, along with fellow believers who hailed from Cyprus, were fleeing from the terrible persecution in Jerusalem.

These Jews *of Cyprus and Cyrene* had lived among Gentiles, perhaps all their lives. They had done business with Gentiles, been friends with Gentiles. They were not so keenly aware of Jewish separation as the Jews of Palestine were. In *Antioch* some of them came in contact with Gentiles and gave the message of Christ to them as they did to Jews. Probably Peter already had preached to the Gentles in Caesarea, but we do not know whether the preachers in Antioch knew about that or not.

C. Success (v. 21)

21. And the hand of the Lord was with them: and a great number believed, and turned unto the Lord.

We are not told just how *the hand of the Lord* worked to help these preachers. Perhaps the Lord guided their speech by the Holy Spirit. Perhaps He gave them good weather for outdoor preaching. Perhaps He worked in ways unknown to us to prevent interruptions and heckling. These men were doing what the Lord wanted them to do. He helped them in ways not described, *and a great number believed, and turned unto the Lord.*

BREAKING THE BONDS OF CULTURE

When Irving Berlin died in 1989 at the age of 101, he had long been recognized as one of the great American songwriters. His songs have been sung by generations of Americans.

One of his most popular songs was written simply as a tune for the 1942 movie, *Holiday Inn.* The song was "White Christmas," and it has become an all-time favorite. And who can forget "God Bless America," as sung by Kate Smith in the dark days of World War II?

Berlin was a Russian Jewish immigrant. His music, however, was American in essence, reflecting as it did the way Americans felt. He broke the bonds of culture to become an artist whose craft has blessed Americans of many and varied backgrounds.

When the gospel first spread out into the Mediterranean world, it was a message preached by Jews to other Jews. But some of those who carried the message realized it could—and should—bless everyone, not just Jews but Gentiles as well. Thus, Jewish Christians from

---

How to Say It

AGABUS. *Ag*-uh-bus.
ANTIOCH. *An*-tee-ock.
BARNABAS. *Bar*-nuh-bus.
CAESAREA. Sess-uh-*ree*-uh.
CYPRUS. *Sye*-prus.
CYRENE. Sye-*ree*-nee.
PHOENICIA. Fih-*nish*-uh.

Cypress and Cyrene came to Antioch proclaiming salvation to anyone who would listen. The blessing of God on their work is a reminder to the church in every age that the gospel must never be bound by any human limitation.

—C. R. B.

II. Help From Jerusalem
(Acts 11:22-26)

If there were some strict Jews from Jerusalem among the disciples in Antioch, they may have been disturbed when they saw many Gentiles becoming disciples. They may have hurried a messenger to Jerusalem to see what the mother church would say about this development. Whether in this way or some other, news of the church in Antioch soon reached Jerusalem.

A. Barnabas (vv. 22-24)

22. Then tidings of these things came unto the ears of the church which was in Jerusalem: and they sent forth Barnabas, that he should go as far as Antioch.

By this time the followers of Jesus in Jerusalem knew about Peter's preaching to the Gentiles, and they were convinced that it was right (Acts 11:1-18). They sent one of their members to Antioch, not to criticize, but to help. Barnabas was a man who could do that. Like the preachers from Cyprus and Cyrene, he was accustomed to living among Gentiles and dealing with them. He would find joy in the salvation of Gentiles, and rejoice in the building of a great church in Antioch. On the other hand, he was thoroughly trained in the way of the Lord. If anything was out of order in the church at Antioch, he would see it. He would move to correct it, but he would move gently and with reason, not with angry accusation.

23. Who, when he came, and had seen the grace of God, was glad, and exhorted them all, that with purpose of heart they would cleave unto the Lord.

Large numbers of people, many of them Gentiles, were turning to the Lord, taking their place among the saints. Very plainly Barnabas could see that *the grace of God* was working in Antioch, and he *was glad.* Happily he *exhorted them all,* and this can be translated *encouraged them all.* Most of Antioch was pagan, and there were many temptations to worldly wickedness. Barnabas urged the new disciples to be loyal to their new Master, Jesus.

24. For he was a good man, and full of the Holy Ghost and of faith: and much people was added unto the Lord.

The record shows that Barnabas was notably unselfish and good at helping and encouraging others. He sold his property to provide for the poor (Acts 4:36, 37). He stood by Saul when the other disciples were afraid of him (Acts 9:26-28). He insisted on giving John Mark a second chance (Acts 15:36-40). With good reason the apostles named him Barnabas, which means exhorter, encourager, helper, or comforter (Acts 4:36). In our text we see him encouraging brethren to be faithful to Christ. Apparently he also encouraged others to come to Christ, *and much people was added unto the Lord.* Barnabas was *full of the Holy Ghost:* he put his selfish wishes aside and followed the leading of the Spirit. He was full *of faith:* he believed in Christ, trusted Him, and was faithful to Him.

B. Saul (vv. 25, 26a)

25. Then departed Barnabas to Tarsus, for to seek Saul.

Here is one more example of help and encouragement given by Barnabas. The growing church at Antioch needed workers as capable and vigorous as Saul, and Saul needed just such a place to work. Barnabas planned to help both the church and Saul by bringing them together.

26a. And when he had found him, he brought him unto Antioch.

It seems that Saul was easily persuaded to go with Barnabas to Antioch. Perhaps he felt indebted to Barnabas because Barnabas had helped him in Jerusalem (Acts 9:26-28); probably he was eager to share his faith in Jesus, and Antioch was a fine place to begin.

C. Progress (v. 26b)

26b. And it came to pass, that a whole year they assembled themselves with the church, and taught much people. And the disciples were called Christians first in Antioch.

For *a whole year* Barnabas and Saul worked together in Antioch, *and taught much people.* Antioch was a big city and many people needed to hear of Jesus. And all who became followers of the Master needed to be taught how to follow Him better. It was a busy year.

And the disciples were called Christians first in Antioch. There is nothing in our English text to tell who first gave the disciples their new name, and scholars have various ideas. Some think the followers of Jesus gave themselves that name, as followers of Luther call themselves Lutherans. Some think the heathen people of Antioch first used the name, perhaps in derision. Some think the Lord himself first gave the name *Christians.* These note that the Greek word used here for *called* is used often in the

New Testament to speak of calls or revelations or warnings from God (Matthew 2:12, 22; Luke 2:26; Acts 10:22; Hebrews 8:5; 11:7; 12:25). Whoever used the name first, the Christians themselves accepted it as an honorable name (1 Peter 4:16).

WHAT'S IN A NAME?

Pulitzer Prize winner Jack Smith, who was a daily columnist in the *Los Angeles Times* for years, was fascinated by unusual names. One column in 1989 told of an obituary in a New Orleans newspaper that noted the passing of Zenda Gloyce Smith, who left sisters Brenda Loyce, Glenda Joyce, Lenda Royce, Renda Floyce, Flenda Boyce, Quanda Doyce, and Benda Noyce.

Some people have names given by parents in a fit of misguided creativity. Others choose an unusual name for themselves to attract attention. The name given to those who accepted Jesus as Savior was certain to attract attention. *Christian*—one who belongs to Christ—says that one has identified oneself with Him who fulfilled God's messianic promise to the Jews. All who follow Christ should be proud to wear that name—and that name alone—as an indication of where their spiritual allegiance lies.

—C. R. B.

III. Help to Jerusalem
(Acts 11:27-30; 12:24, 25)

Men of Cyprus and Cyrene brought to Antioch the good news of salvation (Acts 11:20), but those men learned the good news in Jerusalem and carried it from there to Antioch. So the Christians in Antioch were deeply indebted to those in Jerusalem, and the time came for them to make a payment on their debt.

A. Forecast and Famine (vv. 27, 28)

27. And in these days came prophets from Jerusalem unto Antioch.

Prophets are people whom the Lord chooses to receive messages directly from Him and deliver them to people on earth. Perhaps these men came *from Jerusalem unto Antioch* to add to the help that Barnabas and Saul were giving. In the days before the New Testament was written, Christians needed such inspired prophets to teach them the proper way for Christians to live. The church in Antioch was growing so rapidly that it needed more teachers to give God's word to the new members. So the prophets brought help from Jerusalem, but another result of their coming was help sent back to Jerusalem.

28. And there stood up one of them named Agabus, and signified by the Spirit that there

visual 9

Cleave unto the Lord

with purpose of heart

should be great dearth throughout all the world: which came to pass in the days of Claudius Caesar.

Agabus spoke *by the Spirit;* that is, he said what the Holy Spirit told him to say. Human beings often guess about the future, but the Spirit knows. The prediction was from Heaven, not from Agabus; and it soon proved to be true. A *great dearth* is a severe shortage of food, a famine. It was to be *throughout all the world,* which means the Roman Empire, the world that was known to the people of Antioch. *Claudius Caesar* was emperor from A.D. 41 to A.D. 54.

B. Help Sent (vv. 29, 30)

29. Then the disciples, every man according to his ability, determined to send relief unto the brethren which dwelt in Judea.

The famine was everywhere (v. 28). Food was scarce and expensive. However, the Christians *in Judea* suffered more than others because they had used their savings, and even sold their real estate, to provide a living for all of them while they were listening daily to the apostles' teaching (Acts 2:43-47). The rich among them had been reduced to poverty by caring for the poor. Now they were all poor, and the brethren in Antioch wanted to care for them. Those in Antioch had profited spiritually by receiving the gospel from Judea and being saved from sin and death; now those in Judea would profit materially by receiving funds from Antioch and being saved from starvation. Later Paul would write that such repayment was both a debt and a pleasure (Romans 15:26, 27).

The church did not require a certain amount from each member, but each member gave *according to his ability;* that is, each one gave as much as he thought he could afford.

30. Which also they did, and sent it to the elders by the hands of Barnabas and Saul.

These chosen messengers had lived in Jerusalem and had worked with the Christians there. They were trusted both by the givers in

Antioch and by the receivers in Jerusalem. Still these two did not attempt to distribute the offering among the Christians in Judea. They took the money *to the elders.* There were congregations in many towns of Judea, and probably by this time each congregation had a little group of wise and godly elders to oversee its work. In the earlier days of the church, the apostles had distributed food or money among the needy. Then a committee had been chosen for that important work (Acts 4:34, 35; 6:1-6). Now that the disciples were scattered to many towns in Judea, the elders took up the work of distribution. No doubt they already were distributing such funds as were available in Judea; now the increase in funds would be a blessing to many brethren.

C. Back to Antioch (12:24, 25)

24. But the word of God grew and multiplied.
The first part of chapter 12 tells how Herod began to persecute the Christians in Palestine. This was Herod Agrippa I, grandson of the Herod who was ruling when Jesus was born. He killed the apostle James, and put Peter in prison. But an angel set Peter free, and not long after, Herod died a miserable death. The disciples of Jesus were still preaching the word of God, and that word kept on growing in power and influence. More and more people became Christians.

25. And Barnabas and Saul returned from Jerusalem, when they had fulfilled their ministry, and took with them John, whose surname was Mark.
Barnabas and Saul, having delivered the funds from Antioch to the elders in Judea, went back to Antioch to continue their work there. *John, whose surname was Mark,* went with them. This young man was a relative of Barnabas (Colossians 4:10), though Barnabas came

Home Daily Bible Readings

Monday, Oct. 23—Christian Living (Romans 12:1-13)
Tuesday, Oct. 24—One Body With Many Gifts (1 Corinthians 12:12-20, 27-31)
Wednesday, Oct. 25—Prayer for a Church (Ephesians 1:15-23)
Thursday, Oct. 26—The Church as a Unit (Ephesians 4:1-16)
Friday, Oct. 27—Paul's Care of the Churches (2 Corinthians 12:14-21)
Saturday, Oct. 28—Guidelines for Christian Conduct (Titus 3:1-11)
Sunday, Oct. 29—Guidelines for Church Leaders (1 Timothy 3:1-7)

from Cyprus (Acts 4:36, 37) and John Mark probably lived in Jerusalem with his mother (Acts 12:12). So three good Christian workers went to Antioch, the Christian frontier. This set the stage for our next lesson. Don't miss it.

Conclusion

We have been considering the progress of the early church. It was then directed by apostles of Jesus, and it was tremendously successful. For both these reasons, its activities may well be a pattern for those of the church today. Let's look briefly at three kinds of activity.

A. Growing

Swiftly the church grew till it numbered many thousands in Jerusalem. When those thousands were driven out of town, they took the gospel with them, and growth was increased rather than stopped.

How did they do it? They "went every where preaching the word" (Acts 8:4). If the church is not growing so rapidly today, is it because we are not so vigorous and enthusiastic in spreading the message?

B. Teaching

The first Christians continued in the apostles' teaching, among other things (Acts 2:42). New Christians in Caesarea asked Peter to stay awhile, and no doubt he stayed and taught them (Acts 10:48). Barnabas and Saul spent a year in Antioch, and "taught much people" (Acts 11:26). Teaching is vital in any growing church. Members must learn how to serve Jesus, and how to take His invitation to others.

C. Caring

The Christians in Jerusalem took care of one another, so none among them were without food and clothing and shelter (Acts 4:34, 35). Having "all things common" (v. 32) was not continued in all churches, but generous giving was and is. Christians in Antioch shared with those in Judea, and Christians today share with needy brethren near and far.

D. Prayer

How nobly our early fathers in the faith have given us an example! We are thankful, Heavenly Father, and we pray for guidance and strength as we try to follow their example. In Jesus' name, amen.

E. Thought to Remember

No Christian goes hungry unless all Christians are hungry.

Learning by Doing

This page contains an alternate lesson plan emphasizing learning activities. Classes desiring such student involvement will find these suggestions helpful.

Learning Goals

As a result of participating in today's class session, a student should:

1. Be able to list the characteristics of the church in Antioch that made it "Christian."

2. Choose one of these characteristics to demonstrate in his or her own life this week.

Into the Lesson

Write the word *Christian* on your chalkboard before the class session begins. Ask your class members, "Where did you become a Christian?"

Divide your class members into pairs, and ask the students in each pair to tell each other about the *place* where each became a Christian.

Option. In addition to this introductory activity, or instead of it, ask the students to mention some attitudes and behaviors that would identify a person as a Christian. Give your students ninety seconds to think about this; then ask for their answers. As they offer them, list their suggestions on the chalkboard.

After you have written all the students' suggestions, evaluate the list. How many of the items are complimentary? Are any of the items in the list negative in nature? Poll the class regarding this, then read the list aloud to the class. As you read each attitude and/or behavior that is listed, have the students raise their hands if they have ever been called a Christian because they demonstrated it.

Tell the class that in today's session we will consider the establishment and growth of the church in Antioch of Syria. This study of the church where the followers of Christ were first called Christians will help us identify attitudes and behaviors appropriate for a life modeled after Christ.

Into the Word

Establish the background for today's study by presenting the thoughts under points A. and B. of the "Introduction" section of this lesson. Emphasize the thoughts given in the "Lesson Background" section, which summarize the lessons immediately preceding today's lesson.

Display a poster on which you have written the following words: *Stephen, Phoenicia, Cyprus, Antioch, Cyrene, Barnabas, Tarsus, Saul.* Mention that these are names of key people or places in today's text. Ask a volunteer to

read the text aloud while class members listen for each of these names.

Explain the significance of each name listed on the poster. Begin by asking class members to tell what they know about each one. In the case of place names, locate the places on your classroom map.

Divide the class into groups of about four or five students each. Have each group examine the Scripture text for this lesson and list every principle it contains pertaining to the church. Allot six to eight minutes for them to do this, then let the groups take turns reporting one principle at a time until all have been mentioned. (You may want to write these on a poster or your chalkboard.) The list may include the following principles:

1. Persecution sometimes results in the spreading of the gospel.

2. Christians should share the gospel with all persons.

3. The preaching and teaching of a godly man such as Barnabas can change many lives.

4. Christians should not hesitate to respond to the needs of fellow Christians.

5. Christians should give to the Lord's cause according to each person's ability.

Into Life

Provide a pencil and paper for each student. Have each write this open-ended sentence on the paper and then complete the sentence: "One way the world knows I'm a Christian is—" Ask for volunteers to share their completions.

Lead the class in discussing the following questions: "Was it easy or difficult for you to complete this sentence? We have considered some actions of the Christians in Jerusalem and Antioch. Which of these actions could you emulate in order to make your Christian witness more obvious in our world?"

Option. Use material from the "Conclusion" section of the lesson. Summarize the ideas under the three headings, "Growing," "Teaching," and "Caring." Discuss with the class, "Which of the three does our church do best? What would help us do any of these better?"

Ask each class member to choose one of the three and to write down one specific way he or she could help your congregation demonstrate this characteristic more effectively this month.

Let's Talk It Over

The questions on this page are designed to encourage review of the lesson Scriptures and to promote discussion of the lesson by the class. The answers provided are only discussion starters. Let your class talk it over from there.

1. The introduction of this lesson contains a section entitled, "Problems of a Growing Church," referring to the church in Jerusalem in its early days. What are some problems growing churches encounter today, and how should members respond to them?

One of the most obvious problems is the need for physical facilities to accommodate those who attend the services. All members should see this as a challenge either to increase the number of services, or to plan some new construction, or to take some other bold action to resolve the problem. Another problem area is the challenge of integrating new members into the fellowship and service of the church. Sometimes members of long standing grumble over "all those new people," but they need to see the excitement of opening up new lines of fellowship. One more problem area is the matter of overtaxing the church's leadership. However, this simply raises the exciting challenge of recruiting and preparing additional leaders, those who can help lead the church now and in the future.

2. The experience of the early church demonstrates that persecution can actually contribute to the growth of the church. Why is this true?

Persecution puts Christians face to face with the elements of risk and sacrifice, and brings into sharp focus the difference between the things that are temporal and what is eternal. Although characteristically we tend to shrink from difficult challenges, we are also to some extent drawn to them. To face the risk of being ridiculed, harassed, or worse, because of our faith can strengthen our determination to be faithful disciples and stir up our zeal to witness and win others to Christ. Also, it can heighten our awareness of our fellowship with Christ and the reality of our hope of eternal life in Him (see Philippians 3:10).

3. The lesson writer reminds us that "Barnabas" means "exhorter" or "encourager." How might it help if each member in our church were challenged to be a "Barnabas"?

Such Scriptures as 1 Thessalonians 4:18 and Hebrews 3:13 (see these verses in the *New International Version*) indicate the importance of members' encouraging one another. Perhaps a "Barnabas Award" could be presented to members who excelled in this. A "Barnabas Society" could be formed of members who pledge to dedicate themselves regularly to the ministry of encouragement. These suggestions may sound artificial, but perhaps there would be value in providing some positive reinforcement for members who actively encourage the Lord's people. The church seems to suffer no lack of the opposite—those who are negative and excessively critical.

4. Whatever the origin of the name *Christian*, it is an appropriate name for the followers of Christ to wear. Why is this so?

The name identifies us with Jesus Christ and Him alone. It reminds us that we belong to Christ (Galatians 3:29; 5:24) and that we have certain privileges and responsibilities related to His divine ownership. It serves as a worthy focus for our witness to others. We are not concerned with winning others to ourselves, to our particular religious views, or even primarily to our church. As Christians we represent Jesus Christ, and we are keyed into leading other people to believe in Him and to follow Him.

5. Among the disciples at Antioch "every man according to his ability" gave for the purpose of aiding the Judean Christians. This is in line with Paul's command in 1 Corinthians 16:1, 2 for every Christian to practice giving in proportion to his income. How can we lend excitement to this principle in our church?

We frequently refer to the principle of stewardship (1 Corinthians 4:1, 2). That principle emphasizes God's ownership of all we possess and our responsibility to manage these possessions in accordance with His will. Perhaps other terms to describe this relationship will be helpful. We can be called His "money movers," His "dollar-sign disciples," His "wallet warriors," or His "billfold brigade." Such terms could focus on our privilege of being God's agents in this world, providing the funds for His work in the local church, benevolent institutions, Christian colleges, missions, etc. Furthermore these terms could encourage the going beyond a merely comfortable kind of giving and on to real sacrifice for God's kingdom.

Mission to Gentiles

DEVOTIONAL READING: Acts 13:13-26.

LESSON SCRIPTURE: Acts 13, 14.

PRINTED TEXT: Acts 13:1-5; 14:1-7, 24-27.

Acts 13:1-5

1 Now there were in the church that was at Antioch certain prophets and teachers; as Barnabas, and Simeon that was called Niger, and Lucius of Cyrene, and Manaen, which had been brought up with Herod the tetrarch, and Saul.

2 As they ministered to the Lord, and fasted, the Holy Ghost said, Separate me Barnabas and Saul for the work whereunto I have called them.

3 And when they had fasted and prayed, and laid their hands on them, they sent them away.

4 So they, being sent forth by the Holy Ghost, departed unto Seleucia; and from thence they sailed to Cyprus.

5 And when they were at Salamis, they preached the word of God in the synagogues of the Jews: and they had also John to their minister.

Acts 14:1-7, 24-27

1 And it came to pass in Iconium, that they went both together into the synagogue of the Jews, and so spake, that a great multitude both of the Jews and also of the Greeks believed.

2 But the unbelieving Jews stirred up the Gentiles, and made their minds evil affected against the brethren.

3 Long time therefore abode they speaking boldly in the Lord, which gave testimony unto the word of his grace, and granted signs and wonders to be done by their hands.

4 But the multitude of the city was divided: and part held with the Jews, and part with the apostles.

5 And when there was an assault made both of the Gentiles, and also of the Jews with their rulers, to use them despitefully, and to stone them,

6 They were ware of it, and fled unto Lystra and Derbe, cities of Lycaonia, and unto the region that lieth round about:

7 And there they preached the gospel.

. . . .

24 And after they had passed throughout Pisidia, they came to Pamphylia.

25 And when they had preached the word in Perga, they went down into Attalia:

26 And thence sailed to Antioch, from whence they had been recommended to the grace of God for the work which they fulfilled.

27 And when they were come, and had gathered the church together, they rehearsed all that God had done with them, and how he had opened the door of faith unto the Gentiles.

GOLDEN TEXT: When they were come, and had gathered the church together, they rehearsed all that God had done with them, and how he had opened the door of faith unto the Gentiles.—Acts 14:27.

The Story of Christian Beginnings (Acts)
Unit 3: Spreading the Gospel Into All the World (Lessons 10-13)

Lesson Aims

After this lesson students should be able to:
1. Briefly describe the missionary journey of Paul and Barnabas.
2. Consider their own missionary efforts and those of their congregation.
3. Do a little better.

Lesson Outline

INTRODUCTION
A. Reluctant Outreach
B. Lesson Background
I. SENDING MISSIONARIES (Acts 13:1-5)
A. Abundance in Antioch (v. 1)
B. Call to Share (v. 2)
C. Response (v. 3)
Set Apart and Sent Out
D. Starting the Journey (vv. 4, 5)
II. MISSIONARIES AT WORK (Acts 14:1-7)
A. Successful Preaching (v. 1)
B. Subtle Opposition (v. 2)
C. Preaching and Power (v. 3)
D. Divided City (v. 4)
E. Violent Opposition (v. 5)
F. Moving On (vv. 6, 7)
III. MISSIONARIES BACK HOME (Acts 14:24-27)
A. Preaching on the Way (vv. 24, 25)
B. Reporting to the Home Church (vv. 26, 27)
A Report on a Great Adventure
CONCLUSION
A. Personal Evangelism
B. United Effort
C. Prayer
D. Thought to Remember

Visual 10 of the visuals packet shows that there are to be no limits to the preaching of the gospel. The visual is shown on page 85.

Introduction

Missionary work has long been recognized as an important part of our Christian service. Many of us feel guilty because the money spent in spreading the gospel abroad is only a small fraction of the budget of the local congregation. On the other hand, some Christians would stop mis-

sionary work altogether. "All the money we can raise is needed right here at home," they say. The New Testament does not record that objection by early Christians. Still, something extraordinary was needed to propel them into new fields.

A. Reluctant Outreach

In Jerusalem the first Christians were on fire with the gospel, and the church grew amazingly (Acts 2:41; 4:4; 5:14; 6:1). Yet we do not read that they carried the gospel beyond Jerusalem till persecution came. That misfortune did not lessen their enthusiasm. They took the gospel with them and formed churches all over Judea and Samaria. Philip's great work in Samaria is an example (8:1, 4-8).

Enthusiastic as they were, the scattered disciples offered the gospel only to Jews. It took special acts of God to convince the apostle Peter that salvation was for Gentiles too. With the help of those acts of God Peter then convinced the other Christians, and they rejoiced to know that God wanted to save all of mankind (Acts 10:1—11:18).

B. Lesson Background

It seems that the church at Antioch was the first big congregation among the Gentiles. It was started by Christians scattered from Jerusalem, and helped greatly by others sent from that city. Grateful for such help, the Christians in Antioch were generous in sending help of another kind to their brethren in Judea (Acts 11:19-30). But still a special order from the Holy Spirit was needed to involve the church at Antioch in a great missionary work. That is what we shall see in this week's lesson.

I. Sending Missionaries (Acts 13:1-5)

Barnabas and Saul were the men sent by the Antioch church to carry its offering to the famine-stricken Christians in Judea. When that service was completed they went back to Antioch, taking with them John Mark, a young kinsman of Barnabas (Acts 12:25; Colossians 4:10).

A. Abundance in Antioch (v. 1)

1. Now there were in the church that was at Antioch certain prophets and teachers; as Barnabas, and Simeon that was called Niger, and Lucius of Cyrene, and Manaen, which had been brought up with Herod the tetrarch, and Saul.

Prophets were people to whom God revealed special messages to be delivered to others. They were teachers, of course; but there were other *teachers* who had no special revelations, but taught what they had learned from prophets and from Scripture.

Antioch had capable teachers in abundance. Five of them are named in this verse. *Saul* is named last in this distinguished list, but soon we shall see him becoming the leading character of the book of Acts.

B. Call to Share (v. 2)

2. As they ministered to the Lord, and fasted, the Holy Ghost said, Separate me Barnabas and Saul for the work whereunto I have called them.

It is not clear whether *they* means the five prophets and teachers named in verse 1 or the whole church in Antioch, which also is mentioned in verse 1. Some English versions translate "were worshiping the Lord" instead of *ministered to the Lord*. That translation seems appropriate because fasting often went with earnest prayer (Luke 2:37; Acts 10:30; 14:23). So perhaps we should picture a group, either five prophets and teachers or the whole congregation, engaged in worship. *The Holy Ghost said, Separate me Barnabas and Saul for the work whereunto I have called them.* Perhaps the Spirit also told what that work was. Luke does not record that here, but leaves us to discover it as we read on in the record. The Spirit was calling on the church to give up two of its five fine teachers so they could work in fields where now there were no Christian teachers at all.

C. Response (v. 3)

3. And when they had fasted and prayed, and laid their hands on them, they sent them away.

With fasting and earnest prayer, the two men were set apart, dedicated to the work the Spirit had called them to do. Probably the hands laid on them indicated the approval and blessing of the church. *Sent them away* is more accurately translated "let them go." The Holy Spirit was sending these men (v. 4), but the church was releasing them with its blessing.

SET APART AND SENT OUT

"Greetings!" the letter began. Many citizens received from the draft board a letter with that ominous salutation. The recipient of the letter was being drafted into military service.

Imagine the surprise of Nathan Matt several years ago when he received a letter from Uncle Sam saying, "Greetings! A match of computer files has indicated that you may be required to register with the Selective Service." Mr. Matt was not unwilling to serve his country, but he was seventy-eight years old! The "invitation" to

---

How to Say It

ANTIPAS. *An*-tuh-pas.
ATTALIA. At-uh-*lye*-uh.
CYRENE. Sye-*ree*-nee.
DERBE. *Der*-be.
ICONIUM. Eye-*ko*-nee-um.
LUCIUS. *Lew*-shus.
LYCAONIA. *Lik*-uh-*o*-ni-uh (strong accent on *o*).
LYSTRA. *Liss*-truh.
MANAEN. *Man*-uh-en.
NIGER. *Nye*-jer.
PAMPHYLIA. Pam-*fill*-e-uh.
PERGA. *Per*-guh.
PISIDIA. Pih-*sid*-ee-uh.
SALAMIS. *Sal*-uh-mis.
SELEUCIA. See-*lew*-shuh.
SERGIUS PAULUS. *Sir*-ji-us *Poll*-us.

---

register was later rescinded with the explanation that there had been a computer error.

In response to the guidance of the Holy Spirit, the church at Antioch "drafted" Barnabas and Saul from their midst for special service for Christ. The church set them apart and sent them out as evangelists to distant places.

When mobilizing for a great campaign—whether military or evangelistic—the leaders must recognize and evaluate the need, find the personnel to meet the need, and then give them complete support. The world still needs the gospel. Is the church still willing to make the commitment of personnel and resources?

—C. R. B.

D. Starting the Journey (vv. 4, 5)

4. So they, being sent forth by the Holy Ghost, departed unto Seleucia; and from thence they sailed to Cyprus.

Antioch was about fifteen miles from the coast. *Seleucia* was its seaport. From there, Barnabas and Saul went by ship to the island of *Cyprus,* nearly a hundred miles away. Since the Holy Spirit was sending them, it may be supposed that He told them where to go; but we can hardly think He put money in their pockets for the fare on the ship. Since nothing is said about finances, many students suppose the church at Antioch provided funds for the trip.

Cyprus was the former home of Barnabas (Acts 4:36, 37); but if he now met any relatives or old friends, there is no record of it.

5. And when they were at Salamis, they preached the word of God in the synagogues of the Jews: and they had also John to their minister.

Salamis was the port city on the east side of Cyprus. There the missionaries left the ship and began their work, and now we see what work the Holy Spirit had called them to do. *The word of God* they announced was of course the news of Jesus, the Christ and the Savior. They spoke *in the synagogues of the Jews,* but here in Gentile country probably many in the audiences were not Jews. There were people who were forsaking the old pagan religions in those days, and some of them were learning from the Jews about the real God. In Jewish synagogues the missionaries often found Gentiles who believed in God and worshiped with the Jews.

In writing Acts, Luke did not often tell just what the preachers said. However, he did record three sermons so we can see not only the substance of the Christian message, but also the different ways of presenting it. Acts 2:14-40 records a sermon to Jews in Palestine. Acts 13:16-41 tells how the gospel was presented to an audience of Jews and Gentiles in a synagogue. Acts 17:22-31 shows how Paul preached to intelligent Gentiles who did not believe in God.

Last week we read that John Mark went from Jerusalem to Antioch with Barnabas and Saul (Acts 12:25). This young relative of Barnabas set out with them on their missionary journey. *Minister* here represents a Greek word that means a subordinate worker, a helper.

II. Missionaries at Work
(Acts 14:1-7)

Barnabas, Saul, and John Mark went through the island of Cyprus from east to west. Luke tells us that in part of one sentence, but pauses longer to tell of their encounter with an evil sorcerer (Acts 13:6-12). At this point we see a change that is not fully explained. Barnabas and Saul were teaching a government official called Sergius Paulus. Luke comments that Saul "also is called Paulus," or "Paul," as we have it in English. Through the rest of Acts, the man who has been called Saul is called Paul instead. It seems, too, that Paul now moved into the leadership of the team. We have been reading of "Barnabas and Saul" (13:2, 7); now we shall be reading of "Paul and his company" (13:13) and "Paul and Barnabas" (13:43, 46, 50).

From the west end of the island, the missionaries sailed north to the mainland. At that point John Mark left the party and went back to Jerusalem (Acts 13:13). Paul and Barnabas pushed inland to Antioch, not the Antioch from which they had started, but another city of the same name. In Acts 13:14-52 we have a more complete record of their success there, and the opposition that was aroused. This thrilling story is too long to be included in a single Sunday-school lesson, so we bypass it and go to chapter 14. There a short passage gives a fine example of the kind of work the missionaries were doing and the kind of opposition they faced.

A. Successful Preaching (v. 1)

1. And it came to pass in Iconium, that they went both together into the synagogue of the Jews, and so spake, that a great multitude both of the Jews and also of the Greeks believed.

Iconium was about eighty miles southeast of Antioch. It may have taken three or four days to make the trip on foot. You can trace the missionaries' journey on the map on page 4.

The missionaries found both Jews and Gentiles in the synagogue in Iconium. *Greeks* here means people who were not Jewish, whether they came from Greece or not. The preaching probably was very much like that in Antioch (Acts 13:16-41). It was convincing to *a great multitude both of the Jews and also of the Greeks.* They *believed* the message, *believed* that Jesus is the Christ, the Savior, the Son of God; so of course they were baptized and became Christians.

B. Subtle Opposition (v. 2)

2. But the unbelieving Jews stirred up the Gentiles, and made their minds evil affected against the brethren.

As usual when the gospel was preached, some of the hearers were *unbelieving.* If those unbelievers tried to argue with the preachers, they found themselves defeated by Scripture and reasoning, as unbelieving Jews in Jerusalem had been (Acts 6:9, 10). So *the unbelieving Jews* began a campaign of slander among *the Gentiles,* not only the Gentiles in the synagogue meetings, but Gentiles of influence throughout the city. They were able to convince some that all the excitement produced by these visitors would have bad results.

C. Preaching and Power (v. 3)

3. Long time therefore abode they speaking boldly in the Lord, which gave testimony unto the word of his grace, and granted signs and wonders to be done by their hands.

We can only guess how long Paul and Barnabas stayed in Iconium. Possibly it was several months. They kept on *speaking boldly* in spite of frowns and perhaps threats from leading Jews and influential Gentiles. The missionaries could be bold because they were speaking *in the Lord:* He gave them wisdom and courage. They were speaking *the word of his grace,* the good news of the Lord's grace by which sinners are redeemed. The Lord added His own *testimony:* He *granted signs and wonders to be done by their hands.* Thus He testified that the preachers were His messengers. The *signs and wonders* are not described, so we conclude they were miracles of healing such as the apostles had done in Jerusalem (Acts 5:12-16). These helpful miracles made it more and more difficult for the opponents to discredit the preachers.

D. Divided City (v. 4)

4. But the multitude of the city was divided: and part held with the Jews, and part with the apostles.

No doubt Paul and Barnabas taught people all through the week as well as in the synagogue on the Sabbath. Their miracles attracted attention. Everyone in Iconium knew these preachers had powerful opposition. Naturally many people were loyal to their local leaders who said these strangers were fakers. But more and more were being convinced that Paul and Barnabas were God's messengers. The opponents saw themselves losing, and they became desperate.

E. Violent Opposition (v. 5)

5. And when there was an assault made both of the Gentiles, and also of the Jews with their rulers, to use them despitefully, and to stone them.

An assault here does not mean that there was actual physical violence, but there was a movement toward such violence. The *New International Version* calls it "a plot." Gentiles and Jews who opposed Paul and Barnabas joined in a plan to mistreat and stone them.

F. Moving On (vv. 6, 7)

6. They were ware of it, and fled unto Lystra and Derbe, cities of Lycaonia, and unto the region that lieth round about.

Ware means *aware.* Probably Paul and Barnabas heard from several sources that a plot was being made against them. Probably many new Christians were ready, willing, and able to protect them, meeting violence with violence. But war in the streets has no place in the Christian way of spreading the gospel. Jesus once told His messengers to be "wise as serpents, and harmless as doves." He said, "When they persecute you in this city, flee ye into another" (Matthew 10:16, 23). Wisely, then, Paul and Barnabas flitted away like harmless doves before anyone was injured physically. *Lycaonia* was a region southeast of Iconium. At this time it was included in the Roman province of Galatia. *Lystra* was only

a day's walk from Iconium, and Derbe only a day's walk farther on. The messengers went to both of these cities, and our text seems to suggest that they also spent some time in the villages of *the region that lieth round about.*

7. And there they preached the gospel.

The work of the missionaries was not stopped; it was only moved to other fields. But the opponents followed to Lystra, and this time the preachers did not move on soon enough to escape physical injury (Acts 14:19, 20). Still they continued their work in nearby Derbe (Acts 14:20, 21). From Derbe they turned back to revisit and strengthen the Christians in Lystra, Iconium, and Antioch (Acts 14:21-23).

III. Missionaries Back Home (Acts 14:24-27)

The last part of our text takes up the story as Paul and Barnabas moved southward from Antioch toward the Mediterranean Sea.

A. Preaching on the Way (vv. 24, 25)

24. And after they had passed throughout Pisidia, they came to Pamphylia.

Antioch lay in the region called *Pisidia.* This Antioch is called Antioch of Pisidia to distinguish it from Antioch of Syria, the one from which the missionaries had started on their journey. Pamphylia was south of Pisidia, between it and the sea.

25. And when they had preached the word in Perga, they went down into Attalia.

Perga was a town in Pamphylia. It seems that Paul and Barnabas had passed through the town on the outward journey without stopping to preach (Acts 13:13, 14). Now they did stop to preach the gospel there, but we are not told how long they stayed. Soon they went on to *Attalia* on the coast.

B. Reporting to the Home Church (vv. 26, 27)

26. And thence sailed to Antioch, from whence they had been recommended to the grace of God for the work which they fulfilled.

visual 10

It seems that the missionaries did not revisit the Christians on Cyprus on the way back home. At Attalia they took a ship and sailed directly to *Antioch,* the city in Syria from which they had started their trip, where their fellow Christians had committed them to God's grace as they set out on the work to which the Spirit had called them (Acts 13:1-3). Now they had *fulfilled* the task to which they had been sent and they were going back home.

27. And when they were come, and had gathered the church together, they rehearsed all that God had done with them, and how he had opened the door of faith unto the Gentiles.

We can imagine how joyfully the Christians in Antioch met to hear the report of their missionaries. Modestly and factually, Paul and Barnabas did not tell what they had done; they told what *God had done with them.* It may have taken hours to tell about all their adventures, but Luke summarizes it in a sentence: God *had opened the door of faith unto the Gentiles.* He had opened it earlier in Caesarea (Acts 10:1—11:18). He had opened it wide in Antioch (Acts 11:19-24). Now He had opened that same door of faith to Gentiles in a string of towns in Asia Minor—and there was more to come, as we shall see in later lessons.

A REPORT ON A GREAT ADVENTURE

The Lewis and Clark Expedition blazed a trail westward across an uncharted wilderness. In 1803, President Thomas Jefferson proposed such a venture as a means of exploring the vast region west of the Mississippi River. Much of this area was part of the Louisiana Territory, which was purchased that year from France.

Meriwether Lewis and William Clark and their company left Saint Louis in May, 1804,

and headed up the Missouri River. Late in 1805 they reached the Pacific Ocean. In May, 1806, they began their homeward journey, reaching Saint Louis four months later. The expedition's report contributed enormously to America's knowledge of its new territory.

Whenever a venture into uncharted regions is made, it is fitting that a detailed report of the expedition's findings be given to those who commissioned the venture. So it was with the church's first major missionary effort—Paul and Barnabas's evangelistic tour of Cyprus and Asia Minor. The report of this pioneer mission spoke of momentous accomplishments, as the men described how God had opened the door of faith to the Gentiles.

—C. R. B.

Conclusion

As we consider the church described in the New Testament, we are struck by its rapid growth: both the growth of the local congregation and the beginning of new congregations. If we take that church as a model for the church of today, we need to be concerned about both of these kinds of growth.

A. Personal Evangelism

In former lessons we have seen that Christians from Jerusalem "went every where preaching the word" (Acts 8:4). They were well prepared because they had left their jobs for intensive training by the apostles. Such intensive training was not a model for all the churches: it was not copied in the churches of Judea and Damascus and Antioch. But couldn't your church benefit from a course in personal evangelism taught by someone skilled in that work?

B. United Effort

In our lesson for today we have seen that the church in Antioch had five fine teachers, and ordained two of them to teach where there were no Christian teachers at all. How does the missionary effort of your congregation compare with that?

C. Prayer

Father in Heaven, we are Your children because Your people through centuries passed the gospel on and on till it came to us. We do want to do our part in passing that same gospel on. Help us, then, to see our part more clearly and do it better. Through Christ we ask it. Amen.

D. Thought to Remember

"Go ye into all the world, and preach the gospel to every creature" (Mark 16:15).

Home Daily Bible Readings

Monday, Oct. 30—Witnessing in Cyprus (Acts 13:6-12)

Tuesday, Oct. 31—Witnessing in Antioch in Pisidia (Acts 13:13-25)

Wednesday, Nov. 1—Paul's Sermon Continues (Acts 13:26-39)

Thursday, Nov. 2—Gentiles Happy (Acts 13:40-52)

Friday, Nov. 3—Mistaken Identity (Acts 14:8-18)

Saturday, Nov. 4—Churches Revisited and Strengthened (Acts 14:19-23)

Sunday, Nov. 5—The Christian's Loyalty (Matthew 10:34-39)

Learning by Doing

This page contains an alternate lesson plan emphasizing learning activities. Classes desiring such student involvement will find these suggestions helpful.

Learning Goals

This session will help students to:

1. List the successes and the obstacles to success in the missionary journey of Saul and Barnabas recorded in Acts 13 and 14.

2. Decide how they can more fully participate in the missionary activity of their congregation.

Into the Lesson

Give each of your class members a sheet of paper on which are written the following open-ended sentences. Or, read the sentences to your class members and ask them to write completions on blank paper, which you have provided.

1. When I hear the word *missionary*, my first thought usually is—

2. One way to describe the missionary work of our congregation is—

3. I feel most like a missionary when I—

After class members have completed the sentences on paper, allow several to share them with the class. The purpose of this activity is to get your class members to express their feelings about the missionary enterprise of the church.

Tell the class that today we will consider the missionary activity of the church in its early years to see if there are lessons for the church's missionary efforts today.

Into the Word

Before class prepare nine slips of paper on which you have jotted the following information, one place or person per slip.

Antioch—Seemingly the first large church that included Gentiles in its membership.

Barnabas—A faithful Christian who along with Saul was sent by the church in Antioch to take its offering to the famine-stricken Christians in Judea.

Simeon Niger—A teacher in the Antioch church. *Niger* means "black"; he probably had black hair and dark complexion.

Lucius of Cyrene—A teacher in the Antioch church whose hometown was a city in north Africa.

Manaen—A teacher in the Antioch church, who was brought up as the companion of Herod the tetrarch or who was his foster brother. This Herod also known as Herod Antipas, was the ruler of Galilee and Perea during the earthly ministry of Jesus.

Seleucia—The seaport for Antioch. Antioch lay about fifteen miles inland.

Cyprus—An island in the eastern part of the Mediterranean off the coast of Syria.

Salamis—The port city on the east side of the island of Cyprus.

John—Also known as John Mark, he was a young relative of Barnabas. John had accompanied Barnabas and Saul when they returned to Antioch from Jerusalem after delivering the Antioch church's gift to the needy saints in Judea.

Distribute the slips to class members; then read Acts 13:1-5 aloud. Next, have the class members with the slips read the information on them to the class. Have the slips read in the order shown above.

Ask, "How many teachers were in the church at Antioch?" (Five.) "How did the church know to send Barnabas and Saul on this missionary journey?" (By direction of the Holy Spirit.) "How did the church set them apart?" (With fasting, prayer, and the laying on of hands.)

Connect this passage with Acts 14 by presenting thoughts given in the two paragraphs immediately under the heading "II. Missionaries at Work" in the lesson material. Then read 14:1-7, 24-27 aloud. (If you have time, read all of chapter 14.) Read verse 27 a second time.

Have class members work in groups to list the events of Paul and Barnabas's missionary journey that the two would have been sure to share with their friends in Antioch. As groups report, list their suggestions on the chalkboard.

Into Life

Discuss these questions with the class:

1. How do the obstacles faced by Paul and Barnabas compare with obstacles we face today when we try to spread the gospel?

2. How do you suppose Paul and Barnabas felt about their missionary experience? What aspects of it would make them want to do further missionary work?

3. How do the experiences of Paul and Barnabas affect your feelings about spreading the gospel?

Distribute a list of missionary efforts your congregation sponsors and have the students examine the list. Then close with prayer, asking God to help each person see how he or she can become more involved in these efforts.

Let's Talk It Over

The questions on this page are designed to encourage review of the lesson Scriptures and to promote discussion of the lesson by the class. The answers provided are only discussion starters. Let your class talk it over from there.

1. Missionary work requires financial support. This is an obvious truth, but why does it need to be repeated frequently?

Some people seem to hold a kind of glamorized view of missionary work that obscures for them the practical realities of a missionary's life. Money is needed for transportation costs, language training, living expenses on the field, literature and teaching aids, and various other items. When we hear a missionary tell the amount of funds that are required for the work, we may be shocked at how expensive an enterprise it is. However, in view of the preciousness of human souls (Matthew 16:26) how can we be reluctant to invest the financial resources that are needed to send gospel messengers to foreign lands? And in view of the sacrifices that missionaries make—the physical hardship (if not danger) involved, separation from family and homeland, and the like—how can we begrudge them our generous financial support?

2. In Antioch Paul and Barnabas "had been recommended to the grace of God" before they set forth on their missionary travels (Acts 14:26). How can churches today follow this example when sending out missionaries?

In the *New International Version* this phrase is translated, "had been committed to the grace of God." At least in part this points back to Acts 13:3, where we read that prayer was a prominent feature of the act of sending out Paul and Barnabas. We should give some thought to our prayers for missionaries. It is inadequate merely to append to our prayers the request, "Lord, bless all the missionaries." If we are to commit them to the grace of God, we must pray that their faith will remain strong in the face of disappointment and adversity; we must ask the Lord to remind them that His power can work through their weakness (2 Corinthians 12:9, 10); we must request that He will keep in mind their dependence on His wisdom and guidance.

3. Upon their return to Antioch Paul and Barnabas described "all that God had done with them." Why should a church expect this kind of report from the missionaries it supports?

It is natural for us to want to know something of the land in which missionaries labor or the unusual characteristics of the people among whom they minister. Our main interest, however, should center around their efforts at sowing the gospel seed and the harvest that has resulted from such sowing. If we have prayed for the missionaries in the way described in the previous question, we will want to learn how God has answered our prayers. Their reports should lead us to rejoice anew in the power of the gospel and to praise God for the mighty way in which He works through human instruments to accomplish His will.

4. Should every church provide an ongoing course in which its members can receive training in personal evangelism? Why, or why not?

Some members might feel that such a course would not be necessary on an ongoing basis, since the principles involved and the relevant New Testament Scripture passages could be effectively presented in a few weeks' time. However, since the topic of personal evangelism is so important, and we humans are prone to forgetfulness, it seems that any church would benefit by offering such an ongoing study.

5. It is often a painful experience for a church to lose key members, such as when they leave to help start a new congregation in the area, or depart to prepare for specialized Christian work, or leave to serve on a mission field. How should the remaining members respond to this circumstance?

There is no indication whatsoever that the church at Antioch hesitated or questioned God's plans when the Holy Spirit designated two of their strong leaders to be set apart and sent out to distant lands to preach the gospel there. So today, if in heeding God's call an individual or family moves on to a different place of service, the church can only say, "May the will of the Lord be done!" Even better, the church members should experience a sense of fulfillment and should rejoice that God has allowed them to have a part in preparing men and women for the mission field, new church evangelism, or some other challenging area of service. Because those departing workers are "some of their own," the church members should be pleased to support them with prayer and encouragement.

The Jerusalem Conference

DEVOTIONAL READING: Romans 3:21-31.

LESSON SCRIPTURE: Acts 15:1-35.

PRINTED TEXT: Acts 15:1, 2, 6-18.

Acts 15:1, 2, 6-18

1 And certain men which came down from Judea taught the brethren, and said, Except ye be circumcised after the manner of Moses, ye cannot be saved.

2 When therefore Paul and Barnabas had no small dissension and disputation with them, they determined that Paul and Barnabas, and certain other of them, should go up to Jerusalem unto the apostles and elders about this question.

. . . .

6 And the apostles and elders came together for to consider of this matter.

7 And when there had been much disputing, Peter rose up, and said unto them, Men and brethren, ye know how that a good while ago God made choice among us, that the Gentiles by my mouth should hear the word of the gospel, and believe.

8 And God, which knoweth the hearts, bare them witness, giving them the Holy Ghost, even as he did unto us;

9 And put no difference between us and them, purifying their hearts by faith.

10 Now therefore why tempt ye God, to put a yoke upon the neck of the disciples, which neither our fathers nor we were able to bear?

11 But we believe that through the grace of the Lord Jesus Christ we shall be saved, even as they.

12 Then all the multitude kept silence, and gave audience to Barnabas and Paul, declaring what miracles and wonders God had wrought among the Gentiles by them.

13 And after they had held their peace, James answered, saying, Men and brethren, hearken unto me:

14 Simeon hath declared how God at the first did visit the Gentiles, to take out of them a people for his name.

15 And to this agree the words of the prophets; as it is written,

16 After this I will return, and will build again the tabernacle of David, which is fallen down; and I will build again the ruins thereof, and I will set it up:

17 That the residue of men might seek after the Lord, and all the Gentiles, upon whom my name is called, saith the Lord, who doeth all these things.

18 Known unto God are all his works from the beginning of the world.

Nov
12

GOLDEN TEXT: We believe that through the grace of the Lord Jesus Christ we shall be saved, even as they.—Acts 15:11.

The Story of Christian Beginnings (Acts)
Unit 3: Spreading the Gospel Into All the World (Lessons 10-13)

Lesson Aims

After this lesson a student should be able to:

1. Tell what our text tells about a problem in Antioch and a discussion in Jerusalem.

2. Tell whose will prevailed in solving the troublesome problem.

3. Consider his or her opinions and wishes, and change any that clash with God's will.

Lesson Outline

INTRODUCTION
  A. A Treasured Opinion
  B. Lesson Background
 I. PROBLEM (Acts 15:1, 2, 6)
  A. Dispute (vv. 1, 2a)
  B. Search for Settlement (v. 2b)
  C. Wise Leaders (v. 6)
    Nothing New Allowed
 II. TESTIMONY (Acts 15:7-12)
  A. Simon Peter (vv. 7-11)
    By Law or by Grace?
  B. Paul and Barnabas (v. 12)
III. SCRIPTURE (Acts 15:13-18)
  A. Prophecy of Amos (vv. 13-17)
  B. Comment of James (v. 18)
CONCLUSION
  A. Don't Be Afraid to Change
  B. Let God Decide
  C. Prayer
  D. Thought to Remember

Visual 11 of the visuals packet shows that no one has the right to require more than God requires for a person to be saved. The visual is shown on page 93.

Introduction

A man convinced against his will
Is of the same opinion still

Thus a poet notes what most of us have noted too. People are inclined to cling to their opinions. Sometimes we cling to an opinion because we like it. Why else does anyone ignore the piled-up evidence and say cigaret smoke is not really harmful? Then sometimes we cling to an opinion just because it is ours. We have stated it strongly, and we don't want to admit that we

have been wrong. Years ago Grandpa declared that peanuts will produce more if they are planted in the dark of the moon. He declares it still, even though a neighbor plants when the moon is full and has a better crop.

A. A Treasured Opinion

God chose the Jewish people to be His own. That is a fact, not an opinion. However, many of the Jews took that to mean they were above the rest of the world and must be strictly separate forever. That was their opinion, and they liked it. Not many of them recalled that God chose them for the purpose of bringing a blessing to all the world (Genesis 12:3).

B. Lesson Background

The first Christians were Jews, and for a while they supposed that no one but Jews would ever be Christians. Lesson 8 reviewed how God convinced Peter that Gentiles also would be redeemed. Peter convinced the other Jewish Christians, and they praised God (Acts 11:18). They were convinced, but some of them were convinced against their will. Such Jewish Christians are introduced in this lesson. They did not give up their treasured opinion that Jews must be forever separate and superior.

I. Problem
(Acts 15:1, 2, 6)

After the events recorded in chapters 10 and 11 of Acts, no one could deny that God wanted Gentiles to become Christians. Then the exclusive Jews took a different turn in their thinking. "Certainly Gentiles can become Christians," they said. "That's great. But they must become Jews too." That is the opinion we meet in the first verse of our text.

A. Dispute (vv. 1, 2a)

1. And certain men which came down from Judea taught the brethren, and said, Except ye be circumcised after the manner of Moses, ye cannot be saved.

These men brought a teaching not heard in Antioch before. To *be circumcised after the manner of Moses* is to be converted to the Jewish faith. They said being Christian is not enough, and that Gentile Christians could not be saved unless they would also become Jews.

2a. When therefore Paul and Barnabas had no small dissension and disputation with them.

The new teachers were mistaken. *Paul and Barnabas* knew it, and they said so. The new teachers did not back down. So the debate grew long, and perhaps it grew heated.

B. Search for Settlement (v. 2b)

2b. They determined that Paul and Barnabas, and certain other of them, should go up to Jerusalem unto the apostles and elders about this question.

Probably the new teachers claimed to be giving the true teaching of the original church in Jerusalem. Paul and Barnabas made the same claim, but their teaching was contradictory. The Christians in Antioch thought this question was important enough to deserve a reliable answer. Therefore they sent a delegation to Jerusalem to find out what the original church was teaching. Paul and Barnabas were included. Probably some of their opponents were in the group too, plus some of the Antioch Christians who had taken no part in the debate. *The apostles and elders* could answer the question.

C. Wise Leaders (v. 6)

6. And the apostles and elders came together for to consider of this matter.

In verses 4 and 5 we read that the Christians in Jerusalem met with the apostles and elders to greet their brethren from Antioch. Paul and Barnabas told about their missionary journey. They had brought many Gentiles to Christ, but had not told them to become Jews. Then some Christian Pharisees stood up to agree with the new teachers who had lately gone to Antioch. They said all those Gentile Christians must become Jews and keep the Old Testament laws.

This was the question now to be considered by *the apostles and elders*. Apparently the whole congregation still was present (v. 12), but the leaders *came together* in a little group to talk about *this matter* before the congregation.

NOTHING NEW ALLOWED

In mid-eighteenth-century England, English wool was made into English woolens, and it was done by hand. England's craftsmen took pride in their work. Then came the Industrial Revolution, and with it came social turmoil. Machines were costing people their jobs.

One night in 1811, in England's Spen Valley, two hundred armed men in masks (or otherwise disguised), began what led to a wave of guerilla warfare. They smashed the new textile-making machines that were threatening their way of life. They came to be known as Luddites, after Ned Ludd, who years earlier in a fit of anger had destroyed his father's knitting frame. Their rebellion lasted only five or six years, but the name *Luddite* has been applied to any opponent of new ways of doing things, especially when new technology is involved.

In its early years the church was troubled by spiritual Luddites. They were more concerned with keeping their traditions than they were with what God so obviously was doing in the world. Through His appointed messengers God was leading Gentiles to Christ, but these Jewish Christian "Luddites" could only say, "Everyone has to come to God *our* way."

God clearly has revealed that He seeks the salvation of every person, and He has provided the way. Let us not cling to any tradition that would impede His will. —C. R. B.

II. Testimony
(Acts 15:7-12)

A. Simon Peter (vv. 7-11)

7. And when there had been much disputing, Peter rose up, and said unto them, Men and brethren, ye know how that a good while ago God made choice among us, that the Gentiles by my mouth should hear the word of the gospel, and believe.

It does not seem probable that there was *much disputing* in the little group of apostles and elders; but others were allowed to join in the debate, and there were those who disagreed with the Christian Pharisees. All of those who wished to speak had their opportunities, and then *Peter rose up* to give his testimony. He reminded the gathering that he had been the first to take the gospel to the Gentiles, not by his choice, but by God's.

8. And God, which knoweth the hearts, bare them witness, giving them the Holy Ghost, even as he did unto us.

Peter continued to emphasize the decisive part *God* had played in the matter—God *which knoweth the hearts* and cannot be deceived by outward appearance or pretense. He had given those Gentiles *the Holy Ghost*, just as He had given to the apostles on the Day of Pentecost (Acts 2:1-4; 10:44-46). This was God's own testimony in favor of the Gentiles of Cornelius's household.

9. And put no difference between us and them, purifying their hearts by faith.

In the matter of being saved and becoming children of God, there is *no difference* between Jews and Gentiles. This is indicated by God's own testimony. What makes a difference is *faith*. When one believes in Jesus and obeys

---

How to Say It

ANTIOCH. *An*-tee-ock.

Him as Lord, that one becomes God's child (John 1:12, 13).

10. Now therefore why tempt ye God, to put a yoke upon the neck of the disciples, which neither our fathers nor we were able to bear?

To *tempt* is to test, to try. The Pharisees in the church were putting God on trial. They were contesting His decision, not Peter's or Paul's. God had shown himself ready to accept the Gentiles who came by faith; the Pharisees wanted to require more than God did. The law was *a yoke*, a burden that had proved to be too much for the Jews then present and for all of their ancestors. The Jews who came to Christ came admitting their failure. They were not righteous according to the law. They looked to Jesus to forgive them, to take away their sins, to make them righteous because of their faith. Now Gentiles were coming to Christ in the same way, and the Pharisees wanted to put on them the law that already had proved to be inadequate. That was absurd, preposterous.

11. But we believe that through the grace of the Lord Jesus Christ we shall be saved, even as they.

The grace of the Lord Jesus Christ, His favor that they did not deserve! That was the only hope of the Jewish Christians, even the Pharisees who had been most zealous for the law. The law could not save them. The Lord's grace could, and it could save the Gentiles as well.

BY LAW OR BY GRACE?

We all admit that we need laws. But the average layman is sometimes puzzled by the workings of the legal mind.

A while back the *New Jersey Law Journal* explained in profound "legalese" why an insurance company was legally able to rescind a life insurance policy after the death of the insured. The man's survivors received no benefits from the policy because it was discovered that, in applying for coverage, he had knowingly withheld the information that he had diabetes.

Most of us would say, "Fair enough," if his death had been caused by an undisclosed health problem. But in this case, the man was found in the trunk of his car, *shot to death!* A legal technicality seems—to the layman, at least—to have voided the facts in the case. But then the law seems not to have any room for grace.

The exclusive Jewish Christians were more concerned with points of the law than they were with the grace of God. Apparently they preferred to see Gentile God-seekers crushed by the weight of God's law than to see them enjoy the liberating grace of God in Christ, by which Jews and Gentiles alike are to be saved.

Not even the noblest person can bear the weight of God's law. The fact of our sin mocks our demands that God save us because we have obeyed Him. We simply can't be that good! Only His grace can save us.   —C. R. B.

B. Paul and Barnabas (v. 12)

12. Then all the multitude kept silence, and gave audience to Barnabas and Paul, declaring what miracles and wonders God had wrought among the Gentiles by them.

When Peter had finished his testimony, *Barnabas and Paul* spoke again. They had told about their mission before (v. 4), but now they emphasized the *miracles and wonders* that *God had wrought among the Gentiles by them.* Barnabas and Paul had not done those miracles; God had done them. That was clear evidence that God had been with the missionaries and had given His approval to their work. In that work they had led Gentiles to become Christians without becoming Jews, so it was safe to conclude that God approved of that.

III. Scripture
(Acts 15:13-18)

The testimony of Peter was plain and powerful. It had convinced the Christians in Jerusalem before (Acts 11:1-18), and now it convinced them again. The testimony of Barnabas and Paul added strength to the conviction. Now another speaker added the testimony of the Holy Scriptures. Who could argue with that?

A. Prophecy of Amos (vv. 13-17)

13. And after they had held their peace, James answered, saying, Men and brethren, hearken unto me.

When Barnabas and Paul had finished what they wanted to say, the next speaker was *James.* James the brother of John was no longer living on earth (Acts 12:1, 2), so we conclude that this James was "the Lord's brother" (Galatians 1:19); that is, a half brother of Jesus, a son of Joseph and Mary (Mark 6:3). James became a leader in the Jerusalem church, and author of the book of James. In the meeting we are considering, he rose to bring the discussion to its conclusion.

14. Simeon hath declared how God at the first did visit the Gentiles, to take out of them a people for his name.

Simeon or *Simon* was the original name of the disciple we usually call Peter. James began his speech by recalling what Simon Peter had said in the meeting only a short while before. Peter had recalled *how God at the first did visit the Gentiles.* Before any of the Jewish Christians were ready to welcome Gentiles into the church, God himself had gone to them *to take out of them a people for his name;* that is, to bring some of them to become Christians. How God did that is recorded in Acts 10. It had been thoroughly discussed in the church at Jerusalem, and the Jewish Christians had agreed that God wanted Gentiles to be saved along with Jews (Acts 11:1-18). In the meeting we are now reading about, Peter needed only a few words to remind the brethren of that earlier decision.

15. And to this agree the words of the prophets; as it is written.

James first recalled that God himself had acted to have Gentiles received among His people (v. 14). Then James stated that the same thing was shown in *the words of the prophets* and *written* in the Old Testament that was revered by all Jews, Christian and non-Christian.

16. After this I will return, and will build again the tabernacle of David, which is fallen down; and I will build again the ruins thereof, and I will set it up.

James chose Amos 9:11, 12 as an example of the prophecies that foretold God's acceptance of Gentiles. The first part of that chapter foretells the destruction of Israel, but not total destruction (Amos 9:8-10). In our text we are reading God's promise to rebuild it. The word *tabernacle* means a temporary structure such as a tent or wickiup.

Probably Amos gave his prophecy between 760 and 750 B.C. In 722 or 721 B.C. the Assyrians overcame northern Israel and scattered its people in foreign lands. The southern tribe of Judah survived then, but in 586 B.C. the Babylonians destroyed Jerusalem and took the people of Judah to Babylon as captives. Thus the nation was destroyed, but not utterly. This fulfilled the prophecy of Amos 9:8-10. God preserved a remnant of the nation in Babylon, and about 536 B.C. He brought it back to Jerusalem and rebuilt the nation according to Amos's prophecy quoted in our text. The next verse explains why God rebuilt the ruined nation of Israel.

17. That the residue of men might seek after the Lord, and all the Gentiles, upon whom my name is called, saith the Lord, who doeth all these things.

God did not restore the nation of Israel for its own sake only. He had designed that nation to bring into the world the Savior, Jesus, a man of David's line, who would lead not only Jews, but all the rest of mankind, to seek after the Lord. The non-Jewish people are described as *all the Gentiles.* God intended the good news of salvation for every human creature in the world (Mark 16:15). Of course the offer of salvation

does not rob people of their freedom to choose. Salvation is offered to all, and God wants all to be saved (2 Peter 3:9). Those actually saved are those who accept the Savior, Jesus; those who make Him their Lord and obey Him. God's name is called upon them: that is, they are known as God's people.

Like many prophecies of Scripture, this one from Amos has more than one fulfillment. First, God did rebuild David's tabernacle, his kingdom, his nation, after it had fallen into captivity. He used it to bring the Savior into the world and lead all kinds of people to seek God. But in a second and greater fulfillment, God is even now building up the tabernacle of David, the church that is ruled by Jesus Christ. On the human side, Jesus is David's descendant and heir to his throne. Therefore the kingdom of Christ is fittingly called the tabernacle of David. But now people from all the nations of the world are brought into it.

Verse 17 ends with a reminder that this prophecy is not from Amos, but from *the Lord,* Jehovah, the Creator of Heaven and earth. He is the one *who doeth all these things.* Through Amos He told what He would do; He did it and is doing it still.

B. Comment of James (v. 18)

18. Known unto God are all his works from the beginning of the world.

This is translated in different ways in other versions, but the reading we have here is beautifully appropriate. The quotation from Amos ends with verse 17, and now James adds his comment. *From the beginning of the world* God has known what He was going to do. He foretold much of it through the prophets. People understood the prophecies so poorly that they killed the Son of God, the Savior of the world. God raised Him to life and glory. After that, even the people who knew Christ best and followed Him most eagerly were only gradually coming to understand what God had known all along and had revealed through the prophets. Slowly, and with special urging by the Holy Spirit, Jewish Christians were learning that the offer of salvation is for all people, that the duty of Christians is to take it to all people, and that all people who earnestly follow Jesus are equally acceptable to God. Though that was learned with difficulty, it was learned thoroughly. All around the world today, God is building up "the tabernacle of David," the church of Jesus Christ.

Conclusion

Christians of today are much like those early Christians. We too like our own opinions, and we cling to them vigorously. We had better examine our thinking and be sure we do not cling to any opinion that opposes the will of God.

A. Don't Be Afraid to Change

The first Christians thought only Jews would ever be Christians, but they changed their thinking when God made His will known. Then some of them tried to keep their mistaken opinion in another form. They said, "Sure, Gentiles can become Christians; but they have to become Jews too." That opinion also was abandoned after the discussion we have seen in our lesson text. It was not in accord with God's will.

In our day, not many Christians doubt that God wants all kinds of people to be saved. But do you know of a Christian who has some reservations in his own mind? "Sure," he says, "I'm delighted to have all kinds of people come to Christ, people rich and poor, people educated and illiterate, people of all races and nations—but please, not in our congregation. Let's keep our church like it is." And if we will not do that, some members will move to a congregation that will.

Home Daily Bible Readings

Monday, Nov. 6—Difficulty of Keeping the Law (John 7:14-24)
Tuesday, Nov. 7—Justification by Faith (Galatians 2:11-21)
Wednesday, Nov. 8—Forgiveness of Sins (Acts 10:39-43)
Thursday, Nov. 9—Righteousness Bestowed by Christ (Isaiah 53:7-12)
Friday, Nov. 10—Approval From the Council at Jerusalem (Acts 15:19-29)
Saturday, Nov. 11—Letter Received With Rejoicing (Acts 15:30-35)
Sunday, Nov. 12—Grace for All (Romans 3:21-31)

Let's search the Scriptures. Can we find any indication that God does not want every Christian in our community to be in our church? If any opinion or wish of ours is not in line with God's will, let's change it.

On the other hand, enthusiastic Christians can go too far in demanding that every congregation include all kinds of people in its membership. Some years ago a Christian writer described a church in New Mexico that included Mexican Americans, Chinese Americans, Japanese Americans, Hindu Americans, and some assorted aliens. The description closed with the ringing declaration, "God wants every congregation to be just like that!"

In a rural church in Ohio, an elder chuckled. "Where shall we get all those kinds of people?" he asked. "Shall we hire a bus and bring them fifty miles from Columbus? It just happens that all the people we know have European ancestors —Italian or French or Russian or Norwegian or English."

In our search of the Scriptures, we do not find that God wants our congregation to include any more kinds of people than live in our community; but we do not find that He wants it to exclude any of the kinds of people who do live there.

B. Let God Decide

The Jewish Christians at Jerusalem gave up their treasured opinion because it was not in line with God's will. That is a noble example for us to follow.

Not all of those early Christians so nobly gave up their old opinion, however. There were some who kept on teaching that Christ is not enough, that Gentiles who become Christians must also become Jews and keep the Jewish law in order to be saved.

Paul had a forceful answer for that. If you think Christ is not enough, he said, if you look to the law for salvation, then "Christ is become of no effect unto you . . . ye are fallen from grace" (Galatians 5:2-4). That is a bad example for us to avoid. Let God decide. Accept His will. He is always right.

C. Prayer

Our Father in Heaven, Your love for us is so plain that we can never doubt it. We know every plan of Yours is for our good as well as for Your glory. Help us then to subdue our stubborn wills and bring every thought and word and act in line with the teaching of Your Holy Word.

D. Thought to Remember

God's way is best.

Learning by Doing

This page contains an alternate lesson plan emphasizing learning activities. Classes desiring such student involvement will find these suggestions helpful.

Learning Goals

Students in today's class should:

1. List principles for resolving conflict as demonstrated by the participants in the Jerusalem conference (Acts 15).

2. Choose at least one contemporary conflict and discuss how these principles can help resolve it.

Into the Lesson

Use one of the two following activities to introduce the theme of this study:

• Display a poster on which you have drawn the following diagram:

Conflict Is a Sin and Must Always Be Avoided ⟷ Conflict Is Inevitable and Always Shows Progress

Ask class members to decide which statement best describes their opinion about conflict in the church. If they feel uncomfortable with either extreme, ask them what they *do* believe about conflict between Christians. Divide the students into groups of three and ask each group to write one sentence that describes their thinking about conflict.

• Have a class member read aloud the introduction to this lesson. Then ask, "What are some subjects concerning which there are conflicting opinions among Christians today?" List as many as students identify in ninety seconds. Write their suggestions on sheets of paper, one suggestion per sheet. Tape the sheets to the wall.

Tell the class that in this session we will look at how the church in New Testament times handled conflict, and we will look for principles to help Christians deal with conflict in our time.

Into the Word

Set the stage for Bible study by reviewing last week's lesson.

Divide the class into fourths and assign to each of the fourths a different one of the four persons listed immediately below. As you read today's lesson text aloud, each fourth of the class is to listen to discover the perspective of its character:

1. A Christian who was also a Pharisee
2. A Gentile Christian
3. Paul
4. Peter

After the Scripture is read, have class members further divide into groups of three or four. Each group is to write a brief paragraph retelling the story from the point of view of their assigned character. Allow seven or eight minutes for each group to finish, and then ask to hear some of the paragraphs.

If you are pressed for time, the groups may simply list the thoughts and emotions that they think their character would have had. As the paragraphs or lists are shared, answer questions or fill in gaps with information included in the lesson comments.

Next have members work in pairs or in groups of three to prepare a list of principles for solving church conflicts. They should base their lists on the model set by the apostles and elders as recorded in Acts 15.

Give class members at least ten minutes to make their lists; then, as volunteers share items from their lists, jot them on your chalkboard. As each item is shared, ask other groups or students if they had written down the same or a similar thought.

If time is short, you may want to suggest some principles to your class members and ask them to find how they are demonstrated in this biblical account. Some possible principles from Acts 15 for resolving church conflicts are,

1. Consult church leaders.

2. Confer with leaders from more than one congregation.

3. Keep discussing until consensus is reached; don't take sides or leave a meeting angrily.

4. Analyze what God says about the issue. Keep studying till you can see how all His pronouncements and actions related to an issue agree with each other.

5. Be open to God's will, not committed to your own opinions.

Into Life

Refer to the sheets you taped to the wall earlier (if you chose this introductory activity). Select some of the subjects listed on the sheets and discuss how principles from Acts 15 can help resolve conflicts concerning them; or perhaps you will want to consider issues that have caused disagreement among members of your congregation, and apply these principles to those issues. Close the class session with prayer.

Let's Talk It Over

The questions on this page are designed to encourage review of the lesson Scriptures and to promote discussion of the lesson by the class. The answers provided are only discussion starters. Let your class talk it over from there.

1. There was much disputing and debating in Antioch and in Jerusalem regarding what was to be required of Gentiles in order for them to become Christians (Acts 15:2, 7). The reader may wonder why God did not grant all believers a vision such as Peter's in Acts 10. Was there some benefit gained by the disputing and debating?

It seems that God did not give an excessive amount of visions and dreams. It was His plan that spiritual truth be communicated primarily through human messengers and teachers. The conference in Jerusalem was no doubt a rich learning experience for all who were present. Their minds must have been stimulated to serious thinking as they heard the various viewpoints presented. The lessons they learned would have been made more memorable by the drama of debate. So today we need not fear disagreement and discussion regarding spiritual matters. If they take place in an amiable atmosphere, with a serious effort to arrive at the truth, they can be quite beneficial to learning.

2. What important fact about salvation did the Jerusalem conference establish?

Mankind is saved, not by keeping the law given through Moses, but through "the grace of the Lord Jesus Christ" (Acts 15:11). This shows that salvation is the gift of a loving Father to obedient believers. It removes the self-righteous pride and the hair-splitting of the legalist and recognizes that none are good enough to merit eternal life.

3. Why were Paul and Barnabas determined that Christians not be bound by Jewish law?

Paul taught that Christ died to set us free from the law. For one to return to it, therefore, would signify that that person had no part in the grace of God (Galatians 5:1-4).

4. What are some "yokes" of personal opinion that some believers wish to impose on others?

One such "yoke" has to do with participation in certain forms of recreation—attending movies in theaters, watching television, and many other such matters. Christians hold varying views regarding such activities. If a person treats this as a matter of personal conviction that is one thing;

if, however, one seeks to make his or her conviction binding on others, that is quite another. Observance of certain holidays is another area of diversity. Again some regard such observance as improper; others see it as a matter of personal liberty to participate in the holiday activities. Paul dealt with this problem in Romans 14. There he pointed out that in our differences of opinion we need to seek always to maintain peace and aim at building up one another.

5. The Christian leaders in Jerusalem utilized the Scriptures in trying to resolve this dispute that threatened the church. How can we follow their example?

"What does the Bible say about it?" or more specifically, "What does the New Testament say about it?" are questions that should occur automatically to us whenever disagreement arises in the church. Instead, some church members are inclined to say, "This is the way we have always done it," or, "This is what we must do to compromise and keep the peace at any cost." Of course, many disagreements in the church involve matters for which the Bible has no direct teaching. But even in such cases we must take into account the broad New Testament principles that should govern all Christian activity (see, for example, Romans 15:1, 2; 1 Corinthians 10:31; 16:14). These principles should be recalled regularly when leaders and members sit down for meetings.

6. Some longtime Christians may say, "I have held my opinions for many years, and I am not likely to change them now." What shall we say to this?

To hold firmly for many years to convictions that are centered in biblical doctrines, is commendable. But to cling rigidly to personal opinions that tend to negate Scriptural principles is not. A person of any age who does the latter must be urged to change. And surely change is possible at any age. Occasionally one sees a person of advanced age becoming a Christian after resisting the gospel for many years. On other occasions one witnesses an elderly believer taking on a remarkable new challenge of service in the church. These are evidences that a change of viewpoint can take place at any time in life.

A Gospel for the Whole World

DEVOTIONAL READING: Acts 15:36—16:5.

LESSON SCRIPTURE: Acts 15:36—16:40.

PRINTED TEXT: Acts 16:9, 10, 13-15, 25-34.

Acts 16:9, 10, 13-15, 25-34

9 And a vision appeared to Paul in the night; There stood a man of Macedonia, and prayed him, saying, Come over into Macedonia, and help us.

10 And after he had seen the vision, immediately we endeavored to go into Macedonia, assuredly gathering that the Lord had called us for to preach the gospel unto them.

· · · · · · · · · · · · ·

13 And on the sabbath we went out of the city by a river side, where prayer was wont to be made; and we sat down, and spake unto the women which resorted thither.

14 And a certain woman named Lydia, a seller of purple, of the city of Thyatira, which worshipped God, heard us: whose heart the Lord opened, that she attended unto the things which were spoken of Paul.

15 And when she was baptized, and her household, she besought us, saying, If ye have judged me to be faithful to the Lord, come into my house, and abide there. And she constrained us.

· · · · · · · · · · · · ·

25 And at midnight Paul and Silas prayed, and sang praises unto God: and the prisoners heard them.

26 And suddenly there was a great earthquake, so that the foundations of the prison were shaken: and immediately all the doors were opened, and every one's bands were loosed.

27 And the keeper of the prison awaking out of his sleep, and seeing the prison doors open, he drew out his sword, and would have killed himself, supposing that the prisoners had been fled.

28 But Paul cried with a loud voice, saying, Do thyself no harm: for we are all here.

29 Then he called for a light, and sprang in, and came trembling, and fell down before Paul and Silas,

30 And brought them out, and said, Sirs, what must I do to be saved?

31 And they said, Believe on the Lord Jesus Christ, and thou shalt be saved, and thy house.

32 And they spake unto him the word of the Lord, and to all that were in his house.

33 And he took them the same hour of the night, and washed their stripes; and was baptized, he and all his, straightway.

34 And when he had brought them into his house, he set meat before them, and rejoiced, believing in God with all his house.

GOLDEN TEXT: After he had seen the vision, immediately we endeavored to go into Macedonia, assuredly gathering that the Lord had called us for to preach the gospel unto them.—Acts 16:10.

The Story of Christian Beginnings (Acts)
Unit 3: Spreading the Gospel Into All the World (Lessons 10-13)

Lesson Aims

After this lesson a student should be able to:
1. Retell the stories of Lydia and the jailer.
2. Identify someone who needs Jesus.
3. Try to bring that one to the Master.

Lesson Outline

INTRODUCTION
  A. God's Great Vision
  B. Lesson Background
 I. ANSWERING A CALL (Acts 16:9, 10)
  A. Vision (v. 9)
  B. Response (v. 10)
II. CONVERTING A LADY (Acts 16:13-15)
  A. Prayer Meeting (v. 13)
  B. Attentive Listener (v. 14)
  C. Christian Hospitality (v. 15)
III. CONVERTING A JAILER (Acts 16:25-34)
  A. Big Earthquake (vv. 25, 26)
    Praising God in Strange Places
  B. Narrow Escape (vv. 27, 28)
  C. Important Question (vv. 29, 30)
  D. Important Answer (vv. 31, 32)
  E. Prompt Obedience (vv. 33, 34)
    Meeting Christ in Prison
CONCLUSION
  A. Getting Attention
  B. Giving the Message
  C. Obedience
  D. Joy
  E. Prayer
  F. Thought to Remember

Visual 12 is a photo of the ruins of the Agora in Philippi, where Paul and Silas were hauled before the city magistrates. The visual is shown on page 101.

Introduction

Since the collapse of the Soviet Union, countless missionaries have been flooding into the countries where the Communist government had promoted atheism for many years.

Churches are growing even in China, where the Communist government still rules, and encouraging news comes from countless other fields around the world.

Yet, after two thousand years, how far we are from fulfilling the magnificent vision of the Master! He said, "Go ye into all the world, and preach the gospel to every creature" (Mark 16:15).

A. God's Great Vision

Since the very beginning of the church, how constantly God has been pushing His people to go farther and do more!

The first Christians in Jerusalem won multiplied thousands of people to the Lord, but they seemed to be quite content to stay in that city till persecution drove them out. We wonder if God permitted the persecution for that purpose.

Those who were scattered "went every where preaching the word" (Acts 8:4), but they preached it "to none but unto the Jews only" (11:19). Lesson 8 reviewed the extraordinary methods God used to persuade them that the good news of salvation was for Gentiles too.

Apparently Antioch was the scene of the first great church among the Gentiles. The Christians there were devoted and enthusiastic, but it took a special word from the Holy Spirit to send two of their best workers out through the island of Cyprus and into Asia Minor. Lesson 10 reviewed their trip for us.

B. Lesson Background

Last week's lesson pictured a human effort to restrict church growth by compelling all Christians to become Jews. With the leading of the Holy Spirit, the church repudiated that effort.

Paul and Barnabas then planned a second trip, intending to revisit the churches they had started before. After a sharp difference of opinion, they separated and formed two missionary teams instead of one. Barnabas and John Mark went to Cyprus; Paul and Silas went to the churches on the mainland (Acts 15:36-41).

At Lystra, young Timothy joined Paul and Silas (Acts 16:1-5). After visiting the churches that were started earlier, the three went on to the west, apparently expecting to preach in cities of Asia. This was not the great continent we now call Asia; it was the Roman province at the west end of that continent.

The missionaries must have been surprised when the Holy Spirit told them not to preach in Asia. They thought then of going north to Bithynia, but the Spirit vetoed that idea too. So the trio pressed on to the west till they were stopped by the sea at Troas (Acts 16:6-8). We can imagine that they were greatly puzzled. The gospel was for every creature. Why should they not preach it in Asia or Bithynia? What did the Spirit want them to do?

I. Answering a Call
(Acts 16:9, 10)

Soon the missionaries learned what the Spirit had in mind. As at other times, God's vision was wider than man's. These preachers of the gospel were not only to leave the little province then called Asia; they were to leave the huge continent that now has that name. They were going to Europe!

Some Bible students make much of that, calling it the first coming of the gospel to a new continent. Of that we cannot be sure, for no one knows when or how the gospel first came to Rome.

In any case, the coming of the gospel to Europe proved to be vastly important. From Europe the faith spread to America; from Europe and America came most of the men and money for the great worldwide missionary movement of the nineteenth and twentieth centuries. Thus Europe became an important station on the gospel's journey to "the uttermost part of the earth."

A. Vision (v. 9)

9. And a vision appeared to Paul in the night; There stood a man of Macedonia, and prayed him, saying, Come over into Macedonia, and help us.

Macedonia was not far away, though it was on another continent. It was the country just north of Greece.

B. Response (v. 10)

10. And after he had seen the vision, immediately we endeavored to go into Macedonia, assuredly gathering that the Lord had called us for to preach the gospel unto them.

Paul and his companions had no doubt about the meaning of the vision. It was God's call. He wanted these missionaries to preach the gospel in Macedonia. *Immediately* they began looking for a ship that would take them to the place where God wanted them.

Notice the change in the pronouns. *They*— Paul, Silas, and Timothy— came to Troas (v. 8). But *we* looked for a way to Macedonia, sure that the Lord had called *us*—Paul, Silas, Timothy, and Luke, the writer of this record. Where did Luke come from? Why did he join the party at this point? Was he already known to any of the missionaries? Obviously Luke was a modest historian. He told us nothing about himself.

II. Converting a Lady
(Acts 16:13-15)

The missionaries found the boat they were seeking. It carried them more than a hundred miles northwest across the Aegean Sea to the coast of Macedonia. Landing at Neapolis, they went inland to Philippi (Acts 16:11, 12).

A. Prayer Meeting (v. 13)

13. And on the sabbath we went out of the city by a river side, where prayer was wont to be made; and we sat down, and spake unto the women which resorted thither.

Chief city though it was, Philippi probably did not have enough Jews to maintain a synagogue. But there was a prayer meeting by a river outside the city. The missionaries learned about that and took their message to it. Apparently only women attended, but the visiting teachers were welcomed and given a chance to speak.

B. Attentive Listener (v. 14)

14. And a certain woman named Lydia, a seller of purple, of the city of Thyatira, which worshipped God, heard us: whose heart the Lord opened, that she attended unto the things which were spoken of Paul.

Lydia was a businesswoman. Probably she was a prosperous one, for *purple* is a rare and costly dye obtained from shellfish. Fabric colored by such a dye also is called purple. We cannot tell whether Lydia sold the dye, or the cloth, or finished garments of purple, or all three.

This lady had come from *the city of Thyatira* in the province of Asia, which the missionaries had just left behind. Luke says Lydia *worshipped God.* Probably that means she was not Jewish, but had forsaken the mythical religions of the heathen to worship the real God whom the Jews worshiped. Such Gentiles were described as devout (Acts 10:2, 7; 17:4, 17) or as fearing God (Acts 13:26). Often they were found meeting with Jews in the synagogues.

How to Say It

AEGEAN. A-*jee*-un.
ANTIOCH. *An*-tee-ock.
BITHYNIA. Bih-*thin*-ee-uh.
CYPRUS. *Sye*-prus.
LYDIA. *Lid*-i-uh.
LYSTRA. *Liss*-truh.
MACEDONIA. Mass-eh-*doe*-nee-uh.
NEAPOLIS. Nee-*ap*-o-lis.
PHILIPPI. Fih-*lip*-pie or *Fil*-ih-pie.
THYATIRA. Thy-uh-*tie*-ruh (strong accent on *tie; th* as in *thin*).
TROAS. *Tro*-az.

Lydia's conversion was not accomplished by Paul's personality or Paul's eloquence alone; *the Lord* opened her heart. Some may debate about how God opens a human heart, but in this case one way is obvious. The Lord opened Lydia's heart by means of the message she heard from Paul. It was the Lord's message, and it accomplished His purpose. That message, the gospel, is "the power of God unto salvation to every one that believeth" (Romans 1:16). By means of that message God opened Lydia's heart so that she *attended unto* (she accepted) the message.

C. Christian Hospitality (v. 15)

15. And when she was baptized, and her household, she besought us, saying, If ye have judged me to be faithful to the Lord, come into my house, and abide there. And she constrained us.

In obedience to the message she heard and accepted, Lydia *was baptized.* So was *her household.* This included members of her family, if she had a family living with her. Whether she had a family or not, her household probably included household servants such as cook and housekeeper. It may have included employees who helped with her business. How many there may have been we have no way of knowing. Whoever they were, they too listened to the gospel, and the Lord opened their hearts to receive it. So the mistress of the house and her household became Christians together.

Then Lydia invited Paul, Silas, Timothy, and Luke to stay at her house. Here is another indication that the lady was prosperous. She had room for four houseguests. The four may have been reluctant to accept her generous hospitality. As a rule, Paul liked to make the gospel without cost to those who heard it (1 Corinthians 9:18). But Lydia wouldn't take no for an answer. She *constrained* them, or "persuaded" them, as the *New International Version* has it.

III. Converting a Jailer
(Acts 16:25-34)

A slave girl in Philippi was possessed by a demon. Evil though he was, the spirit knew many things unknown to humans. Using the girl's voice, he made her an excellent fortune-teller, and she earned a lot of money for her owners.

Impelled by the demon, the girl followed the missionaries day after day, shouting, "These men are the servants of the most high God, which show unto us the way of salvation."

Paul was grieved, probably both because the girl was mistreated and because God's servants

do not want the support of demons. In the name of Jesus, Paul ordered the demon to go away and leave the girl alone.

Owners of the girl were furious. Now they had an ordinary slave instead of a high-priced fortune-teller. They dragged Paul and Silas to the marketplace, where judges were sitting to decide whatever cases were brought to them.

Instead of voicing their real complaint, the accusers appealed to racial prejudice. They said these Jews were teaching customs that were not legal for Romans. Without waiting for evidence, the marketplace crowd raised a great cry against Paul and Silas.

Roman authorities liked to prevent rioting at all costs. These judges appeased the crowd by having Paul and Silas stripped, beaten, and put in jail. So these innocent men were sitting in the maximum security cell with their feet locked in the stocks. All this is told in verses 16-24, which are not included in our text.

A. Big Earthquake (vv. 25, 26)

25. And at midnight Paul and Silas prayed, and sang praises unto God: and the prisoners heard them.

At midnight there must have been utter darkness in the inner prison, but Paul and Silas were not sleeping. They could not lie down comfortably because their backs were bruised and bloody from their beating. They could not sit comfortably because their feet were locked in the stocks. So they *prayed, and sang praises unto God.* Other *prisoners* were awake too, and probably they were surprised to hear prayers and praises instead of curses.

PRAISING GOD IN STRANGE PLACES

Most people would not expect to find a church in the trailer of an eighteen-wheel "big rig," but Ken Taylor operates a permanent chapel at a truck stop in Southern California. He drove the open road for thirty years and knows how to speak to the spiritual needs of truckers.

Several ministries to professional drivers have "truck-stop churches" located across the United States and Canada. Drivers who have tired of the irreverent chatter coming over their CB radios, or who are looking for strength to resist the temptations that loneliness brings, find in such chapels a haven where they can praise God and seek His guidance.

Praising God can bring positive change to even the worst of situations. It was so in the prison in Philippi. Jail would seem to be a strange place to praise God, but that is where Paul and Silas were doing it! Even though they were unfairly imprisoned, they gave glory to

God. Their praise not only raised their own spirits but it also had a profound impact on at least one other man and his entire household. Praising God can change lives—our own and others'.

—C. R. B.

26. And suddenly there was a great earthquake, so that the foundations of the prison were shaken: and immediately all the doors were opened, and every one's bands were loosed.

This was no tiny temblor; it was *a great earthquake*. It was strong enough to shake *the foundations of the prison,* but it was a divinely directed quake. Instead of shaking down stone walls, it opened *all the doors* that were locked. It unlocked the stocks from the feet of Paul and Silas and unfastened whatever chains and fetters were restraining other prisoners.

B. Narrow Escape (vv. 27, 28)

27. And the keeper of the prison awaking out of his sleep, and seeing the prison doors open, he drew out his sword, and would have killed himself, supposing that the prisoners had been fled.

Apparently the jailer had an office in the prison and was sleeping there. It was shocking to be wakened by an earthquake; but when he collected his senses and looked around, it was more shocking still to see the open doors. Death was the routine punishment for a guard who let prisoners escape, and this guard preferred suicide to execution. Obviously he was a man of action. Without waiting to be sure the prisoners were gone, he whipped out his sword to kill himself.

28. But Paul cried with a loud voice, saying, Do thyself no harm: for we are all here.

How did Paul know what the jailer was doing? Perhaps the Holy Spirit revealed it to him; or perhaps there was a lamp in the office, and Paul could see through the open doors. In either case, his shout brought a narrow escape to a jailer on the verge of death.

C. Important Question (vv. 29, 30)

29. Then he called for a light, and sprang in, and came trembling, and fell down before Paul and Silas.

If there was a lamp in the office, apparently it was not suitable for carrying. But the jailer had helpers nearby. At his call they quickly brought a torch or lantern. Once again we see the jailer as a man of action. He did not walk, but *sprang* or leaped into the dungeon. Why did he go to Paul and Silas rather than the other prisoners? It seems plain that he knew enough about these

visual 12

two to convince him that they were somehow allied with the power that sent the earthquake. In reverent awe he *fell down* before them. He was *trembling* with fear of the supernatural, and perhaps also because he was unnerved by his narrow escape from death.

30. And brought them out, and said, Sirs, what must I do to be saved?

The jailer did not remain prostrate for long. Probably Paul and Silas told him they were only men and were not to be worshiped. So he rose and *brought them out* of the dungeon. Where did he take them then? We are not told; but as soon as he brought them to a suitable place he asked the question that was on his mind.

What must I do to be saved? What did this pagan mean by that? He was already saved from the earthquake and from suicide, so we know he was not asking about those. He must have been thinking of the kind of salvation that Paul and Silas preached about. This indicates that he already knew something about these men. Perhaps he knew a fortune-teller had said they taught the way of salvation (vv. 16, 17). He may have been told about their preaching; it is even possible that he had heard them preach. Surely he was not yet fully informed about salvation, but he wanted to know how to get it.

D. Important Answer (vv. 31, 32)

31. And they said, Believe on the Lord Jesus Christ, and thou shalt be saved, and thy house.

The preachers gave a short answer that needed a long explanation. See the next verse.

32. And they spake unto him the word of the Lord, and to all that were in his house.

The earthquake came at midnight (vv. 25, 26). Most of the remaining hours of the night may have been used in presenting *the word of the Lord* to the jailer and his family and servants.

E. Prompt Obedience (vv. 33, 34)

33. And he took them the same hour of the night, and washed their stripes; and was baptized, he and all his, straightway.

Ashamed of his part in mistreating these men, the jailer did what he could to make amends. He gave a simple treatment to the backs that had been injured by a savage beating (vv. 22, 23). Now that he and his household had heard the gospel and believed it, they were *baptized . . . straightway.*

34. And when he had brought them into his house, he set meat before them, and rejoiced, believing in God with all his house.

When the baptisms were completed, it was time for brethren to enjoy a happy breakfast together. Preachers and converts *rejoiced* because the jailer and his household had been turned "from darkness to light, and from the power of Satan unto God" (Acts 26:18)—and there was joy in Heaven too (Luke 15:7).

MEETING CHRIST IN PRISON

On June 17, 1972, five men were arrested for breaking into the headquarters of the Democratic National Committee in a Washington, D.C., office building. By midsummer of 1973, what had appeared at first to be a simple burglary had become the Watergate scandal.

Charles Colson was one of the presidential aides who went to prison for his complicity in the Watergate affair. In prison he met Jesus Christ, and Colson's life was turned around. He has since become a highly respected Christian spokesman. He has written several Christian books, is a regular columnist in a major Christian magazine, and is the founder of a Christian ministry to people in prison.

Centuries earlier in Philippi, another prison ministry was conducted. Two innocent men had been imprisoned, but their demeanor in the prison that night was so unusual, so amazing in light of the circumstances, that the jailer was moved to inquire about his own salvation. That very night, through the assistance of Paul and

Silas, the jailer met Jesus. Since we never know what circumstances may incline a person's heart to the gospel of Christ, we should always be ready to share the message whenever the opportunity presents itself.   —C. R. B.

Conclusion

In two sections of our text we see two very different people who became Christians. One was a wealthy and cultured lady who believed in God. The other was a jailer who seemed heartless and unfeeling. There is no indication that he believed either in God or in the mythical deities of the heathen.

Our world likewise has different kinds of people, but they all need Jesus. Our task is to bring all of them to Him. Let's note how that was done in Philippi.

A. Getting Attention

It was easy to get Lydia's attention. She was glad to hear the gospel. There are many like her in the world about us, but they do not come looking for us. We have to go to them.

It was harder to get the jailer's attention, but the Lord did it well. After the earthquake the jailer was very attentive. With no earthquake to help us, we need to think much about how we can get the attention of careless unbelievers.

B. Giving the Message

When people are listening, the same message is for all of them. All have sinned, and salvation is offered to all. There is no salvation except through Jesus.

C. Obedience

Lydia and the jailer heard the same message, and both responded with prompt obedience. First they were baptized. Then they showed their allegiance to their new Master by ministering to the needs of His servants.

D. Joy

In any time and place, there is joy in turning "from darkness to light, and from the power of Satan unto God."

E. Prayer

Our Father, all around us we see people who need Jesus. Help us to get their attention, convince them with the message of salvation, baptize them in the name of Jesus, and teach them to do all He has commanded.

F. Thought to Remember

People need Jesus.

Home Daily Bible Readings

Monday, Nov. 13—Solving a Mother's Need (Exodus 2:1-10)

Tuesday, Nov. 14—God's Response to His People's Cry (Exodus 3:1-8)

Wednesday, Nov. 15—Caring for a Fellow Traveler (Luke 10:25-37)

Thursday, Nov. 16—The Spirit's Response to Our Cry (Romans 8:12-17)

Friday, Nov. 17—Timothy Enlisted as Helper (Acts 16:1-8)

Saturday, Nov. 18—Arrested for Helping a Slave Girl (Acts 16:16-24)

Sunday, Nov. 19—Released for Continued Ministry (Acts 16:35-40)

Learning by Doing

This page contains an alternate lesson plan emphasizing learning activities. Classes desiring such student involvement will find these suggestions helpful.

Learning Goals

As students participate in today's class session, they should:

1. Compare the conversion of Lydia and her household with the conversion of the Philippian jailer and his household.

2. Commit themselves to sharing the gospel with one person they know.

Into the Lesson

Ask your class members to pair off, and have each pair complete one of the following incomplete sentences:

1. "The person who first told me about Christ was—"

2. "The last time I talked with someone else about the gospel was—"

3. "I became a Christian because—"

4. "The main reason people become Christians today is—"

Allow a few class members to share their sentences with the whole class; then tell your group that today we shall study some dramatic conversions to Christ that occurred on one of Paul's missionary trips.

Into the Word

Connect this lesson with last week's by summarizing Acts 15 and 16:1-5. Use the thoughts provided in the "Lesson Background" section.

Write the three major points of the "Lesson Outline" on your chalkboard:

  I. Answering a Call

  II. Converting a Lady

  III. Converting a Jailer

To consider the first point, ask a volunteer to read Acts 16:6-10 aloud while the class listens to hear what the Spirit *wanted* Paul to do, and what the Spirit did not want Paul to do. Then discuss. Refer to maps in your classroom or class members' Bibles to locate the places mentioned in this text. Do the same as you read verses 11 and 12 aloud.

Now consider points II. and III. together. Have one class member read verses 13-15 aloud followed by another class member reading verses 25-34 aloud. As the two read, the rest of the class should listen for *similarities* and *differences* in these two conversion accounts. (Summarize verses 16-24 so class members will understand why Paul and Silas were in prison.)

Divide the class into groups of from three to seven. Each group should list the similarities and differences in the accounts. If you wish you may give these study groups specific questions to get them started. Use questions such as these:

1. How many heard the message?

2. How many responded?

3. What prompted them to respond?

4. How did they respond?

Allow about six minutes for the groups to study; then ask them to share their findings. As they do so, list the similarities and differences on your chalkboard.

Discuss this with your class: "If Acts 16:13-34 were the only passage in the Bible available for your study, what could you learn about—

(a) how to share the gospel message?"

(b) how to become a Christian?"

(c) what it means to a person to become a Christian?"

Into Life

Before class, type the following two quotes on cards, one quote per card. Give the cards to two different class members at this time. Ask each card holder to read his or her quote aloud. After each is read, let the class members comment, basing their comments on today's Bible text. (Appropriate references are provided after each quote for the teacher's convenience.)

• "I don't understand why things are going so badly for me. I was certain that I was doing God's will, but in the last month, all I've had is trouble. I'm tempted to give up on Christ and the church. If I'm doing what God wants me to do, why aren't things going more smoothly for me?" (vv. 19-25)

• Religion is necessary in society, I guess, but the church people I know are sour, sullen, and out-of-touch. Why would anyone want to become a Christian anyway? Aren't a good salary, a decent home, and healthy family enough to bring anyone happiness?" (v. 34).

If you prefer, and if you have time, you could have the students reassemble in the groups in which they did their Bible study earlier. Give each group a copy of one of the quotes and ask them to discuss it. However you discuss them, conclude your class with guided prayer with the theme, "God, help me to understand where You want *me* to share the gospel message."

Let's Talk It Over

The questions on this page are designed to encourage review of the lesson Scriptures and to promote discussion of the lesson by the class. The answers provided are only discussion starters. Let your class talk it over from there.

1. We often hear non-Christian people mention that they pray to God. How can we make that a starting point for presenting the gospel to them?

Perhaps we could take the approach of appealing to their sense of fair play. If their prayers are requests for God to do something for them, they should consider what they are doing for God. To accept His Son as Savior and to follow Him as Lord would not, of course, be a way of earning God's answers to prayer. But it would be a way of responding to God as a gracious Father and not as a glorified genie.

Another approach could be to focus their attention on a biblical prayer they probably already know—the model prayer, which is more commonly referred to as the "Lord's Prayer" (see Matthew 6:9-13). The reference in that prayer to God's will could give us the opportunity to point out that God's will is for all people to be saved (1 Timothy 2:4). Then we could demonstrate how such salvation has been made available through the death and resurrection of Jesus Christ.

2. Lydia's eagerness to provide lodging for Paul and his companions reminds us of the zeal for service that new converts often have. How should the church respond to this zeal?

The church's leadership, in particular, needs to be aware of the new convert's enthusiasm and should challenge that person to serve Christ and the church in ways that are appropriate to his or her capability. Within the new convert's family and circle of friends there may be several unsaved individuals. The new convert should be encouraged and assisted in the task of sharing his or her newfound faith with them. Within the church itself new converts can be given simple responsibilities that will help them become better acquainted with their new brothers and sisters in Christ. Serving as greeters for worship services or making some visits on the sick or shut-ins are examples. One caution to observe is that new converts should not be given too much responsibility too soon. The tasks could be overwhelming and could result in burnout. In general, every member should be alert to the new converts in the church's fellowship and should encourage them in their zeal for Christ.

3. In the midst of cruel and unjust treatment Paul and Silas prayed and praised God. Why is it important that we learn to respond to adversity in a similar manner?

We who are Christians must ask ourselves, "Do we differ from our non-Christian neighbors in the way we handle unpleasant experiences? Or do we complain just as bitterly as they and strike back just as viciously at those who have wronged us?" If we are complaining and vindictive in the face of unpleasant or unfair circumstances, we will be open to the charge, "These Christians are no different from anyone` else!" Our testimony for Christ demands that we respond to adversity with patience, steadfastness, and even praise. Hebrews 13:15 urges us to "offer the sacrifice of praise to God continually." Praise and thanksgiving represent worthy sacrifices to God when they are offered on occasions in which we are tempted instead to complain. Paul exhorted the Thessalonians, "In every thing give thanks: for this is the will of God in Christ Jesus concerning you" (1 Thessalonians 5:18). It hardly needs to be pointed out that "every thing" includes life's unpleasant experiences.

4. If an unbeliever were to ask us, "What must I do to be saved?" would we be able to provide the necessary information? Why should every Christian be prepared to give the biblical answer to this question?

One response that some may be inclined to give to this question is, "Why don't you talk to my preacher or to one of the elders in my church?" But the preacher and the elders may not be available at the particular moment when one who is seeking this information is in the best frame of mind to receive an answer to the question. Furthermore, it may be that the individual would not be comfortable discussing his or her spiritual needs with someone other than us.

Some Christians try to keep themselves prepared for the possibility of being asked this question by writing on the flyleaf of their Bibles the plan of salvation with appropriate Scripture references. Others keep gospel tracts in their pocket or purse at all times. Any of us could follow a similar practice and thus be prepared to provide the saving gospel message to an honest inquirer.

The Power of the Gospel

DEVOTIONAL READING: Acts 18:18-28.

LESSON SCRIPTURE: Acts 18:18—19:41.

PRINTED TEXT: Acts 19:1-6, 11-20.

Acts 19:1-6, 11-20

1 And it came to pass, that, while Apollos was at Corinth, Paul having passed through the upper coasts came to Ephesus; and finding certain disciples,

2 He said unto them, Have ye received the Holy Ghost since ye believed? And they said unto him, We have not so much as heard whether there be any Holy Ghost.

3 And he said unto them, Unto what then were ye baptized? And they said, Unto John's baptism.

4 Then said Paul, John verily baptized with the baptism of repentance, saying unto the people, that they should believe on him which should come after him, that is, on Christ Jesus.

5 When they heard this, they were baptized in the name of the Lord Jesus.

6 And when Paul had laid his hands upon them, the Holy Ghost came on them; and they spake with tongues, and prophesied.

. . . .

11 And God wrought special miracles by the hands of Paul:

12 So that from his body were brought unto the sick handkerchiefs or aprons, and the diseases departed from them, and the evil spirits went out of them.

13 Then certain of the vagabond Jews, exorcists, took upon them to call over them which had evil spirits the name of the Lord Jesus, saying, We adjure you by Jesus whom Paul preacheth.

14 And there were seven sons of one Sceva, a Jew, and chief of the priests, which did so.

15 And the evil spirit answered and said, Jesus I know, and Paul I know; but who are ye?

16 And the man in whom the evil spirit was leaped on them, and overcame them, and prevailed against them, so that they fled out of that house naked and wounded.

17 And this was known to all the Jews and Greeks also dwelling at Ephesus; and fear fell on them all, and the name of the Lord Jesus was magnified.

18 And many that believed came, and confessed, and showed their deeds.

19 Many of them also which used curious arts brought their books together, and burned them before all men: and they counted the price of them, and found it fifty thousand pieces of silver.

20 So mightily grew the word of God and prevailed.

GOLDEN TEXT: So mightily grew the word of God and prevailed.—Acts 19:20.

The Story of Christian Beginnings (Acts)
Unit 3: Spreading the Gospel Into All the World (Lessons 10-13)

Lesson Aims

After the study of this lesson a student should be able to :
1. Recall and retell what is told in our text.
2. Briefly tell what we must do to make God's power effective in saving souls and building the church.
3. Gladly do his or her part.

Lesson Outline

INTRODUCTION
  A. Paul's Second Missionary Journey
  B. Lesson Background
 I. TEACHING NEW DISCIPLES (Acts 19:1-6)
  A. Revealing Question (vv. 1, 2)
  B. Two Baptisms (vv. 3-5)
  C. Power of the Holy Spirit (v. 6)
II. MIRACLES DONE AND ATTEMPTED (Acts 19:11-14)
  A. Miracles Done (vv. 11, 12)
  B. Miracles Attempted (vv. 13, 14)
III. TRIUMPH OF TRUTH (Acts 19:15-20)
  A. Disaster to Fakers (vv. 15, 16)
  B. Honor to Jesus (vv. 17, 18)
  C. From Darkness to Light (vv. 19, 20)
    What Shall We Do With the Past?
CONCLUSION
  A. God and His Son and His Spirit
  B. God's Power and Our Task
  C. Prayer
  D. Thought to Remember

Refer to the map (visual 13) of the visuals packet to retrace the spreading of the gospel to the places mentioned in this quarter's study. The visual is shown on page 109.

Introduction

Last week in our lesson we read that Paul and Silas were midnight prisoners in Philippi; but before morning an earthquake opened the prison, and the jailer became a Christian. City officials then were eager to get those preachers out of their jail and out of their town. After their release Paul and Silas and Timothy moved on; but Luke stayed, probably to continue teaching the new Christians.

A. Paul's Second Missionary Journey

That was early in Paul's second missionary journey. Philippi was his first stop on the European continent. From there he went on to other cities of Macedonia. Souls were won in each place, but unbelieving Jews became so hostile that Paul soon moved on.

From Macedonia he went south to Greece. He taught in Athens for a while, and then spent about two years in Corinth. After that he was ready to bring his second journey to its close.

Paul's good friends Aquila and Priscilla went with him from Corinth to Ephesus. They were tentmakers with whom Paul had worked in Corinth. The two of them stayed in Ephesus while Paul went on to attend a Jewish feast in Jerusalem and spend some time in Antioch before starting his third journey. All this is told in Acts 16:35—18:23.

B. Lesson Background

Before Paul came again to Ephesus, another traveling Jewish teacher arrived. He was Apollos, from Alexandria in Egypt. He was well versed in the Scriptures, enthusiastic, and eloquent. Like Paul, he taught about Jesus; but unlike Paul, he did not understand Christian baptism. He taught baptism as it was taught by Jesus' forerunner, John the Baptist.

Priscilla and Aquila quickly saw the defect in his teaching. They did not oppose him in the synagogue, but took him home with them and "expounded unto him the way of God more perfectly." When he went on to Corinth, he was a better preacher than he had been before (Acts 18:24-28).

I. Teaching New Disciples (Acts 19:1-6)

Meanwhile, Paul was starting his third missionary journey. First the apostle went again to visit the churches he had started on his first journey (Acts 18:23). Then he continued on westward into the province of Asia. On the second journey the Holy Spirit had told him not to preach there (Acts 16:6), but now the time had come.

A. Revealing Question (vv. 1, 2)

1a. And it came to pass, that, while Apollos was at Corinth, Paul having passed through the upper coasts came to Ephesus.

Coasts here does not mean seacoasts. *The upper coasts* were the highlands in the province called Asia. Paul traveled westward through the high country and came to the seacoast at

Ephesus, the principal city of Asia. *Apollos* then had left Ephesus and was at *Corinth.*

1b, 2. And finding certain disciples, he said unto them, Have ye received the Holy Ghost since ye believed? And they said unto him, We have not so much as heard whether there be any Holy Ghost.

Disciples here means Christians, disciples of Jesus. In Ephesus Paul found some of them who were strangers to him. He asked a question that would help him know how much they had been taught. Had they received the Holy Spirit? No, these disciples had not even heard that there was a Holy Spirit.

B. Two Baptisms (vv. 3-5)

3. And he said unto them, Unto what then were ye baptized? And they said, Unto John's baptism.

Again Paul asked a question that would help him understand what these disciples had been taught. Most disciples of Jesus were baptized "in the name of the Father, and of the Son, and of the Holy Ghost" (Matthew 28:19). If these disciples had never heard of the Holy Ghost, what kind of baptism was theirs?

The disciples answered easily. They had been baptized with the kind of baptism John the Baptist taught. That was the only baptism Apollos knew when he came to Ephesus (Acts 18:25). Therefore we suppose these disciples were some that Apollos led to Christ before Priscilla and Aquila taught him more about baptism. After learning from Priscilla and Aquila, Apollos went on to Corinth without giving the added knowledge to all those whom he had converted.

4. Then said Paul, John verily baptized with the baptism of repentance, saying unto the people, that they should believe on him which should come after him, that is, on Christ Jesus.

Now Paul had the opportunity to explain to these disciples what was lacking in their teaching. John baptized people who repented of their sins. So do Christian teachers now. But John told them to believe in a Redeemer who was yet to come. Christian teachers now tell people to believe in a Redeemer who has already come and has given His life to redeem them. Repentant believers now are baptized into Christ (Galatians 3:27) and into His death (Romans 6:3). In Him they are members of His body (1 Corinthians 12:27). This involves much more than John's baptism did.

5. When they heard this, they were baptized in the name of the Lord Jesus.

We need not suppose all this was done in a few minutes. Perhaps Paul talked with these disciples several times, explaining how Christian baptism is different from the baptism John taught. Perhaps they saw some of his miracles (vv. 11, 12), and were convinced that he was truly God's messenger. The outcome was that *they were baptized* again, this time *in the name of the Lord Jesus.*

C. Power of the Holy Spirit (v. 6)

6. And when Paul had laid his hands upon them, the Holy Ghost came on them; and they spake with tongues, and prophesied.

About twelve men were in this group of disciples (v. 7). Some or all of them were given certain miraculous powers, not when they were baptized, but *when Paul had laid his hands upon them.*

It seems that the apostles imparted such powers to selected Christians in this way.

To prophesy is to receive messages directly from God and to pass them on to people on earth. In the early days of the church, it was very helpful to have some prophets in a congregation. They brought divine guidance when as yet there was no New Testament for a guide.

Speaking in tongues is described in Acts 2:1-11. The apostles spoke in languages that they themselves did not know, but people in the audience did. This served two purposes. First, it enabled people to hear the message in their native languages. Second, it was a sign that the speakers were inspired by the Holy Spirit. We do not know whether the disciples in Ephesus were from different countries or not. If not, speaking in tongues still served to show the inspiration of the Holy Spirit.

II. Miracles Done and Attempted (Acts 19:11-14)

Paul taught in the synagogue in Ephesus till the opposition of unbelievers became vigorous. Then he found a schoolroom where he kept on teaching for two years. Many people of the

---

How to Say It

ALEXANDRIA. Al-ex-*an*-dree-ah.
APOLLOS. Uh-*pol*-us.
AQUILA. *Ack*-wih-luh.
DENARIUS. dih-*nair*-ee-us.
DRACHMA. *drak*-ma.
EPHESUS. *Ef*-eh-sus.
MACEDONIA. Mass-eh-*doe*-nee-uh.
PHILIPPI. Fih-*lip*-pie or *Fil*-ih-pie.
PRISCILLA. Pri-*sil*-uh.
SCEVA. *See*-vuh.

province of Asia came to Ephesus on business or on vacations. It seems that some of them listened to Paul and carried his message back home, "so that all they which dwelt in Asia heard the word of the Lord Jesus" (vv. 8-10). Our text goes on with what happened in Ephesus.

A. Miracles Done (vv. 11, 12)

11. And God wrought special miracles by the hands of Paul.

God did the miracles, but He did them *by the hands of Paul* so people could know Paul was God's man. Then they would believe that the message Paul brought was God's message.

12. So that from his body were brought unto the sick handkerchiefs or aprons, and the diseases departed from them, and the evil spirits went out of them.

It was not necessary for Paul to touch or even see the sick and demon-possessed. Bits of cloth that Paul had touched were all that was needed to heal the sick and drive out demons.

B. Miracles Attempted (vv. 13, 14)

13. Then certain of the vagabond Jews, exorcists, took upon them to call over them which had evil spirits the name of the Lord Jesus, saying, We adjure you by Jesus whom Paul preacheth.

The word *vagabond* means that the Jews whom it describes were going from place to place to use their skill as *exorcists*. The Jewish historian Josephus tells of an exorcist named Eleazar. By means of a certain kind of root said to be prescribed by Solomon, along with incantations said to be composed by Solomon, this man claimed to draw a demon out through the nose of an afflicted man. Similar methods may have been used by other Jewish exorcists.

Home Daily Bible Readings

Monday, Nov. 20—Leader of Synagogue Converted (Acts 18:1-11)
Tuesday, Nov. 21—Apollos Strengthens Believers (Acts 18:24-28)
Wednesday, Nov. 22—Idolatry Threatened by the Gospel (Acts 19:21-34)
Thursday, Nov. 23—Order Restored by Clerk's Logic (Acts 19:35-41)
Friday, Nov. 24—Paul's Thanksgiving and Confidence (Romans 1:8-17)
Saturday, Nov. 25—The Spirit's Power in Christ (Luke 4:14-21)
Sunday, Nov. 26—Power to Give Eternal Life (John 17:1-5)

Not all of Paul's miracles were done through handkerchiefs and aprons, as told in verse 12. Sometimes Paul was with someone possessed with a demon. By the authority of Jesus, he ordered the demon to leave. Seeing how effective this was, the exorcists thought Paul had a better incantation than they had. So they tried to use that better incantation.

14. And there were seven sons of one Sceva, a Jew, and chief of the priests, which did so.

We are not told whether these seven were or were not the only ones who tried to use Paul's incantation, but these have special mention because of the startling result of their effort.

III. Triumph of Truth
(Acts 19:15-20)

These vagabond exorcists were not apostles of Christ. They were not even Christians. If they could do the same miracles Paul did, then Paul's miracles would not show that he was God's spokesman. But Sceva's sons soon learned that they could not do what Paul was doing.

A. Disaster to Fakers (vv. 15, 16)

15. And the evil spirit answered and said, Jesus I know, and Paul I know; but who are ye?

The demon knew he had to obey Jesus, and he knew Paul was Jesus' authorized apostle. But the words Paul spoke had no power when they were spoken by an unauthorized person. Power over demons was not in the words, but in Jesus.

16. And the man in whom the evil spirit was leaped on them, and overcame them, and prevailed against them, so that they fled out of that house naked and wounded.

In last week's lesson we read of a demon who gave a girl such superhuman knowledge that she became a fortune-teller (Acts 16:16). Now we are reading of a demon who gave such superhuman strength that it was amazing. That man jumped on the would-be exorcists, tore off their clothes, and gave them such a beating that *they fled out of that house naked and wounded.*

Some of the most valued ancient manuscripts read *overcame both,* and so that reading is seen in some English versions. Some students therefore conclude that only two of Sceva's seven sons were involved in this incident. However, the Greek word for *both* sometimes is used for more than two. For example, see Acts 23:8, where *both* is used of three. Therefore the *New International Version* reads "overpowered them all" in our text, and in Acts 23:8 it reads "acknowledge them all." If this is the correct interpretation, all seven of Sceva's sons were severely beaten by one man—and one demon.

B. Honor to Jesus (vv. 17, 18)

17. And this was known to all the Jews and Greeks also dwelling at Ephesus; and fear fell on them all, and the name of the Lord Jesus was magnified.

News spread swiftly from person to person, especially the spectacular story of seven naked exorcists streaking through the streets. Already the city was buzzing with news of the miracles God did through Paul. Now the buzzing was doubled by added information. Spoken by Paul, the name of Jesus brought healing to the sick and put demons to flight. Spoken by traveling exorcists, the same name brought a beating to the speakers. That was awesome. Reverent fear fell on those who heard about it. One who wanted to speak against Jesus would hardly dare do it, and most were eager to speak in favor of Him. So His name *was magnified;* that is, it was praised, honored, glorified.

18. And many that believed came, and confessed, and showed their deeds.

God's miraculous power working through Paul, coupled with the disaster to Sceva's sons, convinced many people that Paul was telling the truth: that Jesus is indeed the Son of God and the Savior of people on earth. Day after day believers were coming to Paul and other Christians to tell of their faith and to tell also of the wrongs they had done but now intended to do no more.

C. From Darkness to Light (vv. 19, 20)

19. Many of them also which used curious arts brought their books together, and burned them before all men: and they counted the price of them, and found it fifty thousand pieces of silver.

Curious arts seems to be a general term for various kinds of sorcery, divination, and magic. Christians turned away from these superstitious and deceitful practices. *Their books* were scrolls of papyrus or parchment with instructions about those occult practices. Instead of selling the costly books to get their money back, the Christians made a public bonfire of them. Thus they testified that they were renouncing all forms of heathen magic as they embraced the Christian faith. Someone interested in statistics added up the cost of the books that were burned: *fifty thousand pieces of silver.* In Ephesus a piece of silver probably was a Greek drachma. Its value was about the same as that of a Roman denarius. In Jesus' parable in Matthew 20:1-16, a denarius appears as a day's pay for a working man. We see that a man would have to work seven days a week for nearly 137 years to earn the price of all those books.

visual 13

"Mightily grew the word of God and prevailed"

WHAT SHALL WE DO WITH THE PAST?

Some people idealize the past, trying to live in it. An unusual form of this regard for a past era came to light a couple of years ago. At the time a French "performance artist" named Orlan had undergone the fifth of seven cosmetic surgeries scheduled over a four-year period. She called it "art by personal body transformation." Orlan's goal was to change her face and body so that she would be a reincarnation of Renaissance ideals of feminine beauty.

There are other ways to live in the past. Most of us know of people who continue to live in their own past, burdened with guilt for a sin they committed (or some good deed they left undone). We may know others who refuse to change attitudes or actions that have been the cause of trouble for them and their families for many years.

The sorcerers and magicians in Ephesus who became Christians set a good example for us all. In public they destroyed the instruction manuals for the occult practices by which they had made their living. It was a forceful demonstration that they had turned from the past, and were committing themselves to a new way of life in Christ.

In coming to Christ, one should turn from all that was evil or destructive in his or her past. And by making a public commitment to Christ, one places positive moral pressure on oneself to follow through with his or her commitment to Christ.   —C. R. B.

20. So mightily grew the word of God and prevailed.

The books of magic were worthless, but *the word of God* is of eternal worth. The gospel Paul preached was and is "the power of God unto salvation" (Romans 1:16). In Ephesus that word was growing more influential and effective as it was turning souls from darkness to light and from the power of Satan to God (Acts 26:18). The defeat of Sceva's sons helped it grow, and so did the public bonfire of books. Christians sacrificed fifty thousand pieces of silver, but they gained "an inheritance incorruptible, and undefiled, and that fadeth not away" (1 Peter 1:4).

The rest of Chapter 19 in Acts brings further evidence of the growth of the word of God in Ephesus. That word turned many of the Ephesians to the real God, and those who made money from false religions were alarmed. They aroused a mob to chant the praises of Diana, favorite goddess of the heathen city. But their demonstration proved to be as powerless as their goddess. When they had yelled themselves hoarse, the town clerk dismissed the assembly—and the word of God kept on growing.

Conclusion

"The Power of the Gospel"! That is our lesson title, and it is a good one. The gospel, the good news of salvation in Christ, was at work in Ephesus. It was working powerfully, turning people from darkness to light, and from the power of Satan to God.

Yet we must remember that the gospel is God's power (Romans 1:16). God was at work in the gospel, transforming lives, saving souls, building the church. We can give the gospel all the credit it deserves without taking any credit away from God.

In the first part of our text, we read that the Holy Spirit gave to some Christians the miraculous power to speak with tongues and to prophesy—and the Holy Spirit is God. In the middle of our text we read that the name of Jesus defeated diseases and demons—and Jesus is God. In the end of our text we read that the word was growing and prevailing—and it was God's word.

A. God and His Son and His Spirit

There is only one God. There are three divine beings, the Father, Son, and Holy Spirit; but in some way the three are one. This may be too much for us to understand, but it is not too much for us to believe.

The Son is the one who became man and gave His life for us. That seems plain enough. The Spirit is the one who lives in us if we are Christians. That seems plain enough too—or is it? When the Spirit comes to live with us, the Father and Son come too (John 14:23).

Perhaps we can never explain exactly how the three are one even while they are three, nor do we need an explanation. We can be sure they are one in will and purpose. We cannot please one of them without pleasing all of them; we cannot grieve one of them without grieving all of them; we cannot serve one of them without serving all of them. So let us take care to serve and please them, and never to grieve them.

B. God's Power and Our Task

Trying to give God's gospel to a dying world, we find many people who are uninterested and some who are hostile. If only we could heal the sick as Paul did! Then people would listen. God is no respecter of persons. Perhaps a simple illustration will help us understand.

When we plan to build a house, we take our plans to the proper authorities and get a building permit. That authorizes us to build the whole house. When the foundation is laid, we do not need another permit for the walls; when the walls are erected, we do not need another permit for the roof.

"I will build my church," said Jesus (Matthew 16:18); but He is building it through the efforts of His people on earth. As the building began, He gave some of those people His own miraculous power. Like a permit displayed at a building site, that power told everyone that the builders were authorized. As we continue to build according to the original plan, it is not necessary for every worker to display the same evidence of authority. Our task is to be sure we build according to the plan.

If we fail to follow the plan, if we put a wall where there is no foundation, if we substitute wood or straw where stone is called for, we can be sure the building inspector will know (1 Corinthians 3:11-15).

The divine plan is in the New Testament. Let us follow it. Instead of pleading for power God has not given us, let us use the abilities He has given, and use them with the same earnestness and tireless persistence that Paul displayed.

God's power is winning souls and building the church. But in that task God's power is powerless unless we use it. We depend on Him for power; He depends on us to make it effective. If we fail in our task, He must look for other workers—but remember what happens to salt that loses its savor (Matthew 5:13).

C. Prayer

How good it is to know that boundless power belongs to You, our Father! Considering the various abilities that You have given to us, we give You our heartfelt thanks. As we try to use Your gifts for Your glory, we look to You for guidance as well as for power.

D. Thought to Remember

To the work! To the work! We are servants of God,
Let us follow the path that our Master has trod;
With the balm of His counsel our strength to renew,
Let us do with our might what our hands find to do.

—Fanny J. Crosby

Learning by Doing

This page contains an alternate lesson plan emphasizing learning activities. Classes desiring such student involvement will find these suggestions helpful.

Learning Goals

After this session, students should:

1. List ways the power of the gospel was demonstrated through the events recorded in Acts 19:1-20.

2. Commit themselves to sharing the gospel with the lost so those persons may experience its life-changing power.

Into the Lesson

Write this question on your chalkboard before class members arrive: "How do we feel about *power?*" Distribute newspapers and magazines, and ask your students to find advertisements or articles that suggest an answer to the question. After several minutes let volunteers show what they have chosen and tell how their examples answer the question.

Option. Instead of this activity, or after it, conduct two sixty-second brainstorming sessions. In the first, have class members mention everything they can think of that is *good* about power. In the second, have them mention everything they can think of that is *bad* about power. Then ask, "Well, which is it? Is power good or bad?" Discuss.

Tell the class that today's lesson looks at good power, the power of God that was manifested in connection with the preaching of the gospel in the days of the church's infancy.

Into the Word

To connect this lesson's text with that of last week's lesson, deliver a brief lecture based on the information given in the "Introduction" section. After that, your students will be prepared to examine today's Scripture text. Tell them that in this session we will consider Acts 19:1-20 to discover how the power of the gospel was demonstrated in the ancient city of Ephesus.

Divide your class into groups of from three to seven students each. In their groups they are to divide the text into four sections and consider each section separately. The four sections are as follows: verses 1-7; 8-10; 11, 12; and 13-20. For each of these sections, class members should answer these questions:

1. How was the power of the gospel demonstrated?

2. Why was the power needed?

3. What did the power accomplish?

Allot ten to fifteen minutes for group study. Then let the groups share their conclusions and discuss as a class.

As an alternative to small-group study, you may want to try the following approach:

Give each student a sheet of paper on which you have written the three questions (leave plenty of blank space after each question for answers). Or write the questions on the chalkboard and give each student a sheet of blank paper. Read the whole text three times, pausing after each of the incidents recorded (after verses 7, 10, 12, and 20). For each section of the text, class members should write down answers to the first question after the first reading, to the second question after the second reading, and to the third question after the third reading.

After hearing the students' answers, discuss the following questions:

1. How are John's baptism and Christian baptism the same? How are they different?

2. Why did the seven sons of Sceva want to drive out demons? Why were they unable to do so in the incident recorded in our text?

3. How did the failure of the sons of Sceva affect the community? The church?

Into Life

Divide the class into groups of two or three, and ask them to answer these questions:

1. Which example of the power of the gospel in this text strikes you as most remarkable? Why?

2. Why were the Jews and Greeks in Ephesus afraid after the incident with the evil spirit (vv. 15-17)? Why might some people today fear the gospel?

3. Which of the following quotes comes closest to representing how this passage makes you feel?

"When I see how God's power was manifested in New Testament times, I feel dissatisfied. I wish I could see His power unleashed in the same way today."

"This lesson reminds me that the gospel is the only power that can truly change lives today. I'm thankful for the changes the gospel is making in our world."

"I'm reminded of my own need for the gospel's power to rid my life of sin and set me on a productive course."

Let's Talk It Over

The questions on this page are designed to encourage review of the lesson Scriptures and to promote discussion of the lesson by the class. The answers provided are only discussion starters. Let your class talk it over from there.

1. As a result of the preaching of the gospel and the miracles attendant to it, "the name of the Lord Jesus was magnified" in Ephesus (Acts 19:17). How would our worship and witness be affected if we made it our goal always to magnify the name of Jesus?

If we could keep in mind the primary aim of magnifying, honoring, and glorifying Jesus Christ, all of our worship would be enhanced significantly. Our own personal preferences, our desire to glorify self, and our inclination to look for convenience rather than to accept sacrifice would fade in the light of this higher goal. In planning services of worship, the magnifying of the name of Jesus Christ would take precedence over any thoughts of merely "making people feel good." In executing one's duties in the church, it would no longer be adequate simply to "muddle through." In engaging in personal evangelism, the tendency to self-consciousness would be overcome by the desire to focus all attention on the excellencies of Jesus Christ.

2. The believers' destruction of occult literature in Ephesus raises the question of what we should do with spiritually or morally damaging literature that has come into our possession. What shall we say about this matter?

Many Christians are wary of the idea of book-burning. The reason is that the Bible and other Christian writings have at times been subjected to destruction by anti-Christian forces. We do not want to encourage a war of ideas with pagan religions or advocates of immorality that is conducted on that kind of level. Nevertheless, the example of the believers in Ephesus reminds us that immoral, anti-Christian books or magazines have no place in our homes. Community organizations frequently have paper drives. The offensive literature could thereby be recycled into something more useful for our community.

3. By burning their books of sorcery, the Ephesian converts openly declared that the way of Jesus was far superior to their former life-style. Does the life we live declare that Jesus offers a better, happier life than does the world?

Too often a gap exists between our professed allegiance to Christ and the way we live. We must strive to close that gap. We are not to act to be seen by others, but others do in fact see our actions. Let us be a light that will show the way to Christ.

4. How may we increase our appreciation of the power of the gospel?

How well do we know what was involved in the conversions of our fellow church members? It might be very helpful if in our Bible school classes we gave participants an opportunity to speak on the subject, "What was involved in my conversion to Christ?" It would interesting to see what factors contributed to each conversion: the witness of a Christian friend, the effect of attending Sunday services, the example of faithful believers, specific Bible passages, etc. Surely such an exercise would give us a fresh insight into the power of the gospel.

Of course, an even better way to enhance our appreciation of the gospel's power is to become involved in sharing the gospel with those who are outside of Christ. In this way we can witness firsthand the gospel's power to save sinners and transform them into happy, productive citizens of God's kingdom.

5. What concepts that are apparent in the building of a house help us to understand what is involved in building the church of the Lord Jesus?

Although the construction of the former is in the physical realm and the latter the spiritual, there are points of comparison that help us understand the elements involved in building the church. For example, a house must rest on a foundation, and the New Testament tells us that Jesus Christ is the church's foundation (1 Corinthians 3:11). We are aware that a house is constructed according to a plan, and the New Testament provides us with a perfect plan for building the church. There is a great deal of expense in building a house, and likewise the building of the church requires a sacrificial expenditure of time, talents, and treasures. The construction of a house brings together the skills of various workers: masons, plumbers, carpenters, etc. Similarly, in the church people with various talents must blend them in order for the building enterprise to move ahead.

Winter Quarter, 1995-96

God's Promise of Deliverance
(Isaiah)

Special Features

Lessons

Unit 1. The Coming of a New Day

Unit 2. The Ministry of the Suffering Servant

God's Love for All People
(Jonah, Ruth)

About these lessons

Israel's deliverance, the Messiah's kingdom and rule, and the ministry of the Suffering Servant are the focus of the lessons based on the book of Isaiah. The studies in Jonah and Ruth explore God's love for all people.

Dec 3
Dec 10
Dec 17
Dec 24
Dec 31
Jan 7
Jan 14
Jan 21
Jan 28
Feb 4
Feb 11
Feb 18
Feb 25

Quarterly Quiz

The questions on this page may be used in several ways: as a pretest at the beginning of the quarter; as a review at the end of the quarter; or as a review after each lesson. The questions are based on the Scripture text of each lesson (King James Version). ***The answers are on page 119.***

Lesson 1

1. The voice crying in the wilderness said, "Make straight in the desert a ____ for our God." *Isaiah 40:3*

2. The voice said, "The glory of the Lord shall be revealed, and ___ ____ shall see it together." *Isaiah 40:5*

Lesson 2

1. Those among the Jewish exiles who sought the Lord were told to look unto the ____ whence they were hewn and to the hole of the ____ whence they were digged. *Isaiah 51:1*

2. The Lord promised to make Zion's wilderness like (Gilead, Sharon, Eden). *Isaiah 51:3*

Lesson 3

1. Speaking of the Messiah, Isaiah said that the people who walked in darkness had seen what? *Isaiah 9:2*

2. Isaiah prophesied that there would be no end of the increase of Messiah's ____ and ____. *Isaiah 9:7*

Lesson 4

1. The Messiah was identified as a Branch growing out of the roots of whom? *Isaiah 11:1*

2. The angel said that the baby wrapped in swaddling clothes lying in a manger was a ____ to the shepherds. *Luke 2:12*

Lesson 5

1. Prophesying of the Messiah, Isaiah said to Zion, "Arise, (look, stand, shine); for thy (peace, light, salvation) is come." *Isaiah 60:1*

2. Those in Zion would be called ____ of righteousness, the planting of the Lord. *Isaiah 61:3*

Lesson 6

1. Isaiah said that the Lord's servant would not break a bruised ____, and would not quench the smoking ____. *Isaiah 42:3*

2. Isaiah said that God would give His servant for a ____ of the people, for a ____ of the Gentiles. *Isaiah 42:6*

Lesson 7

1. The servant of the Lord lamented that he had labored in vain, and had used up his strength for nothing. T/F *Isaiah 49:4*

2. It was a light thing for the Lord's servant to raise up the tribes of Jacob, and to restore the preserved of Israel; so he was to be God's ____ to the end of the earth. *Isaiah 49:6*

Lesson 8

1. The Lord gave His servant the tongue of whom so he would know how to speak a word in season to the weary? *Isaiah 50:4*

2. Resolved to be faithful to God, the servant set his face like a ____. *Isaiah 50:7*

Lesson 9

1. The Lord's Servant is described as a man of sorrows, and acquainted with what? *Isaiah 53:3*

2. What was the Lord's Servant wounded for? What was He bruised for? *Isaiah 53:5*

3. What has the Lord laid on His Servant? *Isaiah 53:6*

Lesson 10

1. God commanded Jonah to go to what city and preach against its wickedness? *Jonah 1:2*

2. Jonah attempted to flee to what place instead? *Jonah 1:3*

3. What did sailors do to Jonah, and how did God rescue him? *Jonah 1:15, 17; 2:10*

Lesson 11

1. How did the wicked city respond when Jonah announced its destruction? *Jonah 3:5*

2. Taking note of the people's response, God then did what? *Jonah 3:10*

3. How did Jonah then feel about God's action? *Jonah 4:1*

Lesson 12

1. Where did Elimelech, Naomi, and their two sons go when famine struck Judah? *Ruth 1:1*

2. Name the two women the sons married there. *Ruth 1:4*

3. Which members of the family died while they were in that land? *Ruth 1:3, 5*

Lesson 13

1. Whom did Ruth marry after she came to live in Bethlehem? *Ruth 4:13.*

2. Their son was named ____. *Ruth 4:13, 17*

3. Their son was the father of ____, who was the father of ____. *Ruth 4:17*

The Coming of a New Day

by Roger W. Thomas

ANTICIPATION! If there is one word that describes the Christmas season, it is this one. Children grow more and more excited each day. Parents hustle from store to store trying to finish the last minute shopping. Grandparents look forward to the family gatherings and the renewal that comes from seeing the joy and laughter in the faces of the little ones.

Even with all of the commercialism and excessive spending relating to the day, there is still something wholesome and refreshing about looking forward to something with such energy and anticipation. Unfortunately, much of the anticipation is focused on matters of secondary importance.

In part to help correct some of this imbalance, many churches observe Advent, a period of special spiritual emphasis at this time of the year. Advent is not Christmas, but a time to prepare the soul for Christmas. Lasting for nearly a month, Advent provides an opportunity to look toward the coming of the annual celebration of Christ's birth while also drawing attention to the additional promises of Christ's "second coming."

Less formal congregations often accomplish this in a more casual manner. However it is done, anticipating and preparing for the spiritual lessons of Christmas is a worthwhile endeavor.

The lessons of Unit 1 of this quarter's study are all about anticipation, a looking forward with excitement to future events. The lessons are based on the Old Testament prophecies of Isaiah.

Living seven centuries before Christ, the prophet and his people faced difficult times. Political tensions and warring neighbors threatened to engulf tiny Judah. On the home front, religious indifference and even apostasy were destroying the once great faith of Israel.

Into this cauldron the Lord sent Isaiah to deliver a message of impending judgment and future deliverance. Unit 1 concentrates on the promises of deliverance that would come eventually to the faithful of God. Some of the promises were short-term, but most were to be fulfilled in the distant future. All, however, would be fulfilled—that was the important thing!

Lesson 1 examines the words of comfort extended to a people who needed a tender word from Heaven. Times were tough and they were going to become tougher. The prophet already had announced God's judgment. Now a time had come for a word of consolation. The promises of this lesson, as with many in Isaiah, look forward to the day when the Messiah would come. This "anointed one" would be the great fulfillment of all of God's promises. In this lesson, the one who would prepare the way for the Messiah is introduced. The New Testament identifies this "forerunner" as John the Baptist.

Lesson 2 speaks of God's everlasting salvation promised to His people. Isaiah reminded the people that past blessings came because the Lord was faithful in fulfilling His promises to Abraham and Sarah. Just as certain was the fulfillment of His promise of everlasting salvation in the future. Despite the darkness of the moment, the people were told to look forward to a coming day of justice and righteousness that only the Lord could bring about.

Lesson 3 sounds a note of joy and celebration. In this lesson, the promise of the coming Messiah becomes more personal and specific. He is described as a child yet to be born who would usher in a great day of peace, justice, and righteousness. The text will be recognized as one that is frequently read during the Christmas season. We can only imagine the amazement and mystery that surrounded these words when first heard by the people of Isaiah's day.

Lesson 4, the Christmas lesson, starts with Isaiah's promise of a Deliverer coming from the line of David, and moves to a review of the events surrounding the birth of Jesus. Consideration will be given to the qualities possessed by the Messiah as a result of the special endowment of the Holy Spirit, qualities that would enable Him to rule well and to deal fairly with both the wicked and the righteous. The Messiah's righteous dealings with all, and the era of peace He will usher in, are presented in strikingly dramatic terms.

Lesson 5 will move from the promises of Christ's coming to the continuing fulfillment of those promises through the preaching and teaching of the gospel. The study will examine further ways in which Jesus fulfilled the purpose of the Messiah's coming.

These lessons can provide an important part of our preparation for this season, in which Christ's coming is celebrated. In addition, learning the lasting lessons of Isaiah can help prepare us for the great and coming day of Christ's glorious return.

Singing at Midnight

by Stephen M. Hooks

WHEN PAUL AND SILAS CAME TO PHILIPPI, they soon were confronted by a hostile mob. "Jews," the rioters called them, "advocating customs unlawful for us Romans to accept or practice" (Acts 16:21, *New International Version*). Without semblance of a trial, the magistrates ordered them stripped and beaten, and then they threw the two into jail (vv. 22-24).

The prisons in those days must have been dismal, miserable places, designed to enslave the spirit as well as the body. Men had been known to cry and to curse in such jails; and some, in the midst of bleak despair, had even taken their own lives. We venture to say that never in all the dark days of that gloomy old dungeon in Philippi had a prisoner ever been known to sing. And yet, at midnight, in the darkest hour of their darkest night, Paul and Silas sang. Confident that if God was for them no one could stand against them, they gave voice to their faith and filled the prison with the strains of sacred song.

I do not know what song they chose, what lyric or melody they felt best suited the occasion. Perhaps it was one of the psalms that proclaim the Lord "a very present help in trouble"; or maybe it was one of the Servant Songs of Isaiah. These compelling songs (42:1-4; 49:1-6; 50:4-9; 52:13—53:12) were written to be sung in "jail." Anticipating a time when the Jewish nation would be languishing in the Babylonian exile (586-539 B.C.), the Servant Songs were composed by the prophet to reassure the exiles that through obedient submission to the divine will, their suffering would serve a purpose that would reach far beyond their own race and their own generation.

The central figure in the songs is the "Servant of the Lord," an enigmatic character whose exact identity is, at times, difficult to discern. According to the book of Isaiah, the servant is collectively the Israelite nation or, more particularly, the "remnant" of the penitent exiles, whose faithful endurance of their bondage would become the means by which God would redeem His people from their captivity and restore them to the promised land. Yet, at the same time, these prophecies also anticipate some special individual in the future who would arise to suffer for the sins of all humanity. This "Servant," the New Testament tells us, is Jesus the Messiah (Acts 8:34, 35).

Each lesson in this unit is devoted to one of the songs and explores some aspect of the Servant's ministry.

Lesson 6 considers the dynamics of the servant's call—how Israel was chosen by God and empowered by Him to proclaim His truth to all the nations. This servant would not act coercively to perform the Lord's bidding; but gently, through spiritual influences of sacrifice and grace, the servant (Israel) would bring his world to God. Even so, the Servant (Christ) would later say, "And I, if I be lifted up from the earth [crucified], will draw all men unto me" (John 12:32). God's Servant would compel people to righteousness, not by driving them, but by drawing them with the irresistible power of His sacrificial love.

Lesson 7 explains what God was going to accomplish through His servant. According to the prophet, the captivity of Judah would not just punish them for their apostasy; it would also serve a redemptive purpose. Through their suffering, the repentant exiles would "restore" Israel by paying the penalty of the nation's apostasy and thereby pave the way for their reconciliation with God. It would also "save" the nations by illustrating the truth that those who submit to the true and living God will, in due time, be rewarded.

Lesson 8 begins to explore the price the servant must pay to do the Lord's bidding. In spite of rejection and persecution, the servant was determined to see his task through to the end. We will see that the servant was instructed by suffering—taught that those who wait upon the Lord will eventually find the strength to persevere.

Lesson 9 gives the student nothing less than a prophetic glimpse of Calvary. In the final and most compelling of the Servant Songs (52:13—53:12), the prophet predicts the Servant's victory and what it would accomplish. In a paradox only God could construct, suffering and death, the very symbols of defeat, are made the means to victory for the Servant and His people. Rather than overpowering the enemy, the Servant passively submits to him. Instead of smiting His foes, He is smitten by them. Instead of taking lives, He gives His own. And the God who "works in mysterious ways" turns that which appears to be a humiliating defeat into glorious victory.

God's Love for All People

by Ralph E. Sims

"VALENTINE LOVE" is found in the Bible, but not as a description of the attitude of God toward His created beings. God's love is deeper and more encompassing than this kind of affection, and His is a perfect love.

Lessons 10-13 are based on the Old Testament books of Jonah and Ruth. The lessons form a unit entitled, "God's Love for all People."

As we study the books of Jonah and Ruth, we cannot help but understand that God's love causes Him to work for our good at all times. We can also see the hand of God at work, even though the persons in these biblical accounts were not aware of it at the time. If we do not see God's hand as obviously in events of today, we may be sure that it is there. His attitudes toward people are the same as in Bible times, as is His concern for the ways in which His people are to fulfill His will.

Lesson 10 opens with a simple enough picture. We see that Jonah, a prophet of God, was told by God to go to Nineveh and deliver a message of warning against the people's wickedness. Instead, Jonah attempted to run away, hoping to escape from God's presence.

Jonah's disobedience seems to have been prompted by more than an unwillingness to do a particular job. Jonah had a genuine aversion to going to Nineveh. He may have been afraid of "those foreigners." He may have feared a language barrier. He may have been racially prejudiced. He simply may have wanted to stay put in a comfortable ministry. Perhaps, like many today, Jonah just wanted to keep the *status quo*.

Jonah seems to have had the attitude that God would be able to find him if he stayed home in Israel, but that he would be free from the all-seeing eye of God if he fled to the other end of the Mediterranean Sea.

Jonah's reaction to his opportunity revealed much about him, and we will find it instructive to reflect on his reaction. We can learn much about ourselves if we reflect on our responses to the routine things of life, particularly when those events are not of our choosing.

Lesson 11 shows that when the word of God is proclaimed clearly and forthrightly it is effective in bringing the results that God desires. God's will *is* going to be done. The people of Nineveh listened to God's message when Jonah finally delivered it to them, they repented in sackcloth and ashes, and God forgave them.

Although he was physically where God wanted him to be, Jonah was still running from God. For some reason Jonah was displeased because the wicked Ninevites repented of their sins and by so doing escaped destruction. He could not understand why God would "go easy" on these people. God's mercy baffled the prophet. Every Christian would benefit by giving serious attention to the effective power of the Word of God. Some today, like Jonah, have a preconceived notion of what God will do, therefore expect God to do it, and are upset when that expectation is not carried out.

Part of what makes God's grace amazing is that He still loved Jonah, and He loves others like him in spite of themselves.

Lesson 12 presents a picture of the working of God's love in the lives of Naomi and Ruth—two ordinary women of different ethnic backgrounds. This mother and her daughter-in-law became the principals in a story of God's love that involved no miracle, such as in the account of Jonah. Naomi was an Israelite whose love for God and His law was reflected in her everyday life. Ruth was a Moabitess who was drawn into the circle of that love.

Because of famine, Naomi's family left their native land and settled in Moab. In that foreign land Naomi's husband died, and her two sons married daughters of the people of Moab. After some time Naomi's sons died also. From the human standpoint, the young widows would have been wise to return to their own homes. One of them did. Ruth, however, had responded to the love of her mother-in-law, and a great bond based on God's love grew between them. So when Naomi left Moab to return to her homeland, Ruth accompanied her, became part of Naomi's people, and accepted Naomi's God.

Lesson 13 depicts a part of the culture of early Israel that is foreign to us. It was the custom for a brother or the nearest kinsman of a deceased Israelite to care for his widow and to father children in behalf of the deceased member of the family. Although Boaz was not the closest relative of the deceased in this case, he was willing to fulfill that responsibility and provide for Ruth. So through Boaz this woman who was not of Israel was again the recipient of God's love. Through Jesus Christ, the great descendant of Boaz and Ruth, the love of God was shed upon all nations of the world.

The Promise of a Better Day

by Robert C. Shannon

THE JEWISH NATION had a wonderful hymnbook. We call it the book of Psalms. However, ancient Israel did not have a song such as "Standing on the Promises," a song that is precious to many Christian believers. The title of that song does describe Israel's situation, though. Through the long history of Israel, God's people were standing on His promises. More of these promises are found in the writings of Isaiah than in any other prophetic book.

Certainly Isaiah offered warnings to Israel. He spoke of the wrath of God. Even in the stern warnings, however, could be found the underlying principle of God's affection for Israel. Through Isaiah God spoke of "*my* people."

Hope in the Face of Discouragement

Isaiah was haunted by the contrast between the marvelous world God created and the awful mess man made of it. He lifted up two hopes: an intermediate hope and an ultimate hope.

Critical days were ahead for the nation. The prophet saw the need to comfort and console the people who would face those days. He did so by lifting up the rich promises of God. Not all of God's promises given through Isaiah can be confined to the nation of Israel, however. Many reach out to God's people in every generation and in every place.

Whatever your circumstances in life, there is a promise for you in Isaiah. Are you afraid of death? Someday it will be conquered. God "will swallow up death in victory" (25:8).

Are you facing grief and sadness? "The Lord God will wipe away tears from off all faces" (25:8).

Do you feel lonely? "I am with thee" is God's promise in Isaiah (41:10).

Are you weak physically? Are you weak spiritually? God says, "I will strengthen thee; yea, I will help thee" (41:10).

Do you face difficult days or difficult decisions? "When thou passest through the waters, I will be with thee" is God's promise through the prophet (43:2).

Do you long for serenity? "Thou wilt keep him in perfect peace, whose mind is stayed on thee" (26:3).

Do you feel overwhelmed by a rapidly changing world? Do you say with the song writer Henry F. Lyte, "Change and decay in all around I see"? Then Isaiah has this reassurance for you:

"The word of our God shall stand for ever" (40:8).

Reminiscent of Psalm 23 is this promise recorded in Isaiah 40:11: "He shall feed his flock like a shepherd: he shall gather the lambs with his arm, and carry them in his bosom."

What a vivid picture is presented by that last promise! While driving along a highway in Romania, I overtook a large flock of sheep. At the front, leading them, was the shepherd, and he was carrying a young lamb in his arms. I could not help thinking of this precious promise of Isaiah 40. The people to whom Isaiah preached also knew of shepherds and their care of sheep. It made the divine promise vivid and real. Perhaps it would be useful for us to try to match a mental picture with each of the promises listed above. By being able to do this we would fix the promises more securely in our memories and perhaps make them even more precious to us.

First the Darkness, Then the Dawn

Isaiah was a realist. He did not hesitate to say that hard times were coming upon his people. It is generally agreed that Isaiah's prophetic ministry in Judah began the year that the good king Uzziah died. It seems that only a year later, Jotham, who had been coregent with his father, Uzziah, and who had succeeded him, also died. The sixteen-year reign of the wicked king Ahaz followed.

The loss of good leadership was saddening and disheartening, because there was danger from without. Assyria, Syria, and Egypt all threatened the nation. Within, the nation was wracked by corruption. The rich oppressed the poor. People lost land that had been in their family for generations. Government and the courts were corrupt. The rich lived in luxury and idleness and were indifferent to the needs of the poor. Pagan religions were tolerated, thus weakening the worship of Jehovah. This resulted in a new low in moral and ethical standards. For all this a price had to be paid. God's people must pass through a dark night of judgment, and Isaiah pronounced it.

Isaiah spoke of more, however. He spoke of God's mercy and grace. He spoke of a new day, a day of restoration that would follow the people's turning to God. They should not lose heart. Day would follow the night.

God the Promise Keeper

Isaiah had every confidence that God would keep His promises. He based this confidence on his own experience with God. We remember that when Isaiah was called to his prophetic office, he received a divine vision. That vision sustained him through forty years of preaching. We expect no such vision, and we do not need one. We have the record of God's kept promises before us. We can point to prophecy after prophecy fulfilled in Christ, and promise after promise fulfilled in our own lives.

In the Gospel account that bears his name, Matthew shows that many incidents in the life of Jesus were the fulfillment of Old Testament prophecies. "That it might be fulfilled which was spoken by . . . the prophet" is the phrase one reads over and over again in Matthew. In his first letter to the Corinthians Paul asserts that Jesus' death, burial, and resurrection were "according to the Scriptures" (15:3, 4).

Isaiah also based his confidence on the fact that he knew his message was not his own. He wrote, "The Sovereign Lord has given me an instructed tongue, to know the word that sustains the weary" (50:4, *New International Version*).

Isaiah's words did sustain the weary during days of national uncertainty. His words sustained the weary through succeeding centuries as the fortunes of Judah fell. The darker the day of Judah's tribulation, the brighter shone Isaiah's promise of a better day.

The Fifth Gospel

Isaiah's words lift us as well. We cannot think of Jesus without thinking of Isaiah's prophecies that He fulfilled. When we celebrate Jesus' birth, we recall Isaiah's prophecy of the virgin birth (7:14). When we commemorate Jesus' death, we recall Isaiah's prophecy of the Suffering Servant (chapter 53). When we consider Jesus' announcement in the synagogue at Nazareth regarding His ministry (Luke 4:16-21), we recall that He stated that it was the fulfillment of Isaiah's prophecy (see 61:1, 2). In fact, Isaiah's writings contain so many references to Christ that his book is sometimes called the fifth Gospel.

Not only does Isaiah's prophetic picture of Christ embrace His birth and His death; it also interprets each one for us. The birth of Christ is pictured for us in one word: *Immanuel*. The word is found only in Isaiah and Matthew. Yet no other word so clearly summarizes the incarnation. *Immanuel*—God with us. Can you think of any other single word that includes so much about the nature of the Lord Jesus Christ? Can you think of any other one word that so adequately explains the mystery of His divine nature? Wrapped up in that one word is the astounding truth expressed by the apostle Paul, "God was in Christ, reconciling the world unto himself" (2 Corinthians 5:19).

Immanuel has its practical, as well as its theological, implications. We are not alone (John 14:23; Romans 8:35-39; Hebrews 13:5). God will never abandon us. He did not abandon Israel, though the people sometimes felt abandoned. We too may sometimes feel forsaken, but our feelings are unreliable. God is with us.

If we find a brief mention of the birth of Christ in Isaiah, we find much more about the death of Christ. Chapter 53 gives us a detailed account of Jesus' suffering for our sake. That prophetic picture of Calvary is as accurate and as moving as any of the eyewitness accounts of Jesus' crucifixion that are given in the four Gospels. The theological interpretation of the cross is as clear in Isaiah as it is in any of Paul's letters. When we read Isaiah 53 we are truly "at the cross." It is no wonder that that passage has become so precious to so many believers.

Of all the Old Testament books, none offers us a stronger foundation for our faith in Christ, or a stronger foundation for our hope, than the book of Isaiah. As we study this book, let us build on this sure foundation.

Answers to Quarterly Quiz on page 114

Lesson 1—1. highway. 2. all flesh. **Lesson 2**—1. rock, pit. 2. Eden. **Lesson 3**—1. a great light. 2. government, peace. **Lesson 4**—1. Jesse. 2. sign. **Lesson 5**—1. shine, light. 2. Trees. **Lesson 6**—1. reed, flax. 2. covenant, light. **Lesson 7**—1. true. 2. salvation. **Lesson 8**—1. the learned. 2. flint. **Lesson 9**—1. grief. 2. our transgressions, our iniquities. 3. the iniquity of us all. **Lesson 10**—1. Nineveh. 2. Tarshish. 3. They threw him into the sea; God prepared a great fish that swallowed Jonah and vomited him out on dry land after three days and nights. **Lesson 11**—1. They believed God and repented, fasting and wearing sackcloth. 2. He turned from the evil He said He would do to them. 3. He was very angry. **Lesson 12**—1. to the country of Moab. 2. Orpah and Ruth. 3. Naomi's husband, Elimelech, and her two sons. **Lesson 13**—1. Boaz. 2. Obed. 3. Jesse, David.

A Love Like God's

by Paul S. Williams

"I DON'T EVER WANT TO RETURN to that place!" That is not an uncommon response from people heading home after a visit to New York City. While some are energized by its pace and vibrancy, others see only the crime-riddled streets and graffiti-stained concrete canyons. They can't wait to get away from New York and its dizzying collection of 178 ethnic groups and 116 languages.

After my first visit to New York City, I was one of those who vowed never to return. And now I live and work in the New York City metropolitan area! I never intended to work in or near a city, or to be involved in cross-cultural ministry. I always thought I would stay in the Midwest, remaining comfortably in the culture in which I was reared. God seemed to have other plans. In that regard I am not alone.

Comforting the Afflicted, and Afflicting the Comfortable

As Jonah discovered, the call of God is not always what one might expect or desire. While God comforts the afflicted, He may find it necessary to afflict the comfortable! Jonah didn't want to go to Nineveh. God had other plans.

It is difficult to see beyond our own fences to distant fields, rich and ready for cultivation. It is difficult to leave the comfort and familiarity of home to move to a new land or a foreign culture. It is difficult to do the work necessary to see others as God sees them. But it is only when we attempt that task that we begin to understand and reflect the true character of Christ.

The churches of the New York City metropolitan area meet annually for several gatherings. It is always a rich experience to see five or six languages spoken and music presented in seven or eight distinctly different cultural styles. When participating in such a gathering, one begins to realize that we can never understand the fullness of Christ until we see His fullness reflected through cultures other than our own. It is only as we come together that we understand the richness of the unity we have in the midst of such cultural diversity.

It is a fact, however, that resistance to change and hesitancy to embrace people and things that are strange and unfamiliar, run deep. I understand Jonah's reluctance to go to Nineveh. I also understand God's purpose for sending him. There was a need, and Jonah was God's man to meet that need. Did Jonah ever warm up to the idea of being in Nineveh? We really don't know. We do know, however, that God was concerned about the hundreds of thousands of people who lived in that city, just as He is concerned about the more than nineteen million people of metropolitan New York City and six billion people in the world today, each one of them.

To show concern for those of another culture does not always require a public presence in their midst, such as Jonah's. At different times in their lives, both Naomi and Ruth had to learn to live in a foreign land. But their experience was deep and rich, because they made the effort to cross cultural barriers to reach out to understand and appreciate one another. In the process they both received great joy.

Reaching out to those of another culture may mean giving oneself in service to others, such as feeding the hungry in the teeming city of a developing nation. It may mean using vacation time to build a mission hospital abroad. It may mean a public and visible proclamation of the Word of God after the manner of Jonah. Or, like Ruth and Naomi, it may mean finding the courage to care for that person whom God has already placed in your path whose cultural background differs from yours.

Called to Be Faithful

Whether it takes place in the public arena or in the quiet events of everyday life, God wants us to make the effort to "cross over" to others. He has chosen only one method to bring the good news to those who need to hear. God's word must come through us—Christian people—culturally bound and woefully inadequate vessels that we are. Yet he has chosen us to take the good news to the cities and villages of the world, from America to Asia to Africa. He has chosen us to announce the good news that Jesus came to make crooked ways straight. He has given us the ministry of reconciliation: to tell everyone that God was reconciling the world to himself in Christ. May we have the courage to move beyond our cultural limitations and zones of comfort to respond to His awesome and mighty call.

At times I still am uncomfortable in New York City. In those times I am reminded that God did not issue the call to an easy life. He did not call us to be successful. He called us to be faithful. May we be faithful indeed.

A Time of Comfort

December 3
Lesson 1

DEVOTIONAL READING: 2 Corinthians 7:2-7.

LESSON SCRIPTURE: Isaiah 40:1-11.

PRINTED TEXT: Isaiah 40:1-11.

Isaiah 40:1-11

1 Comfort ye, comfort ye my people, saith your God.

2 Speak ye comfortably to Jerusalem, and cry unto her, that her warfare is accomplished, that her iniquity is pardoned: for she hath received of the LORD's hand double for all her sins.

3 The voice of him that crieth in the wilderness, Prepare ye the way of the LORD, make straight in the desert a highway for our God.

4 Every valley shall be exalted, and every mountain and hill shall be made low: and the crooked shall be made straight, and the rough places plain:

5 And the glory of the LORD shall be revealed, and all flesh shall see it together: for the mouth of the LORD hath spoken it.

6 The voice said, Cry. And he said, What shall I cry? All flesh is grass, and all the goodliness thereof is as the flower of the field:

7 The grass withereth, the flower fadeth; because the spirit of the LORD bloweth upon it: surely the people is grass.

8 The grass withereth, the flower fadeth: but the word of our God shall stand for ever.

9 O Zion, that bringest good tidings, get thee up into the high mountain; O Jerusalem, that bringest good tidings, lift up thy voice with strength; lift it up, be not afraid; say unto the cities of Judah, Behold your God!

10 Behold, the Lord GOD will come with strong hand, and his arm shall rule for him: behold, his reward is with him, and his work before him.

11 He shall feed his flock like a shepherd: he shall gather the lambs with his arm, and carry them in his bosom, and shall gently lead those that are with young.

GOLDEN TEXT: Comfort ye, comfort ye my people, saith your God. Speak ye comfortably to Jerusalem.—Isaiah 40, 1, 2.

God's Promise of Deliverance (Isaiah)

Unit 1: The Coming of a New Day
(Lessons 1-5)

Lesson Aims

This lesson is designed to help the student:

1. Recognize God's promises to strengthen and comfort in hard times.

2. Anticipate the fulfillment of God's promises to His people.

3. Persevere in the midst of adversity, knowing that God's redemption is certain.

Lesson Outline

INTRODUCTION
  A. The Power of Hope
  B. Lesson Background
  I. THE VOICE OF PARDON (Isaiah 40:1, 2)
  A. The Source of Comfort (v. 1)
  B. The Means of Comfort (v. 2)
  II. THE VOICE OF PREPARATION (Isaiah 40:3-5)
  A. The King Announced (v. 3)
  B. The King Anticipated (v. 4)
  C. The King Revealed (v. 5)
  III. THE VOICE OF PROTECTION (Isaiah 40:6-8)
  A. Things Temporary (vv. 6, 7)
  B. Things Permanent (v. 8)
    Sustaining Life
  IV. THE VOICE OF POWER (Isaiah 40:9-11)
  A. Good News: God Is Here (v. 9)
  B. Good News: God Is Great (v. 10)
  C. Good News: God Is Good (v. 11)
    Shepherd King
CONCLUSION
  A. Never Give Up!
  B. Let Us Pray
  C. Thought to Remember

Visual 1 of the visuals packet (shown on page 123) calls to mind the teaching of Isaiah 40:8. Visual 14 is a timeline for use throughout this quarter.

Introduction

A. The Power of Hope

People come in two basic models. The big difference in people is not that some are rich and others are poor, or that some are learned and others less so. It is that some have hope and others do not. This is the difference that makes all the difference in the world.

One who has hope knows that the world is not an accident governed by chance or luck, but is the careful product of a wise and caring Creator. One who has hope is convinced that every person has a purpose and a place in the scheme of things.

Without hope, there are no better tomorrows. Hope means believing that "what is" need not determine "what will be."

Hope is the conviction that as long as God is here even darkness can be turned into light. Hope is the secret that keeps some people going when others have long since quit.

Some interesting information has been discovered by scientists who research human nature and the keys to survival under difficult circumstances. One research project investigated coal mine disasters in an effort to discover why some men survived and others did not. One common thread seemed to stand out among survivors. Generally, those who survived were those who expected to escape. Most who believed they were doomed seldom lived. Interestingly, even with miners in the same cave-in under the same circumstances, those who gave up often died first. Those who kept trying to dig their way out because they thought it possible often lasted longer, even though they used more precious oxygen and energy in the effort.

The difference was not in the circumstances, or in the miners' physical condition, but in their attitude. Some had hope, a reason to hang on. Others did not!

When we are faced with difficulties or hardships, the key to overcoming is often not so much the depth of the problems but the degree of our hope. People of faith who believe that God will deliver them often can endure far more than those who believe that they are at their own devices.

The message of this season of anticipation and preparation for Christmas is hope. These weeks are a time to look forward and know that something is going to happen, that God is going to act. It is a reminder that God's promises are worth waiting for.

B. Lesson Background

Isaiah the prophet lived in Jerusalem in the eighth century B.C. He prophesied in the days of four kings of Judah: Uzziah, Jotham, Ahaz, and Hezekiah. These were difficult times for Judah. Relations were not good with their sister nation, Israel, to the north. Assyria to the east and Egypt to the south were casting threatening shadows across the entire Middle East. During Isaiah's lifetime, Israel would fall to Assyria, and her people would be carried away into captivity.

The politicians in Judah thought that their nation would survive only if they made peace with their more powerful neighbors. Isaiah, on the other hand, insisted that survival depended on the nation's making peace with God. Treaties and alliances with the military powers of the day would prove futile, he preached. If Judah refused to return to God, she would surely follow the way of Israel. In fact, Isaiah prophesied that Judah would indeed be carried away into captivity by Babylon (Isaiah 39:5-7), a nation yet to rise as a dominant world power. Isaiah also prophesied that Judah's punishment in captivity would be followed by their return to their own land (1:25-27).

The captivity that Isaiah prophesied concerning Judah would not begin until more than one hundred years had passed, and the return would occur seventy years after that. It is little wonder that his countrymen scoffed at his prediction of defeat and captivity. Likewise, his assurance of a return from captivity had no meaning for them. However, a hundred and fifty years later the Jews were actually captives in Babylon. There that prediction from an ancient book came to them as a word of comfort, providing hope in a time of despair.

Isaiah's prophecy was partly fulfilled when God took the Jews back to Jerusalem. It was partly fulfilled when Jesus came to redeem mankind from sin's bondage. It will be completely fulfilled when Jesus comes again and God's new order is fully manifested.

Rightly has Isaiah been called the great "gospel" prophet of the Old Testament. He more than any other Old Testament prophet points to the coming Messiah. To read Isaiah is to read a preview of Matthew, Mark, Luke, and John.

The book of Isaiah divides into two basic sections: chapters 1-39 and 40-66. The messages of the two sections are vastly different. The first section deals largely with the themes of judgment and doom. The latter section, which opens with our lesson text, promises blessings that will eventually follow the years of captivity and that will extend not only to the Jewish people, but to all the nations of the earth.

visual 1

Chapter 40 begins the latter section of Isaiah, with a promise of comfort and deliverance. Our text serves as an introduction to the entire second half of Isaiah. The text divides into four parts, representing four voices, or messages, about the future of God's people.

I. The Voice of Pardon
(Isaiah 40:1, 2)

A. The Source of Comfort (v. 1)

1. Comfort ye, comfort ye my people, saith your God.

The previous chapter, which concluded the first section of Isaiah, ended with the prediction that at some point in the future Judah would suffer captivity in Babylon. This chapter jumps ahead to the promise of release and restoration that would eventually follow.

The Hebrew word rendered here as *comfort* literally means "to breathe again." It perfectly describes the sensation of relaxing and taking a deep breath after a period of peril and difficulty. It is repeated twice for emphasis. The prophet, writing many years earlier, exhorted the people in captivity to be comforted. God, however, was the real Comforter of His people (Isaiah 12:1; 49:13; 51:3, 12).

My people and *your God* are reminders of the Lord's faithfulness to His people, even though Judah had been judged by Him and sent into exile. He was "their" God, not a stranger. Judah had not ceased to be His people.

B. The Means of Comfort (v. 2)

2. Speak ye comfortably to Jerusalem, and cry unto her, that her warfare is accomplished, that her iniquity is pardoned: for she hath received of the LORD's hand double for all her sins.

Speak ye comfortably is literally "speak to the heart." This was a message for the soul, for the innermost needs and desires of the people. The expression was meant to quiet the people's fears and anxieties as they languished in captivity. There was nothing superficial about it. *Jerusalem* is used as a personification of the people of God.

The term *warfare* stands for the long period of hardship that Judah experienced in her captivity. Remember, Isaiah was speaking of a time more than a century into the future. Because of the certainty of God's faithfulness, he spoke as if the events had already occurred.

Judah's greatest comfort would come from pardon. The God of grace and mercy would forgive the sins of the past. *She hath received of the Lord's hand double* is not intended to suggest that Judah was punished with twice the severity that she deserved. It means, instead, that she had received her full measure of suffering and that she need not fear further vengeance (compare Isaiah 61:7).

This promise of God was the basis for the people's hope. Knowing that His punishment for their sins was complete, they could live in hope that better times would be coming. They could "keep on keeping on."

Likewise, the gospel of Christ is a message of hope to a lost world. It gives assurance that God offers forgiveness and grace for a person's sin. Only those who refuse to avail themselves of the offer of the Savior are doomed.

II. The Voice of Preparation (Isaiah 40:3-5)

A. The King Announced (v. 3)

3. The voice of him that crieth in the wilderness, Prepare ye the way of the LORD, make straight in the desert a highway for our God.

In ancient times, a visit by a king would be preceded by his messenger announcing the event. Preparations were to be made for his coming. The way was to be cleared, and the people properly attired.

Using this image, the prophet indicated that God's people in captivity must ready themselves for His coming to them to restore them to the homeland. The prophet spoke figuratively. The preparation they needed to make was spiritual. Whatever hindrances—political, spiritual, or others—that stood in the way of the return were to be removed.

Students of the New Testament know that there was a deeper meaning in this prophecy of Isaiah. His words were also prophetic of John the Baptist, the herald who prepared a people to receive the Messiah (Matthew 3:1-17). John came in a literal wilderness to announce the coming of the King and to call the nation to prepare for His coming. John made it clear that only repentance properly prepares one for a visit from the King. According to John, sins must be abandoned, wrongs righted, and commitments made to follow the way of the master.

How to Say It

AHAZ. *A*-haz.
ASAPH. *A*-saf.
HEZEKIAH. Hez-eh-*kye*-uh.
JOTHAM. *Jo*-tham.
UZZIAH. Uh-*zye*-uh.

B. The King Anticipated (v. 4)

4. Every valley shall be exalted, and every mountain and hill shall be made low: and the crooked shall be made straight, and the rough places plain.

The prophet continues the figure regarding the preparations that were to be made for the visit of royalty. The rough and uneven places were to be smoothed out and leveled to facilitate the monarch's coming. So, captive Judah was to prepare herself to receive the Lord and the redemption He was bringing. The proud and the self-righteous must be humbled. The poor and weak, the downcast and oppressed, must be raised up and encouraged. The crooked and wicked must be called to change their ways. They must "straighten up."

Likewise, Christ Jesus is ready and waiting to come into any life that is prepared for His coming. However, into the life that desires Him not, He will not come.

C. The King Revealed (v. 5)

5. And the glory of the LORD shall be revealed, and all flesh shall see it together: for the mouth of the LORD hath spoken it.

When all of the preparation was completed, God's glory would be revealed. Judah would be delivered from Babylon by the power of God, and by this act God's glory and majesty would be shown to the nations.

All flesh shall see it clearly suggests a work of God that would go far beyond the return of the Jews to Jerusalem. When Christ came to earth, He revealed the glory of God (John 1:14; 2:11; 2 Peter 1:16). This "revealing" will be completed when He comes again (Matthew 16:27; Revelation 1:7).

III. The Voice of Protection (Isaiah 40:6-8)

A. Things Temporary (vv. 6, 7)

6. The voice said, Cry. And he said, What shall I cry? All flesh is grass, and all the goodliness thereof is as the flower of the field.

The voices falling on the prophet's ear are not identified. Perhaps they were angels. The first point of their discourse was that all human conditions are only temporary. *All flesh* is finite. There are no exceptions.

On the surface this might seem to be anything but a word of comfort and encouragement (v. 1). Quite the contrary! In the context it is good news, because even the power of the Babylonians and the captivity in which Israel would be held would pass away.

Goodliness refers to the outward beauty and attractiveness of human life. Physical strength diminishes with time. Eventually, frailty rules where power once reigned.

7. The grass withereth, the flower fadeth; because the spirit of the LORD bloweth upon it: surely the people is grass.

The illustration given here is repeated for emphasis. *The spirit of the Lord* or "breath of Jehovah" (the same Hebrew word is translated "spirit," "breath," or "wind"). This brings to mind the force of the hot east wind that can blow out of the desert and quickly wither the heartiest of crops. When the Spirit of the Lord blows in judgment upon men, they will perish.

B. Things Permanent (v. 8)

8. The grass withereth, the flower fadeth: but the word of our God shall stand for ever.

Here is the second and most important element in the discourse of the voices (see comment under verse 6). Whereas everything in the world is finite, God is infinite. Nations, rulers, and governments come and go, but what God says stands forever. He is completely dependable.

The word of our God refers to the promises of the Lord. Here is the great comfort for a people facing adversity. The powers that create the troubles will fade, but the God who delivers will remain.

Peter quotes this passage and applies it to the gospel (1 Peter 1:23-25). Jesus used a similar image to call His disciples to greater dependence on the everlasting Lord (Matthew 6:30; also see 1 John 2:17).

SUSTAINING LIFE

Where I live, lawn mowing is normally a once-a-week job. One recent summer, however, it was different. The weather was so dry in July and August I didn't have to mow my lawn for six weeks! Without water, grass withers quickly and flowers fade fast.

Even with adequate moisture, plant life grows through a predictable and comparatively short cycle of "bud, blossom, fruit"—and then dies. In cold climates, the whole process, from green to brown, lasts only a few weeks.

With this analogy, the prophet makes a point about mortality: "All flesh is grass." Human life is short—here today, gone tomorrow. And all the good we do is soon forgotten, like a fading corsage taped to a dresser mirror. As wise King Solomon wrote, "That which now is in the days to come shall all be forgotten" (Ecclesiastes 2:16).

Christians, however, can survive the "Solomon syndrome." Flesh is mortal, but God's Spirit in us is eternal. And "the word of our God shall stand for ever." Even Solomon admitted, "Whatsoever God doeth, it shall be for ever" (Ecclesiastes 3:14). Let us live our brief span keeping eternity's values in view.   —R. W. B.

IV. The Voice of Power (Isaiah 40:9-11)

A. Good News: God Is Here (v. 9)

9. O Zion, that bringest good tidings, get thee up into the high mountain; O Jerusalem, that bringest good tidings, lift up thy voice with strength; lift it up, be not afraid; say unto the cities of Judah, Behold your God!

Here begins the great news of comfort to which the previous verses of this text have been leading. The preparation spoken of in them is complete. God was returning to reign in Jerusalem. The fallen city and nation would be restored.

The message was to be heralded from the highest mountains. It was to be proclaimed with the strongest possible voice and without fear. The Lord was with His people once again, and this good news was for all of Judah.

The message sounds strikingly like that of John the Baptist, who, when identifying the Messiah, declared to those from Jerusalem and the villages of Judah, "Behold the Lamb of God" (John 1:29). At the heart of John's preaching was the good news, "The kingdom of heaven is at hand" (Matthew 3:2).

B. Good News: God Is Great (v. 10)

10. Behold, the Lord GOD will come with strong hand, and his arm shall rule for him: behold, his reward is with him, and his work before him.

God would come in power to His people, assembling His flock and taking it back to Jerusalem. *His reward is with him.* This may be a reference to the salvation bestowed upon the people, or it may refer to the fact that the accomplishment of His purposes is God's own reward.

The great consolation for God's people is that at the time God deems it appropriate, He will act and make all things right and just.

C. Good News: God Is Good (v. 11)

11. He shall feed his flock like a shepherd: he shall gather the lambs with his arm, and carry them in his bosom, and shall gently lead those that are with young.

Many in our time may be unfamiliar with a gentle, caring shepherd, but it was not unfamiliar to the ancients. Even for those who know little of shepherds and sheep, the message of a gentle, compassionate guardian comes through loud and strong. The Lord has special concern for those who are unable to care for themselves.

In these closing verses of our text we see two aspects of the Lord's coming to rescue His people from their captivity in Babylon and to lead them back to their homeland—namely, His strength and His gentleness. In a larger way this prophecy speaks of the coming of the Lord in the person of Christ—in His first and in His second coming.

His first coming revealed His meekness and humility, for He came as "the Lamb of God, which taketh away the sin of the world" (John 1:29). Jesus referred to himself as the Good Shepherd, who was concerned for His sheep.

Christ's second coming will reveal His "strong hand." Then He will "reign for ever and ever" (Revelation 11:15), not as the Lamb, but as "the Lion of the tribe of Judah" (Revelation 5:5). In this the people of God can take comfort.

SHEPHERD KING

People don't always stay in the pigeonholes that our stereotypes build for them. Example: some Americans were surprised that a peanut farmer from Georgia could become president of the United States. Is that the stuff of which presidents are made? Harry Truman also rocked

Home Daily Bible Readings

Monday, Nov. 27—Shortsighted Behavior (Isaiah 39:1-8)
Tuesday, Nov. 28—Declaration of Sin (Micah 3:1-8)
Wednesday, Nov. 29—Prayer for Blessing on the King (Psalm 72:1-14)
Thursday, Nov. 30—The Appeal of Good Tidings (Isaiah 52:1-10)
Friday, Dec. 1—The Lord Will Restore (Isaiah 49:1-10)
Saturday, Dec. 2—Gift of Abundant Life (John 10:1-11)
Sunday, Dec. 3—Prayer for Deliverance (Psalm 86:8-17)

millions back on their heels when he came from humble beginnings to win the Oval Office. Presidential candidates are stereotypically wealthy and prestigious professional people.

We are thrown a bit off balance, it seems, when someone becomes what we never expected. Israel was surprised when David, a mere shepherd boy, became king. How could a gentle shepherd hope to rule and lead a nation?

Significantly, David is described as "a man after God's own heart." We note with interest that in our text Isaiah pictures God as a *shepherd king*, ruling with a strong hand, yet feeding His flock, gathering His lambs, and gently leading the vulnerable ones. He is Lord of lords, but still the Good Shepherd who leads us beside still waters and makes us lie down in green pastures. His name is wonderful! —R. W. B.

Conclusion

A. Never Give Up!

Winston Churchill agreed to deliver a speech to the students at the boys' school he had once attended as a youngster. The subject of his address was to be the secret of his success. When the hour came for his much-heralded address, the statesman mounted the podium, noted the topic for the day, spoke only five words, and then returned to his seat. His message? "Never, never, never, give up!"

Indeed, the secret of success in most important matters is simply perseverance—refusal to give up. The difference between perseverance and defeat is often the conviction that victory is just around the corner.

The people of God are comforted, and they comfort one another, with the certainty that God is faithful. No matter how dark the moment seems, He will eventually bring His promised deliverance. His greatest deliverance has already come in Jesus, and it will be brought to completion in His final return.

B. Let Us Pray

Lord, there is much about life and the troubles of this world that we don't understand. Sometimes the problems seem just too big to handle. But we know that You are concerned about Your people, and that if we trust You, all will be well one day. Help us to be faithful through good days and bad. In Jesus' name we pray. Amen.

C. Thought to Remember

The difference between defeat and victory is often perseverance. The key to perseverance is hope!

Learning by Doing

*This page contains an alternate lesson plan emphasizing learning activities. Classes
desiring such student involvement will find these suggestions helpful.*

Learning Goals

This lesson should enable students to:

1. Explain how Isaiah's prophecy is a message of comfort to God's people today.

2. Indicate several of the text's phrases that are words of comfort.

3. Use the various comforting truths in a personal ministry to the discouraged.

Into the Lesson

The first four sessions in this study have titles beginning with the words, "A Time of." On the wall at the front of your classroom, display a clock and the heading, "A TIME OF—." Have also the words COMFORT, ENCOURAGEMENT, JOY, and RIGHTEOUSNESS AND PEACE prepared so you can display them with the respective studies.

As class members arrive and are seated, greet each one and ask, "Are you comfortable?" Have a few throw pillows around the room. If anyone mentions discomfort from the "too-hard" seats, offer him or her a pillow. You might also have a large comforter available for one who suggests it is a bit chilly in the classroom. As you get your class members thinking about and discussing physical comfort, ask, "What do we usually think about when we are discussing 'being comfortable'?" Then make the transition from physical comfort to spiritual comfort, the essence of today's text

Into the Word

The opening portion of Handel's *Messiah* is based on Isaiah 40:1-5. Bring a recorded version of this oratorio to class and play this section for your students. Again, perhaps a class member would bring a small sound system for the occasion. Direct your class members to follow the verses in Scripture as the passage is sung.

Provide paper and pens for the following activity. Working individually, your students are to examine today's text to find comforting truths that are contained in it. Instruct them to condense each truth to three words. For example, "warfare is accomplished" (v. 2) and "word stands forever" (v. 8).

Be prepared with your own list. Here are several you might include: "iniquity is pardoned" (v. 2); "glory is revealed" (v. 5); "all shall see" (v. 5); "Lord hath spoken" (v. 5); "Behold your God!" (v. 9); "God will come" (v. 10); "He shall feed" (v. 11); "He shall carry" (v. 11).

Allot five minutes for your students to prepare their lists; then go through the text and ask if anyone found any comforting words from each verse as you come to it.

Give each student a copy of the following antiphonal devotional reading. Divide your students into two groups. One group is to read the parts of the "discouraged," and the other the parts of the "comforters." It would be ideal for the two groups to face each other. After allowing a short time for your students to skim through the reading, lead them in reading it aloud.

Discouraged: "The struggle with the devil is so long and so hard."

Comforters: "But the warfare is completed in Christ's death and resurrection."

Discouraged: "The sins of the nation are so many."

Comforters: "But her iniquity can be pardoned."

Discouraged: "God seems so far away."

Comforters: "But the glory of the Lord has been revealed!"

Discouraged: "Oh, how can we be sure?"

Comforters: "The mouth of the Lord has spoken it!"

Discouraged: "Human beings are like grass that withers and fades and dies."

Comforters: "But the word of our God—its truth and its hope—stands forever."

Discouraged: "But the city of God is surrounded by vicious and evil warriors."

Comforters: "Look! God comes with a strong hand, and His arm will rule!"

Discouraged: "We are like feeble sheep, wandering, helpless, hungry."

Comforters: "He will feed His flock like a shepherd; He will gather you with His arm and carry you in His bosom."

Discouraged: "But—"

Comforters: "The Word of our God stands—*forever!*"

Into Life

Ask your students to identify some church members and friends they know who are struggling. Urge them to communicate comforting words to these persons this coming week by phone, by note, and by visit.

Let's Talk It Over

The questions on this page are designed to encourage review of the lesson Scriptures and to promote discussion of the lesson by the class. The answers provided are only discussion starters. Let your class talk it over from there.

1. The promises of comfort and hope found in Isaiah 40 must have seemed incredible to Judah in captivity. It is not surprising that they had lost hope. What are some of the factors that can cause a person to lose hope?

In the midst of difficult and painful experiences, we may lose our perspective. When suffering is intense over time, it tends to distort reality. Our difficult circumstances seem so overwhelming that we are unable to keep things in perspective. We lose sight of God's faithfulness. Our view of God gets smaller and smaller; thus our problems grow larger and larger. Also we lose hope when we begin to *confuse the temporary with the eternal.* We feel as if our suffering will never end. God reminded His people that their "hard service" had ended. We also lose hope when we *limit our resources to our strength alone.* Isaiah 40:21-31 and 41:10 provide clear reassurance for the discouraged and hopeless.

2. It is difficult for us to see any value in pain or suffering. What possible benefits might one find in these experiences?

One of the most obvious benefits is that we may grow in the virtue of patience. We live in a society that expects instant gratification. This may be due, in part, to the good fortune most persons have enjoyed. Patience comes from enduring difficulty (1 Peter 2:20). In addition, hardship and difficulty can produce a strength and firm resolve in our character, qualities essential for growth and maturity (1 Peter 5:10).

3. When we experience serious discouragement, it is not uncommon to find ourselves somewhat paralyzed emotionally. What constructive steps can a person take to deal with such discouragement?

There are several positive things one can do. First, *make a clear distinction between the temporary and the permanent.* Check your vocabulary. Do you often use the words *never* and *always?* These words speak of permanence, and they are self-defeating. Second, *remember to do only what you can do today.* Discouraged people are usually anxious people. They worry a lot. When we are anxious, we are attempting to solve tomorrow's possible problems today. Jesus teaches us to focus on what can be done today

(see Matthew 6:31). Third, *deliberately remember instances of God's faithfulness in the past.* We must allow the intellect to override the emotions. Emotionally we are unable to reconstruct positive experiences, but intellectually we can affirm them. Read Deuteronomy 7:9; Psalm 89:1 and 1 Peter 4:19. Fourth, *focus on those realities that do not change.* The God who delivered His people still does. Consider Isaiah 40:8; Malachi 3:6; Hebrews 1:12; 13:8; and James 1:17.

4. All about us are people who appear to be helpless and hopeless, powerless to change their circumstances. Although they may have made some poor choices that have contributed to their situation, as Christians we have a responsibility to offer them a message of hope and comfort. How can we do this?

The promise of God's love and care can be communicated best when it is expressed in tangible ways. Once we have given help in this way, we may encourage their endurance in the midst of the circumstances. Though the nights may seem endless and the days hopeless, God does not forget us. He understands our suffering (James 5:11). He makes special provision for us in the times of our weakness and helplessness, if we endure (Isaiah 40:10, 11). We can also help these persons choose the best of the alternatives available to them. Life is much more a matter of choice than of circumstance. Discouraged people need to remember that choices still are available to them.

5. It is not uncommon for mature Christians to experience pain and suffering. The apostle Paul is an example. Consider 2 Corinthians 1:3-7. In what sense is our suffering related to the suffering of Christ?

We share many of Jesus' experiences. He faced hostility. Our world is still hostile to Christianity. He did not receive justice. Injustice is still widespread. He was misunderstood, rejected, and persecuted; so are Christians today. Sometimes when Christians experience such suffering, they wonder why. Paul suggests the answer: (see v. 4, *New International Version*). One of the blessings of being part of the body of Christ is that we can share in one another's sufferings and in one another's comfort (v. 7).

A Time of Encouragement

DEVOTIONAL READING: Acts 27:14-26.

LESSON SCRIPTURE: Isaiah 51:1-8.

PRINTED TEXT: Isaiah 51:1-6.

Isaiah 51:1-6

1 Hearken to me, ye that follow after righteousness, ye that seek the LORD: look unto the rock whence ye are hewn, and to the hole of the pit whence ye are digged.

2 Look unto Abraham your father, and unto Sarah that bare you: for I called him alone, and blessed him, and increased him.

3 For the LORD shall comfort Zion: he will comfort all her waste places; and he will make her wilderness like Eden, and her desert like the garden of the LORD; joy and gladness shall be found therein, thanksgiving, and the voice of melody.

4 Hearken unto me, my people; and give ear unto me, O my nation: for a law shall proceed from me, and I will make my judgment to rest for a light of the people.

5 My righteousness is near; my salvation is gone forth, and mine arms shall judge the people; the isles shall wait upon me, and on mine arm shall they trust.

6 Lift up your eyes to the heavens, and look upon the earth beneath: for the heavens shall vanish away like smoke, and the earth shall wax old like a garment, and they that dwell therein shall die in like manner: but my salvation shall be for ever, and my righteousness shall not be abolished.

GOLDEN TEXT: My salvation shall be for ever, and my righteousness shall not be abolished.—Isaiah 51:6.

God's Promise of Deliverance (Isaiah)
Unit 1: The Coming of a New Day (Lessons 1-5)

Lesson Aims

This lesson is designed to help the student:

1. View God's blessings in the past as the harbinger of a glorious future.

2. Build their lives and hopes on what is permanent, not on what is temporary.

3. Look to God as the only source of eternal salvation.

Lesson Outline

INTRODUCTION

   A. The Way Out Is Up

   B. Lesson Background

  I. THE FOUNDATION OF THE FAITHFUL (Isaiah 51:1-3)

   A. Remembering Their Beginnings (v. 1)

   B. Recalling Their Ancestors (v. 2)

   C. Receiving Former Blessings (v. 3)

     Too Good to Be True?

 II. THE FUTURE OF THE FAITHFUL (Isaiah 51:4-6)

   A. The Lord's Righteous Promises (v. 4)

   B. The Lord's Universal Promises (v. 5)

   C. The Lord's Everlasting Promises (v. 6)

     Hope and Caution

CONCLUSION

   A. Seeing Through the Dark

   B. Let Us Pray

   C. Thought to Remember

God's promise to transform Zion (Isaiah 51:3) is pictured by visual 2 of the visuals packet. The visual is shown on page 132.

Introduction

A. The Way Out Is Up

The smallest obstacles sometimes can thwart living creatures. For example, it is said that a bumblebee can be held captive in an open tumbler. The bee will bounce around the sides of the glass until it dies. The only way of escape, so it thinks, is horizontally through the transparent glass near the bottom of the container. It either cannot or will not look up and escape through the opening at the top.

People also can be held prisoner by things that they at first view as small and inconsequential matters—a habit that they should break, but

don't; an attitude that needs correcting, but is allowed to continue and harden. They remain captives to these things, partly because they either do not know there is a way out, or having been told about it, don't believe it will work for them.

Judah's downward slide away from God may have begun with what some might regard as "little" things—failure to observe and remember God's blessings in the past, disrespect for elders, disregard of a bothersome law that restricted one's pursuit of pleasure, etc. In time, these "little" things formed a life-style that forged spiritual shackles the people could not break. By the time of Isaiah's prophetic ministry, Judah was faced with a future filled with real problems. There was nothing make-believe about them. God's judgment was coming upon them; captivity and slavery lay ahead. They would find themselves in the pit of despair. Isaiah stated that at that time their escape would come, from looking up to the Lord. Their salvation would come from above or not at all. Seeking their own solutions, or just looking down and around, would never lead to their release. The only way out would be up!

The same holds true for many who are battling life's problems today. The way out is still up. To seek a solution apart from God leads to discouragement and failure. Knowing that the Lord of Heaven offers the way of escape provides the encouragement needed to "keep on keeping on," even during the darkest of times.

B. Lesson Background

In the chapters preceding Isaiah 51, several themes are seen. One is the greatness of God. The Lord, Isaiah insisted, is more powerful than all false gods and idols combined. A second theme is Israel's unfaithfulness. It was Israel's unfaithfulness that would bring God's judgment, which would take the form of the Babylonian captivity. Standing over against Israel's unfaithfulness is the faithfulness of God. God would remain faithful to His promises. Someday He would deliver the people from their captivity.

Eventually, Babylon, the chosen instrument of God's judgment against Israel, would fall. Its fall would show to everyone the impotence of the false gods and idols. After that, Israel would be restored as a nation, and the people would receive abundant blessings of the Lord.

Intertwined with the message of the fall and restoration of Israel are Isaiah's prophecies regarding the Servant of the Lord. This Servant will be the subject of the second unit of lessons in this quarter's study (lessons 6-9). The Servant's identity and mission will be considered in detail at that time.

The words of this lesson's Scripture text, written by Isaiah well over one hundred years before the Babylonian captivity actually occurred, were intended for that generation of God's people who in the future would languish as captives in Babylon. The prophet's words would come as an encouragement for the captives to remain faithful in the midst of those dark days. They were to understand that the Lord had not forgotten Israel. His promises of a great and glorious future would surely come to pass.

I. The Foundation of the Faithful (Isaiah 51:1-3)

A. Remembering Their Beginnings (v. 1)

1. Hearken to me, ye that follow after righteousness, ye that seek the LORD: look unto the rock whence ye are hewn, and to the hole of the pit whence ye are digged.

The prophet was directing God's message to a dispirited people. The command for them to *hearken* or "listen" is repeated three times in this chapter. This was a divine "wake-up call." The Lord was calling His chosen people to look at their glorious past to learn lessons about the future he had in store for them.

The call was given to those who *follow after righteousness*. The phrase is further defined as those *that seek the Lord*. Righteousness is defined by the nature and character of God. In this context, "following righteousness" is contrasted with pursuing the passing, temporary things of this world (v. 6).

Look unto the rock . . . pit was a call for those who would seek the Lord in the Babylonian captivity to look back at their past history, especially at their beginning. They would be reminded of their humble origins and of their growth into a great multitude of people. From such lowly beginnings they had become a mighty nation. And how had this come about? There was but one explanation—it was due to the blessing of God. Israel as a people was a creation of God. The people could no more claim credit for their beginning and their development as a nation than a lifeless statue could claim to have given itself form out of a shapeless rock. The purpose for this reflection on their past history is seen in verse 3.

B. Recalling Their Ancestors (v. 2)

2. Look unto Abraham your father, and unto Sarah that bare you: for I called him alone, and blessed him, and increased him.

A review of Israel's past would lead one all the way back to Abraham and Sarah. The entire nation issued from these two, who were beyond

the age of having a child by natural means when God's promise that they would have a son was fulfilled in them. Read Genesis 12:1-7 and 17:1-21 for a review of how this beginning took place.

I called him alone; or, "when he was but one I called him" (*American Standard Version*). God called Abraham out of Ur of the Chaldees before he had any children. God promised to bless him, and He fulfilled His promise (Genesis 12:2; 24:1, 35). Not only did God give Abraham material blessings, but He also *increased him*. He made Abraham "a father of many nations" (Genesis 17:5).

If the Lord could begin with one man and make a great nation, surely He could begin again with a faithful remnant of the exiles (who numbered in the thousands—see Ezra 2:64) and cause His people to flourish. Truly God's "track record" is one of the greatest incentives to faith.

C. Receiving Former Blessings (v. 3)

3. For the LORD shall comfort Zion: he will comfort all her waste places; and he will make her wilderness like Eden, and her desert like the garden of the LORD; joy and gladness shall be found therein, thanksgiving, and the voice of melody.

The Lord shall comfort Zion . . . and he will make her wilderness like Eden. Literally, the text reads, "The Lord hath comforted Zion: he hath comforted all her waste places; and hath made her wilderness like Eden." This future condition of God's people was so certain that Isaiah could speak of it as if it had already been accomplished. Indeed, in the mind of God it was as good as done!

At the time of Judah's fall to the Babylonians, great destruction would take place in the land. Because virtually all of the people would be removed to other lands, much of Judah would be untended and would become a wilderness. One can only imagine what the land would look like after seventy years of neglect. Ezekiel described the abandoned land as a "desolate land" and the cities as "waste and desolate and ruined cities" (36:34-36).

Like Eden. The land's desolate condition would change. Isaiah said that the land would once again flower and bloom and be fruitful—so much so that he compared it to the Garden of Eden in the very beginning. The prophet Joel used this imagery in describing the land of

Judah before the ravages of the Babylonian invasion occurred (2:3). Ezekiel, like Isaiah here, prophesied that the land would once again be "like the garden of Eden" (36:35). Such would be the blessings God would bestow on the land when the Babylonian captivity ended and the exiles returned home.

The voice of melody. Music stops when a land is afflicted, for music is associated with times of happiness, joy, and peace (see Isaiah 24:8). Even so, when affliction ceases, music is heard in the land once again. Therefore, in stating that music would be found again in Zion, Isaiah was prophesying that Judah's affliction would end and the people would one day live happily in their homeland. Thus the thought of this verse reinforces the message contained in verses 1 and 2—the people in captivity should take heart; God had not forgotten them; brighter days lay ahead. This would all come to pass for those among God's people who would look to Him in faith and continue to trust in Him, even though the days of their captivity were very dark.

TOO GOOD TO BE TRUE?

These may be momentous times. Israel and Palestine (PLO) have signed a peace treaty of sorts—a covenant of mutual acknowledgement. Most of the world is not "holding its breath," however. Considering the hatred that has manifested itself in violence for decades between these peoples, it is understandable that one might wonder how long this compatibility will continue. By the time you read this, they could be fighting again.

Judah in exile, to whom Isaiah's prophecy was directed, likely received his promises of peace and restoration with guarded optimism too. Sometimes good news seems too good to be true. The prophet foretold a time of "joy and gladness . . . thanksgiving, and the voice of melody." The prospects of a return to good old days of peace and prosperity must have seemed incredible.

Could the shepherds, centuries later, truly grasp the implications of the good news brought by God's angel: "For unto you is born this day in

the city of David a Saviour, which is Christ the Lord"? Did they dare to believe what the heavenly host proclaimed: "Glory to God in the highest, and on earth peace, good will toward men"? (Luke 2:11, 14). At least they mustered enough hope to seek out the Christ child, as did sages from the East. Wise men still seek the Savior.

—R. W. B.

II. The Future of the Faithful (Isaiah 51:4-6)

A. The Lord's Righteous Promises (v. 4)

4. Hearken unto me, my people; and give ear unto me, O my nation: for a law shall proceed from me, and I will make my judgment to rest for a light of the people.

Hearken unto me. The Hebrew term here is a stronger term than that used in verse 1. The meaning is not just "listen to me," but "give me your undivided attention." The previous section promised the restoration of Judah after the captivity. Verse 4 and those that follow in our text look to something greater than the return of the land to abundance and prosperity. They describe the glorious future when the Lord would send forth His *light* to the nations. This, too, was a part of the original promise of blessing to Abraham (Genesis 12:2, 3).

A law shall proceed from me. The *law* here probably refers to the gospel of redemption. This law, or instruction, would go forth from God into all nations (see Isaiah 2:4; compare Isaiah 42:4).

Earlier, Isaiah had spoken of a time when the glory of the Lord would be revealed, and said that "all flesh" would see it (Isaiah 40:5). This was fulfilled in the coming of the Messiah, Jesus. Simeon, the aged resident of Jerusalem, sang at Jesus' coming, "For mine eyes have seen thy salvation, which thou hast prepared before the face of all people; a light to lighten the Gentiles, and the glory of thy people Israel" (Luke 2:30-32).

To rest describes the forming of a standing place, a firm foundation, from which the *judgment* (justice) of the Lord would shine forth. That place was Jerusalem, and the light was to be the gospel, which would come forth from it. That light would shine upon *the people.* This term in the Hebrew is plural and is best understood as "the peoples" or "the nations."

B. The Lord's Universal Promises (v. 5)

5. My righteousness is near; my salvation is gone forth, and mine arms shall judge the people; the isles shall wait upon me, and on mine arm shall they trust.

The Lord shall comfort Zion.
He will make her wilderness like Eden
and her desert like the garden of the Lord.
Isaiah 51:3

visual 2

The prophet continues to speak of the great day of the Messiah's coming, and he describes it as being *near.* In other prophecies as well, Isaiah makes it appear as though the coming of the messianic kingdom would immediately follow the restoration of Israel. In fact, the events would be separated by more than five hundred years. The prophets received God's messages and delivered them to His people. It is obvious that not all was divulged to the prophets in this process. (See 1 Peter 1:10-12.) From God's standpoint, the coming of the Messiah *was* near, just as it was certain. And so God could say through the prophet Isaiah, *my salvation is gone forth.* In this statement we are reminded once again that the Lord's timing is not man's. Peter reminds his readers that "one day is with the Lord as a thousand years, and a thousand years as one day" (2 Peter 3:8).

My righteousness refers to the great plan that God would put into effect with the Messiah's coming. That plan consists of two parts. The first is His righteous plan to redeem His people through Christ. This thought is touched on by the apostle Paul in his statement, "For I am not ashamed of the gospel of Christ: for it is the power of God unto salvation to every one that believeth; to the Jew first, and also to the Greek. For therein is the righteousness of God revealed from faith to faith: as it is written, The just shall live by faith" (Romans 1:16, 17).

The second part of God's righteousness has to do with the punishment given to those who resist His will and reject His offer of grace through Christ. If God's righteousness is seen in the salvation of those who accept His offer of pardon, it is seen no less in the punishment directed to those who despise His gracious offer and who, in so doing, show that they even despise Him who makes the offer.

The expression *mine arms* refers to the strength or might by which the Lord would accomplish His purposes. For many, the result will be judgment and punishment, but not for all. For those who believe the great news and accept the Christ, God's arm will bring blessing and salvation. (See 2 Thessalonians 1:5-10.)

The isles are the most distant lands. Even peoples scattered to the farthest reaches of the earth will be blessed by this great act of God. These peoples *shall wait* on the Lord. This means that these distant peoples will look to God for deliverance and will accept the salvation that He offers. The record in the book of Acts reveals with what readiness the Gentiles received the gospel of Christ when it was preached to them (see Acts 11:21; 13:42; 14:1; 17:4; 18:8-10, etc).

C. The Lord's Everlasting Promises
(v. 6)

6. Lift up your eyes to the heavens, and look upon the earth beneath: for the heavens shall vanish away like smoke, and the earth shall wax old like a garment, and they that dwell therein shall die in like manner: but my salvation shall be for ever, and my righteousness shall not be abolished.

God's people are called to look up *to the heavens,* that is, to the vast expanse of the firmament. They are also to look down on the earth. The material universe seems to us to be stable, dependable, that which will just go on and on.

The word *for* introduces the reason why we are to look at the material universe. In truth, it is not permanent. Isaiah states that the *heavens shall vanish away like smoke.* This presents a picture of the vast universe disintegrating and disappearing like a house consumed by fire. It first falls apart, crashes in on itself, and is consumed until finally its ash is carried away in the wind.

The prophet changes the metaphor when describing the fate of the earth, though the truth he is conveying is the same. He says *the earth shall wax old like a garment.* The figure of a garment is used similarly by the psalmist when he writes, "They [the heavens and earth] will perish, . . . they will all wear out like a garment. Like clothing you will change them and they will be discarded" (Psalm 102:26, *New International Version*; see also Hebrews 1:11).

The entire created universe will not last forever. It is only a matter of time until it will not exist as we know it. This material universe does not provide a lasting foundation for anyone. Security must be found elsewhere. Jesus' admonition in the Sermon on the Mount sets forth a similar concept; "Lay not up for yourselves treasures upon earth, where moth and rust doth corrupt, and where thieves break through and steal" (Matthew 6:19).

The Hebrew phrase rendered *in like manner* in the *King James Version* is translated in more recent versions as "like flies" or "like gnats." The meaning is that humanity (*they that dwell therein*) is just as frail and finite as the smallest insect. Whatever the correct translation, the idea is clear. Mankind is subjected to the same law of perishableness as the physical universe; our physical bodies shall die. It is readily apparent, therefore, that anyone who trusts in the flesh as though it were permanent is foolish indeed.

Over against the temporal nature of all things related to the physical universe stands God, the One who is eternal. And He offers us *salvation.* Though we die in the flesh, by God's gift we may live eternally. We can have full confidence in the promises of God, for He is the righteous one. (See Isaiah 40:8.)

The verse following our text gives a practical application that may be drawn from God's truth contained in verses 1-6: "Fear ye not the reproach of men, neither be ye afraid of their revilings." God's enemies will come to nothing, and He will remain faithful to His promises. Let us take courage and remain faithful to Him.

HOPE AND CAUTION

How old is Earth? Some scientists speculate that the age of our planet is millions, even *billions*, of years. Some Christians, on the other hand, would measure the earth's age in thousands of years. Archeology, geology, and carbon-dating notwithstanding, the exact age of the universe is known only to God. And God has not revealed to us the birth date of the universe.

God has, however, outlined the events of creation, and He has described the end-time demise of the heavens and the earth. Through Isaiah He indicates that the world may simply die of old age, like a worn-out garment. Other Scriptures predict more cataclysmic events: "The earth . . . and the works that are therein shall be burned up" (2 Peter 3:10).

Whatever the details, the material world will someday cease to be; it is temporal. But we have God's promise that salvation and righteousness "shall not be abolished." The spiritual world is everlasting. Let us rejoice because of this truth, and let us be prepared for that day. Peter concludes rightly that we should be holy and godly, "looking for . . . the coming of the day of God" (2 Peter 3:11, 12).   —R. W. B.

Conclusion

A. Seeing Through the Dark

Everyone sat spellbound by the courage of the circus animal trainer. Armed with nothing more than a wooden chair and a small whip, he stepped into a cage filled with ferocious tigers.

Once inside the cage, he barked orders at the huge animals and cracked his whip. Each animal growled ominously and pawed the air, but then they jumped through flaming hoops and over barrels, just as the trainer commanded.

Suddenly the unexpected happened—all of the lights in the arena went out. The trainer was trapped in the cage with the tigers.

No one knew for sure what to expect. When the lights were restored moments later, the trainer was standing with whip and chair in hand in the same place where he had been when the lights went out. Each animal seemed just as much under his control as before. The audience erupted in a standing ovation.

When interviewed later, the trainer was asked if he was afraid when he was stranded in the dark with the animals. He admitted to being more afraid than ever before. "After all," he told the reporters, "I knew the cats' night vision was much better than mine. I was at their mercy."

He then explained how he was able to maintain his composure. "I remembered," he added, "that the tigers didn't know that I couldn't see them! I just cracked my whip and talked to them until the lights came on. They never knew the advantage they had over me."

In life, when surrounded by the forces of darkness and evil, we who are God's children may feel overwhelmed and at the mercy of our enemy. But this we know and are assured of: He who is in us is greater than he who is in the world (1 John 4:4). We have the advantage.

Isaiah encouraged Judah in exile to look through their dark and depressing situation to the glorious future God had in store for them—their return to their homeland. May we look to Christ, the light of the world, and find assurance for our eternal future in the presence of God.

B. Let Us Pray

Our Father, the spiritual darkness around us seems overwhelming at times. In our discouragement Your faithfulness sustains us. Strengthen our trust in Your great promises. Build in us a faith that lives for the coming of Your kingdom. In Jesus' name we pray. Amen.

C. Thought to Remember

The hope of God's glorious tomorrow gives one courage and strength to walk through today's darkness.

Home Daily Bible Readings

Monday, Dec. 4—Encouraged to Trust (Exodus 14:10-18)
Tuesday, Dec. 5—God's People Liberated (Isaiah 41:11-16)
Wednesday, Dec. 6—Joy of Being Forgiven (Matthew 9:1-8)
Thursday, Dec. 7—Cheered by a Friend (Matthew 14:13-27)
Friday, Dec. 8—God's Support in Prison (Acts 23:1-11)
Saturday, Dec. 9—Comfort From an Unexpected Source (Acts 27:21-25)
Sunday, Dec. 10—God Is With His People (Isaiah 43:1-7)

Learning by Doing

This page contains an alternate lesson plan emphasizing learning activities. Classes desiring such student involvement will find these suggestions helpful.

Learning Goals

Having participated in this study of Isaiah 51:1-6, each adult disciple will:

1. Identify the elements of encouragement that a Christian has from God, according to the lesson outline used below.

2. Recall and ponder these encouraging truths when discouraged.

3. Encourage a disheartened Christian with these thoughts, at the earliest opportunity.

Into the Lesson

(If you are using the clock and title idea suggested in lesson 1, add the label "A Time of ENCOURAGEMENT" for this week's session.)

Recruit an artistic member of your class to prepare a life-size paper head. By means of a simple line drawing have a face drawn on the front. On the back of the head include a pair of eyes. Attach the head to a stick, such as a ruler.

As class begins, show the head—front and back—and ask, "What is this person able to do?" ("He can look back as well as ahead.") When you receive the answer, display two signs you have prepared with print large enough to be seen by all: "LOOKING BACK: The Foundation of the Faithful" and "LOOKING AHEAD: The Future of the Faithful." Display these respectively to the left and right at the front of your room. Identify the two ideas as being the basic outline of today's text, Isaiah 51:1-6.

Into the Word

Write the following Scripture references on triangular pieces of paper shaped like pennants, one reference per piece. Attach each piece to a different pencil so that they look like flags. The references are Genesis 2:8, 9; Genesis 12:1-7; Psalm 102:25, 26; Isaiah 24:8; Jeremiah 31:33, 34; Joel 2:3; Luke 2:30-32; 2 Peter 3:8.

Distribute these eight "flags" to eight of your students, one flag for each. Have each of these students take a moment at this time to find the Scripture that is identified on his or her flag and read it silently to become familiar with its content.

After they have done this, invite one of your better readers to stand before the class and read aloud the six verses of today's Scripture text. After this reading, ask the reader to read the text aloud once again, going slowly this time. During this second reading, those who are holding the "flags" are to "flag the reader down" when the reader reads a phrase of the lesson text that relates to a passage held by a flag holder. Each time the text reader is "flagged down," have the flag holder read his or her passage and note how it relates to what the text reader has just read.

Before the class session, print the following headings on separate strips of paper, using letters large enough to be read by all in the class: "Remembering Their Beginnings," "Recalling Their Ancestors," "Receiving Former Blessings," "The Lord's Righteous Promises," "The Lord's Universal Promises," and "The Lord's Everlasting Promises." Then roll up each strip.

At this point in the session, hand these six rolled phrases to six of your class members and have the strips read randomly. The phrases relate to the two posters that you displayed earlier at the front of the room. Ask your class first to decide which three of the phrases relate to "Looking Back" and which to "Looking Ahead." Then ask the class to decide which phrase goes with each verse of today's text. As the matches are made, mount each strip under the correct heading and in verse order. Point out that the six phrases and the six verses contain six reasons to be encouraged in the Lord.

Into Life

Divide your students into groups of four. Provide each group with a pen and a sheet of paper, at the top of which is written, "Be encouraged, Christian, because—" Have each group write down as many reasons for encouragement as they can that are related to the verses of the lesson text, and ask them to give the verse number. Then let the groups share their suggestions. Here are two examples: "you are standing on the Rock" (v. 1); "God keeps His promises" (v. 1).

Read verse 3 of the text aloud. Emphasize the last clause: "joy and gladness shall be found therein, thanksgiving, and the voice of melody." Note that you have been discussing reasons we have for joy and singing. Ask the class members to identify songs, hymns, and choruses that are expressions of joy and encouragement to them. Do one yourself to get the list started, such as "On Christ the Solid Rock I stand!" Suggest that they use these in their own devotional times this coming week.

Let's Talk It Over

The questions on this page are designed to encourage review of the lesson Scriptures and to promote discussion of the lesson by the class. The answers provided are only discussion starters. Let your class talk it over from there.

1. If anyone had reason to be discouraged and to give up, Abraham and Sarah did. Yet, it was out of their barrenness that God produced a nation. Can you think of other situations of "barrenness" and "hopelessness" out of which came great blessing?

You may want to ask the class to share some personal experiences in this regard. Several biblical examples may be given also. When Joseph was a slave in Egypt, his situation looked rather hopeless. However, Genesis 39:2 states, "The Lord was with Joseph and he prospered" (*New International Version*). His faithfulness ultimately resulted in great blessing for himself and his family.

Moses and the Israelites at the Red Sea were in desperate circumstances, but God provided deliverance. In his song after the Red Sea crossing, Moses expressed this beautifully: "In your unfailing love you will lead the people you have redeemed. In your strength you will guide them to your holy dwelling" (Exodus 15:13, *New International Version*).

King Jehoshaphat of Judah, when faced with overwhelming enemy forces, prayed, "O our God . . . we have no power to face this vast army that is attacking us. We do not know what to do, but our eyes are upon you" (2 Chronicles 20:12, *New International Version*). He was reminded by the prophet, "The battle is not yours, but God's" (2 Chronicles 20:15, *New International Version*). How we need to remember this!

2. When life looks desolate and bleak, it is not easy to believe that beauty and joy are in our future. How can we live with anticipation of the "best" when we are experiencing what seems to be the "worst"?

It seems Isaiah was trying to help the people do some "faith imaging." He reminded them of how it was before sin had so marred the beauty of God's creation and man himself. What God has done, He can and will do. In this sense the past is prologue to the future. We need to reach back into our memory, and, placing the Word of God alongside our experiences, reflect on those occasions when He has brought light to dispel our darkness, companionship to ease our loneliness, harmony to erase our discord, and joy to replace our sadness. This seems to be what men and women of faith have always done. They have affirmed what they could not deny—the faithfulness of God in keeping His promises. "Now faith is being sure of what we hope for and certain of what we do not see. This is what the ancients were commended for" (Hebrews 11:1, 2, *New International Version*). They viewed life and its experiences through the eyes of faith. When we do that, we are more likely to see beyond the immediate. If winter is here, can spring be far away?

3. What resource do we have as Christians to control our fearful feelings and attitudes, and how can we gain help from that resource?

Our resource is God himself. We should begin by affirming that He is greater than anything we may fear. Meditating on a Scripture passage such as Isaiah 41:8-10 gives much comfort, especially as we focus on the phrases, "I have," "I am," and "I will." In the light of these statements, what is the logical conclusion? Paul states it in Romans 8:31: "What, then, shall we say in response to this? If God is for us, who can be against us?" (*New International Version*).

Our problem is that we fail to distinguish between the facts as clearly stated in God's Word, and our feelings as we often identify them. Our feelings fluctuate as the circumstances of life change, but God's purposes and promises are not subject to the winds of change. They are sure and certain. We need not fear, for He is our God!

4. What, then is the real source of the Christian's confidence and joy?

Certainly it is not found in the improvement of our physical environment or in the change of our circumstances, as important as these may seem to be. The circumstances of life change so rapidly that we dare not put our confidence in these things. Verse 6 of our text makes it abundantly clear that there is no permanence in this material world. The daily news is a constant reminder that it is foolish to seek lasting security here. Our only source of confidence and lasting joy is to be found in the righteousness and salvation of the Lord (Isaiah 51: 6, 8). We must place our trust in the One who remains, when all else perishes (see Hebrews 1:10-12).

A Time of Joy

December 17
Lesson 3

DEVOTIONAL READING: Luke 1:46-55.

LESSON SCRIPTURE: Isaiah 9:1-7.

PRINTED TEXT: Isaiah 9:1-7.

Isaiah 9:1-7

1 Nevertheless the dimness shall not be such as was in her vexation, when at the first he lightly afflicted the land of Zebulun, and the land of Naphtali, and afterward did more grievously afflict her by the way of the sea, beyond Jordan, in Galilee of the nations.

2 The people that walked in darkness have seen a great light: they that dwell in the land of the shadow of death, upon them hath the light shined.

3 Thou hast multiplied the nation, and not increased the joy: they joy before thee according to the joy in harvest, and as men rejoice when they divide the spoil.

4 For thou hast broken the yoke of his burden, and the staff of his shoulder, the rod of his oppressor, as in the day of Midian.

5 For every battle of the warrior is with confused noise, and garments rolled in blood; but this shall be with burning and fuel of fire.

6 For unto us a child is born, unto us a son is given: and the government shall be upon his shoulder: and his name shall be called Wonderful, Counselor, The mighty God, The everlasting Father, The Prince of Peace.

7 Of the increase of his government and peace there shall be no end, upon the throne of David, and upon his kingdom, to order it, and to establish it with judgment and with justice from henceforth even for ever. The zeal of the LORD of hosts will perform this.

GOLDEN TEXT: For unto us a child is born, unto us a son is given: and the government shall be upon his shoulder: and his name shall be called Wonderful, Counselor, The mighty God, The everlasting Father, The Prince of Peace.—Isaiah 9:6.

God's Promise of Deliverance
(Isaiah)
Unit 1: The Coming of a New Day
(Lessons 1-5)

Lesson Aims

After the completion of this lesson, students should:

1. Understand the historical and geographical background of the prophecy in today's text.

2. Be aware of the New Testament's use of this text and how Jesus Christ fulfilled Isaiah's description of a joyous future.

3. Resolve that they will become bearers of Christ's light in a world of spiritual darkness.

Lesson Outline

INTRODUCTION
    A. A Time for Children
    B. Lesson Background
  I. A TRANSFORMED LAND (Isaiah 9:1-5)
    A. From Darkness to Light (vv. 1, 2)
       Carry the Light
    B. From Grief to Joy (v. 3)
    C. From Oppression to Deliverance (vv. 4, 5)
       Joy to the World
 II. A TRIUMPHANT LAD (Isaiah 9:6, 7)
    A. His Accolades (v. 6)
    B. His Achievements (v. 7)
CONCLUSION
    A. Christmas Lights
    B. The Kingdom of Kingdoms
    C. Let Us Pray
    D. Thought to Remember

The central message of visual 3 of the visuals packet is that the light that dispels the shadow of death (Isaiah 9:2) came to earth in the incarnate Son of God. It is shown on page 142.

Introduction

A. A Time for Children

In spite of the fact that it has continued to keep children at the heart of its observance of Christmas, American society has become an increasingly difficult place for children to live and grow up. The impact of the nation's moral and spiritual decline has wrought havoc in the lives of countless innocent children, particularly through the breakup of their families.

The Scripture text for today is one of the most stirring messianic prophecies in all of the Old Testament. It describes through impressive titles and elevated language the Child whose birth is the reason for genuine celebration at Christmas. We should remember, however, that this prophecy was delivered during a difficult period for children in Judah's' history. Ahaz, king of Judah, had sacrificed his own children in the fire as part of his devotion to pagan gods (2 Chronicles 28:1-4). Because of the king's blatant disobedience, other children were seized as captives by invading nations (vv. 5, 8, 17-19; 29:9).

Perhaps it was only fitting, then, that Ahaz should have been the recipient of the prophecies concerning Immanuel (Isaiah 7:14) and the child promised in today's text. Both prophecies were foretelling the coming of Jesus Christ, the King who encouraged little children to come to Him and rebuked anyone who hindered them.

May the children in our families and our neighborhoods know not only that Christmas is for them, but that Christ is as well.

B. Lesson Background

The hope and joy promised in Isaiah 9:1-7 must be considered against the backdrop of the gloom and misery present in Judah when Isaiah spoke this message. Judah was being threatened by an alliance between the northern kingdom of Israel and Syria, and King Ahaz and his people were terrified.

Isaiah (accompanied by one of his sons) approached Ahaz and told him not to fear the alliance, for it would not stand. He urged the king to trust God to provide deliverance for Judah. The nation's problems were spiritual in nature, not political. Isaiah then challenged the king to ask God for a sign to verify Isaiah's message. But the unbelieving Ahaz refused to ask, at which point Isaiah uttered the virgin birth prophecy found in Isaiah 7:14. Instead of turning to God, Ahaz preferred to seek help from Assyria. In no uncertain terms Isaiah told Ahaz that the Assyrian military machine would eventually turn on Judah and leave behind extensive damage (Isaiah 7:18-25). The Lord would, in effect, hide His face from His people (8:17).

The final verses of chapter 8 describe conditions that would exist in Judah as a result of the Assyrian invasion. The people would actually consult mediums and spiritists for assistance rather than "the law and the testimony" (vv. 19, 20). Instead of looking inwardly and assessing their own guilt, they would curse God and the king (v. 21). The people would be engulfed in spiritual darkness, and their land would be turned into a curse. However, God, whom they were cursing, would not forever turn His back upon His people.

I. A Transformed Land
(Isaiah 9:1-5)

A. From Darkness to Light (vv. 1, 2)

1. Nevertheless the dimness shall not be such as was in her vexation, when at the first he lightly afflicted the land of Zebulun, and the land of Naphtali, and afterward did more grievously afflict her by the way of the sea, beyond Jordan, in Galilee of the nations.

Nevertheless indicates a link with the material at the close of chapter 8. So also does the word *dimness* (rendered "gloom" in the *New International Version*), which appeared in 8:22. In the time of affliction, the message of hope was proclaimed. A dramatic change from the depressing scenario of disobedience and despair was on the horizon. Those who heard the message probably understood it to mean relief from oppression by the Assyrians. Prophecy can have more than one fulfillment, however, and we shall see that Isaiah also had in mind the later deliverance from sin by the power of Christ.

The lands of *Zebulun* and *Naphtali* were mentioned first in Isaiah's description of future events. These were two of the twelve tribes of Israel, neither of which was of great significance in the history of the nation. This was due in part to their geographical location. Zebulun and Naphtali were neighboring tribes situated within the northernmost sector of the nation of Israel, with the Sea of Galilee serving as part of Naphtali's eastern border.

These two tribes were far removed from the influence of Jerusalem, which under David became the political and religious center of the nation. Residents of Zebulun and Naphtali felt the influence of the peoples immediately to their north, which included the pagan Phoenicians. (Some pagan influence was in the midst of these tribes because of their failure to remove the Canaanites completely during the conquest, as Judges 1:30, 33 indicates.) Furthermore, armies invading Israel would tend to come from the north, meaning that tribes such as Zebulun and Naphtali would be among the first to experience any hardship that would occur. In the time of Isaiah it was they especially who suffered during the Assyrian invasion under Tiglath-pileser (2 Kings 15:29).

All of these factors contributed to a feeling of contempt in which the more central and southern tribes held the northerners. This was reflected in the title, *Galilee of the nations* (or Gentiles), used by Isaiah in this verse.

The latter part of this verse presents a problem in translation, involving in particular the phrase, *and afterward did more grievously afflict her by the way of the sea.* The verb translated *grievously afflict* is more correctly rendered "honor." The verse is describing the great contrast between the turmoil that Zebulun and Naphtali had suffered and the blessing that God had in store for them. The *New International Version* conveys this understanding as follows: "In the past he humbled the land of Zebulun and the land of Naphtali, but in the future he will honor Galilee of the Gentiles, by the way of the sea, along the Jordan."

2. The people that walked in darkness have seen a great light: they that dwell in the land of the shadow of death, upon them hath the light shined.

So certain is the accomplishment of God's word that Isaiah speaks as though he were standing in the day of the fulfillment of God's promise. How was this formerly despised region of Zebulun and Naphtali to be honored? The answer is given by Matthew, who quotes this verse (Matthew 4:15, 16) after recording that Jesus settled in the town of Capernaum (which was located in the territory of Naphtali). Thus, this area that held a long-entrenched reputation as a place of "darkness" (spiritual as well as political) became the residence of the "light of the world." The *land of the shadow of death,* where much suffering inflicted by invaders had occurred, became host to Life personified.

This illustrates the Scriptural principle that God's ways are far different from man's. He tends to use people, places, and objects of little value in the eyes of the world to accomplish His purposes. It was as unlikely that Jesus should have made Galilee His headquarters as it was that He should have made a stable in Bethlehem the place of His birth.

CARRY THE LIGHT

I'm afraid of the dark. Actually, I fear what is *in* the dark. The bogeymen of childhood no longer frighten me, but the darkness of ignorance and sin hides scores of modern monsters

---

How to Say It

AHAZ. *A*-haz.
CANAANITES. *Kay*-nan-ites.
CAPERNAUM. Kuh-*per*-nay-um.
NAPHTALI. *Naf*-tuh-lye.
PHOENICIANS. Fih-*nish*-unz.
TIGLATH-PILESER. *Tig*-lath-pih-*lee*-zer (strong accent on *lee*).
ZEBULUN. *Zeb*-you-lun.

that are very threatening. Lurking in the darkness of secularism are doubt and fear. Humanism is casting dark shadows into every corner of our culture. Homosexuals have come out of their "closets," and they have brought the darkness of their perversions with them. The midnight madness of carnal corruption seems to engulf us.

Jesus said that the doers of evil love darkness (John 3:19, 20). He also said, "I am the light of the world: he that followeth me shall not walk in darkness, but shall have the light of life" (John 8:12). In so saying He showed that He is the light prophesied by Isaiah, the light that shined upon those "in the land of the shadow of death."

It is the Christian's privilege to reflect the light of Christ. Twila Paris has written a challenging song, *Carry the Light*. It asks, "Who will tell the children . . .? Who will preach the Gospel . . .?" The answer is imperative: "Carry the Light!"   —R. W. B.

B. From Grief to Joy (v. 3)

3. Thou hast multiplied the nation, and not increased the joy: they joy before thee according to the joy in harvest, and as men rejoice when they divide the spoil.

Thou hast multiplied the nation, and not increased the joy. This seems to be a contradiction, since increasing the nation would be expected to cause an increase in joy. Some manuscripts of Isaiah omit the *not*, and scholars are agreed that this is the better reading. The translation should read something like, "Thou hast multiplied the nation and increased its joy."

The prophet sees God's people multiplied and rejoicing in the days of the "great light," like people rejoicing in the days of a bountiful harvest, or when dividing the spoil taken from a conquered enemy. Jesus most certainly increased the nation by creating an entirely new nation in which both Jews and Gentiles could be included (Ephesians 2:14-17; 1 Peter 2:9). Perhaps this gave added significance to Jesus' appearance in an area that was scornfully known as "Galilee of the nations (Gentiles)." From many nations believers in Jesus have joined the "holy nation" and have added their testimonies to the company of the joyful.

C. From Oppression to Deliverance (vv. 4, 5)

4. For thou hast broken the yoke of his burden, and the staff of his shoulder, the rod of his oppressor, as in the day of Midian.

Isaiah elaborated further on the effects of the light in eliminating the people's darkness. Their oppression and enslavement would cease. *The yoke, the staff,* and *the rod* were all items used to control animals, so that they might do the bidding of their masters. Israel was reduced to such a condition under the Assyrian onslaught, and it is likely that those who heard these words spoken would have thought in terms of deliverance from the Assyrians.

The reference to *the day of Midian* brought to mind the victory that God gave Israel over the oppressive Midianites during the days of Gideon (Judges 7:19-25). This incident would have held special meaning for the tribes of Zebulun and Naphtali, since it occurred in the vicinity of that section of Israel.

The removal of the Assyrian menace would have been a marvelous event to witness. Yet, at best it could deal with only part of Israel's misery, and not the main part at that. Another form of oppression lay at the root of Israel's woes. This was the tyranny of sin. See Isaiah's indictment against the people (Isaiah 1:1-8). Sin was the yoke, staff, and rod that was degrading the nation and leading it to destruction. Israel never could be really free until it was rid of this greater burden.

There is only one way anyone can have this yoke broken and this burden lifted. God alone has the power to accomplish such a deliverance. It is as impossible for man to do this as it was for Gideon to conquer Midian in his own strength.

JOY TO THE WORLD

Serendipity is a happy word. A serendipity is an unsought fortunate discovery. It is finding a quarter in a public telephone change cup, or winning a sweepstakes, or receiving an unexpected promotion. If Hebrew vocabulary had a counterpart, it surely would appear in this text. Isaiah was given a joyous message of hope for his people, when all seemed hopeless!

God's prophets did not often have good news to announce. For the most part, they issued warnings of "gloom and doom." Isaiah, however, was privileged to tell of the coming of the Messiah, who would bring peace and joy and hope. He predicted a brighter future for Judah, and for all people of all times and all places.

Countless people live "in quiet desperation." Disappointment, discouragement, and depression foster unbearable personal pain. Psychiatrists, analysts, therapists, and ministers carry huge counseling loads, trying to help clients find a life that is tolerable.

For all who despair, Christ is joy. He is the reason for this joy-filled season. We who believe in Him "rejoice with joy unspeakable" (1 Peter 1:8), for He has broken sin's shackles and has brought us salvation.   —R. W. B.

5. For every battle of the warrior is with confused noise, and garments rolled in blood; but this shall be with burning and fuel of fire.

For every battle of the warrior is with confused noise. A better translation is, "Every boot of tramping warrior." These, along with the soldiers' garments *rolled in blood* were to become the *fuel of fire.* This verse reinforces the fact that the real battle facing Israel was not to be fought as battles are normally fought. The battle was spiritual in nature, aimed at addressing Israel's real problem; thus, vast armies and man-made weapons of war were useless. God had another strategy in mind. His primary and most powerful weapon was to be a Child.

II. A Triumphant Lad (Isaiah 9:6, 7)

A. His Accolades (v. 6)

6. For unto us a child is born, unto us a son is given: and the government shall be upon his shoulder: and his name shall be called Wonderful, Counselor, The mighty God, The everlasting Father, The Prince of Peace.

Here was the glorious climax of Isaiah's picture of future deliverance and joy. He had described the conditions of the transformed land and its people, the defeat of the oppressor, and the nature of the accompanying conflict. Now he turned his prophetic spotlight on just whom God planned to use to bring these magnificent things to pass. While the distraught King Ahaz was preoccupied with alliances, battle tactics, and political maneuvers, God had Israel's future resting squarely upon the shoulders of a Child.

Every child is born; this Child was, in addition, to be *given.* The stage had been set for the coming of One who would secure for Israel (and for mankind) deliverance from sin, which would indeed multiply the nation and increase its joy. No greater commentary on this thought can be found than that within the timeless proclamation of John 3:16.

The government shall be upon his shoulder. Rather than describing His rule as a burden He must carry, this phrase more likely referred to an insignia (such as a key) that sometimes was laid upon the shoulder of a ruler to symbolize authority. (See Isaiah 22:22.)

The most striking feature of this passage is the series of titles to be associated with the Child. While it is true that Jesus was never actually called by any of these names, it is also true that He was never called "Immanuel" either. These titles should be taken as indicative of the characteristics of the promised Child. In other words, He would be worthy to receive such honors.

Wonderful. As He would be God as well as man, the Messiah would be "wonderful" in His nature. "Wonderful" describes the circumstances of His birth, death, resurrection, and ascension. His teaching "astonished" those who heard it (Matthew 7:28). *Counselor.* This name is well suited to the One who is wisdom itself. It is He who says, "Counsel is mine, and sound wisdom: I am understanding; I have strength" (Proverbs 8:14). Some, however, understand the title *Wonderful* as a description of the word *Counselor* and thus translate "Wonderful Counselor." It is pointed out that in Isaiah 28:29 the words "wonderful in counsel" are used of "the Lord of hosts." With either translation, the Child's divinity is indicated.

The mighty God. Here the Child's divine character becomes even more apparent. The Hebrew term used for God (*El*) appears also in the name "Immanu-el" (God with us.) The phrase itself appears in Isaiah 10:21 as another name for the Lord (see also Jeremiah 32:18).

The everlasting Father or "Father of eternity" highlights the promised One's gentleness and tenderness. He would possess these fatherly qualities eternally. It is not possible to find adequate fulfillment of a description of this magnitude in anyone other than Jesus Christ. No other one could show us the mighty God and at the same time exemplify the kind of tenderness that any father would do well to emulate.

The Prince of Peace is perhaps the title most heralded at Christmas, mainly because at Jesus' birth the heavenly host announced peace on earth. Jesus created peace by triumphing over "principalities and powers" (Colossians 2:15) and by destroying the devil (Hebrews 2:14, 15). The "battle of Calvary" was the most intense struggle in the history of the world, despite the

Home Daily Bible Readings

Monday, Dec. 11—Suffering Servant Serves Others (Isaiah 50:4-10)
Tuesday, Dec. 12—Oppressors Defeated (Isaiah 10:20-27)
Wednesday, Dec. 13—God's Love Declared (John 3:16-21)
Thursday, Dec. 14—Messiah Reigns as King (Jeremiah 23:1-6)
Friday, Dec. 15—My Name Is Beyond Understanding (Judges 13:15-20)
Saturday, Dec. 16—All Authority (Matthew 28:11-18)
Sunday, Dec. 17—He Is Our Peace (Ephesians 2:11-18)

absence of conventional weapons of warfare. The Prince of Peace paid the price of peace, which was His own blood (Colossians 1:20). This peace remains the only true and lasting peace, for it is peace with God.

B. His Achievements (v. 7)

7. Of the increase of his government and peace there shall be no end, upon the throne of David, and upon his kingdom, to order it, and to establish it with judgment and with justice from henceforth even for ever. The zeal of the LORD of hosts will perform this.

Of the increase of his government and peace there shall be no end. Earthly governments usually expand through war, but the kingdom portrayed here thrives by means of peace, justice, and righteousness. The Messiah's kingdom shall have no end, either in time or extent.

The mention of the *throne of David* is another signpost marking this passage as messianic. David had been promised an everlasting kingdom (2 Samuel 7:12-16), a promise fulfilled in his greatest descendant, Jesus Christ (compare Luke 1:31-33). The Messiah's kingdom would be firmly established. Furthermore, it would be upheld and characterized by justice and righteousness, for ever. *The zeal of the Lord of hosts will perform this.* God's "jealousy" for His own honor, which involves His people's final triumph over the forces of evil, will cause all that is promised here to be fulfilled.

Conclusion

A. Christmas Lights

While Christmas is ideally a season of joy and celebration, a quick reality check will tell us that some amount of darkness envelops the lives of many people. Because of a serious illness, a financial crisis, a death in the family in the past year, or a similar experience, these persons may find the sounds of seasonal tunes and greetings of "Merry Christmas!" shallow and even a bit offensive.

As Christians we must remember that we are more than followers of the Light of the world;

visual 3

we *are* the light of the world (Matthew 5:14). We possess the power to dispel darkness. We must be especially sensitive to the concerns of those whose condition is reminiscent of the people in our text for today. These also have "walked in darkness," and their residence has become "the land of the shadow of death." The "light" of a visit, a card, a meal, or a gift can have an impact far beyond the Christmas season.

Someone has observed, "In Christ we move from P.M. to A.M." We who are His followers are called to have the same effect on others.

B. The Kingdom of Kingdoms

If Jesus Christ is the King of kings, then His church deserves to be regarded as the "Kingdom of kingdoms," or the greatest of all kingdoms. Many earthly kingdoms have sought justice and peace, but the methods they have used to achieve these often have been anything but just and peaceful. The kingdom of Jesus seeks justice, peace, and righteousness. Unlike the world, the church believes that only in a relationship with God through the Child promised by Isaiah can these become realities. Without God they are noble ideals, but remain like the carrot on the stick, ever out of reach.

Whenever the church has failed to sound a distinct message on behalf of Jesus Christ, it has lost the kind of impact it was meant to have in the world. When it has allowed the world to define peace, justice, and righteousness, the church has failed to be the bearer of "good tidings of great joy."

The hostility we see toward the Christian message today is in essence no different from that of Ahaz in Isaiah's day, Herod in Jesus' day, or Communism in this century. Psalm 2:2 reminds us, "The kings of the earth set themselves, and the rulers take counsel together, against the Lord, and against his Anointed." Let us remember that Ahaz, Herod, and Communism have come and gone; of the increase of Christ's government and peace, "there shall be no end."

C. Let Us Pray

Father in Heaven, thank You for sending Your Son as the light to dispel sin's darkness and gloom. Help us to understand that we must reflect Christ's light in the world today. May we not be overcome by the darkness of our time, but overcome the darkness with light. In the name of Jesus, amen.

D. Thought to Remember

Those who walk in the light of Jesus know true and lasting joy.

Learning by Doing

This page contains an alternate lesson plan emphasizing learning activities. Classes desiring such student involvement will find these suggestions helpful.

Learning Goals

As a result of this study of Isaiah 9:1-7, each adult learner will:

1. Be able to describe the conditions of the geographical area mentioned in Isaiah's prophecy.

2. Be able to draw a distinction between earthly kingdoms, and the Messiah's kingdom.

3. Reflect in mood and in deed the joy of the Christmas season.

Into the Lesson

(If you are using the clock/label idea from lesson 1, remember to add "A Time of JOY.")

Provide paper and pens for your students so they may take the following "Negative/Positive" test. Have each student write the numbers 1 through 29 down the left side of his or her sheet. After they have done that, tell them that you are going to read aloud a list of twenty-nine words. As you read each word, the students are to put a plus or minus sign on their sheets to indicate whether each word has a positive or negative connotation. Read this list clearly, but not too slowly: *dimness, vexation, afflict, darkness, light, shadow, death, shined, yoke, burden, rod, oppressor, battle, warrior, confused, noise, blood, burning, government, wonderful, counselor, mighty, everlasting, prince, peace, increase, throne, justice, forever.*

After you have completed the reading, ask your students to characterize their list of symbols; that is, to tell where most of the pluses and minuses are. They will indicate that most of their first symbols are minuses and that only at the end is there a significant number of pluses. Mention that these words are taken directly and in order from today's text and that the pattern of minuses and pluses reflects the nature of the content. Isaiah first describes the sad state of affairs, especially among the northern tribes of Israel, and only then follows the glorious future as the Messiah's light comes to that very area.

Into the Word

A map of the Holy Land in the time of Isaiah is important for an understanding of today's text. Such a map should show the kingdoms of Judah and Israel, the location of the areas occupied by the tribes of Zebulun and Naphtali, and the nation of Syria to the north. Refer to this map as you present the historical and geographical information included in the Lesson Background section and in the comments of explanation of today's text.

Have your students write the following statement on the back of the sheets used in the opening activity: "A Transformed Land: from ____ to ____ (vv. 1, 2); from ____ to ____ (v. 3); from ____ to ____ (vv. 4, 5)."

The lesson outline provides a sample of appropriate terms, but expect learners to suggest others. Have them give reasons for their choices. Having these verses read aloud in several versions may encourage a variety of answers as well as help the students' understanding of the verses.

For your consideration of verses 6 and 7, display eight unlit candles in simple candleholders. Have a ninth candle already lit for the purpose of lighting the other candles. Then darken your room as much as possible.

Use these candles for a reverent, worshipful reading of verse 6 in the following manner. Ask eight class members to come forward one at a time and light a candle as you slowly read the eight phrases relating to verse 6: "Unto us a child is born"; "Unto us a son is given"; "The government shall be upon his shoulder"; "His name will be Wonderful"; "His name is Counselor"; "His name is mighty God"; "He is everlasting Father"; "He is Prince of Peace." Once the verse is read and all the candles lit, turn the lights on again. Use the lesson writer's notes to explain the significance of each phrase. Separate each relevant candle from the rest as you discuss each phrase.

Then read verse 7 aloud. Ask how many put a minus sign for the word *government* in the initial class activity. Probably many did. Ask if they would change that minus for the context of verse 7. Ask them to explain why.

Into Life

Close with a prayer circle. Darken the room and have eight class members hold the candles and give God the thanksgiving He deserves for each of the eight truths of verse 6. If those who pray need direction, be prepared to hand them a slip of paper with the appropriate clause and prayer directive. For example, "A child is born"; thank God for the marvel of the incarnation: God became flesh and lived among us.

Let's Talk It Over

The questions on this page are designed to encourage review of the lesson
Scriptures and to promote discussion of the lesson by the class. The answers
provided are only discussion starters. Let your class talk it over from there.

1. What is our responsibility as Christians living in a spiritually darkened world, and how can we fulfill our responsibility?

The Scripture calls us to live as children of the light. Paul writes, "For you were once darkness, but now you are light in the Lord. Live as children of light" (Ephesians 5:8, *New International Version*). This means that we are to "shine as lights in the world," doing what we can to dispel the spiritual darkness that surrounds us (Philippians 2:15). We are to recognize the darkness for what it is, and live in stark contrast to that darkness. The purpose of this walk in the light is very similar to Israel's responsibility in ancient times. God's people were to be a light for the nations to come to know God, and we are to be a light to bring men to a knowledge of Jesus Christ. Paul quoted Isaiah in his response to the Jews who rejected the gospel, which he preached first to them: "For this is what the Lord has commanded us: 'I have made you a light for the Gentiles, that you may bring salvation to the ends of the earth'" (Acts 13:47, *New International Version*). To His followers Jesus said, "Ye are the light of the world" (Matthew 5:14). Israel failed. We must not fail!

2. One of the problems the people of Judah experienced was that they began to question God's faithfulness and the validity of His word. When God's word is rejected, something must fill the void. What are people turning to today?

Isaiah tells us in chapter 8 that the people eventually strayed so far from God as to consult mediums and spiritists. This is not unlike the current interest in New Age teaching. We humans need to experience a sense of transcendence, of rising above the normal limits of our existence, and if we do not find it in worship, prayer, and meditation on the Word of God, then we will seek it elsewhere. We are living in an era in which technology has become an extremely significant aspect of life every day. It provides great benefits to us, but it cannot meet our need in the spiritual dimension. It tends to leave us cold and calculating, insensitive and indifferent. As a result, people are searching elsewhere for personal meaning. In the course of that search, they often delve into the realm of spiritualism. The tragedy of all this is that it does not bring light to the darkness of our spiritual state. It only brings more darkness, and the results for us will be as unpleasant as they were for rebellious Judah (Isaiah 8:20-22).

3. Few expected that any help in their time of distress would come out of Galilee, yet that is precisely what happened. God has a way of bringing light out of darkness and hope out of hopelessness. What are some situations in your own life in which this has happened? Mention some examples from the Bible.

Allow your class members to share a few personal instances. Here are some biblical examples that might be mentioned: Ruth, the Moabite widow whose plight seemed hopeless, told Naomi, her mother-in-law, who was of Israel, "Your God shall be my God." Soon Ruth became the wife of Boaz and the mother of Obed, an ancestor of Jesus. Esther, the Jewish orphan girl who became the queen of Persia, ultimately saved Mordecai and the Jewish people. She could not have anticipated that she might be the one used to turn the course of history for the Jewish people. From the darkness of their circumstances, they experienced "light, and gladness, and joy, and honor" (Esther 8:16). That certainly was an unexpected turn of events. The Samaritan woman at the well in Sychar, whose life was filled with disappointment and disillusionment, never would have believed that her testimony could result in many Samaritans becoming believers (John 4:39).

4. The search for peace in our world is unending. Why is peace so elusive? What will be necessary for real peace to be achieved?

For most persons, peace is defined as the cessation of conflict, whether it be between individuals or nations. However, such a state is only conditional. The circumstances or conditions that currently exist make peace possible, but if there is any change in those circumstances, peace may vanish very quickly. Real peace is possible only when justice and righteousness are in the land. (See Isaiah 59:8, *New International Version*.) This begins in the heart of man. Until we come to the place where our hearts are right with God, they will never be right with others.

A Time of Righteousness and Peace

DEVOTIONAL READING: Hebrews 8:6-12.

LESSON SCRIPTURE: Isaiah 11:1-9; Luke 2:1-20.

PRINTED TEXT: Isaiah 11:1-6; Luke 2:10-14.

Isaiah 11:1-6

1 And there shall come forth a rod out of the stem of Jesse, and a Branch shall grow out of his roots:

2 And the Spirit of the LORD shall rest upon him, the spirit of wisdom and understanding, the spirit of counsel and might, the spirit of knowledge and of the fear of the LORD;

3 And shall make him of quick understanding in the fear of the LORD. And he shall not judge after the sight of his eyes, neither reprove after the hearing of his ears:

4 But with righteousness shall he judge the poor, and reprove with equity for the meek of the earth: and he shall smite the earth with the rod of his mouth, and with the breath of his lips shall he slay the wicked.

5 And righteousness shall be the girdle of his loins, and faithfulness the girdle of his reins.

6 The wolf also shall dwell with the lamb, and the leopard shall lie down with the kid; and the calf and the young lion and the fatling together; and a little child shall lead them.

Luke 2:10-14

10 And the angel said unto them, Fear not: for, behold, I bring you good tidings of great joy, which shall be to all people.

11 For unto you is born this day in the city of David a Saviour, which is Christ the Lord.

12 And this shall be a sign unto you; Ye shall find the babe wrapped in swaddling clothes, lying in a manger.

13 And suddenly there was with the angel a multitude of the heavenly host praising God, and saying,

14 Glory to God in the highest, and on earth peace, good will toward men.

GOLDEN TEXT: The wolf also shall dwell with the lamb, and the leopard shall lie down with the kid; and the calf and the young lion and the fatling together; and a little child shall lead them.—Isaiah 11:6.

God's Promise of Deliverance (Isaiah)

Unit 1: The Coming of a New Day
(Lessons 1-5)

Lesson Aims

As a result of this lesson, students should:

1. Understand how Jesus fulfilled Isaiah's prophecy.

2. Distinguish between the peace Jesus came to bring and the peace the world seeks.

3. Sense the atmosphere of wonder surrounding the night in which Jesus was born.

Lesson Outline

INTRODUCTION
  A. The Christmas Presence
  B. Lesson Background
 I. THE PROMISED MESSIAH (Isaiah 11:1, 2)
  A. His Human Side (v. 1)
  B. His Heavenly Side (v. 2)
 II. THE PRIORITIES OF MESSIAH'S REIGN (Isaiah 11:3-5)
  A. Impartial Judgment (v. 3)
  Circumstantial Evidence
  B. Compassion for the Needy (v. 4a)
  C. Condemnation for the Wicked (v. 4b)
  D. Righteousness and Faithfulness (v. 5)
 III. THE PEACE OF MESSIAH'S KINGDOM (Isaiah 11:6)
 IV. THE PROMISE HAS COME! (Luke 2:10-14)
  A. A Savior for All (vv. 10, 11)
  B. A Sign for the Shepherds (v. 12)
  C. A Message for the Ages (vv. 13, 14)
  Harold, the Singing Angel
CONCLUSION
  A. Jesus Makes the Difference
  B. Let Us Pray
  C. Thought to Remember

Isaiah's description of the Messiah's peaceful reign is illustrated by visual 4 of the visuals packet. The visual is shown on page 149.

Introduction

A. The Christmas Presence

Today's lesson falls on the Sunday before Christmas, which this year also is Christmas Eve. By this time, many households have had a Christmas tree up for a number of days or even weeks. All that is missing now are the presents that will be placed under the tree.

One of the most enchanting and heartwarming Christmas traditions is a brightly and beautifully decorated tree. Many persons have joyous memories of family members trudging through the snow to track down just the right tree. Today the varied lights and ornaments available for decorating the tree produce some dazzling displays.

Let us now consider the "tree" mentioned in today's lesson text from Isaiah 11. From the standpoint of appearance, it hardly seems worth comparing with the richly adorned trees that we have come to associate with Christmas. The tree of which Isaiah spoke was but a mere stump.

Let us not be fooled by appearances, however. Isaiah's ordinary stump sent out an extraordinary shoot, the "Branch" who would grow to become "beautiful and glorious" (Isaiah 4:2). It should not surprise us, therefore, to learn that the announcement of the birth of the One who was that Branch was first made to lowly shepherds, or that He was born amid humble surroundings.

Every person, no matter what his or her status in this life may be, can take encouragement from the fact that Jesus was born into the simplest of surroundings. Those surroundings help to draw our attention to the real message of this season. Christmas has never depended upon the *presents* one receives, but only on the *presence* of Jesus.

B. Lesson Background

In last week's lesson, we saw the importance of considering the context of a Scripture passage. Isaiah's prophecy of a "great light" (Isaiah 9:2) was spoken only after he had painted a vivid picture of the darkness produced by Israel's sin (8:19-22). Likewise, the prophecy in today's lesson text of a coming "Branch" is related to what precedes it. It was the climax to a series of messages using trees (or a similar type of vegetation) to symbolize nations.

Following the prophecy of the Child who would reign upon David's throne (9:6, 7), Isaiah returned to the theme of judgment, addressed chiefly to the kingdom of Israel and its irresponsible leadership (vv. 8-17). As early as 9:18, he was laying the groundwork for the prophecy to appear in chapter 11: "For wickedness burneth as the fire: it shall devour the briers and thorns, and shall kindle in the thickets of the forest, and they shall mount up like the lifting up of smoke." The nation of Israel was going to be overrun by the Assyrians; the devastation inflicted on the land would be most severe. And God would use the Assyrians to chastise the kingdom of Judah as well.

With chapter 10, verse 5, Isaiah's oracle of judgment takes a sudden turn eastward and comes down with full force upon the Assyrian empire. Assyria, whom God had chosen to use as an instrument to punish His people, has become intoxicated with a desire to ravage as many nations as possible, including Judah with its capital city, Jerusalem (v. 11). Assyria's lust for conquest has gone out of control. God will not stand for such a "stout heart" (v. 12), and He promises to rise up and put a stop to the Assyrian war machine. The divine judgment that will fall upon Assyria is the subject of verses 15-19. Note the imagery Isaiah uses in verse 19 to describe the outcome of that judgment: "And the rest of the trees of his forest shall be few, that a child may write them."

In verse 20, the prophet turns his attention once again to Israel, in order to compare its destiny with the fate of Assyria. Here his words carry a tone of optimism and hope, in anticipation of what the beginning of chapter 11 will promise. In 10:20-22, Isaiah refers to a "remnant" of Israel who will return to God following His judgment of them that would be carried out by the Assyrians. And although Judah will suffer greatly at the hands of the Assyrians, God's people are not to fear them. God will rescue His people (vv. 24, 25).

God's people needed to remember that He is the Master Forester, with the power to uproot and plant trees (nations) as He desires. Within one century from the time of Isaiah, the curtain fell on Assyria, ending her role in the history of empires. For His people, however, God had other plans.

The second part of our lesson text comes from a very familiar portion of Scripture. In fact, Luke's account of the birth of Jesus has become so familiar that we may fail to appreciate the astonishing content of the angel's message to the shepherds. May we in this season recapture the sense of wonder the shepherds felt when they received the good news of the Savior's birth.

I. The Promised Messiah
(Isaiah 11:1, 2)

A. His Human Side (v. 1)

1. And there shall come forth a rod out of the stem of Jesse, and a Branch shall grow out of his roots.

In chapter 10 mighty Assyria was compared with a forest that was to be cut down by God's judgment, never again to rise (vv. 17-19, 33, 34). Israel too was cut down as a result of the judgment of God, but there was hope for Israel's future—the time would come when new life

would spring up from that which appeared dead. A *rod* or "tender shoot" would come *out of the stem* [or more accurately, "stump"] *of Jesse*. The *stem of Jesse* refers to the house of David, for there is but one Jesse mentioned in Scripture, and that is David's father.

The nation eventually recovered from the devastation brought on by the invasions of the Assyrians and later the Babylonians. Clearly, however, an individual is spoken of in this verse, and that one is Jesus Christ, who was David's greatest descendant. The New Testament attests to this (see Revelation 22:16; compare Romans 15:12). When Jesus was born, Herod was king of Judea; and the line of David, once the line of nobility, was reduced to common life. From an ancient family whose glory was all but gone arose One more glorious than David had ever been.

B. His Heavenly Side (v. 2)

2. And the Spirit of the LORD shall rest upon him, the spirit of wisdom and understanding, the spirit of counsel and might, the spirit of knowledge and of the fear of the LORD.

After indicating that the Messiah would be descended from the human line of David, Isaiah began to focus upon those divine qualities that would distinguish Him from all others and would prove the Messiah to be the perfect Ruler.

The Spirit of the Lord shall rest upon him. Isaiah was clearly referring to how God would equip the Messiah for His task. Certainly leaders throughout the Old Testament (such as the judges) were given the Holy Spirit for specific purposes, but the Spirit would *"rest upon"* or continually lead the promised Branch. Thus did Jesus possess the Spirit "without limit" (John 3:34, *New International Version*).

The qualities that would be manifested in the Messiah through the power of the Spirit are named in a series of pairs. The first is "wisdom and understanding." The One who described himself as "greater than Solomon" (Matthew 12:42) possessed wisdom "without limit." This embraces intellectual power and the ability to perceive moral truth.

The terms *counsel and might* bring to mind last week's Scripture text, which indicated that the promised Child was to be called "Counselor" and "The mighty God." The Messiah would have practical knowledge, enabling Him to instruct and guide His people, together with the power to execute His decisions. Concerning the final pair, *knowledge* and *the fear of the Lord,* the prepositional phrase *of the Lord* can be understood as applying equally to both the knowledge and the fear. To fear God and to know Him was at the heart of Old Testament religion. Proverbs 1:7 says, "The fear of the Lord is the beginning of knowledge." For Jesus to have possessed these two qualities distinguished Him as the truly godly man and as the sum total of what the Old Testament described as a righteous individual.

II. The Priorities of Messiah's Reign (Isaiah 11:3-5)

A. Impartial Judgment (v. 3)

3. And shall make him of quick understanding in the fear of the LORD. And he shall not judge after the sight of his eyes, neither reprove after the hearing of his ears.

Of quick understanding in the fear of the Lord. The Hebrew text literally reads, "and his smelling [will be] in the fear of the Lord." The *New International Version* renders this, "He will delight in the fear of the Lord." Desiring something or finding delight in it was often expressed by means of the symbolism of smelling. It may be compared with the intensely competitive athlete who speaks of "smelling victory." Old Testament sacrifices were said to provide a "sweet savor" or aroma to the Lord (Leviticus 1:17, for example), indicating His approval of them. The phrase, therefore, describes the Messiah's high degree of commitment to pleasing God.

Isaiah then highlighted the Messiah's work as judge. It is interesting, in light of the preceding explanation of "smelling," that Isaiah mentioned two other senses, seeing and hearing. For the Messiah to judge accurately He would have to know more than what was available by means of the eyes and ears. Being empowered by God's Spirit, He would be able to discern the hearts of people (1 Samuel 16:7; John 2:24, 25). His judgment would be just (John 5:30).

Home Daily Bible Readings

Monday, Dec. 18—No Love, No Kinship (1 John 4:1-12)

Tuesday, Dec. 19—Love Perfected (1 John 4:13-21)

Wednesday, Dec. 20—Memory With Hope (Genesis 9:8-17)

Thursday, Dec. 21—Immanuel, God With Us (Isaiah 7:10-17)

Friday, Dec. 22—Preparation of Zechariah (Luke 1:5-17)

Saturday, Dec. 23—Announcement to Mary (Luke 1:26-38)

Sunday, Dec. 24—A Marvelous Birth (Luke 2:1-7)

CIRCUMSTANTIAL EVIDENCE

Good mystery writers keep readers off balance by leading them wrongly to believe that various innocent characters committed the crime (usually murder), until a surprise ending reveals "whodunit" (usually someone the reader never suspected).

Sometimes readers are led on "wild goose chases" by circumstantial evidence. A character is seen at the scene of the crime; her fingerprints are discovered on the murder weapon; or his car is identical to the one supposedly driven by the killer. None of these bits of evidence is proof sufficient to convict a defendant in court. Smart judges and juries regard such evidence as inconclusive.

True justice requires consideration of more than incriminating appearances. The Messiah prophesied by Isaiah "seeth not as man seeth; for . . . the Lord looketh on the heart" (1 Samuel 16:7). His justice is perfect. And His followers are cautioned: "Judge not according to the appearance, but judge righteous judgment" (John 7:24). Christians must overcome personal biases. Circumstantial evidence is not trustworthy.

—R. W. B.

B. Compassion for the Needy (v. 4a)

4a. But with righteousness shall he judge the poor, and reprove with equity for the meek of the earth.

Throughout history the poor have been victims of injustice and oppression. They have been discriminated against in favor of the wealthy and powerful. The Messiah, however, would not side with the rich against the poor; He would see to it that the poor received impartial judgment. The humble and downtrodden would receive from Him consideration equal to that accorded any others.

In the Sermon on the Mount, Jesus referred to the "poor in spirit" and the "meek" as those who would be "blessed" (Matthew 5:3, 5). There may be a reference here to these persons. But the main idea of the verse is that Jesus would be a friend of the poor, the oppressed, the downtrodden, and would treat them with fairness.

C. Condemnation for the Wicked (v. 4b)

4b. And he shall smite the earth with the rod of his mouth, and with the breath of his lips shall he slay the wicked.

The Hebrew word for *rod* is used in the Old Testament to describe a tool of chastisement or punishment. The prophet Isaiah used the word when speaking of Assyria, the "rod" of divine anger (10:5). The verse before us tells us that the very words of Christ will bring judgment upon *the wicked*. He will speak with authority, and what He says will be carried into effect instantly. In the last day, His spoken word will seal the eternal destiny of all the nations (see Matthew 25:31-46).

D. Righteousness and Faithfulness (v. 5)

5. And righteousness shall be the girdle of his loins, and faithfulness the girdle of his reins.

Isaiah concluded his description of the Branch's personal characteristics by saying that *righteousness* (already mentioned in verse 4) and *faithfulness* would be as a girdle or belt tied around His waist. In ancient times a man who was about to engage in an activity that required physical exertion and freedom of movement would gather up his loose outer garment and tuck it under his belt so his garment would not hinder Him. All of Jesus' actions were characterized by commitment to His Father's righteous purpose and faithfulness to truth (compare Ephesians 6:14). These were always as close to Him as the belt or sash around His waist, and they characterized His nature.

III. The Peace of Messiah's Kingdom (Isaiah 11:6)

6. The wolf also shall dwell with the lamb, and the leopard shall lie down with the kid; and the calf and the young lion and the fatling together; and a little child shall lead them.

Isaiah's fondness for images taken from the created world produced a wide range of striking word pictures throughout his book. This verse contains one of the most memorable of them. It served to emphasize the degree of change that the Messiah of whom he has been writing would bring about through His labors. Animals that no one would dream of placing in pairs were pictured as living in a state of harmony and bliss. Supervising this incredible transformation of character would be a little child.

How should this scene be understood? It is important to observe the manner in which the New Testament interprets Isaiah's imagery. For example, the changes of land features that are described in Isaiah 40:3, 4 are declared fulfilled in the ministry of John the Baptist (Luke 3:1-6). There the language of Isaiah is viewed as symbolic of the impact that John the Baptist's ministry would have. Perhaps the same could be said of the verse before us now. The changes wrought in people's lives through the gospel of Jesus Christ and the once-impregnable barriers that have crumbled by the power of His love have produced friends and comrades among

visual 4

people whose animosity at one time seemed permanent.

At the same time, there is something to be said for a view that sees verse 6 of our text as a portrayal of conditions under the reign of the Messiah, when the gospel shall have accomplished its full effects in all the nations, when "the earth shall be full of the knowledge of the Lord" (Isaiah 11:9). The Scriptures indicate that the created world is waiting "on tiptoe" (Romans 8:19, J. B. Phillips) for its liberation from bondage (8:21). The establishment of peace between animals that have long been bitter enemies may be included in Isaiah's prophecy, thus constituting part of the restoration of a sin-cursed world to divine wholeness.

IV. The Promise Has Come! (Luke 2:10-14)

The final portion of our printed text is taken from Luke's timeless account of the birth of Jesus. This was He of whom the prophet Isaiah had spoken nearly seven hundred years earlier, and of whom we have been studying in the preceding portion of our Scripture text. To lowly shepherds tending their flocks at night in a field near Bethlehem came the wonderful news of the Messiah's birth.

A. A Savior for All (vv. 10, 11)

10, 11. And the angel said unto them, Fear not: for, behold, I bring you good tidings of great joy, which shall be to all people. For unto you is born this day in the city of David a Saviour, which is Christ the Lord.

The words *Fear not* make up one of the most important watchwords in the Gospels. The same angelic command was issued on the morning of Jesus' resurrection (Matthew 28:5). Thus the ministry of Jesus to the world was introduced and climaxed with the banishment of fear.

Good tidings. The good news was that a *Saviour* had been born unto them. It was He who would "save his people from their sins" (Matthew 1:21). Through His death and resurrection Jesus made it possible for *great joy* to come to *all people*. Both the empty cross and the empty tomb are signs that He is the Savior and that He reigns as *Christ the Lord* (Acts 2:36).

The mention of the *city of David* (Bethlehem) here and in verse 4, plus the reference to the "house and lineage of David" in verse 4, testified to the important link between David and Jesus. Luke was identifying this newborn child as the One who would fulfill such prophecies as those we have been studying.

B. A Sign for the Shepherds (v. 12)

12. And this shall be a sign unto you; Ye shall find the babe wrapped in swaddling clothes, lying in a manger.

The angel gave the shepherds a way by which they would know the message was true. At one and the same time it would unmistakably identify which baby born in Bethlehem that day was the Messiah. (It would seem that in a small town the size of Bethlehem few babies would have been born on any given day.) *Ye shall find the babe wrapped in swaddling clothes, lying in a manger.* It would not have been unusual to find a baby wrapped in swaddling clothes. They were the ancient equivalent of the modern receiving blanket. However, the sight of a new baby obviously cared for with love and tenderness yet cradled in the feed trough of a stable would be so unusual as to make identity of the Christ child absolutely certain.

C. A Message for the Ages (vv. 13, 14)

13, 14. And suddenly there was with the angel a multitude of the heavenly host praising God, and saying, Glory to God in the highest, and on earth peace, good will toward men.

The wondrous news of the birth of God's Son was so exciting that Heaven's angels could not keep silent. It was impossible for only one of them to announce it! But the real impact of the coming of Jesus was to be experienced on earth. The phrase translated *good will toward men,* is literally "to men of good will." The angels were announcing the arrival of peace "in men"—that is, peace that an individual can possess if one chooses to order one's life according to God's *good will* or purpose.

In this season, "peace on earth" is treated as a highly noble and desirable ideal that is somehow in the power of man to attain. This is a perspective in direct opposition to what the angels declared in the fields near Bethlehem. Jesus came for the very reason that man cannot achieve real peace through his own agenda.

Without Jesus Christ, peace will remain ever in the realm of elusive possibility. With Him, any person can possess a peace that "passeth all understanding" (Philippians 4:7).

HAROLD, THE SINGING ANGEL

Kids are a "trip." No wonder they are precious in God's sight. Their innocent, literal interpretation of life is charming, and sometimes disarming. Often we are unaware that they have misunderstood what we simply take for granted.

Small children frequently mistranslate hymns. You may have heard of one young Sunday school scholar who went home singing, "what Harold, the angel, sang!"

To be technically correct, the "herald angels" were "praising God, and *saying. . . .*" Whether they spoke or sang, however, is not important. But their message is of utmost significance. "Peace" and "good will"—that's the good news that we celebrate at Christmas. The announcement of Christ's coming captured the imaginations of shepherds and kings. The reality of His peace thrills the hearts of all who receive Him.

His *presence* is the best of all presents!

—R. W. B.

Conclusion

A. Jesus Makes the Difference

We know the Christmas story so well; we have heard it so often! But is the story so familiar to us that we lose our sense of wonder at the events of that remarkable night in Bethlehem? Consider the surroundings: a smelly stable, the usual farm animals, common shepherds, a simple peasant couple, a manger filled with hay. And lying on that hay in the feed trough was Jesus, in the middle of it all. The stable became a sanctuary.

The circumstances of our lives may not always be pleasant. If Jesus is enthroned in our hearts, however, even the dire situations we face will undergo change. If the Savior is at the center of our lives, turmoil will give way to peace, sadness will turn to joy, and despair will be replaced by hope. Jesus makes the difference.

B. Let Us Pray

Father, may we in this season of giving remember to *receive* the gift that you placed in Bethlehem's manger. Thank You for sending just the gift we needed. In His name we pray. Amen.

C. Thought to Remember

"May we keep Christmas in our hearts, that we may be kept in its hope."

—PETER MARSHALL

Learning by Doing

This page contains an alternate lesson plan emphasizing learning activities. Classes desiring such student involvement will find these suggestions helpful.

Learning Goals

As a result of studying and comparing the two texts in this lesson, the learner will:

1. Highlight the texts' matched and mismatched pairs (as defined in this lesson plan).

2. Be able to explain how Jesus fulfills the characteristics Isaiah noted regarding the Messiah who was to come.

3. Notice the matched and mismatched pairs in contemporary Christmas celebration.

Into the Lesson

Sometime during the week before class, ask one of the amateur horticulturists among your class members to bring a variety of plants to display as class begins. Make the suggestion that this person bring one or more of the following kinds of plants: a rhizome, a bulb plant, a seed plant, and/or a bonsai. Have the person briefly explain how each plant regenerates itself and grows. Ask the person to speak of the role of pruning in order to enhance the growth of plants. Such a brief discussion will provide a helpful background for your consideration of verse 1 of the Scripture text for this lesson. Picture Israel as a tree, cut to stump, but with a new shoot growing up.

As an alternate introduction, bring enough flower bulbs to leave one on each seat. As the members arrive and notice or pick up the bulbs, direct their attention to the words "DEAD or ALIVE?" that you have displayed prominently in large letters at the front of the classroom. As class begins, ask the question, "Are these bulbs dead or alive?" Anticipate the students' comments on the bulbs' dormancy and their *potential* for new growth. Read verse 1 of the text and note that Isaiah prophesied that Israel would be in that same dormant, seemingly dead but potentially alive, condition. Read Galatians 4:3, 4 and note that when all conditions were just right, God reintroduced life for Israel in the person of Jesus Christ.

Into the Word

The student book that accompanies this series contains the following puzzle and activity. If you do not use the student book, reproduce this puzzle, either on poster board or on an overhead transparency. Have today's Scripture texts read aloud, and then ask your group to find the pairs

of words that are, in some manner, connected in the texts. Each pair of words either crosses or "touches" in the puzzle. Here are the pairs to be found: animals *and* child, branch *and* roots, calf *and* lion, counsel *and* might, ear *and* eye, fear *and* joy, kid *and* leopard, knowledge *and* fear, judge *and* reprove, good *and* great, loin *and* reins, manger *and* babe, mouth *and* lips, poor *and* meek, rod *and* stem, sight *and* hearing, wisdom *and* understanding, wolf *and* lamb.

```
H L I P S W R I G H T E O
T U S N K I D R A P O E L
U N D E R S T A N D I N G
O F E S T D S P E R A E C
M E J O Y O E B R A Y I G
B A O L H M A N G E R P T
E R O D S B L E S N U O C
S I A T E D M K E E M O A
N O E N O U S I F E A R L
I M N O C E S S G P E I F
E A G C E H S D R H O I G
R E P R O V E L R N T P T
E H T E E L O A A U S H C
G N E S W A S P R M G H E
D A C O E O T R I I I G H
U T N B M A L E S L N N O
J K U S N E S F D S P G A
```

As the pairs are found and identified, write them where all can see them. When all are found, ask your learners to label each with the verse number where each pair is found. Also ask if each is a "matched" or "mismatched" set. For example, babe *and* manger is a mismatched set, because these two do not normally "go together."

Into Life

Have your students work in groups of four to make two lists: "Christmas Matched Pairs" and "Christmas Mismatched Pairs." For example: Worship *and* Carols (matched—they "go together"; "Santa *and* Stable" (mismatched); "Gifts *and* Christmas Day" (matched). Have the groups share their lists and see if there is general agreement. Direct your adults to take notice of such matched and mismatched pairs this Christmas season.

Let's Talk It Over

The questions on this page are designed to encourage review of the lesson Scriptures and to promote discussion of the lesson by the class. The answers provided are only discussion starters. Let your class talk it over from there.

1. The description in Isaiah 11:2-4 of the Messiah includes characteristics long considered desirable in any leader: wisdom, understanding, knowledge, strength of character, impartial judgment, and the fear of the Lord. Which of these characteristics are considered important in leadership today? To what extent?

If we are thinking of Christian leadership, it is clear that each of these qualities is absolutely essential. A church is unlikely to rise above the level of the character and commitment of its leadership. If we are to fulfill the mission Christ has given us, then we must model His leadership character and style. He describes that style in Matthew 20:24-28 and 23:1-12.

In the world, however, these qualities are not always thought of as important. Many seem to be more impressed with shrewdness than with wisdom and understanding, with positional power rather than strength of character, and with corporate and political influence rather than with impartial judgment. When leaders in the world are selected, rarely is it considered important that they possess a "fear of the Lord." In fact, some consider it to be a handicap in today's society. This may explain why national and world affairs are in such disarray today.

2. Isaiah stated that the Spirit of the Lord would rest upon the Messiah (11:2), enabling Him always to exhibit the qualities mentioned in question 1. To what extent do you think these qualities are available to the Christian who is "filled with the Spirit"? (Ephesians 5:18).

Isaiah clearly indicated that the Messiah would possess these qualities in a superior way. Jesus' knowledge and understanding were definitely beyond the limits that even the most mature Christian possesses. His understanding of what was in a person's heart, and His ability to know what was beyond ordinary knowledge were apparent many times during His ministry. These abilities were all a part of His messianic credentials and confirmed His mission and role on earth.

Jesus' promise that He would ask the Father to send us another Comforter "the Spirit of truth" (John 14:17)—assures us that we do not have to rely solely upon our own resources. And Paul stated that there were those in the early church to whom the Spirit had given the special gifts of wisdom and knowledge (1 Corinthians 12:8). However, Galatians 5:22, 23 suggests that the presence of the Holy Spirit in a Christian's life will be shown more by that person's character and personality traits than by the possession of supernatural gifts. For the most part, the New Testament teaches that we are diligently to seek to develop these traits of character and personality in our lives (2 Peter 1:5-7). Our effectiveness as Christ's ambassadors depends on it.

3. One of the characteristics of the Messiah's ministry was His compassion for the needy. How can we, the church, emulate Christ in expressing this same concern?

Jesus was able to identify the whole need of persons. He was not unwilling to respond to their physical and material needs, but He was unwilling to limit His response to those needs. This may be the missing dimension in much of what the world offers in terms of compassion. People may have homes to live in, food on their tables, clothes on their backs, and still be terribly lonely, empty, and unfulfilled. We may need to check our ministry to those in need to be certain that their spiritual needs, as well as material needs, are being met.

4. In Isaiah 11:6-9 the prophet paints a picture of the Messiah's kingdom when His reign is complete. It is a picture of tranquillity, trust, and peace. It is a world without fear. How different is that world from our present reality, even though the desire for that ideal world seems universal! What must we do as individuals to experience personally a measure of the blessing of such a perfect state?

We must come to Christ in faith, trusting Him implicitly. We must begin to exhibit those qualities in our relationships that build trust and harmony. We must model to the world the kind of character and values that encourage integrity and mutual concern. We must return good for evil, kindness for indifference, and love for hatred. In short, we must be like Jesus!

A Time for Sharing Good News

DEVOTIONAL READING: Romans 15:15-21.

LESSON SCRIPTURE: Isaiah 60, 61.

PRINTED TEXT: Isaiah 60:1-4; 61:1-4.

Isaiah 60:1-4

1 Arise, shine; for thy light is come, and the glory of the LORD is risen upon thee.

2 For, behold, the darkness shall cover the earth, and gross darkness the people: but the LORD shall arise upon thee, and his glory shall be seen upon thee.

3 And the Gentiles shall come to thy light, and kings to the brightness of thy rising.

4 Lift up thine eyes round about, and see: all they gather themselves together, they come to thee: thy sons shall come from far, and thy daughters shall be nursed at thy side.

Isaiah 61:1-4

1 The Spirit of the Lord GOD is upon me; because the LORD hath anointed me to preach good tidings unto the meek; he hath sent me to bind up the brokenhearted, to proclaim liberty to the captives, and the opening of the prison to them that are bound;

2 To proclaim the acceptable year of the LORD, and the day of vengeance of our God; to comfort all that mourn;

3 To appoint unto them that mourn in Zion, to give unto them beauty for ashes, the oil of joy for mourning, the garment of praise for the spirit of heaviness; that they might be called Trees of righteousness, The planting of the LORD, that he might be glorified.

4 And they shall build the old wastes, they shall raise up the former desolations, and they shall repair the waste cities, the desolations of many generations.

GOLDEN TEXT: The LORD hath anointed me to preach good tidings unto the meek; he hath sent me to bind up the brokenhearted, to proclaim liberty to the captives, and the opening of the prison to them that are bound.—Isaiah 61:1.

God's Promise of Deliverance (Isaiah)
Unit 1: The Coming of a New Day
(Lessons 1-5)

Lesson Aims

As a result of this lesson, students should:

1. Understand that the redeemed are to share the good news of Christ with those living in the darkness of sin.

2. Explain how Jesus fulfilled the prophecy in Isaiah 61:1-4, and how Christians in turn are continuing its fulfillment.

3. Resolve to take the good news of salvation to a world besieged by bad news.

Lesson Outline

INTRODUCTION

    A. The Reason for *All* Seasons

    B. Lesson Background

I. THE BENEFICIARIES OF GOOD NEWS (Isaiah 60:1-4)

    A. The Lord's People (vv. 1, 2)

    B. The Nations of the World (vv. 3, 4)

    Power of Light

II. THE BEARER OF GOOD NEWS (Isaiah 61:1-4)

    A. Compelled by Divine Power (v. 1a)

    B. Committed to Rebuilding People (vv. 1b-3)

    God's New Year

    C. Committed to Rebuilding Places (v. 4)

CONCLUSION

    A. "So Send I You"

    B. Let Us Pray

    C. Thought to Remember

Visual 5 of the visuals packet conveys the good news that lives broken by sin can be repaired by God's anointed One. The visual is shown on page 156.

Introduction

A. The Reason for *All* Seasons

When the holidays have passed, many who made the effort to "put Christ back into Christmas" will slip back into their former routines. Perhaps they wish deep down that somehow the "spirit of Christmas"—the feelings of love, joy, peace, and goodwill—could last the entire year.

As Christians we know that such a wish *can* come true, because Christmas is much more than a season or a spirit; it is God's good news

concerning the Savior. Because He himself is the very source of life, His influence cannot be confined to any one month or segment of the year. Jesus is not just the reason for the season; He is the reason for living itself.

More than seeing Christ put back into Christmas, the world needs to see Him put into daily life on a consistent basis. That responsibility falls on the shoulders of us who are called to overcome the darkness with His light in His name.

B. Lesson Background

Today's lesson is taken from the second part of Isaiah's prophetic writings (chapters 40-66). The important themes that characterize Isaiah's prophecies in chapters 1-39 are present with equal power in chapters 40-66. Among them are the "bad news" of God's judgment on Israel and the "good news" of His deliverance and salvation. These themes are prominent in the chapters preceding the printed text for this lesson. Isaiah 57 and 58 dwell on various sins and abuses in Israel that produced her sad condition. Chapter 59 contains Isaiah's declaration that the burden of responsibility in addressing Israel's plight lay with Israel.

Following Isaiah's summary of Israel's sins, God is pictured as surveying His chosen nation's desperate condition. Isaiah 59:16 describes what the Lord saw. There was no one to champion the cause of the weak and innocent against the oppressors in Israel, much less anyone to deliver Israel from its heathen enemies. The verse carries the reader from the depth of man's sinfulness to the heights of divine grace. Clearly, God was pledging himself to do for His people what they were unable to do for themselves.

After God's "adversaries" and "enemies" had been punished, penitent Israel would be saved by the coming of the Messiah (vv. 18, 20). Isaiah takes no note of periods of time, and his prophecy of the deliverance of Israel blends into a vision of triumphant deliverance and continuing spiritual life in the Redeemer's (Messiah's) kingdom (v. 21). The beginning of chapter 60 elaborates upon the glorious results of the execution of God's plan of human redemption. The beginning of chapter 61 focuses on the unique individual who would fulfill the plan.

I. The Beneficiaries of Good News (Isaiah 60:1-4)

A. The Lord's People (vv. 1, 2)

1, 2. Arise, shine; for thy light is come, and the glory of the LORD is risen upon thee. For, behold, the darkness shall cover the earth, and gross darkness the people: but the LORD shall

arise upon thee, and his glory shall be seen upon thee.

The people addressed in Isaiah 59:2 as those whose sins separated them from God are now encouraged to bask in the divine light that has arisen to dispel their darkness. Their former pitiful condition is described in 59:9: "Therefore is judgment far from us, neither doth justice overtake us: we wait for light, but behold obscurity; for brightness, but we walk in darkness." It is a scenario reminiscent of that found in the text of our lesson two weeks ago: "The people that walked in darkness have seen a great light: they that dwell in the land of the shadow of death, upon them hath the light shined" (Isaiah 9:2).

The source of this wondrous light is captured in the phrase, *"the glory of the Lord."* Although there is a sense in which "the whole earth is full of [God's] glory" (Isaiah 6:3), Isaiah also predicted a time when the glory of God would be "revealed" to all mankind (Isaiah 40:5). Such exalted language as this must find its true fulfillment only in that historic moment recorded in John 1:14: "And the Word was made flesh, and dwelt among us, (and we beheld his glory, the glory as of the only begotten of the Father,) full of grace and truth."

For, behold, the darkness shall cover the earth. Not just Israel, but the whole earth and all the nations were enshrouded in spiritual darkness. Upon Israel, however, a glory dawned, coming from God himself. In this glory Israel was to stand, and then the results indicated in the following verse would occur.

B. The Nations of the World (vv. 3, 4)

3. And the Gentiles shall come to thy light, and kings to the brightness of thy rising.

When Isaiah announced the coming of God's light to dispel sin's darkness, he went on to describe the light's global impact. The *"The Gentiles"* or "nations" would be astonished by the glory radiating from Israel and they would be drawn to it. Isaiah had spoken earlier of the conversion of the Gentiles in coming to Jerusalem: "And it shall come to pass in the last days, that the mountain of the Lord's house shall be established in the top of the mountains, and shall be exalted above the hills; and all nations shall flow unto it" (Isaiah 2:2; see also verses 3, 4).

Among those turning to the light of the Lord would be *kings.* In Old Testament times, kings, even those who ruled God's people, often corrupted or openly opposed the worship of God. The psalmist observed, "The kings of the earth set themselves, and the rulers take counsel together, against the Lord, and against his Anointed" (Psalm 2:2). The New Testament

records Herod the Great's attempts to destroy the Christ child, whom he saw as a threat.

Isaiah predicted a radical transformation in the attitude of kings toward the Lord. In so doing, he touched on the power of the gospel to change even the most proud and rebellious individuals. The apostle John, in his description of the new Jerusalem, saw the consummation of Isaiah's prophecy: "And the nations of them which are saved shall walk in the light of it: and the kings of the earth do bring their glory and honor into it" (Revelation 21:24).

POWER OF LIGHT

Has anyone ever discovered why flying insects are attracted to light? Moths destroy themselves flying through flame. A modern device attracts winged insects to its light and exterminates them on contact.

Bright lights attract human interest, too. Neon lights, strobes, lasers, and even candlelight—they all have peculiar fascination, particularly when seen against stark darkness.

Isaiah heartened Judah (and us) with his prophecy of the coming light—"the glory of the Lord" (v. 1). The "light of the world," Jesus Christ, appeared in the black midnight of man's sin and despair. He showed us the way out; indeed, He was, and is, the only way out. In Him is forgiveness and hope.

This "light" continues to attract all nations, for, as Jesus predicted, "And I, if I be lifted up from the earth, will draw all men unto me" (John 12:32). In Christ we see the great light of God. And when we follow that light, we do not fly to our destruction, but to our salvation.

—R. W. B.

4. Lift up thine eyes round about, and see: all they gather themselves together, they come to thee: thy sons shall come from far, and thy daughters shall be nursed at thy side.

Here Isaiah uses one of his many touching word pictures to elaborate on the procession of peoples streaming toward Zion. Zion is compared to a mother looking about with joy as her family gathers around her. Earlier Zion's condition was so bad that it was likened to blindness (59:10). Because of the appearance of the true Light, however, Zion's standing has reversed dramatically. Everywhere she looks there is evidence of God's goodness and blessing.

Thy daughters shall be nursed at thy side, rather, "shall be carried upon the hip." This was the common manner of carrying children in the Near East. Elsewhere Isaiah pictures the Gentiles carrying Zion's sons in their arms and her daughters on their shoulders (49:22).

The symbolism of this is very powerful. Whereas Israelites had been forcibly taken from their homeland by Gentiles, now, as the nations flock toward Zion, they bring with them her children who had long been scattered. While Gentiles (such as the Persians) did assist Israelites in returning home following the Babylonian captivity, Isaiah's language again directs our attention to a fulfillment of far greater impact. His words paint an inspiring picture of the collapse of the barriers that once separated Jew and Gentile. This reconciliation was a result of the death of Jesus Christ at Calvary (Ephesians 2:14-18).

II. The Bearer of Good News (Isaiah 61:1-4)

A. Compelled by Divine Power (v. 1a)

1a. The Spirit of the Lord God is upon me; because the Lord hath anointed me.

In chapter 61, Isaiah turns his attention to the specific individual who would accomplish all of the marvelous things described in chapter 60. Most important for our understanding of this passage is the fact that Jesus, in a synagogue service at Nazareth, applied Isaiah's words to himself (Luke 4:16-21). Verse 21 of Luke's account records that Jesus declared, "This day is this Scripture fulfilled in your ears." Clearly, Jesus was pointing to himself as the one who could lay claim to Isaiah's words and speak them as His own.

The Spirit of the Lord God is upon me. In Old Testament times God gave His Spirit to many persons whom He called to serve Him in various ways. Such expressions as the one that follows are found in the Old Testament: "And the Spirit of God came upon him [Saul], and he prophesied among them" (1 Samuel 10:10). For other examples see Exodus 31:3; Numbers 24:2; Judges 3:10; 6:34; 11:29; 13:25. Upon His Son, however, God poured out His Spirit more abundantly. Speaking of the Messiah, who would arise from the line of David, Isaiah earlier said the Spirit of the Lord would rest upon Him continually (Isaiah 11:2). Elsewhere, Jesus affirmed His unmeasured possession of God's Spirit (see John 3:34).

The Lord hath anointed me. Among the Jews, a person was set apart for divine service by the act of anointing, which involved the pouring of oil upon the person's head. Kings were thus consecrated to office (1 Samuel 16:1, 13) as were priests (Leviticus 8:12). There is one instance of the anointing of a prophet (1 Kings 19:16). From the Hebrew word for *anoint* comes the *Messiah,* or "anointed one." God himself anointed the

Messiah (Psalm 45:7), and the writer of Hebrews testifies that Jesus is the Messiah (Hebrews 1:8, 9). This anointing was not with oil, but with the Holy Spirit, and was openly manifested at the time of Jesus' baptism (Luke 3:21, 22), shortly before His visit to the synagogue in Nazareth, mentioned above. (See also Acts 10:38.)

B. Committed to Rebuilding People (vv. 1b-3)

1b. To preach good tidings unto the meek; he hath sent me to bind up the brokenhearted, to proclaim liberty to the captives, and the opening of the prison to them that are bound.

To preach good tidings unto the meek or "the poor" (compare Isaiah 11:4; Matthew 11:5). Jesus' ministry was to include the poor, the unfortunate, the needy. His good news was not limited to a few, but included all persons. *He hath sent me.* "God sent forth his Son" (Galatians 4:4), but the Son did not come into the world by compulsion. He came of His own will and desire when He was sent (see Philippians 2:5-7). Isaiah then listed the things the Messiah would be *sent* to do. The first of these, *"to bind up the brokenhearted,"* portrayed Him as someone with a heart for people, particularly those whose lives were badly in need of repair. In another passage, Isaiah captured the Messiah's gentleness with the promise, "A bruised reed shall he not break" (Isaiah 42:3). Jesus' ministry to the brokenhearted is clearly seen in the record of His life.

The next two phrases focus on the freedom that the Messiah would proclaim and grant to the imprisoned. The words *"proclaim liberty"* call to mind the language contained in the regulations concerning the Israelites' jubilee (Leviticus 25:10). This special year occurred every fifty years, at which time land was to be returned to the family that had originally owned it and those in bondage were to be set free.

When Jesus quoted this passage in the Nazareth synagogue and applied it to himself, He was declaring the institution of a new kind of jubilee. Just as the New Covenant is better than the Old, so is the new jubilee far superior

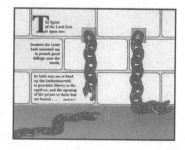

visual 5

to the old. The jubilee inaugurated by Jesus accomplished goals that were similar to those of the old one, but on a much grander scale. Jesus made it possible for mankind to return to its original owner—namely, God himself. He came to bring freedom from sin to those long held captive in its tyranny. Today Christians are called to *proclaim liberty* in Jesus' name to all the world.

2. To proclaim the acceptable year of the LORD, and the day of vengeance of our God; to comfort all that mourn.

The fact that the Messiah would *proclaim the acceptable year of the Lord* also indicates that Isaiah had in mind a new kind of jubilee that the Messiah would bring to pass. Jesus came to proclaim God's "year of acceptance," that is, a period of time during which God would be pleased to accept those who repented and turned to Him. The word *"acceptable"* or "pleasing" may provide an interesting link to the message of the heavenly host to the shepherds on the night Jesus was born. Isaiah's text literally reads, "the year of the favor of the Lord." Perhaps the heavenly host's announcement of "on earth peace, good will toward men" (or, more accurately, "peace in men of favor") constituted a declaration that the *year* (that is, the time) prophesied by Isaiah had come.

In contrast to this was the further announcement of *the day of vengeance of our God.* Some think that the comparatively much shorter time period for God's wrath (*day* as opposed to *year*) highlights the fact that in the Messianic era, grace would predominate over wrath. This is certainly at the heart of the gospel message, but it should not make us lax regarding the fact that a day of vengeance is inevitable. For now, those who *mourn* in repentance of their sins can still find the *comfort* of forgiveness (Matthew 5:4; James 4:9).

GOD'S NEW YEAR

Today is New Year's Eve. Many persons around the world will be reflecting on the year just ending. All will look forward to the new year with the hope that it will be a good year.

Isaiah announced a new "year of the Lord"—a year (or era) of God's favor. The remnant of Judah, who, some 150 years later were in captivity in Babylon, may have interpreted this prophecy to mean that they would be released from captivity and allowed to return to their homeland to restore their holy city and national heritage. Good news, indeed!

Students of the New Testament see in the announcement a second prophecy—one fulfilled by the coming of Christ (Luke 4:21), who ushered in the present era of peace and possibilities. The most recent "year of God's favor" began when in the fullness of time "God sent forth his Son" (Galatians 4:4, 5).

Is it possible to find a third meaning in Isaiah's prophecy? The New Testament tells of Christ's return in terms of *day* rather than *year.* We read that God "hath appointed a day, in the which he will judge the world in righteousness" (Acts 17:31). The Jerusalem restored by the returning remnant of Judah can hardly be compared to the "new Jerusalem, coming down from God out of heaven" (Revelation 21:2), to usher in the ultimate "year of the Lord."   —R. W. B.

3. To appoint unto them that mourn in Zion, to give unto them beauty for ashes, the oil of joy for mourning, the garment of praise for the spirit of heaviness; that they might be called Trees of righteousness, The planting of the LORD, that he might be glorified.

In this verse Isaiah uses a number of striking images to describe the impact of the Messiah's ministry. To those who "mourn" in repentance for their sins, promises signaling divine favor were given. These "mourners" would receive *beauty for ashes.* The term *beauty* actually refers to a coronet or turban, an ornamental covering for the head signifying joy and gladness. (The *New International Version* reads, "crown of beauty".) This would replace the ashes that were sprinkled on one's head during a period of mourning.

Similar is the expression, *the oil of joy for mourning.* The pouring of oil on someone was associated with times of celebration (Psalm 23; Ecclesiastes 9:8). Because of the Messiah's ministry the tears of those who mourn would be wiped away and replaced by joy.

The next figure, *the garment of praise for the spirit of heaviness,* calls to mind other references in Isaiah to clothing as symbolic of one's characteristics and attitudes. (See Isaiah 11:5; 59:16, 17.) Sackcloth was the traditional dress for those in grief or mourning. The prophet here points out that a spirit of praise would characterize people in the day of the Messiah's coming. No more would a drooping, feeble spirit characterize the people of God. Released from the bondage of sin, they would praise God for His grace bestowed upon them.

Those who accept the Messiah's good tidings are identified by the figure *Trees of righteousness.* The Speaker of verse 1, who would preach, bind up, proclaim liberty, etc., is the One who states that these persons are righteous. Although this righteousness is their own, it comes from God (see Isaiah 60:21). The New Testament indicates that this righteousness is credited to us through faith in Jesus Christ (Romans 3:22). In other words, this righteousness is a gift (Romans 5:17). Consequently, we become the trees of God's planting, designed to bring forth fruit that is in keeping with the righteousness that He has bestowed upon us. As trees of righteousness, we will bear righteous fruit, and this will be to the glory and honor of God. Using a different figure, but with the same thought in mind, Jesus said, "Let your light so shine before men, that they may see your good works, and glorify your Father which is in heaven" (Matthew 5:16).

C. Committed to Rebuilding Places (v. 4)

4. And they shall build the old wastes, they shall raise up the former desolations, and they shall repair the waste cities, the desolations of many generations.

Now Isaiah's emphasis shifts to a consideration of the work to be done by God's renewed people, "that he might be glorified" (v. 3). At first glance this language may seem to refer to the return of the Jews from captivity in Babylon and the rebuilding of Jerusalem and Judah that followed. But in light of the context, both preceding and following this verse, it is clear that we must look for something in line with a messianic interpretation and with Jesus' application of the opening words of the chapter to himself. Help is obtained by examining Acts 15:13-17, where James was speaking about the inclusion of Gentiles into the church. James stated that the prophets were in agreement with this action, and then he quoted from Amos 9:11, 12 to illustrate. Acts 15:16 is especially noteworthy: "After this I will return, and will build again the tabernacle of David, which is fallen down; and I will build again the ruins thereof, and I will set it up."

The rebuilding of ruins was associated with the activity of the church in expanding her outreach and bringing the gospel message to others. That rebuilding process is still going on through the faithful witness of committed followers of Jesus. All around us each day are people who could very easily summarize their lives with words such as *wastes* and *desolations*. They need to hear and know that "the year of the Lord" has not yet run out. The Rebuilder and Repairer of broken lives is still "on call."

Conclusion

A. "So Send I You"

According to today's Scripture text, the Messiah came to earth because He was "sent" by the Lord God with a particular mission to fulfill. He never lost sight of this task: "For I came down from heaven, not to do mine own will, but the will of him that sent me" (John 6:38).

On the day of His resurrection, Jesus appeared to His disciples and spoke these words to them: "Peace be unto you: as my Father hath sent me, even so send I you" (John 20:21). While this passage is not usually referred to as Jesus' Great Commission, it is filled with meaning for disciples of Jesus today. Jesus says that His disciples are sent by Him just as He was sent by the Father. We who have received the marvelous benefits of the Messiah's ministry are also "sent" to share the same good news with others.

How is this done? One answer to this question lies in a study of Isaiah 61, which states the objectives of the Messiah's ministry. If Jesus' mission was aimed toward the brokenhearted, the prisoners, the mourners, and the wasted and desolate ones, then so must ours be. Each of us likely has contact with persons who fall into these categories. Perhaps their lives have consisted of one round of bad news after the other. Perhaps they wonder, "Is there any good news out there?" We know that the answer to that question is yes. Let us commit ourselves to sharing God's good news with them.

B. Let Us Pray

Father, thank You for those who faithfully taught us the gospel and helped us to grow in Christ. Help us to renew our enthusiasm for sharing the gospel. In His name, amen.

C. Thought to Remember

"So send I you to bind the bruised and broken,
O'er wand'ring souls to work, to weep, to wake,
To bear the burdens of a world a-weary—
So send I you to suffer for My sake."

—E. Margaret Clarkson

Home Daily Bible Readings

Monday, Dec. 25—Heavenly Choir (Luke 2:18-20)

Tuesday, Dec. 26—A Bright Future (John 6:41-47)

Wednesday, Dec. 27—The Glory of Christ (2 Corinthians 8:16-24)

Thursday, Dec. 28—Receive Your Brother (Philemon 10-18)

Friday, Dec. 29—Honest Reasoning (Luke 5:1-11)

Saturday, Dec. 30—Infirmities Healed (Luke 5:12-15)

Sunday, Dec. 31—God's Glory in Evidence (Isaiah 60:15-22)

Learning by Doing

This page contains an alternate lesson plan emphasizing learning activities. Classes desiring such student involvement will find these suggestions helpful.

Learning Goals

After today's lesson, each adult will be:

1. Able to show that the lesson texts predominantly contain "good news."

2. Able to explain how these prophecies were fulfilled in Old Testament history as well as in the coming of Christ.

3. Able to describe an evangelist's task.

Into the Lesson

Prepare index cards as directed below and give each of your students one as they arrive. Print in large letters BN on one side of each card, GN on the other side. On half of the cards print *cap* in small letters at the bottom; likewise print *cro* on the other half of the cards. Explain that GN represents "Good News," and BN, "Bad News."

Bring some daily newspapers to class. As you read headlines from them, have your learners hold up either GN or BN, based on whether the article appears to be good or bad news. Typically there will be more bad than good news.

Into the Word

Read aloud the clauses of today's text as listed here. Have students respond to each with their GN/BN cards. Discuss any over which there is disagreement.

1. "Arise, shine; for thy light is come."
2. "The glory of the Lord is risen upon thee."
3. "For, behold, the darkness shall cover the earth, and gross darkness the people."
4. "But the Lord shall arise upon thee, and his glory shall be seen upon thee."
5. "The Gentiles shall come to thy light."
6. "Kings [shall come] to the brightness of thy rising."
7. "[Zion], lift up thine eyes round about, and see: all they gather themselves together, they come to thee."
8. "Thy sons shall come from far."
9. "Thy daughters shall be nursed at thy side."
10. "The Spirit of the Lord God is upon me."
11. "The Lord hath anointed me to preach good tidings unto the meek."
12. "He hath sent me to bind up the broken-hearted."
13. "[He hath sent me] to proclaim liberty to the captives."

14. "[He hath sent me] to proclaim the opening of the prisons to them that are bound."
15. "[He hath sent me] to proclaim the acceptable year of the Lord."
16. "[He hath sent me] to proclaim the day of vengeance of our God."
17. "[He hath sent me] to comfort all that mourn."
18. "[He hath sent me] to give unto them beauty for ashes, the oil of joy for mourning, [and] the garment of praise for the spirit of heaviness."
19. "They might be called Trees of righteousness, The planting of the Lord, that he might be glorified."
20. "They shall build the old wastes, they shall raise up the former desolations."
21. "They shall repair the waste cities, the desolations of many generations."

Have your learners form groups of four each, based on whether *cap* or *cro* is at the bottom of their cards. The *cap* groups are to list ways Isaiah's prophecies were fulfilled when God delivered Israel from Babylonian *cap*tivity; the *cro* groups are to show how they were fulfilled with the coming of Christ, His death on the *cro*ss, and His resurrection. Allot five to eight minutes for this; then have someone from each group report the group's ideas to the class.

Into Life

Lead the class in preparing an evangelist's job description based on Isaiah 61:1-3. Give each student a worksheet with the heading "Evangelist's Job Description" and the page divided into two parts: "Qualifications" and "Responsibilities." Have each student fill in his or her own sheet as the class works.

Ask the class to state the elements of the text in modern terms. For example, "to bind up the brokenhearted" becomes "to comfort those grieving a loss" (to include visits to funeral homes and sending sympathy cards to the bereaved). If your group needs help, ask such questions as, "If the person being addressed is *meek*, what attributes does the evangelist need?" or "What is implied of one who is called a 'Tree of righteousness'?" Suggest that the students read their job description sheets each day this week so they can be more effective bearers of the light of Christ in our spiritually dark world.

Let's Talk It Over

The questions on this page are designed to encourage review of the lesson Scriptures and to promote discussion of the lesson by the class. The answers provided are only discussion starters. Let your class talk it over from there.

1. Chapters 57-59 of Isaiah describe the darkened spiritual condition of the people of Israel in Isaiah's day. Briefly consider the groups of verses indicated below and identify the sinful behavior described in each.

57:1-4 (A loss of moral and spiritual conscience)

57:5-7 (Widespread immorality and idolatry)

57:10, 11 (Spiritual poverty and godlessness)

58:3-7 (Blatant hypocrisy)

59:1-11 (A lack of integrity and justice)

59:12, 13 (A rebellious spirit and treacherous behavior)

2. In what way may Israel's condition be compared with that of our nation? What is the widely accepted approach in dealing with the problems we face?

In general, the sins of which Israel was guilty are found in our society also, although in some instances they are manifested differently. Simply stated, we as a nation have shown disregard for God's moral and ethical laws and we are spiritually sick as a result. Admitting that things are not as they ought to be in our society, many turn to remedies that are inadequate to treat the real sickness. They are convinced that more money, more social programs, more law enforcement, more education, more legislation, etc., will bring about a healthy society. In truth, these do not get at the real sickness—our sin and rebellion against God.

3. In view of the "darkness" that covers our society and the world community, what should we as Christians be doing personally to fulfill the mission Christ has given us?

Isaiah suggests that we begin with the acknowledgment that the One who is the "light" has come (Isaiah 60:1). John identifies Jesus as "the true light that gives light to every man" (John 1:9, *New International Version*). Jesus spoke of himself as the light of the world (John 8:12). Once we acknowledge Him as the true light, we are to live as reflections of that light in the world. (See Matthew 5:14; Ephesians 5:8; and Philippians 2:14-16.) We are to penetrate our culture with the gospel so that the light of Christ may shine in the spiritual darkness there. Many Christians, however, are so intimidated by the indifference and antagonism of the non-Christian world that they retreat into their sanctuaries or small groups and find their security there. Some associate with groups whose aggressive tactics hardly reflect the spirit of Jesus. This is a far cry from the description given of the early church in its non-Christian environment. There must be an attractive contagion about our lives and witness, and we must manifest a gentle firmness in the expression of that witness.

4. In Luke 4:16-21, Jesus identifies himself as the one described by Isaiah in chapter 61, verses 1 and 2. If the church is to carry on the mission of Christ in the world, as expressed in these verses, what should be the focus of its ministries?

Over the years one of the problems with the church has been its tendency to lose its clear sense of mission and to substitute in its place the maintenance of the institution. The measurement of a church's effectiveness is often the number of people present for programs, the size of budgets, and the investment in real estate. As important as these may be in our culture, they can easily change our focus from the needs of people to the needs of the organization. The church becomes program-centered instead of people-oriented. More and more, each congregation needs to ask the question, "What is our mission, our purpose?" and then take a hard look at how it is investing resources, structuring programs, and developing ministries to assure that the mission is being accomplished.

5. In Isaiah 61:3, the prophet describes God's redeemed people as "Trees of righteousness, The planting of the Lord, that he might be glorified." This is a symbol of strength and productivity. Jesus, the living vine, describes our relationship to Him as that of "branches" (John 15:5). How are we to manifest this relationship?

Obviously, there is the expectation of Jesus to His disciples to be alive, dynamic, growing, and bearing fruit. This fruit is to be the fruit of His Holy Spirit (see Galatians 5:22, 23). He is the one who energizes us and makes us productive. Our task is to keep the relationship with Him strong.

The Servant's Call

DEVOTIONAL READING: John 7:37-44.

LESSON SCRIPTURE: Isaiah 42:1-9.

PRINTED TEXT: Isaiah 42:1-9.

Isaiah 42:1-9

1 Behold my servant, whom I uphold; mine elect, in whom my soul delighteth; I have put my Spirit upon him: he shall bring forth judgment to the Gentiles.

2 He shall not cry, nor lift up, nor cause his voice to be heard in the street.

3 A bruised reed shall he not break, and the smoking flax shall he not quench: he shall bring forth judgment unto truth.

4 He shall not fail nor be discouraged, till he have set judgment in the earth: and the isles shall wait for his law.

5 Thus saith God the LORD, he that created the heavens, and stretched them out; he that spread forth the earth, and that which cometh out of it; he that giveth breath unto the people upon it, and spirit to them that walk therein:

6 I the LORD have called thee in righteousness, and will hold thine hand, and will keep thee, and give thee for a covenant of the people, for a light of the Gentiles;

7 To open the blind eyes, to bring out the prisoners from the prison, and them that sit in darkness out of the prison house.

8 I am the LORD; that is my name: and my glory will I not give to another, neither my praise to graven images.

9 Behold, the former things are come to pass, and new things do I declare: before they spring forth I tell you of them.

GOLDEN TEXT: Behold my servant, whom I uphold; mine elect, in whom my soul delighteth; I have put my Spirit upon him: he shall bring forth judgment to the Gentiles.—Isaiah 42:1.

God's Promise of Deliverance (Isaiah)
Unit 2: The Ministry of the Suffering Servant (Lessons 6-9)

Lesson Aims

As a result of studying this lesson, each student should:

1. Understand how God raises up people to accomplish His purposes.
2. Be open to God's call to service.

Lesson Outline

INTRODUCTION
 A. Called to Serve
 B. Lesson Background
 I. GOD COMMISSIONS HIS SERVANT (Isaiah 42:1-4)
 A. The Servant Chosen by God (v. 1a)
 B. The Servant Empowered by God's Spirit (v. 1b)
 C. The Nature of the Servant's Ministry (vv. 2, 3a)
 D. The Goal of the Servant's Ministry (vv. 3b, 4)
 II. GOD ASSURES HIS SERVANT'S SUCCESS (Isaiah 42:5-9)
 A. The God Who Sends the Servant (vv. 5, 6a)
 B. The Universal Ministry of the Servant (v. 6b)
 C. The Deliverance That Comes Through the Servant (v. 7)
 D. The Truth Revealed by the Servant's Work (vv. 8, 9)
 Happy New Year!
CONCLUSION
 A. "A Tale of Two Servants"
   "There Ain't No Justice"?
 B. Let Us Pray
 C. Thought to Remember

Visual 6 of the visuals packet is a chart based on Isaiah 42:1-4. The visual is shown on page 165.

Introduction

A. Called to Serve

"This Is a Service Organization," read the sign in front of the church building. For this congregation these words were more than an empty slogan. A drug rehabilitation center, an orphanage, a nursing home, a lunch-hour Bible study for businessmen, and a halfway house for troubled youth were just a few of the ways these believers had found to meet the needs of people in the name of Christ. When I asked the minister what inspired the church's many ministries, he replied, "We believe that when God calls us, He calls us to serve."

When these believers answered that call, they joined a great host of saints whom God has raised up to accomplish His purposes on earth. Throughout the history of God's kingdom on earth God has honored His children by inviting them to share in the unfolding of His will. In this text from the book of Isaiah we are introduced to one who personifies this biblical concept of "servanthood."

This is the first lesson of a four-lesson study of the Servant of the Lord, one who is presented in four passages in the latter portion of Isaiah's writings. Some Bible students understand the Servant to be the Messiah, and see the Servant's mission fulfilled only in Jesus Christ.

The writer of these four lessons feels that the Servant passages speak first of the nation of Israel, specifically the faithful among the exiles in Babylonian captivity, and that they find their ultimate and complete fulfillment in Jesus Christ. These lessons are presented, therefore, from that point of view.

B. Lesson Background

The Servant Songs of Isaiah (42:1-4; 49:1-6; 50:4-9; 52:13—53:12) belong to a section of the book of Isaiah (chapters 40—55) that has as its backdrop the Babylonian captivity of the nation of Judah. In this setting the exiled Judean nation is portrayed as the servant of the Lord.

According to the prophet the Babylonian captivity (586-538 B.C.) would serve three purposes. First, by it God would punish Judah for her sins. In a manner typical of God's dealings with His people, He would use a hostile nation as an instrument of His judgment upon His people's apostasy. Second, the Babylonian captivity would purge Judah of her idolatry. Throughout her national history Judah had been drawn to idol worship. After a series of more limited judgments, God would use the Babylonian captivity to demonstrate, once and for all, the catastrophic consequences of following false gods. The third and final purpose for the captivity would be to prepare the Israelite nation to become a "light of the Gentiles" (42:6; 49:6). By dispersing His people among the nations God would position them to become a universal witness to the message of the one true God.

In the Servant Songs of Isaiah God sought to minister to His exiled nation by reassuring them that through obedient submission to the divine will their suffering would serve a purpose that would reach far beyond their own race and their own generation. These prophecies ultimately anticipated a period in the future when Jesus himself would emerge from Israel as God's Servant, whose sufferings would save the world.

I. God Commissions His Servant (Isaiah 42:1-4)

A. The Servant Chosen by God (v. 1a)

1a. Behold my servant, whom I uphold; mine elect, in whom my soul delighteth.

Behold my servant. With these words God announced His selection of Israel as the servant He would raise up to accomplish His purposes on earth. The Hebrew term translated *servant* means "one who performs some deed in obedience to the command of another." In the Bible and throughout the ancient world the word was often used as a formal title for an officer of the royal court (for example, 2 Kings 22:12). For those who bore the title "servant" it implied both honor as the king's representative and at the same time complete subservience to the king's command. In similar fashion the Christian's service to the heavenly King brings honor to God's servants and expects submission to His commands.

Abraham, Moses, and David were among important biblical personalities who were referred to as God's "servant" as they performed deeds at His command. In the book of Isaiah the term *servant* is used once to describe the prophet himself (20:3), but most commonly it refers collectively to the nation of Israel (41:8; 44:2, 21; 45:4; 48:20). The exiled Israelite nation, as they submitted to God's commands and performed His will, would become a faithful "remnant" (see 46:3) and function as His servant.

Mine elect. In Old Testament times servants rarely initiated their own positions. Whether in a royal court or the household of a common citizen, those who served were normally chosen or commissioned by their superiors. This explains why in this verse, and in many others, the title *servant* is accompanied by the term *elect* or *chosen* (see 41:8; 44:2). As with the role of being God's servant, being His *elect* brought with it a

---

How to Say It

BABYLONIAN. Bab-uh-*low*-nee-un.
JEPHTHAH. *Jef*-thuh (*th* as in *thin*).
PISIDIA. Pih-*sid*-ee-uh.

---

balance of privilege and responsibility. For the people of Israel, the privilege consisted of their being selected, lovingly and graciously, from among the nations to be a special people to God. Their responsibility included the challenge of representing the one true God among the nations and of being held to the higher standards expected of such a position. Our relationship with Christ is likewise a position of great privilege and serious responsibility.

B. The Servant Empowered by God's Spirit (v. 1b)

1b. I have put my Spirit upon him: he shall bring forth judgment to the Gentiles.

In the New Testament the Spirit of God (Holy Spirit) is described as abiding in the believer as a permanent resident, producing "fruits" of character and service. In the Old Testament God's Spirit (God's empowerment) is said to have related to His people in a different manner. It is described as an external force or power that came "upon" individuals to equip them temporarily for some specific service. In such fashion Jephthah and Samson were empowered with courage or strength by God's Spirit (Judges 11:29; 14:6) without necessarily becoming "spiritual" people. The same is true for the effect that the Spirit would have upon the nation of Israel. The prophet simply meant that God would equip His people to perform the task to which He commissioned them.

C. The Nature of the Servant's Ministry (vv. 2, 3a)

2, 3a. He shall not cry, nor lift up, nor cause his voice to be heard in the street. A bruised reed shall he not break, and the smoking flax shall he not quench.

By studying the Servant Songs we gain insight into the way God works in His world. We see that God accomplishes His will through spiritual influences of sacrifice and grace, rather than through aggressive, coercive, and manipulative tactics such as lie behind much of human achievement. This is the emphasis of these verses as they describe the servant's ministry. Israel would not assume a posture of self-promotion but one of genuine humility. Rather than exploiting the weakness of broken humanity, the servant would show compassion toward those whose lives were broken and nearly extinguished. Rather than attempting to force God's justice and impose His peace, the exiled Israelite nation would wait for God to accomplish His will in His own way and in His own time. As they endured the sufferings of the Babylonian captivity and were then subsequently restored to their homeland, this generation of exiled Judeans would bear witness to all peoples that they who submit to the one true God will eventually receive His vindication and reward. It was the nation's task to bring their world to God by means of a spirit of obedience and grace. Later, Jesus Christ, the Lord's Servant par excellence, would say, "And I, if I be lifted up from the earth [that is, crucified], will draw all men unto me" (John 12:32). The Servant would compel people to righteousness, not by driving them, but by drawing them with the irresistible power of His sacrificial love.

D. The Goal of the Servant's Ministry (vv. 3b, 4)

3b, 4. He shall bring forth judgment unto truth. He shall not fail nor be discouraged, till he have set judgment in the earth: and the isles shall wait for his law.

The phrase *bring forth judgment* and the similar *set judgment* appear three times in this brief song (vv. 1, 3, 4). They spell out the goal of the servant's ministry. The *judgment* was not some punishment that God was prepared to enforce upon the nations. It was rather a new "justice," which He was prepared to offer them. It was a verdict, a *truth*, revealed by his *law* (notice the parallel between *judgment* and *law* in verse 4) and leading to a new basis for interpersonal and international relationships. This truth was that there is but one true God who rules His world by righteousness and justice (v. 6). As the nations embrace this truth they will learn to live together in equity and peace.

The verbs *bring forth* and *set* mean to "decree" or "proclaim." The servant role of Israel was to be, therefore, much like that of a prophet who would carry God's liberating message to the world.

II. God Assures His Servant's Success (Isaiah 42:5-9)

A. The God Who Sends the Servant (vv. 5, 6a)

5, 6a. Thus saith God the LORD, he that created the heavens, and stretched them out; he that spread forth the earth, and that which cometh out of it; he that giveth breath unto the people upon it, and spirit to them that walk therein: I the LORD have called thee in righteousness, and will hold thine hand, and will keep thee.

Thus saith God the Lord. These words seem to indicate the beginning of a new prophetic utterance, independent of the Servant Song in verses 1 through 4. The theme of Israel's role as

God's representative among the nations, however, is continued in these verses. First, God who commissioned the servant is described. He might have been identified as the God who raised up Abraham or who brought Israel out of Egypt. But, since the ministry of the servant was to be universal, God is described in terms of two of His roles that equally affect all peoples and all nations: that of Creator and Provider. God's claim to control the events of history is established by virtue of the fact that He made the world and continually gives life to all of its inhabitants. He who *spread forth* (literally, "beat out") the earth as a smith shapes a bowl from a lump of silver is capable of shaping history as well. He who *giveth breath* to humanity can raise a nation from its ranks to accomplish His purposes and fulfill His will.

I the Lord have called thee in righteousness. It seems that the prophet continues to speak of the captive Israelite nation collectively and the role they would play in teaching the peoples of the earth about the one true God. The phrase *in righteousness* refers not to the qualifications of the Lord's chosen one but to the purpose of the Lord's calling. In this usage the expression should be rendered "unto righteousness" or, even better, "unto justification." The basic idea behind the term employed here is "to render normal." The Lord's people were to have a part in "normalizing" relations between God and the peoples of the earth. The God who called His people to this mission would also *hold* and *keep* them as they participated in its unfolding.

B. The Universal Ministry of the Servant (v. 6b)

6b. And give thee for a covenant of the people, for a light of the Gentiles.

From the beginning, God's election of Israel as His chosen people had a universal goal. One of the promises God made to Abraham when He first called him was that through him all families of the earth would be blessed (Genesis 12:3). Though the ultimate fulfillment of that promise would await the coming of Christ (Acts 3:25, 26; Galatians 3:8), the prophet makes it clear that this generation of exiled Israelites would play a role in moving this part of God's unfolding plan toward its goal.

Israel's intercessory role in the conversion of the nations is characterized in two ways. First, Israel is described as *a covenant of the people* (see also Isaiah 49:8). In biblical times covenants reconciled or bound one party to another. In this case God was one party and the non-Jewish nations were the other. Israel, or more particularly the exiled Judeans, would have a part in the reconciliation of the two. The way this would be accomplished is suggested by the phrase *for a light of the Gentiles.* By this expression the prophet probably meant that as the foreign nations witnessed Israel's patient submission to the will of God and the positive benefits that came of it, they would be convinced that the God of Israel is, indeed, the one true God.

There is a truth here that is applicable to the Christian. God uses people to spread His truth to the world. As was the case for ancient Israel, our relationship with God as it is witnessed by those around us has the power to enlighten people spiritually and invite them to seek the true and living God. By submitting to His will and living according to His precepts we can help to mediate a reconciliation between a lost world and the saving God.

C. The Deliverance That Comes Through the Servant (v. 7)

7. To open the blind eyes, to bring out the prisoners from the prison, and them that sit in darkness out of the prison house.

These metaphors of the spiritual enlightenment and liberation that the nations would experience as they learned the truth taught by Israel's exile and subsequent return to Canaan had special meaning to the Judean captives. They themselves were liberated from their *prison* of captivity by the mighty hand of God as He conquered Babylon and secured their release through Cyrus in 538 B.C. Even as God used Cyrus to liberate them from a physical, political bondage, God would use them in the liberation of the nations from the bondage of spiritual darkness. Sin binds a soul in the darkest prison of all—a prison of guilt and alienation from God. It is from such bondage that Jesus came to deliver mankind.

D. The Truth Revealed by the Servant's Work (vv. 8, 9)

8, 9. I am the LORD; that is my name: and my glory will I not give to another, neither my praise to graven images. Behold, the former things are come to pass, and new things do I declare: before they spring forth I tell you of them.

Here we see the culmination of the prophet's message to the nations. From the beginning of this chapter the prophet has been speaking of the role that would be played by the faithful remnant of the Israelite exiles (God's servant) in the enlightenment and the liberation that God would bring to the nations of the earth. He now defines the great spiritual truth that forms both the basis and goal of that spiritual deliverance:

visual 6

there is but one true God and Yahweh (Jehovah) is His name (v. 8). Indeed, this truth constitutes the goal of all of God's revelation to mankind. This is the truth God wanted the Egyptians to learn from the ten plagues (see Exodus 7:5; 8:22). Isaiah repeatedly says that this truth would be learned from God's punishment and subsequent restoration of His people (see Isaiah 49:23, 26).

Monotheism (the worship of one God to the exclusion of all others) is a concept that is taken for granted by most modern Westerners, but not so the peoples of the ancient world. Predominantly polytheists (those who worship many gods), the people surrounding tiny Israel deified virtually all objects and forces of material creation. It would be difficult for them to abandon their *graven images,* but such would be required if they were to embrace the one true God (see Exodus 20:1-5). It is likewise essential for us to abandon any object, person, ambition, or ideology that might function as a god in our lives if we are to truly worship God as He intends and deserves to be worshiped.

Before they spring forth I tell you of them. This final statement is meant to stand as proof of the claim that Jehovah alone is God. In the previous chapter (41:22, 23) He challenged the false gods to declare the future ahead of time as proof that they truly were gods. Only One who is in control of history can declare what will be before it happens. By declaring the fate of His exiled people ahead of time and then bringing it to pass, God demonstrated that He is the sovereign Lord of the universe.

HAPPY NEW YEAR!

New Year's Day may be my favorite holiday. I like new beginnings—new years, new weeks, new days. I even get excited over the beginning of new months, despite the inevitable bill-paying. In fact, that is one reason I like "day 1"—I can balance accounts, clean the slate, and start budgeting all over again.

Solomon was a cynical mid-lifer when he said, "There is no new thing under the sun" (Ecclesiastes 1:9). He was suffering from boredom and frustration, disillusioned by his own mortality. Often we forget to embrace the newness of ordinary events, such as the dawn of each day, or the first day of each week. Much excitement surrounds the first day of the year, but the same kind of excitement can be generated over any new start, any fresh beginning.

The prophet Isaiah spoke of "new things." Today is the first Sunday of a new year and the first day of a new week. It is an appropriate time for reflection, repentance, renewal, and resolution. New beginnings are possible with God. "If any man be in Christ, he is a new creature: old things are passed away; behold, all things are become new" (2 Corinthians 5:17).

—R. W. B.

Conclusion

A. "A Tale of Two Servants"

In Matthew 12:18-21 the gospel writer tells us that what Isaiah predicted of the servant (Israel) was ultimately "fulfilled" in the life and ministry of Jesus of Nazareth. This reveals to us another capacity of prophetic literature. It is the power of the word of God to leap beyond its historical, contextual meaning to anticipate the unfolding of God's will in ways that perhaps even the prophet himself never could have anticipated. Not only would Israel serve as God's servant, but, in a deeper and fuller sense, another Servant, One "whose goings forth have been from of old, from everlasting" (Micah 5:2), would arise to accomplish God's eternal purposes. What God began in creation and continued in Israel was completed through the ministry of Jesus Christ.

Other New Testament Scriptures reveal that Isaiah's prophecy concerning the Lord's Servant pointed to Christ Jesus for its ultimate fulfillment. When the Jews in Antioch of Pisidia railed against Paul and Barnabas's preaching of the gospel, the two took that message to the Gentiles. In doing so, they stated that their action was governed by divine directive and offered as proof Isaiah's prophecy in 42:6 and 49:6 (see Acts 13:46, 47). In the preaching of the gospel, therefore, was the ministry of the Lord's Servant continued: light was given to the Gentiles, the light that brings salvation to all persons everywhere.

Wherever His gospel is proclaimed today, Christ, the Lord's Servant, continues to be the light of life to those who are lost in sin's darkness.

"THERE AIN'T NO JUSTICE?"

Life's Not Fair, But God Is Good! The title of Robert Schuller's book speaks to the frustration experienced by many of God's people as they struggle to understand and accept the injustices of our existence. The rich get richer, the poor get poorer. Drunk drivers, drug dealers, prostitutes, pornographers, and rapists go free after only a "slap on the wrist" administered by our judicial system. Babies die, millions of them before birth. Good people get sick; hard workers lose their jobs. People live longer, but many without quality; some die without dignity. Life is not fair!

But God is good. Through His prophet God announced that His justice would be established in the earth (v. 4). His Servant, the Messiah, would bring to fulfillment God's eternal purpose. His purpose of redemption—a plan of salvation for the righteous and judgment for the wicked—that's more than fair.

"Shall not the Judge of all the earth do right?" asked Abraham before Sodom was destroyed (Genesis 18:25). The implicit answer is yes. Perfect justice is inherent in God's nature. That truth will be understood when the Servant Christ returns as the ruling King.   —R. W. B.

B. Let Us Pray

Father in Heaven, thank You for honoring us with the privilege of participating in the unfolding of Your will. When You call us may we answer as willing servants, ready to do Your bidding. In Jesus' name, amen.

C. Thought to Remember

God accomplishes His will through spiritual influences of sacrifice and grace. We serve Him best when we so live.

Home Daily Bible Readings

Monday, Jan. 1—Song of Victory (Isaiah 42:10-17)

Tuesday, Jan. 2—Israel—Deaf and Blind (Isaiah 42:18-25)

Wednesday, Jan. 3—Israel's Redemption (Isaiah 43:1-7)

Thursday, Jan. 4—Israel, the Lord's Witness (Isaiah 43:8-13)

Friday, Jan. 5—God as Redeemer (Isaiah 43:14-21)

Saturday, Jan. 6—The Greatness of His Power (Ephesians 2:1-10)

Sunday, Jan. 7—Jesus' Power (Matthew 12:22-32)

Learning by Doing

This page contains an alternate lesson plan emphasizing learning activities. Classes desiring such student involvement will find these suggestions helpful.

Learning Goals

As a result of this study of Isaiah 42, the adult student will:

1. Explain how Israel was to serve God as His servant to the nations.

2. Understand his or her personal role as a servant of God and serve Him in the manner and ways suggested in this text.

Into the Lesson

As your class members arrive, have on prominent display a large copy of the standard telephone key pad with this number alongside: 737-8268. This is not an actual phone number. Ask the class to figure out what word the corresponding letters on the phone key pad spell. (737-8268 reads S-E-R-V-A-N-T.)

Arrange in advance with one of your class members who enjoys doing drama to act out the following short "dialogue." Your actor, seated at a table with a telephone, answers the phone, and says the following lines, pausing when appropriate:

"Hello, this is ____." "Oh, hello, Sam(antha), how can I help you?" "The three-year-olds?" "A trip to the zoo?" "I don't know; I'm not very patient with young children." "Bruised reed? . . . huh?" "Smoking flax? . . .huh? "Oh, I know it would please you . . . but would it please me?" "Yes, I know they would delight in God's creation, but . . . but. . ." "So, you'll put my name in the church paper if I go?" "Well, that would be an honor . . . I guess." "I *suppose* I can serve in this way. Thank you for all the support I know you'll give me."

After the phone conversation has ended, ask the class to scan today's text to see how many of its words or ideas were represented in the call. Such ideas as reference to God as Creator (v. 5), and the caller's delight in His servant (v. 1), and others may be noted.

Into the Word

The lesson writer uses the following sentences in his development of today's lesson. Read each aloud, in the order given, and ask your adults to match the idea with a verse of the text. (You may want to assign each learner a verse to keep special attention to.) If a wrong "match" is chosen, indicate the error but ask, "How do you see the idea of this statement as related to the verse you

have identified?" Verse numbers are given, but, of course, do not read those.

"As the foreign nations witnessed Israel's patient submission to the will of God and the positive benefits that came of it, they would be convinced that the God of Israel is, indeed, the one true God" (v. 6).

"For the people of Israel, the privilege consisted of their being selected, lovingly and graciously, from among the nations to be a special people to God" (v. 1).

"God accomplishes His will through spiritual influences of sacrifice and grace" (v. 3).

"Only One who is in control of history can declare what will be before it happens" (v. 9).

"Predominantly polytheists (those who worship many gods), the people surrounding tiny Israel deified virtually all objects and forces of material creation" (v. 8).

"Rather than exploiting the weakness of broken humanity, the servant would show compassion toward those whose lives were broken and nearly extinguished" (v. 3).

"Sin binds a soul in the darkest prison of all— a prison of guilt and alienation from God" (v. 7).

"Since the ministry of the servant was to be universal, God is described in terms of two of His roles that equally affect all peoples and all nations: that of Creator and Provider" (v. 5).

"The prophet simply meant that God would equip His people to perform the task to which He commissioned them" (v. 1).

You may prefer to add or substitute other statements from the lesson.

Into Life

Have your class work together to prepare an acrostic using today's key word: *servant*. Write the word vertically on the chalkboard. Ask your students to note characteristics of the Servant as given or implied in this text. For example, S (spirit-filled); E (elect); R (righteous); V (valuable); A (approved); N (not discouraged); T (tenderhearted).

Sometime before class have someone with a standard labelmaker prepare enough labels of today's "servant's number" (737-8268) to give one to each member of the class. Suggest to them that it be kept near their own phone as a reminder of the concept.

Close with prayer.

Let's Talk It Over

The questions on this page are designed to encourage review of the lesson Scriptures and to promote discussion of the lesson by the class. The answers provided are only discussion starters. Let your class talk it over from there.

1. Ancient Israel had difficulty accepting and fulfilling its role as "servant of the Lord." Why do you think this was true?

The nation of Israel seemed to have a limited understanding of what it meant to be God's "chosen people." God chose them and blessed them above all peoples, but it was not because of their goodness or special merit. Nor were they chosen so that they *alone* would live forever in God's favor. God chose them and cared for them because He would be faithful to His covenant with Abraham and bring to fulfillment His promise of blessing for the whole world (Genesis 12:1-3; Deuteronomy 7:7, 8; 9:5, 6). The blessings God bestowed upon Israel were not simply an expression of favoritism, as some suppose, but were given to enable them to carry out His loving purpose for all peoples. Isaiah 1 describes their failure to understand this call to servanthood.

Isaiah 42:18-25 reveals that Israel had deliberately chosen not to hear God's call or to see the great privilege and responsibility He had given them. In time Israel became as spiritually blind and deaf as other nations. The people's self-interest and idolatrous disobedience left them without any testimony and ultimately vulnerable to the very nations to whom they were supposed to be a witness.

2. What parallel, if any, may be seen between ancient Israel and the church in our nation today regarding the concept of being God's servant?

In effect, Israel asked God, "But, what have you done for me lately?" Again and again they defaulted in their responsibility as the Lord's servant and blamed their plight on God's failure to meet their needs.

Many Christians today seem to have the attitude that the church exists to serve them and to meet their needs, when in fact we exist as the body of Christ in the world, not to be served, but to serve (Matthew 20:28). When the Lord's people turn their focus inward in a self-centered manner, they lose the sense of urgency of reaching out to the lost of the world and giving evidence of the new life in Christ. Then the concept of being the Lord's servant is lost, just as in ancient Israel.

3. Servant leadership and the leadership style of the world are vastly different. What characteristics of servant leadership are suggested in Isaiah 42:1-4?

Jesus contrasted worldly leadership with servant leadership (see Matthew 20:24-28). Worldly leaders seek authority and status (v. 25). Servant leaders desire no position, but give themselves in the interest of others, following the example of Jesus (vv. 27, 28).

Isaiah 42:1-4 describes the Lord's servant, and the characteristics included there are similar to those mentioned by Jesus. The servant leader works quietly in unassuming ways (v. 2). He is gentle and compassionate with those who are weak or wounded emotionally or spiritually (v. 3). And he is not easily discouraged by difficulty or criticism, because he is not seeking honor or self-glory (v. 4).

4. The Lord affirmed that He would take hold of His servant's hand (v. 6), which was a promise intended to instill confidence and encourage perseverance. Why is this promise of God so important to one who serves Him?

Two of the greatest enemies of effective Christian service are fear of failure and discouragement in the presence of adversity. These twin killers destroy confidence and weaken our endurance. When we focus on our own inadequacies, we set up a self-defeating context for our service. God would remind us that we serve Him "that created the heavens" and "spread forth the earth" and who gives "breath unto the people upon it" (v. 5). Surely He can be trusted to accomplish through us what He calls us to do in His name. *We do not take hold of His hand; He takes hold of ours.* That is security in serving!

5. As a group, list some things your congregation could do to serve God in the manner suggested in Isaiah 42:6, 7.

How might you be "a light of the Gentiles"? How could you help "open the blind eyes"? In what ways could you help to "free captives" and "release . . . those who sit in darkness?" (*New International Version*).

Put these phrases into contemporary settings and discuss how your church might be a "service organization" in your ministry area.

The Servant's Mission

DEVOTIONAL READING: Malachi 3:1-5.

LESSON SCRIPTURE: Isaiah 49:1-6.

PRINTED TEXT: Isaiah 49:1-6.

Isaiah 49:1-6

1 Listen, O isles, unto me; and hearken, ye people, from far; The LORD hath called me from the womb; from the bowels of my mother hath he made mention of my name.

2 And he hath made my mouth like a sharp sword; in the shadow of his hand hath he hid me, and made me a polished shaft; in his quiver hath he hid me;

3 And said unto me, Thou art my servant, O Israel, in whom I will be glorified.

4 Then I said, I have labored in vain, I have spent my strength for nought, and in vain: yet surely my judgment is with the LORD, and my work with my God.

5 And now, saith the LORD that formed me from the womb to be his servant, to bring Jacob again to him, Though Israel be not gathered, yet shall I be glorious in the eyes of the LORD, and my God shall be my strength.

6 And he said, It is a light thing that thou shouldest be my servant to raise up the tribes of Jacob, and to restore the preserved of Israel: I will also give thee for a light to the Gentiles, that thou mayest be my salvation unto the end of the earth.

GOLDEN TEXT: I will also give thee for a light to the Gentiles, that thou mayest be my salvation unto the end of the earth.—Isaiah 49:6.

God's Promise of Deliverance (Isaiah)
Unit 2: The Ministry of the Suffering Servant (Lessons 6-9)

Lesson Aims

Participation in this lesson should enable the students to:

1. Understand the nature of the servant's ministry to Israel and the world.

2. Appreciate the role that all Christians in the world today can play in continuing the work of God's Servant.

Lesson Outline

INTRODUCTION
    A. Things Are Not Always As They Seem
    B. Lesson Background
  I. THE SERVANT'S REFLECTIONS (Isaiah 49:1-4)
    A. The Servant's Credentials to Minister on God's Behalf (vv. 1-3)
      Prenatal Destiny
    B. The Servant's Misunderstanding of His Ministry (v. 4)
      By Faith, Not by Sight
  II. THE PURPOSE OF THE SERVANT'S CALLING (Isaiah 49:5, 6)
    A. The Servant's Ministry to Israel (vv. 5, 6a)
    B. The Servant's Ministry to All the World (v. 6b)
CONCLUSION
    A. Misunderstanding God
    B. Let Us Pray
    C. Thought to Remember

The fragment of the Isaiah scroll pictured in visual 7 of the visuals packet is one of the Dead Sea Scrolls, the first of which was discovered in 1947 in a cave a few miles south of Jericho. The visual is shown on page 172.

Introduction

A. Things Are Not Always As They Seem

There is a Chinese parable about an old man who lived with his son in a tiny cottage. One night the old man's horse—the only horse he had—wandered away, and his neighbors all came to say how sorry they were about his misfortune. "How do you know this is ill fortune?" he replied.

A week later the horse came home, bringing with him a whole herd of wild horses. The neighbors then congratulated him on his good fortune. The old man smiled and asked, "How do you know this is good fortune?"

The man's son began to ride the new horses. One day he was thrown from a horse, and the fall left him with a crippled leg. Right on cue the neighbors approached the old man to express their regrets over his bad luck, but the old man asked, "How do you know it is bad luck?"

A few days later a Chinese warlord came by and conscripted all able-bodied men for a bloody war, but the old man's son, being crippled, was passed over in the draft. Once more the neighbors came to congratulate the old man on his good luck, and once more he replied, "How do you know this is good luck?"

The story ends there, though it could have gone on forever. The point of the parable is that things are not always as they seem. In the long run, some immediate circumstance, good or bad, may ultimately lead to a most unexpected outcome.

Today's text was written to a people who were convinced that their immediate circumstance was the worst of fortunes. The message of the prophet, however, enabled them to see that their temporary suffering would lead to a glorious future. Unlike the Chinese parable, however, which pictured a life driven by fate, this prophetic message declared that Israel's negative circumstance would be turned into something good by the power of a sovereign God.

B. Lesson Background

The text of this lesson comprises the second of the four "Servant Songs" of Isaiah. These songs were written to encourage that generation of Judeans who were exiled to Babylon (586-538 B.C.). The destruction of Jerusalem and the subsequent deportation of her citizens to Babylon had long been foretold by the prophets as the means by which God would punish His people for their idolatrous ways. The Servant Songs, however, revealed to these exiles that their suffering would be more than punitive. Their suffering would "restore" Israel by paying the penalty of the nation's apostasy and thereby paving the way for the reestablishment of the state of Israel in the land of promise. These repentant exiles would "save" the nations by becoming a living illustration of the truth that those who submit to the true and living God will, in due time, find their vindication and reward. As the nations witnessed the obedient suffering of the exiled Judeans and the positive benefits it brought to the Israelite nation, they too would desire to know the God who brought this to pass.

I. The Servant's Reflections (Isaiah 49:1-4)

A. The Servant's Credentials to Minister on God's Behalf (vv. 1-3)

1. Listen, O isles, unto me; and hearken, ye people, from far; The LORD hath called me from the womb; from the bowels of my mother hath he made mention of my name.

Whereas in the first Servant Song (Isaiah 42:1-4) God was the speaker, in the second, the speaker was the servant (the exiled Judeans).

Listen . . . hearken. In the first three verses of the song, the servant spoke of his call to servanthood and the credentials that qualified him to speak authoritatively on God's behalf. This language bears some resemblance to other texts in Scripture that record prophetic calls. For example, of the prophet Jeremiah it was said that he too was commissioned from the womb and had his mouth equipped to speak for God (see Jeremiah 1:5, 9). To the *isles* and *people, from far* the servant affirmed his calling, because that which God would accomplish through His servant Israel would take place before the eyes of the nations and would ultimately be for their benefit.

The Lord hath called me from the womb. Interpreters disagree over the exact intent of this statement. Some suggest that it is poetic hyperbole, an exaggeration for the sake of emphasis. It seems better, however, to regard it as an actual statement of fact. In a manner similar to the commissionings of Jeremiah and Paul, God consecrated Israel to His service before Israel was even born (see Jeremiah 1:5; Galatians 1:15; Isaiah 44:2, 24; 46:3). This reference to mother and child could refer to God's actual use of Abraham and Sarah to produce the chosen people (compare Isaiah 51:2). Above all it is clear from the prophet's language that Israel's appearance on the world scene was no accident, but was the unfolding of the predetermined will of God. Isaiah punctuated this truth by placing *The Lord* in the emphatic position in the Hebrew text. This great work was the Lord's doing, not man's. Only God can determine the future and announce it before it comes to pass.

2. And he hath made my mouth like a sharp sword; in the shadow of his hand hath he hid me, and made me a polished shaft; in his quiver hath he hid me.

And he hath made my mouth like a sharp sword. With these words the prophet began to describe Israel's role as the spokesperson of the Lord. God's word (spoken through the servant) was like a *sharp sword* and *polished shaft* (arrow) in its power to announce and execute the will of God. In similar fashion Ephesians 6:17 speaks of "the sword of the Spirit, which is the word of God" (see also Hebrews 4:12). Israel would proclaim the authoritative word of the King of Heaven and earth. It would constitute a sharp and penetrating word as it announced judgment upon the Babylonians and liberated Israel from her bondage.

The references to the Lord's servant being hidden *in the shadow of his hand* and *in his quiver* are of particular interest. At one level this language undoubtedly refers to God's protection of His people during their years of captivity. The stories of Daniel and his companions illustrate how God vindicated those who remained faithful to Him during the exile (see Daniel 1, 3, 6). It is possible, however, that the prophet had an additional thought in mind. This may be his way of saying that the word of judgment that God would announce through Israel would come quickly and unexpectedly as a blow from a concealed weapon. Israel, like a sheathed sword or a quivered arrow, was hidden away until the time came for it to become an instrument of God's will. Certainly no one expected the defeated and devastated Israelite nation to have any power to bring about the destruction of mighty Babylon. But God, who is the Lord of history, in His own time and in His own way unsheathed the sword of His servant's word to announce Babylon's doom and to bring about the return of His people from their captivity. Sacred history reveals that God has made a habit of taking that or those whom men think obscure or unimportant and using them as the instruments of His will.

3. And said unto me, Thou art my servant, O Israel, in whom I will be glorified.

Thou art my servant, O Israel. This is but one of several places in chapters 40-55 of Isaiah where the servant is identified as *Israel* (see 41:8, 9; 44:1, 2; 48:20). In the literary and historical context of chapters 40-55, "Israel" (Jacob) most specifically refers to the penitent Judean exiles who learned the sad lessons of the exile and who, as a faithful "remnant," obediently endured their suffering as they expectantly waited for the Lord's deliverance (compare 46:3-13; also 43:1-13; 44:1-5; 49:8-13). The idea of the "servant" as one (group) from the nation whose

---

How to Say It

ACHAN. *A*-kan.
ZERUBBABEL. Zeh-*rub*-uh-bul.

action saved the nation is an important theme in the Servant Songs (49:5; 52:13—53:12) and ultimately anticipated the vicarious suffering and death of Jesus Christ (see Acts 8:30-35; 1 Peter 2:21-25).

In whom I will be glorified. In the Old Testament the concept of "glory" carries with it the idea of "honor," "beauty," or "splendor." With reference to God it often manifested itself in the form of a brilliant, radiating light that evoked a sense of awe in those who beheld it. In this text the prophet suggests that the servant Israel would function like a mirror to reflect God's splendor to the world. This analogy is an important one and is particularly instructive to the modern church. A mirror is nothing in itself. It can only reflect the light that strikes it. Likewise, the church has no glory of its own. It serves only to reflect the glory of God revealed in His Son. The church is what God intended it to be when it reflects glory rather than receives it.

PRENATAL DESTINY

If our first grandchild is a boy, he surely is destined to be a sports fan, for my son-in-law is not only an avid sports spectator but a participant as well. If our grandchild is a girl, she surely will be a brilliant student and a gifted musician, like her mother!

Neither of these predictions necessarily will come true. Most gifts and interests are possibilities for both males and females, especially since today's children are being "freed" from gender-specific stereotypes. We may have a granddaughter who plays ball, or a grandson who plays piano, or twins (wouldn't that be grand!) who both do all things well. We can only guess what their personal inclinations may be.

God's call of Israel to be His servant nation had to do with more than genetic traits and parental predispositions. It was by divine design that Israel would be the agent to carry out God's eternal will for the human race. Even before God's nation was born, He promised Abraham that it would be so. In Canaan as sojourners, in Egypt as slaves, in Judah as a people, in Babylon as exiles, and back in Judah as only a remnant—

The Living Word

visual 7

God's chosen servant was brought along toward their ultimate destiny. Through Israel all the nations of the earth would be blessed, for Israel was to be progenitor of the Messiah.

As "new Israel," Christians have inherited the destiny of God's chosen. Jesus calls us, and those who follow Him are to be servants of His salvation.   —R. W. B.

B. The Servant's Misunderstanding of His Ministry (v. 4)

4. Then I said, I have labored in vain, I have spent my strength for nought, and in vain: yet surely my judgment is with the LORD, and my work with my God.

For the expression *then I said,* one might substitute "but I thought to myself." Israel is speaking. The people were reflecting upon their recent history, and the statement reveals that they misunderstood what happened to them and how God could use it to accomplish His purposes in His world. It was part of a consistent pattern of "deafness" and "blindness" that the servant demonstrated toward the role of God in the Babylonian captivity (see Isaiah 42:18-25). As the exiles looked back over more than fifty years of captivity, they saw only shame and humiliation. The servant Israel's presence in Babylon appeared to be just the opposite of what he had been called to become. The one who was called to be the sharp sword of the Lord and the mirror of His glory was instead an outcast among the nations. Stripped of their freedom and their dignity, these exiled Judeans felt helpless to achieve their own agenda, much less accomplish the work of the Lord. The repetition of the word *vain* punctuated their sense of futility. This is the same term that is used so often in Ecclesiastes, where it describes a life that is completely empty and meaningless. Measured by circumstance alone, the servant's life appeared to have served no purpose.

It was faith, and faith alone, that enabled the servant to find meaning in life when there appeared to be none. This is what he meant when he said, *yet surely my judgment is with the Lord.* With these words the servant expressed his unshakable confidence that God who promised him vindication was capable of bringing it to pass.

These words of the servant illustrate the capacity of faith to empower life. While faith expects much of the believer, it also supplies much to the believer. It enables us to see life as something far more than a trip through time controlled by chance or circumstance. We can see it rather as a pilgrimage, a spiritual journey with an eternal destination. The events along the way, positive or negative, do not dictate life's meaning. They are part of a process controlled by the will of a sovereign God, which unfolds in our lives as we submit to Him by faith. For us, as for the servant, faith can give meaning to life even in its most empty hours.

BY FAITH, NOT BY SIGHT

Laborers who work diligently with few or no visible results have to be admired. Egyptians who first labored to build the pyramids did not live long enough to see the project completed. Though they could observe progress year-to-year, they could only imagine what the finished structures would look like.

Assembly line workers usually see only a small part of the product they work on. Soldiers risk limbs and life in battle, as they advance into enemy territory or stand off enemy attacks, even though they do not know how things are going in the larger war effort. Teachers, social workers, and other "people persons" often work with little visible proof of their effectiveness. All of these folk are motivated by some degree of faith that they are making a contribution in the advancement toward a significant goal. Reflecting on his situation, the Lord's servant began to feel that he had labored in vain. His confidence in God, however, carried him through. He stated, "Surely the justice due to me is with Jehovah" (v. 4, *American Standard Version*).

Christians often must do kingdom work without perceptible positive results. But "we walk by faith, not by sight" (2 Corinthians 5:7). Jesus taught that a significant portion of gospel seeds scattered never produce fruit (Matthew 13:1-23). Yet we must keep believing that our "labor is not in vain in the Lord" (1 Corinthians 15:58).

—R. W. B.

II. The Purpose of the Servant's Calling (Isaiah 49:5, 6)

A. The Servant's Ministry to Israel (vv. 5, 6a)

5, 6a. And now, saith the LORD that formed me from the womb to be his servant, to bring Jacob again to him, Though Israel be not gathered, yet shall I be glorious in the eyes of the LORD, and my God shall be my strength. And he said, It is a light thing that thou shouldest be my servant to raise up the tribes of Jacob, and to restore the preserved of Israel.

Our search for the meaning of this passage must begin with two important considerations: one involves the wording of the Hebrew text, and the other centers on interpretation. The textual issue centers in the phrase *though Israel be*

not gathered. In the original Hebrew, the word *not* is identical in sound and almost identical in written form with the expression *to him*. The Dead Sea Scrolls and most ancient versions suggest that the latter is correct and that this phrase should read, *and that Israel should be gathered to him* (as it is translated in most of the more recent Bible versions). Thus restored, this phrase simply affirms what the text elsewhere says—that the servant's goal was to restore Israel to her preexilic status as an independent state in Palestine.

The second and far more difficult issue is how to interpret the meaning of the important term *servant* in verses 5 and 6. The most obvious answer is supplied in verse 3, where Israel is clearly identified as the servant. As most interpreters have noted, however, the expression *And now* at the beginning of verse 5 suggests a break with what has preceded it. Further, it is noted in these verses (5, 6) that the servant's task was to bring back or restore Israel. If the servant was Israel, how could Israel restore Israel?

Commentators have gone in at least three directions in their attempts to solve this interpretive difficulty. Some suggest that the servant here was not the Israel of verse 3, but rather the prophet Isaiah who delivered God's liberating word concerning the restoration of Israel (see Isaiah 20:3). Others suggest that the reference was to Cyrus the Great, the Persian king whom God would actually use to accomplish Israel's liberation (see Isaiah 44:24—45:4). While either of these interpretations is possible and is within the range of meanings assigned to the term *servant* by the prophet Isaiah, there is another interpretation that is possible, and perhaps preferable, to the immediate context.

As suggested in the comments on verse 3, in Isaiah 40-55 "Israel" sometimes refers to the exiled Judeans or, even more specifically, to those among them who constituted a faithful "remnant" of penitent believers who accepted God's judgment upon their apostasy and who obediently suffered through the captivity in faith that God would eventually restore them (Isaiah 46:3-12; see also 1:27, 28). This notion has the support of the opening lines of the section in Isaiah devoted to the servant of the Lord (40:1, 2) and also best explains the primary meaning of the final Servant Song (52:13—53:12) in its immediate, historical context, namely, that the servant (the penitent Judean exiles) would suffer for the entire nation, paving the way for their restoration to Canaan.

This is but one example of the larger Old Testament concept of the "one (or few) for the many," which is behind such texts as Abraham's bargaining for the citizens of Sodom (a few righteous being able to save the evil many, Genesis 18:16-33) and the furor over the sin in Israel's camp (Achan's sin resulting in judgment for the army of Israel, Joshua 7). The idea behind the one for the many is that the righteousness (or sin) of an individual member of the community has the power to benefit (or harm) the entire community. Other examples may be found in the Old Testament system of sacrifice, where the slaughter of unblemished animals had the power to "make atonement" (remove the consequences) for the sins of the entire nation (Leviticus 16). In similar fashion the death of the high priest had the capacity to clear the guilt of the manslayers who had been exiled to the cities of refuge (Numbers 35:25, 28).

B. The Servant's Ministry to All the World (v. 6b)

6b. I will also give thee for a light to the Gentiles, that thou mayest be my salvation unto the end of the earth.

God's election of Israel to be His chosen people was never an end, in and of itself. It was rather a means to a greater end that had implications for the whole world (see Genesis 12:3; 22:18; 26:4; 28:14). Though the complete fulfillment of this universal mission was not accomplished until the coming of Christ and the spread of His church (Luke 2:32), this generation of exiled Judeans would yet participate in its gradual unfolding by bearing witness to what can happen to a people who submit to the Lord God of the universe. The vindication and restoration that followed their suffering are held out as a promise of what God will do for all peoples who bow before Him.

Home Daily Bible Readings

Monday, Jan. 8—God Is Everywhere (Psalm 139:7-14)
Tuesday, Jan. 9—God Is All-Knowing (Psalm 33:13-22)
Wednesday, Jan. 10—God Is All-Powerful (Jeremiah 32:17-22)
Thursday, Jan. 11—The Source of Mercy (Psalm 130)
Friday, Jan. 12—The Promise of Peace (Isaiah 26:1-8)
Saturday, Jan. 13—Message of Salvation (Isaiah 48:9-16)
Sunday, Jan. 14—Message of Joy (Isaiah 48:17-22)

Paul and Barnabas quoted this part of verse 6 to explain their turning to the Gentiles after the Jews had rejected their message in Antioch (Acts 13:47). There is a sense in which the ministry of the Servant, begun in Israel and fulfilled in Jesus Christ, continued on in the work of the early church. Not only was Jesus of Nazareth the personified Servant of the Lord, but also His followers could be identified with God's Servant as they spread the gospel, which brought light to the nations. In the same way, Christians today can participate in the ministry of God's Servant as they proclaim the good news that Jesus saves.

Conclusion

A. Misunderstanding God

The pages of Scripture are full of the stories of people who misunderstood what God was seeking to do in their lives. Abraham misunderstood how God was going to provide him a son through Sarah; so Abraham produced another son through Hagar instead. In his suffering, Job thought God was unjustly punishing him for some sin he had not committed, when in reality God was permitting his faith to be tested. Jacob thought his life had been a struggle against men, when all along he had really been wrestling with God. Jonah resisted, then resented his mission to Nineveh because he mistakenly thought only Israel should be saved. Peter believed he was helping Jesus when he vowed to defend Him against harm, only to learn from Jesus himself that such an act would actually play into the hands of Satan. Paul mistakenly believed that Christianity posed a threat to the worship of the one true God and thought it his duty to persecute the church.

All of these incidents illustrate the danger of hastily drawn conclusions about the will of God for human life. As today's lesson indicates, the servant too misunderstood the purpose of what God had brought about in his life. As those who seek to serve God today, we should faithfully follow His will as revealed in Scripture and wait patiently for Him to disclose the meaning of the individual events of our lives.

B. Let Us Pray

Father in Heaven, grant us the courage to complete the mission to which You have called Your church. May we have the patience to wait upon You to fulfill Your promises and to accomplish Your will in Your own time. In Jesus' name we pray. Amen.

C. Thought to Remember

Human extremity is God's opportunity.

Learning by Doing

This page contains an alternate lesson plan emphasizing learning activities. Classes desiring such student involvement will find these suggestions helpful.

Learning Goals

Following today's study, each adult will:

1. List what God does for His servant to prepare and support him for his assigned tasks.

2. Affirm the purpose of God's servant.

3. Be able to quote verse 6b of the text.

Into the Lesson

Before class, trace on paper the outlines of various nations of the world and then cut out the outlines. Among them include these island nations: Australia, Cyprus, Japan, Indonesia, Madagascar, Great Britain, New Zealand, Philippines, Cuba. If your time for preparation is limited, simply put the outlines on sheets and do not cut them.

As class members arrive, give each an outline. To begin the session, ask if anyone recognizes the shape he or she holds. If a clue is needed, identify them as nations. If a second clue is necessary, note that some are islands. Have all the nations identified, and then direct your learners to skim today's text and explain how these nations relate to Isaiah's revelation.

Into the Word

If possible, find and display a large map of the Old Testament world of the sixth century B.C. Highlight Jerusalem and Babylon, the capital city of the empire in which the Jews were held captive. From this land God's people were to be gathered and restored to their homeland.

Write the following truth statements on slips of paper, one per slip, and distribute the slips randomly to your class members. Do *not* include the numbers with the statements.

(1) "He has called me." (2) "He knows and calls me by name." (3) "He has sharpened my tongue for truth." (4) "He hides me in His hand." (5) "He calls me His servant." (6) "He will reward me for my work for Him." (7) "He formed me in the womb." (8) "He expects me to restore Israel." (9) "He sees me as glorious." (10) "He is my strength." (11) "He expects me to be light to the Gentiles." (12) "He makes me His vessel of salvation to the ends of the earth."

Direct those who hold these truth statements regarding God's servant to come to the front and line themselves in the order of the Scripture verses in which the truths are revealed. Then have the twelve read the statements in their

order. Then, have another class member read today's Scripture text aloud so the entire class can either confirm the sequence of the twelve statements or rearrange them as necessary.

Now ask your group of truth holders to separate themselves into two groups: group one indicating what God does for His servant, and group two indicating what God wants His servant to do. Have them reread the truths aloud, first group one, then group two. (Probably only numbers 8, 11, and 12 will be in the second group.)

Let the truth holders be seated. Now have the whole class identify truths from the text *not* used in the preceding activity. Such ideas as the following should be noted: 1. God expects all nations to heed His servant (v. 1). 2. God uses His servant as an arrow (v. 2b). 3. God is glorified *in* the servant (v. 3). 4. The servant acknowledges his feelings of futility (v. 4a). 5. The servant's role to save Israel is the lesser of his roles (v. 6a). Write these ideas on the chalkboard as they are suggested. When the list is complete, ask, "Are these truths any less significant than those highlighted in the previous group activity? Explain."

Discuss the following questions as review of this study. (1) What was the task of God's servant Israel? (2) What did God do to prepare His servant? (3) What did God do to support His servant? (4) How does the task God gives the church differ from the task of God's servant Israel?

Into Life

Verse 6 is the heart of today's lesson. The servant's task was to spread the light of God's salvation to the whole world. Christians today are to join in that task. Help your class memorize verse 6b as a way the Holy Spirit can daily urge each to fulfill his or her servant's task.

Write the two parts of verse 6b on two lines, the second line under the first. The word *that,* begins the second line, which should be offset to the left. Point out the parallels: *I* (God) is over *thou* (servant); *to the Gentiles* is over *of the earth.* Ask for volunteers to say it solo; then have the class read the verse together two or three times. Divide the class. Let one half say the first line, and the other half the second line. When general familiarity is gained, close the session by reminding your students of their privilege and duty to be God's servants.

Let's Talk It Over

The questions on this page are designed to encourage review of the lesson Scriptures and to promote discussion of the lesson by the class. The answers provided are only discussion starters. Let your class talk it over from there.

1. In the text for this lesson, the Lord's servant acknowledged his doubts concerning his usefulness in accomplishing the mission to which he had been called (v. 4). What doubts did he express? How may Christians relate to this?

The servant's primary doubts seem to have been centered in a sense of futility. He felt that he had "labored in vain" and spent his strength for nothing. In spite of it, *there were no results.* Few things are more discouraging. When we put our best effort into something in which we really believe, but nothing comes of it, we begin to question our own usefulness. A sense of futility may then overtake any servant of God.

2. What can we learn from the way the servant handled his feelings of futility?

First, he openly acknowledged them. He didn't deny or hide them from himself or the Lord. They were honest feelings of frustration and discouragement. This is always a good first step for anyone struggling with such feelings.

Second, what he could not control he left in God's hands (v. 4). Faithfulness, not success or failure, was the real issue here. Likewise, we who are Christians are called to be faithful, not successful. Our discouragement often is linked to our pride. We evaluate our service from the world's perspective of personal success, rather than God's perspective of integrity and faithfulness. Our responsibility is to engage wholeheartedly in the task to which God has called us, to do the best that we can, to learn and grow as we serve, and to leave the results with Him. He will reward us according to our faithfulness rather than our success as determined by human standards.

3. As suggested by today's text, what attitudes and/or perspectives tend to foster doubt and discouragement in us as we seek to live for Christ and serve Him?

One attitude that may be mentioned is our tendency to evaluate life by outward circumstances rather than by our relationship with God. Evidence of this attitude may be seen by examining the focus of our prayer life. For the most part, our prayers are requests for God to change the circumstances of our lives—whether it be health, finances, or relationships. A far better focus would be to pray for growth in the areas of our lives that would lead us to have a stronger, more mature, personal relationship with our Lord.

A perspective to consider is that our view of the mission to which we have been called may be too limited. When the servant expressed his sense of frustration and futility in not seeing results, God simply enlarged his perspective of the task. Hence, the servant's responsibility was not just to "restore the tribes of Jacob" but to be "a light for the Gentiles" so that he might bring God's salvation "to the ends of the earth" (v. 6, *New International Version*). Sometimes small complaints and frustrations vanish in the presence of tasks so huge that only God can accomplish them. Let us enlarge our vision—broaden our perspective—and stretch our faith so far that we cannot possibly expect victory unless God is in the undertaking. Then, trusting God to be our strength (v. 5), we will avoid the discouragement that can come from trusting in our own.

4. To what extent is your local congregation committed to the universal mission of "making disciples of all the nations"? What might you be able to do to enlarge the church's vision in this regard?

No congregation of Christians will ever be what Christ intended until they begin to act on His command to go "into all the world" with the gospel of salvation. This means not only giving generously to cross-cultural mission causes and church-planting efforts, but also sending out its own to the lost of the world. The place to begin is with a fresh understanding of the church's purpose. Only when we focus on this mission and set goals that are unattainable unless we are in partnership with God, will we begin to change disheartened disciples into faithful servants. Perhaps your class might set an example in outreach by sending out one of your own, underwriting a significant portion of a church planter's needs, or entering into a support relationship with a missionary or a recruit serving on a mission field.

The Servant's Steadfast Endurance

January 21
Lesson 8

DEVOTIONAL READING: Hebrews 12:1-11.

LESSON SCRIPTURE: Isaiah 50:1-11.

PRINTED TEXT: Isaiah 50:4-11.

Isaiah 50:4-11

4 The Lord GOD hath given me the tongue of the learned, that I should know how to speak a word in season to him that is weary: he wakeneth morning by morning, he wakeneth mine ear to hear as the learned.

5 The Lord GOD hath opened mine ear, and I was not rebellious, neither turned away back.

6 I gave my back to the smiters, and my cheeks to them that plucked off the hair: I hid not my face from shame and spitting.

7 For the Lord GOD will help me; therefore shall I not be confounded: therefore have I set my face like a flint, and I know that I shall not be ashamed.

8 He is near that justifieth me; who will contend with me? let us stand together: who is mine adversary? let him come near to me.

9 Behold, the Lord GOD will help me; who is he that shall condemn me? lo, they all shall wax old as a garment; the moth shall eat them up.

10 Who is among you that feareth the LORD, that obeyeth the voice of his servant, that walketh in darkness, and hath no light? let him trust in the name of the LORD, and stay upon his God.

11 Behold, all ye that kindle a fire, that compass yourselves about with sparks: walk in the light of your fire, and in the sparks that ye have kindled. This shall ye have of mine hand; ye shall lie down in sorrow.

Jan 21

GOLDEN TEXT: The Lord GOD will help me; therefore shall I not be confounded: therefore have I set my face like a flint, and I know that I shall not be ashamed.—Isaiah 50:7.

God's Promise of Deliverance
(Isaiah)
Unit 2: The Ministry of the Suffering Servant
(Lessons 5-9)

Lesson Aims

This lesson should encourage students to:

1. Appreciate the servant's faithful commitment to his difficult mission.

2. Have greater confidence in the power of God to vindicate those who serve Him.

3. Strive toward the faithful completion of the Christian calling.

Lesson Outline

INTRODUCTION
    A. "Should Such a Man as I Flee?"
    B. Lesson Background
  I. THE SERVANT ENDURES PERSECUTION (Isaiah 50:4-6)
    A. The Servant Is Instructed by God (v. 4)
      A Word Fitly Spoken
    B. The Servant Is Obedient in Spite of Persecution (vv. 5, 6)
      Hearing Aids
  II. THE SERVANT HAS CONFIDENCE IN THE LORD'S HELP (Isaiah 50:7-9)
    A. The Servant Believes God Will Deliver Him (v. 7)
    B. The Servant Challenges His Enemies to Compete Against God (vv. 8, 9)
 III. THE SERVANT EXTENDS THE CALL OF GOD (Isaiah 50:10, 11)
    A. The Servant Encourages the Godly (v. 10)
    B. The Servant Warns the Ungodly (v. 11)
CONCLUSION
    A. "Finishing the Race"
    B. Let Us Pray
    C. Thought to Remember

Visual 8 of the visuals packet conveys the thought that each new day brings renewed opportunities to serve others in the name of God. The visual is shown on page 180.

Introduction

A. "Should Such a Man as I Flee?"

Our world is full of fleeing people. Rather than face life's challenges and endure life's hardships they run from them. "Move on" is their motto—to a new school, a new job, a new town, a new "life."

In striking contrast to this fleeing spirit stand the strong words of Nehemiah, the wall builder of old Jerusalem: "Should such a man as I flee?" (Nehemiah 6:11). These words were offered in response to a threat raised against him by the enemies of God's people. Wanting no strong Jerusalem they resisted all of his efforts to reconstruct its walls. Refusing to be distracted by their interruptions or deterred by their opposition, Nehemiah remained true to his calling and completed the task that God assigned him. Aware of who he was and, more importantly, of who God was, Nehemiah simply refused to quit.

This same spirit of faithful devotion to God's calling was displayed by the servant of the Lord in today's text. In spite of rejection and persecution, the servant was determined to see his task through to the end God desired.

B. Lesson Background

The third of the four "Servant Songs" of Isaiah is the subject of this lesson. Though the speaker in this song is not identified, the language and context suggest that he is the "servant" of the previous two songs (42:1-4; 49:1-6). As noted in the two previous lessons, there is some debate over who the servant is in these texts. The broader context of Isaiah 40—55 favors an interpretation that the title "servant" refers to the nation of Israel (see 41:8; 44:2, 21; 45:4; 48:20; 49:3) or, more particularly, to that generation of penitent Judean exiles who obediently endured the suffering of the Babylonian captivity and became the faithful remnant from whom God would rebuild His nation (see Isaiah 10:20-22). This particular song begins to explore the servant's faithfulness to his calling in spite of persecution from those who opposed him.

I. The Servant Endures Persecution (Isaiah 50:4-6)

A. The Servant Is Instructed by God (v. 4)

4. **The Lord GOD hath given me the tongue of the learned, that I should know how to speak a word in season to him that is weary: he wakeneth morning by morning, he wakeneth mine ear to hear as the learned.**

The servant (the faithful remnant) was speaking either to his fellow Judean exiles or, perhaps, as in the the case of the previous Servant Song (49:1-6), to the nations at large. He began by describing how the Lord prepared him to speak a comforting word to those who were weary of suffering, even as he was.

The Lord hath given me. The first words that came out of the servant's mouth revealed his understanding of who controlled his life and of at least one of the purposes that his suffering had served. The servant saw himself as a pupil, enrolled in the "school of hard knocks." Experience had been his teacher. It was not an experience dictated by chance, but one shaped by the unfolding will of a sovereign God. His suffering was not accidental; it was providential. It was used by God to equip him to minister effectively to his fellow exiles.

The servant's suffering resulted in a *tongue of the learned* (literally, "tongue of pupils"). The idea behind this unique expression (it is used only here and in 8:16, 17) is that before the servant (the faithful remnant) could become a teacher, he first had to become a student. He was to speak not only what he had been told, but also what he had personally experienced. Taught daily (*morning by morning*) by the captivity that those who wait upon the Lord will eventually find their strength, the servant was uniquely qualified to speak an appropriate word (*a word in season*) to the *weary*.

Among other things, this text teaches the unique value of knowledge gained by experience. This kind of knowledge has at least two advantages over theoretical knowledge. First, it is typically more empathetic toward the student. The teacher has already gone where he or she wishes to take the pupil. Second, it is frequently more respected by the student. It has been authenticated by life, tried and proved true in the real world. It seems that God had this in mind when He sent His Son to earth. The author of Hebrews in 2:10-18 declared that Jesus was uniquely qualified to be the supreme messenger of God's truth because, unlike the angels, He came to earth and spoke as a human to humans: "For in that he himself hath suffered being tempted, he is able to succor them that are tempted" (v. 18). There is also a sense in which Christians, after the model of Christ, are prepared by suffering to minister more effectively to their fellow humans.

A WORD FITLY SPOKEN

Shopping for greeting cards can take a long time. One reason is that many cards make interesting reading; more important, however, searching for just the right verse or sentiment to fit the recipient and the occasion deserves careful consideration. And that translates into time.

Saying the right words to the right person at the right time is a gift. Friends with that kind of intuition and initiative are very special. For one who is on the receiving end of such communication, there is great comfort and encouragement. And those who speak (write, send) the messages

---

How to Say It

BAAL. *Bay*-ul.
NEHEMIAH. *Nee*-heh-*my*-uh (strong accent on *my*).
PHARAOH. *Fair*-o or *Fay*-ro.
ZECHARIAH. Zek-uh-*rye*-uh.

---

experience great satisfaction and blessing, too. "A word fitly spoken is like apples of gold in pictures of silver" (Proverbs 25:11).

Israel the servant was given the ability to speak "a word in season" to the "weary"—the discouraged and downtrodden exiles in captivity. This honor and opportunity has been passed on to Christians, the church, God's servant in this age.

The gospel is the *right word*, the lost are the *right audience*, and now is the *right time*. "A word spoken in due season, how good is it!" (Proverbs 15:23).   —R. W. B.

B. The Servant Is Obedient in Spite of Persecution (vv. 5, 6)

5, 6. The Lord GOD hath opened mine ear, and I was not rebellious, neither turned away back. I gave my back to the smiters, and my cheeks to them that plucked off the hair: I hid not my face from shame and spitting.

Not every child of God who suffers profits from the experience. Some are broken by suffering. Others are embittered by it. In this verse the servant expressed the attitude that enabled him to turn suffering into a springboard for spiritual growth. This same attitude enables the believer today to grow spiritually as a result of enduring life's hard blows.

The Lord God hath opened mine ear. The servant was able to remain faithful in the face of suffering because, by faith, he saw it as God's will that he should suffer. He believed God was in his suffering, using it as a stimulus to his spiritual awakening. Earlier Isaiah characterized the servant (Israel) as spiritually "blind" and "deaf," having failed to learn from the Lord's chastening (Isaiah 42:18-25). This passage confirms that what Israel had not learned from previous plagues, famines, and invasions they finally learned from the destruction of their nation by the Babylonians: that God would hold His people accountable for their rebellion against Him (see 42:24). Accepting his suffering as the Lord's chastening, the servant did not recoil against it but obediently submitted to it, hearing its message and learning its truth as for the first time (50:4, 5). Smarting from his suffering, the servant submitted to God, as if saying to Him, "I hear you." There is a sense in which the servant's experience illustrates the claim that "sometimes God has to get our attention before He can instruct us."

Of course, it was not God who actually smote the servant's *back* or *plucked off the hair* of his *cheeks*. These cruel acts, meant to be humiliating as well as painful, were perpetrated against Israel by their Babylonian oppressors. Recognizing this, the reader can understand how the servant could both nobly endure the suffering that his adversaries inflicted upon him and then later condemn them and pronounce their doom (v. 11). He could endure it because he knew God was using it to awaken him spiritually and instruct him. Yet he could condemn his oppressors because they persecuted him for their own evil and vindictive reasons. For this they should and would be held accountable.

HEARING AIDS

Communication fails more often, it seems, because of poor listening skills than because of poor speaking skills. Ask almost any wife. Some complain that their husbands won't talk to them, but most accuse their mates of *not listening*.

Actually, the fault of poor listening habits is not gender related; females probably are just as guilty as males. Good listeners are hard to find. Effective counselors, successful salespeople, and happily married couples have learned the great importance of intentional listening. It is a gift in some persons, yet a skill that can be developed by anyone to *everyone's* benefit.

God gave servant Israel "the tongue of the learned, that I should know how to speak" (v. 4). He also gave him the gift of discernment through listening: "The Lord God hath opened mine ear" (v. 5). Both speaking and listening were essential to the servant's mission.

Successful communication continues to require clear speaking and attentive listening. God's people are advised, "Be swift to hear, slow to speak" (James 1:19). The emphasis is upon hearing. As many have cleverly observed, that is why God gave us two ears, but only one mouth!

Morning
by morning,
he wakeneth mine ear to hear.

visual 8

Christians must listen with their *hearts*, too, ever sensitive to nonverbal expressions of pain and unspoken cries for help. "Open my ears, Lord, and teach me to listen."   —R. W. B.

II. The Servant Has Confidence in the Lord's Help (Isaiah 50:7-9)

A. The Servant Believes That God Will Deliver Him (v. 7)

7. For the Lord GOD will help me; therefore shall I not be confounded: therefore have I set my face like a flint, and I know that I shall not be ashamed.

For the Lord God will help me. The confidence that the servant expressed did not come from "within" but from "above." It grew out of a faith that God would not abandon him to his foes. This faith was well founded. The pages of Scripture are filled with the accounts of persons who have stood up for God in the face of opposition and found Him to be "a very present help in trouble" (Psalm 46:1). Moses before Pharaoh, Elijah before Ahab and the prophets of Baal, and Daniel and his companions before the Babylonians are familiar examples of well-placed faith in God's power to protect His children.

Therefore I shall not be confounded. With these words the servant's expectations of God are clarified. The servant did not envision help in the form of freedom from suffering. Rather, he expected help to enable him to endure suffering. The sting was taken out of the blow and the humiliation out of the abuse because the servant knew that it ultimately would not stand, it would not carry the day. The servant was able to endure because he understood that the future was not in the hands of the ruthless; it was in the hands of the sovereign Lord of the universe.

The same resource that God provided His servant is available to the struggling saint today. The power of suffering to undo us is overcome by the realization that God will not allow us to suffer more than we can endure, and that He has prepared a destiny for us where suffering no longer can intrude to rob us of our joy.

I set my face like a flint. This metaphor of resolve describes the determination of the servant to carry out his task in spite of all obstacles and opposition. He was not the first to do so. Throughout the history of Israel many who answered God's call faced opposition and even persecution in their efforts to serve Him. Sometimes this opposition came from a foreign source, such as a belligerent king or a hostile foe. In the case of Israel's prophets, opposition often came from the Israelites themselves. As the prophets proclaimed a message that God's people did not want to hear, they were persecuted by kings and commoners alike. In preparing Ezekiel to go to the rebellious house of Israel to speak His words to them, God had to make the prophet's face "harder than flint" in order to withstand the opposition he would receive from his countrymen (Ezekiel 3:8, 9). It is possible, therefore, that at least part of the persecution the servant faced likewise came from his own countrymen.

B. The Servant Challenges His Enemies to Compete Against God (vv. 8, 9)

8, 9. He is near that justifieth me; who will contend with me? let us stand together: who is mine adversary? let him come near to me. Behold, the Lord GOD will help me; who is he that shall condemn me? lo, they all shall wax old as a garment; the moth shall eat them up.

The language of these verses is that of the law court. The servant envisioned himself as the accused in a legal tribunal. The exact identity of his *adversary* is unclear. The adversary could be those who are described in verse 6, the Babylonian oppressors of the Judean exiles; or the adversary could be skeptical Jews who remained unconvinced that God was about to do a great thing through His servant (the faithful remnant of Israel), as verses 10 and 11 may imply. The fact that the adversary came to *contend* and *condemn* rather than physically harm the servant would seem to favor the view that these were fellow exiles who were slow to believe that anything good would come out of Israel's suffering in the Babylonian captivity.

It seems that the remnant's claim to servanthood had not gone unchallenged. To all appearances the faithful exiles seemed more abandoned by God than chosen by Him. Here they were, helpless captives of a pagan nation, without their temple and without their land, broken and humiliated by their devastating defeat. In the minds of many Judeans, the stigma of their captivity was so great that they would never be able to live it down. Never again would they be worthy to bear the title, "the chosen people."

This same claim was made against them even after they returned to the promised land. The prophet Zechariah was later to answer that objection by relating a vision he had from God. It depicted Satan accusing Joshua (the high priest of the postexilic community) of being defiled by the captivity and disqualified to preside over the temple worship. It was the Lord himself who came to Joshua's defense, purifying him and pronouncing him qualified to lead the worship of the restored nation (Zechariah 3:1-10).

In similar fashion the *Lord God* was *near* to justify the servant. He functioned as the servant's legal advocate. Though many, including some skeptical Jews, did not think the faithful remnant worthy to represent God, the Lord did. He declared them innocent and defended them against their detractors.

The Lord was brought into the proceedings with the dramatic, *Behold*. The servant's confidence swelled because he had a Vindicator who was more than a match for any would-be accuser. What adversary would dare approach to challenge him now? If they dared to accuse him, they would only grow old trying to make the charge stick, wasting away like a moth-eaten garment.

With similar words the apostle Paul expressed the confidence of the Christian: "If God be for us, who can be against us? . . . Who shall lay any thing to the charge of God's elect? It is God that justifieth. Who is he that condemneth?" (Romans 8:31-34).

III. The Servant Extends the Call of God (Isaiah 50:10, 11)

A. The Servant Encourages the Godly (v. 10)

10. Who is among you that feareth the LORD, that obeyeth the voice of his servant, that walketh in darkness, and hath no light? let him trust in the name of the LORD, and stay upon his God.

In this verse the servant addressed his fellow exiles or those who feared the Lord. In the Old Testament the "fear of the Lord" was the Hebrew equivalent to our idea of "piety" or "being sincerely religious." To "fear the Lord" meant to live reverently before God. It meant to live by a world view that saw God at the center of all of life. The ethics, the values, the priorities of the person who feared God were all shaped by the belief that there is one true God who made all things and to whom all are accountable.

It is important to note here that the prophet equated the person *that feareth the Lord* with one *that obeyeth the voice of his servant*. Reverence expects obedience. Though worship is one way in which a believer expresses reverence for God, the ultimate test of a believer's reverence for God is submission to His will. By calling for obedience to the servant's word, the prophet was equating the message that the servant delivered with the very will of God. As noted in the comments under verses 8 and 9, not all of the Jews accepted the notion that God was active in the remnant's suffering and that He was going to use them to provide release for the captives and restoration to the state of Israel. By placing these two phrases side by side, the prophet meant to equate reverence for God with acceptance of the prophet's explanation of the servant's (the faithful remnant's) mission.

Commentators differ over the meaning of the phrases, *that walketh in darkness, and hath no light.* It is not clear in the Hebrew text if these phrases refer to the servant or to the fellow exiles he was addressing. It seems more probable that the language describes those whom the servant was addressing. If this is correct, the *darkness* could describe the exiles' lack of enlightenment concerning all that God was going to achieve through His faithful remnant. The exiles had yet to accept the proclamation that the glory of the Lord would be revealed through the servant's patient endurance of his suffering and his subsequent vindication and restoration. They saw no end to their misfortunes and had no hope for the future.

The key to finding such a hope is expressed in the invitation that the prophet extended: *let him trust in the name of the Lord, and stay upon his God.* These phrases are essentially two different ways of saying the same thing. To trust in the Lord's name means to "place confidence in" or "rely upon" (*stay upon*) God. It means to take God at His word.

In this same way Christians find hope. Our hope, like the servant's, rests in the promises of God. Though our present circumstance may not suggest that we have a glorious future, God's Word yet declares it. We step out of the darkness of fear and despair when we trust in God's promises and take Him at His word.

B. The Servant Warns the Ungodly
(v. 11)

11. Behold, all ye that kindle a fire, that compass yourselves about with sparks: walk in the light of your fire, and in the sparks that ye have kindled. This shall ye have of mine hand; ye shall lie down in sorrow.

This final verse of the chapter is in the form of a prophecy of judgment. It is filled with a kind of irony that is typical of many prophetic threats of punishment. The idea is that the opponents of the servant would be destroyed by the very arguments that they used against him. The *fire* they kindled and the *light* in which they walked was their belief that they could have a secure future only by carving one out for themselves. And this they would do by accommodating themselves to their pagan captors, their beliefs and life-style. They had built an ideological and ethical *fire* that said, "When in Babylon, do as the Babylonians do." They

warmed themselves in its false sense of security. The sad irony is that by identifying with the pagan Babylonian nation they would end up suffering its fate—destruction and sorrow.

This final warning balances God's grace with His justice. Though the invitation to deliverance is generous and merciful, those who reject it will have to answer to God.

Conclusion
A. "Finishing the Race"

In Philippians 3:12-14 the apostle Paul describes the Christian life as a race, and calls the church to run it to the finish. It is clear from his words that the "race of life" is not a sprint; it is a distance run, and requires great endurance.

Paul was an outstanding example of one who was committed to finishing the race of life. In spite of stoning, beatings, shipwrecks, and imprisonment he continued to "press toward the mark." Like the servant of today's lesson he gave his "back to the smiters" and bore his suffering with grace, knowing ultimately that he would be vindicated by the Lord. Paul understood that when it comes to the race of life, it is not how fast the Christian runs but how far.

B. Let Us Pray

Father, we are thankful for the Christ who was willing to suffer on our behalf. Give us the strength to bear the burdens of servanthood with the confidence that You will sustain us and receive us to yourself. In Jesus' name, amen.

C. Thought to Remember

Those who serve God do so often at the cost of opposition and persecution. God will not abandon those who suffer in His name.

Home Daily Bible Readings

Monday, Jan. 15—God's Faithfulness (Isaiah 49:7-13)

Tuesday, Jan. 16—God Does Not Forget (Isaiah 49:14-18)

Wednesday, Jan. 17—God's Restoration (Isaiah 49:19-26)

Thursday, Jan. 18—God Reaches Out to All People (Isaiah 56:1-8)

Friday, Jan. 19—God Against Idolatry (Isaiah 57:1-13)

Saturday, Jan. 20—God Ready to Heal (Isaiah 57:14-21)

Sunday, Jan. 21—God Chooses Compassion (Isaiah 58:1-14)

Learning by Doing

This page contains an alternate lesson plan emphasizing learning activities. Classes desiring such student involvement will find these suggestions helpful.

Learning Goals

With this study of steadfast endurance, an adult student of the Word will:

1. Recall Isaiah 50 as the "no-matter-what" chapter about God's servant and his completion of duty.

2. Give at least three reasons for the servant's steadfast endurance, based on the chapter.

3. Move closer to a lifelong commitment to steadfast endurance in his or her own life.

Into the Lesson

Put the following letters on sheets of paper, one letter per sheet: A, A, E, H, M, N, O, R, T, T, T, W. Display them randomly at the front of your classroom, but in such a manner that you can rearrange them for correct wording. Tell your class that if they "belong to the right club," they will figure out the three-word phrase these letters can be rearranged to form. (The phrase is "NO MATTER WHAT.")

Let students guess either the whole phrase or individual words. After a short time, if they need help, move the first letters of the three words—N, M, W—into place and continue. Give more letter placement clues as you deem necessary. Emphasize that today's study is a reminder of a basic truth regarding all of God's servants: they serve no matter what comes.

Prepare the following descriptions of three members of God's "No-Matter-What Club." Recruit three members to read them one line at a time until someone guesses who each is.

PAUL: 1. No matter what, even if I am imprisoned, I will still do right. 2. No matter if close friends forsake me, I will be true to God. 3. No matter if I should be threatened with death, God still rules my life. 4. No matter what happens to me, I will preach the gospel in Asia and Europe.

JOSEPH: 1. No matter what, even if I am imprisoned, I will still do right. 2. No matter if those as close as brothers rise up against me, I will finish my job. 3. No matter if I am falsely accused, I will persist in righteousness. 4. No matter what, I will save my family in Egypt.

NEHEMIAH: 1. No matter what, I want to do the right thing for God. 2. No matter if men falsely accuse me to the authorities, I will be true. 3. No matter, if I have to carry a weapon while I work, I will continue. 4. No matter what, the wall will be built to God's glory!

Into the Word

Divide your class into groups of three or four students each. Tell the groups that the theme of this lesson is the steadfast endurance of the Lord's servant. Give each group a sheet of paper containing the following questions and have them examine today's Scripture text for the answers:

1. What support does God give to His servant to help him remain faithful to his task?

2. What are the circumstances that often interfere with endurance, and what response to each can be found in the text?

3. By what slogans, suggested by the text, can the servant of God be encouraged to endure?

Allot about ten minutes for the groups to work. As they share their answers to question 1, list them on the chalkboard. Expect some of these ideas (and others):

1. God's servant can endure because God is there every morning (v. 4).

2. Your enemies will grow old, weaken, and die (v. 9).

3. No servant of God will ultimately be ashamed (v. 7).

4. God's servants will speak the right word when you need it (v. 4).

5. God is your constant companion (v. 8).

For sample slogans, "One person and God are a majority," is close to the thought of verses 7 and 8. "Set your jaw and stiffen your lip—God is your helper!" is based on verse 7.

Into Life

Prepare several copies of the checklist below for learners to mark "on their own" and to keep to encourage or challenge them in the coming days.

SELF-CHECK OF MY STEADFAST ENDURANCE

Mark each statement with A for *always*, U for *usually*, O for *often*, S for *sometimes*, N for *never*. Decide how you are doing!

____ I speak the right words to weary ones.

____ I am aware of God's presence every morning.

____ I listen diligently to God's Word.

____ I tolerate abusive language from others.

____ I am determined to follow God no matter what.

____ I am committed to being God's servant.

Let's Talk It Over

The questions on this page are designed to encourage review of the lesson Scriptures and to promote discussion of the lesson by the class. The answers provided are only discussion starters. Let your class talk it over from there.

1. We who are Christians have opportunities frequently to "speak a word in season to him that is weary" (Isaiah 50:4). The discouraged, wounded, and defeated are all around us. How can we speak these words most effectively?

Our lesson today suggests that the Lord's servant had learned through experience how to live in the face of adversity and hardship. The providential care of the Lord was reality for him. Daily ("morning by morning") he depended on the Lord. He knew that God cares for and helps His faithful servants, because he had experienced that help..

Paul prayed that the Ephesians might "know the love of Christ, which passeth knowledge" (Ephesians 3:19). Christ's love is immeasurable and incomprehensible. Yet it can be known by experience. When it is thus known, it can be shared with others. The person who has experienced Christ's love and who daily trusts God and depends on Him is the person who best can lead others to do likewise.

2. Many people seek to escape hardships in life, thinking this will enable them to experience personal happiness. Why does this fail?

We are living in a time when the pursuit of personal happiness has been elevated to the supreme good. The assumption is that if only we can escape pain, suffering, hardship, and restricted freedoms, we will be happy. We fail to realize that life's circumstances, no matter how desirable, do not in themselves produce lasting happiness. The person who knows real joy in life is the person who loves God, trusts Him, and learns to grow through life's circumstances, whatever they may be.

The Lord's servant said, "I was not rebellious, neither turned away back . . . I set my face like a flint" (vv. 5, 7). He knew that ultimately the person who fears the Lord and remains faithful in the face of any circumstance will know true joy.

3. The resolve of the Lord's servant to stand by his convictions and to accomplish his purpose in the face of rejection or persecution is expressed in his statement that he had set his face "like a flint" (v. 7). In what situations are Christians today called upon to express such resolve?

We are living in times of change, not only material change, but social and spiritual change as well. Christian standards of morality and ethical behavior, so long upheld by the majority in our society, are characterized by many as archaic. We are being told that the Christian understanding of marriage and family is no longer tenable.

Some change, of course, is good. For example, methods that once were regarded as expedient may no longer be effective. Moral and spiritual truth, however, does not change. When social custom or moral practices violate what the Word of God teaches, then we must resolutely determine that we will refuse to compromise regardless of the cost. God's truth is eternal; it stands unchanging, even in changing times.

4. How should we who are Christians respond when we are ridiculed for our convictions or are unjustly characterized as being self-righteous and out of touch with social realities?

Our first inclination is to counterattack, using tactics not unlike those of our accusers. The servant of the Lord, however, refused to take up his own defense (vv. 8, 9). He was willing to face his accusers and to hear the charges brought against him, but he was unwilling to make a case for himself. His responsibility was to be faithful and live with integrity. He would allow the Lord God to be his advocate.

Likewise, Christians today should patiently walk in the light of God's truth and allow Him to deal with His enemies.

5. In the presence of persistent difficulties and dangers, why is it so hard to rely on God as advocated in verse 10?

In such situations, the intensity of our feelings often overrides thoughtful reason and good judgment. We may reach a point where fear takes over and we react on the basis of our doubts rather than our faith.

In the darkest moment of His life, Jesus gave us the supreme example of reliance on the unseen God. When it seemed that evil would prevail over righteousness, Jesus said, "Father, into thy hands I commend my spirit" (Luke 23:46). As a result, hope was born out of hopelessness, and light sprang forth out of darkness.

The Servant's Victory

DEVOTIONAL READING: Revelation 3:14-21.

LESSON SCRIPTURE: Isaiah 52:13—53:12.

PRINTED TEXT: Isaiah 53:1-6, 10-12.

Isaiah 53:1-6, 10-12

1 Who hath believed our report? and to whom is the arm of the LORD revealed?

2 For he shall grow up before him as a tender plant, and as a root out of a dry ground: he hath no form nor comeliness; and when we shall see him, there is no beauty that we should desire him.

3 He is despised and rejected of men; a man of sorrows, and acquainted with grief: and we hid as it were our faces from him; he was despised, and we esteemed him not.

4 Surely he hath borne our griefs, and carried our sorrows: yet we did esteem him stricken, smitten of God, and afflicted.

5 But he was wounded for our transgressions, he was bruised for our iniquities: the chastisement of our peace was upon him; and with his stripes we are healed.

6 All we like sheep have gone astray; we have turned every one to his own way; and the LORD hath laid on him the iniquity of us all.

. . . .

10 Yet it pleased the LORD to bruise him; he hath put him to grief: when thou shalt make his soul an offering for sin, he shall see his seed, he shall prolong his days, and the pleasure of the LORD shall prosper in his hand.

11 He shall see of the travail of his soul, and shall be satisfied: by his knowledge shall my righteous servant justify many; for he shall bear their iniquities.

12 Therefore will I divide him a portion with the great, and he shall divide the spoil with the strong; because he hath poured out his soul unto death: and he was numbered with the transgressors; and he bare the sin of many, and made intercession for the transgressors.

Jan 28

GOLDEN TEXT: He shall see of the travail of his soul, and shall be satisfied: by his knowledge shall my righteous servant justify many; for he shall bear their iniquities.—Isaiah 53:11.

*God's Promise of Deliverance
(Isaiah)*
Unit 2: The Ministry of the Suffering Servant
(Lessons 6-9)

Lesson Aims

After studying this lesson a student should:
1. Understand how God can bring salvation from suffering and victory through defeat.
2. Become even more appreciative of Christ's suffering on our behalf.

Lesson Outline

INTRODUCTION
  A. "A Tale of Two Servants"
  B. Lesson Background
I. THE APPEARANCE OF GOD'S SERVANT (Isaiah 53:1-3)
  A. An Unlikely Savior (vv. 1, 2)
  B. A Rejected Savior (v. 3)
    Squares, Nerds, and Geeks
II. THE SUFFERING OF THE SERVANT (Isaiah 53:4-6)
  A. Burdens Borne (v. 4)
  B. A Sacrifice for Sin (vv. 5, 6)
    "All We Like Sheep"
III. THE VINDICATION OF THE SERVANT (Isaiah 53:10-12)
  A. The Lord's Will Achieved (vv. 10, 11)
    Pain and Gain
  B. The Servant Glorified (v. 12)
CONCLUSION
  A. "Behold the Lamb"
  B. Let Us Pray
  C. Thought to Remember

The mission of the Lord's Servant was to rescue willful, fallen humanity. Visual 9 of the visuals packet (based on Isaiah 53:6) presents this truth. The visual is shown on page 189.

Introduction

A. "A Tale of Two Servants"

"Of whom speaketh the prophet this?" asked the Ethiopian eunuch upon reading from the fifty-third chapter of Isaiah (Acts 8:34). His confusion is understandable. In the book of Isaiah, the servant is identified with the prophet himself (20:3), and with the Israelite nation, or, more particularly, with that generation of Israelites who suffered through the Babylonian captivity and remained faithful to God (41:8; 44:2, 21; 45:4; 48:20; 49:3). Philip answered the

eunuch's question by preaching "unto him Jesus" (Acts 8:35).

The answer offered in this lesson will be one that, this writer believes, is most consistent with both the book of Isaiah and the later statements of the New Testament. In Isaiah, the servant is collectively the repentant Israelite exiles who faithfully suffered through the Babylonian captivity and who became the righteous remnant through whom God would restore the Israelite nation (see 49:5; 46:3). Yet the words of this text describe a Servant who suffers in a manner and for a purpose that is ultimately beyond that of the exiled Israelites. He is One not identical to Israel, but One who came out of Israel and died to save the world—Jesus Christ (Acts 8:34, 35).

If this answer seems confusing or contradictory, the student should be aware that Old Testament prophecy is sometimes given to dual or multiple applications or "fulfillments." For example, the expression, "out of Egypt I called my son" (Hosea 11:1, *New International Version*), referred historically to God's calling Israel out of Egypt in the Exodus; at the same time, the expression anticipated prophetically Jesus' being taken to Egypt so as not to be killed by Herod, and His subsequent return to Israel (Matthew 2:15). In other words, the "son" in Hosea was "Israel" but, as the Gospel of Matthew informs us, the son was also in a fuller and unique sense "Jesus" (Matthew 2:15). It is our understanding that a similar phenomenon is at work in this Servant Song from Isaiah.

B. Lesson Background

Today's text is taken from the fourth and final of the Servant Songs of Isaiah (52:13—53:12). The first two songs acquainted us with the servant's call and his mission. Last week's lesson on the third song introduced us to another aspect of the servant's ministry, which is more fully developed in this final song. It is the unique and compelling concept that the servant's suffering would accomplish the Lord's purposes and save His people. This suffering, which in a limited and somewhat symbolic way referred to the struggles of the exiled Israelites, ultimately anticipated the vicarious suffering of the Messiah for the sins of all humanity.

I. The Appearance of God's Servant (Isaiah 53:1-3)

A. An Unlikely Savior (vv. 1, 2)

1. Who hath believed our report? and to whom is the arm of the LORD revealed?

Isaiah prophesied to an unbelieving people (see 30:9-11; 42:23). In light of what follows, it seems that his complaint centered on the people's rejection of his prophecy concerning what God would accomplish through His suffering servant. As both Jesus and Paul revealed in their quotations of this text, these opening questions were meant to imply that few believed (see John 12:38; Romans 10:16). The questions addressed the unbelief of the people toward the unlikely prospect that God was going to achieve His purposes through the suffering and defeat of His servant. It was hard for both the nations and even some Israelites to understand how *the arm of the Lord* (the power of God) could be *revealed* through Israel's humiliating defeat and subjugation at the hands of the Babylonians. Harder still was it for Jew and Gentile alike to believe that victory over sin and death would be achieved through the death of the Messiah (see 1 Corinthians 1:18-23).

2. For he shall grow up before him as a tender plant, and as a root out of a dry ground: he hath no form nor comeliness; and when we shall see him, there is no beauty that we should desire him.

He shall grow up . . . as a tender plant, and as a root out of a dry ground. The comparison of the servant to a *tender plant* and a *root* has messianic overtones. By use of these terms, Isaiah prophesied the rise of the Messiah (Isaiah 11:1-5). The main thrust of this verse, however, is clarified in the latter half of it. The servant was as unattractive and unappealing to men às the formless shoot of the scrub brush that springs up in the desert. The thought is that on the basis of appearance, there was nothing that would recommend the servant to men as a champion and savior. In Psalm 118:22, 23 a similar idea is expressed regarding Israel: "The stone the builders rejected has become the capstone; the Lord has done this, and it is marvelous in our eyes" (*New International Version*; see also Matthew 21:42 where Jesus applies it to himself). In Deuteronomy 7:7 the Israel God chose is described as the least significant of all peoples, and in Ezekiel 16:1-7 the citizens of Jerusalem are characterized as an abandoned baby, whom only the Lord pitied. The point of all these texts is that Israel was an unlikely candidate to be the people of God through whom He would achieve His purposes on earth. If this was true of Israel in general, it was even more so of that generation of exiles who endured the humiliation of the captivity.

What has been said of Israel is even more true of Jesus Christ, the ultimate Suffering Servant of the Lord. He was born to peasants in an insignificant town, and a feeding trough was His bed. He lived the life of an itinerant preacher, and

died like a common criminal. His whole "appearance" on earth was not of the kind to which people normally gravitate in search of a Savior. "Who would have believed" that God would come to save us in such a One?

B. A Rejected Savior (v. 3)

3. He is despised and rejected of men; a man of sorrows, and acquainted with grief: and we hid as it were our faces from him; he was despised, and we esteemed him not.

The point of these poignant words is that not only did the servant's appearance make him an unlikely savior, it even repulsed those who looked upon him. The key to understanding the source of this repulsive appearance is found in the words *sorrows* and *grief*. These words can also mean "pains" and "wounds." They describe the effects that his suffering had upon his appearance (see verses 4-6). The language remembers the observation near the beginning of the song: "His visage was so marred more than any man" (52:14).

For the servant Israel this refers to the wretched state of the exiles (see Isaiah 42:22). In her humiliated defeat at the hands of the Babylonians, Israel was *despised and rejected of men.* As Lamentations 2:15 clearly shows, the shame of this defeat was felt deeply by the Israelites: "All that pass by clap their hands at thee; they hiss and wag their head at the daughter of Jerusalem, saying, Is this the city that men call The perfection of beauty, The joy of the whole earth?" Though this verse is not directly quoted in the New Testament and applied to Christ, it is yet a fitting description of how men would reject Him in His humiliating death. When we understand that Christ's death was made necessary because of our sins, our guilt and shame make it even more difficult for us to look upon the Suffering Servant.

SQUARES, NERDS, AND GEEKS

Depending on the decade in which you lived as a teenager, social misfits were called *squares* or *nerds*. Webster defines *nerd* as "a person regarded as contemptibly dull"; a *square* is one who is "old-fashioned, unsophisticated." The latest such term seems to be *geek*. (My dictionary has no definition for that word.)

All such terms, however, are reserved for those who don't conform in one way or another to popular trends and expectations. Isaiah knew that God's Servant would be "despised and rejected," because He would refuse to be molded by the image-makers among His contemporaries. The Suffering Servant did not measure up to the erroneous standards established by misguided religious types of His day. He was held in contempt by the very ones He came to serve and save.

Christ continues to be rejected by a populace that despises His claims, His demands, His warnings, and His promises. In our culture, He generally is not considered to be worthy of the social register.

Being Christian does not guarantee popularity. Indeed, Jesus warned that His followers "shall be hated of all men" (Matthew 19:22). But being *saved* is far better than merely being socially approved by those whose standards and values are based on this temporal, material world. Therefore, "be not conformed to this world: but be ye transformed by the renewing of your mind" (Romans 12:2).   —R.W.B.

II. The Suffering of the Servant (Isaiah 53:4-6)

A. Burdens Borne (v. 4)

4. Surely he hath borne our griefs, and carried our sorrows: yet we did esteem him stricken, smitten of God, and afflicted.

The people of God at first misunderstood the suffering of the servant. As the latter part of the verse suggests, they thought it was something God had sent merely as punishment for sin. This understanding of servant Israel's suffering was correct as far as it went, as the prophet's earlier statements make clear: "Who gave Jacob for a spoil, and Israel to the robbers? did not the Lord, he against whom we have sinned? for they would not walk in his ways, neither were they obedient unto his law" (Isaiah 42:24). What the Israelites now realized was that God used the servant's suffering for an additional purpose—their emotional and physical healing.

Interestingly, the New Testament quotes only the first half of the verse and applies it to Jesus' healing ministry. Matthew states that this part of the Servant's role was fulfilled by Jesus in His being sent to heal the sick (Matthew 8:16, 17). This further illustrates the phenomenon that an Old Testament prophecy may have one meaning in its own context yet find a "fulfillment" of a different type in the life of Christ.

At the same time, however, it is clear from what follows that Christ's sufferings were borne for mankind, and that His sufferings were the remedy for all the ills that come upon flesh.

B. A Sacrifice for Sin (vv. 5, 6)

5, 6. But he was wounded for our transgressions, he was bruised for our iniquities: the chastisement of our peace was upon him; and with his stripes we are healed. All we like sheep have gone astray; we have turned every one to his own way; and the LORD hath laid on him the iniquity of us all.

In this powerful passage we are allowed to behold the nature of the servant's suffering. The preposition *for* (used twice in verse 5; also in verse 8) means "because of," "on account of." The emphasis in these texts is that the servant paid the penalty for sin. The first of the two words the prophet uses to describe sin is particularly instructive. The word *transgressions* literally means "rebellions." At the heart of the biblical concept of sin is the idea of rebellion against God. Motivated by pride the sinner chooses to place his or her will above God's and thereby rise up against Him.

The chastisement of our peace was upon him. By this phrase is meant "the punishment that brought us peace was borne by him." As many commentators note, it is difficult to see how this could refer to Israel. Yet, as Isaiah proclaimed at the beginning of the section in which the Servant passages are found (Isaiah 40—55), the suffering of the captivity was in some sense a payment for Israel's sins: "Speak tenderly to Jerusalem, and proclaim to her that her hard service has been completed, that her sin has been paid for, that she has received from the Lord's hand double for all her sins" (Isaiah 40:2, *New International Version*). In other words, the same God who brought the Babylonian captivity as a punishment of Israel's sins, now, in consideration of the suffering that the exiles endured, considered their sin paid for and announced their pardon. What this text suggests is what Isaiah 53 confirms.

If the suffering of the penitent exiles paid for the sins of Israel in a figurative manner, the suffering of Jesus on the cross paid for the sins of all mankind in reality. He was sinless, yet He suffered for sin (Hebrews 4:15; 1 Peter 2:22), not His own sin, but ours. He suffered in our place. He was wounded even to death, as verses 8 and 9 make clear, and it was all for us, not for any sin He had committed. He offered himself as a sacrifice, and His sacrifice made atonement for our sins. We can be restored to God and have peace with Him because upon Jesus is laid *the iniquity of us all.* (See Romans 3:25; 2 Corinthians 5:21; 1 John 2:2; 4:10.)

"ALL WE LIKE SHEEP"

The Bible often uses the metaphor of sheep to describe the Lord's people. Christ himself is called the Good Shepherd. The idea of being protected, guided, fed, and cared for like helpless wooly lambs is a warm and cozy thought. Snuggling down in the shelter of the shepherd's love is a comforting analogy. Psalm 23 and John 10 are favorite texts for all Christians, because they assure us that the Lord is our Shepherd, and He is willing to give His very life for our safety and salvation.

Another aspect of the sheep metaphor, however, is disquieting, to say the least. Sheep are prone to go astray, to go their own way, as it were; thus the need for constant shepherding. And despite the vigilance of the shepherd, sheep often choose wrong and dangerous paths.

Isaiah compares man's spiritual waywardness with the straying of sheep. We are inclined to wander off the narrow way that leads to abundant life. Whenever we insist on going our own way, disregarding the directions and leadership of the Good Shepherd, we sin and place our souls in serious jeopardy. Hear His voice and follow Him.　　　　　　　　　　—R. W. B.

III. The Vindication of the Servant (Isaiah 53:10-12)

A. The Lord's Will Achieved (vv. 10, 11)

10, 11. Yet it pleased the LORD to bruise him; he hath put him to grief: when thou shalt make his soul an offering for sin, he shall see his seed, he shall prolong his days, and the pleasure of the LORD shall prosper in his hand. He shall see the travail of his soul, and shall be satisfied: by his knowledge shall my righteous servant justify many; for he shall bear their iniquities.

Yet it pleased the Lord to bruise him. The opening line of this verse informs us that it was God's will that the Servant should suffer. The Servant's suffering was not accidental, it was providential. In the context of Isaiah, this means that the suffering that the penitent exiles endured in their captivity was not simply the result of international politics or military aggression. It was the unfolding of the divine will. Their suffering was more than punishment. God was also going to use it as a means by which to pave the way for Israel's restoration to Canaan. This is how the *pleasure of the Lord shall prosper* in the servant's hand.

When thou shalt make his soul an offering for sin. The Hebrew text is unclear as to whether the Lord or the Servant is doing the offering. Most translations take it to mean that the Lord is doing it, and that seems to fit best with the idea expressed in the preceding clause. As applied to Jesus, either idea is appropriate. The New Testament affirms that God purposed Christ's death on the cross (Acts 2:23) and that Christ willingly offered himself for the sins of all the world (John 10:17, 18).

visual 9

The backdrop to this language is the Old Testament system of sacrifice. The type of *offering* referred to by Isaiah is described in Leviticus 5:14-19. The text prescribes the offering up of a ram from the flock in order to achieve the forgiveness of the person guilty of the sin. The idea is that God accepts the life of the sacrificial animal as a substitute for the life of the sinner. The consequences of the sin are thus atoned for, and the sinner is spared the "wages of sin" (death).

The new and compelling idea that Isaiah 53 adds to this sacrificial concept is the startling revelation that the Lord will offer a person (the Servant), not an animal, for sin.

It is obvious how this applies to Christ. Speaking of Jesus, the author of Hebrews says, "He did not enter by means of the blood of goats and calves; but he entered the Most Holy Place once for all by his own blood, having obtained eternal redemption" (Hebrews 9:12, *New International Version*). Jesus literally gave up His life as a sacrifice for the sins of all humanity.

Less obvious is how this sacrificial idea applies to the servant identified as "Israel" in the book of Isaiah. The answer seems to be that God accepted the suffering of the penitent exiles as a sacrifice for the collective sins of the Israelite nation. Thus, God's servant (the repentant exiles) would *justify many* (the entire nation of Israel) and make it possible for them to be restored to God. It is also possible that by *many* the prophet meant to include the Gentiles. Of the servant the Lord said, "I will also make you a light for the Gentiles, that you may bring my salvation to the ends of the earth" (49:6, *New International Version*). As was noted in last week's lesson, this "salvation" would occur as the nations witnessed what God did through the penitent exiles and came to believe in Him.

PAIN AND GAIN

Paul Brand has written a book entitled *PAIN: The Gift Nobody Wants.* He relates the startling statistic that the people of the United States spend $63 billion per year on pain relievers. The irony is that, while we have greater ability to manage pain, it seems increasingly difficult for us to find activities and experiences that make us feel good. We have lost sight of the interdependent relationship of pain and pleasure. Simply put, to have a rainbow there has to be a little rain. A Chinese philosopher points out that in order to feel the exquisite sensation of scratching, one must first endure the discomfort of a big itch.

If gain follows pain, it follows that the greater the pain the greater the gain. And no greater pain has ever been experienced than the torture of Christ on the cross. The physical torment was very real, but the spiritual dimensions of the agony were greater still. No wonder Jesus cried out, "My God, my God, why have you forsaken me?" (Matthew 27:46, *New International Version*). He bore our sins at Calvary, and at that moment our iniquities separated the sinless Son from the forgiving Father.

No pain ever achieved greater gain. By His sacrifice we are justified—perceived by God to be righteous in spite of our transgressions.

His pain was/is our gain!   —R. W. B.

B. The Servant Glorified (v. 12)

12. Therefore will I divide him a portion with the great, and he shall divide the spoil with the strong; because he hath poured out his soul unto death: and he was numbered with the transgressors; and he bare the sin of many, and made intercession for the transgressors.

This final Servant Song concludes with a prediction of the Servant's victory. Normally suffering and death lead to defeat. But in a paradox only God could construct, these very symbols of defeat are made the means to victory for the Servant and all people. Rather than overpowering the enemy, the Servant passively submits to him (v. 7). Instead of smiting them, He is smitten by

Home Daily Bible Readings

Monday, Jan. 22—A Righteous Remnant in Israel (Zephaniah 3:8-13)

Tuesday, Jan. 23—Children of Light Produced (Ephesians 5:6-14)

Wednesday, Jan. 24—Gratitude for What God Has Done (1 Peter 1:3-9)

Thursday, Jan. 25—Faith Produces Good Works (Galatians 5:1-12)

Friday, Jan. 26—Rising Above Persecution (Acts 5:33-42)

Saturday, Jan. 27—God's Ultimate Authority (Revelation 21:22-27)

Sunday, Jan. 28—God Reigns (Isaiah 52:7-15)

them. Instead of taking lives, He gives His own. And the God who "works in mysterious ways" turns that which appears to be a humiliating defeat into a glorious victory.

For the people of Isaiah's day this meant that the humiliation of the Babylonian captivity would ultimately lead to the restoration of a glorified Zion in the land of Canaan. For those of us this side of Calvary, the prophet's words hold even greater promise. They anticipate the death, burial, and resurrection of Jesus Christ, by which all humanity may find forgiveness of sins and the promise of eternal life.

Conclusion

A. "Behold the Lamb"

When John the Baptizer saw Jesus coming to the Jordan, he announced His arrival by saying, "Behold the Lamb of God, which taketh away the sin of the world!" (John 1:29). There are other words he might have chosen. He might have said, "Behold the Son of David, who has come to restore the kingdom to Israel!" or, "Behold the Master Teacher, who has come to proclaim the truth of God!" or, "Behold the Great Physician, who has come to heal the sick!" or, "Behold the Great Reformer, who has come to show us a new way to live!" He might have said any of these, for they were all true. But he reached instead for the very purpose for which Christ had come and said, "Behold the Lamb of God, which taketh away the sin of the world."

This, the most powerful of the Servant Songs, anticipates better than any other Old Testament prophecy the significance of Christ's coming. In some way the suffering of the servant Israel led to God's redeeming the nation from the bondage of the Babylonian captivity. But that pales in comparison to the sacrifice of Jesus Christ, God's ultimate Servant, at Calvary. There the very Son of God offered himself as the sacrificial Lamb. Allowing himself to be slain He paid the penalty for the sins of all mankind so that we all might be brought back to God.

B. Let Us Pray

Thank You, merciful Father, for sending Your Son to suffer and die in our place, that we might have victory over sin and death. Help us to give of ourselves sacrificially that others may know of Your saving grace. In Jesus' name, amen.

C. Thought to Remember

The message of the Servant Songs ultimately anticipates the message of the cross. The sovereign Lord of the universe can turn suffering into salvation and defeat into victory.

Learning by Doing

*This page contains an alternate lesson plan emphasizing learning activities. Classes
desiring such student involvement will find these suggestions helpful.*

Learning Goals

As a result of this lesson, a student will:

1. Identify Jesus Christ as the ultimate Suffering Servant of the Lord.

2. Be able to use the text as evidence from prophecy of the person and work of Jesus.

Into the Lesson

The following verses are based on the printed text for this lesson. A week before class, ask a singer to practice these lyrics to the tune of "Joy to the World" and to come prepared to sing them to your class as today's session begins.

Who has believed our strong report?
To whom is He revealed?
For He shall grow
Up as a tender plant
And root out of dry ground,
And root out of dry ground,
And root, and root, out of dry ground.

He has no form nor comeliness,
No beauty of desire.
He is despised,
Rejected of men,
A man of sorrows full,
A man of sorrows full.
We hid, we hid our faces from Him.

He surely bore our griefs and pain.
Although we did not know
His wounds and His bruises
Were taken for our sins.
He suffered for our peace,
He suffered for our peace,
And by His stripes we are healed.

All we like sheep have gone astray;
We turned to our own way.
The Lord gave Him
Our sins and shame.
And by His death He saves,
And by His death He saves,
And by His death He saves all men.

Joy to the world because He poured
His soul out unto death.
He stood with men
Of transgression.
He bare the sin of men,
He bare the sin of men,
He makes the plea to God for us.

Next have a class member read Isaiah 53:1-6, 10-12 aloud. Then lead a discussion of these questions:

1. What is the general tenor of this passage of Scripture? (It is gloomy, dealing as it does with the suffering of the Lord's Servant.)

2. Why might the tune possibly be considered inappropriate? (It is a joyous, upbeat tune, which is normally associated with a happy event.)

3. Why might the tune be considered appropriate? (The suffering and death of Christ, the ultimate Servant of the Lord, brought true joy to the world!)

Into the Word

Write the following nine Scripture phrases on slips of paper, one phrase per slip. Do the same with the nine Scripture references in the following paragraph. Distribute them randomly. The references match the phrases in the order given.

Phrases: (1) "He opened not his mouth"; (2) "He was numbered with the transgressors"; (3) "With his stripes we are healed"; (4) "He shall grow up . . . as a tender plant"; (5) "We like sheep have gone astray"; (6) "[He was] with the rich in his death"; (7) "a man of sorrows, and acquainted with grief"; (8) "[He] made intercession for the transgressors"; (9) "My righteous servant [will] justify many."

References: Matthew 26:62, 63; Luke 23:32; Mark 15:15; Matthew 2:23; Psalm 119:176; Matthew 27:57-60; John 11:35; Luke 23:34; Romans 3:24.

Have the holders of the Scripture references read their verses aloud. As each is read, let the holder of a matching phrase from Isaiah 53 read it aloud. Comment on how this great Servant Song finds its ultimate fulfillment in Jesus, the Servant Messiah.

Into Life

Give each class member a copy of the lyrics your soloist sang earlier. Sing the song together. Point out that singing these truths to the tune of "Joy to the World" can be a reminder of how God's Servant, who suffered and died, has given us reason to rejoice.

Ask if any in your class would like to compose a stanza for this hymn based on verses 7-11, which were not used in the hymn sung today. Have the class sing the stanzas next Sunday.

Let's Talk It Over

The questions on this page are designed to encourage review of the lesson Scriptures and to promote discussion of the lesson by the class. The answers provided are only discussion starters. Let your class talk it over from there.

1. What is there about the concept of redemption through suffering that is so difficult for many to accept?

In modern society, suffering is generally viewed as a form of weakness rather than strength. It makes little sense to us that anything of real worth can be achieved through suffering, so we desire to avoid it, if at all possible.

Reflecting on Isaiah 29:14, the apostle Paul explains that "the message of the cross is foolishness to those who are perishing" (1 Corinthians 1:18, 19, *New International Version*). The worldly-wise see Christ's death as a sign of defeat, not victory. However, God's "foolishness" is "wiser than man's wisdom, and the weakness of God is stronger than man's strength" (1 Corinthians 1:25, *New International Version*). Christ's death accomplished what man in all his wisdom and power could never accomplish—the defeat of sin and death. So in reality the suffering of Christ the Servant was not a display of weakness, but of power. Because His sacrifice reveals our weakness and our desperate need of a Savior, the proud foolishly reject the redemption He offers.

2. Verse 3 of today's text describes the Servant as one "acquainted with grief." How might this relate to the fact that He was "despised and rejected"?

Most persons relate suffering to the darker side of life. We conclude that if it is not a consequence of divine displeasure, at least it must be considered the result of our poor choices. Job's friends insisted that his suffering and his sins were related. For example, see Job 11:14, 15. In the latter part of verse 4 of our text, Isaiah states that those who beheld the Suffering Servant of God felt that God was punishing Him for His sins. The contemporaries of Jesus could not understand how He could truly be the sinless One if He had to endure such suffering. When encountered by the risen Christ, two of His followers acknowledged that their faith had been shattered by the reality of His suffering. They said, "We had hoped that he was the one who was going to redeem Israel" (Luke 24:21, *New International Version*). Jesus responded, "How foolish you are, and how slow of heart to believe all that the prophets have spoken! Did not the Christ have to suffer these things and then enter his glory?" (Luke 24:25, 26). The suffering of Jesus was part of His victory. Instead of turning the apostle Paul away, Christ's suffering drew him to the Lord (Philippians 3:10, 11). May we as appreciative disciples say with the hymn writer, "In the cross of Christ I glory."

3. Why is it so difficult for many persons to accept the fact that Jesus suffered and died for them?

It is a characteristic of modern man that he does not want to admit guilt for his actions. He has made a science of blame. To acknowledge that we need another to make atonement for us is to admit our guilt, something that only a humble heart can do. And that strikes at the heart of the issue—our pride. Yet this fact is crystal clear from Scripture, and human experience attests to it: "All we like sheep have gone astray; we have turned every one to his own way" (Isaiah 53:6). The apostle Paul affirms, "All have sinned, and come short of the glory of God" (Romans 3:23). It may be difficult for a person to admit that he or she has sinned against God, but it is a necessary step if one would be free of sin's guilt and penalty.

4. How can we make use of Isaiah 53 to strengthen our faith?

To realize that this magnificent chapter was written some seven centuries before Christ and yet that it offers a vivid description of what took place at Calvary provides a solid underpinning for faith. It may not be too much to say that every Christian should come to know this chapter better than any other in the Old Testament.

5. How can we make use of Isaiah 53 to increase our appreciation of what Jesus Christ has done for us?

Many preachers and teachers have pointed out that we can legitimately substitute our own names for the pronouns "our" and "we" in Isaiah 53:5. And to a great extent we can personalize much more that appears in the chapter. Like the Ethiopian eunuch (Acts 8:27-35), we would do well to ponder these words and to discover afresh that joy we experienced when we first partook of the benefits of Jesus' death.

Jonah Flees From God

DEVOTIONAL READING: Jonah 2:2-9.

LESSON SCRIPTURE: Jonah 1, 2.

PRINTED TEXT: Jonah 1:1-4, 10-15, 17; 2:1, 10.

Jonah 1:1-4, 10-15, 17

1 Now the word of the LORD came unto Jonah the son of Amittai, saying,

2 Arise, go to Nineveh, that great city, and cry against it; for their wickedness is come up before me.

3 But Jonah rose up to flee unto Tarshish from the presence of the LORD, and went down to Joppa; and he found a ship going to Tarshish: so he paid the fare thereof, and went down into it, to go with them unto Tarshish from the presence of the LORD.

4 But the LORD sent out a great wind into the sea, and there was a mighty tempest in the sea, so that the ship was like to be broken.

. . . .

10 Then were the men exceedingly afraid, and said unto him, Why hast thou done this? For the men knew that he fled from the presence of the LORD, because he had told them.

11 Then said they unto him, What shall we do unto thee, that the sea may be calm unto us? for the sea wrought, and was tempestuous.

12 And he said unto them, Take me up, and cast me forth into the sea; so shall the sea be calm unto you: for I know that for my sake this great tempest is upon you.

13 Nevertheless the men rowed hard to bring it to the land; but they could not: for the sea wrought, and was tempestuous against them.

14 Wherefore they cried unto the LORD, and said, We beseech thee, O LORD, we beseech thee, let us not perish for this man's life, and lay not upon us innocent blood: for thou, O LORD, hast done as it pleased thee.

15 So they took up Jonah, and cast him forth into the sea: and the sea ceased from her raging.

. . . .

17 Now the LORD had prepared a great fish to swallow up Jonah. And Jonah was in the belly of the fish three days and three nights.

Jonah 2:1, 10

1 Then Jonah prayed unto the LORD his God out of the fish's belly.

. . . .

10 And the LORD spake unto the fish, and it vomited out Jonah upon the dry land.

Feb
4

GOLDEN TEXT: Jonah rose up to flee unto Tarshish from the presence
of the LORD.—Jonah 1:3.

God's Love for All People
(Jonah, Ruth)
(Lessons 10-13)

Lesson Aims

After studying this lesson, students should:

1. Be aware that no excuse is adequate for failing to attempt to fulfill the will of God that has been made known to us.

2. Know that even in the worst of circumstances God is at work for the good of those called according to His purpose.

3. Give their time and money to support the church's effort to share the gospel with all people.

Lesson Outline

INTRODUCTION
    A. Fish Story?
    B. Lesson Background
  I. THE CALL (Jonah 1:1-4)
    A. Nineveh's Need (vv. 1, 2)
    B. The Major Problem (v. 3)
      The God and Run Club
    C. God in Control (v. 4)
 II. THE TESTING (Jonah 1:10-15, 17)
    A. Pointed Question (v. 10)
    B. Painful Solution (vv. 11-15)
      Man Overboard!
    C. God Cares (v. 17)
III. THE DELIVERANCE (Jonah 2:1, 10)
    A. Prayer (v. 1)
    B. Deliverance (v. 10)
CONCLUSION
    A. The Problem—Evasion
    B. Let Us Pray
    C. Thought to Remember

One's freedom to choose to obey or disobey God's commands is the theme of visual 10 of the visuals packet. The visual is shown on page 198.

Introduction

A. Fish Story?

During the depression of the 1930s a stuffed whale transported by a freight car was exhibited in many cities of the United States. The man in charge of the exhibit carefully pointed out that while the mouth of the whale certainly was large enough to envelop a man, the opening in the whale's throat was not large enough to allow the man to pass into the whale's stomach. To that exhibitor, the biblical account of Jonah was a "fish story"—unreliable, untrue.

To the discerning, however, the exhibitor's attempts to discredit the biblical account of Jonah don't hold water. The book of Jonah says that God prepared "a great fish" to swallow Jonah in order to preserve the prophet's life. The person who believes in the Creator God has no difficulty believing that He could accomplish this.

Instead of "a fish story," the account of Jonah is a story of God's love and human responsibility. It has its miraculous element, and in that regard is no different from many of the biblical accounts of God's dealings with His chosen people. The fact that the book of Jonah is included in the Bible gives it the full force of a message that God wants us to have. It speaks of His relationship to His chosen people and the rest of the world. Specifically, it emphasizes God's love for all people and His desire for all to be saved from the terrible consequences of wickedness. And, in a forceful manner, it depicts the importance of carrying out God's assigned tasks, even if a task has unpleasant or difficult overtones.

B. Lesson Background

Little is known of the prophet Jonah. Our principal source of information concerning him is the book that bears his name. Additional personal information about him is found in the notice given in 2 Kings 14:23-25. From this brief reference we gather several things.

First, the identity of the prophet is confirmed. Verse 25 corroborates the statement of identification given in Jonah 1:1—he was the son of Amittai. From the reference in 2 Kings we discover that Jonah was from the town of Gath-hepher. Joshua 19:10, 13, 16 indicates that this town (there called "Gittah-hepher") was in the part of the land that had been assigned to the tribe of Zebulun. Gath-hepher was situated about three miles northeast of Nazareth. Jonah, therefore, was a prophet of the northern kingdom, the kingdom of Israel.

The reference in 2 Kings also gives us some indication of the time of Jonah's prophesying, although nothing very definite. Jeroboam II, who is named in these verses as the king of Israel, ruled from about 789 to 748 B.C. The lands that he restored to Israel in fulfillment of Jonah's prophecy (v. 25) were those east of the Jordan, which were taken from Israel during the reign of Jehu (see 2 Kings 10:32, 33), most probably near the close of that king's reign (about 815 B.C.). So this prophecy of Jonah would have been delivered some time after 815 B.C. It may be deemed certain that the prophecy was given some time before Jeroboam's conquests, either near the end of the reign of his predecessor or about the beginning of Jeroboam's reign. If Jonah flourished in the reign of Jeroboam II, he was a senior contemporary of the prophets Amos and Hosea.

During this time Israel had its battles with Syria to the north. But a far more potentially dangerous foe lay farther to the east—the nation of Assyria, whose capital city was Nineveh. From the Assyrian inscriptions, we learn that Jehu, the great-grandfather of Jeroboam II, had been forced to pay tribute to Assyria. The people had been required to pay that tribute continually ever since. Furthermore, the Assyrians were a strong, fierce, warlike people, noted for their cruelty. Jonah was a good patriot and lover of Israel. The combination of these factors, it would seem, led him to respond the way he did when God called His prophet to take a very important message to that heathen nation.

Israel was God's chosen nation, and yet the people had grievously transgressed against Him and had gone after other gods. The people were steadily moving toward their destruction, and God's prophets were sent to them to try to call them back to Him. In spite of the people's gross wickedness, God loved them, and the prophets were chosen to deliver His message of love.

Jonah, it seems, could accept the fact that his own people could sin terribly against God and still be worthy of His love and forgiveness. But he could not bring himself to extend God's love and mercy to a people who had never known Him. The dominant purpose of the book of Jonah seems to be, therefore, to expose and rebuke in Jonah the tendency to bigotry, and to show that God, the Creator of all, has a tender, compassionate care for every living person.

I. The Call
(Jonah 1:1-4)
A. Nineveh's Need (vv. 1, 2)

1. Now the word of the LORD came unto Jonah the son of Amittai, saying.

We are not told the manner in which God communicated with Jonah, whether audibly or by means of a dream or vision. But there was no question in Jonah's mind that God was the one giving him the commission.

2. Arise, go to Nineveh, that great city, and cry against it; for their wickedness is come up before me.

Go to Nineveh. Most of God's prophets delivered His messages to the people of Israel. Jonah, however, was directed to go to Nineveh, Assyria's capital city, which was about 750 miles east of Israel.

How to Say It

AMITTAI. Uh-*mit*-eye.
GATH-HEPHER. Gath-*he*-fer.
GITTAH-HEPHER. *Git*-a-*he*-fer (strong accent on *he*).
JEHU. *Jee*-hew.
JEROBOAM. Jair-o-*bo*-um.
NINEVEH. *Nin*-uh-vuh.

That great city. Nineveh was called *great*, it seems, because of its size and the influential place it held as the capital of the dominant nation in the regions east of Israel. Jonah 4:11 tells us that Nineveh was home to one hundred twenty thousand young children. The entire population of the city may have been as large as six hundred thousand.

Cry against it; for their wickedness is come up before me. God was fully aware of the wicked life-style of the Ninevites, and Jonah himself was not unaware of their reputation. Unpleasant as the task may have seemed to Jonah, he knew he was to be God's agent to help the Ninevites change—for the good.

We today who have been commissioned to take the gospel of God's grace to the world may at times be hesitant to warn people of the danger that awaits them if they live wicked lives. Perhaps we are afraid of offending them; or perhaps we fear an unpleasant response from them. Whatever, God's message of warning is always for man's ultimate good, and that should spur us on to do the work He has commissioned.

B. The Major Problem (v. 3)

3. But Jonah rose up to flee unto Tarshish from the presence of the LORD, and went down to Joppa; and he found a ship going to Tarshish: so he paid the fare thereof, and went down into it, to go with them unto Tarshish from the presence of the LORD.

God told Jonah to arise, and Jonah *rose up,* but that was the extent of the prophet's obedience. He was to go east to Nineveh, but instead he went in the opposite direction. It is believed that *Tarshish* was Tartessus, a Phoenician city on the south coast of Spain, some two thousand miles west of Israel.

Jonah's intention was to flee *from the presence of the Lord.* This may mean that Jonah imagined he could flee to a place where God would be unaware of his presence. Some students point out that the expression "to be" or "stand in a king's presence" is often used to mean acting as the king's official minister (see Genesis 41:46;

1 Kings 17:1; 2 Kings 3:14; Luke 1:19). The phrase as it is used here, therefore, may mean that Jonah was renouncing his office as the Lord's prophet so he would not have to carry out the mission he was given. So he *went down* out of the hill country *to Joppa,* a seaport about fifty miles away on the Mediterranean coast. Finding a ship that would take him where he wanted to go, he *paid the fare* and went aboard.

Although much of the narrative in the book of Jonah centers around the prophet, the Lord is the key figure of action in the book. The purpose of this opening scene will have been achieved if the reader inquires how God is going to proceed. But we will be missing much if we ask only how the Lord will frustrate Jonah's plan to flee. This is not just a biblical "cops and robbers" account about how God gets His man. It has to do with the fulfilling of a specific commission from God.

There are important truths that may be learned from God's dealings with Jonah, not the least of which is that we should carefully consider our devotion to God, the demands of Christian discipleship, and our willingness to serve Him.

THE GOD AND RUN CLUB

Young faces pictured on milk cartons and on the back of carpet-cleaning ads tell a tragic story. Some of these youngsters were abducted by strangers with evil intent. Others have been "kidnapped" by noncustodial parents after a bitter divorce. Many, especially the teens, are simply runaways—seeking freedom from control.

Jonah tried to run away from God to avoid the distasteful task of preaching to the Ninevites. Like a teen fleeing the control and discipline of parents, Jonah tried to hide from the chief authority figure of life, the omnipotent God.

The spiritual descendants of Jonah are legion. Among the children of God, countless runaways turn up missing every year. They want Christianity without a commission, discipleship without discipline, freedom without faithfulness.

Our heavenly Father is loving, but never permissive. He guides us, not with *suggestions,* but by *commandments.* His authority is supreme, and His children must submit to Him. As Jonah learned, one cannot hide from God; we run from Him to our own peril.   —R. W. B.

C. God in Control (v. 4)

4. But the LORD sent out a great wind into the sea, and there was a mighty tempest in the sea, so that the ship was like to be broken.

Sent out. The verb in the Hebrew text here has a stronger meaning than the reading of our text suggests. It actually means "cast" or "threw." It is the same word that is used of King Saul's casting a spear at David, and later at Jonathan (1 Samuel 18:11; 20:33). It denotes a hard throw as opposed to a gentle toss such as a parent tossing a sponge ball.

To picture what type of storm the Lord caused to arise, think of what happens when we throw a large stone into the water. Only the water relatively close to the stone is disturbed to any large degree. So it seems that the Lord "threw" this storm only where this particular ship was sailing and that the sea around was calm. This would explain the sailors' conviction that this storm was far beyond what was natural (v. 7). Added to the destructive force of the fierce wind was the terrible weight of the driven water, which threatened to destroy the ship. God was making life exceedingly difficult on that one ship in that spot at that time.

II. The Testing
(Jonah 1:10-15, 17)

The intervening verses describe the terror experienced by the seamen on the ship and the steps they took to avert disaster. Apparently they all agreed that they would be saved only by divine intervention, so each of these heathen crewmen frantically cried out to his god, all the while throwing the cargo overboard.

Suspicion was raised toward Jonah's being in some way connected with this disastrous situation when the chief officer found him below deck sleeping instead of calling upon his God. That suspicion was strengthened when the sailors decided to cast lots to find out who was responsible, and the lot fell on Jonah. Upon interrogation by the sailors, Jonah identified himself and told them what he had done.

A. Pointed Question (v. 10)

10. Then were the men exceedingly afraid, and said unto him, Why hast thou done this? For the men knew that he fled from the presence of the LORD, because he had told them.

Then were the men exceedingly afraid. To this point the sailors had had a general suspicion that there was something about the storm that was supernatural. But now Jonah's confession convinced them that the wrath of the Most High God was coming upon them. *Why hast thou done this?* This was not so much a question of inquiry as it was of wonder—"How *could* you provoke the wrath of so powerful a God?" Implied also is the question, "And how could you involve us in your guilt?" Distressed as the seamen were, apparently some kind of respect, or perhaps fear, caused them to be careful how they treated this person who had such powerful connections!

Again we see that God was in control. He wanted the people of Nineveh to be brought to repentance. He wanted Jonah to be His messenger, but Jonah had acted in self-interest. Jonah needed to face the truth about himself in God's eyes.

The sailors sought more than Jonah's name when they asked his identity. His purpose for being on the ship, his country of origin, and the identity of his God were all important parts of the cause of the problem they all faced. Many times one's relationship to God is the key factor in the development *and* in the resolution of a problem.

Isn't it entirely possible that our efforts to avoid responsibilities by excuses, finding other things to do, or just closing our eyes to a situation, grieve God as much as did Jonah's flight? What do you suppose would happen if God made direct and obvious corrections in our man-made plans today? Would God's mission for the church be accomplished more thoroughly and more quickly by more people?

B. Painful Solution (vv. 11-15)

11. Then said they unto him, What shall we do unto thee, that the sea may be calm unto us? for the sea wrought, and was tempestuous.

The situation was becoming dire, for the turbulence of the sea was increasing. Feeling certain that Jonah was responsible for their plight, the sailors also felt that he must make some sort of restitution to appease Jehovah so He would not destroy them all. Because Jonah was the prophet of Jehovah, perhaps these men felt Jonah could reveal Jehovah's will in this regard, so they asked him, *What shall we do unto thee?*

12. And he said unto them, Take me up, and cast me forth into the sea; so shall the sea be calm unto you: for I know that for my sake this great tempest is upon you.

It would seem that Jonah spoke these words under divine direction, for it was God's plan to have Jonah rescued by a great fish He had prepared. At the same time, however, Jonah recognized his fault in this matter and assumed the responsibility for it. He was willing to sacrifice himself so that all the persons on board the ship would be spared. Speaking as God's prophet, Jonah assured the sailors that if they threw him into the sea, the troubled waters would become calm.

13. Nevertheless the men rowed hard to bring it to the land; but they could not: for the sea wrought, and was tempestuous against them.

Whether it was because these sailors (undoubtedly heathen) were of tender heart or they stood in awe of Jonah because of his relation to Jehovah, whose mighty power was being proved to them, they were reluctant to throw Jonah overboard. So they tried their best to row the ship to land. But the wind, which was coming from shore, was too strong for them to make any headway.

14. Wherefore they cried unto the LORD, and said, We beseech thee, O LORD, we beseech thee, let us not perish for this man's life, and lay not upon us innocent blood: for thou, O LORD, hast done as it pleased thee.

No longer calling upon their own gods, these heathen called upon Jehovah, the God of Jonah. They recognized His hand in all that had happened. Now, as they finally prepared to carry out what they understood to be the divine sentence, they pleaded that Jehovah would not hold them guilty of murder.

15. So they took up Jonah, and cast him forth into the sea: and the sea ceased from her raging.

The scene ends with Jonah's being thrown into the sea, followed by the immediate calming of the sea. The experienced seamen knew immediately that God was at work.

MAN OVERBOARD!

Pirates used to make prisoners and incorrigible crew members "walk the plank." It was a prearranged (and premature) burial at sea. These days, incidents of people being intentionally drowned in the sea are few. Everything possible usually is done to rescue "men overboard."

Jonah's case was a unique situation. Many sailors' lives were at risk due to his disobedience. Apparently he experienced great remorse

Home Daily Bible Readings

Monday, Jan. 29—Israel's Disobedience Recalled (Psalm 78:1-8)

Tuesday, Jan. 30—God's Care for His People (Psalm 78:9-16)

Wednesday, Jan. 31—Faithlessness Disapproved (Psalm 78:17-31)

Thursday, Feb. 1—God's Steadfast Love (Psalm 78:32-41)

Friday, Feb. 2—Easy to Forget (Psalm 78:42-55)

Saturday, Feb. 3—Davidic Dynasty (Psalm 78:67-72)

Sunday, Feb. 4—An Unproductive Flight (Jonah 1:5-10)

for his sin, for he penitently confessed it to the sailors; and he actually requested that he be thrown overboard.

Despite his disobedience, Jonah had not lost his prophetic perception: he knew he was responsible for the life-threatening storm, and he knew it would cease if he were sacrificed to the sea. The gambling guesses of the crew were confirmed by Jonah's admission of guilt. Even so, the sailors were reluctant to harm him and made valiant effort to bring the ship to shore. Finally, however, they were forced to admit that they were fighting against Jehovah to their own potential destruction. So, after a brief invocation, they threw Jonah in the brink without further ceremony.

Retribution for sin is not always as swift as that, but God does have ways to get our attention. Earthquakes, hurricanes, and other "acts of God" remind us of who is in control, and can bring us to our knees in gratitude and/or repentance. At least they should!   —R. W. B.

C. God Cares (v. 17)

17. Now the LORD had prepared a great fish to swallow up Jonah. And Jonah was in the belly of the fish three days and three nights.

Many efforts have been made to discredit this account of *a great fish* because man has never observed a fish such as is mentioned here. The biblical record is that God specially *prepared* a great fish to swallow Jonah, to keep him from drowning or being digested, and to give him time to think about the predicament his disobedience had gotten him into. Who is man to say what God can and cannot do?

In this episode, God's care for both the pagan seamen and His unwilling prophet is demonstrated. The fact that God is at work for our good at all times (Romans 8:28) is a promise illustrated here. Every Christian should find continuous comfort by this thought.

III. The Deliverance (Jonah 2:1, 10)

A. Prayer (v. 1)

1. Then Jonah prayed unto the LORD his God out of the fish's belly.

The following verses (2-9) indicate the sentiments Jonah felt and expressed to God at this time, among which were fear, admiration, thanksgiving, and recommitment. Only one's imagination can put the specific words in his prayer. We may be certain, however, that it was a heartfelt communication with God about his situation. Can we pray otherwise or even less and still expect God to help us?

B. Deliverance (v. 10)

10. And the LORD spake unto the fish, and it vomited out Jonah upon the dry land.

What an unpleasant way to be brought back to the starting point! Now that Jonah was back on dry ground, it would seem natural that he would be ready to obey the Lord wholeheartedly. Next week's lesson will show that Jonah still had faults. But it will also show that his prayer was not the kind that some people make while in a hospital bed: "If I get well, I'll be in church every Sunday"; or, "I'm going to give a tithe of all my income"; or, "I'm not going to refuse to serve the next time!"

Conclusion

A. The Problem—Evasion

From childhood up, people who attend Bible study classes are taught the story of Jonah and the "whale." The emphasis normally is on God's power, evidenced in Jonah's miraculous preservation in and rescue from the "belly of the whale." This emphasis is proper.

There is more to be learned from this account, however. Although the circumstances of our lives are certainly different from Jonah's, we are no more excused from obeying God's directions than he was.

We may not be named to carry out a specific task as Jonah was, but there is no question that every Christian has work to accomplish for God, which no one else on earth is to do. This lesson reveals God's displeasure when His servants try to evade their responsibility.

B. Let Us Pray

Help us, our heavenly Father, to search the Scriptures to know what You want us to do. Then help us, by Your power, to do it. In Jesus' name, amen.

C. Thought to Remember

"[Jonah] found that desertion, however possible, can never be satisfactory. God's authority is not to be run away from."   —J. E. Henry

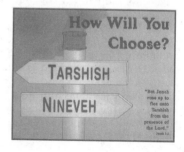

visual 10

Learning by Doing

This page contains an alternate lesson plan emphasizing learning activities. Classes desiring such student involvement will find these suggestions helpful.

Learning Goals

As a result of this study, adults will:

1. Be able to enumerate the good and bad choices recorded in Jonah 1 and 2.

2. Be able to compare their attitudes and behavior with Jonah's.

3. Commit themselves to more active involvement in ministry to other peoples.

Into the Lesson

Give your learners the following true/false quiz. (This quiz is included in the student's book that accompanies this series.)

1. The book of Jonah has only two chapters. (*false*)

2. Jonah sailed on a ship to go to Tarshish. (*true*)

3. Heathen sailors offered sacrifices to Jehovah. (*true*)

4. Only one miracle is pictured in the book of Jonah. (*false*)

5. Jonah was inside the great fish three days and nights. (*true*)

6. The citizens of Nineveh were given only a seven-day notice of coming destruction. (*false*)

7. Though many Ninevites repented, most did not, including the hardhearted king. (*false*)

8. Jonah was delighted with the success of his preaching. (*false*)

9. Jonah became so uncomfortable in the Assyrian heat, he wished he were dead. (*true*)

10. God expressed His concern for the animals of Nineveh as well as the people. (*true*)

This quiz deals with the text of this lesson and next week's lesson, giving you opportunity to survey the whole story with your learners.

Write CHOISES on the chalkboard. Ask how this word represents today's lesson. (This misspelled word suggests that some *bad* choices were made in this episode involving Jonah.)

Into the Word

Have five copies of the entire text of Jonah 1 and 2 available for readers whom you have recruited during the week before class. Have each copy highlighted appropriately for each of five parts to be read: narrator, God, shipmaster, sailors, and Jonah. The narrator reads all the words not spoken by the others, including preface words to their dialogues. Provide a name tag on a neck cord for each reader to wear to iden-

tify his or her part. Have the group stand in front of the class and read the entire text.

Place these two column headings on your chalkboard: *Choices God Made* and *Choises Men Made*—deliberate misspelling, once again. Divide your class into two groups. Have one group examine Jonah 1 and 2 and list the choices God made; the other group is to list the bad choices men made. After five minutes let the groups report their findings. Write them under the appropriate headings on the chalkboard. As each entry is offered, ask for a Bible verse that confirms it.

It may prove profitable to let the groups alternate in offering their findings. Occasionally ask, "Do you others have a related *choice/choise* to the one given by the other group?" For example, the first group may note, "God chose Jonah to be His preacher to Nineveh"; to which the second group could respond, "Jonah chose not to do what God commanded" (from verses 2 and 3, respectively, of chapter 1. Though lists may vary significantly, choices may run all the way from "God chose to attempt to convert the wicked Ninevites" to "God chose to rescue Jonah from the fish's stomach." (Next week's study will emphasize that even the utterly wicked, such as the Ninevites, can *still* choose to do right!)

Into Life

Write each of the following phrases on a separate strip of paper and attach each to the wall:

"Escaping to Tarshish"

"Sleeping Through the Storm"

"Flying Head Over Heels Into the Deep"

"Sitting in the Whale's Belly"

"Praying in a Dark Place"

Ask your students to do one of the following: "Describe how a Christian occasionally gets into one of these Jonah-like predicaments," or, "Pick the one that best characterizes you and your Christian life, and share with us how it relates."

Ask the class to list ten places they definitely would not want to go with God's good news. As each place (situation, city, country) is named ask, "Why?" Note any similarities to the circumstances of Jonah. Have your adults copy the list of places; encourage them to pray for God to send a messenger for each one. If someone knows a Christian or agency working there, note the name(s) for your learners' prayer lists.

Let's Talk It Over

The questions on this page are designed to encourage review of the lesson Scriptures and to promote discussion of the lesson by the class. The answers provided are only discussion starters. Let your class talk it over from there.

1. Jonah attempted to evade his responsibility as God's prophet by running away. How do some Christians evade their responsibilities as disciples of Jesus? What does the account of Jonah teach us regarding the failure to do what God commands?

Some simply deny that discipleship has any responsibilities. When asked to perform some task in the ministry of the church, they may respond by saying, "It's not my job," or, "Isn't that what the preacher is hired to do?" Others, like Jonah, attempt to run away from them. This they do by getting busy with other, less important, activities. Some may make excuses as to why they can't take on a certain job, or why someone else could do it so much better.

What we must learn from the account of Jonah is that all efforts to evade the responsibility of doing what the Lord has commanded us to do will fail. Jesus asked a penetrating question: "Why call ye me, Lord, Lord, and do not the things which I say?" (Luke 6:46). He then made it clear that such a person will suffer utter ruin.

2. How are the church and those who are not part of the family of God affected by the failure of Christians to fulfill the responsibilities of discipleship?

In his discussion of Christian responsibility recorded in 1 Corinthians 12, the apostle Paul drew his readers' attention to the human body. He reminded them that the body has great diversity—it has many members, and each member has its unique function. When each member of the body does what it is designed to do, the body can move, and work, and accomplish things. If, however, any of the body's members cannot function normally, that lack diminishes the body's ability to do what a body does.

The same is true of the church, the body of Christ. It is made up of many members to whom the Holy Spirit has given differing gifts, which are to be used so the body can do Christ's work. If Christians ignore their responsibilities as members of Christ's body and do not use the gifts given them, the ability of Christ's body to accomplish its work on earth is hampered. The effect on those outside the family of God will be that they may remain *eternally* outside God's family. The church has been given the commis-

sion to take the gospel of salvation to the whole world. We who are members of Christ's church must take our responsibilities seriously!

3. When the sea stopped raging after the sailors threw Jehovah's prophet overboard, the sailors realized that Jehovah was a powerful God. How can our lives be a testimony for the power of God?

We can give testimony to God's power by the way we conduct ourselves every day. The way we respond to persons and situations should demonstrate God's control over our minds and hearts. If we are unjustly criticized, do we respond in kind, or do we hold our tongue? If illness strikes, do we abandon faith, or do we trust God all the more? Christians should respond in a manner that reflects their confidence in God's ability to take care of them.

4. Jonah prayed fervently from inside the great fish, and God heard his prayer. How does the time we spend in prayer affect our relationship with God?

Our standing with God in Christ is an objective fact, based on His grace. But the subjective part of that relationship, that is, how close we feel to God at any particular moment, is affected dramatically by our prayer life. This seems reasonable. Can a husband and wife experience a sense of unity if they never talk to each other? How, then, can we expect to really sense God's presence in our lives, if we do not communicate with him? Talking to God seems the most natural thing in the world for a Christian to do. And let us remember that God *wants* us to talk to Him!

5. How can we determine what God would have us to do to advance His kingdom on earth?

We can consider our spiritual gifts, and see how God has equipped us to serve Him. We can see where our heart is; that is, in what areas of ministry do we have a particular burden? Are there physical requirements that would prohibit our serving in some area? What abilities have we developed that may not be a "spiritual gift" as such, but that may be used in service? Above all, we can be sensitive to doors God has opened and be ready to walk through them to render service for His glory.

God Shows Mercy

DEVOTIONAL READING: **Genesis 18:20-33.**

LESSON SCRIPTURE: **Jonah 3, 4.**

PRINTED TEXT: **Jonah 3:1-5, 10; 4:1-5, 11.**

Jonah 3:1-5, 10

1 And the word of the LORD came unto Jonah the second time, saying,

2 Arise, go unto Nineveh, that great city, and preach unto it the preaching that I bid thee.

3 So Jonah arose, and went unto Nineveh, according to the word of the LORD. Now Nineveh was an exceeding great city of three days' journey.

4 And Jonah began to enter into the city a day's journey, and he cried, and said, Yet forty days, and Nineveh shall be overthrown.

5 So the people of Nineveh believed God, and proclaimed a fast, and put on sackcloth, from the greatest of them even to the least of them.

. . . .

10 And God saw their works, that they turned from their evil way; and God repented of the evil, that he had said that he would do unto them; and he did it not.

Jonah 4:1-5, 11

1 But it displeased Jonah exceedingly, and he was very angry.

2 And he prayed unto the LORD, and said, I pray thee, O LORD, was not this my saying, when I was yet in my country? Therefore I fled before unto Tarshish: for I knew that thou art a gracious God, and merciful, slow to anger, and of great kindness, and repentest thee of the evil.

3 Therefore now, O LORD, take, I beseech thee, my life from me; for it is better for me to die than to live.

4 Then said the LORD, Doest thou well to be angry?

5 So Jonah went out of the city, and sat on the east side of the city, and there made him a booth, and sat under it in the shadow, till he might see what would become of the city.

. . . .

11 And should not I spare Nineveh, that great city, wherein are more than sixscore thousand persons that cannot discern between their right hand and their left hand; and also much cattle?

Feb 11

GOLDEN TEXT: I knew that thou art a gracious God, and merciful, slow to anger, and of great kindness, and repentest thee of the evil.—Jonah 4:2.

God's Love for All People
(Jonah, Ruth)
(Lessons 10-13)

Lesson Aims

This lesson should help students:

1. Become aware of God's patience in dealing with persons who do not measure up to the standards of which they are capable.

2. Give priority in life to those matters that are of eternal significance.

3. Renew their efforts to live more completely in harmony with the revealed will of God.

Lesson Outline

INTRODUCTION
    A. We Must Change
    B. Lesson Background
  I. A SECOND CHANCE (Jonah 3:1-5, 10)
    A. The Unchanging Word (vv. 1, 2)
    B. Obedience (v. 3)
    C. Proclamation (v. 4)
    D. Results (vv. 5, 10)
      Saving the City
  II. UNEXPECTED OUTCOME (Jonah 4:1-5)
    A. Anger Expressed (vv. 1, 2)
    B. How Wrong Can You Be? (vv. 3, 4)
      Unhappy Are the Unmerciful
    C. Jonah Still Unconvinced (v. 5)
      A Kind Kind of God
 III. FINAL QUESTION (Jonah 4:11)
CONCLUSION
    A. Our Mission
    B. Let Us Pray
    C. Thought to Remember

Visual 11 of the visuals packet is a reminder of God's loving and compassionate nature. The visual is shown on page 206.

Introduction

A. We Must Change

Not everyone immediately accepts an idea that is new. "We've never done it that way before" is adequate reason to keep some persons from considering a different approach to an area of service in the church. Few people are willing to admit that their minds are that closed, however. So they give other reasons (excuses): "I'm too busy"; "I've had my turn; let somebody else do it"; "Somebody else can do it better than I can." These are among the responses given by many who are asked to take part in the church's ministry. Sometimes a person accepts an assignment and then just doesn't fulfill it because "something came up."

The fact is that some people are just not willing to step out from the familiar and do what needs to be done to further the Lord's work. This reluctance is widespread, in spite of the Bible's teaching to the contrary.

Perhaps the greatest challenge to the teacher of this lesson will be to get the members of the class to identify ways in which people today demonstrate the attitudes of Jonah. To get them to see the "Jonah" in themselves will usher in a new day in their lives and create a new wave of interest in the life-saving ministry of Christ's church. Personal participation is essential if the student expects to benefit from what the church, under God's direction, is doing.

B. Lesson Background

Last week's lesson provides the background for this lesson. The first part of the account of Jonah—his futile attempt to flee from God's presence, his being swallowed by a specially prepared fish, and his unusual escape from it—is dramatic and powerful. The second half of the account (this lesson) is equally powerful.

The text for this lesson emphasizes Jonah's attitude while carrying out and viewing the results of the mission God gave him. Jonah's attitude needed to be changed. Our study will reveal God's efforts to effect that change in His prophet.

I. A Second Chance
(Jonah 3:1-5, 10)

A. The Unchanging Word (vv. 1, 2)

1, 2. And the word of the LORD came unto Jonah the second time, saying, Arise, go unto Nineveh, that great city, and preach unto it the preaching that I bid thee.

God spoke to the fish that had swallowed Jonah, and the fish vomited him upon the dry land. We are not told where Jonah was when the Lord gave him his commission *the second time,* nor when it came. It may well be that *the word of the Lord came unto Jonah* while he was on that beach pondering his terrifying, yet amazing, experience. Patiently the Lord dealt with His disobedient prophet. In His first commission, God had instructed Jonah to "cry against" Nineveh because of the people's wickedness (1:2). In the second, the prophet Jonah was told that he was to proclaim the message that God would give him.

Christ gave His disciples the commission to take His gospel into all the world. There should be no misunderstanding about His wishes in this regard. We *know* that God wants the world to be redeemed, and yet many Christians are reluctant to speak to others about Christ. Particularly in these days of college-educated preachers, many members of the church are more than willing, if not anxious, to have the "professionals" do that kind of work. Is there any doubt that there is a direct correlation between how well we know the Bible and how willing we are to teach it to another? Many reasons can be given to show the value of daily study of the Bible. Not the least of them is the fact that in so doing we will be better equipped to fulfill this commission that the Lord Jesus has given to us all.

Nineveh was a grossly wicked city. God alone knew the fateful results if a word of warning and the opportunity to repent were not given to it. So He would not release Jonah from the duty that was his. And what shall we say about the great urban centers of our land? More and more voices are being raised concerning the escalating signs of the spiritual and moral decay that is occurring there. Shall we ignore it, hoping it will go away? Shall we, like Jonah, flee from any responsibility to bring change? At the very least we must pray that God will raise up people who will take Christ's message of hope and life to these influential yet troubled places. And as He does, we must be ready to support those persons in any and every way we can.

B. Obedience (v. 3)

3. So Jonah arose, and went unto Nineveh, according to the word of the LORD. Now Nineveh was an exceeding great city of three days' journey.

With the results of his effort to evade God's commission still fresh in his mind, Jonah *arose* this time to do as he was commanded.

An exceeding great city. The Hebrew text literally reads *a city great unto God.* The exact meaning of this expression is unclear. Perhaps included in it is the thought that God regarded Nineveh with interest because of the part it would play in carrying out His purposes.

Of three days' journey. This phrase is a description of the size of the city. Some think it means the city was large enough that it took three days to walk straight across it; others, that it was a three days' journey in circumference; still others, that it took three days to walk through the city, traversing the main streets and marketplaces. Of these, the second seems most probable. This much we can be safe in saying:

Nineveh was a very large city, and the task given Jonah would have been overwhelming were not God directly involved in it.

The evangelization of the world is a formidable undertaking. Nevertheless, we have the responsibility, under the same God to whom Jonah was accountable, to take the first step with every intention of continuing the "three-days' walk" in sharing the gospel of Christ with everyone.

The enormity of the task should cause all Christians to be more responsible and generous in their support of world evangelization through missionaries. Going one step further, all should be seeking and encouraging capable young Christians to consider the challenge of taking the gospel into all the world as their life's work.

C. Proclamation (v. 4)

4. And Jonah began to enter into the city a day's journey, and he cried, and said, Yet forty days, and Nineveh shall be overthrown.

A day's journey. Heedless of the danger he faced, Jonah entered the capital city of this enemy of his nation and began to sound God's warning. He did not travel one whole day *before* beginning to preach. Rather, as he made his way from one gathering place to another during the day, he preached. We learn from Isaiah 36:11, 13 that there would have been people in this Assyrian city who would have understood the language Jonah spoke. Word of his message, therefore, would have spread among the citizens of Nineveh.

Yet forty days, and Nineveh shall be overthrown. The message was one of warning, of doom. Nineveh's destruction would be as complete as that of Sodom and Gomorrah. (The same word for "overthrow" is used in each case—see Genesis 19:21, 25; Deuteronomy 29:23.) If these words were the only ones spoken by Jonah, they were impressive enough to cause the people to believe and to repent of their sins and to hope that God would not carry out the announced destruction. Some, however, think that Jonah would have elaborated on this statement, specifying Nineveh's sins and telling them that the destruction would not come if they repented. In light of Jonah's attitude and subsequent actions, he probably was not even considering the possibility that the people would repent. He appears to have been more interested in delivering the message of doom and making a hasty retreat! Unfortunately, most of us know or have known people who have delighted in being the bearer of bad news.

D. Results (vv. 5, 10)

5. So the people of Nineveh believed God, and proclaimed a fast, and put on sackcloth, from the greatest of them even to the least of them.

The people listened to Jonah's message and believed God. They proclaimed a fast; and citizens from all walks of life put on sackcloth, indicating sorrow and penitence.

Verses 6-9 record that when the king heard of Jonah's preaching, he put off his royal garments and put on sackcloth and sat in ashes. Expressing grief by sackcloth and ashes was practiced by various peoples of the Middle East. The king and the nobles took the lead in this citywide revival, proclaiming that every person, and even all livestock, should neither eat nor drink, but wear sackcloth in the hope that God would not carry out the threatened destruction.

10. And God saw their works, that they turned from their evil way; and God repented of the evil, that he had said that he would do unto them; and he did it not.

God, never out of touch with the world, saw the deeds of Nineveh as indicative that they were turning away from their harmful and evil ways. So God did not follow through on the threats that had been made about the city. The key factor was the change in the people's conduct. Because *they turned from their evil way*, God withheld the threatened destruction.

God promises blessing or punishment according to the principle stated in Jeremiah 18:7-10. In each case, God's actions are conditional—they are called forth by the actions of people. This is an unchanging truth concerning God's nature. If, as in the case of the Ninevites, people change and obey God, His threatened punishment will be withheld.

SAVING THE CITY

Only two short verses are given to Jonah's preaching and Nineveh's extraordinary response. His sermon, especially, was abbreviated. It would seem that he said more than, "In forty days Nineveh will be destroyed."

In any case, when an entire city of many thousands repents simultaneously after hearing only one sermon—that is phenomenal. We could wish that saving cities were that easy today! Urban evangelism is the greatest challenge for the church in America. Evangelistic

methods must change to reach the highly educated, economically privileged, and very private people of the new culture in this technological era.

The cities, however, are made up of more than those in the "uptown." There are also the teeming masses of economically underprivileged in the "downtown." These too need the gospel of Christ.

Accommodating culture without compromising God's message is the balancing act that Christians must perfect to save our cities. What would Jonah's approach be today?

Lord, help us!   —R. W. B.

II. Unexpected Outcome (Jonah 4:1-5)

A. Anger Expressed (vv. 1, 2)

1. But it displeased Jonah exceedingly, and he was very angry.

For disobeying the direct command of the Lord, Jonah had been thrown into the raging sea and had been swallowed by a great fish. For three frightful days and nights he lived in the belly of that fish. From there he cried to God, and God heard his cry and rescued him. Oh, how thankful Jonah was for the Lord's salvation! (See Jonah 2:2-9.) How strange, therefore, and how selfish for him to think that he could be a recipient of God's grace but that that same grace should not be extended to other sinners who, like himself, had repented of their evil deeds!

Jonah had obeyed God by finally going to Nineveh and delivering the message God had given him to speak. Clearly, however, Jonah's heart was not in it. Assyria was the enemy of Israel, and Jonah wanted Nineveh to be destroyed (compare verse 11). When that didn't happen, Jonah grew angry.

2. And he prayed unto the LORD, and said, I pray thee, O LORD, was not this my saying, when I was yet in my country? Therefore I fled before unto Tarshish: for I knew that thou art a gracious God, and merciful, slow to anger, and of great kindness, and repentest thee of the evil.

By this statement Jonah showed that his thinking was not lined up with God's concerning the people of Nineveh. Jonah wanted them wiped off the face of the earth, and he knew that God would be merciful and spare them if he went and preached to them. So, he explained, that was why he had fled to Tarshish after receiving God's first call. Jonah's manner of expression suggests that he felt he had been justified in disobeying God. He saw nothing wrong with putting his will above God's will regarding who should receive God's mercy.

B. How Wrong Can You Be? (vv. 3, 4)

3, 4. Therefore now, O LORD, take, I beseech thee, my life from me; for it is better for me to die than to live. Then said the LORD, Doest thou well to be angry?

It is better for me to die than to live. Perhaps Jonah felt this way because of wounded vanity, since he had predicted a destruction that was not going to be carried out. It may be that he felt like a traitor, since he had had a part in sparing Nineveh from destruction. Whatever the reason, he had much to learn about the kind of attitudes God wants His people to have in their hearts.

God's response to Jonah's fierce anger was tender kindness. His question called for Jonah to examine his own heart and life to see how graciously God had dealt with him. Couldn't Jonah see that that same grace and mercy could be extended to persons of another nationality or race as well?

In many instances, honest searching of our hearts reveals that the problems we attribute to God or others are actually in us.

UNHAPPY ARE THE UNMERCIFUL

A celebrated psychologist says, "Happy people are good people, and good people are happy people." Such a statement, of course, must be qualified by definition of terms. What is meant by *happy?* What is the connotation of *good?*

Jesus said, "Blessed (happy) are the merciful" (Matthew 5:7). We can discern what He meant. In this instance, *happy* is "deeply content," "at peace with oneself." *Merciful* is "sensitive, kind, forgiving, understanding, patient."

We know it's true. This beatitude is verified by our personal experience. A satisfied mind is our reward when we behave mercifully, especially

Home Daily Bible Readings

Monday, Feb. 5—Sin's Punishment (Genesis 19:24-29)
Tuesday, Feb. 6—Test of a True Prophet (Deuteronomy 18:15-22)
Wednesday, Feb. 7—God Is in Charge (Lamentations 3:31-39)
Thursday, Feb. 8—Moral and Social Abuses (Micah 1:1-10)
Friday, Feb. 9—Steadfast Compassion (Exodus 34:1-9)
Saturday, Feb. 10—Recipe for Discouragement (1 Kings 19:1-8)
Sunday, Feb. 11—God's Logic (Jonah 4:6-10)

toward our enemies, those who have offended us in one way or another. Good people are happy people.

Jonah learned the truth of the negative corollary: *unhappy are the unmerciful.* Even when he finally preached in Nineveh, it seems that he did so without compassion. It appears that he relished the destruction that he foretold concerning the city. He was disappointed and unhappy when the citizens of Nineveh repented and were saved —so unhappy in fact, he wished he could die.

The merciful obtain mercy. "Be ye kind . . . even as God for Christ's sake hath forgiven you" (Ephesians 4:32).   —R. W. B.

C. Jonah Still Unconvinced (v. 5)

5. So Jonah went out of the city, and sat on the east side of the city, and there made him a booth, and sat under it in the shadow, till he might see what would become of the city.

Jonah left the city and made a *booth* in which he could live while he waited to *see what would become of the city.* The booth would have been a tent-like structure made of interlaced scrub branches, which did not entirely keep the sun off Jonah. It seems that he still clung to the hope that Nineveh would be destroyed. Did he misinterpret God's question in verse 4? Did he mistakenly think God meant by it that Jonah was too hasty in his judgment—that because God did not bring destruction upon Nineveh immediately did not mean that He would not bring destruction at all?

Verses 6-10 are omitted from our text, but they contain information necessary for our understanding of the conclusion of this account.

As Jonah sat in his Spartan structure, God showed mercy to him once again by preparing a special plant that grew quickly up over Jonah's booth and provided shade for him. The shade delivered him "from his grief," both of body and spirit, and Jonah was very glad for the relief it brought him. The next morning, however, after Jonah had come to depend on the shade, God prepared a worm that attacked the plant, causing it to wither as quickly as it had grown.

The next agent God used in His effort to instruct Jonah was the east wind. The combination of the blazing sun and the scorching wind made Jonah want to die. At this point God spoke to him about his feelings for the plant that had been destroyed. Jonah openly admitted his anger at the loss of it, for it had been a blessing to him. God then came to the heart of the matter, attempting to get Jonah to have a better understanding of God's love for human beings. Jonah had pity on, that is, he was loath to lose, a senseless plant, which he neither planted nor caused to grow, a plant that made its appearance in a day and departed just as quickly. From there God drove home the lesson with unanswerable force.

A KIND KIND OF GOD

J. B. Phillips is the author of a classic little book entitled, *Your God Is Too Small*. In it he explores some of the erroneous conceptions people have about God. Some, for example, imagine that God is some kind of celestial cop, vigilant to catch His creatures in wrongdoing. Others may picture God as a grandfather type, permissive and indulgent, a regular softy. We usually assign to God human characteristics, for they are all we know. With our material, finite minds we cannot accurately conceive of a spiritual being.

Phillips urges us to expand our thinking and stretch our imaginations to believe in the God of the Bible. Jehovah not only exists above and beyond the material universe, but He also is with us here and now. Justice and mercy, grace and truth are inherent elements of His being.

Jonah knew in part what God is like—"gracious . . . merciful, slow to anger, and of great kindness" (4:2). But his God was too small if he believed that Jehovah would exclude Nineveh, or any people, from His love and grace.

God "is . . . not willing that any should perish" (2 Peter 3:9). Do we have such a lofty spirit? Do we feel responsible for sharing the gospel with unreached people groups? Do we take global, cross-cultural evangelism seriously? Our God is big enough and kind enough to love the whole world and every generation.   —R. W. B.

III. Final Question
(Jonah 4:11)

11. And should not I spare Nineveh, that great city, wherein are more than sixscore thousand persons that cannot discern between their right hand and their left hand; and also much cattle?

Spare. The Hebrew word here is the word for "pity." If Jonah could become fondly attached to a plant of little worth that had grown up without

visual 11

his help, wasn't it fitting for God to look upon the people of Nineveh in the same way? The difference was that this *great city* was God's; He had permitted it to grow into a great power, and He sustained it. Therefore, he had all the more reason to be concerned for the people there.

Another reason God gave for His desire to spare Nineveh was the fact that living in the city were a hundred and twenty thousand persons who could not *discern between their right hand and their left hand.* This is generally taken to mean small children, those who were innocent of serious wrongdoing. Given this number of such children, it is estimated that the total population of the city was around six hundred thousand. Even the presence of *much cattle* in Nineveh evoked God's compassion.

This verse gives us a glimpse of the heart of God and reveals His tender mercy over all His works. It teaches us that God loves all people and that He is displeased with the narrow-minded attitude that would lead anyone to exclude those of another race or nationality from His kingdom.

We don't know how Jonah responded to God's final question. More important to us, however, is, do *we* understand how deep God's love for mankind is and how wide His mercy? And are we willing to do what we can to see that all persons learn of them?

Conclusion

A. Our Mission

Jesus said, "Go ye into all the world, and preach the gospel to every creature" (Mark 16:15). That is our mission, just as Jonah's mission was to go to Nineveh. Christ's commission was intended for all of His followers. We are to make known the gospel; we are to spread the word of God's concern for all mankind. The message of the book of Jonah is that God's love knows no ethnic nor racial boundaries. It is inclusive. Let us do all we can to fulfill our mission, and rejoice when lost souls anywhere turn to Him.

B. Let Us Pray

Our Father in Heaven, we thank You for Your unfailing love for us. May we show our gratitude by sharing Your gospel of love with people everywhere who don't know You and who do not know that You love them too. In Jesus' name, amen.

C. Thought to Remember

"For as the heaven is high above the earth, so great is [the Lord's] mercy toward them that fear him" (Psalm 103:11).

Learning by Doing

This page contains an alternate lesson plan emphasizing learning activities. Classes desiring such student involvement will find these suggestions helpful.

Learning Goals

With this study adult learners will:

1. Affirm this doctrinal truth: God accepts sincere repentance.

2. Identify the differences between God's and Jonah's attitudes toward sinners.

3. See and name similarities between their own attitudes and those of Jonah.

Into the Lesson

Before class, prepare a sign that reads, "The End Is Near," and attach it to a yardstick. Recruit someone to enter your classroom on cue and walk through with the sign over his shoulder, all the while announcing, "Prepare to meet thy God!" Once the person passes through, ask your class what name society commonly gives such a person. (Answer: "Prophet of Doom," or the like.) When you receive that answer, indicate that that is what Jonah wanted to be and what he actually was.

Into the Word

Begin by reading chapters 3 and 4 responsively with your class. The alternating verse pairs work quite well overall as idea and response.

Then, divide your class into groups of three persons each. For each student, prepare a sheet on which you have written the following six questions. List them in the order shown and allow space for answers to be written in.

1A. What does God expect His preacher to do regarding the message he is given?

2B. How (well) did Jonah fulfill his responsibilities?

2A. What result does God want when His word is preached?

3B. How (well) did the Ninevites respond when they heard God's message?

3A. How do you think God wants His preacher to react when his audience hears and obeys God's word?

1B. How (well) did Jonah react when his preaching accomplished what God intended?

Have the members in each group number themselves 1, 2, and 3. Direct each student to examine the text to answer question A with his or her number, and to list responses. After two or three minutes, direct group members to pass their sheets to the next member (1 to 2, 2 to 3, 3

to 1). Each person should now answer question B by his or her number, using the previous person's response as well as the text. After two or three minutes, have the sheets passed once more.

Now have the class reassemble. Ask the six questions in the sequence shown. As you ask each question, have someone who is holding the answer to it share the answer with the class. Encourage others holding the same answer to respond also. The purpose in this study is to emphasize God's expectations and His character. For example, in answer to questions 1A and 2B, anticipate such responses as these: "God expects His preacher to preach the message he has been given" (see 3:2b) and, "It seems that Jonah spoke what God directed" (see 3:4b). Also, "God expects His preacher to preach whenever opportunity allows," and "Jonah preached in Nineveh as soon as he arrived."

As an alternative to the preceding activity, or in addition to it, consider the following: Bring two photo albums you have conspicuously marked "Pretty Pictures" and "Ugly Pictures." Suggest that what you have inside are pictures from the events described in Jonah 3 and 4. Ask your class to describe pictures they would expect to see in each volume. An example of a "pretty" picture would be Jonah headed away from the seashore, walking by a sign that says, "Nineveh, This Way," with an arrow pointing the direction Jonah is walking. An "ugly" picture would be Jonah sitting on a hillside overlooking Nineveh, with his hands shading his head and his lip stuck out in a pout. Challenge your adults to cover Jonah 3 and 4 as comprehensively as they can and to be as creative in specific details as possible.

Into Life

Bring to class large, full leaves cut out of green paper, one for each of your learners. As you distribute them, mention that Jonah's plant and its death represent well the differences between God's concern for the Ninevites and Jonah's selfish concerns. Have your learners write on one side, "God's Concerns," and on the other, "My Concerns." Ask them to take the leaf home. Suggest that they turn it over once a day and ponder whether their concerns of the day are selfish or selfless. This should reinforce the teaching of the book of Jonah.

Let's Talk It Over

The questions on this page are designed to encourage review of the lesson Scriptures and to promote discussion of the lesson by the class. The answers provided are only discussion starters. Let your class talk it over from there.

1. The message Jonah proclaimed to the people of Nineveh was not of his own devising; it came from God. Christians too have a message from God that is to be delivered to the people of their generation. That message is found in the Bible. What implication does this have for us?

The obvious implication is that we must be thoroughly acquainted with the Bible if we are to present God's message accurately to the people of our day. At the heart of this message is God's love, mercy, and grace, all of which find their highest expression in the atoning death of God's Son on our behalf. Part of the message, however, deals with man's response to God's grace, and this includes the need to repent of sin and to turn from it. Warning of certain judgment for rejecting God's gracious offer is part of the message also. Peter encourages his readers to "grow in grace, and in the *knowledge* of our Lord and Saviour Jesus Christ" (2 Peter 3:18). Knowledge of Christ, salvation, and the principles of Christian living comes only from the careful study of the Word of God.

2. Compare Jonah's commission and message with those given to Christians.

Jonah was instructed to deliver God's message to one city. Christians are instructed by Jesus to go into all the world (Mark 16:15). Jonah's message emphasized Nineveh's physical destruction. From the biblical record, it would seem that hope of escape from that destruction may have been only implied. The gospel we preach majors in hope—the hope of escaping the punishment we deserve for our sins, the hope of living eternally in Heaven. But the gospel contains the clear and direct warning of a punishment much worse than physical destruction for those who choose to reject God's offer of escape. While the church's task may be much more enormous than Jonah's, we have two advantages: the fellowship of the church and the presence of the Lord himself (Matthew 28:20).

3. The need for messengers to take the gospel to a lost world is great. What can the church, and specifically Christian parents, do to help fill that need?

We must first recognize the need for workers in the Lord's harvest field and be willing to follow the Lord's leading as He calls us to serve Him. Christian parents must be challenged to encourage their children to devote their lives to service for the Lord. Entering the ministry or mission work is not seen as a way to "get ahead" in life, so, unfortunately, many Christian parents discourage their children from going in this direction. But those who do commit their lives in service to Christ can testify that they are on the cutting edge of the Lord's blessings. Not only so, but in choosing a life of sacrificial service for Christ, they will reap eternal reward. So at a time when the demand for Christian workers is increasing, it is crucial for parents to understand that the Lord's harvest is ready, and to encourage their children to become reapers.

4. Things did not go the way Jonah expected or wanted, either with the city of Nineveh or with the gourd vine that provided shade for him in the blistering heat. How should we respond when our prayers are not answered in the way we would like?

The Christian life is based on trust that God will always do what is best for us. We may *think* we know what is best for us, but God, in fact, *knows* what we need. We would do well to meditate often on God's majestic statement recorded by the prophet Isaiah: "For my thoughts are not your thoughts, neither are your ways my ways, saith the Lord. For as the heavens are higher than the earth, so are my ways higher than your ways, and my thoughts than your thoughts" (Isaiah 55:8, 9). When the circumstances of our lives are not in accord with our wishes, let us trust that God will work all things for the good of those who love Him and are called according to His purpose (Romans 8:28).

5. What is the fundamental truth that is taught by the account of Jonah?

Underlying the entire account is the truth that God's love is universal. Jonah's reaction to the possibility of Nineveh's salvation was an expression of the attitudes and perspectives of his own people, who wanted to build a wall around God's love and mercy and claim them only for themselves. This book stands as a testimony against all who make exclusive claims regarding God's love and mercy.

The Loyalty of Ruth

February 18
Lesson 12

DEVOTIONAL READING: Psalm 119:59-72.

LESSON SCRIPTURE: Ruth 1.

PRINTED TEXT: Ruth 1:1-8, 16-18.

Ruth 1:1-8, 16-18

1 Now it came to pass in the days when the judges ruled, that there was a famine in the land. And a certain man of Beth-lehem-judah went to sojourn in the country of Moab, he, and his wife, and his two sons.

2 And the name of the man was Elimelech, and the name of his wife Naomi, and the name of his two sons Mahlon and Chilion, Ephrathites of Beth-lehem-judah. And they came into the country of Moab, and continued there.

3 And Elimelech Naomi's husband died; and she was left, and her two sons.

4 And they took them wives of the women of Moab; the name of the one was Orpah, and the name of the other Ruth: and they dwelt there about ten years.

5 And Mahlon and Chilion died also both of them; and the woman was left of her two sons and her husband.

6 Then she arose with her daughters-in-law, that she might return from the country of Moab: for she had heard in the country of Moab how that the LORD had visited his people in giving them bread.

7 Wherefore she went forth out of the place where she was, and her two daughters-in-law with her; and they went on the way to return unto the land of Judah.

8 And Naomi said unto her two daughters-in-law, Go, return each to her mother's house: the LORD deal kindly with you, as ye have dealt with the dead, and with me.

. . . .

16 And Ruth said, Entreat me not to leave thee, or to return from following after thee: for whither thou goest, I will go; and where thou lodgest, I will lodge: thy people shall be my people, and thy God my God:

17 Where thou diest, will I die, and there will I be buried: the LORD do so to me, and more also, if aught but death part thee and me.

18 When she saw that she was steadfastly minded to go with her, then she left speaking unto her.

GOLDEN TEXT: Entreat me not to leave thee, or to return from following after thee: for whither thou goest, I will go; and where thou lodgest, I will lodge: thy people shall be my people, and thy God my God.—Ruth 1:16.

Feb
18

God's Love for All People
(Jonah, Ruth)
(Lessons 10-13)

Lesson Aims

After this lesson, a student should:

1. See the value of loyalty in human relations as demonstrated by Ruth.

2. Understand how God uses people of loyalty to accomplish His purposes.

3. Develop loyalty as a Christian trait in interpersonal relations.

Lesson Outline

INTRODUCTION
  A. Skeletons in the Closet
  B. Lesson Background
I. A FAMILY COPES WITH TRAGEDY (Ruth 1:1-5)
  A. Famine in Bethlehem (vv. 1, 2)
    Gotta Keep Movin'
  B. Death in the Family (vv. 3-5)
II. NAOMI GOES HOME (Ruth 1:6-8)
  A. Good News From Home (v. 6)
  B. Going Home (v. 7)
    Thinkin' 'Bout Home
  C. Naomi's Kindness (v. 8)
III. RUTH'S LOYALTY (Ruth 1:16-18)
  A. Ruth's Vow (vv. 16, 17)
  B. Naomi's Response (v. 18)
CONCLUSION
  A. Love and Loyalty
  B. Let Us Pray
  C. Thought to Remember

Visual 12 of the visuals packet reveals the principle that lies at the very heart of loyalty. The visual is shown on page 213.

Introduction

A. Skeletons in the Closet

What king of Israel and Judah can you name who was greater than David? The prophets viewed his kingdom as Israel's golden age and the model for the coming messianic glory. They called the Messiah "Son of David" and occasionally simply "David" (Jeremiah 30:9, for example). David was described as a man after God's own heart (1 Samuel 13:14), but David's life certainly had its darker side. This is seen in his adultery with Bathsheba and in the deterioration within his own family as a result of rape, mur-

der, and rebellion among his children. But there was another "skeleton" in David's closet. His great-grandmother was a Gentile. Her name? Ruth, the Moabitess.

Ruth, however, has become the personification of loyalty and fidelity, a powerful example for all generations in developing character and godly values. We associate her nobility with the good Samaritan in Jesus' parable. Her commitment and conduct lifted her from the category of being a "skeleton in the closet" to that of being a respected role model.

Ruth's transformation arose from a series of promises she made to Naomi. Central among these was her vow, "Thy people shall be my people, and thy God my God" (Ruth 1:16). Arising from this foundational commitment to Naomi and to Naomi's God, she struck out on a new path that changed her life forever and contributed significantly to Israel's future. What a wonderful "skeleton" to have in one's closet!

B. Lesson Background

This lesson and the next are based on the book of Ruth. This biblical short story takes its title from the main character of the story, Ruth of Moab. In our English Bible, the book follows Judges, which provides its historical setting. This connection is seen in the opening statement of the book, "Now it came to pass in the days when the judges ruled."

The small book seems to have several purposes. Besides showing how difficult times were during the era of the judges, it teaches qualities that God endorses: courage, duty to family, fear of God, honor, loyalty, and love. The main characters (Naomi, Ruth, and Boaz) display these noble traits even under stress. The book also warns God's people against dismissing foreign people simply because they are foreign. It shows that conversion, even by enemies, is possible and can bring blessing in unexpected ways. As we shall see, a foreigner became an ancestress of King David himself, and she was the very model of what an Israelite wife should be. Another purpose of the book may be to show that David's sterling qualities could be traced to notable and honorable characters, among whom was Ruth.

The story of Ruth touches us because it gives us realistic glimpses of life in Judah prior to the time of the kings. Literary analysis shows us the artistic quality of the book as a short story making use of a semipoetic style, wordplay, symmetry, character development, and dialogue. Theological subtleties abound. Though God as a character does not speak in the book as He does in the books of Judges and Samuel, His providential mercy lies behind the entire story and remains prominent in the minds of all the characters. Though we are hearing a tale of simple villagers, in an agricultural setting, we find much to teach us about God's ways among His people and the qualities He values.

As the story opens, a severe famine has come to Judah during the time of the judges. Elimelech and Naomi, along with their two sons, Mahlon and Chilion, leave their home in Bethlehem and journey to Moab where, presumably, food was available. There the family settles. In time, however, Elimelech dies. The two sons marry Moabite girls, and within ten years Naomi's two sons also have died. Naomi decides to return to Bethlehem and seek help from her family, and her daughters-in-law offer to go with her. She tries to dissuade them by saying that she can offer them no help. Orpah reluctantly turns back, but Ruth will not leave her mother-in-law. The two women come to Bethlehem at harvesttime.

Ruth gleans in the fields of Boaz, a man of prominence who was related to Elimelech. Ruth's hard work and determination stand out. Boaz treats her kindly when he hears the sad story of Ruth and Naomi. Naomi later advises her how to behave toward Boaz at the threshing floor (chapter 3). Boaz promises to handle Naomi's and Ruth's affairs with honor. The next day he calls the village court into session (chapter 4) and confronts the "kinsman-redeemer" with Naomi's situation. The man agrees to redeem Elimelech's land, but refuses to marry Ruth. Boaz seizes the opportunity to redeem the land and to marry Ruth to continue the family line. A son, Obed, is born to Boaz and Ruth; so Naomi finds joy in her advanced years. The story ends with a genealogy running from Pharez, son of Judah, through Boaz and Ruth to King David. The same, or similar, genealogies appear in Matthew 1, Luke 3, and 1 Chronicles 2:5-15.

How to Say It

CHEMOSH. *Kee*-mosh.

CHILION. *Kil*-e-on.

ELIMELECH. E-*lim*-eh-leck.

EPHRATH. *Ef*-rath.

EPHRATAH. *Ef*-rah-tah.

EPHRATHITES. *Ef*-rah-thites.

HESED (Hebrew). *hes*-ed.

MAHLON. *Mah*-lun.

MOABITESS. *Mo*-ub-*ite*-ess (strong accent on *ite*).

PHAREZ. *Fa*-rez.

ZEBULUN. *Zeb*-you-lun.

We notice movement in the plot development geographically, from Judah into Moabite exile and back in the safety of the promised land. Also the character development moves from Elimelech as the dominant person to Naomi, to Ruth, then to Boaz, and finally to David. The tension in the plot moves through deepening danger and distress to emerging hope, and finally to a bright future.

I. A Family Copes With Tragedy (Ruth 1:1-5)

A. Famine in Bethlehem (vv. 1, 2)

1, 2. Now it came to pass in the days when the judges ruled, that there was a famine in the land. And a certain man of Beth-lehem-judah went to sojourn in the country of Moab, he, and his wife, and his two sons. And the name of the man was Elimelech, and the name of his wife Naomi, and the name of his two sons Mahlon and Chilion, Ephrathites of Beth-lehem-judah. And they came into the country of Moab, and continued there.

The book of Ruth opens by using the typical narrative expression, "And it was," or, "It came to pass." This opening statement identifies the time frame as *the days when the judges ruled*. Judges sometimes presided over court cases, but their most important duty was to organize and lead their people in war against an enemy. They were sometimes called "saviors."

The era of the judges stretched from the time of Joshua and Caleb to the monarchy of Saul. The books of Judges and 1 Samuel describe this period of Israel's history. The genealogy in chapter 4 suggests the second generation before Samuel as the generation of Boaz and Ruth.

The cause for the famine that came upon the land is not stated, but drought or warfare was the probable cause. Southern Palestinian farmers lived on the margin of subsistence, so that several bad harvests in a row could make life difficult for them. Towns such as Bethlehem, situated on the eastern side of the Judean watershed, would receive significantly less rain than those on the western side; so they were especially susceptible to drought conditions.

Bethlehem-judah is located about six miles south of Jerusalem. Ephrath and Ephratah are other names for the town (see Genesis 35:19 Micah 5:2). Thus the members of the family in this account are called Ephrathites. *Judah* in the name distinguishes this Bethlehem from the town of the same name located in the territory of the tribe of Zebulun (Joshua 19:15). For the "country of Moab" the Hebrew text has the "fields of Moab," the pastoral territory of that country. Moab was located just east of the Dead Sea.

The name *Elimelech* signifies "The King (meaning Jehovah) is my God." Nothing more is known of this man other than what is recorded here. Seemingly, Elimelech had done all that he could to keep the wolf of hunger from his door, but it was a losing battle. When it became apparent that conditions were not going to improve immediately, he took his family to Moab *to sojourn* there, that is, to stay there awhile.

The fact that the Moabites accepted Elimelech and allowed this foreigner to dwell in their midst in peace speaks well of him. The period of the judges was a time of social and moral degeneration in Israel, a time when "every man did that which was right in his own eyes" (Judges 21:25). However, at the time when many were doing their own thing, there were others seeking to walk in the ways of God. It would seem that Elimelech and his family were among the latter.

GOTTA KEEP MOVIN'

Americans, on average, change residence every three to five years. Ours is a mobile society. Moving is neither good nor bad of itself, but the motivations and results are often negative. We are a restless people. Many of us are without roots, family ties, or close friends.

Sometimes, of course, people move for very practical reasons. Elimelech and Naomi moved their family to Moab to escape a famine. Work, income, food, and shelter—chasing the necessities still keeps people on the move. Ruth's inlaws were by no means transient or vagrant. Once they were settled in Moab, they stayed at least ten years. When the land of Judah once again was productive and prosperous, Naomi chose to return to familiar surroundings and reestablish her home there.

Christians today must rediscover the church-family values of fellowship, loyalty, and faithfulness. "Church shopping" and "church hopping" have hurt the body. The spirit of community has suffered. Let us remember and return to our religious roots and be glad we are part of the family of God.   —R. W. B.

B. Death in the Family (vv. 3-5)

3. And Elimelech Naomi's husband died; and she was left, and her two sons.

The story moves along swiftly at this point, and embellishing details are omitted. How much time passed before the death of Elimelech we are not told. Nor are we told how Naomi, now a widow away from her own country, survived. We presume that the people of Moab were hospitable toward her and her sons.

4. And they took them wives of the women of Moab; the name of the one was Orpah, and the name of the other Ruth: and they dwelt there about ten years.

The sequence of the biblical text makes it seem that Naomi's sons took Moabite wives after their father's death. Taking these wives suggests their intention to remain permanently in Moab. From verse 10 of chapter 4 we learn that Ruth was the wife of Mahlon.

They dwelt there about ten years. It is uncertain whether the ten years is marked from the time when Elimelech and his family entered Moab until the death of the sons, or only from the time of the marriages of the sons until their deaths. The former seems preferable.

5. And Mahlon and Chilion died also both of them; and the woman was left of her two sons and her husband.

The author continues to make a long story short, omitting details. Up to this point in the narrative, the emotions of the characters are not described. Think, however, of the sorrow Naomi felt at the loss of her mate and then of both her sons. And think of the hardship she now faced as a result. She was destitute in a foreign culture. The expression, "the woman was left of her two sons and her husband," means that she was left behind by the departure of her husband and sons in death. In ancient patriarchal society a woman seldom functioned apart from a male agent, whether her father, brother(s), husband, or son(s). Naomi's situation suddenly turned desperate, being as she was in a foreign land away from the support of near family and clan structure. With her sons dead, she was left with only her two daughters-in-law. And since these two Moabite women themselves now were widows, they might be expected to return to their own parents for the support that they could give them. But what was Naomi to do?

II. Naomi Goes Home (Ruth 1:6-8)

A. Good News From Home (v. 6)

6. Then she arose with her daughters-in-law, that she might return from the country of Moab: for she had heard in the country of Moab how that the LORD had visited his people in giving them bread.

She arose with her daughters-in-law. Naomi, as it were, had been "sitting" where her family had settled (see verse 4), and now she rose up to depart. The impression is given that her daughters-in-law were in close contact with her, perhaps even living with her. *That she might return* means that she began making preparations to return to her homeland. The reason given is that she had heard that the famine in her homeland had ended.

The expression, *the Lord had visited his people,* may seem strange to us. It usually designates God's punishment, but sometimes it refers to God's blessing. The term in Hebrew primarily means "to review, take note of, inspect" and secondarily "to take action appropriate to the results of the inspection." The Lord, so to speak, had reviewed His people's condition and had taken steps to improve it. Crops were growing on the farmlands again. This was taken as God's blessing upon His people.

B. Going Home (v. 7)

7. Wherefore she went forth out of the place where she was, and her two daughters-in-law with her; and they went on the way to return unto the land of Judah.

Naomi left her home of many years in Moab and began the journey back to Judah. No doubt she had mixed feelings prompted by fear of the uncertain future that lay before her. She may have wondered if anyone from her family or her husband's family would remember her or bother to help. Regardless, there was no future for her in Moab, so she must push on in faith.

Naomi's character commanded such respect and love from her Moabite daughters-in-law that they wanted to stay with her, even though to do so meant they would have to leave their native land. And so Orpah and Ruth joined Naomi for the walk to Bethlehem. The strength and courage of all three is remarkable.

THINKIN' 'BOUT HOME

For most of us, *home* is still a nostalgic word. We remember the warmth and love of family togetherness, the laughter and joy of childhood experiences, and the closeness and security we felt in times of trouble. Our senses continue to flash back memories of the smells and tastes of home-cooked meals, the feel of blankets "tucked in" at night, the sounds of clocks and radios, and the sights of Mother's apron, Dad's saw or fishing pole, or sunlight streaming through a window, illuminating the imaginary world of our personal toylands.

Sometimes we yearn to go home, to return to that safe place of refuge from the toils and cares of adult life, to find again the family and friends who gave us such contentment in our youth.

During the years she spent in Moab, Naomi must have thought often about going home. No doubt she reminisced about good people and good times in Bethlehem, and longed for the comfort and security of native customs. We are

visual 12

"Loyalty means nothing unless it has at its heart the absolute principle of self-sacrifice."
—Woodrow Wilson

not surprised to read that "she went forth . . . to return unto the land of Judah" (v. 7).

Christians are comforted by thoughts of going to their spiritual home, the heavenly place prepared by the Lord for the faithful. Terry Toler expressed it musically:

> I'm thinkin' 'bout home,
> Thinkin' 'bout goin' home;
> Dreamin' 'bout leavin' here . . .
> Thinkin' 'bout home.
>
> —R. W. B.

C. Naomi's Kindness (v. 8)

8. And Naomi said unto her two daughters-in-law, Go, return each to her mother's house: the LORD deal kindly with you, as ye have dealt with the dead, and with me.

This verse and verses 9-15, which are not included in the printed text, give indication of Naomi's kind and generous spirit. She was old and would do what she must, but her daughters-in-law were young. So Naomi urged them to turn back and remain with their people. Both girls protested that they would go with her. After more persuasion by Naomi, however, "Orpah kissed her mother-in-law" (v. 14). Naomi then turned to Ruth and encouraged her also to return.

Ruth's response is recorded in verses 16 and 17. Her words of devotion to Naomi are among the most beautiful in the Bible.

III. Ruth's Loyalty (Ruth 1:16-18)

A. Ruth's Vow (vv. 16, 17)

16, 17. And Ruth said, Entreat me not to leave thee, or to return from following after thee: for whither thou goest, I will go; and where thou lodgest, I will lodge: thy people shall be my people, and thy God my God: where thou diest, will I die, and there will I be buried: the LORD do so to me, and more also, if aught but death part thee and me.

Ruth's reply has the character of a personal plea, a confession, and an oath. She was so moved by the love she had experienced from Naomi that she begged her not to press her to go home. She could not face a future apart from this trusted friend. She vowed to go with Naomi no matter where she might travel. She confessed her commitment to Naomi's people and to Naomi's God. There is a threefold commitment here. Ruth pledged herself and her future to Naomi as a person who could be trusted, to Naomi's people and their social customs, and to Naomi's God and His goodness. Ruth's commitment to Naomi's God equaled a rejection of the religious tradition in which she had been reared. Ruth's sense of loyalty to Naomi led her to make life-altering alignments that cut to the very core of her heart. Something about Naomi's manner of life and her trust in God drew Ruth to her decision. Her entire future hung on this decision.

The last clause of Ruth's vow took the form of the familiar self-curse seen elsewhere in the Old Testament (1 Samuel 20:13, for example). This was the ancients' strongest form of affirmation similar to what a person today would mean by saying, "May God strike me dead if . . . !"

Ruth was making an irrevocable pledge, meant to be lifelong and beyond. Even when she died she would be buried where Naomi was buried. Seldom have words of such determination and strength of purpose been spoken. They are a marvelous testimony to Ruth's character.

B. Naomi's Response (v. 18)

18. When she saw that she was steadfastly minded to go with her, then she left speaking unto her.

Steadfastly minded means Ruth was firmly resolved. The strength of Ruth's declaration

Home Daily Bible Readings

Monday, Feb. 12—A Forefather's Generosity (Genesis 50:15-26)

Tuesday, Feb. 13—Provision of Food (Exodus 16:9-21)

Wednesday, Feb. 14—God's Care for the Earth (Psalm 104:10-18)

Thursday, Feb. 15—Bread for the Poor (Psalm 132:11-18)

Friday, Feb. 16—God's Faithfulness (Psalm 145:11-20)

Saturday, Feb. 17—Loyal Commitment (2 Timothy 2:1-7)

Sunday, Feb. 18—Naomi's Considerate Behavior (Ruth 1:9-15)

proved her loyalty and her determination. She would not take "no" for an answer. Naomi's sensitive perception told her not to pressure Ruth further. Ruth's decision was made just as much for Ruth's good as it was for Naomi's welfare. Ruth's act of sacrifice became her means for development and making a contribution to God's purposes.

The last verses of chapter 1 describe Naomi and Ruth's arrival in Bethlehem, and the stir it caused. Soon the townsfolk knew of the sorrow Naomi had experienced during the years since she had last seen her friends there.

Conclusion

A. Love and Loyalty

The Hebrew term *hesed* is one of the Bible's most powerful terms describing God's divine nature. The *King James Version* employs ten different English words to convey the meaning of this Hebrew term. Primary among these are *lovingkindness, mercy, kindness,* and *goodness.* Other versions add *loyalty* and *steadfast love.*

When Naomi urged her daughters-in-law (Orpah and Ruth) to return to their families, she pronounced a benediction of God's kindness (*hesed*) upon them, even as they had shown to their deceased husbands, her sons. Later in the account (Ruth 3:10) another mention is made of Ruth's kindness (*hesed*).

Orpah returned to her people, but Ruth refused to leave her mother-in-law. When Ruth spoke her vows to Naomi, she was expressing her love, loyalty, and concern for her. She was committing herself wholly to the interests and welfare of her deceased husband's mother. Ruth possessed and practiced *hesed.*

Hesed has been defined as "covenant love," such as that of friend with friend, marriage partners with each other, and child of God with God. The significance of this quality is such that none of these relationships is ideally possible without it. Without loyal love, these relationships go sour or many times they are broken altogether. May this divine quality characterize each of us.

B. Let Us Pray

Merciful heavenly Father, we thank You for the steadfast love You have for us. May the love we have for You and for one another remain strong and loyal always. Through Jesus Christ we pray. Amen.

C. Thought to Remember

Remember God's wish, "I desired mercy [*hesed*], and not sacrifice" (Hosea 6:6).

Learning by Doing

This page contains an alternate lesson plan emphasizing learning activities. Classes desiring such student involvement will find these suggestions helpful.

Learning Goals

This study enables students to use Ruth as a:
1. Model of loyalty for their relationships with others and with God.
2. Source of inspiration in difficult times.

Into the Lesson

As class members arrive, have on display a collection of large boxes taped or tied shut. Begin class by asking, "What does a stack of boxes make you think of?" Once someone says, "Moving," mention that today's study is a "moving" lesson in both the geographical and emotional sense of the word.

A map of Israel during the time of the judges, showing the location of Moab also, will aid your learners' understanding of this lesson.

Into the Word

As an overview of the lesson, do the following: Before class obtain twenty opaque sheets (8½ by 11 inches) and number them one through twenty. On half sheets of paper (5½ by 8½ inches) print in large letters the following twenty words, one word per sheet: *adequacy, Bethlehem, Bethlehem, Boaz, faith, fame, family, famine, Hebrew, joy, Judges, Kings, Mahlon, Moab, Moab, Moabitess obscurity, solitude, sorrow, superstition.* Tape the numbered sheets as liftable flaps to the front wall of your classroom or to the chalkboard. Arrange them in numerical order in five rows of four each. Tape the twenty words under the flaps in the order the words are shown above, one word per flap.

To begin, have your learners count off by fours. Have the "ones" skim chapter one, the "twos" skim chapter two, etc. Allow three minutes for this. Then hold up to your class a strip on which you have written "FROM ____ TO ____." Tell your learners that you want them to find the ten pairs of words under the flaps that represent ten "moving" experiences (from ____ to ____) in the book of Ruth. Ask a volunteer to choose two numbers from one through twenty; then show the words under those two flaps. Recover the words and have another volunteer choose two numbers from one through twenty. Continue doing this until all the matches are made.

Here are the pairs of words to be found. A brief explanation accompanies each: (1) from *Bethlehem* to *Moab*, the original move of Naomi's family; (2) from *famine* to *adequacy*, the reason for the move of Naomi's family to Moab; (3) from *joy* to *sorrow*, Naomi's change from her delight in her family to her loss of husband and sons; (4) from *family* to *solitude*, Naomi's situation; (5) from *Moab* to *Bethlehem*, Naomi's return home (6) from *Moabitess* to *Hebrew*, Ruth's change of national identity; (7) from *superstition* to *faith*, Ruth's religious change; (8) from *Mahlon* to *Boaz*, from Ruth's first husband to her second; (9) from *obscurity* to *fame*, Ruth's move from remote Moabitess to grandmother of King David; (10) from *Judges* to *Kings*, the historical setting of the book of Ruth.

Have a volunteer read Ruth 1:1-19a aloud to the class. Then lead the class in discussing the following *why* questions: (1) Why did the family move to Moab? (2) Why was Naomi's predicament so dire when her sons died? (3) Why did Naomi decide to return to Bethlehem? (4) Why did Naomi's daughters-in-law accompany her on the first part of her journey? (5) Why did Naomi urge her daughters-in-law to return to their homes in Moab? (6) Why did Ruth decide to accompany Naomi to Bethlehem?

Develop an acrostic on the word *loyalty* to emphasize Ruth's character and choices. Because the word has two Ls and two Ys, you may want to get the group started by giving an example for one of those two letters. Here are samples: L (love for another); O (obedience); Y (yielding to another's best interests); A (attachment to principle); L (lifetime decision); T (total commitment); Y (yearning for relationship). Whatever words or phrases are suggested, be certain to relate the concept to what is seen in Ruth's relationship to Naomi and to God.

Into Life

No doubt Ruth learned much of what she knew of Jehovah and godly behavior from her mother-in-law, Naomi. Encourage each of your learners who has a living, godly mother-in-law to write her a note of thanks for the ways she reflects the love and grace of God, and for the ways she taught that love and grace to her child (the class member's spouse). Others may be encouraged to identify an older person who exemplifies the values of a godly lifestyle and to write that person a note of appreciation

Let's Talk It Over

The questions on this page are designed to encourage review of the lesson Scriptures and to promote discussion of the lesson by the class. The answers provided are only discussion starters. Let your class talk it over from there.

1. What are some modern world problems that demonstrate how much people of the world need each other?

The growing problem of feeding the world's hungry indicates how dependent upon the great agricultural nations the other countries are. On the other hand, oil, rubber, sugar, and certain other vital products come from nations that are lacking in agricultural resources. The general problem of ecology, the cause of world peace, and the battle against poverty, ignorance, and disease are matters of concern for all nations.

2. Naomi experienced great grief because of the deaths of her husband and her two sons. How should we who are Christians deal with the grief that we experience when a loved one is taken from us by death?

First Thessalonians 4:13 speaks to the issue of a Christian's grieving for those who have died. In that passage the apostle Paul does not instruct Christians *not* to grieve at all, but rather not "to grieve like the rest of men, who have no hope" (*New International Version*). Some of "the rest of men" would tell the bereaved not to cry. Others of "the rest of men" may tell us not to give any kind of expression to our grief. These praise the stoicism of persons at the time of bereavement. Grief, however, is a person's natural response to the loss of a loved one or dear friend, and the expression of grief should not be discouraged; it is necessary to the mental and emotional healing process. The Christian knows that Jesus himself wept when He arrived at the tomb of a dearly loved friend, although we are not told why (see John 11:35). The Christian knows also that God has given us each other for support and sympathy during times of grief (Romans 12:15). The Christian knows further that when Christians are separated by death, that separation is only temporary. There will be a joyful reunion eventually in Heaven. We have this hope. That is why we are not to grieve like "the rest of men."

3. Why may loyalty be considered the most significant element of any meaningful relationship?

Loyalty connotes reliability, steadfastness, certainty. It becomes the predictable in the midst of the unpredictable. Loyalty affirms, "I'll stand by you." For example, in a friendship it says, "When circumstances go sour, when others turn on you, when life seems to cave in—you can count on me!" It is not common blood that bonds a family together—it is loyalty. Loyalty is the variable in our relationship to Christ. *He* is dependable; the question is, can He count on us? Ruth exhibited a strong loyalty to Naomi.

4. Naomi attempted to talk Ruth out of coming with her to Israel, but finally accepted her solemn declaration of lifelong loyalty. In so doing, Naomi was accepting the offer of help implied in Ruth's statement of commitment. Why do some persons today have difficulty accepting offers of assistance from other persons?

We are an independent people, and many persons cherish their independence to a fault. To admit that they need help is to them a confession of inadequacy, and few people want to admit that they are inadequate. However, one's willingness to admit personal inadequacy must be cultivated. First and foremost it is an attitude of heart that is essential to one's correct relationship to God. Furthermore, only as we admit our inadequacies, our needs, are we able to minister to one another as the members of the body of Christ are supposed to do. When we allow another to minister to us, our needs are met, and the one who helps us is given opportunity for spiritual growth. Thus the needs of both giver and receiver are met at one and the same time. This is the beauty of Christian fellowship (see Galatians 6:2).

5. What perspective does today's lesson provide for contemporary marriage and family relationships?

The prime perspective is that of faithfulness, of loyalty. The current trend among many in these relationships is that they forsake commitments when problems arise. Loyalty tends to be conditional. *If* everything goes well, *if* I feel happy, then I'll be loyal and faithful. Another perspective asserts, *because* you're good to me, *because* we've not encountered hard times, therefore I'll be faithful and loyal. Loyalty affirms *regardless* of what happens, I'll be faithful and loyal. *Unconditional* is the key word!

The Kindness of Boaz

February 25
Lesson 13

DEVOTIONAL READING: Ruth 2:14-20.

LESSON SCRIPTURE: Ruth 2—4.

PRINTED TEXT: Ruth 2:1, 8-12; 4:13-17.

Ruth 2:1, 8-12

1 And Naomi had a kinsman of her husband's, a mighty man of wealth, of the family of Elimelech; and his name was Boaz.

. . . .

8 Then said Boaz unto Ruth, Hearest thou not, my daughter? Go not to glean in another field, neither go from hence, but abide here fast by my maidens:

9 Let thine eyes be on the field that they do reap, and go thou after them: have I not charged the young men that they shall not touch thee? and when thou art athirst, go unto the vessels, and drink of that which the young men have drawn.

10 Then she fell on her face, and bowed herself to the ground, and said unto him, Why have I found grace in thine eyes, that thou shouldest take knowledge of me, seeing I am a stranger?

11 And Boaz answered and said unto her, It hath fully been showed me, all that thou hast done unto thy mother-in-law since the death of thine husband; and how thou hast left thy father and thy mother, and the land of thy nativity, and art come unto a people which thou knewest not heretofore.

12 The LORD recompense thy work, and a full reward be given thee of the LORD God of Israel, under whose wings thou art come to trust.

Ruth 4:13-17

13 So Boaz took Ruth, and she was his wife: and when he went in unto her, the LORD gave her conception, and she bare a son.

14 And the women said unto Naomi, Blessed be the LORD, which hath not left thee this day without a kinsman, that his name may be famous in Israel.

15 And he shall be unto thee a restorer of thy life, and a nourisher of thine old age: for thy daughter-in-law, which loveth thee, which is better to thee than seven sons, hath borne him.

16 And Naomi took the child, and laid it in her bosom, and became nurse unto it.

17 And the women her neighbors gave it a name, saying, There is a son born to Naomi; and they called his name Obed: he is the father of Jesse, the father of David.

GOLDEN TEXT: Blessed be he of the LORD, who hath not left off his kindness to the living and to the dead.—Ruth 2:20.

God's Love for All People
Jonah, Ruth
(Lessons 10-13)

Lesson Aims

After the completion of this lesson the student should:

1. Value loyalty in human relations, as did Boaz.

2. Become kinder in dealing with fellow believers and with all people.

Lesson Outline

INTRODUCTION
    A. Help Needed
    B. Lesson Background
  I. BOAZ AS KINSMAN (Ruth 2:1)
    A. Israel's Redeemers (v. 1a)
    B. Boaz Fits the Part (v. 1b)
 II. THE KINDNESS OF BOAZ (Ruth 2:8-12)
    A. Boaz Provides Protection (vv. 8, 9)
    B. Ruth Responds (v. 10)
    C. Boaz Answers Graciously (vv. 11, 12)
      Mercy for the Merciful
III. THE REWARDS OF KINDNESS (Ruth 4:13-17)
    A. God Blesses Boaz and Ruth (v. 13)
    B. God Blesses Naomi (vv. 14, 15)
      Surviving the Mid-life Crisis
    C. God Blesses Obed (vv. 16, 17)
      Unpredictable Potential
CONCLUSION
    A. Who Holds the Future?
    B. Let Us Pray
    C. A Thought to Remember

The kindness Boaz showed to the foreigner Ruth stands as an example for all generations. Visual 13 of the visuals packet depicts one of his acts of kindness. It is shown on page 222.

Introduction

A. Help Needed

Life was uncertain in the days of the judges. With the death of Joshua, strong central leadership over the tribes soon disappeared. Animosities developed, and on occasion fighting broke out among the tribes. Read chapters 19-21 of Judges for the details of how eleven of the tribes of Israel nearly annihilated the tribe of Benjamin when it tried to defend one of its villages where a murder occurred.

Ever present was the danger of raids by bandits who would attack villages without warning. These bandits would seize crops, property, women, and children. To defend themselves against such attacks, a cluster of villages might coordinate their defense efforts.

During these times Israel was subjected also to invasion by the peoples round about them. When Israel's situation became dire, God raised up a Spirit-filled leader to rally groups of citizen soldiers to attack the enemy. We know these mighty warriors as "judges." Such God-directed leaders might not hold any official position within the village power structure, but they were recognized as God's leaders in times of emergency.

Just as the nation at times needed the strong leadership the judges provided, and the villages needed protection against raiders, even so there were the weak in Israelite society who needed protection from those who might take advantage of them. It becomes clear that in a society such as Israel's in the time of the judges, the family unit was of vital importance. In the family one enjoyed protection and the provision of physical and spiritual needs. The untimely loss of a husband and father dealt a devastating blow to the welfare of the remaining members of the family. They then looked to the extended family for help and protection. In today's lesson we read of an instance when such help was sought and received.

B. Lesson Background

In last week's lesson we were told of a Hebrew family from Bethlehem in Judah who moved to the country of Moab to escape a severe famine. While they were there the husband and father, Elimelech, died. The widow, Naomi, was left with her two sons. The two sons married Moabite wives, but later both sons died also.

The widow Naomi decided to return to her home in Bethlehem, and her two widowed daughters-in-law determined to return with her. Naomi urged both to return to their families in Moab. One did so, but the other, Ruth, would not. So the two women came to Bethlehem: Naomi, bereft of husband and sons, embittered; Ruth, a young widow, a stranger in a foreign land, perhaps fearful of her reception by the citizens of Bethlehem.

The two women were in financial straits when they arrived in Bethlehem, but industry was no stranger to this young Moabitess who was devoted to her mother-in-law. Barley harvest was just beginning, so Ruth set about to find food for their table.

I. Boaz as Kinsman
(Ruth 2:1)

A. Israel's Redeemers (v. 1a)

1a. And Naomi had a kinsman of her husband's, a mighty man of wealth, of the family of Elimelech.

Naomi had a kinsman. The word translated *kinsman* primarily means "known," "well known," "an acquaintance." Its usage here, and in the feminine form in Ruth 3:2, denotes a person with whom one is intimately acquainted, one's "relation." In Ruth 3:9—4:14, however, the Scripture uses a special expression in both noun and verb forms to describe the relation of Boaz to Naomi and Ruth. That term is translated "near kinsman" in our version. The *New International Version* translates it "kinsman-redeemer." In Israelite society in the time of the judges, the kinsman-redeemer had the responsibility to maintain his extended family. It was his duty to represent and protect the family's poor, widows, and orphans. Also, he was to buy back ancestral land that had passed from the family's possession. Boaz's responsibility toward Naomi and Ruth is emphasized by the statement that he was *of the family of Elimelech.*

The expression *a mighty man of wealth* is properly translated "mighty man of valor" (see Judges 6:12; 11:1; 1 Kings 11:28) and "a mighty man of power" (1 Samuel 9:1). In 2 Kings 15:20 the phrase is used of the heads of households who were taxed by King Menahem so Israel could pay the tribute imposed by the Assyrians. We conclude, therefore, that Boaz was a man of some wealth, vigor, and good reputation, a man of full standing as the head of a household in Bethlehem.

B. Boaz Fits the Part (v. 1b)

1b. And his name was Boaz.

The name *Boaz* literally means, "in him is strength." We usually think of strength in terms of physical might or fighting prowess. However, it is measured in other ways as well. The position as redeemer and protector in Israel's society

---

How to Say It

BOAZ. *Bo*-az.
ELIMELECH. E-*lim*-eh-leck.
MENAHEM. *Men*-uh-hem.
MOABITE. *Mo*-ub-ite.
MOABITESS. *Mo*-ub-*ite*-ess (strong accent on *ite*).

---

required a man of many unusual qualities. Boaz was such a man. He directed his estate with efficiency. He showed respect for the law and customs of his people. He took charge of difficult situations. He was resourceful, as was shown in his dealing with the kinsman-redeemer who was a closer relative than he to Naomi and Ruth. He showed respect for those working for him. He was generous and kindhearted. He rose above bigotry. He showed concern for Ruth's reputation. He was careful not to embarrass Naomi or Ruth. The Scripture thus describes Boaz as a man of moral strength and nobility of character.

II. The Kindness of Boaz
(Ruth 2:8-12)

Verses 2-7, which are not included in the printed text, describe how Boaz and Ruth met. Ruth proposed to Naomi that Ruth should go to the fields and gather grain, and Naomi gave her approval. The field Ruth chose to glean in happened to belong to Boaz, Naomi's relative. Boaz came from the town and greeted the workers cordially. Noticing Ruth, he inquired of his overseer as to who she was. The overseer identified her as the Moabite girl who had come back with Naomi from Moab, and he stated that she had worked very hard all day with only a brief rest. Boaz then approached Ruth and spoke to her. His kindness to her at this first meeting was based on the fact that already he had heard about the plight of Naomi and Ruth's dedication to her (v. 11).

A. Boaz Provides Protection (vv. 8, 9)

8, 9. Then said Boaz unto Ruth, Hearest thou not, my daughter? Go not to glean in another field, neither go from hence, but abide here fast by my maidens: let thine eyes be on the field that they do reap, and go thou after them: have I not charged the young men that they shall not touch thee? and when thou art athirst, go unto the vessels, and drink of that which the young men have drawn.

Hearest thou not, my daughter? This means, "Please listen to the advice I am giving you." *My daughter.* The term *daughter* is used here as a term of respect and at the same time suggests his mature age.

Go not to glean in another field. At harvesttime the reapers went through the grainfields and cut down the standing grain with hand sickles. They were followed by those who tied up the sheaves. Following these were the gleaners, needy folk who were permitted by law to pick up the grain that was missed or dropped. The practice is explained and its rules defined in

Leviticus 19:9, 10; 23:22; Deuteronomy 24:19-22. Ruth was gleaning in Boaz's field, and as an indication of his concern for her welfare he urged her to stay in his field near where his *maidens* were working. Seemingly, Boaz's maidens were those who were tying up the bundles of grain.

Have not I charged the young men that they shall not touch thee? More recent versions render this "molest" or "harm" or "bother." As long as Ruth stayed in Boaz's fields, she would be under his protection. Another expression of his kindness and concern for Ruth was his permission for her to drink of the water reserved for the workers. Normally, gleaners were not given such a privilege.

B. Ruth Responds (v. 10)

10. Then she fell on her face, and bowed herself to the ground, and said unto him, Why have I found grace in thine eyes, that thou shouldest take knowledge of me, seeing I am a stranger?

Then she fell on her face, and bowed herself to the ground. This act was in accord with the customs of people in that time and in that part of the world. By prostrating herself before Boaz, Ruth was showing very high respect for him. She was overwhelmed by the kindness of this man whom she now met for the first time. Her act of obeisance was an expression of beautiful humility and modesty, and by it she demonstrated her profoundest gratitude for the provisions Boaz was making for her.

Why have I found grace in thine eyes . . . seeing I am a stranger? Ruth, *a stranger,* that is, a foreigner, hardly ever would have thought that she would receive such preferential treatment as Boaz was bestowing on her! She was surprised, amazed, bewildered.

C. Boaz Answers Graciously (vv. 11, 12)

11. And Boaz answered and said unto her, It hath fully been showed me, all that thou hast done unto thy mother-in-law since the death of thine husband; and how thou hast left thy father and thy mother, and the land of thy nativity, and art come unto a people which thou knewest not heretofore.

Boaz had received a full account of this young widow's life since her bereavement. Whether he had learned it from his servants or his neighbors in town we are not told. And he had witnessed with his own eyes how this young Moabitess was toiling in the field to provide food for her mother-in-law and herself. Boaz had also taken note of Ruth's bravery in leaving her parents and

her native land to come and be a part of a people whom she had never known before. He had good reason to respect this young woman. Being the man of noble character that he was, he wanted to help her.

12. The LORD recompense thy work, and a full reward be given thee of the LORD God of Israel, under whose wings thou art come to trust.

Boaz acknowledged that in the long run only God can truly reward courageous living. Sensitive humans may recognize goodness in others sometimes, but they might not. God alone fully knows the intent behind actions and words, and He will reward those who are compassionate, caring, and committed to serving and helping others.

This statement of Boaz should be read as expressing a strong wish, "May *the Lord recompense thy work.*" Boaz recognized that Ruth had done more than change her residence. She had left behind the idolatry of her native people and had come to faith in the living God. This was a decision reached at the deepest level of the heart and involved attitudes, values, and ways of thinking and ways of responding to people and situations. She had cast her lot with Naomi's people and with their God.

Under whose wings thou art come to trust. Psalm 91:4 is a beautiful illustration of this expression. By his words and actions Boaz may have been subtly acknowledging that someone in the family had the responsibility of aiding Ruth. However, by his call for God's protection of her, Boaz recognized that in the last resort Ruth's strongest redeemer was the God of Israel in whom she had placed her trust.

MERCY FOR THE MERCIFUL

"You get what you pay for" is a common expression among consumers. It is generally expected that higher priced goods and services will be superior in quality. When we pay "top dollar," we expect the best in products and labor. And though it doesn't always work out that way, the principle generally holds true.

Such a reciprocal dynamic is definitely at work in spiritual matters. Solomon suggested it: "Cast thy bread upon the waters: for thou shalt find it after many days" (Ecclesiastes 11:1). Jesus was more explicit. He said, "Blessed are the merciful: for they shall obtain mercy" (Matthew 5:7). Whatever you give, you receive in kind; and the more you give, the more you receive.

That's the way it worked for Ruth. She selflessly ministered to Naomi, then received generous and merciful treatment from Boaz.

Of course, *receiving* mercy must not be the primary motivation for *giving* mercy. Ruth struck no bargain with God when she chose to be a blessing to her mother-in-law. She pledged her loyalty on the "regardless" level. Likewise, whatever we do for God should not be done to earn personal reward, but to honor Him and to help others. Then rich rewards and personal happiness will be ours. "What goes around, comes around." —R. W. B.

III. The Rewards of Kindness (Ruth 4:13-17)

Chapter 3 records how Ruth acted on Naomi's advice to put herself into the hands of Boaz, her kinsman-redeemer. She thereby showed her trust in him to act honorably in her behalf and in behalf of her dead husband.

In the background of this episode was the "law of the brother-in-law" (levirate), which required the brother of a man who had died childless to marry the deceased's widow and raise up children for him. (See Deuteronomy 25:5-10.) It is clear here in Ruth that the kinsman-redeemer was to take over this responsibility in the absence of a brother of the deceased.

Boaz indicated to Ruth that he was willing to fulfill the role of kinsman-redeemer to her. There was a member of Elimelech's family, however, who was a closer relative to Naomi, and thus to Ruth, than Boaz was. If that man desired to accept the responsibility of kinsman-redeemer to Naomi and Ruth, he was to be given the first opportunity to do so (3:12, 13).

Without delay, Boaz met at the city gate with the closer relative and ten elders of the city. The negotiations that followed revealed Boaz's resourcefulness, but they also underscored his true concern for Naomi and Ruth and the continuation of the names of their deceased husbands in Israel. When the closer relative declined to fulfill the role of kinsman-redeemer for the two women, Boaz made it officially known that he would accept that responsibility. He purchased all that had belonged to Elimelech, Naomi's deceased husband, and their two deceased sons; and he took as his wife, Ruth, the widow of one of the sons (4:1-12).

A. God Blesses Boaz and Ruth (v. 13)

13. So Boaz took Ruth, and she was his wife: and when he went in unto her, the LORD gave her conception, and she bare a son.

God blessed the union of Boaz and Ruth, and Ruth gave birth to a son. From the opening pages of Scripture God's covenant promises focused on the gift of children. Seth, born to Adam and Eve after Abel was slain, extended God's blessings into the future. Abraham's hope lay with Isaac. Hannah's earnest and faithful life was rewarded with the birth of Samuel. Every new generation was a sure sign of God's keeping His promise never to forsake His people.

B. God Blesses Naomi (vv. 14, 15)

14, 15. And the women said unto Naomi, Blessed be the LORD, which hath not left thee this day without a kinsman, that his name may be famous in Israel. And he shall be unto thee a restorer of thy life, and a nourisher of thine old age: for thy daughter-in-law, which loveth thee, which is better to thee than seven sons, hath borne him.

God had blessed Naomi with a daughter-in-law who risked everything for her, and with a son-in-law redeemer/protector/kinsman. The greatest gift of all, however, was an infant grandson to carry on Elimelech's line of descent. Again the underlying theme of future hope emerges. Since Naomi herself would not be able to have more children, this child would bring her great joy and happiness and be a comfort in her old age.

SURVIVING THE MID-LIFE CRISIS

Middle age used to be about thirty-five or forty, if the average life span was "threescore and ten." Now people live longer, so what is called "mid-life crisis" generally occurs around age fifty. Whenever it happens, the symptoms are clear. As their nests empty, lonely middle-agers, who at the same time may be caring for aging parents, may become preoccupied with their own mortality. They review their past, and regret failures and "wasted time"; they become cynical about the future, realizing that some of their dreams will never be fulfilled. Depression sets in, and zest for living goes out.

Home Daily Bible Readings

Monday, Feb. 19—Gleaning the Field (Ruth 1:19—2:7)
Tuesday, Feb. 20—Befriended and Protected (Ruth 2:13-23)
Wednesday, Feb. 21—Aggressive Behavior (Ruth 3:1-13)
Thursday, Feb. 22—Giving Encouragement (Ruth 3:14-18)
Friday, Feb. 23—Nearest Kinsman Declines (Ruth 4:1-6)
Saturday, Feb. 24—Making a Formal Claim (Ruth 4:7-12)
Sunday, Feb. 25—Blessed Descendants (Psalm 128)

Naomi was suffering something like mid-life crisis. Her husband and sons were gone, her age precluded remarriage and childbearing, and she had no grandchildren to perpetuate her family heritage. If she were to die, nothing would remain to validate her existence. She was sadly resigned to a gloomy future.

But then Ruth and Boaz had a baby! Naomi became a grandmother, and, as her friends predicted, baby Obed became the "restorer" of her life and the "nourisher" of her old age.

Grandchildren can be such a blessing. Soon, my wife and I will be grandparents, the Lord willing. We are looking forward to it. We will have a new reason to be and do, and there will be a bright future for our family. Grandparenthood is one of God's best ideas!   —R. W. B.

C. God Blesses Obed (vv. 16, 17)

16, 17. And Naomi took the child, and laid it in her bosom, and became nurse unto it. And the women her neighbors gave it a name, saying, There is a son born to Naomi; and they called his name Obed: he is the father of Jesse, the father of David.

The duty of nurturing the child fell not to Boaz and Ruth only. It also became Naomi's joyful responsibility. The community also participated in this joyful occasion by naming the baby *Obed.* This was an acceptable Hebrew name that means "servant." No reason is given for the choice of this particular name, but the townsfolk may have been thinking of the service of love and duty that he would render to his grandmother Naomi.

God blessed Obed in several ways. He had parents of noteworthy character, and a loving and grateful grandmother. The community in which he grew up seems to have been a caring and supportive one. Perhaps the greatest, however, is the fact that his own grandson was David, the great king of Israel.

UNPREDICTABLE POTENTIAL

Great-grandmothers have little way of knowing how great their descendants might become. They may have dreamed of it, but they could not predict it.

Naomi did not suspect that many generations later Jesus, the Christ, would be born to the wife of her descendant, Joseph (Matthew 1). Mary gave birth to *Immanuel,* God incarnate. Little Obed was truly a temporal blessing to his grandmother, but beyond that he became progenitor of One who brought eternal blessing for all mankind.

Who knows what your great-grandchildren and their great-grandchildren will achieve and contribute to mankind? Perhaps through you, too, generations to come will find salvation in Christ. Pray that you and yours will remain faithful.   —R. W. B.

Conclusion
A. Who Holds the Future?

Many persons believe that the events that occur are strictly the result of natural or human causes. Believing that brute force controls what happens in life, these persons become uncertain, perhaps even terrified, of what the future holds.

The book of Ruth shows, however, that there is another power at work in our world. It is the power of God, and although that power itself is invisible, its results may be seen. Those who see with the eyes of faith know that these words of the apostle Paul are true: "And we know that all things work together for good to them that love God, to them who are the called according to his purpose" (Romans 8:28). The power of God works in the lives of godly people. We have seen that in our lessons from Ruth. Naomi's godly character had a profound influence on her daughter-in-law Ruth, the Moabitess. Ruth loved Naomi and she came to love Naomi's God. It is obvious that Boaz loved God.

Although Naomi and Ruth had experienced great tragedy and sadness, God worked through their kinsman-redeemer, Boaz, to accomplish His will, to replace their sadness with joy, and to secure a happy future for them all. The kindness of Boaz has a powerful message for our skeptical age. Who holds the future? God does.

B. Let Us Pray

Holy Father, we honor You as our divine Protector and Redeemer. Help us to emulate You in these ways as we relate to all other persons. Through Christ we pray. Amen.

C. A Thought to Remember

"Be ye kind one to another" (Ephesians 4:32).

visual 13

Learning by Doing

This page contains an alternate lesson plan emphasizing learning activities. Classes desiring such student involvement will find these suggestions helpful.

Learning Goals

As a result of participating in this session, the students will:

1. Recognize and appreciate Boaz's godly character.

2. Strive to be more godly in their associations with others.

Into the Lesson

Hold up several "cents off" coupons and ask, "What do we do with these?" When someone responds, "Redeem them," read from a major dictionary its complete definition for the word *redeem*. One of its definitions will relate to coupon uses; another will relate to the Old Testament concept of kinsman-redeemer. Ask your class which definition best matches the role of Boaz in the life of Ruth. Then move to the next activity.

Into the Word

In the week before class recruit a male class member or another man in your congregation to "be Boaz" and deliver the monologue that follows this paragraph. Biblical costuming will add interest to the presentation. Introduce "Boaz" with enthusiasm and drama. Here is the monologue:

"She was simply there one day . . . in *my* fields. I could not help but notice her; she was a stranger, and she was beautiful. When I found out who she was, I had to speak to her; she was of the family of Elimelech, my deceased relative. Of course, I told her she was welcome to glean in my fields anytime . . . all the time! I had heard of her outstanding character and integrity. When I left the field that day, I gave special instructions to my harvesters: they were to 'accidentally' drop extra grain for her; she was to have full access to the water and the treats in the fields for my laborers.

"I don't remember how many days later it was. I was sleeping at the threshingfloor after a hard day's work. Sleep was easy. But during the night I awoke. Ruth was lying at my feet. As we talked that night, I acknowledged that I was her kinsman-redeemer. Yet I knew that there was one, my uncle Amminoah, who was a closer relative than I. I had to ask him if he would fulfill his obligation to Ruth and make her part of his family.

"The very next day I sat at the city gate. I gathered ten elders, as the custom was, and then called to Amminoah as he came, 'Ho, kinsman, come, sit; we have business.' When I explained his obligation to take Naomi and Ruth, he would have none of it. 'You do it, my kinsman,' he said, 'I yield my rights to you.' Oh, what joy I felt!

"As soon as it could be arranged, Ruth became my wife. And in due time—may the Lord be praised!—we had a son. *Obed* our neighbors named him. He would be famous in Israel!"

When your dramatist finishes, ask your adults to compare "Boaz's story" with the text of Ruth. Notice what details are added and omitted.

Copy the following word-find puzzle on a large poster board for group use. Have the class find the following words, which highlight Boaz's character: *careful, discreet, generous, gentle, gracious, honest, kind, lovesick, meek, perceptive, prayerful, respected, spiritual, wealthy, wise.*

```
B O A D I S C R E E T
E V I T P E C R E P S
S Z M R B W L S O R E
U A Z E I B U P O A N
O K A S E O F I Z Y O
I C E P R K E R B E H
C I D E B E R I O R A
A S N C Z L A T B F O
R E I T A T C U Z U B
G V K E O N A A Z L B
O O A D W E A L T H Y
Z L B O A G Z B O A Z
```

As the words are found, ask your group to suggest verses of the text related to each.

Into Life

Assign these texts to your students, one per student: 1 Corinthians 16, 2 Corinthians 13, Ephesians 6, Philippians 4, Colossians 4, 1 Thessalonians 5, 2 Thessalonians 3. Repeat until each student has one. Direct your adults to skim through his or her assigned chapter to find a verse that is an admonition to act in a way Boaz acted. Make the point that godly behavior does not change from era to era. Such ideas as bearing one another's burdens or being kind to one another are right behaviors because they reflect the eternal nature of God.

Let's Talk It Over

The questions on this page are designed to encourage review of the lesson Scriptures and to promote discussion of the lesson by the class. The answers provided are only discussion starters. Let your class talk it over from there.

1. Instead of waiting for God to supply their needs, Ruth and Naomi determined that Ruth would go out and glean in the harvest fields. When they followed through with that, God's providence took over to bless them in a remarkable way. How does God's providence work in similar fashion in our lives?

It is possible to get in God's way by trying too hard to solve our own problems and supply our own needs. The popular counsel, "Let go, and let God," is legitimate if we find that in relying on our own cleverness and power we have failed to trust God for the supply of all our needs. But we do need to put ourselves into position to receive God's help. If we need financial help, we may need to seek a better job; if we have personal problems we are unable to solve, we may need to talk to a counselor; if we want to have new friends, we may have to take the initiative in forming friendships. As we step boldly in the direction of self-help, God may then meet our faith and courage with His providential care, as He did with Naomi and Ruth.

2. Boaz showed great kindness to Ruth in protecting her and in fulfilling the role of kinsman-redeemer. What can motivate us to show kindness to others?

Whatever we may feel about another person, treating him or her with kindness is right in the sight of God. Kindness is a fruit of the Spirit (Galatians 5:22, *New International Version*). Also, the example of Jesus should motivate us to acts of kindness. One may say that such acts characterized His earthly ministry. Because He is our Lord, we want to follow His example in this regard. Our sense of duty and our desire to follow the Lord's example will be aided immeasurably if we cultivate a spirit of compassion for those who are in need.

3. Ruth and Naomi accepted the kindness and generosity of Boaz, apparently without any reluctance. How should we react when others do acts of kindness for us?

We gratefully accept the kindness of God, because we know that without His favor and grace we are totally lost. Regarding expressions of kindness by other persons, however, often we do not accept them so graciously. We may act as

though we have no need. The truth is, however, that we do need each other. This is especially so in the church, whose members are described by Paul as being interdependent. Therefore, when an act of kindness is done for us, we should accept it in the same spirit of grace in which the kindness is given. By doing so, we are blessed, the giver is blessed, and the body of Christ is strengthened.

4. Ruth was from a nation and culture different from Boaz's, yet she received many benefits and blessings from her association with Israel. In what ways can Christians from differing backgrounds and cultures benefit from their association with each other?

People from differing cultures worship the Lord differently. Each can learn from the others, and the worship of God by each can be enriched thereby. The same holds true in the individual lives of Christians. The tendency for most persons quite naturally is to associate with those who are like themselves. This leads people to become set in their ways and perhaps even unwilling to consider varying viewpoints. Association with Christians who are from cultures or groups different from one's own allows for new experiences in Christ, new appreciation for others and their perceptions, and new possibilities for one's own spiritual growth and development.

5. The book of Ruth contains several valuable lessons for us today. For example, in the actions of Naomi, Ruth, and Boaz we see the blessings that result from the unconditional loyalty of one human being to another. The book also teaches an important lesson about God's workings in the world. What do you think that lesson is?

The story of Ruth teaches that God works through the events of people's lives to carry His will forward. Naomi and Ruth experienced much sadness in the deaths of their loved ones. Yet those very circumstances led to Ruth's meeting Boaz, their subsequent marriage, and the birth of their son, who took his place in the lineage of Christ. The conclusion we must draw from this is that God oversees our lives and can bring good from our experiences if we continue to trust and obey Him.

Spring Quarter, 1996

Teachings of Jesus

Special Features

Lessons

Unit 1: Teachings About the Kingdom of Heaven

Unit 2: Teachings About God

Unit 3: Teachings About Living

About these lessons

The lessons of the Spring Quarter are based on texts taken from the Gospels of Matthew, Luke, and John. Unit 1 is a study of five of Jesus' parables, each of which considers a different truth concerning the kingdom of Heaven. The four lessons of Unit 2 focus on the nature of God and Christ. Unit 3 has four lessons, all dealing with teachings taken from the Sermon on the Mount and with emphasis on living a Christian life-style.

Mar 3
Mar 10
Mar 17
Mar 24
Mar 31
Apr 7
Apr 14
Apr 21
Apr 28
May 5
May 12
May 19
May 26

Quarterly Quiz

The questions on this page may be used in several ways: as a pretest at the beginning of the quarter; as a review at the end of the quarter; or as a review after each lesson. The questions are based on the Scripture text of each lesson (King James Version). ***The answers are on page 232.***

Lesson 1

1. If one doesn't understand the word of the kingdom that is sown in his heart, who snatches away the word that is sown? *Matthew 13:19*

2. What chokes the word of the kingdom of Heaven, causing one who hears the word to become unfruitful? *Matthew 13:22*

Lesson 2

1. The man who was forgiven a ten-thousand-talent debt did what to a man who owed him a hundred pence? *Matthew 18:30*

2. When the lord of the first servant heard of what he had done, what did the lord call him and what did the lord do? *Matthew 18:32, 34*

Lesson 3

1. In Jesus' parable of the workers in the vineyard, each worker received pay based on how many hours he worked. T/F *Matthew 20:9, 10*

2. By giving wages to the workers as he did, the householder demonstrated that he was (good, evil). *Matthew 20:15*

Lesson 4

1. In Jesus' parable, the man who was given one talent hid his lord's money in the earth because he said he was _____. *Matthew 25:25*

2. What did the lord do to this unprofitable servant? *Matthew 25:30*

Lesson 5

1. Jesus told a parable about a man who invited many persons to a banquet. What did they do when the banquet time arrived? *Luke 14:18*

2. How did the host feel when he learned about what the invitees did? *Luke 14:21*

Lesson 6

1. On the day of His resurrection, Jesus joined two disciples going where? *Luke 24:13*

2. One was named _____. *Luke 24:18*

3. Beginning at _____ and all the _____, Jesus taught the two disciples what the Scriptures said about Him. *Luke 24:27*

Lesson 7

1. When the publicans and sinners drew near to hear Jesus, what was the complaint of the Pharisees and scribes against Him? *Luke 15:2*

2. Jesus responded by telling the parables of the lost sheep and lost coin, which emphasize the joy in Heaven over what? *Luke 15:7, 10*

Lesson 8

1. Jesus said that sheep follow their shepherd because they know what? *John 10:4*

2. Jesus came so that the sheep might have _____ and might have it more _____. *John 10:10*

3. Jesus is the Good Shepherd. The Good Shepherd gives what for the sheep. *John 10:11*

Lesson 9

1. Jesus compared himself to a vine and God to a vinegrower. Jesus' followers are branches pruned by God so they may do what? *John 15:2*

2. Jesus declared that His Father is glorified when Jesus' disciples bear much fruit. T/F *John 15:8*

Lesson 10

1. In the Beatitudes Jesus said that certain persons should rejoice and be exceeding glad. What persons are they? *Matthew 5:11, 12*

2. Why should they rejoice? *Matthew 5:12*

3. What persons of an earlier time had the same experience? *Matthew 5:12*

Lesson 11

1. Jesus told His followers to give more than the law required of them. T/F *Matthew 5:40, 41*

2. Jesus said, "Love your _____, bless them that _____ you, do good to them that _____ you, and pray for them which despitefully _____ you, and persecute you." *Matthew 5:44*

Lesson 12

1. Jesus advises His followers to lay up for themselves _____ in Heaven. *Matthew 6:20*

2. Why shouldn't Jesus' disciples worry about obtaining life's necessities? *Matthew 6:31, 32*

3. Jesus' disciples should give first place to seeking what? *Matthew 6:33*

Lesson 13

1. When we pray, we are not to do it in order to be seen of whom? *Matthew 6:5*

2. We may be certain that our heavenly Father will not forgive our trespasses if we refuse to do what? *Matthew 6:15*

Your Teacher!

by Edwin V. Hayden

TEACHER!
What pictures, thoughts, and emotions does the word call to your mind? The impressions should be associated pleasantly with home, Sunday school, and with school at its various levels. Someone there led you through the adventures of learning to tie your shoes, to read, to know Jesus, to enjoy songs and poetry, to share with others the things you enjoyed, to appreciate the works and the Word of God, to earn and manage money, to respect the intimacies of family living, and all the other things that have brought lasting joy and solid accomplishment to your life.

Among your favorite teachers, no doubt, were the ones who loved you, loved the material they taught, and exercised imagination and enthusiasm in bringing you and the subject matter together. Your parents were probably your most effective, as well as your earliest, teachers.

You may, on the other hand, be among the unfortunate ones to whom *teacher* is not a love-inspiring word; hence, it does not immediately draw you to Jesus as Master Teacher. If so, you stand to gain the greatest benefit from this quarter's study, entitled "Teachings of Jesus." He is what the best of teachers strive to be, and He teaches what the wisest of persons still need to know.

Jesus Our Teacher

In the Gospels Jesus is referred to most often as *Master* or *Teacher*. Occasionally He is called *rabbi*, which refers to Jewish teachers. He heralded God's kingdom, but His activity is called *teaching* almost three times as often as it is called *preaching*.

This quarter's lessons present major aspects of His teaching about the kingdom of Heaven (lessons 1-5), about God (lessons 6-9), and about living as citizens in God's kingdom (lessons 10-13). He invited His disciples to "learn of me" (Matthew 11:29). That may mean, "Learn *from me.*" It is a twofold exhortation: to become acquainted with Him and learn by His *example*, that is, from what He *is*; and to hear His words and learn by His *instruction*, that is, from what He *says*. Our lessons of Jesus' "teachings about" various subjects point to His words more than His being, but the person and works of Jesus cannot be excluded from any study of His words. He demonstrated before He described.

Teachings About the Kingdom of Heaven
(Unit 1)

The five lessons to be studied in March exemplify a teaching method used most effectively by Jesus—the parable, or story based on circumstances familiar to the hearers, but setting forth eternal truths the people needed yet to learn. The texts point to these facts about the kingdom of Heaven: it centers in God as the divine King; it is made up of citizens who choose to live under God's authority; and the citizens are responsible for definite commitments in relation to their King.

Lesson 1. Parable of the Sower (Matthew 13:1-9, 18-23). The blessings of God's kingdom are available to all who hear the gospel as good seed broadcast by a faithful messenger. Growth and fruitfulness from the sowing depend on the soil into which the seed falls; that is the hearer. God's kingdom, then, is made up of those who receive the gospel into good and honest hearts, permitting it to produce the works of God.

Lesson 2. Parable of the Unforgiving Servant (Matthew 18:21-35). As God forgives and welcomes penitent sinners to His kingdom, so He requires that the ones welcomed shall forgive their fellow citizens of any wrong that has been done between them. Jesus taught this in the story of a servant who was forgiven a huge debt by his royal master and then dealt harshly with a fellow servant who owed him a pittance.

Lesson 3. Parable of the Vineyard Workers (Matthew 20:1-16). God's generous mercy will be extended to all mankind on God's own terms. He gives to everyone what He has promised, but does not limit himself to what has been specified in the promises. This Jesus taught in the story of laborers paid according to contract, but some far beyond the promised wage.

Lesson 4. Parable of the Three Servants (Matthew 25:14-30). God's kingdom will offer to each citizen unlimited opportunities to serve to the extent of one's willingness and capacity. Jesus taught this through a story of stewards entrusted with their master's assets, and who, afterward, were dealt with according to their faithfulness, or lack of it, in conducting their master's business.

Lesson 5. Parable of the Great Feast (Luke 14:15-24). Folk who think they have an "inside track" to God's kingdom by reason of their lifelong association with things religious are in special danger of becoming careless and preoccupied with other matters, and therefore of losing out entirely. This Jesus taught in His story of guests who reneged on their early acceptance of a great man's invitation to his feast, and so were replaced by strangers invited at the last minute.

Teachings About God
(Unit 2)

Who and what kind of being is the King in Heaven? The four lessons for April deal with that question. They do not try to prove that God exists. They demonstrate it. The teacher is Jesus, who could say, "No one knows the Father except the Son and those to whom the Son chooses to reveal him" (Matthew 11:27, *New International Version*). Jesus revealed the Father much more fully by what He was than by what He said.

Lesson 6. The Living Lord (Luke 24:13-27). Our Easter lesson brings us to the afternoon of Resurrection Day, and the risen Lord in conversation with two otherwise unknown disciples. To them He unfolded the Scriptures showing that Messiah's suffering death and triumphant resurrection were in God's plan from the beginning. His way is a matter of death and life, with life final and eternally victorious.

Lesson 7. The Loving God (Luke 15:1-10). Criticized for being too receptive of social and moral outcasts, Jesus responded that He was doing as the loving heavenly Father does, rejoicing at the finding and rescue of that which was lost. His critics themselves would rejoice similarly, He said, at the rescue of one of their sheep that strayed.

Lesson 8. The Good Shepherd (John 10:1-18). Jesus was like God not only in His care for the lost; He himself was the one in whom "dwelleth all the fulness of the Godhead bodily" (Colossians 2:9). Thus He fit David's declaration, "The Lord is my shepherd" (Psalm 23:1). Not only would He seek the one lost sheep until He found it; He would lay down His life to save the flock or any of its members. In saying, "I am the good shepherd," He was saying He was God on earth.

Lesson 9. The True Vine (John 15:1-17). As God is the source of all life through creation and provision, so Jesus is He who makes spiritual life possible to His followers by their vital contact with Him. This lesson is conveyed by means of the figure of a branch that flourishes or withers, depending on whether it draws its life forces through a firm, natural relationship with the plant. Jesus not only gives and sustains one's spiritual life, but He makes His followers to be like himself in their character.

Teachings About Living
(Unit 3)

Our lessons for May are found in Jesus' great Sermon on the Mount, as recorded in Matthew 5-7. Sometimes called the constitution of the Kingdom, it describes the life and character of those who follow Jesus, draw their spiritual being from Him, and so partake of His personality. Persons not acquainted with Him nor committed to Him cannot achieve the life-style He describes.

Lesson 10. Teachings About Happiness (Matthew 5:1-12). The "Blesseds," or "Beatitudes," with which the Sermon opens hold up a joy-filled experience that everybody fervently desires, but few attain because they are looking in the wrong places, like looking for roses on broomsticks. Many persons expect the blessings of God while denying the God who blesses. Jesus shocks His hearers into listening and remembering, while assuring the earnest seekers of truth that the love of God will bring joys that they are neither expecting nor seeking.

Lesson 11. Teachings About Loving Your Enemies (Matthew 5:38-48). Right relationship with God will lead us naturally into becoming more like God in His attitude toward mankind in general—toward our friends and our enemies as well as toward ourselves. Here again Jesus taught first by example, in extending mercy to all, in dying for those who approached Him as enemies, and in praying for forgiveness for His persecutors. His followers will go with Him in this direction also.

Lesson 12. Teachings About Riches and Anxiety (Matthew 6:19-21, 24-34). This lesson brings us to Jesus' teaching about material possessions and their influence on one's attitude toward life as a whole. One's ownership of things is temporary at best, Jesus taught. Wealth will go off and leave us, or we will go off and leave it. We need, therefore, to be focused on what is eternally meaningful, and to have our trust firmly established in Him who provides for both time and eternity. Doubt and fear must yield to faith.

Lesson 13. Teachings About Prayer (Matthew 6:5-15). A fitting climax to Jesus' teaching comes with a study of the Christian's communication with God. That communication is the lifeline of our relationship with God. Jesus taught about prayer both by praying and by describing the attitudes and expressions that are appropriate to prayer. These are modeled in the Lord's prayers and in "The Lord's Prayer."

Our Teacher's instruction focuses on Him whose is the kingdom, and the power, and the glory forever. He demands that we have that same focus.

Jesus the Master Teacher

by Henry E. Webb

THEY CALLED HIM "Rabbi." This was a title of respect, and Jesus accepted it. The title meant "teacher" and it pointed to one of Jesus' major activities. For centuries the Jewish people were instructed to hold their teachers in high esteem. Because the law was the holiest object in the life of the people, those who taught from the Law or expounded on its provisions were naturally held in high regard.

A Traveling Teacher

We think of a teacher as one who gives instruction in a school where there are classrooms and a library and where everything operates on a schedule. In Jesus' day there were few formal schools of this type. Jesus was what we now call a "peripatetic" teacher; that is, one who walks around. His classroom was the world. There was no formal schedule; His students (called "disciples") lived with Him day and night. When Jesus said to a person, "Follow me," He was inviting that person to be a part of His school and thus join His band of traveling students. Acceptance of this invitation meant leaving family and occupation to accompany those who lived with, listened to, and observed the Master Teacher.

Without faith in Jesus, one would hardly abandon one's normal activity or business to become a full-time follower. One had to believe that Jesus could impart some valuable insights to justify the investment of time and energy that discipleship demanded. Some, like the rich young ruler (Luke 18:18-30), declined Jesus' invitation. Others, however, had faith in Him, and became His disciples.

The Nature of Great Teaching

What made Jesus such an exciting teacher? Often He had to teach outdoors because no building could hold the crowds that came to hear Him. How can we account for the multitudes that were drawn to Him in such numbers? A look at Jesus' teaching gives several insights into what made Him the greatest teacher the world has ever known.

(1) *Jesus' teaching was directed at the major issues of life.* He discussed matters such as hypocrisy, lying, anxiety, and many of the other problems that plague people every day. He addressed the issues of life after death, relationships with one's neighbors and associates, and the ways a person can approach God—matters that are of utmost importance. He took no interest in the obscure interpretations of rabbinic traditions that so preoccupied the religious teachers of the day. Jesus was able to distinguish between important and trivial issues. All humans struggle with the problems that Jesus discussed. In this sense, His teachings are timeless.

(2) *Jesus utilized concrete imagery in teaching.* The Sermon on the Mount contains many excellent examples of this. At times He taught by means of parables, simple stories that illustrated spiritual truth in concrete terms that even the unlearned could readily understand. For example, to illustrate the various receptions that people give the word of God's kingdom, Jesus told a story of a sower whose seeds fell on different types of soil, an occurrence easily visualized by every person who heard Him speak. In telling of God's love He told of a father who welcomed home a son who was a prodigal sinner. All who heard Him could visualize the drama and sense the joy of the father as he embraced the distraught youth. Concrete pictures such as these are worth hundreds of words of abstract theory.

Students today who are preparing for a teaching career should study the methods of Jesus. The most gifted teacher of this writer's college experience often answered questions by telling a graphic story that presented a parallel situation, thus throwing light on the student's question. Instantly the student would see the connection and discover the answer.

(3) *Jesus was a master in the use of questions.* The Gospels record more than a hundred questions that He posed. Some of Jesus' questions were clearly rhetorical. One example is, "Is not life more important than food, and the body more important than clothes?" (Matthew 6:25, *New International Version*). While the answer to a question such as this is very obvious, posing the question opens for discussion the important subject of human priorities.

Jesus also utilized more direct questions to open a topic for discussion. He asked, "To what can I compare this generation?" (Matthew 11:16, *New International Version*) At other times He used a question to drive home a point: "Do men gather grapes of thorns, or figs of thistles?" (Matthew 7:16). The skillful use of questions is an effective way not only to open a topic for discussion but also to maintain interest and keep the attention of students at an optimum level.

(4) *Jesus dealt with theological issues in language people could understand.* Theology is the study of God, and we all need to learn about Him. Many theologians, however, confuse people with their abstract jargon. In contrast, Jesus taught about His Father in such a positive and simple way that anyone could understand that God is a loving Father who cares about all of His children.

A Different Kind of Rabbi

God's law given through Moses was often at the center of Jesus' teaching, and always loomed in the background. Jesus, however, was not an ordinary expositor of the law. He differed from the rabbis in that He saw the deeper meaning of the law, while they mostly were concerned with outward conformity to its precepts. This was so apparent in the Sermon on the Mount that Matthew noted that the people were amazed at how different His teaching was (7:28, 29). Since He was the Son of the Author of the law, He knew the law's intent. He could speak with genuine authority about its purpose and aims, opening treasures of meaning that other teachers often missed entirely.

Speaking of the law, Jesus was forthright to affirm that He had come to fulfill it (Matthew 5:17). Nobody could ever suggest, however, that Jesus failed to keep or obey the law. Just the opposite was true. It was in obeying the law perfectly that He fulfilled it, thus making it possible for all persons to be freed from the penalty that breaking the law demanded.

The Purpose of Teaching

Fundamentally, a teacher is one who imparts knowledge. Jesus did this as He instructed His disciples concerning the kingdom of Heaven, His own nature, and His oneness with His Father in Heaven. Jesus once said, "Ye shall know the truth, and the truth shall make you free" (John 8:32). He revealed truth that we must learn. Learning is at the very heart of discipleship. Knowledge is most useful when it makes a difference in the way we live. Regarding His teaching on one occasion Jesus stated, "Now that you know these things, you will be blessed if you do them" (John 13:17, *New International Version*).

Jesus not only imparted knowledge, important as that is. He also taught about attitudes and motives, which have great bearing on people's actions. First and foremost, Jesus was concerned with people's relationship with God. We are to love Him with all our being, and we are to seek His kingdom above all else. After that is Jesus' stress on how people deal with each other,

and on the values people adopt to guide them through life. The joys and sorrows, the satisfactions and the hurts of life are located primarily in the realm of human relationships. This is where one finds both love and hate, right and wrong, benevolence and crime. In the realm of morality human beings rise to God-like beauty of character or stoop to the level of demons. Nobody ever probed the mysteries of ethical motivation as Jesus did in the Sermon on the Mount. Here, again, He discussed profound issues of human conduct in terms so simple that even the unlearned person can comprehend.

The teachers of Jesus' day insisted that mere compliance with the law regarding stipulated actions and ceremony was adequate ethical behavior. Jesus went deeper. He indicated that it was right to obey the law in all that it commanded in matters of ceremony and human conduct. However, He showed that the focus of ethical behavior rests on the vital considerations of motive and intent. Jesus' insight centered on the sources of human conduct.

No person can legitimately say that Jesus' teaching is irrelevant to the critical issues that every human confronts in the ordinary course of living. The Master Teacher doesn't waste time on the peripheral issues of life; He goes straight to the heart of human problems. With rapier-like precision, He cuts away the chaff of legalistic tradition and exposes the underlying motives of pride and greed that cause mayhem in the life of family and society. The Master Teacher is always "on target." Those who hear Him are not belabored with the unimportant; they are always confronted with vital themes that deal with life's central issues. Two millennia have passed since He taught, but the world still listens to the words and respects the insights of the Master Teacher.

The Personal Dimension

Finally, we must not fail to note that teaching is a highly personal activity. It was particularly so with those teachers who, in former times, lived every day with their disciples, but it is also true of others. What a teacher *is* is as important to teaching as what the teacher *says*; the force of personality reinforces (or detracts from) what the teacher says.

We can sense the appeal of Jesus' personality by the way little children were drawn to Him. Such winsomeness is a trait not usually found in adult teachers, but it is one that all should seek to develop. The attracting power of God's truth is only enhanced when it is presented through a winsome personality. Let the love of God shine through you!

Toward a Better Life

by Victor Knowles

POLYCARP WAS A DEVOUT CHRISTIAN who served Christ for many years as bishop (elder) of the church at Smyrna. This church is mentioned in Revelation 2:8-11. Polycarp is thought to have been a disciple of the apostle John.

In A.D. 155 Rome's terrible persecutions reached the city of Smyrna. When some of the faithful Christians were delivered to wild beasts, the bloodthirsty crowd called for the leader of the Christians, Polycarp. Two poor slave boys were cruelly tortured until they at last revealed the whereabouts of Polycarp.

Upon hearing of the impending arrest of their beloved leader, friends of Polycarp wanted to spirit him away. He refused, however, saying, "God's will be done." When the authorities arrived, Polycarp provided a meal for them, thus heaping "coals of fire" upon their heads. His one request was granted: an hour alone to pray.

When Polycarp was brought into the crowded stadium, the proconsul told him, "Swear, and I will set thee at liberty, reproach Christ."

Polycarp replied, "Eighty and six years have I served Him, and He never did me any injury: how then can I blaspheme my King and my Saviour?"

The pagan proconsul tried to convince the aged Christian to swear by the genius (spirit) of the emperor. Again Polycarp refused, boldly declaring that he was a Christian. The proconsul then threatened to throw Polycarp to the wild beasts if he would not repent.

"Bring them forth," said Polycarp. "I would change my mind if it meant going from the worse to the better, but not to change from the right to the wrong."

Enraged, the proconsul threatened to have Polycarp burned alive.

To this Polycarp responded, "Thou threatenest me with fire which burneth for an hour, and after a little is extinguished, but art ignorant of the fire of the coming judgment and of eternal punishment, reserved for the ungodly."

Before he was consumed in the flames, Polycarp prayed, "O Lord God Almighty, . . . I give Thee thanks that Thou hast counted me worthy of this day and this hour, that I should have a part in the number of Thy martyrs, in the cup of Thy Christ. . . . Among whom may I be accepted this day before Thee as a fat and acceptable sacrifice."

The Christian life, though many have paid the supreme price to live it, is the most rewarding life on earth, and ultimately leads to eternal life with Christ himself. Why was Polycarp willing to pay the supreme sacrifice? Because he was fully committed to Jesus Christ. The life and teachings of Jesus had produced the conviction in Polycarp that Jesus was indeed the Son of God. Jesus Christ has had similar influence on the lives of millions of other Christians.

Testimony to Christ

The impact that Christ has had upon the masses through the centuries cannot be overestimated. Napoleon marveled that Jesus Christ ruled from the grave. (This is an impressive statement, attesting to the influence that Christ exerts over the lives of men and women, but it is not a totally accurate one. Christians believe that Jesus did not remain in the grave, but after three days rose from the dead, ascended to Heaven, and reigns in the hearts of men and women yet today.)

The division of time has been influenced by Jesus Christ. The initials B.C. stand for "before Christ," and A.D. represents the Latin *anno Domini*, which means "in the year of the Lord." Calendars virtually everywhere are silent witnesses to the power of Jesus Christ.

Transformation by Christ

Before Jesus came, life was as cheap as a stick of wood. Not only was abortion routinely practiced, infant abandonment was common. In Rome and Greece special "high places" were built where newborn babies, especially little girls, were exposed to the mercy of the elements and the birds of prey. The gospel of Christ brought new meaning to life. In ancient Rome the early morning mists swirled around the Christians and the pagan pimps, each of them frantically searching for these little ones before the other found them. In time "infanticide" itself was abandoned by the Roman Empire.

Who can deny that the status of women was raised to new heights by the influence of Christ and His teachings? Even supposedly cultured men such as Aristotle and Plato wrote degrading things about women. Radical opponents of Christianity today are misinformed when they say that Christianity has suppressed and held back women. Had it not been for the influence of British missionaries, the heathen practice of suttee might still be common in India. (Suttee was the horrible practice of burning—voluntarily or involuntarily—the widow of a husband on his funeral pyre.)

In time the teachings of Christ helped to abolish the cruel practice of slavery. In Paul's day a master treated his dog with more compassion than his slave. Yet Paul wrote a Christian brother, Philemon, to receive his runaway slave, Onesimus, as "a brother beloved" (Philemon 16). Only Christ could make such a difference! In England, William Wilberforce, a devout believer in Christ, fought long and hard for the abolition of slavery.

Our Lord declared that human life is of inestimable value. He stated that human beings are of more value than the birds of the air (Matthew 6:26). So precious is a human being, according to the teaching of Jesus, that one's possessing the world supply of oil, timber, precious metals, or any other vital commodity pales in significance to the inherent value of that person's soul (see Mark 8:36).

The teachings of Christ are not mere words or meaningless psychobabble. They have dramatically and radically altered people's lives, and those changed men and women have changed the world!

Francis of Assisi left all to care for the poor and downtrodden. General William Booth founded the Salvation Army, an army of "soldiers" committed to Christ, and this organization continues to touch the lives of countless souls. George Mueller housed and fed more than ten thousand orphans in England because he had been touched by the teachings of Christ. Hospitals were started by people who believed in the teachings of Christ. (Can one name a hospital atheism ever started?) Today in filthy Calcutta a frail and bent woman stoops again and again to minister to the diseased, the orphan, and the widow.

On and on we could go, recounting the many wonderful things Christ and His divine teachings have done to raise the quality of life in this world. D. James Kennedy has listed many of these changes in his book *What If Jesus Had Never Been Born?* Kennedy writes, "Despite its humble origins, the Church has made more changes on earth for the good than any other movement or force in history." Countless lives have been drastically changed by the gospel of Jesus Christ. Among them were Saul of Tarsus, Augustine, John Newton, C. S. Lewis, and many, many more.

Touching Others for Christ

What a privilege it is to stand before men and women, boys and girls, and teach the teachings of Christ—teachings that have changed the lives of millions, teachings that have indeed changed the course of world history! There is no greater calling in life than to declare this wonderful story of love!

G. Campbell Morgan was one of the greatest expositors of the Bible during his lifetime (1863-1945). In time he became recognized as the "Prince of Expositors." In his classic volume *The Teaching of Christ,* Morgan observed, "The greatest human teachers have always been reticent as to the ultimate authority of their teaching. They have always admitted that there is room for interpretation, for question, for further investigation. That note is entirely absent from the teaching of Christ. There is no apology. He never said: 'It is natural therefore to suppose'; 'It may probably be'; or 'Consult the authorities.'"

On one occasion officers were sent to arrest Jesus, but they came back empty-handed. When their superiors demanded to know why they had failed in their mission, the officers responded, "No one ever spoke the way this man does" (John 7:46, *New International Version*). May those of us who have been assigned the mission to teach the message of Christ in the spirit of Christ never fail in our mission. Rather, may our subjects themselves be arrested by the powerful claims of Christ as we teach His matchless Word!

Answers to Quarterly Quiz
on page 226

Lesson 1—1. the wicked one. 2. the care of this world, and the deceitfulness of riches. **Lesson 2**—1. cast him into prison. 2. wicked servant, delivered him to the tormentors. **Lesson 3**—1. false. 2. good. **Lesson 4**—1. afraid. 2. cast him into outer darkness. **Lesson 5**—1. began to make excuse. 2. he was angry. **Lesson 6**—1. to a village called Emmaus. 2. Cleopas. 3. Moses, prophets. **Lesson 7**—1. He receives sinners and eats with them. 2. one sinner who repents. **Lesson 8**—1. his voice. 2. life, abundantly. 3. his life. **Lesson 9**—1. bring forth more fruit. 2. true. **Lesson 10**—1. those who are reviled, persecuted, and falsely spoken against for Jesus' sake. 2. their reward in Heaven is great. 3. the prophets. **Lesson 11**—1. true. 2. enemies, curse, hate, use. **Lesson 12**—1. treasures. 2. our heavenly Father knows we need these things. 3. the kingdom of God. **Lesson 13**—1. men. 2. forgive men their trespasses.

Parable of the Sower

March 3
Lesson 1

DEVOTIONAL READING: Matthew 13:10-17.

LESSON SCRIPTURE: Matthew 13:1-23.

PRINTED TEXT: Matthew 13:1-9, 18-23.

Matthew 13:1-9, 18-23

1 The same day went Jesus out of the house, and sat by the sea side.

2 And great multitudes were gathered together unto him, so that he went into a ship, and sat; and the whole multitude stood on the shore.

3 And he spake many things unto them in parables, saying, Behold, a sower went forth to sow;

4 And when he sowed, some seeds fell by the wayside, and the fowls came and devoured them up:

5 Some fell upon stony places, where they had not much earth: and forthwith they sprung up, because they had no deepness of earth:

6 And when the sun was up, they were scorched; and because they had no root, they withered away.

7 And some fell among thorns; and the thorns sprung up, and choked them:

8 But other fell into good ground, and brought forth fruit, some a hundredfold, some sixtyfold, some thirtyfold.

9 Who hath ears to hear, let him hear.

. . . .

18 Hear ye therefore the parable of the sower.

19 When any one heareth the word of the kingdom, and understandeth it not, then cometh the wicked one, and catcheth away that which was sown in his heart. This is he which received seed by the wayside.

20 But he that received the seed into stony places, the same is he that heareth the word, and anon with joy receiveth it;

21 Yet hath he not root in himself, but dureth for a while: for when tribulation or persecution ariseth because of the word, by and by he is offended.

22 He also that received seed among the thorns is he that heareth the word; and the care of this world, and the deceitfulness of riches, choke the word, and he becometh unfruitful.

23 But he that received seed into the good ground is he that heareth the word, and understandeth it; which also beareth fruit, and bringeth forth, some a hundredfold, some sixty, some thirty.

GOLDEN TEXT: He that received seed into the good ground is he that heareth the word, and understandeth it; which also beareth fruit.—Matthew 13:23.

Teachings of Jesus
Unit 1: Teachings About the
Kingdom of Heaven
(Lessons 1-5)

Lesson Aims

This study should help the student:
1. Summarize and explain the Parable of the Sower to someone not familiar with it.
2. Accept responsibility for listening and responding to Christian teaching.

Lesson Outline

INTRODUCTION
  A. Hear! Hear!
  B. Lesson Background
I. PEOPLE AND PROCEDURES (Matthew 13:1-3a)
II. THE PARABLE (Matthew 13:3b-8)
  A. Sower, Seed, and Sowing (v. 3b)
    Which Seed Will Grow?
  B. Seed-Proof Soil (v. 4)
  C. Shallow Soil (vv. 5, 6)
  D. Preoccupied Soil (v. 7)
  E. Productive Soil (v. 8)
III. THE POINT (Matthew 13:9, 18)
IV. THE APPLICATION (Matthew 13:19-23)
  A. Hearers Without Understanding (v. 19)
  B. Hasty Hearers (vv. 20, 21)
  C. Too Busy Hearers (v. 22)
    Seeds and Weeds
  D. Fruitful Hearers (v. 23)
    The Power of a Seed
CONCLUSION
  A. Demonstration
  B. Broadcasting
  C. Prayer
  D. Thought to Remember

The key verse for today is both printed and illustrated on visual 1 of the visuals packet. The visual is shown on page 237.

Introduction

A. Hear! Hear!

Because her hearing is severely impaired, a veteran missionary resident in our retirement home is seldom able to enjoy the biblical preaching and teaching she so greatly loves. She searches for a teacher who speaks with a voice she can hear and understand.

A more common hearing problem is addressed by Jesus in the parable before us today (see also Mark 4:1-20; Luke 8:4-15). It afflicts even persons who can hear small sounds, but do not know what to do with the sounds that come to them. They seem not to be aware of what they hear, so as to understand and respond. Conversation is lost on them, except as an opportunity to say what is on their own minds. In church or Bible school they may attend but not pay attention. They have not learned to listen.

Listening is a skill not sufficiently taught in churches, schools, and colleges. The students who will become public speakers and teachers are instructed in their craft, but the hearers are not taught how to listen. It is a lack that Jesus addressed in His story leading to its logical conclusion, "Consider carefully how you listen" (Luke 8:18, *New International Version*).

B. Lesson Background

Jesus' ministry in Galilee was nearing its height in popular acclaim, with great crowds gathering to hear Him and to benefit from His miracles. Not everyone was pleased, though, with what they saw and heard. The nation's religious leaders felt threatened by His popularity and therefore stubbornly opposed Him. His words were examined for traces of false doctrine, leading to charges of blasphemy. His deeds, especially His miracles of healing, scrutinized for wrongdoing, resulting in charges of Sabbath violation.

Even among His admirers were many who were not prepared to understand and follow the teaching He urged upon His disciples. The multitudes were fascinated, but not ready to accept the "hard teachings."

I. People and Procedures (Matthew 13:1-3a)

1. The same day went Jesus out of the house, and sat by the sea side.

The *day* already had been marked by stress and conflict. Jesus had been teaching, perhaps in the house belonging to the brothers, Simon (Peter) and Andrew (Mark 1:29), located in the town of Capernaum on the northern shore of the Sea of Galilee. On this day some of the scribes and Pharisees had demanded a supernatural "sign" to establish Jesus' right to teach as He did. He rebuked the demand and offered a "sign" that they would see only later—the sign of the prophet Jonah, whose three days inside the great fish would become a symbol of Jesus' time in the tomb before rising on the third day.

The *day* also had seen the arrival of Jesus' earthly family, perhaps by a day's journey from Nazareth. The Lord had declined to receive them, preferring rather to serve His spiritual family of believers (Matthew 12:38-50).

Did Jesus seek rest and relaxation as He went alone to sit beside the lake, or did He anticipate the gathering of a crowd larger than any He could address in the house? In any event, His day of teaching was far from over.

2. And great multitudes were gathered together unto him, so that he went into a ship, and sat; and the whole multitude stood on the shore.

This was to be a teaching session, so Jesus did not stay on the shore where eager seekers for miracles would press upon Him, and where He would be in danger of being pushed into the water. Besides, where on the shore could He sit in the manner of teachers in the synagogue (Luke 4:20), as the multitude *stood* to be taught? On an earlier occasion Jesus taught from a similar arrangement (Luke 5:1-3). He may even have used the same boat both times. It would be hard to find better acoustics than in speaking from open water to the slope of the shoreline. The Lord of lands and lakes—the great lover of all mankind—knew how to bring them all together in glorifying their Maker!

3a. And he spake many things unto them in parables, saying.

Matthew 13 records seven parables, some very brief, out of the many things Jesus taught concerning the kingdom of God. Four of the seven deal with growing things and seem to apply to His hearers generally. Three deal with priorities in value, and apply especially to His disciples.

Parables (the word signifies a comparison, or casting one thing alongside another) are stories of common matters involving common people, but illustrating eternal truths. In telling them Jesus dealt with subjects so familiar to His hearers that they became interested and involved. The story-comparisons served a purpose for three different groups in Jesus' audience. First, the Lord's *critics* could find no solid ground in the parables or accusations against Him. Second, the parables formed a test of the moral state of His hearers. The *multitudes* could listen and remember, then perhaps listen again and

VISUALS FOR THESE LESSONS

The *Adult Visuals/Learning Resources* packet contains classroom-size visuals designed for use with the lessons in the Spring Quarter. The packet is available from your supplier. Order no. 392.

learn, if they had interest in things spiritual and were willing to exert the effort to understand the parables. If not, their lack of interest would be readily apparent. The *disciples*, who were interested, could seek out applications for their immediate instruction and spiritual growth. So Jesus explained why He taught in parables (vv. 10-17) and provided His own commentary on certain of the stories (vv. 18-23, 36-43).

II. The Parable
(Matthew 13:3b-8)

A. Sower, Seed, and Sowing (v. 3b)

3b. Behold, a sower went forth to sow.

Sowing grass seed, including grains such as wheat, rye, and barley, is very different from planting larger seeds, such as corn and beans, where the seeds are placed in the soil and covered. Ground may be prepared for sowing by loosening the surface. The seed is broadcast—scattered by handfuls so as to be spread evenly over the area. Light raking afterward may help the seed to penetrate the soil and take root.

In Bible lands the farmers did not live on separate farms. They lived among others in villages, and *went forth* to work their unfenced fields. Autumn seeding would be done for the spring and early summer harvest of barley and wheat. It is suggested that the events before us took place in October and that a seed-sowing workman may have been visible in the background as Jesus spoke. The *sower* in Jesus' parable is replaced almost immediately by Jesus' emphasis on the seed and the soil.

WHICH SEED WILL GROW?

In Shakespeare's play *Macbeth*, the character Banquo consults a trio of fortune-telling witches with these words: "If you can look into the seeds of time, And say which grain will grow and which will not, Speak then to me." It's a good question. Which seed will grow and which will not? Perhaps all of us at one time or another have wished we could look into the future. It may be we desired information that would help us choose the right career move, the best investment, or the perfect mate.

When thinking about sharing their faith with others, Christians are often tempted to ask the question, "Which seed will grow?" Yet the question never appears in Jesus' parable of the sower. The sower's responsibility was to sow seed, not test soil.

None of us knows for sure which seed will grow and which will not. Sometimes our witness will bear fruit by leading someone to Christ. Sometimes it will not. It is possible to

influence people whose response to Christ will be made many years and many miles from us. Our job is to sow the seed and trust God to bring the increase.
—C. B. Mc.

B. Seed-Proof Soil (v. 4)

4. And when he sowed, some seeds fell by the wayside, and the fowls came and devoured them up.

Paths, packed hard by the feet of people and burdened beasts, led alongside, and even through, the unfenced fields. Some of the scattered seed would fall on the pavement-like surface, where it would lie unprotected until it was picked up and eaten by hungry birds.

C. Shallow Soil (vv. 5, 6)

5. Some fell upon stony places, where they had not much earth: and forthwith they sprung up, because they had no deepness of earth.

The ground described here is not that which is littered with loose stones. That can be productive. Here, rather, is shallow soil over layers of limestone. Seed here would be warmed with heat reflected by the underlying rock, and would spring up quickly.

6. And when the sun was up, they were scorched; and because they had no root, they withered away.

Attention shifts naturally here from the seed to the sprouts from the seed. The same sun that warmed the seeds into life would dry the thin soil and wither the almost rootless plants.

D. Preoccupied Soil (v. 7)

7. And some fell among thorns; and the thorns sprung up, and choked them.

Here is recognized the curse that came upon the ground because of Adam's sin (Genesis 3:17-19). Sixteen different kinds of thorn-producing plants have been identified in Palestine, and their seeds would be present in the soil. No farmer or gardener needs to be reminded that noxious weeds seem always more vigorous than the desirable growths.

E. Productive Soil (v. 8)

8. But other fell into good ground, and brought forth fruit, some a hundredfold, some sixtyfold, some thirtyfold.

The ground where seed found lodging to sprout and grow with adequate rootage, moisture, and light produced the harvest for which the total investment of seed and labor was made. An Iowa farmer who harvested no more than a hundred bushels of corn for every bushel of seed he planted would not be pleased with the crop, but harvests vary with different kinds of

grain as well as different growing conditions. Jesus' estimates are accurate to the local circumstances. Genesis 26:6, 12 reports that when Isaac planted crops in Gerar, God blessed him with a hundredfold harvest. Christians must remember that in every instance God gives the increase (1 Corinthians 3:6, 7).

III. The Point
(Matthew 13:9, 18)

9. Who hath ears to hear, let him hear.

This is the point of the whole parable. Jesus was talking to His hearers about hearing. The sentence construction is emphatic. Luke's account of the parable says that the Lord raised His voice to emphasize the admonition: "When he had said these things, he cried, He that hath ears to hear, let him hear" (Luke 8:8). Listen and think about what you hear!

18. Hear ye therefore the parable of the sower.

The intervening verses, 10-17, contain Jesus' response to His disciples when they asked Him privately why He had begun to address the crowds in parables rather than in plain and literal terms. The plain teachings and the explanations, He said, were for them rather than for the general public. Quoting from Isaiah 6:9, 10, He said that hardhearted persons were not presently prepared to hear, see, and understand His message. If they would understand the parables, the understanding would come later with remembering, pondering, and observing the truth of what was said. For now, the explanation of the parable would be given to none but the Lord's faithful followers. Let them listen and consider.

IV. The Application
(Matthew 13:19-23)

The Parable of the Sower becomes immediately a lesson about the kinds of soil into which the seed fell. These kinds of soil were the hearers of the Word.

A. Hearers Without Understanding
(v. 19)

19. When any one heareth the word of the kingdom, and understandeth it not, then cometh the wicked one, and catcheth away that which was sown in his heart. This is he which received seed by the wayside.

The hard-packed pathway represents the hearer whose mind is fixed on other, and perhaps opposing, interests. This hearer may listen only to scoff at the speaker or the message. Such a hearer may be so completely absorbed with self and the world that the kingdom message makes no sense to him or her. This person may even have heard and rejected the gospel so many times that rejection has become a habit. The Word simply does not soak in. The wicked one—Satan (Mark 4:15) or the devil (Luke 8:12)—has ready access to this person's mind, and removes the message.

Lest we too readily assume that we are not that hardhearted, we might well measure the time it takes for a Bible lesson or sermon to disappear from our own mind or memory.

B. Hasty Hearers (vv. 20, 21)

20, 21. But he that received the seed into stony places, the same is he that heareth the word, and anon with joy receiveth it; yet hath he not root in himself, but dureth for a while: for when tribulation or persecution ariseth because of the word, by and by he is offended.

The Lord seems here to be describing the kind of excitable person who is easily impressed by promises and just as easily depressed by disappointment. This person may be "tossed to and fro, and carried about with every wind of doctrine" (Ephesians 4:14). The church that offers "help, healing, and hope" will attract such a one, but may finally cause rejection of the message altogether because it led this person to expect more of health and happiness than is consistent with Christian teaching and experience. Such a person's early zeal and enthusiasm may lead to burnout and desertion, especially if the person's zeal is not sufficiently applauded by fellow Christians.

Not thoroughly "rooted and grounded in love" (Ephesians 3:17), this hearer still lives and serves in Christ long enough to experience trouble and persecution because of his or her faith. The same heat of hardship that strengthens the mature Christian destroys the shallow one.

C. Too Busy Hearers (v. 22)

22. He also that received seed among the thorns is he that heareth the word; and the care of this world, and the deceitfulness of riches, choke the word, and he becometh unfruitful.

The hearer represented here may be a solid citizen, involved in community affairs. He likes what he hears of the gospel and concludes that Christ can add to his satisfying life. He may be able to wedge some church activities into his full schedule. For a time it may seem that he does rather well at worshiping both God and mammon (Matthew 6:24). But then some emergency arises to demand all-out commitment one way or the other. Unable finally to put the

visual 1

But he that received seed into the good ground is he that heareth the word, and understandeth it; which also beareth fruit.

Matthew 13:23

kingdom of God foremost above either the worries of poverty or the pleasures of wealth, the too busy hearer lingers half-alive in Christ. Incapable of producing either the fruit of the Spirit (Galatians 5:22, 23) or the reproductive fruit of evangelism, he falls under the Master's judgment on the barren fig tree (Luke 13:7).

SEEDS AND WEEDS

Anyone who has ever tried to keep a lawn or a garden has faced his or her share of crabgrass and dandelions. Since the day God drove Adam from the Garden of Eden, people who work in the soil have contended with thorns, thistles, and weeds.

Some weeds are more than just a nuisance—they are harmful, perhaps even deadly. Many species of milkweed, for example, contain a compound that produces severe muscle spasms, seizures, and profound weakness in animals that consume them.

Not all dangerous weeds grow along roadsides or in abandoned fields. The most dangerous are the weeds of the spirit that choke out the life-giving message of the gospel. Food, shelter, clothing, and human companionship are all necessities of life. But when our physical passions and possessions become the focus of our lives, they become weeds and thorns that choke off the influence of God's Word. Be careful that the soil of your heart is free of weeds.—C. B. Mc.

D. Fruitful Hearers (v. 23)

23. But he that received seed into the good ground is he that heareth the word, and understandeth it; which also beareth fruit, and bringeth forth, some a hundredfold, some sixty, some thirty.

The good-ground hearer is normal! Such a person does not have the faults that characterize the others. He or she listens and lets the truth soak in, then acts according to it. (See Luke 8:15.) Honesty forbids that the hearer should claim to receive the message and then neglect to follow it. Patience is found in one's willingness to undergo the period of growth and development through good times and bad, allowing God to work on His own schedule to produce His fruits of character and influence. The *good ground* is not all equally productive, but is acknowledged *good* if it produces to its capacity.

What is the significance of the multiplied harvest? Is it the spreading of God's Word from each one to many others? If so, it is not enough that "each one win one." How many persons have you helped to win to Christ? And how many were involved in winning you? On a harvest report, what would be the record for your acreage?

THE POWER OF A SEED

Seeds are simple but powerful objects. They vary in size from the dustlike seeds of the epiphytic orchids—thirty-five million of which weigh only one ounce—to the forty-four pound seed of the double coconut that grows in the Seychelles Islands in the Indian Ocean. Some of the smallest seeds have the power to produce very large plants.

The most massive living thing on earth is the General Sherman tree in California's Sequoia National Forest. Standing 275 feet tall, it has a girth of just over eighty-three feet and its estimated weight, including roots, is 2,756 tons. Yet the tree starts from a tiny seed that weighs only 1/6000th of an ounce.

God's Word is also a powerful seed. When we open our hearts to His Word, we become fertile ground for that seed. Like the good ground in the parable, we become fruitful and effective. God's Word produces an abundant harvest of righteousness in our lives. How receptive is the soil of your heart?   —C. B. Mc.

Conclusion

A. Demonstration

Just as the time of growth and harvest revealed the kinds of soil that Jesus described, so the months of His developing ministry revealed the kinds of hearers in His audiences. There were the rulers of the people, hardened by prejudice so that any impression made by His words was a negative impression.

There were the eager short-time followers who thronged Jesus to receive His words and His miracles, but they turned away when He refused to be their kind of king (John 6:60-66).

There was the rich young ruler, who was seriously interested in life eternal, but had too much in this present life to make the exchange.

Then there were various kinds of good ground among the apostles and their contemporaries. We don't know much about most of them. And the same is true about any effort to identify "soil samples" among our own contemporaries. Most important is the quality of our own hearing and response to the Word.

B. Broadcasting

How is the Parable of the Sower to become clear to folk who have no experience with seeds and soils and growing things? Perhaps there is a helpful linking word, *broadcasting*. The gospel message, like the seed, is broadcast (spread abroad) with little awareness of where it may land or which tiny bit may sink in and bring results. The messenger broadcasts in faith, and the hearer must listen responsibly. There are hardened hearers, mentally and emotionally deafened by the noise and repetition of commercial promotion. There are excitable hearers, swept one way and then another by the most recent emotional appeal. There are preoccupied hearers, absorbed with business, pleasure, and daily problems, so they have scant time for serious contemplation. And there are still thoughtful hearers, who listen carefully, consider thoughtfully, and respond appropriately. Any of us can increase his or her own responsiveness by the spiritual exercises of prayer, Bible study, and thoughtful conversation with others about God and His purposes.

C. Prayer

We are grateful, dear God, for the capacity to receive Your Word. May we treasure the ability, and protect it, and use it to Your glory, for Jesus' sake. Amen.

D. Thought to Remember

"Consider carefully how you listen" (Luke 8:18, *New International Version*).

Home Daily Bible Readings

Monday, Feb. 26—Trouble With the Law (Matthew 12:1-8)

Tuesday, Feb. 27—A Day Separate From Others (Exodus 20:8-11)

Wednesday, Feb. 28—Regard for Human Need (1 Samuel 21:1-6)

Thursday, Feb. 29—Parable of the Weeds (Matthew 13:24-30, 36-43)

Friday, Mar. 1—Ripened Wickedness (Joel 3:13-20)

Saturday, Mar. 2—Sowing Goodness (Galatians 6:1-10)

Sunday, Mar. 3—Understanding and Faith (Matthew 13:10-17)

Learning by Doing

This page contains an alternate lesson plan emphasizing learning activities. Classes desiring such student involvement will find these suggestions helpful.

Learning Goals

This lesson is designed to help the students:

1. Distinguish the variety of responses to the gospel presented in the parable.

2. Identify the admirable qualities of "good soil."

3. Identify an area of life in which he or she will bear more fruit for Christ.

Into the Lesson

Have the students work in pairs to name several qualities or characteristics of a good listener. After two minutes ask for their results. Write their answers on a chalkboard, poster paper, or overhead transparency. Here are some possible answers: acting interested, caring, being empathetic, maintaining good eye contact, giving feedback, being willing to get involved, allowing adequate time, and not interrupting. (Other responses are possible, and all answers should be accepted).

Make the transition into the study of today's Bible text by explaining that listening is a critical issue in our response to the gospel and to the will of God every day.

Into the Word

Ask for a volunteer to read Matthew 13:1-9 aloud to the class. Explain Jesus' use of parables as you feel it necessary for your class. Ask another volunteer to read Matthew 13:18-23 to the class.

After the second reading divide the class into four groups, assigning each group a type of soil: the path (vv. 4, 19); the rocky soil (vv. 5, 6, 20, 21); the thorny soil (vv. 7, 22); and the productive soil (vv. 8, 23). Tell the class that each of these types of soil represents a different type of hearer of the gospel of Christ. Ask each group to determine the qualities or characteristics lacking in the hearer that its soil represents. They can consider items in the list developed at the beginning of class and any other qualities they can think of. Examples are, the *hard-packed soil* lacks understanding and does not give adequate time to listening; the *rocky soil* lacks commitment and endurance; and the *thorny soil* lacks proper priorities and is not committed. Encourage each group to discuss the qualities of its soil (hearer) in the context of listening to the gospel, not only initially but also on a continuing basis.

After allowing seven minutes for discussion, have a spokesperson from each group summarize the group's conclusions for the entire class. Accept each response and be ready to probe where necessary. (For example, "So what are the priorities of those identified as thorny soil?")

Move into a discussion of the hearers represented as *good soil* by reading Matthew 13:23 and asking this question: Is the secret to being "good soil" the absence of the negative qualities of the other soils? Lead the discussion to the conclusion that these hearers of God's Word have sincerity of heart, patience, a desire to apply God's truth personally, a willingness to change, and endurance.

Into Life

Jesus points out that the good soil is productive, bringing forth a harvest. Ask the students to work in pairs once more to make an acrostic using the word *listen*. The words chosen should be qualities appropriate for the Christian who has heard, understood, and applied the Word of God in his or her life. The following acrostic is an example:

A person who hears the gospel and responds in faithful obedience will bear fruit such as:

L—love, learning
I—interest in others, initiative
S—sanctity (holiness), Spirit-led living
T—trust in God, telling others
E—enthusiasm, evangelism, endurance
N—needs-meeting, nurturing others

As students share their entries, write them on the chalkboard, poster paper, or overhead transparency. Encourage a variety of responses and accept them all (even if oddly phrased).

Ask the class members to reflect on the following: In what way, if any, have you demonstrated the qualities or characteristics of any of the four soils of the parable? Encourage specific responses. Guide the discussion toward the realization that each person is responsible for how he or she listens to God's Word.

Conclude the session by having the same pairs of students share their answers to the following question: In what way this week will I improve how I listen to God's direction and bear fruit for Him?

Let's Talk It Over

The questions on this page are designed to encourage review of the lesson Scriptures and to promote discussion of the lesson by the class. The answers provided are only discussion starters. Let your class talk it over from there.

1. What are some principles that would help a person be a better listener to the presentation of God's Word in lessons and sermons?

One key principle is that listeners need to be at their physical and mental best. Staying up late on a Saturday night to watch television or visit with friends is not conducive to good listening on Sunday morning. Another principle is that one should practice active rather than passive listening. If a copy of the speaker's outline is not available, it is helpful to try to discern the message's main points and subpoints. The listener may want to anticipate where the speaker is headed in a particular line of thought. And it could be beneficial for the listener to take notes on the above features and others. James reminds us that hearing must be combined with doing (James 1:22-25). As a person listens to a lesson or sermon, he or she will do well to keep in mind the question, "What am I going to do about the truths I am hearing?"

2. What are some steps that can be taken in the church to ensure that worshipers can hear clearly during the services of worship?

There are some actions that the church's leadership can take to enable the members to hear clearly the messages presented from God's Word. One may be to purchase and maintain a high quality sound system. Another may be to install special listening devices in designated areas for those with special hearing problems. There are some things, however, that the worshipers themselves can do to make it easier for all to hear. Each worshiper should practice "worship etiquette." This simply means that one will not engage in any kind of behavior, such as whispering or rustling papers, that might distract those who are seated nearby. And if a person has difficulty hearing, the problem may be solved by something as simple as one's sitting a bit closer to the front.

3. What can we do to help "pathway hearers" develop into good hearers of the word?

Surely we know people who are unresponsive to the word of God. They may exhibit some superficial interest in matters of the Spirit, but they quickly resist if we try to press them about faith, repentance, and obedience to the

Lord. It may be that only an occasion of personal crisis can cause them to "break up [their] fallow ground" (Hosea 10:12). Like the jailer in Philippi they may have to undergo a soul-shaking experience before they are ready to ask, "What must I do to be saved?" (Acts 16:30). Perhaps we can get through to them by reminding them of their human frailty and mortality. Then, they may at last recognize the wisdom of paying heed to the God who gives strength and life.

4. What can we do to help "stony-places hearers" develop into good hearers of the word?

In speaking of the "stony-places hearer," perhaps Jesus was describing the person who makes only a shallow, emotional response to the gospel. Of course, a merely intellectual person also may be shallow. God looks for a response that involves all the heart, all the soul, and all the mind (Matthew 22:37). If we know of believers who have come to the Lord on the basis of a vivid emotional experience, we should encourage them to engage in the kind of study of the Word that will stimulate their thinking. We should also hold before them the principle that the Lord wants every believer to grow to maturity in Him, and to help them to understand that this involves changes in attitude and behavior. Thus they may move beyond a commitment that rises or falls with the ever-fluctuating levels typical of human emotion. In so doing they will have something to keep them steadfast when trials, discouragements, and doubts arise.

5. What can we do to help "thorny-soil hearers" develop into good hearers of the word?

It is clear that these hearers attempt to follow Christ while still clinging to the treasures and values of this world. These persons need to hear the New Testament equivalent of Elijah's challenge to the Israelites on Mount Carmel: "How long will you waver between two opinions? If the Lord is God, follow him; but if Baal is God, follow him" (1 Kings 18:21, *New International Version*). Perhaps James 4:4, which equates friendship with the world with spiritual adultery and becoming God's enemy, will help. Strong words such as these may be required to awaken "thorny-soil hearers" to the foolishness of their pursuing the things of this world.

Parable of the Unforgiving Servant

DEVOTIONAL READING: Ephesians 4:25—5:2.

LESSON SCRIPTURE: Matthew 18:21-35.

PRINTED TEXT: Matthew 18:21-35.

Matthew 18:21-35

21 Then came Peter to him, and said, Lord, how oft shall my brother sin against me, and I forgive him? till seven times?

22 Jesus saith unto him, I say not unto thee, Until seven times: but, Until seventy times seven.

23 Therefore is the kingdom of heaven likened unto a certain king, which would take account of his servants.

24 And when he had begun to reckon, one was brought unto him, which owed him ten thousand talents.

25 But forasmuch as he had not to pay, his lord commanded him to be sold, and his wife, and children, and all that he had, and payment to be made.

26 The servant therefore fell down, and worshipped him, saying, Lord, have patience with me, and I will pay thee all.

27 Then the lord of that servant was moved with compassion, and loosed him, and forgave him the debt.

28 But the same servant went out, and found one of his fellow servants, which owed him a hundred pence: and he laid hands on him, and took him by the throat, saying, Pay me that thou owest.

29 And his fellow servant fell down at his feet, and besought him, saying, Have patience with me, and I will pay thee all.

30 And he would not: but went and cast him into prison, till he should pay the debt.

31 So when his fellow servants saw what was done, they were very sorry, and came and told unto their lord all that was done.

32 Then his lord, after that he had called him, said unto him, O thou wicked servant, I forgave thee all that debt, because thou desiredst me:

33 Shouldest not thou also have had compassion on thy fellow servant, even as I had pity on thee?

34 And his lord was wroth, and delivered him to the tormentors, till he should pay all that was due unto him.

35 So likewise shall my heavenly Father do also unto you, if ye from your hearts forgive not every one his brother their trespasses.

GOLDEN TEXT: Judge not, and ye shall not be judged: condemn not, and ye shall not be condemned: forgive, and ye shall be forgiven.—Luke 6:37.

Lesson Aims

This study should prepare the student to:
1. Relate in his or her own words the story of the parable.
2. Compare the relationship of the first debtor to his king with our relationship to God.
3. Make a prayerful beginning toward complete forgiveness of someone who has wronged him or her.

Lesson Outline

INTRODUCTION
   A. Of Debts and Debtors
   B. To Forgive Is Divine
   C. Lesson Background
  I. How MANY TIMES? (Matthew 18:21, 22)
 II. THE PARABLE (Matthew 18:23-34)
   A. A Forgiven Debtor (vv. 23-27)
   B. An Unforgiving Creditor (vv. 28-30)
   C. No Mercy for the Merciless (vv. 31-34)
    Measure for Measure
III. A SOLEMN WARNING (Matthew 18:35)
    How God Forgives
CONCLUSION
   A. The Answer in Action
   B. Praying to Forgive
   C. Thought to Remember

Visual 2 of the visuals packet highlights forgiveness, the theme of today's lesson. It is shown on page 246.

Introduction

A. Of Debts and Debtors

Debt—the obligation to pay for a benefit already received—is variously viewed. Some people spend without considering anything beyond the present benefit. They seem not to recognize that other folk must bear the losses of unpaid debt. Others limit their expenditures to what they can pay for immediately. Even they face the continuing obligation noted in Romans 13:8: "Owe no man any thing, but to love one another."

This brings us to another kind of obligation, or debt, incurred when we offend, injure, or mistreat another person, including God himself. But how do we pay that debt? Money can be returned, or property damage can be paid for, but how shall we unsay hurtful words, or unbruise a black eye, or undo a thoughtless, sinful act? Those are the debts that we never can pay. They remain unpaid until they are forgiven. So the Lord teaches us to pray, "Forgive us our debts, as we forgive our debtors" (Matthew 6:12), and in today's lesson He speaks of wiping out social, emotional, and moral obligations in terms of canceling money debts.

B. To Forgive Is Divine

"To forgive what he (or she) did to me is just impossible. It's too much to expect of any human being." Most of us have heard something like that more than once, and perhaps we have even said it ourselves. And it is not all wrong. The essayist Alexander Pope was never more right than when he wrote, "To err is human, to forgive divine." The first clause is a short form of Romans 3:23: "For all have sinned, and come short of the glory of God." The second clause is a short form of Psalm 103:8-13, which includes this: "The Lord is merciful and gracious, slow to anger, and plenteous in mercy. . . . As far as the east is from the west, so far hath he removed our transgressions from us."

Forgiveness is a quality of God, who cannot tolerate wickedness, but who can remove it by forgiving the penitent sinner. That divine quality was fully expressed in Jesus, whose mission was to bring God's forgiveness to mankind (Romans 8), and who prayed for His murderers, "Father, forgive them; for they know not what they do" (Luke 23:34). That divine quality of forgiveness enables the child of God, through the indwelling Holy Spirit, to do what is humanly impossible, even as the dying evangelist Stephen prayed, "Lord, lay not this sin to their charge" (Acts 7:60).

That is not to say that non-Christians can never forgive offenses against them. Through the influence of teaching and example the human tendency of those who do not know the Lord Jesus is sometimes overcome by the divine quality of forgiveness. Occasionally, however, the appearance of forgiveness is simply tolerance of evil by one who doesn't care. Genuine forgiveness requires a person to recognize evil for what it is, to reflect the divine abhorrence of any wickedness, and yet to throw the mantle of patient love over the confessing offender.

C. Lesson Background

Jesus' public ministry in Galilee had passed its peak of popularity. No longer was He addressing the multitudes and demonstrating His deity by many miracles. His closest disciples were now convinced of His deity, as indicated by Peter's confession (Matthew 16:13-20), and by the transfiguration event and Heaven's confession (Matthew 17:1-8). Now He was teaching the twelve concerning His coming death and resurrection, with the attendant difficulties they would face (Matthew 16:21-28).

Some stresses and tensions had become evident among the apostles. They were arguing about position and preference among themselves, while Jesus was urging humility and care for others (Matthew 18:1-10). Recognizing differences of opinion—even hard feelings—among His followers, the Lord set forth a plan, which the offended person was to follow in reestablishing a right relationship (Matthew 18:15-18). The offender might not even know that he had committed any offense; or he might be a habitual offender, who apologized repeatedly for repeated offenses.

I. How Many Times?
(Matthew 18:21, 22)

21. Then came Peter to him, and said, Lord, how oft shall my brother sin against me, and I forgive him? till seven times?

The teaching session before us began with a personal question. Had Peter become the object of jealousy and unkind remarks because following his confession he had received Jesus' compliment (Matthew 16:17, 18), or because he was one of the "inner circle" witnessing the transfiguration? (Matthew 17:1-4). No indication is given regarding the reason for Peter's question.

Jewish tradition of a later date declared that the extent of required forgiveness was three times. If this was the teaching of the spiritual leaders in Jesus' day, Peter undoubtedly felt that he was being quite generous in offering to forgive an offender seven times.

22. Jesus saith unto him, I say not unto thee, Until seven times: but, Until seventy times seven.

Seventy times seven (that is, 490)—or even seventy-seven times, as some translations render it—was an inclusive and indefinite number. To make a tally of injuries, ending at either number, would violate the principle of 1 Corinthians 13:5: "[Love] keeps no record of wrongs" (*New International Version*). It would also misrepresent the infinite grace of God, which is the theme of Jesus' ministry.

This teaching of personal forgiveness for personal offenses should not be applied, however, to public affairs of criminal justice (see Romans 13:1-7). Unlimited judicial clemency for habitual crimes is no part of Jesus' program.

II. The Parable
(Matthew 18:23-34)

What began as a conversation between Jesus and Peter became immediately a teaching session directed first to all the apostles and then to all who would become followers of the Christ.

A. A Forgiven Debtor (vv. 23-27)

23. Therefore is the kingdom of heaven likened unto a certain king, which would take account of his servants.

In response to Peter's question Jesus instructed His disciples to practice unlimited forgiveness (v. 22). That introduced the infinities of God and led Jesus to tell a parable about *the kingdom of heaven*. Couched in terms of this world, the parable deals with a royal relationship with citizen-slaves. It deals with a king-sized debt, kingly compassion, and kingly judgment. It is an awesome story.

Luke 19:12-27 and Matthew 25:14-30 tell of royal personages who left their countries for an extended period of time, during which they entrusted their business to responsible servants. Upon their return they demanded an accounting of the servants' business activities. An occasion for taking account might occur, however, without an owner's prolonged absence (see Luke 16:1, 2). Such an occurrence might be compared with our experience at the end of the month, or when one's job performance comes up for review. The accounting that took place in the parable for our study in this lesson was of this type.

24. And when he had begun to reckon, one was brought unto him, which owed him ten thousand talents.

A man so debt-ridden, or guilt-ridden, might have been reluctant to come; but come he must. One estimate of the man's debt is that it was enough to pay a thousand Roman soldiers' daily wages for a hundred years. This debtor was no unimportant person. He could have been a high official appointed by the king to rule over a great part of his domain and to bring into his treasuries the revenues of one of the provinces (compare Daniel 2:48, 49). Let us consider, then, our responsibility to God for handling the spiritual treasures of Heaven! Our unpayable debt to God gives point to the parable.

25. But forasmuch as he had not to pay, his lord commanded him to be sold, and his wife, and children, and all that he had, and payment to be made.

Whatever the man may have done with his king's money, it was gone, and he was as helpless to pay his vast debt as we are helpless to pay God for our used-up blessings and our sins.

The sale of a man and his family, along with whatever possessions he may have, to satisfy his debts is a fact recognized—not necessarily approved—in Leviticus 25:39, 40; Nehemiah 5:4, 5; and 2 Kings 4:1. The last passage quotes the plaint of a widow: "My husband is dead . . . and the creditor is come to take unto him my two sons to be bondmen."

26. The servant therefore fell down, and worshipped him, saying, Lord, have patience with me, and I will pay thee all.

The debt that might have been admitted lightly in conversation with someone else was now seen in its hopeless enormity when settlement was required. So is man's debt to God. Too often it is dismissed with the observation that "nobody is perfect"; but in the divine presence, that debt is devastating.

In desperation the debtor prostrated himself before his king and begged for a delay in judgment. Even so, his pride prevented an honest confession of helplessness. Instead, he made the ridiculous promise to pay all if only given enough time. Depicted again is the pride of man trying to establish his own terms for gaining God's approval. Pressed to the limit he will beg desperately and promise anything—anything but complete dependence on God's mercy.

27. Then the lord of that servant was moved with compassion, and loosed him, and forgave him the debt.

Pity for the man's hopeless condition, including his failure even to recognize his hopelessness, led the king to totally cancel the debt. Thus the king accepted to himself the loss it represented and paid the debt. In like manner, God, through Christ, paid the penalty for our sins.

Home Daily Bible Readings

Monday, Mar. 4—Warning Against Wrong Teaching (Matthew 16:5-12)
Tuesday, Mar. 5—Declaring One's Belief (Matthew 16:13-20)
Wednesday, Mar. 6—Sharing a Vision (Matthew 17:1-13)
Thursday, Mar. 7—Healing a Child (Matthew 17:14-21)
Friday, Mar. 8—Paying the Tax (Matthew 17:22-27)
Saturday, Mar. 9—Determining Greatness (Matthew 18:1-14)
Sunday, Mar. 10—Handling a Grievance (Matthew 18:15-20)

The words of the verse before us suggest that the debtor had arrived bound before his king. Now he was loosed from his bonds as well as from his debt. In thus granting freedom, the king was most like the God he represents.

A country doctor who canceled all bills owed to him was complimented for his unselfishness. He responded that it had been a totally selfish act; he was tired of his debtor friends' avoiding him on the street. God—represented by the king in this parable—recognizes forgiveness as the only way to maintain friendly relations with those who have committed offenses. Not selfishness, however, but divine compassion is the motivating force of God's forgiveness.

B. An Unforgiving Creditor (vv. 28-30)

Here the parable turns from good news of God to bad news of man who rejects God's way.

28. But the same servant went out, and found one of his fellow servants, which owed him a hundred pence: and he laid hands on him, and took him by the throat, saying, Pay me that thou owest.

Like some people who are "converted" through a traumatic experience, this man was frightened and made marvelous promises, but he was not truly converted. Instead, he used his newly found freedom to "lord it" over another of his king's servants. Proverbs 30:21-23 mentions among the things the earth "cannot bear" these two: "a servant when he reigneth" and "a handmaid that is heir to her mistress." This servant suddenly thought he should reign. The same pride that prevented his asking forgiveness prevented also his granting forgiveness to another.

By one estimate the amount the first servant had owed the king was more than a million times greater than the *hundred pence* that he was owed by his fellow servant. Yet his actions in demanding payment were violent and merciless. They portray the attitude of one who expects a merciful God to overlook his sins, but is unforgiving toward another child of the same Savior.

29, 30. And his fellow servant fell down at his feet, and besought him, saying, Have patience with me, and I will pay thee all. And he would not: but went and cast him into prison, till he should pay the debt.

By action and by words, the hapless small debtor made the same plea this merciless creditor had made to his king. One might expect the similarity to stir sympathy in the one now making the demand. But reason was as far from him as was mercy. The small debt was not enough to justify selling the victim into slavery. A debtor's prison was chosen as the alternative.

What did he gain by it? Nothing but a strange satisfaction of his own arrogant pride and lust for power. It is the same satisfaction sought and gained by the one who says, "I'll never forgive that kind of treatment from anybody. They don't get away with walking all over me!"

Not many of us have opportunity to exercise the kind of royal generosity found in the forgiving king, but we can do small favors and forgive small injuries. That is where the meaningful tests of Christian living begin. This is another way to apply Jesus' words about being "faithful in that which is least" (Luke 16:10).

C. No Mercy for the Merciless
(vv. 31-34)

31. So when his fellow servants saw what was done, they were very sorry, and came and told unto their lord all that was done.

Others of the king's servants were shocked and distressed by the rough treatment that was given to one of their colleagues by another. They acted properly in laying the matter before their lord for correction. Romans 12:19 recommends that Jesus' followers in similar manner leave acts of punishment to God. But there is a difference—He does not need to be told what has happened.

32, 33. Then his lord, after that he had called him, said unto him, O thou wicked servant, I forgave thee all that debt, because thou desiredst me: shouldest not thou also have had compassion on thy fellow servant, even as I had pity on thee?

Here is the central point of the parable. God's infinite mercy demands that His people also be merciful.

The king lost no time in addressing the problem. He called the culprit into his presence and pronounced judgment. The sin he condemned was not dishonesty and financial default; it was the man's despising and rejecting the king's example in dealing with a debtor. The man had asked for time to pay, and the king had canceled the debt. The man's victim had asked for time to pay, and the man had cast him into prison. Wicked as the offender was, the king knew that the man had enough moral sense to reply to the king's question, "Shouldn't you have had compassion on your fellow servant?" and thus pronounce his own guilt.

Even as I had pity on thee. This is a parable of the kingdom. It speaks of God's infinite mercy in Christ, and that mercy is the basis of God's requirement that His children be merciful to one another. Elsewhere the Scripture speaks directly of the requirement for mutual forgiveness: "Be ye . . . forgiving one another, even as God for Christ's sake hath forgiven you" (Ephesians 4:32; see also Colossians 3:12, 13). That principle was flagrantly violated by the forgiven but unforgiving debtor/creditor.

MEASURE FOR MEASURE

In Shakespeare's *Measure for Measure*, the severe and upright Lord Deputy, Angelo, presides over the case of a poor young man condemned to death because he seduced his sweetheart before they were able to wed. The man's sister, Isabella, approaches Angelo and pleads for her brother's life. While admitting his wrong, she asks that Angelo have mercy and rescind the stern sentence of death for her brother's crime. The unbending Angelo is deaf to Isabella's plea, declaring, "Your brother is a forfeit of the law, and you but waste your words."

Isabella responds with this beautiful appeal: "Alas! alas! Why, all the souls that were were forfeit once; and He that might the vantage best have took found out the remedy. How would you be, if He, which is the top of judgment, should but judge you as you are? O, think on that; and mercy then will breathe within your lips, like man new made."

Can one who has received God's mercy be so unfeeling as to refuse to show mercy to others? God has chosen not to punish us as we deserve, but by His grace through Christ to forgive the magnitude of our transgressions. Because we are condemned prisoners set free from Hell, God's mercy, grace, and love should flow to others from us like persons "new made."   —C. B. Mc.

34. And his lord was wroth, and delivered him to the tormentors, till he should pay all that was due unto him.

Wroth is a term precisely describing the judicial and punitive anger of God, a king, or a judge. *Tormentors* (jailers) could add affliction to confinement. Torture was not used by Jews or Romans as punishment for debt, but an Eastern despot would use it to make a debtor reveal where he had hidden assets that could be applied toward payment. In this case the sentence was of indefinite duration. Earlier the servant had escaped being sold into slavery, only now to be sentenced to endless punishment.

How shall we explain the reactivation of the forgiven debt? Does God's computer include a memory file that can be used at any time to call up deleted material? Is His forgiveness, then, truly complete? Let us remember, though, that the offender was not punished for old debt; he was punished for the new offense of withholding mercy from another. Given the example of grace and mercy, he had chosen instead the way of law and punishment. So to the way of law and punishment he was returned. It is, of course, impossible to depict our infinite God fully in human terms.

III. A Solemn Warning (Matthew 18:35)

Jesus made His own application of the human story to the divine reality.

35. So likewise shall my heavenly Father do also unto you, if ye from your hearts forgive not every one his brother their trespasses.

If one is looking for the unpardonable sin, here is where it will be found. It is in the heart of one who prays, "Forgive us our debts, as we forgive our debtors," while harboring malice and plotting revenge for some perceived insult or injury. Such a one belittles God, who offers pardon for king-sized transgressions, while the unforgiving one closes the gates of Heaven against himself by nursing a king-sized rage over his neighbor's pint-sized offenses.

Judgment frequently arrives in early installments to the unforgiving one, as the body, mind, and spirit suffer the erosions of an acid disposition. Hence Jesus' requirement that forgiveness must come from the heart. God knows, and our own bodies and spirits know, exactly how much or how little it means when we say, "I forgive." The unforgiving are, by the very nature of their attitude, incapable of receiving forgiveness (Matthew 6:14, 15).

HOW GOD FORGIVES

In Ephesians 4, Paul describes our new life in Christ. Among the qualities he mentions are kindness and compassion. He calls on us to demonstrate those qualities by forgiving each other, just as God forgave us (4:32). God forgives us completely. How can this be described?

The prophet Micah painted a word picture of God's removal of Israel's sin. He said that God would hurl their iniquities "into the depths of the sea" (7:19). Imagine all your sins, every wrong you have ever done, buried in the depths of the sea!

visual 2

The deepest place in the ocean is the Marianas Trench, southwest of Guam in the Pacific Ocean. This undersea depression reaches a maximum depth of 36,201 feet, nearly seven miles. By comparison, the world's tallest building, the Sears Tower in Chicago, rises 110 stories from the street. So deep is the Marianas Trench that it would take a stack of twenty-five Sears Towers to reach from the ocean floor to the surface above the trench.

Anything dropped into the ocean at such a depth would be covered with so much water it would never again see the light of day. That's how God forgives; and that's how He calls us to forgive others—deeply, completely, permanently.
        —C. B. Mc.

Conclusion

A. The Answer in Action

Jesus spoke His parable in reply to a question from the apostle Peter: "How often should I forgive?" The answer in brief was this: "As often as God forgives you." Consider the night when Peter boasted to Jesus, "Though all men shall be offended because of thee, yet will I never be offended" (Matthew 26:33). Within a few hours, three times he vehemently denied knowing Jesus. Moments later Peter was weeping, and within hours Jesus was dying. Immediately after the Lord's resurrection, however, Peter was included by name in an invitation to meet Jesus in Galilee (Mark 16:7). Then in Galilee the Lord made a special point of accepting Peter's acknowledgment of personal devotion, and giving to Peter a shepherd's appointment over His flock (John 21:15-17). Peter knew what he was talking about when he preached Christ as Savior, "To give repentance to Israel, and forgiveness of sins" (Acts 5:31). He was not counting the sins, nor worrying whether there would be enough forgiveness to go around.

B. Praying to Forgive

O God, You have made us in Your image, and we praise You. We have marred that likeness in many ways, but especially in our failure to forgive as You have forgiven us. May we see again Your perfect likeness in Jesus our Lord, and may we learn from Him to forgive. Free us, please, from any unforgiving spirit that hinders our being fully forgiven and offering acceptable praise in His name. Amen.

C. Thought to Remember

"Be ye kind one to another, tender-hearted, forgiving one another, even as God for Christ's sake hath forgiven you" (Ephesians 4:32).

Learning by Doing

This page contains an alternate lesson plan emphasizing learning activities. Classes desiring such student involvement will find these suggestions helpful.

Learning Goals

As a result of participating in today's lesson, a student will be able to:

1. Relate in his or her own words the story of the parable.

2. Compare the relationship of the first debtor to his king with our relationship to God.

3. Make a prayerful beginning toward complete forgiveness of someone who has wronged him or her.

Into the Lesson

As far in advance of class time as possible, ask two class members to be prepared to engage in a short, friendly debate on how debt should be handled. Ask one to present the view that buying things on credit is the normal way of doing business in today's society. Ask the other to take the view that debt should be avoided entirely. Introduce the debate and allow each debater to speak for one minute. Allow for brief rebuttals.

Make the transition to the study of the text by asking, "How do we handle the debt incurred when we offend or are offended by someone? Is there a difference in the way we handle our financial debt and our interpersonal debts?"

Into the Word

Lead the class in a brainstorming session for a list of biblical passages that relate to our forgiving our fellowmen. As time allows, find the passages and have volunteers read them aloud to the class. The list could include the following: Matthew 6:12-15; Matthew 18:15-18; Luke 17:3, 4; 1 Corinthians 13:5 *(New International Version)*; Ephesians 4:32; and Colossians 3:12, 13.

Give each class member a pencil and a blank sheet of paper. During the first part of this study activity, the class members are to work individually. Ask them to read the first part of the Parable of the Unforgiving Servant (Matthew 18:23-27) and write down in what ways the events of the parable parallel our forgiveness by God in Christ. Answers should include these or similar thoughts: the servant was totally unable to repay his debt, and we cannot pay for our debt of sin; the servant's debt would lead to slavery, and our sin leads to spiritual slavery; the king canceled the debt, and our sin-debt is canceled or paid for in Christ; the result is freedom. After four or five minutes, ask students to work in groups of three

to share their answers with one another. Allow about two minutes for this sharing.

Now read verses 28-30 aloud to the class. Point out that ten thousand talents was an enormous amount of money in that day and perhaps one million times the value of one hundred pence. Ask the class members to write a short paragraph on the following questions: How could the first servant treat his fellow servant so cruelly after receiving such grace? What was he thinking and feeling—or *not* thinking and feeling? Allow several minutes for individual reflection and writing; then ask for volunteers to share their written paragraphs with the class.

Next, read verses 31-35 aloud to the class. Summarize the study by stating the point of the parable: God's infinite mercy demands that His people also be merciful.

Into Life

Introduce an activity of role-playing. Have volunteers act out briefly the following scenes:

• A husband comes home from work late again, and the wife is angry because he did not bother to call her.

• A person driving his new car has just been hit from behind by another driver.

• A worker who has just been fired by an unfair boss is telling a friend, who is trying to be sympathetic.

After the scenes have been played, ask the class to comment on each of them. What attitudes were expressed? What insights to our own behaviors do these give us?

If time allows, ask one or two of the pairs to replay their roles, with the offended party attempting to maintain a spirit of forgiveness. Afterward, take note of the difficulty many persons have in forgiving those who offend them. Point out also that the results—physical, emotional, social, and spiritual—of a person's unforgiving spirit can be profound and severe. (See the comments in the second paragraph under verse 35.) Everyone benefits from godly forgiveness.

Conclude the class with prayer, asking the Lord for guidance in what each person can do to begin the process of forgiving someone who has offended him or her. Allow a time of silent prayer, encouraging the class members to begin praying for the will and ability to forgive others as God has forgiven them.

Let's Talk It Over

The questions on this page are designed to encourage review of the lesson Scriptures and to promote discussion of the lesson by the class. The answers provided are only discussion starters. Let your class talk it over from there.

1. What are some ways in which people put conditions on the forgiveness they extend, as Peter was apparently tempted to do?

We may say, "I'll forgive him if he gets down on his knees and begs for forgiveness," or "I'll forgive her if she proves to me she is really sorry for what she has done." If we follow the example of Jesus, we will forgive even when we are not asked to forgive. While He hung on the cross, Jesus said, "Father, forgive them; for they know not what they do" (Luke 23:34). Apparently His entreaty was not made in response to anyone's request for forgiveness. Sometimes a person wants to make an offender "squirm" a bit before extending forgiveness. That is a mild form of revenge, which Christians are forbidden to take (Romans 12:19-21). And sometimes, like Peter, we are inclined to set limits on the number of times we will forgive. But we forget how long-suffering the Lord must be with us.

2. How can we better appreciate the magnitude of our indebtedness to God because of our sins?

It is helpful to ponder man's first sin and its terribly damaging effects. At first glance, what Adam and Eve did seems trivial. They ate fruit that "was good for food, and . . . pleasant to the eyes" (Genesis 3:6). But it was fruit that God had expressly forbidden them to eat. Thus, their act was a sin, and we today still suffer the effects of that sin. When we see the destructive power of that sin, and we add up all the sins we have committed, we begin to realize the immensity of the debt we have accumulated before God. Furthermore, when we widen our viewpoint to take in the sins of the billions of other human beings who have lived on this earth, it staggers our minds to think of what was involved in Jesus' sacrifice on the cross to bring about our reconciliation with God.

3. In Jesus' parable the debtor promised the king, "I will pay thee all." How is this an illustration of the common misunderstanding of sin and our ability to deal with it?

Human beings generally underestimate the seriousness of sin. One frequently gains the impression that many people picture God as a kindly grandfather, who witnesses human sins and says, "Why those little rascals! Well, boys will be boys, and girls will be girls. I'll just have to overlook their shortcomings." As we noted in the previous question, sin is a tremendously destructive reality, and God cannot merely shrug it off as though it were inconsequential. Because of a defective view of sin's seriousness, human beings tend to think it can be resolved easily. A few good deeds done, a little money given to a church or charitable organization, some well-expressed prayers—these should balance the ledger, so some think. In truth, nothing we can do will make payment for our sins. The death of God's Son was required to pay our sin-debt.

4. How can thinking of God's forgiveness of us help us to forgive those who wrong us?

We may say of one who has offended us, "He does not deserve to be forgiven," or "What she did to me is beyond forgiveness." But when we review our own circumstances, we find that in no way do we deserve God's forgiveness, and yet He gives it. We may lament, "How can I forgive him when he continues to hurt me in the same way?" But do we not persist in certain sinful attitudes and actions and expect God's grace to cover us? We may find it difficult to forgive when the effects of an offense remain with us. A physical scar, a recurring painful memory, the loss of a friend—these remind us of what was done to us. But the damaging effects of our own sins are abundantly evident to God, and in spite of them He forgives us.

5. How can prayer help remove bitterness that remains in our hearts as a result of a wrong done to us?

Paul wrote, "Be ye kind one to another, tender-hearted, forgiving one another, even as God for Christ's sake hath forgiven you" (Ephesians 4:32). If God has commanded us to forgive one another, surely it must be something He will help us accomplish. We can pray, "Lord, make me more aware of how much You have forgiven me, so that I may be inspired to forgive." As we think of the offender and the offense, we can pray, "Lord, make me more tenderhearted and compassionate, so that I can better understand why this wrong was done to me and thereby be able to let go of my bitterness."

Parable of the Vineyard Workers

DEVOTIONAL READING: Matthew 19:23-30.

LESSON SCRIPTURE: Matthew 19:27—20:16.

PRINTED TEXT: Matthew 20:1-16.

Matthew 20:1-16

1 For the kingdom of heaven is like unto a man that is a householder, which went out early in the morning to hire laborers into his vineyard.

2 And when he had agreed with the laborers for a penny a day, he sent them into his vineyard.

3 And he went out about the third hour, and saw others standing idle in the market place,

4 And said unto them; Go ye also into the vineyard, and whatsoever is right I will give you. And they went their way.

5 Again he went out about the sixth and ninth hour, and did likewise.

6 And about the eleventh hour he went out, and found others standing idle, and saith unto them, Why stand ye here all the day idle?

7 They say unto him, Because no man hath hired us. He saith unto them, Go ye also into the vineyard; and whatsoever is right, that shall ye receive.

8 So when even was come, the lord of the vineyard saith unto his steward, Call the laborers, and give them their hire, beginning from the last unto the first.

9 And when they came that were hired about the eleventh hour, they received every man a penny.

10 But when the first came, they supposed that they should have received more; and they likewise received every man a penny.

11 And when they had received it, they murmured against the goodman of the house,

12 Saying, These last have wrought but one hour, and thou hast made them equal unto us, which have borne the burden and heat of the day.

13 But he answered one of them, and said, Friend, I do thee no wrong: didst not thou agree with me for a penny?

14 Take that thine is, and go thy way: I will give unto this last, even as unto thee.

15 Is it not lawful for me to do what I will with mine own? Is thine eye evil, because I am good?

16 So the last shall be first, and the first last: for many be called, but few chosen.

GOLDEN TEXT: The last shall be first, and the first last: for many be called, but few chosen.—Matthew 20:16.

Teachings of Jesus
Unit 1. Teachings About the
Kingdom of Heaven
(Lessons 1-5)

Lesson Aims

This study should enable students to:
1. Tell in their own words the Parable of the Vineyard Workers.
2. Understand the relationship between trusting God's promises and doing God's work.
3. Adjust their own priorities so as to be in agreement with what God regards as first.

Lesson Outline

INTRODUCTION
  A. What Would You Save?
  B. What Did Jesus Have in Mind?
  C. Lesson Background
 I. A PERSISTENT EMPLOYER (Matthew 20:1-7)
  A. Employing Under Contract (vv. 1, 2)
    Looking for Workers
  B. Employing With a Promise (vv. 3-5)
  C. Employing the Unemployed (vv. 6, 7)
 II. A GENEROUS EMPLOYER (Matthew 20:8-10)
III. A JUST EMPLOYER (Matthew 20:11-16)
  A. Presumptuous Complaint (vv. 11, 12)
    Newcomers
  B. Promises Are Kept (vv. 13, 14)
  C. Priorities Are Established (vv. 15, 16)
CONCLUSION
  A. Who Is Number One?
  B. Prayer for Understanding
  C. Thought to Remember

Visual 3 of the visuals packet explains terms dealing with money in today's lesson. It is shown on page 253.

Introduction

A. What Would You Save?

"You must leave your home within the hour and take with you only what you can carry!" Faced with that ultimatum, what would you take?

Thousands of American families have had to make that choice in recent years as they have been faced with hurricanes, floods, or fires. What have these folk carried away with them? Usually not "big-ticket" items, such as entertainment centers, though these may have occupied much of their time and attention. Instead, the number-one item was frequently the family photo album—not very expensive, but priceless because it never could be replaced and it was personally treasured. When it comes time to make ultimate decisions, amazing changes may take place regarding one's priorities. Then, what is usually first suddenly becomes last, and what is usually last suddenly becomes first.

Jesus was always dealing with ultimate values in His teachings about the kingdom of Heaven, where moth and rust do not corrupt, and where tornado, flood, or fire do not destroy. That kingdom has its own set of values, which often contrast sharply with those recognized in this world.

B. What Did Jesus Have in Mind?

The Parable of the Vineyard Workers is introduced by this statement: "Many that are first shall be last; and the last shall be first" (Matthew 19:30). The parable is concluded with the same thought (Matthew 20:16). That theme applies to just about every subject Jesus discussed, and its principle applies to a lot of things the first-century Christians never heard of.

The principle applied to the apostles, who had ambitions to be front-runners in the kingdom; Jesus warned that if they failed to overcome their ambition, they wouldn't even be in the race (Mark 10:15). It applied to the nation's religious leaders versus the social outcasts with regard to entering the kingdom (Matthew 21:31; Luke 18:10-14), and likewise to the Jews in general versus the Gentiles (Acts 13:44-48). And God will make His own adjustments to popular choices of "first citizens" in our communities.

C. Lesson Background

The parable in today's text was spoken by Jesus after the one in last Sunday's lesson. Both illustrate the grace of God. Last week we learned of God's mercy, expressed in forgiveness; this week God's mercy is seen in generosity to the poor. In both, our minds are stretched to see the dimensions of the divine kingdom.

Today's story was told during a stressful time in Perea shortly before Jesus' death. The religious leaders did not like His rebukes of their pretensions to superior wisdom, character, and authority. His own disciples were still displaying some selfish ambitions.

Matthew 19 records a series of related events. Verses 13-15 tell of the Lord's blessing little children as examples of the humility that should characterize His followers. Verses 16-26 tell of the rich young ruler who desired eternal life, but not enough to make it his first priority. Verses 27-30 relate a conversation in which Peter wanted to know what reward would be coming to him and the others because, in leaving all to follow Christ, they had done as the rich young man had not. The Lord assured them of rewards on earth and in Heaven, but warned that "many that are first shall be last; and the last shall be first" (v. 30). The parable in today's lesson develops that theme.

I. A Persistent Employer (Matthew 20:1-7)

A. Employing Under Contract (vv. 1, 2)

1. For the kingdom of heaven is like unto a man that is a householder, which went out early in the morning to hire laborers into his vineyard.

The introductory *for* links the narrative firmly to the warning just spoken.

Obviously, the householder owned and managed a considerable estate. The *vineyard* is important only as background for the owner's concern to harvest its grapes before the autumn rains came and ruined the crop.

Since the working day occupied some twelve hours from sunrise to sunset, the landowner went *early* to the marketplace, where he could expect day laborers to be looking for employment. He would hire workers for this day's needs.

2. And when he had agreed with the laborers for a penny a day, he sent them into his vineyard.

The agreement seems to have involved some negotiation, and assumed the force of a binding contract. The *penny* is an old English translation indicating a *denarius*—a Roman silver coin accepted as the daily wage for a soldier or laborer.

There are, of course, rewards other than money for one who works for God and men. One is the deep satisfaction of being useful. For the Christian, there is joy in serving Jesus!

LOOKING FOR WORKERS

In studying the Parable of the Vineyard Workers, our attention usually centers on the wages the landowner paid to the laborers. But let us concentrate for a few moments on the fact that the Master gives out work as well as wages.

Genesis 2:15 says that God put Adam in the Garden of Eden "to work it and take care of it" *(New International Version)*. Man was created to do something, not simply to pass his days idly. The Bible extols the value and dignity of work.

The apostle Paul encouraged the Corinthians to be "always abounding in the work of the Lord, forasmuch as ye know that your labor is not in vain in the Lord" (1 Corinthians 15:58).

How to Say It

DENARIUS. dih-*nair*-ee-us.
PEREA. Peh-*ree*-uh.

To the Ephesians Paul wrote that Christian leaders are "to prepare God's people for works of service, so that the body of Christ may be built up" (Ephesians 4:12, *New International Version*). The New Testament speaks of the work of the gospel, the work of evangelism, the work of preaching, the work of teaching, the work of leading. There is plenty of work to do in the kingdom. No matter when a person comes to Christ, or what abilities that person possesses, there is work that he or she can, and should, do.

Work that one does to make a difference in other people's lives brings satisfaction and joy. Our Lord honors us by allowing us to experience the special joy that comes through sharing in the most important work in the world.

—C. B. Mc.

B. Employing With a Promise (vv. 3-5)

3, 4. And he went out about the third hour, and saw others standing idle in the market place, and said unto them; Go ye also into the vineyard, and whatsoever is right I will give you. And they went their way.

It was about nine o'clock when the landowner, still needing help to harvest his grapes, went looking for more workers. How did the men feel about their idleness? Did they know that other workers had already been hired? Anyway, this time there was no dickering over their wage. Whatever they received would be better than nothing. They showed a meaningful faith in their employer, and acted on it. The *way* they went was the way he directed.

5. Again he went out about the sixth and ninth hour, and did likewise.

Here is reflected the urgency expressed in Jesus' reference to His Father's harvest: "The harvest truly is plenteous, but the laborers are few; pray ye therefore the Lord of the harvest, that he will send forth laborers into his harvest" (Matthew 9:37, 38). So at midday and again in mid-afternoon the lord of this harvest repeated his search for workers, with the same results.

C. Employing the Unemployed (vv. 6, 7)

6. And about the eleventh hour he went out, and found others standing idle, and saith unto them, Why stand ye here all the day idle?

At this point the parable strains the probabilities of human experience to convey the realities of God's kingdom. The landowner would need to be desperate for help to go seeking for workers one hour before quitting time. And the laborers would have to be desperate for work to pursue job-hunting at that hour. One condition would bring them together: the employer's consideration for the laborers' need. And that is characteristic of the kingdom of Heaven.

How, though, would the landowner know that the job-hunters had stood there all the day idle if he had not seen them on his previous visits? Had they rejected his earlier offer, but now thought better of it? Had he begun to wonder if those poor chaps had found any work? There is a note of rebuke in his question. He was looking for workers, and not for drones.

7. They say unto him, Because no man hath hired us. He saith unto them, Go ye also into the vineyard; and whatsoever is right, that shall ye receive.

Who, if anyone, was at fault in the workmen's predicament? Had they been job-hunting seriously all day? Such questions are left unanswered. Anyway, the landowner accepted their explanation and sent them to work. The weight of manuscript evidence leads the newer versions to omit the landowner's promise of fair payment to these workers. From this it would appear that the workers were tired of loafing and would welcome the activity, even without the pay.

II. A Generous Employer
(Matthew 20:8-10)

8. So when even was come, the lord of the vineyard saith unto his steward, Call the laborers, and give them their hire, beginning from the last unto the first.

Deuteronomy 24:14, 15 directs, "Thou shalt not oppress a hired servant that is poor and needy . . . at his day thou shalt give him his hire, neither shall the sun go down upon it; for he is poor, and setteth his heart upon it." Bread for the evening meal in the laborer's home might be bought with that day's wages. The steward perhaps had acted as foreman in the field; now he became the paymaster.

The last unto the first. For purposes of the parable, the all-day workers had to know how much the one-hour workers were paid.

9. And when they came that were hired about the eleventh hour, they received every man a penny.

We can only imagine the feelings of these men. They had received no assurance of payment, and had worked for only an hour, yet they received a full day's wage! We should not expect them to be quiet about it.

What could have been the employer's motives in directing such generosity? He must have been thinking more of the workers' need than he was of his own gain. If reward was involved, it was reward for their faith and willingness to work without assurance of payment, rather than for what they were able to accomplish. Romans 4:4, 5 shows the similarity of this situation and the grace of God regarding our salvation: "Now when a man works, his wages are not credited to him as a gift, but as an obligation. However, to the man who does not work but trusts God who justifies the wicked, his faith is credited as righteousness" *(New International Version)*. So the last are *first*, and the *first*, last. But don't wait for an eleventh-hour call that may not come.

10. But when the first came, they supposed that they should have received more; and they likewise received every man a penny.

What about the workers who were called at the third, sixth, and ninth hours of the day? The purpose of the parable was served by considering the payment given to the one-hour workers and the all-day laborers. That purpose would have been clouded by noting that the half-day workers could compare their per-hour payment with those ahead of them in the line.

They supposed. The supposition of those who worked all day was based on comparisons that would come out to their advantage. Some of their neighbors had received a day's wage for an hour's work; at that rate, they may have reasoned, they should receive two weeks' wage for their day's work! Forgotten was the commitment they had negotiated in the morning.

III. A Just Employer
(Matthew 20:11-16)

A. Presumptuous Complaint (vv. 11, 12)

11, 12. And when they had received it, they murmured against the goodman of the house, saying, These last have wrought but one hour, and thou hast made them equal unto us, which have borne the burden and heat of the day.

The workers' complaint was brought against the owner who had directed the manner of payment. Their objection was centered not in what the landlord had done *to them*, but in what he had done *for someone else*. They were saying, "These who have done so little to earn it have been made equal to us who have done so much. We worked not only all day, but in the blistering heat of noon, while they enjoyed the relative cool of late afternoon."

What was the offensive quality? Why, the amount of money paid to those who had worked only one hour, of course. No factor other than money seemed worthy of consideration by these all-day workers. That was made rather plain in the morning's bargaining for a contract. Thoughts about the satisfaction of being useful, or gratefully participating in God's provision, had no place in their thinking.

You made them equal to us who are really superior! So complained the Pharisees when Jesus spent time with sinners. So cries the athlete on learning that another has been given an equally favorable contract. So wails the church worker who finds another recognized for unimpressive service. The elder brother in Jesus' Parable of the Prodigal Son utters this same complaint.

Human nature does not take kindly to equal treatment for lesser personages, but that is the way of God's kingdom.

NEWCOMERS

When Israel entered Canaan, the people were instructed to drive out the idol-worshiping peoples who inhabited the land, to have no dealings with them. Through the centuries, the Jews maintained separateness from the people of other nations, to greater or lesser degrees. By the first century A.D., the separation was quite distinct.

When the gospel was first preached to Gentiles, some Jewish Christians had difficulty accepting them. This was in spite of the fact that the gospel plainly declares that all persons, whether Jews under the law or Gentiles outside the law, are in need of God's grace, His mercy, His forgiveness, which no one merits.

The apostles and elders of the Jerusalem church met to consider this issue. The discussion boiled down to this: "Are we going to let those people into our church?" Their Holy Spirit-inspired answer was, "Yes, we are."

Like the workers in the parable, some members of a church may feel resentment toward new converts to the Lord's kingdom. If your church is seeing the addition of "strangers" or "newcomers," thank God that lost people are coming to know Christ, and rejoice that the Lord's work force is being strengthened.

—C. B. Mc.

B. Promises Are Kept (vv. 13, 14)

13. But he answered one of them, and said, Friend, I do thee no wrong: didst not thou agree with me for a penny?

The *one* addressed may have been the spokesman for the group, or simply the most persistent complainer. The singular and personal response, however, applied equally to each one.

Friend translates the Greek word for comrade. Jesus used this word when He addressed Judas

visual 3

in Gethsemane (Matthew 26:50). It is a term of indifference, not a term of affection.

I do thee no wrong. "I am not being unfair to you," the landowner stated. The bargainers had established their price, and that price was paid. They had no right to complain. The landowner had not reduced his payment to them in order to overpay the workers who came later.

14. Take that thine is, and go thy way: I will give unto this last, even as unto thee.

The interview was ended, and the plaintiff was dismissed. He should take his money and go. Let him make the most of it. Even a denarius or a dollar is more or less valuable, depending on the way it is used. So also even God's blessings are enhanced or reduced by the way they are received and used. We are reminded of the parables of the pounds and of the talents with their indication of rewards based on levels of faithful performance (Luke 19:11-27; Matthew 25:14-30). Even in today's parable there is nothing to encourage faithlessness or delay in response to the Lord's invitation. Each worker went to work when he was summoned.

Final and undebatable was the landowner's *I will*. For his own sufficient reasons he would give to the one-hour worker the same as he gave to the laborer first employed. He did not expect the all-day worker to agree or even understand.

Folk who insist on justice will receive justice, and no more. They are slow to appreciate mercy, generosity, or grace, all of which seem to them like injustice. It is hard for them to see that any of us are blessed, not because we are good, but because the Lord is good.

C. Priorities Are Established
(vv. 15, 16)

15. Is it not lawful for me to do what I will with mine own? Is thine eye evil, because I am good?

Two questions, answered automatically in their context, are addressed first to the grumbling day laborers, then to the apostles, to the

Jewish faultfinders, and to Jesus' total audience, then and now.

Human organizations and secular governments have come increasingly to challenge the common law that recognizes an owner's right to do as he wishes with his property. Regulations and restrictions of various kinds now apply. But Jesus spoke in a simpler time of the more natural application of common law. More importantly, He was teaching about the kingdom of heaven and God's right to rule in it. Those who believe in God as Jesus revealed Him still acknowledge His total authority there, even in matters they cannot understand. They will say with the patriarch Job, "Though he slay me, yet will I trust in him" (Job 13:15).

An *evil eye*, or hostile glare, often indicated a spirit of envy or enmity. So the second of the two questions may be rendered, "Are you envious because I am generous?" or "Do you hate your neighbors because I show compassion to them?"

The focus here is on God's right to dispense grace and salvation on His own terms. Those terms are clearly set forth to be accepted or rejected by any and every person. God never gives less than He has promised. Sometimes He gives infinitely more than anyone has a right to expect.

16. So the last shall be first, and the first last: for many be called, but few chosen.

Jesus had said this previously to His disciples in the conversation that led to the Parable of the Vineyard Workers (Matthew 19:30); the principle appears again as the conclusion to which the parable led. The *last* and *first* might be people, with the greatest being the ones who have been servants of all. The *last* and *first* could be in items of importance, with small-coin offerings being more significant than large gifts (see Luke 21:1-4). In all things God will make the final determination, often reversing the order recognized by the world.

Many be called, but few chosen. This suggests that from the multitudes who are called into the Lord's service very few persons will be chosen for special favors or rewards, and that the basis for divine approval may be very different from what we expect.

Conclusion

A. Who Is Number One?

If we find the Parable of the Vineyard Workers a bit difficult to understand and apply, we are in very good company, beginning with the disciples to whom it was first delivered. It warned against presumptions of importance, but shortly afterward the apostles James and John were applying for positions of preference in the coming kingdom (Matthew 20:20-28). The other apostles objected, and Jesus had to remind them all that "whosoever will be chief among you, let him be your servant" (v. 27). Demonstration came in time, as Paul, last to become an apostle, came to labor "more abundantly than they all" (1 Corinthians 15:8-10).

Reversal of the order is seen dramatically in Jesus' parable of the rich man and the beggar Lazarus (Luke 16:19-31). "Wherefore let him that thinketh he standeth take heed lest he fall" (1 Corinthians 10:12).

Let the charter member of a church learn to welcome earnestly the newest convert. Let the one who has labored fruitfully in former years seek out and encourage the one whose fruitful labors lie mostly in the future. And let every Christian build on that number-one priority that will not be reversed, because it comes from God in the first place: "Seek ye first the kingdom of God, and his righteousness; and all these things shall be added unto you" (Matthew 6:33).

B. Prayer for Understanding

Thank You, O God, for the wisdom with which Jesus taught the deep truths of Heaven from the common experiences of earth. Be patient, please, with our slowness to understand, and our greater slowness to put into practice the truths we do understand. May we be faithful workers in Your vineyard. Through Christ our Lord, we pray. Amen.

C. Thought to Remember

"My thoughts are not your thoughts, neither are your ways my ways, saith the Lord" (Isaiah 55:8).

Home Daily Bible Readings

Monday, Mar. 11—God's Concern for the Poor (Deuteronomy 24:10-15)
Tuesday, Mar. 12—A Disappointing Harvest (Isaiah 5:1-7)
Wednesday, Mar. 13—God's Right to Choose (Romans 9:14-24)
Thursday, Mar. 14—A Day Fixed for Judgment (Acts 17:24-34)
Friday, Mar. 15—A Way to Behave (Leviticus 19:9-14)
Saturday, Mar. 16—A Sad Decision (Matthew 19:16-26)
Sunday, Mar. 17—A Change of Mind (Matthew 21:28-32)

Learning by Doing

This page contains an alternate lesson plan emphasizing learning activities. Classes desiring such student involvement will find these suggestions helpful.

Learning Goals

After today's lesson, students will be able to:

1. Tell in their own words the Parable of the Vineyard Workers.

2. Discuss the role of God's grace in the kingdom of Heaven.

3. Give thanks to God for His grace extended to us through His Son Jesus Christ.

Into the Lesson

To begin hand out sheets of paper to your class members. Ask each to write about a time when he or she received something that was not deserved, or did not receive something that was deserved. Following that have each write a definition of *grace*. After a short time, ask for volunteers to share briefly their stories of "unfair" treatment. (Mention that their definitions of grace will be considered later in the session.)

To establish the background for today's Scripture text, point out that Peter expressed interest in receiving what he thought he deserved for being a follower of Jesus. Read Matthew 19:27-30 and explain that Jesus told the Parable of the Vineyard Workers to enlarge on His comment in verse 30.

Into the Word

Read Matthew 20:1-16 aloud to the class. Before the reading, instruct the class to listen for elements of *trust*, *envy*, and *graciousness* in the parable of the workers in the vineyard. After the text has been read, explain that Jesus made the point that there is a vast difference in the way God deals with us in His kingdom and the way people expect to be treated in this life.

Now discuss the elements of the parable that class members listened for: (a) trust (the workers recruited at the third, sixth, ninth, and eleventh hours trusted the man to pay them "whatsoever is right"); (b) envy (the "evil eye" of the all-day workers is the Jewish idiom for envy); and (c) graciousness (the vineyard owner gave all the servants what they needed, a full day's wage, though many had not worked for it).

Remind the class that Peter desired to receive what he deserved (Matthew 19:27). Jesus responded by teaching that God, through His grace, gives us much more.

Ask for volunteers to share their definitions of grace written earlier. Move them beyond the cliche of "unmerited favor." Help them to see that God gives us what we need, rather than what we deserve. God's grace is seen most plainly in the death of His Son. We were lost in sin, unable to save ourselves. God knew our need and sent His Son to die for us, even though we did not deserve such love (see Romans 5:8; Ephesians 2:1-10).

Give the class members copies of the true/false quiz below (minus the answers):

1. In the kingdom of God, one's rewards must be earned. *False.*

2. The benefit of being in God's kingdom is the same for all—eternal life. *True.*

3. While salvation is a free gift from God, we may expect Him to reward us in this life for our Christian service. *False* (the problem word is *expect*).

4. The wisdom of God seems like foolishness to men. *True* (see 1 Corinthians 1:18-29).

Ask the class members to respond as a group, raising their hands to indicate whether they think each statement is true or false. Encourage a brief discussion of each as time allows. The major point is that rewards are not earned in the kingdom of Heaven. We deserve eternal punishment for our sin; but by His grace God offers us eternal life instead. When we begin to expect a "bonus" for our work as Christians, we lose sight of God's grace.

Into Life

Have your class divide into groups of four or five students each and discuss the following questions: "What would life be like if always we were given what we deserved? Would we be content? What else might we desire?"

After about seven minutes, ask someone from each group to summarize the group's conclusions. Emphasize the fact that God does not promise us health, wealth, and quick fixes to the problems we face in this life. Life is not always fair, but God graciously gives us everything we need, no matter when, how, or where we enter His kingdom. And in the end, those who accept His Son as their Savior receive eternal life.

Next, have each class member write a response to this question: "What adjustments do I need to make in my thinking to more fully appreciate God's grace?" After a few minutes, conclude the session with prayer.

Let's Talk It Over

The questions on this page are designed to encourage review of the lesson Scriptures and to promote discussion of the lesson by the class. The answers provided are only discussion starters. Let your class talk it over from there.

1. Should people derive their personal sense of worth from the work they do? Why, or why not?

From a biblical standpoint our sense of worth should come from realizing that we are created in the image of God (Genesis 1:27) and that God loves us so much that He gave His Son to be our Savior (John 3:16). It seems true, however, that for a great number of people, how they feel about themselves is closely related to what they do for a living. Some social observers, noting the segment of our society that relies on public welfare, advocate the abolishing of this connection between work and self-worth. But, the Bible speaks approvingly of honest labor, and it teaches that every person who is capable should work to contribute to the betterment of his family and society (see Proverbs 10:4; 12:11; 22:29; Ephesians 4:28; 1 Timothy 5:8). Of course, the Bible recognizes that some people will be unable to do adequate work and will require benevolent assistance.

2. When we read the parable of the workers in the vineyard, we may find ourselves sympathizing with the day-long workers. Why is this?

From childhood we learn to voice the complaint, "That's not fair!" when we feel that rewards or punishments have been disproportionately allotted to us. Also from childhood we learn that life is not always fair, and it is not helpful to lament over the unfairness. Some may accuse God of unfairness, because He distributes different blessings, talents, or rewards, to each of us. But we are assured by the Bible that God does extend to each of us the same offer of salvation and the same invitation to eternal life in Heaven. So while we may feel some identification with the day-long workers in their complaint, it is a sign of spiritual maturity when we can also acknowledge that God is just and wise, that His wisdom and His ways are far above us (Isaiah 55:8; Romans 11:33-36), and that we must humbly submit to His arrangements as far as blessings and rewards are concerned.

3. The lesson writer points out that "God never gives less than He has promised. Sometimes He gives more than anyone has a right to expect." Why is this a truth we should ponder?

If we are inclined to feel that God has treated us unfairly in some matter, it is well to consider how He has been more than fair with us in other ways. Concerning salvation, for example, had God merely been fair or just with us, we sinners would have no hope of eternal life. But God has gone beyond fairness—He has extended His grace to us through the death and resurrection of Jesus Christ. Regarding life's physical necessities, most persons have abundantly more than the bare minimum. God has provided a variety of nourishing foods; fabrics for clothing that keep us warm, dry, and comfortable; and homes filled with various comforts and labor-saving devices. Truly God "is able to do exceeding abundantly above all that we ask or think" (Ephesians 3:20).

4. There is quite an emphasis in our society on being "number one." How can we who are Christians avoid being caught up in this pursuit of preeminence?

In sports, in politics, in the business world, and elsewhere, the goal of being "number one" frequently fosters excessive competitiveness, slander and name-calling, and bending of the rules. Obviously, these are practices in which Christians are not to participate. However, this ultracompetitive mind-set sometimes shows up in the church and produces friction and conflict. Colossians 1:18 speaks of the greatness of Christ and expresses the goal "that in all things he might have the preeminence." We need to program our minds with this goal. Perhaps as a counterpart to what the crowds often do to support their favorite athletic team we should lift our index fingers Heavenward and cry out, "Christ is number one! Christ is number one!"

5. What are some dangers that are inherent in the habit of envying the prosperity of others?

This habit may lead us to minimize our own blessings and to lose the spirit of gratitude and praise to God for what we possess. If we persist in the habit of envy, we may fall into the even more dangerous habits of covetousness and lust and the sinful acts that issue from them. And, most frighteningly, it may lead us to the point of attributing evil to God for failing to bring us a similar level of prosperity.

Parable of the Three Servants

DEVOTIONAL READING: Matthew 25:1-13.

LESSON SCRIPTURE: Matthew 25:14-30.

PRINTED TEXT: Matthew 25:14-30.

Matthew 25:14-30

14 For the kingdom of heaven is as a man traveling into a far country, who called his own servants, and delivered unto them his goods.

15 And unto one he gave five talents, to another two, and to another one; to every man according to his several ability; and straightway took his journey.

16 Then he that had received the five talents went and traded with the same, and made them other five talents.

17 And likewise he that had received two, he also gained other two.

18 But he that had received one went and digged in the earth, and hid his lord's money.

19 After a long time the lord of those servants cometh, and reckoneth with them.

20 And so he that had received five talents came and brought other five talents, saying, Lord, thou deliveredst unto me five talents: behold, I have gained beside them five talents more.

21 His lord said unto him, Well done, thou good and faithful servant: thou hast been faithful over a few things, I will make thee ruler over many things: enter thou into the joy of thy lord.

22 He also that had received two talents came and said, Lord, thou deliveredst unto me two talents: behold, I have gained two other talents beside them.

23 His lord said unto him, Well done, good and faithful servant; thou hast been faithful over a few things, I will make thee ruler over many things: enter thou into the joy of thy lord.

24 Then he which had received the one talent came and said, Lord, I knew thee that thou art a hard man, reaping where thou hast not sown, and gathering where thou hast not strewed:

25 And I was afraid, and went and hid thy talent in the earth: lo, there thou hast that is thine.

26 His lord answered and said unto him, Thou wicked and slothful servant, thou knewest that I reap where I sowed not, and gather where I have not strewed:

27 Thou oughtest therefore to have put my money to the exchangers, and then at my coming I should have received mine own with usury.

28 Take therefore the talent from him, and give it unto him which hath ten talents.

29 For unto every one that hath shall be given, and he shall have abundance: but from him that hath not shall be taken away even that which he hath.

30 And cast ye the unprofitable servant into outer darkness: there shall be weeping and gnashing of teeth.

GOLDEN TEXT: Unto every one that hath shall be given, and he shall have abundance: but from him that hath not shall be taken away even that which he hath.—Matthew 25:29.

Teachings of Jesus
Unit 1. Teachings About the Kingdom of Heaven
(Lessons 1-5)

Lesson Aims

This study should prepare the student to:

1. Summarize the parable.

2. Apply the parable to our responsibilities and to Jesus' return in judgment.

3. Identify some God-given asset that he or she will put to work for the kingdom of Heaven.

Lesson Outline

INTRODUCTION
    A. Weighty Matters
    B. Lesson Background
I. SERVANTS RECEIVE AND RESPOND (Matthew 25:14-18)
    A. Assignments According to Ability (vv. 14, 15)
    B. Activities and Results (vv. 16, 17)
       Something to Stake Your Life On
    C. Inactivity (v. 18)
II. SERVANTS REPORT AND ARE JUDGED (Matthew 25:19-27)
    A. Return and Reckoning (v. 19)
    B. Praise and Promotion (vv. 20-23)
    C. Excuse Rejected (vv. 24-27)
       Reproduce or Die
III. SERVANTS REASSIGNED (Matthew 25:28-30)
    A. Reassignment by Results (vv. 28, 29)
    B. Rejection and Remorse (v. 30)
CONCLUSION
    A. What Did I Do Wrong?
    B. Faithful or Fearful
    C. A Servant's Prayer
    D. Thought to Remember

Visual 4 highlights the verse from Matthew 25:21 concerning the Christian's reward. It is shown on page 259.

Introduction

A. Weighty Matters

A *talent* seems to have been first a unit of weight, applied principally to precious metals. In New Testament times a talent of silver was worth approximately six thousand denarii. Since a denarius was considered a fair day's wage, it would take a working man in those days almost twenty years to earn a full talent!

The other significance of *talent* appears in the parable with the distribution of moneys to responsible servants, each according to his *ability* (v. 15). The master considered each man's intelligence, energy, aptitude, and character. The most capable servant was trusted with the most money. He was *talented* in both ways.

Our lesson title emphasizes persons. The money or the ability is but the tool with which the person does his work in relation to his opportunities. On that he will be judged.

B. Lesson Background

Shortly after Jesus' final ministry in Perea (last week's parable was given during that time) He entered Jerusalem, welcomed by a throng present for the Passover. For two days He taught in the temple, opposed but not attacked by the Jewish leaders. On the afternoon of the second day He went with His disciples to the Mount of Olives (Matthew 24:3), where He taught them many things in preparation for His death and resurrection. He emphasized the responsibilities that would be theirs after His departure.

Then came three great teachings recorded in Matthew 25, all dealing with the judgment at His coming again. The parable of ten bridesmaids (vv. 1-13) taught the need for watchfulness in preparation for His arrival. The parable of three servants (vv. 14-30) urged diligence in working for Him until He comes. In vivid description of judgment itself (vv. 31-46), Jesus showed that caring for those He loves is a requisite of loving service to Him. The parables develop the warning: "Watch therefore; for ye know neither the day nor the hour wherein the Son of man cometh" (Matthew 25:13).

I. Servants Receive and Respond (Matthew 25:14-18)

The parable opens with the introduction of *persons* who bring out the relationship between King and citizens in the kingdom of Heaven.

A. Assignments According to Ability (vv. 14, 15)

14. For the kingdom of heaven is as a man traveling into a far country, who called his own servants, and delivered unto them his goods.

For. This word relates to the warning that Christ's coming in judgment will be sudden and unannounced (v. 13). The phrase *the kingdom of heaven* is not in the Greek manuscripts, but the idea is carried from verse 1.

Travel to distant places was common, but a long journey took a long time. A wealthy man would need to arrange for his business interests

visual 4

to be carried on during his absence (compare Matthew 21:33-41). This man's possessions included much money, which he wanted to be productive. So he entrusted it to certain of his servants to manage in his absence. This was a customary practice in ancient times. Trusted servants were put in positions of responsibility where they would have control over their master's money to use for their master's profit.

Jesus' teaching here is plain. Soon He was to be separated from His disciples, and He needed to correct a notion then current that "the kingdom of God should immediately appear" (Luke 19:11). In the Lord's absence, His business on earth would claim the attention of His servants. Christ has honored His people, then and now, with a great trust, and that should be motivation enough for energetic dedication to the task He has given.

15. And unto one he gave five talents, to another two, and to another one; to every man according to his several ability; and straightway took his journey.

The master's acquaintance with his servants enabled him to know each one's capacity to carry out an assignment. The one with superior ability was given enough to keep him busy, and the less capable one was not loaded down with an impossible task. These principles are appropriate to any administrator anywhere: can, and will, this candidate do this job as it should be done?

Three servants are enough to serve Jesus' purposes in the parable. They provide samples for the limitless variety of persons involved in the Lord's business between His giving of the Great Commission (Matthew 28:18-20) and His coming in glory to judge those to whom He gave it.

B. Activities and Results (vv. 16, 17)

16, 17. Then he that had received the five talents went and traded with the same, and made them other five talents. And likewise he that had received two, he also gained other two.

Two of the three servants went to work immediately doing business with the money entrusted to them. Both exercised the same faithfulness in using what was given, and both achieved the same rate of return. Each servant had doubled his master's investment by the time he returned.

How shall we apply the faithful servants' example to our work in serving our Lord in Heaven? We have been entrusted with immeasurable gifts of the gospel and the blessing of our own abilities. Applied faithfully, both of these treasures will increase. Any skill will become greater with exercise, and gospel power will grow with application. Neglected, though, any of these gifts will stagnate or shrink. The time to go into business for the Lord is when we receive the treasure, and the time to close shop is when He comes to call us home.

SOMETHING TO STAKE YOUR LIFE ON

Douglas MacArthur served as a brigadier general in World War I. In October, 1918, the allied forces faced the German stronghold along the Hindenberg Line in France. MacArthur, who commanded the 42nd Brigade, was chosen to advance against the heights of the Hindenberg Line and take a fortified knoll, the Cote-de-Chatillon. This was the toughest link in the enemy's position, the one part the Germans could not yield and still win the war.

On October 12, MacArthur met with his commander, General Summerall, to receive his orders. So crucial was this assignment that Summerall closed by telling MacArthur, "Give me Chatillon, or a list of five thousand casualties."

MacArthur replied, "If this brigade does not capture Chatillon, you can publish a casualty list of the entire brigade with the brigade commander's name at the top."

MacArthur took Chatillon because he was willing to stake his life on his success in carrying out his orders. The successful servants in the parable pleased their master because they were willing to assume some risk for his sake.

Are you willing to enter into the Lord's work wholeheartedly, to take risks, in order to carry out the responsibility He has entrusted to you?

—C. B. Mc.

C. Inactivity (v. 18)

18. But he that had received one went and digged in the earth, and hid his lord's money.

The burying of treasure in the ground was a common means of safe-keeping in ancient times (compare Matthew 13:44). A clay jar would be appropriate for underground storage.

This man committed no crime. He did not use the money as his own or treat it carelessly. He simply took the easiest way of getting out of his responsibility. He is represented in our society, including the church, by those who don't want anyone to know that they can render necessary service. It's easier that way, especially if they can convince themselves and others that they have so little ability that there is no use exercising it.

II. Servants Report and Are Judged (Matthew 25:19-27)

The parable makes its point in the fact that each servant gives his own account of what he did, and is judged according to his own words.

A. Return and Reckoning (v. 19)

19. After a long time the lord of those servants cometh, and reckoneth with them.

The *long time* of the master's absence allows for the accomplishment of the two faithful servants, and emphasizes the other servant's long avoidance of responsibility. It also warned the earliest Christians against expecting an immediate return of Jesus to the earth.

The present tense of *cometh* and *reckoneth*, on the other hand, emphasizes the certainty of the Lord's coming in judgment. As the master's last item of business before his departure was the assignment of responsibility to his servants, so his first item of business at his return was to learn how they had carried out that assignment.

B. Praise and Promotion (vv. 20-23)

20. And so he that had received five talents came and brought other five talents, saying, Lord, thou deliveredst unto me five talents: behold, I have gained beside them five talents more.

There is a clear note of joy in the servant's report. With enthusiasm he welcomed his master's return. He recognized that his opportunity had come from his lord; now his accounts were ready for inspection. He rejoiced in giving the report. Revelation 22:20 reflects the same kind of joy in the saints' anticipation of the Lord's coming in glory: "Even so, come, Lord Jesus."

21. His lord said unto him, Well done, thou good and faithful servant: thou hast been faithful over a few things, I will make thee ruler over many things: enter thou into the joy of thy lord.

The master's approval was related specifically to the man's fulfillment of his given task. He had served well in doing what was asked of him. Other elements of his character might be judged differently, but that is not germane to the parable.

Few things . . . many things. We might hesitate to call five talents *a few things*, but the master's total estate obviously was a great deal more. If the servant expected a long vacation as reward for his efforts, he was in for a surprise. Success at one level brought opportunity at high levels. Good service brought larger assignments to serve. One had better enjoy serving that kind of master, or that kind of reward is no reward at all!

The joy of thy lord. Come and share your lord's happiness. Having participated in the success of the lord's business, the servant would participate with his master in the enjoyment of its benefits.

As a foreshadowing of final judgment, this surely indicates disappointment for those persons who love self-indulgence and only occasionally nod toward piety in the expectation of limitless self-indulgence in Heaven. But for those who fervently love God and thoroughly enjoy serving Him, the prospect of limitlessly expanding areas of service is marvelous.

22, 23. He also that had received two talents came and said, Lord, thou deliveredst unto me two talents: behold, I have gained two other talents beside them. His lord said unto him, Well done, good and faithful servant; thou hast been faithful over a few things, I will make thee ruler over many things: enter thou into the joy of thy lord.

The second servant was equal to the first in faithfulness, performance, commendation, and reward. Having two talents to begin with, he was not expected to produce ten. "He that is faithful in that which is least is faithful also in much" (Luke 16:10). In terms of a homely little rhyme,

> It's not what you'd do with a million,
> If a million should e'er be your lot;
> It's what you're doing right now
> With the dollar and dime that you've got.

The same principle applies to ability/talents. So says a meaningful gospel song:

> Our talents may be few;
> These may be small,
> But unto Him is due
> Our best, our all!

C. Excuse Rejected (vv. 24-27)

24. Then he which had received the one talent came and said, Lord, I knew thee that thou art a hard man, reaping where thou hast not sown, and gathering where thou hast not strewed.

The one-talent man knew he was in trouble. He resorted to an all-too-human ploy—blaming someone else. It began with Adam and Eve (Genesis 3:11-13). Like Adam (v. 12), this man pointed to his judge.

I knew thee. He didn't know his master at all, but saw in him a reflection of his own self-serving traits (compare Romans 2:1). So he called his lord cruel and unreasonable, given to using other people to his own advantage. Assuming that he could expect no mercy if anything went wrong with the investment entrusted to him, the man decided to play it safe and went out and buried the treasure.

Reaping . . . sown . . . gathering . . . strewed. References to the grain harvest depict a person living from others' efforts, reaping the harvest that others have labored to produce, and gathering from the threshing floor the grain that others have threshed out. To the complainer, his master was a thieving, heartless capitalist.

Almost any of us can become expert in discovering scapegoats on whom we can blame our failures. What did this servant gain by blaming his master? And likewise what can we gain from blaming—outwardly or inwardly—our failures on God?

25. And I was afraid, and went and hid thy talent in the earth: lo, there thou hast that is thine.

Was it fear of punishment if he lost some of his master's money that prevented any productive effort by this servant, or was it fear of doing the wrong thing that kept him from doing anything at all? To prevent such paralyzing fears, the apostle Paul heralded, "God hath not given us the spirit of fear; but of power, and of love, and of a sound mind" (2 Timothy 1:7). John adds, "There is no fear in love; but perfect love casteth out fear: because fear hath torment" (1 John 4:18).

There thou hast that is thine. "Here is your money." The third servant could not be accused of any crime. He returned his lord's money, promptly and intact. But he had failed to carry out his assignment as a steward.

26, 27. His lord answered and said unto him, Thou wicked and slothful servant, thou knewest that I reap where I sowed not, and gather where I have not strewed: thou oughtest therefore to have put my money to the exchangers, and then at my coming I should have received mine own with usury.

Wicked and *slothful* contrast directly with the *good* and *faithful* of verses 21 and 23. The man's wickedness consisted in his not exercising the positive goodness found in the others. His slothful laziness contrasted with the active faithfulness seen in them.

Thou knewest. This does not necessarily admit that the man was right in what he said about the master. But if the description had been accurate, that very fact should have impelled the servant to do all he could to placate that kind of a master. So he stood condemned by his own words.

Put my money to the exchangers, or on deposit with bankers. If the man himself could not do business profitably in the lord's interest, he should at least get help from those who could and would do so. (If you can't go to others with the gospel, you can help send someone who will.)

Usury is interest paid for the use of money. It is not necessarily excessive, though now the word usually indicates an illegal rate of interest. Any return would have been better than the inaction that thwarted the master's purpose in distributing his funds.

REPRODUCE OR DIE

Reproduction is one of the essential functions of every organism. Every living thing must reproduce or cease to exist. The most prolific single-cell animals can reproduce themselves in as little as three hours. In a single day, a lone protozoan can become a great-great-great-great-great-grandparent with 510 descendants. Potatoes reproduce by sprouts that come from the plant's "eyes." The leaves of ferns release spores that are spread by the wind to germinate new plants.

The most prolific warm-blooded animal is the New Zealand white rabbit, which produces five to six litters each year with an average of eight to twelve baby rabbits per litter. From protozoa to the rabbits, the means vary, but the object is the same: reproduce or die.

The church must reproduce or it too will die. The seed of the gospel must be scattered abroad in the hope that it will find lodging in receptive hearts. Only then will spiritual birth occur; only then will there be new believers added to the church.

The Lord has entrusted us with the task of sowing the gospel seed throughout the world. When He returns, will He find the increase He desires?   —C. B. Mc.

III. Servants Reassigned (Matthew 25:28-30)

At this point the master's judgment turns from commendation or condemnation to the servants, and becomes instruction to other helpers.

How to Say It

PEREA. Peh-*ree*-uh.
TALANTON (Greek). *tal*-ahn-tahn.

A. Reassignment by Results (vv. 28, 29)

28, 29. Take therefore the talent from him, and give it unto him which hath ten talents. For unto every one that hath shall be given, and he shall have abundance: but from him that hath not shall be taken away even that which he hath.

The non-serving servant had shown himself unworthy of trust. He had blown his opportunity. Now the money formerly assigned to him would be removed and put in the hands of the one who had shown himself most capable and trustworthy. In this action there appears for the first time a difference in the treatment accorded the two faithfully active servants.

The principle of removing from the "have-nots" and adding to the supply of the "haves" is an inescapable fact of life. It applies alike to material substance and to physical, mental, and spiritual growth. Matthew 13:12 applies it to the hearers of Jesus' parables—those who understood would gain in knowledge, and those who lacked understanding would go away empty. Learning becomes progressively easy as one learns, and spiritual—or even physical—development accelerates with advancement. This does not excuse prosperous Christians from being generous to those in need (James 1:27; 1 John 3:17), materially or spiritually. That is an important part of their own development!

B. Rejection and Remorse (v. 30)

30. And cast ye the unprofitable servant into outer darkness: there shall be weeping and gnashing of teeth.

The same attendants who took the one talent from the lazy servant and gave it to the industrious one were instructed to evict the wretch from the master's presence, where alone in the darkness he could weep and wail over the stupidity that cost him his great opportunity forever.

This agrees with Jesus' other teachings concerning judgment, in which angels are shown to be attendants in the heavenly court. Angels are to accompany the Lord at His coming in glory (Matthew 16:27; 24:30, 31; 25:31), and angels are to carry out the Lord's judgments (Matthew 13:39-42). The hopeless state of the condemned —cast out, shut out from God's presence forever in burning darkness—is everywhere the same.

Conclusion

A. What Did I Do Wrong?

Did the unprofitable servant of Jesus' parable complain, "What did I do wrong?" or "Don't blame me; I didn't do anything." That, of course, is just what was wrong with what he did. He did nothing with what his master had given him to use. He fell under the judgment of James 4:17: "To him that knoweth to do good, and doeth it not, to him it is sin."

This servant knew the purpose for which his talent was bestowed, and he thwarted that purpose. Do we not similarly thwart the purposes of God's goodness when we use His gifts for our own pleasure, complaining that it is just too much for anyone to expect us to spend our time, our money, and our energy for Christ and His church? Where did we get all those good things anyway? And for what purpose?

B. Faithful or Fearful

The faithful servants in our parable were commended; the fearful one was condemned. Faith and fear are not natural companions. Jesus impressed that on His disciples one stormy night on the Sea of Galilee (Mark 4:40). Revelation 21:8 includes the "fearful" in the lake of fire. But to Christians the Lord has promised, "Be thou faithful unto death, and I will give thee a crown of life" (Revelation 2:10).

"Faithful servant . . . enter."

C. A Servant's Prayer

We thank You, our God, for offering us a partnership in Your kingdom, and for providing us with what we need for faithful service. Give us, we pray, a clearer view of our responsibility and a new sense of joy in fulfilling our assignments. In Jesus' name, amen.

D. Thought to Remember

"I must work the works of him that sent me, while it is day: the night cometh, when no man can work" (John 9:4).

Home Daily Bible Readings

Monday, Mar. 18—Greatest Commandments (Matthew 22:34-40)

Tuesday, Mar. 19—Greatness Seen in Serving (Matthew 23:1-12)

Wednesday, Mar. 20—Hypocrisy Condemned (Matthew 23:13-26)

Thursday, Mar. 21—The Pain of Rejection (Matthew 23:29-39)

Friday, Mar. 22—Unpredictable Event (Matthew 24:36-44)

Saturday, Mar. 23—Punishment for Unfaithfulness (Matthew 24:45-51)

Sunday, Mar. 24—Poor Preparation (Matthew 25:1-13)

Learning by Doing

This page contains an alternate lesson plan emphasizing learning activities. Classes desiring such student involvement will find these suggestions helpful.

Learning Goals

This lesson will enable students to:

1. Present a sketch of the Parable of the Three Servants in his or her own words.

2. Explain the parable in relation to our own faithfulness as servants of God.

3. Identify some God-given asset that he or she will put to work for the kingdom of Heaven.

Into the Lesson

In advance of class time, ask four class members to prepare to act out the parable of the three servants recorded in Matthew 25:14-30.

Before the four class members act out the parable, explain that a *talent* was a unit of weight in New Testament times by which metal, especially precious metal, was measured. A talent of silver, for example, was equal in value to nearly twenty years' wages of a day laborer. Our use of the word for an ability or skill comes directly from this parable.

Into the Word

Ask the class members to follow along in Matthew 25:14-30 as the four actors present the parable, with you providing needed narration. When the four are finished, lead the class in applause for their talents.

Give each class member a sheet of paper on which you have copied the following five questions (minus the answers shown here), and with space allowed for answers. These questions are included in the student book also. Ask your class members to answer briefly these questions about the parable:

1. In what way is the man's traveling to a distant country and leaving his business in the care of others like the kingdom of Heaven? *(Jesus would soon go to Heaven and entrust the work of the kingdom to His disciples until His second coming.)*

2. On what basis did the master give his servants differing amounts of money? *(The distribution was based on their abilities. See verse 15.)*

3. In what ways did the "good and faithful" servants qualify for the master's commendation? *(Apparently they went to work immediately, using what they were given. They did what was asked of them. The implication is that they continued to work till their master returned. They were productive.)*

4. What do you think might have been the true motive of the "wicked and slothful" servant? *(Perhaps he wanted to avoid responsibility. He was more concerned about his own comfort and convenience than he was about pleasing his master.)*

5. In what ways are Christians now in the role of the servants? *(We have God-given talents and the priceless gospel entrusted to us while Jesus is away. We are to be productive in evangelism and spiritual growth until He returns.)*

Encourage the class members to share their responses to questions one through four. Discuss them briefly. Emphasize the fact that faithfulness and productivity are equated.

Question five provides the transition to life application. Discuss their responses at this time.

Into Life

Divide the class into groups of three or four students each, who know each other fairly well. Each person in the group takes his or her turn being on the "hot seat," as the other members of the group take turns saying what they think are the talents, skills, and special qualities of the person on the "hot seat." Make it clear that the person on the "hot seat" may not talk, make faces, or in any way interrupt the others while they are sharing. When the first person has received all the input from the others, the "hot seat" rotates to the next person, and the process repeats itself. Do this until all the members in the group have been on the "hot seat."

Take care to involve visitors and new members, even allowing them to talk about themselves if no one else knows them. Circulate among the groups, giving additional instructions and encouragement as necessary. This has been an affirming and enlightening exercise for those who have experienced it. Allot five to ten minutes for this activity.

When all the groups have finished, ask each person to identify one of his talents that he would like to use to become more productive in ministry for Jesus. Ask for volunteers to share their responses. Then ask each person to consider what the first step would be for him or her to do so. Again, seek volunteer responses.

Ask the students to assemble in their groups again and pray for the Lord's guidance as they use their talents for Him.

Let's Talk It Over

The questions on this page are designed to encourage review of the lesson Scriptures and to promote discussion of the lesson by the class. The answers provided are only discussion starters. Let your class talk it over from there.

1. Why should a person not be hasty to insist that he or she does not possess any specific talents?

Talents can lie hidden within any individual's personality. A talent needs only to be recognized and developed to become a tool for the cause of Christ. In many churches there are people who can testify that at one time they were convinced they could never stand before an assembly of worshipers and speak, but now they do it; there are others who once would have thought it impossible that they could enter a near-stranger's home and share the gospel with that person, but now they do it; there are still others who, in the past, would have denied having any leadership ability, but now they lead in the church. It can be said that assessing our talents is not merely determining what we are presently capable of doing, but envisioning what we could become capable of doing. Much prayer and the encouragement of fellow Christians may be needed to help us do this.

2. The servants who received five talents and two talents seem to have taken immediate action to put their master's money to work. What does this suggest about us and our talents?

How much work in the church is left undone as a result of procrastination? We may say that someday we are going to serve as a deacon or sing in the choir or volunteer to help with youth programs. While "someday" tarries, however, these areas of service may suffer because we are not already there investing our talents. Putting our talents to work ties in with the overall subject of obedience to God. God expects prompt obedience, and we may bring ourselves trouble if we fail to give it to Him.

3. One may rightly find motivation for service to Christ in the anticipation of hearing the Master's words, "Well done, thou good and faithful servant." Why is this so?

To be commended for our work is always a sweet experience. While we do not serve in the church simply to receive the commendation of others, we must admit that it is gratifying when a fellow member praises us for some service we have rendered. But to be commended by our heavenly Father, by the Creator of the universe

—what an awesome and wonderful prospect that is! That may rightly motivate us to do our work prayerfully, thoroughly, and joyously, anticipating that moment when we will hear those glorious words of approval.

4. Why is it important to note that Heaven will be a place of service, and not just a place of ease and self-indulgence?

We sympathize with those hard-working people who envision Heaven as a place providing an extended rest, but it will be more than that. We understand why individuals who have suffered through severe conflict may view Heaven as the haven of perfect peace, but it will be more than that. Revelation 22:3 informs us that "the throne of God and of the Lamb shall be in it; and his servants shall serve him." We will be serving in Heaven, not merely resting and not merely renewing fellowship with family and friends. Exactly what that service involves is not detailed, but we need now to prepare ourselves for it. While we are still on earth, we have the opportunity to learn to find our richest joy and delight in serving God and our fellow human beings. We can enhance our fellowship with Jesus even now by sharing His purpose while He was on earth: "not to be ministered unto, but to minister" (Mark 10:45).

5. The parable of the three servants makes it clear that the protest, "I'm afraid," is not an acceptable excuse for avoiding Christian service. How do we deal with the fear that often accompanies the challenge to serve?

What is the reason for our fear? Are we afraid of failure, of embarrassment, of rejection, or of something else? We can deal with it better if we know precisely what it is, and we can also pray more specifically about it. If we fear failure, we must learn to focus on the God who "giveth us the victory through our Lord Jesus Christ" (1 Corinthians 15:57). If we fear embarrassment, we must concentrate on doing our best to "serve the Lord Christ" (Colossians 3:24) and forget about ourselves. Perhaps our prayers will be more effective if we approach the matter positively—instead of asking for fears to be silenced, we can pray for the opposite quality of boldness (note Ephesians 6:18-20).

Parable of the Great Feast

DEVOTIONAL READING: Luke 14:7-14.

LESSON SCRIPTURE: Luke 14:1-24.

PRINTED TEXT: Luke 14:15-24.

Luke 14:15-24

15 And when one of them that sat at meat with him heard these things, he said unto him, Blessed is he that shall eat bread in the kingdom of God.

16 Then said he unto him, A certain man made a great supper, and bade many:

17 And sent his servant at supper time to say to them that were bidden, Come; for all things are now ready.

18 And they all with one consent began to make excuse. The first said unto him, I have bought a piece of ground, and I must needs go and see it: I pray thee have me excused.

19 And another said, I have bought five yoke of oxen, and I go to prove them: I pray thee have me excused.

20 And another said, I have married a wife, and therefore I cannot come.

21 So that servant came, and showed his lord these things. Then the master of the house being angry said to his servant, Go out quickly into the streets and lanes of the city, and bring in hither the poor, and the maimed, and the halt, and the blind.

22 And the servant said, Lord, it is done as thou hast commanded, and yet there is room.

23 And the lord said unto the servant, Go out into the highways and hedges, and compel them to come in, that my house may be filled.

24 For I say unto you, That none of those men which were bidden shall taste of my supper.

GOLDEN TEXT: The lord said unto the servant, Go out into the highways and hedges, and compel them to come in, that my house may be filled.—Luke 14:23.

Lesson Aims

This study should equip the student to:
1. Summarize the parable.
2. Show how this parable relates to the Lord's invitation for us to participate in "the marriage supper of the Lamb" in Heaven (Revelation 19:9).
3. Recognize the importance of God's provision and give it top priority in his or her life.

Lesson Outline

INTRODUCTION
    A. Banquet Time
    B. Lesson Background
  I. WHAT BANQUET? (Luke 14:15)
 II. PREPARATION AND INVITATION (Luke 14:16, 17)
    Celebrate
III. PREFERRING SOMETHING ELSE (Luke 14:18-20)
    A. Fields (v. 18)
    B. Facilities (v. 19)
    C. Family (v. 20)
    "No Excuse, Sir"
IV. PLACES TO BE FILLED (Luke 14:21-23)
    A. By Hungry People Nearby (v. 21)
    B. By Hungry People Farther Away (vv. 22, 23)
 V. PERMANENCE OF CHOICE (Luke 14:24)
CONCLUSION
    A. Please Reply
    B. Prayer of an Invited Guest
    C. Thought to Remember

Use visual 5 of the visuals packet as a humorous way to illustrate today's lesson about excuses. It is shown on page 268.

Introduction

A. Banquet Time

If you were among those brought up in the "clean plate" tradition at home, you will not soon forget your first banquet and learning that you were not required to eat all your vegetables before accepting the dessert. You came to understand that an oversupply of rich food is an expected part of the celebration at weddings, political rallies, fund raisings, and receptions for notable visitors.

Big dinners are not limited to any one time, place, or circumstance. They are perhaps more notable among people whose daily fare is not plentiful, but banquets can be exciting events even among royalty (Esther 5; Daniel 5:1-4; Matthew 22:1-14). So they are mentioned prominently throughout the Bible, from Abraham's hospitality toward heavenly messengers (Genesis 18:1-8) to the "marriage supper of the Lamb" in Heaven itself (Revelation 19:9).

It is not surprising, then, that when God's Son came to dwell among men, He attended feasts in the homes of the well-to-do as well as quiet dinners in the homes of His friends (Luke 10:38-42). Neither is it surprising that He used these occasions as opportunities for teaching.

B. Lesson Background

Two of Jesus' banquet parables are so much alike that they are sometimes thought to be two reports of the same event. Luke 14:15-24 says that a man made a great supper, invited many, and made one servant his agent in notifying the guests, who excused themselves more or less politely and were replaced by others who would accept last-minute summonses to the dinner.

Matthew 22:1-14 says that a king invited many to the marriage celebration for his son and sent notifications through groups of servants, who were treated roughly and contemptuously by those who had been invited; whereupon the king punished the offenders and replaced them at his feast with other guests.

The account in Matthew relates to a time of public conflict in Jerusalem during the final week of Jesus' ministry. Luke's account relates to an earlier and somewhat less stressful occasion. The settings account for the differences in details and nature of the stories. Jesus occasionally set forth the same principles at different times and places.

Chapter 14 of Luke begins with the account of a prominent Pharisee's Sabbath dinner, which Jesus attended, and notes that the Pharisee and others were watching Jesus, apparently with the purpose of finding occasion against Him. Verses 2-6 tell that a man suffering with dropsy appeared in the Pharisee's house, and that Jesus healed him, after first noting the intent of the Pharisees and lawyers to accuse Him of thus violating the Sabbath. Clearly, Jesus had observed the persons around Him as they had been observing Him!

Verses 7-11 record Jesus' good-natured advice to the guests who had crowded to the most honorable seats at the table, noting that they might be embarrassed by being asked to give way to latecomers higher on the guest list.

Verses 12-14 follow with similar advice to the host, that he should make up his guest list from among those who were poor and needy, rather than those who could be expected to reward him with returned favors. If he would do so, the greater reward would come "at the resurrection of the just."

I. What Banquet?
(Luke 14:15)

15. And when one of them that sat at meat with him heard these things, he said unto him, Blessed is he that shall eat bread in the kingdom of God.

The fellow diner obviously was interested in the Lord's reference to rewards in the resurrection. Some Bible students think that this man was expressing approval of Jesus' advice as to the kind of behavior that would please God, rather than what would yield material advantage now. Others think that the speaker was a self-righteous Pharisee who was fully convinced that he would have a favored place at the table in Heaven, where the approved ones would "sit down with Abraham, and Isaac, and Jacob, in the kingdom of heaven" (Matthew 8:11). At least his comment sparked interest in the discussion and provided Jesus a great starting point for His parable. The ones first invited to the feast might not share in it, after all.

II. Preparation and Invitation
(Luke 14:16, 17)

16. Then said he unto him, A certain man made a great supper, and bade many.

Jesus' response was made to the one who spoke up, but clearly it was intended for all.

A certain man. The man, not otherwise identified, obviously possessed great resources and authority. In application, it is God himself, preparing limitless blessing for those who accept His invitation.

Made a great supper. This story was surely appropriate at a dinner party, where the invitation and conduct of guests had already been mentioned. *Made.* Preparation for this feast seems to have been going on for some time and to be continuing. Even so, God had been engaged for centuries in the preparation of men's salvation.

Supper translates a word that signified the principal meal of the day, usually in the evening. This one was to be great in every dimension. Great preparation is the key to the whole parable.

Why, in fact, does one prepare a dinner and invite guests? That could be asked concerning the Pharisee who hosted this dinner. Does he owe invitations to others who have entertained him? Does he wish to impress people? Does he enjoy the company of his guests? Does he want to put them under obligation for future favors? Does he want to feed folk who are hungry, in body, mind, or spirit?

God, our ultimate host, loves us, wants to supply our needs, and desires our company. For hundreds of years, through the patriarchs, the law, and the prophets, He had been issuing His invitation to the Jewish people.

CELEBRATE

People love to celebrate. From ancient times people of every culture and nation have had their festive celebrations, and these celebrations have been accompanied by lavish feasts. The oldest American day of celebration, Thanksgiving, dates from 1621. In that year the Plymouth colonists, rejoicing over the first corn harvest, joined with the neighboring Indians as all brought food and shared their bounty. Now, American families gather every fourth Thursday of November around tables of turkey, dressing, cranberries, and other delectable foods, to enjoy and give thanks for God's bountiful provisions.

From Thanksgiving hymns and turkeys to Fourth of July hot dogs and fireworks, Americans love to celebrate. Of all the things Americans, or people from any nation, could celebrate, salvation in Jesus Christ is the greatest. Perhaps that is why the Lord often referred to the kingdom of Heaven in terms of a banquet. While Christianity involves the death of our sinful selves, being part of God's family is not a perpetual funeral, but a feast.   —C. B. Mc.

17. And sent his servant at supper time to say to them that were bidden, Come; for all things are now ready.

To them that were bidden. It seems that all who were invited accepted the invitation. However, the precise time of the feast had not been set. The summons to "come and get it" awaited until everything was ready. Esther 5:8 and 6:14 reveal a similar pattern.

Why should only one servant be mentioned as bearing the last-minute summons to the guests who were expected to fill the host's great banquet hall? (Compare verses 21-23.) Perhaps one responsible servant was charged with directing many others who must go to the homes of the guests throughout the city.

When we apply the parable to God's long preparation and invitation to His people, and when we learn that He sent His Son in the "fulness of the time" (Galatians 4:4, 5), and when we observe that Jesus took on the "form of a servant" (Philippians 2:7), the mystery tends to disappear. God's one and only Son becomes the sole authoritative voice to say, "Come!" That does not rule out the necessity for many messengers to carry His invitation.

III. Preferring Something Else (Luke 14:18-20)

Up to this point Jesus' parable followed a common course, telling of customs familiar to His hearers. Now the parable moves away from the norm of human experience. Although it is possible, it is rather unlikely that all the guests invited to a feast would find other things more enticing and decide not to come. But this deviation is necessary to add force to the truth Jesus makes concerning the realities of Heaven.

A. Fields (v. 18)

18. And they all with one consent began to make excuse. The first said unto him, I have bought a piece of ground, and I must needs go and see it: I pray thee have me excused.

How great was the feast to which these folk had been invited? And how greatly did they respect the host? Enough, it seems, for them to have accepted the invitation when it was given, but not enough to overcome some new and compelling interests.

Consent does not appear in the original; but as *one*, the many invited guests expressed a similar disposition. Had they all changed their minds about accepting the invitation, so that now they were looking for, or inventing, excuses for getting out of the appointment?

Jesus' hearers may have smiled at the thought of a man's buying real estate without first seeing it. It is not so unusual, though, for even a careful buyer to be fascinated with an important new purchase. And real estate is important! We are reminded of Jesus' earlier reference to a new convert's faith being choked out by the cares of this world, and by the deceitfulness of riches (Matthew 13:22).

The land buyer's apology was at least politely worded: "Please let me be excused." Would his reasoning appear as sound to the host as it did to him?

B. Facilities (v. 19)

19. And another said, I have bought five yoke of oxen, and I go to prove them: I pray thee have me excused.

The humor here is heightened by the fact that there were *five* yoke of oxen, that is, ten draft animals in teams fitted for heavy pulling. And

the man said he was on his way right now to see how well they would work! Can anyone believe that he would have made such a purchase if he had had any serious doubts about the quality of these animals? And if he had bought them, he could have tried them out at another time.

A farmer's fields would be rendered more valuable by the presence of heavy equipment for clearing and plowing the land. That seemed important enough for this invited guest to cancel an evening's company with the generous host.

C. Family (v. 20)

20. And another said, I have married a wife, and therefore I cannot come.

Another. This implies that the pattern of excuses from the guest roster could be extended indefinitely. The ones quoted are representative samples. The blunt, covers-it-all nature of the third man's statement, however, heightens the comic aspect of this dinner time commentary.

Deuteronomy 24:5 cites a bridegroom's exemptions from certain duties in ancient Israel in order to establish the pattern of marital joys, but nothing is said about avoiding festive celebrations with one's friends.

Jesus was talking about God's invitation to the spiritual feast provided through the gift of His only Son, and the invited guests' response to that invitation. And immediately after the parable we find this plain statement: "If any man come to me, and hate not his father, and mother, and wife, and children, and brethren, and sisters, yea, and his own life also, he cannot be my disciple" (Luke 14:26). For the Christian, Christ is more important than kin. First Corinthians 7:29-33 agrees in warning that marriage might come between the believer and service to the Lord.

Just why did the guests go back on their commitment to be present for the feast? They named other interests that seemed more important at the time. The items they named were important, but their real reasons could have been things they would have been ashamed to name. And in every instance they could have come if their desire to do so had been strong enough. Basic to their decision was their attitude toward the host.

visual 5

They respected him enough to accept his first invitation; but not enough to give first place to his wishes. And that is what determined his response to their excuses.

"NO EXCUSE, SIR"

Visitors to the United States Army post at Fort Benning, Georgia, were observing a training exercise involving recruits of the Army's famed airborne troops, the Green Berets. The most striking thing about these young soldiers was their "esprit de corps," their spirit of comradeship, enthusiasm, and devotion to their cause.

The guests watched as a platoon of Green Beret trainees parachuted into a large field, then quickly assembled into fighting formation in front of the grandstand where the guests were seated. It was a blustery day, and the wind caught the parachute of one young private, slamming him hard into the ground on the far end of the field. Though he had suffered a severely sprained ankle, the soldier rose to his feet and attempted to run to his place in the formation. Limping with great effort across the field, he was the last man to take his position. The private obviously was injured; nonetheless, the sergeant in charge loudly demanded why he was the last man to arrive. Though it was clear to the civilian guests that the soldier had good reason to be late, he nevertheless answered his sergeant with the words, "No excuse, Sir."

When the invitation comes for us to be part of God's kingdom and to be used in His service, may we do our best to obey the Master in whatever He calls us to do and, in the spirit of that young soldier, offer no excuses.   —C. B. Mc.

IV. Places to Be Filled
(Luke 14:21-23)

A. By Hungry People Nearby (v. 21)

21. So that servant came, and showed his lord these things. Then the master of the house being angry said to his servant, Go out quickly into the streets and lanes of the city, and bring in hither the poor, and the maimed, and the halt, and the blind.

Having received the invited guests' negative responses, the faithful servant reported their rejections to his master. That gentleman's reaction was predictable in one who had gone all out to provide a banquet for his friends and found that they did not respect him enough to set aside other activities for the evening. Disappointed and angry, he still would not sit alone at home and let the banquet food go to waste. He would find other guests—the kind who did not have fields and oxen and weddings to occupy their attention—the kind whom Jesus had advised His pharisaic host to invite to his next dinner party (v. 13). Bring the *poor*; bring folk limping along on crutches; lead, and be prepared to feed, the ones unable to see—those persons who could not return the invitation. Bring them from the city streets and alleys where they made their homes and searched for scraps of food.

These are the kinds of people who had turned most eagerly to Jesus in their need when He was rejected by the religious establishment. Having little or no holdings in the present world, they had time to learn about the kingdom of Heaven (compare Matthew 21:31, 32).

B. By Hungry People Farther Away
(vv. 22, 23)

22, 23. And the servant said, Lord, it is done as thou hast commanded, and yet there is room. And the lord said unto the servant, Go out into the highways and hedges, and compel them to come in, that my house may be filled.

To scour a city for prospective guests and to bring them into the banquet hall would take time, but the accomplishment is made and reported.

Yet there is room . . . that my house may be filled. Here is the thrust of the parable, not in the material limits of an evening in a banquet hall, but in the outreach of a generous and loving God, who would have all men to be saved, and who is not content as long as there is a vacancy in His "many mansions" (John 14:2).

The invitation, therefore, is to be taken beyond the city to outlying areas (beyond Jerusalem and Judea to Samaria and the uttermost parts of the earth—Acts 1:8), where the roadways and the paths along the hedgerows are to be searched and folk to be found. It will not be easy for the peasant poor to believe that an invitation to a grand banquet in town, right now, is something more than a cruel joke. So they must be compelled by the most earnest persuasion and consistent demonstration of the master's genuine care for every man, woman, and child.

This is the spirit of Christ's church: "We are ambassadors for Christ, as though God did beseech you by us: we pray you in Christ's stead, be ye reconciled to God" (2 Corinthians 5:20).

V. Permanence of Choice
(Luke 14:24)

24. For I say unto you, That none of those men which were bidden shall taste of my supper.

The parable closes with the banquet host announcing his decision concerning the guests who have rejected his invitation to dine at his table; but here a transition occurs. The word *you* is plural, and so it seems that Jesus is directing this statement to all who were present at this meal in the Pharisee's home. These words ring with the judgment of God on Israel's religious leaders and the presumptuous nationals who assumed that, as God's chosen people, they had no further need to honor God with their life choices. Particularly intolerable was their rejection of God's Son, who came to announce and establish the kingdom that had been prepared and prophesied through the ages. To them it would happen as to the guests who didn't want to come to the host's banquet: "The kingdom of God shall be taken from you, and given to a nation bringing forth the fruits thereof" (Matthew 21:43). Paul and Barnabas spelled it out to some unbelieving Jews in Asia Minor: "It was necessary that the word of God should first have been spoken to you: but seeing ye put it from you, and judge yourselves unworthy of everlasting life, lo, we turn to the Gentiles" (Acts 13:46).

Nothing in the parable indicates that the invited guests were bad people. They offended the host by their indifference to him and his preparations for them. The depth of that offense is reflected in the emotion that burns in those final words.

The absentees would miss out because they chose not to come. They said they couldn't come, each for his own reason. The host's final message to them was, "It shall be as you have said."

Conclusion

A. Please Reply

A formal invitation to almost any kind of event will probably conclude with a request for a reply. The request will be made with the letters RSVP, which abbreviate a phrase borrowed from the French, *repondez s'il vous plait*—"reply, if you please." The host or hostess wants to know how many places to reserve for how many people.

On what basis does one reply? Several kinds of questions will influence a person's decision: Who is offering the invitation? What advantage could I gain, either by attending or by staying away? Do I have any conflicting prior commitments? Is there something else I would rather be doing at the time?

The first and last questions probably influence our decisions more than we realize. They are vital in respect to activities involving the church. The stranger comes or not, depending on who extends the invitation and how enjoyable the experience is perceived to be. The church member participates or not, depending on what he or she thinks of God in relation to the other elements involved.

Church members today, like the invited guests in Jesus' parable, have said yes to the Lord's formal RSVP. However, that does not guarantee they will show up when the time actually comes to render service or even to attend the worship services. New or compelling personal affairs may get in the way of their full participation in God's banquet.

How does such a person answer questions about the matter? Usually by giving reasons that can be made to seem important. Seldom does one admit having a preference to do something else with his or her time and assets. Almost never will one say plainly, "I just don't care that much about God and my Savior."

What is God to say about it? "I invited him (her) to my banquet in Heaven, and he said yes. Now, however, he has decided that he is more interested in something else, and he won't come. I'll have to get along with others less occupied with things of this present world. But in the place marked with his name at my table, there will be a full plate and an empty chair."

B. Prayer of an Invited Guest

All praise to You, O God in Heaven, for the glorious love that provides through Christ Jesus blessings that are beyond our imagination. We thank You for Your invitation to share in Your glory. We pray Your forgiveness for the times when we have forgotten You in our absorption with lesser things. Give us a winsome faith, we pray, to extend to others Your invitation to Your banquet table in Heaven. Through Jesus our Lord. Amen.

C. Thought to Remember

All things are ready; come to the feast!

Home Daily Bible Readings

Monday, Mar. 25—Always Prepared (Luke 12:35-40)

Tuesday, Mar. 26—Satisfaction in Obedience (Luke 12:41-48)

Wednesday, Mar. 27—Produce or Die (Luke 13:1-9)

Thursday, Mar. 28—Misplaced Emphasis (Luke 13:10-17)

Friday, Mar. 29—The Narrow Gate (Luke 13:22-30)

Saturday, Mar. 30—Determining Priority (Luke 14:1-6)

Sunday, Mar. 31—Humility Honored (Luke 14:7-14)

Learning by Doing

This page contains an alternate lesson plan emphasizing learning activities. Classes desiring such student involvement will find these suggestions helpful.

Learning Goals

This lesson will enable students to:

1. Retell the parable of the great feast in their own words.

2. Begin to bring their priorities in line with the importance of God's invitation extended through Jesus Christ.

3. Be ready to share with others God's invitation to eternal life.

Into the Lesson

Ask your students how they decide whether or not to attend an event to which they have been invited. Write their responses on a chalkboard or poster board. Expect answers such as: Acceptance depends on who is extending the invitation, conflicting commitments, cost, whether the activity is enjoyable, other things they would rather do. Then ask, "Which of these reasons would have the most bearing on your decision?" As you lead a brief discussion, remember that there are no "right" answers.

Into the Word

Briefly summarize Luke 14:1-14, the background for today's text. Jesus was at a dinner in the home of a Pharisee, and the lawyers and Pharisees who were there were watching Him, probably in hopes of finding fault. After Jesus healed a man who had dropsy, however, they remained silent. Jesus then spoke about humility (vv. 7-11) and compassion (vv. 12, 13). When He mentioned that those who have compassion for the poor and unfortunate will be rewarded "at the resurrection of the just" (v. 14), one of the guests responded that it will be a blessing to eat at the feast in the kingdom of God. That statement evoked Jesus' parable recorded in our text.

Have a volunteer read Luke 14:15-24 aloud. Then give each student a list of the elements of the parable and verse references as shown below (omit the italicized words). Have your students write who or what they think each element represents.

- "A certain man" (v. 16)—*God*
- "A great supper" (v. 16)—*Heaven, salvation*
- The "many" invited (v. 16)—*Israel*
- The call to come (v. 17)—*to accept Christ*
- "His servant" (v. 17)—*Jesus*
- Three respondents (vv. 18-20)—*those originally invited, but who reject God's Son*

- Second group invited (v. 21)—*the truly humble in Israel*
- Third group invited (vv. 22, 23)—*the Gentiles*

After five or ten minutes ask for volunteers to share their answers. Help the students make the associations given above.

Briefly discuss why the host in the parable was so angry. Make it clear that the invitation to the dinner had been extended previously, according to the custom of that day. The servant was notifying those who already had accepted the invitation that it was time to come. All the expense and effort regarding the preparation already had been made. Point out that the people of Israel had professed allegiance to God for many centuries, but when He sent His Son (the Messiah) to announce the coming of the kingdom of God, Israel, as a whole, rejected Him. This parable also speaks to those who accept Christ and then refuse to give first place to His wishes.

Into Life

Ask, "What does this parable teach about a person's refusing God's invitation extended through Christ?" (Read and discuss verse 24.) Ask, "On the basis of this parable, is there any need for urgency in responding to God's invitation?" (Consider Hebrews 3:7-15 and 2 Corinthians 6:1, 2. The parable emphasizes the need to accept when one has the opportunity, and not becoming sidetracked after accepting.)

In the parable the respondents' reasons for not attending the host's banquet are seen to be empty pretexts. Many today who have accepted Christ have allowed worldly interests to have priority in their lives, and they offer flimsy excuses for not doing as God wishes. Ask the class to name some things that Christians allow to crowd God out of their lives. List them on your chalkboard. In this connection have your students consider Demas, who was a co-worker of the apostle Paul (2 Timothy 4:10). Ask what his example teaches us about priorities in life.

Close the session by allotting a minute or so for the students to ponder the list on the chalkboard to see if they are allowing any of these things to become too important in their lives. Ask, "Do you need to make any adjustments regarding the priorities in your life? If so, what adjustments will you begin to make this week?"

Let's Talk It Over

The questions on this page are designed to encourage review of the lesson
Scriptures and to promote discussion of the lesson by the class. The answers
provided are only discussion starters. Let your class talk it over from there.

1. In what ways is it significant that Jesus compared His kingdom with a great supper?

Many things have changed since Jesus' time, but it is still true that people gain great enjoyment in coming together to eat. Probably all of us can count banquets, church fellowship dinners, and family dinners among our richest experiences. So Jesus must have been depicting the tremendous joy that His kingdom affords. Another consideration here is the amount of preparation involved in hosting such a supper. We are thereby reminded of the extensive plans and preparations God made in order to provide us salvation and eternal life. A third aspect to consider is the invitation. We seldom greet an invitation to a banquet or a supper with indifference or revulsion. Why is it, then, that people frequently regard the invitation to follow Christ as something to be put off or spurned?

2. The parable of the great feast is one of the teachings of Jesus in which he featured a bit of humor. Why is Jesus' use of humor an aspect of His personality worthy of note?

Bible scholars have pointed out that Jesus was using a form of humor when he spoke of the man who was offended by a speck of sawdust in his brother's eye, while having a plank in his own eye (Matthew 7:3-5). Another example is Jesus' charge against the nation's religious leaders that they would carefully strain something they were going to drink in order to remove a gnat, and then swallow a camel (Matthew 23:24). To think of our Savior as a person who appreciated humor gives us an insight into His humanity. It reminds us that there is a place for laughter in the Christian life. And it encourages teachers to find appropriate ways of injecting humor into their teaching.

3. The invited guests who made excuses for not attending the host's banquet may represent persons who allow their possessions and their families to come ahead of God. How can one help these persons reorder their priorities?

In light of the previous question, perhaps light humor could be used to reveal the absurdity of people's misplaced priorities. With a bit of imagination one should be able to show how foolish are some of the choices that people make. Many devote much time and attention to material treasures, all of which in some way are susceptible to deterioration or destruction, while neglecting what cannot fade; others center their lives around family relationships that can end in an instant, while ignoring God's invitation to become a member of His eternal family. If we approach these people in this way, we may be more successful than if we approach them in a critical, threatening manner.

4. God wants all persons to be saved and to enter His heavenly home. What effect should this truth have on one's evangelistic efforts?

It is legitimate to warn people of God's wrath and of the realities of Hell. Some sinners need to hear this to be shaken out of their preoccupation with this world's values. Paul said, "Knowing therefore the terror of the Lord, we persuade men" (2 Corinthians 5:11). Jude 22, 23 suggests that some persons will respond better to an emphasis on God's love and benevolence. These persons may be acutely aware of their sinfulness and may consider themselves hopelessly unworthy of God's favor. To tell them that God does not want them to perish and that He desires an eternal fellowship with them can have a powerful effect on them.

5. "For I say unto you, That none of those men which were bidden shall taste of my supper." The tragedy of rejecting the gospel is depicted in these words of Luke 14:24. How can we gain a stronger sense of this tragedy?

We use the word *tragedy* to describe a variety of circumstances: an airplane crash that results in a great number of deaths, an automobile accident that leaves a young man or woman paralyzed, a storm that destroys scores of homes and businesses. But no earthly tragedy can begin to compare with the loss of a soul through rejection of the gospel. We remember Jesus' soul-searching question: "For what is a man profited, if he shall gain the whole world, and lose his own soul?" (Matthew 16:26). No earthly gain can begin to offset the loss of one's soul, for that is an eternal, irrevocable loss. How powerfully should this tragedy move us to urge those who have rejected God's gracious invitation to reject it no longer!

The Living Lord

DEVOTIONAL READING: Luke 24:1-12.

LESSON SCRIPTURE: Luke 24:1-36.

PRINTED TEXT: Luke 24:13-27.

Luke 24:13-27

13 And, behold, two of them went that same day to a village called Emmaus, which was from Jerusalem about threescore furlongs.

14 And they talked together of all these things which had happened.

15 And it came to pass, that, while they communed together and reasoned, Jesus himself drew near, and went with them.

16 But their eyes were holden that they should not know him.

17 And he said unto them, What manner of communications are these that ye have one to another, as ye walk, and are sad?

18 And the one of them, whose name was Cleopas, answering said unto him, Art thou only a stranger in Jerusalem, and hast not known the things which are come to pass there in these days?

19 And he said unto them, What things? And they said unto him, Concerning Jesus of Nazareth, which was a prophet mighty in deed and word before God and all the people:

20 And how the chief priests and our rulers delivered him to be condemned to death, and have crucified him.

21 But we trusted that it had been he which should have redeemed Israel: and beside all this, today is the third day since these things were done.

22 Yea, and certain women also of our company made us astonished, which were early at the sepulchre;

23 And when they found not his body, they came, saying, that they had also seen a vision of angels, which said that he was alive.

24 And certain of them which were with us went to the sepulchre, and found it even so as the women had said: but him they saw not.

25 Then he said unto them, O fools, and slow of heart to believe all that the prophets have spoken:

26 Ought not Christ to have suffered these things, and to enter into his glory?

27 And beginning at Moses and all the prophets, he expounded unto them in all the Scriptures the things concerning himself.

GOLDEN TEXT: Beginning at Moses and all the prophets, he expounded unto them in all the Scriptures the things concerning himself.—Luke 24:27.

Teachings of Jesus
Unit 2. Teachings About God
(Lessons 6-9)

Lesson Aims

When this lesson has been completed, the students should be able to:

1. Summarize the conversation of Jesus with the two on the way to Emmaus.

2. Identify four Old Testament Scriptures that were prophecies concerning the Christ.

3. Have a stronger faith in Jesus as the Christ.

Lesson Outline

INTRODUCTION
   A. Not Was, But Is!
   B. Lesson Background
  I. THE LORD WALKS WITH MEN (Luke 24:13-16)
   A. Important News Discussed (vv. 13, 14)
   B. Shared Experience (vv. 15, 16)
 II. THE LORD LISTENS TO MEN (Luke 24:17-24)
   A. Absorption With Current Events (vv. 17, 18)
    A Matter of Public Record
   B. Bad News of Canceled Hopes (vv. 19-21)
   C. Good News of Resurrection (vv. 22-24)
    The Witness of the Women
III. THE LORD TEACHES THE TRUTH (Luke 24:25-27)
   A. Lack of Understanding Rebuked (vv. 25, 26)
   B. The Scriptures Explained (v. 27)
CONCLUSION
   A. A Good Way to Be Known
   B. Prayer of an Unknown Disciple
   C. Thought to Remember

Visual 6 of the visuals packet pictures Jesus sitting to eat with the men from Emmaus. It is shown on page 276.

Introduction

A. Not Was, But Is!

Who and what was Jesus?

A Christian can't answer that question as it is presented. The living Lord is not a has-been, to be described in the past tense. The testimony of the apostles, sustained by the Holy Spirit, is couched in an unchanging present, and that testimony is vital: "No one can say, 'Jesus is Lord,' except by the Holy Spirit" (1 Corinthians 12:3, *New International Version*).

The apostle Paul affirmed the resurrection as the central fact in establishing Jesus' identity. Jesus was "declared to be the Son of God with power, according to the Spirit of holiness, by the resurrection from the dead" (Romans 1:4).

"Resurrection from the dead!" Those four words compress the bad news/good news core of the gospel. "Christ died for our sins according to the Scriptures" (1 Corinthians 15:3). The four Gospels detail the bad news of that death, which left even the material world in quake-torn darkness. Jesus' death was necessary as the atonement for our sin. Its necessity saves it from the ultimate tragedy of being without meaning, but does not provide genuine relief. That relief awaited the dawn of the third day, when Christ "rose again . . . according to the Scriptures" (1 Corinthians 15:4). The good news of resurrection provides hallelujahs that begin with the final chapters of the four Gospels, continue as a theme for the book of Acts and the New Testament epistles, and furnish a background for triumphant Revelation. So Jesus is the Lamb of God—"he that liveth, and was dead; and, behold, I am alive for evermore, Amen" (Revelation 1:18).

B. Lesson Background

Our studies in March dealt with five parables teaching about the kingdom of Heaven. We turn now to four (April) lessons teaching about God, as living, and loving, and caring, and life-sustaining. These qualities are presented not only in the words of Jesus, but especially in His works and His being. In this lesson, the lesson for Easter, we find "The Living Lord" in Jesus, risen from the dead.

Before there could be a resurrection, there had to be a death—a real, stone-cold death. Jesus spent much time and effort in teaching His disciples that He must die at the hands of His enemies, but that He would rise again. Luke 19:28—22:46 details the events of Jesus' final week, and 22:47—23:49 tells of His arrest, trials, and crucifixion.

Luke 23:50-56 tells of Jesus' burial. Two believing members of the Jewish high court took His body down from the cross, prepared it hastily for burial before the Sabbath began at sundown on Friday, and laid it in the new tomb belonging to one of them (John 19:38-40; Matthew 27:59, 60). The tomb was sealed by the Roman authority and soldiers were posted to guard it (Matthew 27:62-66).

The burial of Jesus was observed by women who had followed Him and supported His ministry. They left the place and spent the Sabbath at rest according to the Jewish law (Luke 23:56).

They were back at the burial place early on the first day of the week, however, and found the stone closure rolled away from the opening, and the tomb empty. Two men "in shining garments" were present to tell them that Jesus was alive, and the women carried the message to His apostles. Peter and John (John 20:3-10) came to the sepulchre and found it as reported (Luke 24:1-12).

At this point Luke introduces the Emmaus incident, mentioned also in Mark 16:12, 13: "Afterward Jesus appeared in a different form to two of them while they were walking in the country. These returned and reported it to the rest" (*New International Version*).

I. The Lord Walks With Men (Luke 24:13-16)

A. Important News Discussed (vv. 13, 14)

13. And, behold, two of them went that same day to a village called Emmaus, which was from Jerusalem about threescore furlongs.

The *two* were followers of Jesus, and probably numbered among the 120 mentioned in Acts 1:15, but they are not mentioned otherwise in Scripture. They had been in Jerusalem long enough to know about recent events there. Their walk to *Emmaus* took place on the day of Jesus' resurrection, evidently some time after noon.

We know nothing about Emmaus except what appears here. The village was about seven miles from Jerusalem, and most Bible students think it was northwest of the city.

The two evidently were friends, or perhaps members of the same family. It seems reasonable to infer that they lived in Emmaus (see verses 28, 29).

14. And they talked together of all these things which had happened.

There was much news for the two to discuss. In fact, the events of those days in and around Jerusalem have been the subject for discussion among many of the world's people ever since. Virtually everyone in Palestine in those days knew at least something about Jesus, but there was much disagreement as to who He really was. Many had seen His mighty works and heard His amazing words, but very few understood fully what they had seen and heard. When they reported it, they were not believed. Even among the closest witnesses and believers there were many unanswered questions. How could things come to such an end for such a one as Jesus? The pieces just didn't seem to fit together. The travelers' conversation was surely not boring; neither was it trivial small talk.

B. Shared Experience (vv. 15, 16)

15. And it came to pass, that, while they communed together and reasoned, Jesus himself drew near, and went with them.

The intensity of their discussion would have made it easy for almost anyone to approach, either from behind them or by an intersecting path, without being noticed. Jesus joined them as an interested listener to their discussion.

Mark 16:9-11 and John 20:11-18 tell that Jesus had appeared that morning to Mary Magdalene. Matthew 28:9, 10 tells of His appearing to other women. But this is the first appearance of the risen Lord mentioned by Luke. Even after the resurrection Jesus companied readily with common folk. When thought and conversation center on Him, we are most likely to enjoy His presence.

16. But their eyes were holden that they should not know him.

Others also were slow to recognize Jesus after the resurrection. Mary Magdalene mistook Him for the gardener at the tomb (John 20:14-16). That evening He had difficulty persuading the eleven apostles that it was really He, and not just a ghost, before them (Luke 24:36-43). Later in Galilee, fishermen/apostles recognized Jesus on the shore only after He had directed them to a miraculous catch (John 21:4-7).

We can only guess how and why the two on the road were prevented from recognizing the Lord. His appearing in "another form" (Mark 16:12) suggests why they did not recognize Him. And if they had recognized Jesus immediately, they might have been so excited that they would have been unable to receive the teaching they so greatly needed and the Lord desired to give.

II. The Lord Listens to Men (Luke 24:17-24)

A. Absorption With Current Events (vv. 17, 18)

17. And he said unto them, What manner of communications are these that ye have one to another, as ye walk, and are sad?

How to Say It

ANASTROPHE (Greek). ahn-ah-strah-*fay*.
CHUZA. *Kew*-za.
CLEOPAS. *Klee*-uh-pass.
EMMAUS. Em-*may*-us.
MAGDALENE. *Mag*-duh-leen or Mag-duh-*lee*-nee.

The lively discussion between the two disciples would have been evident to the most casual observer. *Communications* here translates a word depicting a back-and-forth exchange like the volleying of a ball in a tennis match. In it we can hear a frequent "on the other hand," probably emphasized with gestures. They clearly were disturbed by what they were talking about. The *American Standard Version* renders the final clause, "and they stood still, looking sad." So Jesus' question stopped them in their tracks.

18. And the one of them, whose name was Cleopas, answering said unto him, Art thou only a stranger in Jerusalem, and hast not known the things which are come to pass there in these days?

The name *Cleopas* appears in Scripture only here and in John 19:25. There is no evident connection between the two. The companion of Cleopas is nowhere identified or described. They could not understand how anyone even visiting briefly in Jerusalem could be unaware of what had happened there. And what else could they be talking about? That was the news of the day!

A MATTER OF PUBLIC RECORD

"Are you only a visitor to Jerusalem and do not know the things that have happened there in these days?" Cleopas asked the stranger on the Emmaus road. The question reveals an important fact that fortifies the credibility of the New Testament accounts of the crucifixion and resurrection of Jesus. These events were not the product of a closely held myth that time and distance made more plausible, but were widely known in the city where they took place.

Fifty days later amid the miraculous manifestations of the Holy Spirit on Pentecost, Peter stood in Jerusalem to proclaim the good news about the risen Lord. "Men of Israel, listen to this: Jesus of Nazareth was a man accredited by God to you by miracles, wonders and signs, which God did among you through him, *as you yourselves know*" (Acts 2:22, *New International Version*). Peter appealed to the common knowledge of his listeners as independent confirmation of his message that Jesus had risen from the dead.

A person can lie about the shape of the St. Louis arch, but one can't get away with it in St. Louis. One can lie about the height of the Sears tower, but one can't get away with it in Chicago. Of all the places in the world where no one could have gotten away with saying that the death and resurrection of Jesus did not occur, that place was Jerusalem. These earthshaking events were a matter of public record.

—C. B. Mc.

B. Bad News of Canceled Hopes
(vv. 19-21)

19. And he said unto them, What things? And they said unto him, Concerning Jesus of Nazareth, which was a prophet mighty in deed and word before God and all the people.

Jesus did not pretend to be ignorant; the two must put into words what they were thinking. And they did it marvelously. Luke has recorded briefly what is probably a summary of statements by both men. The subject was identified accurately as the man *Jesus* who grew up in *Nazareth* of Galilee. He is the proper center of all our life, thought, and behavior. They acknowledged Him properly as a supremely great spokesman for God, but they fell short of affirming His messiahship. They saw in Him a perfect balance of power in what He said and what He did. They found in Him also a complete integrity, as seen by God and also by men, whether in personal contact or before a multitude. In His life on earth, He showed himself to be Lord, and that they properly acknowledged. What a confession!

20. And how the chief priests and our rulers delivered him to be condemned to death, and have crucified him.

As Jews, Cleopas and his friend recognized the responsibility of the politically oriented *priests* and the recognized religious *rulers* of the Jews for delivering Jesus to the Roman authorities and persuading them to execute Jesus in the Roman style. They told it as it was. It was bad news, overshadowing all the good news of Jesus' life, character, and influence.

21. But we trusted that it had been he which should have redeemed Israel: and beside all this, today is the third day since these things were done.

There is a dismal past tense in *trusted*. Their trust was shattered when Jesus died. That was at least partly because they expected the wrong things of their Messiah. They expected Him to

visual 6

redeem the nation Israel, apparently by a military deliverance from Rome. For that kind of Messiah to die, betrayed by His own people and executed by the authorities He was supposed to overthrow, just could not happen!

Three days was time enough for the incredible facts to soak in and be accepted as final. If it all had been a horrible nightmare, they would have awakened before now. Did they know that Jesus had predicted His resurrection after three days? If so, the time was up!

C. Good News of Resurrection
(vv. 22-24)

There was another place for "the other hand" in the complicated, puzzling report, though.

22, 23. Yea, and certain women also of our company made us astonished, which were early at the sepulchre; and when they found not his body, they came, saying, that they had also seen a vision of angels, which said that he was alive.

Luke 8:2, 3 mentions women whom Jesus had "healed of evil spirits and infirmities, Mary called Magdalene, out of whom went seven devils, and Joanna the wife of Chuza Herod's steward, and Susanna, and many others, which ministered unto him of their substance." Luke 24:10 provides a similar list, adding "Mary the mother of James," as being those who witnessed the burial of Jesus, and then returned to the sepulchre early on the first day of the week. There they saw and heard the angels who said, "Why seek ye the living among the dead? He is not here, but is risen."

Cleopas and his friend identified themselves as being in the *company* of Jesus' followers. But, like Peter and John, to whom the women brought the same report, these two were not convinced. They were sufficiently impressed, though, to discuss it between themselves and to report it to this interested stranger.

THE WITNESS OF THE WOMEN

Because of the Jewish culture of the first century, the resurrection accounts in the New Testament are given a special credibility as a result of the part the women played in them. If the resurrection were a hoax, the perpetrators of it would *not* have made women the primary witnesses.

In that time and place the testimony of women was regarded as invalid. Describing the Jewish legal system, the first-century Jewish historian Josephus says, "Put not trust in a single witness, but let there be three or at the least two, whose evidence shall be accredited by their past lives. From women let no evidence be accepted,

because of the levity and temerity of their sex." While we would disagree with this ancient bias against female witnesses, the fact remains that the bias was a strong part of that culture. Yet all four Gospel accounts say that the women were first to discover that the tomb was empty, and the Gospel record indicates that it was to women that Jesus first showed himself alive after His resurrection.

If the disciples of Jesus fabricated the story of His resurrection, would they have made women the primary witnesses under the circumstances? Hardly. The best answer as to why the New Testament has the women as the first witnesses of Jesus' resurrection is that it really happened just that way.
—C. B. Mc.

24. And certain of them which were with us went to the sepulchre, and found it even so as the women had said: but him they saw not.

Here is evident reference to Peter and John, with whom Cleopas and his friend felt a close association. John 20:1-8 and Luke 24:12 tell of their visiting and entering the empty tomb, where they observed the grave clothes neatly abandoned. There they were almost, if not entirely, convinced that Jesus had risen. Jesus actually appeared to Peter some hours later (Luke 24:34; 1 Corinthians 15:5). The women's account was supported by all the evidence, but to Cleopas and his friend it still came short of being fully proved.

We may be grateful for the skepticism with which the first reports of Jesus' resurrection were met—especially by the men among His followers. His disciples were not easily convinced. They had to be shown. But when provided with proof beyond question, they committed themselves and all they possessed to spreading the ultimate good news. How silly, in contrast, is the "scholarship" of persons who come along thousands of years later with fabricated theories to explain how the gospel story was started, believed, and followed for centuries without being true!

III. The Lord Teaches the Truth
(Luke 24:25-27)

A. Lack of Understanding Rebuked
(vv. 25, 26)

25. Then he said unto them, O fools, and slow of heart to believe all that the prophets have spoken.

"How could you possibly not know about this?"

Now it was Jesus' turn to express amazement that these good friends did not know or understand the Scriptures with which they were supposedly familiar. They were not hard-headed, stupid fools. They were just slow to catch on to the meanings of messianic Scriptures. They had accepted popular political ideas about the Messiah rather than study what God's messengers said. The *prophets* here included all the inspired Old Testament writers—Moses, David, and Solomon, as well as those known as prophets, such as Isaiah, Jeremiah, Micah, and Daniel.

What really is the basis of our religious beliefs and practices, and our daily choices? Is it a conviction arising from our own careful study of what the Bible says, or do we simply rest upon the tradition in which we were reared? Could we be guilty of a foolishness similar to what Jesus found in these friends?

26. Ought not Christ to have suffered these things, and to enter into his glory?

The Messiah had to suffer—even die—on the way to His glory. Clearest indication is in Psalm 22, portraying crucifixion from the viewpoint of the crucified, and Isaiah 53, with its extended description of the Servant's suffering for the sins of others. Then, "He was cut off out of the land of the living. . . . And he made his grave with the wicked, and with the rich in his death" (Isaiah 53:8, 9). The glory, however, was to follow. God would not abandon Him to the grave, nor let His Holy One see decay (Psalm 16:10, 11, *New International Version*).

New Testament writers show the theme fulfilled in Jesus (see Philippians 2:5-11), and trace that same course for those who would follow Him: "If we be dead with him, we shall also live with him: if we suffer, we shall also reign with him" (2 Timothy 2:11, 12).

B. The Scriptures Explained (v. 27)

The walk from Jerusalem to Emmaus would take some two hours. Were Cleopas and his friend halfway there when Jesus joined them? We may be sure that He did most of the talking as they went on. Perhaps they slowed their pace and wished that they had longer to be with this stranger.

27. And beginning at Moses and all the prophets, he expounded unto them in all the Scriptures the things concerning himself.

The Lord was talking about Jesus of Nazareth, the Messiah, but His hearers didn't yet know who was talking. Afterward they said, "Did not our heart burn within us, while he talked with us by the way, and while he opened to us the Scriptures?" (Luke 24:32). The written Word of God was explained to them by the living Word. They weren't bored by the lecture!

Beginning at Moses, that is, the part of the Scriptures written by Moses. Jesus surely mentioned Satan's bruising of the woman's offspring (Genesis 3:15), and the symbolism of the Passover lamb (Exodus 12), and the promise of the coming prophet to whom the people must give heed (Deuteronomy 18:15, 18). He surely noticed David's prophetic references and Isaiah's promise of the virgin-born ruler (7:14) and the serving messenger (61:1-3). He may have mentioned the ruler coming from Bethlehem (Micah 5:2), the son called out of Egypt (Hosea 11:1) and many others.

Jesus had profound respect for the Old Testament Scriptures, but He did not hesitate to declare to the Jewish leaders, "Search the Scriptures; for in them ye think ye have eternal life: and they are they which testify of me" (John 5:39). The life is in the living Lord.

Conclusion

A. A Good Way to Be Known

Readers of Luke 24 are introduced to unknown walkers on their way to an unknown village. They benefit from the introduction because of an hour spent with the risen Lord. Is there a better claim to fame than to be numbered among those who walk with the resurrected Savior?

B. Prayer of an Unknown Disciple

Thank You, Lord Jesus, for the blessed privilege of walking with You on the way home. Thank You for listening to my concerns and uncertainties and teaching me Your way. Amen.

C. Thought to Remember

"Whosoever will save his life shall lose it: and whosoever will lose his life for my sake shall find it" (Matthew 16:25).

Home Daily Bible Readings

Learning by Doing

This page contains an alternate lesson plan emphasizing learning activities. Classes desiring such student involvement will find these suggestions helpful.

Learning Goals

As a result of participating in today's lesson, a student will be able to:

1. Summarize the conversation of Jesus with the two disciples on the way to Emmaus.

2. Explain how Jesus' suffering, death, and resurrection were the fulfillment of Old Testament prophecy.

3. Describe his or her own view of Jesus.

Into the Lesson

Before class time prepare a matching quiz to give to your class members as class begins. Type the following references in a column down the left side of a sheet of paper: Genesis 3:15; Psalm 16:10; Psalm 22:1a; Psalm 22:16; Isaiah 53:5. Type the actual verses in scrambled order in a column to the right. Ask the students to match each Scripture reference with its corresponding text by drawing a line to connect the two.

Allow a few minutes for your class members to complete the exercise, but do not discuss or reveal the correct matches at this time. Ask for several volunteers to share briefly some examples of when they have felt skeptical, when they have said in effect, "I must see it to believe it."

Into the Word

Have the class members read Luke 24:13-27 silently. When they have finished, give each a sheet of paper on which the following questions are listed. Ask them to answer the questions without looking at the text.

1. On what day of the week did this event occur? (The "same day" as the resurrection, the first day of the week—v. 13)

2. Where were the two men going? (Emmaus —v. 13)

3. What were the two discussing before Jesus joined them? (The events associated with Jesus' death and the reports of His resurrection—v. 14)

4. Why didn't they recognize Jesus? (In some manner they were kept from recognizing Him.)

5. What was the state of mind of the disciples? (They were sad—v. 17.)

6. As they talked with this stranger on the road, how did they identify Jesus of Nazareth? ("A prophet mighty in deed and word"—v. 19)

7. What phrase that they used indicated their skepticism regarding Jesus' resurrection? ("But him they saw not"—v. 24)

8. According to Jesus, what was necessary before Christ could enter His glory? (Suffering—v. 26)

Point out that these two disciples were acquainted with those who went to the empty tomb (vv. 22, 24). They probably had heard Jesus teach and seen His miracles. But they, like Jesus' closest disciples, did not understand that He would suffer death and rise again.

Have each class member discuss these two questions with a person sitting beside him or her: What had kept them from understanding? Why were they now so sad and skeptical? After a few minutes, ask for volunteers to share their answers. Lead the class to the following: Though the text does not say, they probably were looking for a political leader to set up an earthly kingdom, just as others were (see Mark 10:35-45; Luke 19:11; John 6:15; Acts 1:6). Their inaccurate expectations had not been met, so they became sad and lost hope. So today, when one's expectations are based on mistaken interpretation of Scripture, one may miss the wonderful blessings of God!

Into Life

Refer back to the matching quiz given earlier and reveal the correct references for each passage. State that the Old Testament indicated that the Christ would suffer, die, and be raised from the grave. Mention also that Jesus made it clear that He is the Christ (Matthew 16:16, 17). The two disciples on the road to Emmaus lacked understanding about what the Scriptures taught about the Christ, so Jesus made it plain to them.

The two disciples gave a superb description of Jesus, although they fell short of acknowledging His messiahship. Ask each class member to use the back of the initial handout to write a paragraph that summarizes how he or she views Jesus. Have each include reasons for his or her belief. After five minutes (or more as time allows), ask for volunteers to share their paragraphs. If the class is large, have class members work in smaller groups for this sharing. Allow for questions and discussion. Probe the respondents gently with questions of when or how their view of Jesus came to be their own.

Conclude by reading verse 27 aloud. Urge the class members to study God's Word regularly and make it the sole basis of their faith in Jesus.

Let's Talk It Over

The questions on this page are designed to encourage review of the lesson Scriptures and to promote discussion of the lesson by the class. The answers provided are only discussion starters. Let your class talk it over from there.

1. What reasons may be given to explain why several of Jesus' followers were slow to recognize Him when He appeared to them after His resurrection?

One may be that they were not expecting to see Him. Even though He had foretold His death and resurrection, their faith was not strong enough to cause them to believe His words. Another reason may be that His resurrected body still showed the effects of crucifixion. John 20:25, 27 demonstrate that the nailprints in His hands and the spear wound in His side were still visible. Perhaps the torture He suffered produced other effects that altered His normal appearance (Isaiah 52:14). The best answer may be that Jesus somehow hid His identity until He had time to give His followers the teaching they needed to receive (Luke 24:27). Had they recognized Him sooner, they might have been too excited to hear what He had to tell them.

2. The two on the way to Emmaus were amazed that the stranger could have been unaware of the events in Jerusalem concerning Jesus of Nazareth in recent days. This reminds us of how much the teachings and actions of Jesus were a matter of public notice. Why is this important?

After relating to King Agrippa the facts concerning the death and resurrection of Christ, the apostle Paul told Festus, "I am persuaded that none of these things are hidden from him; for this thing was not done in a corner" (Acts 26:26). Jesus was no obscure prophet. The Jewish leaders in Jerusalem took note of Him early in His ministry (see John 3:1, 2); His deeds and words came to the attention of Herod Antipas (Matthew 14:1, 2); Peter asserted that the Roman officer Cornelius knew of Jesus' teaching and healing ministry (Acts 10:36-38). Jesus was very much a public figure. It was impossible, therefore, that a fabricated myth concerning His life, death, and resurrection could have been passed off on that society and accepted by it.

3. "But we trusted that it had been he which should have redeemed Israel." What a terrible sense of disillusionment is expressed in these words! What was the reason for this disillu-sionment? **What parallels do you see in people today?**

Jesus was not the Messiah many of His followers expected Him to be! It seems that many hoped He would lead a political and military effort to free Israel from Rome's domination. His shocking death on the cross ended those hopes. People today may become disillusioned when God doesn't do what they want Him to do. They may pray as never before, make an extra effort to be good, attend worship services more regularly, and even give a larger-than-usual offering. But as long as they are seeking *their* will and not *God's* will, they will be disillusioned.

4. Why should we be thankful that the disciples were slow to believe the reports of Jesus' resurrection?

Some have suggested that Jesus' disciples were ignorant, superstitious, gullible people and would have been eager to believe reports that He had risen from the dead. But this is not the picture the Gospels give us. Instead, Peter and John rushed to the tomb to investigate the reported disappearance of Jesus' body; the general skepticism of the entire band of disciples was reflected by the two disciples in our lesson; and Thomas stubbornly resisted belief in the resurrection until he had firsthand evidence (John 20:24, 25). Did the church's faith in the resurrection result from a raging hysteria on the part of the earliest of His followers? We can answer firmly: "No!"

5. The lesson writer asks this probing question: "What really is the basis of our religious beliefs and practices, and our daily choices?" Why should we make such a self-examination?

Some of us were blessed to have godly parents. They taught us who Jesus was, and we came to trust Him, to love Him. This was good, of course; but if we have not proceeded as adults to develop our own faith, building on what our parents gave us, we may not yet have a faith that will sustain us through all of life's pressures and temptations. Perhaps we came to faith in Christ as an adult, but on the basis of a deeply emotional experience. That kind of faith, too, may not last unless we strengthen it through a careful study of the Scriptures.

The Loving God

DEVOTIONAL READING: Luke 15:11-24.

LESSON SCRIPTURE: Luke 15:1-10.

PRINTED TEXT: Luke 15:1-10.

Luke 15:1-10

1 Then drew near unto him all the publicans and sinners for to hear him.

2 And the Pharisees and scribes murmured, saying, This man receiveth sinners, and eateth with them.

3 And he spake this parable unto them, saying,

4 What man of you, having a hundred sheep, if he lose one of them, doth not leave the ninety and nine in the wilderness, and go after that which is lost, until he find it?

5 And when he hath found it, he layeth it on his shoulders, rejoicing.

6 And when he cometh home, he calleth together his friends and neighbors, saying unto them, Rejoice with me; for I have found my sheep which was lost.

7 I say unto you, that likewise joy shall be in heaven over one sinner that repenteth, more than over ninety and nine just persons, which need no repentance.

8 Either what woman having ten pieces of silver, if she lose one piece, doth not light a candle, and sweep the house, and seek diligently till she find it?

9 And when she hath found it, she calleth her friends and her neighbors together, saying, Rejoice with me; for I have found the piece which I had lost.

10 Likewise, I say unto you, there is joy in the presence of the angels of God over one sinner that repenteth.

GOLDEN TEXT: I say unto you, there is joy in the presence of the angels of God over one sinner that repenteth.—Luke 15:10.

Teachings of Jesus
Unit 2. Teachings About God
(Lessons 6-9)

Lesson Aims

This study should prepare the student to:
1. Cite the circumstances of Jesus' telling the parables of the lost sheep and the lost coin.
2. Tell which character in the parables he or she is most like, and in what way.
3. Join the "search party" and the "cheering section" to find and welcome the lost ones who may be brought home.

Lesson Outline

Visual 7 of the visuals packet illustrates the joy of finding that which once was lost. It is shown on page 286.

Introduction

A. Introducing the Father

"Dad, this is the work crew I have been telling you about. Fellows, meet my father." That's a plain introduction. There shouldn't be anything hard about it.

Jesus had been working for years at just that kind of introduction; but on the evening before He must leave to go back home, one of His crew said they would be satisfied if only the Lord would show His Father to them (John 14:8). Jesus had just been talking about preparing lodg-ings for them in His Father's house, and providing the way for them to get there. By His words, works, and character He had revealed His Father to them; and He had assured them that He was not only like His Father, He was totally one with Him. A more thorough introduction would be impossible.

The essential character of the Father in Heaven is love (1 John 4:8). It was love that led Him to give His only begotten Son for the salvation of mankind (John 3:16). It is love that impels Him to seek out and invite sinners to the eternal banquet He has prepared for them (Luke 14:15-24). That searching and rejoicing love is the central quality of the Father to whom Jesus introduces us in Luke 15.

B. Lesson Background

The teachings recorded in Luke 14 and 15 are closely tied in time and subject. They were given during Jesus' later ministry in Perea, east of the Jordan, before He went to Bethany to raise Lazarus from the dead (John 11).

The subject discussed in Luke 14 and 15—the conflict between the religious leaders' proud superiority and Jesus' ministry among the people they despised—is not limited, however, in time or in location. That conflict had surfaced many months earlier in Galilee when Jesus accepted Matthew's invitation to a dinner with many of his "disreputable" friends (Luke 5:27-32). It was the conflict between Jesus and those who "trusted in themselves that they were righteous, and despised others" (Luke 18:9). That conflict reached a final severity in Jerusalem when Jesus told those leaders that publicans and prostitutes would precede them in God's kingdom because those "disreputable" folk had repented at the preaching of John the Baptist, and the priests and rulers had rejected it (Matthew 21:31, 32).

Luke 15 includes two special and significant elements. First is the *thrust of a question*: what farmer among them would refuse to look for one of his sheep if it were lost? The second special element is *rejoicing*. God's pleasure at the sinner's repentance sounds throughout the chapter, both overshadowing and emphasizing His disappointment in the loveless self-satisfaction of the "righteous" ones.

I. Receiving the "Wrong People" (Luke 15:1-3)

1. Then drew near unto him all the publicans and sinners for to hear him.

Publicans were tax collectors, usually Jewish, employed by the Roman authorities. They were despised as traitors to their own nation and for

How to Say It

CAESAREA. Sess-uh-*ree*-uh.
PEREA. Peh-*ree*-uh.

making themselves rich by charging more than they were authorized to collect (Luke 3:12, 13).

Sinners were "those people" who for any of several reasons were outside the Jewish religious community. Persons of loose morals and bad behavior, and irreligious persons would be included. These were not welcomed in the synagogues. But Jesus would talk *with* them—not just *at* them—and what He said made sense. They came from great distances to hear Him. Having come with that purpose, they listened attentively to what He had to say. Church folk should bring the same serious purpose to their church attendance—to hear the word of God.

2. And the Pharisees and scribes murmured, saying, This man receiveth sinners, and eateth with them.

Pharisees. The name means "separated." They were zealous keepers and advocates of the Mosaic law. Jesus came into conflict with their legalism, which emphasized outward conformity to ceremonies and practices, often to the neglect of spirit and purpose. The joyous love of God was foreign to them.

Scribes were craftsmen who made hand-lettered copies of the Scriptures. Their interest in the Scriptures led naturally to their being teachers of the law. Their skills and interests made them natural partners with the Pharisees, and therefore critical of Jesus' departures from legalistic tradition.

Luke's language here describes the critics' *murmuring* as a continuous grumbling among themselves against Jesus. *This man receiveth sinners.* In the thinking of the scribes and Pharisees, to welcome any contact with a sinner would seem like approval of the sin; it would defile the person accepting the sinner's company, and would bring condemnation.

Eateth with them. Here was the scribes and Pharisees' chief complaint against Jesus. Eating with another person still indicates a measure of acceptance and intimacy that is not found in casual conversation, or even social visiting in another's home. The idea is strong in the roots of our word, *companion*, which comes from the Latin for bread eaten together. When the apostle Peter was rebuked by the Jewish Christians in Jerusalem for being too friendly with the Gentile household of Cornelius (Acts 11:3), the chief complaint was that he had *eaten* with them.

What determines our choices of dinner companions? Business advantage? Social advancement? Convenience? The advancement of Christ's kingdom? How comfortable are we with Jesus' way of doing things, such as making up our guest lists among the homeless? (Luke 14:12-14).

3. And he spake this parable unto them, saying.

Jesus did not need to be informed about what the Pharisees and scribes were thinking and saying among themselves. He knew, just as on other occasions (Luke 5:22; 6:8). We must never think that our God does not know what we are doing, or saying, or thinking, or suffering. He knows all too well our dissatisfaction with His way of doing things.

The parable that follows occupies the rest of the chapter and falls into three parts, all emphasizing the concern of the loving God for that which is lost, and His joy at the recovery of such a one. The first two parts, occupying verses 4-10, are not the kind of stories we usually identify as parables, but still provide commonplace comparisons with eternal truth.

II. Joy at Finding a Lost Sheep (Luke 15:4-7)

Jesus' parable dealt with matters familiar to His audience. But many today may not grasp the full meaning in the imagery He used. How many of us have owned or tended sheep?

Here we need the Bible to help us understand the Bible! We might start with Psalm 23, and learn to depend on the Lord as Shepherd for leading, protecting, and the finding of daily nourishment. We need to ponder the Good Shepherd who lives with and protects His sheep, even to laying down His life for them (John 10:1-18). Jeremiah 31:10-20 and Ezekiel 34:11-16 will instruct us both in the shepherd's care for his flock and in God's care for His people. We need that instruction, too, in order to understand the church leader's responsibility among the people he serves (Acts 20:28-31; 1 Peter 5:1-5).

A. Care for One in a Hundred (v. 4)

4. What man of you, having a hundred sheep, if he lose one of them, doth not leave the ninety and nine in the wilderness, and go after that which is lost, until he find it?

"What man among you" (*New American Standard Bible*). If Saul of Tarsus, a rigid Pharisee (Acts 26:5), was also a maker of tents (Acts 18:3), we may suppose that some of the scribes and Pharisees now facing Jesus were keepers of sheep. At least they lived among shepherds enough to appreciate their intimate involvement with their flocks. These men might be heartless in their application of the law toward their fellowmen, but they had a tender feeling toward their animals. Jesus made His appeal to that tender spot. His hearers' response, in feeling if not in words, would indicate the nature of God and answer their grumblings against himself.

If he lose one. The loss of one percent of any possession would not seem important until the owner recognizes the individuality and the peculiar value of what is lost. The good shepherd calls his sheep by name (John 10:3), and does not regard any a mere statistic. So it is with God.

Anything lost may assume a peculiar quality. Almost any of us will become deeply disturbed and spend important time looking for relatively unimportant items. When, on the other hand, the lost item is not replaceable, as an heirloom or a child, the concern takes on a whole new aspect. With God, no person is replaceable.

Leave the ninety and nine in the wilderness. Jesus raised no questions about the shepherd's putting the flock at risk by leaving them in the open pasture land. That was not an issue in the parable. Jesus' focus was on finding the lost. The search for a missing child may leave the rest of the family feeling neglected, but they will be cared for when the emergency has been met.

Go after that which is lost, until he find it. The search acknowledges only one purpose, and is not complete until it is successful. The parable is not truly understood until we feel the wrench of lostness as it applies to a person out of contact with Christ, "the Shepherd and Bishop of your souls" (1 Peter 2:25).

B. Celebrating the Return (vv. 5, 6)

5, 6. And when he hath found it, he layeth it on his shoulders, rejoicing. And when he cometh home, he calleth together his friends and neighbors, saying unto them, Rejoice with me; for I have found my sheep which was lost. Celebration begins with the recovery of the lost sheep. Luke 15 is filled with happy endings, except for those persons who refuse to join in Heaven's rejoicing (Luke 15:25-30).

The laying of the lost one on the shepherd's shoulders provides a natural, vivid, and tender detail. Even if the lost one was able to walk, the carrying would provide comfort and assurance, besides speeding the trip home. Back home, the celebration goes beyond personal gladness to become a neighborhood party. "Come and celebrate with me!" Such rejoicing has to be shared. "Rejoice with them that do rejoice, and weep with them that weep," wrote Paul (Romans 12:15).

The Lord did not say how the shepherd's invitation might have been accepted by the neighbors, or how many would join in the celebration. Some might come because they were glad the sheep was found; some because they were glad the shepherd felt so good about it; some for a "good time." And some would stay at home, talking about the shepherd's foolishness in going to so much trouble over one sheep.

The neighbors' responses would certainly depend on their regard for the shepherd. The ones who loved him most would join most heartily with him in his rejoicing. And that brings us to the conclusion Jesus presented.

CARRIED TO SAFETY

Most of us have heard or read of accounts of dogs that have shown great courage in protecting human beings or in rescuing them from life-threatening situations.

One such dog was a Chesapeake Bay retriever owned by the Homme family of Livingston, Montana. One day in 1978, Mrs. Homme was washing dishes as she watched her five-year-old son, Kenny, who was playing in the backyard. Suddenly Mrs. Homme noticed that Kenny was gone. She ran outside and heard Kenny shouting for help from a surging creek in back of their house. The boy had fallen down an embankment and into a creek swollen from recent rains.

The Hommes's dog, Chester, was already in the water trying to save the boy. As the dog swam toward Kenny, the water swept the child into a culvert. Chester fought the raging current for ten minutes before finally reaching the boy. Kenny grabbed Chester's fur twice but lost his grip both times. Finally Kenny was able to climb onto the dog's back, and Chester carried him out of the culvert to shore.

Mankind was drowning in the surging current of sin, headed toward the endless tunnel of Hell. Had Jesus not entered this world to carry us to safety, we surely would have perished in the flood.   —C. B. Mc.

C. Heaven's Rejoicing (v. 7)

7. I say unto you, that likewise joy shall be in heaven over one sinner that repenteth, more than over ninety and nine just persons, which need no repentance. Up to this point Jesus' argument had been developed in the minds of the hearers as they responded to His question about any shepherd among them. Such a one would surely find *pleasure* in possessing a sizable flock, safe and sound; but *celebration*, beginning with the shepherd and involving his neighbors, would attend the recovering of one that had been lost.

The Lord spoke now on His own authority, declaring that the loving God feels the same way about His people. He is pleased with dependable good behavior on the part of any, but His greater rejoicing—shared with the angels in Heaven and His loving friends on earth—attends the return of a penitent sinner to His care and presence.

Just persons, which need no repentance might include persons such as the parents of John the Baptist, "righteous before God, walking in all the commandments and ordinances of the Lord blameless" (Luke 1:6), or Cornelius of Caesarea, devout and generous (Acts 10:1, 2); yet even these would acknowledge their need of constant care, guidance, and correction from their heavenly Shepherd. It seems clear that Jesus was thinking of the Pharisees, scribes, and persons like them, those who trust in themselves that they are righteous (Luke 18:9) and recognize no need for repentance. God has no pleasure, of course, in such pride. These persons are represented in the older brother of the returned wanderer (Luke 15:25-32), who may have been as virtuous as he thought he was, but had no loving rapport with his father and refused to share with him in celebrating the wanderer's return.

III. Joy at Finding a Lost Coin (Luke 15:8-10)

To emphasize the point He was making, Jesus continued His parable and changed the scene and the actors. The person suffering the loss and celebrating the return is now a woman at home. The loss is a possession misplaced. The course of action is the same, and the conclusion the same.

A. Concern for One in Ten (v. 8)

8. Either what woman having ten pieces of silver, if she lose one piece, doth not light a candle, and sweep the house, and seek diligently till she find it?

The silver piece was a Greek coin called a drachma. It seems the drachma was equivalent to the Roman denarius, which amounted to a day's wage for a soldier or laborer. The fact that there were ten coins may have no special significance. This simply may have been the woman's (perhaps widow's) available household funds. One student of customs in Bible lands has pointed out, however, that a woman's marriage dowry could include coins worked into a dress or a circlet around the head. These would establish her status as a married woman and would remain as her possession even if the marriage were dissolved by divorce. The loss of one coin

in such case could seriously mar the symbolism as well as the value of her possession.

Members of the Akha tribe in the hills of northern Thailand in 1992 showed special interest in this parable. There an Akha woman wears a headdress including a circlet of nine silver coins. This identifies her marriage status, and the loss of even one coin would be a great embarrassment. It would also reduce the "good" odd number nine to the "bad" even number eight. In any such circumstance the loss of one coin would be regarded very seriously.

In a modest house familiar to Jesus' hearers the candle and broom would be appropriate tools for an all-out search. If the house had any windows, they would have been few and small. Most likely it would have a dirt floor.

As in the case of the shepherd, the search would continue until the lost was found.

B. Celebrating the Find (v. 9)

9. And when she hath found it, she calleth her friends and her neighbors together, saying, Rejoice with me; for I have found the piece which I had lost.

In the preceding parable a man experienced the loss; when he found the sheep, his male friends and neighbors rejoiced with him. Here a woman lost a coin, and women rejoiced when she found it. Jesus didn't want to leave out anyone as He exhorted all to join with Him and the Father in seeking and saving the lost.

Did the woman accept responsibility in speaking of *the piece which I had lost*? Perhaps so, but the loss was hers, whether by carelessness, by accident, or by the act of another person. Similarly, God experiences the loss in His family and seeks the return of the absentee, whatever or whoever caused the departure.

Home Daily Bible Readings

Monday, Apr. 8—The Importance of One (Matthew 18:10-14)

Tuesday, Apr. 9—Lost Sheep Returned (1 Peter 2:18-25)

Wednesday, Apr. 10—Sinners Called to Repentance (Luke 5:27-32)

Thursday, Apr. 11—Sought and Saved (Luke 19:1-10)

Friday, Apr. 12—Freely Restored (Luke 15:11-24)

Saturday, Apr. 13—Petty Self-Righteousness (Luke 15:25-32)

Sunday, Apr. 14—Contending Loyalties (Luke 16:1-13)

C. Heaven's Rejoicing (v. 10)

10. Likewise, I say unto you, there is joy in the presence of the angels of God over one sinner that repenteth.

Like verse 7, this verse speaks of the joy in Heaven over one sinner who repents and returns to God's family. Unlike verse 7, there is no comparison here with any other circumstance. Does Jesus mean to say that the angels themselves rejoice when a sinner is converted? Perhaps so. There are Scriptures that indicate the angels' interest in our salvation (see Matthew 18:10; Luke 2:10-14; 1 Peter 1:12; Revelation 3:5). The main point of Jesus' teaching in this chapter, however, is that God, in whose presence the angels dwell, seeks sinners and rejoices when one who was lost is found.

Contrary to some popular opinions, Heaven is not dull. It is characterized by celebration of God's victorious goodness, now and forever. Don't stay away!

LOST FOREVER

The English mathematician and physicist Sir Isaac Newton gave the world many of its most important scientific discoveries. He invented calculus, advanced the field of optics, and devised the laws of motion and of universal gravitation. The publication of his works marked an epoch in the history of science.

Newton authored one manuscript that the world will never see, however, for it was accidentally destroyed. While teaching at Cambridge University, Newton once left his rooms and forgot that a burning candle remained on his desk. It is thought that his pet dog overturned the candle and set the papers on fire. By the time Newton returned to his rooms, the manuscript had been consumed in the flames.

The parables of the lost sheep and the lost coin are two of several stories Jesus told about lost objects, all designed to convey God's concern for lost people. The loss of money, property, or even a valuable scientific manuscript may make us poorer, but nothing can compare with the tragedy of a soul eternally lost. Understandable, then, is the rejoicing in Heaven when one sinner returns to God. —C. B. Mc.

Conclusion

A. The Rest of the Story

Our loving God cares for the lost. He rejoices when they are found. His people are expected to share in His rejoicing. This is the message spoken and demonstrated by Jesus to answer the objections raised against His spending time with "those people" not qualifying for approval in the synagogue. To the lost sheep the shepherd stands in the relationship of God to a lost sinner. To the lost coin the searching woman likewise stands in the relationship of God to a lost sinner. But that relationship is more forcefully represented in a father who permitted his younger son to take his inheritance to waste it far from home, and then welcomed him with celebration when he came home (Luke 15:11-24). Jesus' reply to His critics was not complete until He identified them as the stay-at-home son who refused to join in that celebration (Luke 15:25-32).

We have seen the character and concern of the loving God as shown in Christ, who came "to seek and to save that which was lost" (Luke 19:10). We must determine how we are going to relate to Him in those concerns. That is the rest of the story.

B. Draw Your Own Conclusions

Jesus' skill as a teacher is uniquely demonstrated in the questions He asked, bringing out from others the principles, conclusions, and judgments they would not accept if He presented them. His questions, explicit and implied, were the vehicle for His teaching that we are considering in this lesson. How shall we respond to Him? To which will we give more attention: a lost wallet or a lost neighbor? Draw your own conclusions.

C. Prayer of a Reluctant Rejoicer

Help us, please, our loving God, to see Your world and Your people as You see them—their lostness when separated from You, and their loveliness when they come home. May we learn to share Your concern over anyone who strays and Your celebration at that person's return. In Jesus Your Son, amen.

D. Thought to Remember

Friends of the Good Shepherd will rejoice with Him when a lost sheep is brought home.

Rejoice with me; for I have found my sheep which was lost. Luke 15:6

visual 7

Learning by Doing

This page contains an alternate lesson plan emphasizing learning activities. Classes desiring such student involvement will find these suggestions helpful.

Learning Goals

This lesson will enable the student to:

1. Cite the circumstances under which Jesus taught the parables in Luke 15:1-10.

2. Identify one member of the lesson text's "cast of characters" whom he or she is most like, and say how it is so.

3. Join the "search party" and the "cheering section" to find and welcome the lost ones.

Into the Lesson

During the week before class, recruit two of the class members to be ready to act out the two "seeking and finding" roles of Jesus' parables in Luke 15:1-10. Suggest that they be creative, dramatizing the stories as the text allows. Tell them that they will perform their roles during the Bible study part of the session.

To begin this session, read the following statement aloud and ask the class members to indicate, by show of hands, whether they agree or disagree with it: "If Jesus were ministering on earth today, He would spend time in the inner city with crooks and prostitutes." As class members share their points of agreement or disagreement, encourage as many as possible to get involved in the discussion. The point is to get everyone thinking about the context of these parables of Jesus.

Into the Word

Have everyone read Luke 15:1, 2 silently; then ask this series of questions:

Who were these people who came to hear Jesus? ("Publicans" were tax collectors who routinely cheated the people; "sinners" were those who violated the law in some way. See comments under verse 1.)

Why were the Pharisees and scribes upset? (They believed that it was sinful to associate with sinful people and that by eating with such persons Jesus gave approval to their sins.)

Should a Christian isolate himself or herself from all who are not righteous? (This should arouse some discussion, including such points as whether or not it is possible to do so, and how it would affect evangelism.)

Tell the class that the two short parables of Jesus that form our lesson text bear on this subject. Introduce the class member who at this time will portray the shepherd seeking one lost sheep. After his performance, lead the class in applause. Next, introduce the class member who now will portray the woman searching for her lost coin. When she has finished, express appreciation for both performances.

Have a volunteer read Luke 15:3-10 aloud to the class. Then ask the class members to work in pairs to develop three questions the Pharisees and scribes might have wanted to ask concerning the parables. (Examples: Weren't the ninety-nine sheep in danger in being left alone? Isn't God happy that there already are good people? Why would the woman spend so much time and effort over a little coin?) After several have shared their questions, point out that all such questions miss Jesus' point. Then ask, "What *is* Jesus' point?" (The loving God is seeking His lost people, and their return is cause for great joy.)

Into Life

Give each student a copy of the chart shown below. By circling a number from one to five, each student is to indicate to what extent he or she identifies with the "characters" in today's text. One means "I'm not at all like this one," and five means "I'm very much like this one":

The tax collectors/sinners	1 2 3 4 5
The Pharisees/scribes	1 2 3 4 5
The lost sheep	1 2 3 4 5
The shepherd	1 2 3 4 5
The woman who lost the coin	1 2 3 4 5
The friends/neighbors	1 2 3 4 5

When all have completed their charts, divide the class into groups of three or four students each. Ask each person in each group to take thirty seconds to explain his or her highest scores (for example, why he or she identifies with the shepherd, the friends/neighbors, etc.).

Mention that today's text has to do with seeking the lost and restoring them to fellowship with God. Divide the class into two groups: the "Search Party" and the "Cheering Section." Have the class members in the former group discuss ways Christians today can reach out with the gospel to those lost and dying in sin. Have those in the other group discuss ways new Christians can be made to feel welcome in the church. After five or ten minutes let all share their conclusions. Close with the prayer that each class member will become involved in both efforts.

Let's Talk It Over

The questions on this page are designed to encourage review of the lesson Scriptures and to promote discussion of the lesson by the class. The answers provided are only discussion starters. Let your class talk it over from there.

1. Are we tempted to regard scornfully certain kinds of persons as "sinners," similar to the way the Pharisees and scribes looked upon the publicans and other social outcasts in Jesus' time? If so, how can we overcome this attitude?

Some may be inclined to brand as "sinners" those who practice homosexuality or adultery, those who indulge in excessive use of alcoholic beverages, and those who engage in any kind of criminal activity. Of course, such behavior is sin; but for one to look upon such persons in a proud, scornful way as "sinners" unworthy of one's consideration or God's love is to possess the kind of attitude Jesus condemned. It would be wise if every redeemed person cultivated the thought, "There but for the grace of God go I." How can one be certain that if one's environment, opportunities for sin, and temptations were the same as these "sinners," he or she would not fall into the same practices? This consideration should lead to appropriate humility and sympathy for those caught up in sin.

2. In various ways Jesus attempted to illustrate the preciousness of every human soul. How can we increase our awareness of this truth?

We remember that Jesus asked, "For what is a man profited, if he shall gain the whole world, and lose his own soul? or what shall a man give in exchange for his soul?" (Matthew 16:26). It would be well for us to list all kinds of objects that human beings consider valuable, and then after considering each one to say, "But one human soul is more valuable than this." The list could include precious gems, priceless works of art, private airplanes and yachts, fabulous holdings of stocks and bonds and real estate, and the like. The clear meaning of Jesus' words is that no material treasurers are as valuable as a person's soul. In today's Scripture text the shepherd's diligent searching for the one lost sheep reveals the value God places on a human soul.

3. What can we do to increase our awareness of the tragedy of a human soul's being lost?

It is said that the famous evangelist Billy Sunday made it his aim to put as much emphasis as possible on two words: *lost* and *eternity* We use the word *lost* in many trivial contexts: Our favorite baseball team lost a big game; we may have become temporarily lost while driving through an unfamiliar city. To be eternally lost, however, is definitely no trivial matter. We struggle to comprehend the concept of eternity. It is clear enough, though, to bring us a chill when we think of any person's being separated forever from the God who made him or her, and who is the only true source of love, joy, and hope. Furthermore, we have the biblical warnings regarding an eternal Hell (for example, Mark 9:42-48; 2 Thessalonians 1:7-9; Revelation 20:11-15), which we must not neglect.

4. Why is it important that we probe the significance of the lost coin in Jesus' parable?

For most of us the loss of a single coin would be a minor problem. Some Bible readers may glance at this parable and say, "Why all the fuss over a missing coin?" A closer look would reveal that the coin in question was worth more than a dime or quarter would be to us. If we were to lose fifty dollars or so, which is closer to the value of the coin in the parable, we would go to some effort to find that. But if, as some Bible teachers believe, the coin was part of the woman's dowry, its value would have been even greater. It, therefore, would have been a symbol of her married status. Thus the woman would have prized the coin very highly and indeed would have searched desperately to reclaim it. When we dig deeper into this parable, therefore, we discover how well it illustrates the specialness and preciousness of our souls to God.

5. What is the importance of knowing that our life in Heaven will be characterized by joy and rejoicing?

Christians may dampen their enthusiasm for Heaven by fretting over questions such as: "How will we know each other there?" "How will we feel if loved ones are missing from Heaven?" "How will we escape the embarrassment of remembering our earthly sins?" It is impossible now to answer such questions. However, if Heaven is a place of eternal rejoicing, it is clear that we will not be troubled by such matters. Revelation 21:4 assures us that those things that mar our joy on earth—death, sorrow, crying, pain—will be forever gone.

The Good Shepherd

April 21
Lesson 8

DEVOTIONAL READING: John 10:31-42.

LESSON SCRIPTURE: John 10:1-30.

PRINTED TEXT: John 10:1-18.

John 10:1-18

1 Verily, verily, I say unto you, He that entereth not by the door into the sheepfold, but climbeth up some other way, the same is a thief and a robber.

2 But he that entereth in by the door is the shepherd of the sheep.

3 To him the porter openeth; and the sheep hear his voice: and he calleth his own sheep by name, and leadeth them out.

4 And when he putteth forth his own sheep, he goeth before them, and the sheep follow him: for they know his voice.

5 And a stranger will they not follow, but will flee from him; for they know not the voice of strangers.

6 This parable spake Jesus unto them; but they understood not what things they were which he spake unto them.

7 Then said Jesus unto them again, Verily, verily, I say unto you, I am the door of the sheep.

8 All that ever came before me are thieves and robbers: but the sheep did not hear them.

9 I am the door: by me if any man enter in, he shall be saved, and shall go in and out, and find pasture.

10 The thief cometh not, but for to steal, and to kill, and to destroy: I am come that they might have life, and that they might have it more abundantly.

11 I am the good shepherd: the good shepherd giveth his life for the sheep.

12 But he that is a hireling, and not the shepherd, whose own the sheep are not, seeth the wolf coming, and leaveth the sheep, and fleeth; and the wolf catcheth them, and scattereth the sheep.

13 The hireling fleeth, because he is a hireling, and careth not for the sheep.

14 I am the good shepherd, and know my sheep, and am known of mine.

15 As the Father knoweth me, even so know I the Father: and I lay down my life for the sheep.

16 And other sheep I have, which are not of this fold: them also I must bring, and they shall hear my voice; and there shall be one fold, and one shepherd.

17 Therefore doth my Father love me, because I lay down my life, that I might take it again.

18 No man taketh it from me, but I lay it down of myself. I have power to lay it down, and I have power to take it again. This commandment have I received of my Father.

GOLDEN TEXT: I am the good shepherd: the good shepherd giveth his life for the sheep.—John 10:11.

Even without that game, we will probably never cease following leaders. In that respect we resemble sheep, whose tendency to move in flocks of followers is well known.

What leader shall we follow? That question is best answered in today's lesson, introducing Jesus as the Good Shepherd, who not only leads by direction and example, but gives His very life to caring for those who elect to follow Him.

B. Of Sheep and Shepherds

Domestic sheep need a great deal of care. They are virtually helpless against wild beasts. They are subject to disease, and to wandering far from sources of food and water. In unfenced areas they need the constant care of shepherds, who come to know the animals even by name.

Scripture abounds in references to God's people as His sheep needing and receiving His care: "We are his people, and the sheep of his pasture" (Psalm 100:3); "The Lord is my shepherd; I shall not want" (Psalm 23:1). The prophets Isaiah (40:11), Jeremiah (23:1-4), Ezekiel (34:1-19), and Zechariah (11:17) expand on the theme of God's shepherding of His people.

C. Lesson Background

Our lesson today continues the story that occupied John 9: the healing of a man born blind. John 9:39-41 tells that certain Pharisees who were following Jesus objected to His suggestion that they were spiritually blind. He responded by talking about the Good Shepherd in contrast to sheep-stealers and hirelings, and they didn't understand (John 10:6). When He finished, some of them thought He was crazy; but others disagreed, arguing that a crazy man couldn't give sight to a man who was born blind (John 10:19-21). So we look at what Jesus said that caused His hearers to argue as they did.

I. Thieves and the Shepherd (John 10:1-5)

A. The Intruder Versus the Owner (vv. 1, 2)

1, 2. Verily, verily, I say unto you, He that entereth not by the door into the sheepfold, but climbeth up some other way, the same is a thief and a robber. But he that entereth in by the door is the shepherd of the sheep.

The *you* who were addressed here had been discussing Jesus' healing of the man born blind (John 9:39-41).

The *sheepfold*—or sheep pen—was typically a walled enclosure providing nighttime protection for several flocks at a time. The walls could be of rock, high enough to keep wild animals from

---

Teachings of Jesus
Unit 2: Teachings About God
(Lessons 6-9)

Lesson Aims

This lesson should enable the student to:

1. Cite three Scriptures that help him or her to understand the relationship of sheep to shepherds in Bible lands.

2. Name three ways in which Jesus qualifies as the one completely Good Shepherd.

Lesson Outline

INTRODUCTION
  A. Follow What Leader?
  B. Of Sheep and Shepherds
  C. Lesson Background
I. THIEVES AND THE SHEPHERD (John 10:1-5)
  A. The Intruder Versus the Owner (vv. 1, 2)
  B. The Shepherd Known and Followed (vv. 3, 4)
    Somebody Knows Your Name
    Recognizing the Master's Voice
  C. Strangers Are Rejected (v. 5)
II. TEACHING NOT UNDERSTOOD (John 10:6)
III. THE DOOR AND THE INTRUDERS (John 10:7-10)
  A. Wrong Entrance and Rejection (vv. 7, 8)
  B. What Is the Purpose? (vv. 9, 10)
    I Am the Gate
IV. THE GOOD SHEPHERD (John 10:11-18)
  A. Caring Shepherd, Cowardly Hireling (vv. 11-13)
  B. Shepherd Knows and Is Known (vv. 14, 15)
  C. Welcomes the Larger Flock (v. 16)
  D. Gives His Life for the Sheep (vv. 17, 18)
CONCLUSION
  A. Who Follows Whom?
  B. Prayer of a Faulty Follower
  C. Thought to Remember

Visual 8 of the visuals packet shows the risk a shepherd takes to rescue a lost sheep. The visual is shown on page 291.

Introduction

A. Follow What Leader?

Do you remember an old game called "Follow the Leader"? The leader liked to choose a course or perform feats that others couldn't accomplish, and so they would have to fall out.

leaping over, and topped with thorns to keep thieves from climbing them. One opening, closed with a door or gate, would be guarded by a gatekeeper in the shepherds' absence.

Penalties for sheep-stealing were written early into the law of Moses (Exodus 22:1). The *thief* comes to steal by surprise or in secret. The *robber* comes with violence openly, as marauding bands of Midianites plundered Israel in the time of Gideon (Judges 6:1-6). The owner-shepherd of any flock in the fold could come openly to the gate to be recognized and admitted.

B. The Shepherd Known and Followed (vv. 3, 4)

3. To him the porter openeth; and the sheep hear his voice: and he calleth his own sheep by name, and leadeth them out.

The shepherd comes each morning to the sheep pen. He is admitted by the gatekeeper and starts to call out his own sheep *by name*. They recognize his voice and respond to their names.

To the leader of men it is surely not less important to know and call by name those whom one would lead. It is a skill sometimes used by charlatans, but priceless when it expresses a genuine regard for the person.

SOMEBODY KNOWS YOUR NAME

The same technology that gave us space travel, interplanetary probes, and communication satellites flows into our daily lives through cable television, cellular phones, and bar-coded supermarket check-out lines.

However, as progress has enriched us, it has raised our anxieties. There is in modern life a sense that we have ceded some vital control over our own destinies to impersonal forces. To the Social Security Administration, the IRS, and countless other bureaucracies, you are a nine-digit number. To your state's Department of Motor Vehicles you are a number such as QA916592.

Yet there is Someone who doesn't want to process you as a number, but to know and care for you as a person. Speaking of himself as the Good Shepherd, Jesus said that He calls His own sheep by name and leads them out. No matter how complicated modern life becomes, you have a Savior who knows your name and watches over you as one of His own.   —C. B. Mc.

4. And when he putteth forth his own sheep, he goeth before them, and the sheep follow him: for they know his voice.

Once a shepherd's flock is outside the pen, he goes ahead of it and *leads* on to the places of pasture, shade, and water, talking as he goes.

In the church the true shepherd leads by example, doing what the sheep have not yet learned to do (1 Peter 5:3); also by teaching, saying what the sheep do not yet know or believe. The false teacher, on the other hand, will drive the flock from behind (Matthew 23:4), or say only those things the people already know and wish to hear (2 Timothy 4:3).

RECOGNIZING THE MASTER'S VOICE

Imagine being able to tell your computer to program your VCR, pay the phone bill, schedule a lunch date, or fetch your electronic mail. Such technology will be widely available at work and at home in the near future. Already AT&T has begun installing computerized voice recognition systems that can recognize words like "collect" and "person to person" about as well as a human operator can.

Though a computer that recognizes human voices will bring revolutionary changes to the way we work and transact business, a more revolutionary change takes place when a person learns to recognize the voice of Jesus in his or her own life. The Lord said that His sheep would know His voice and would follow Him. Later on in the Gospel of John (14:25, 26 and 16:12-14), Jesus promised that the Holy Spirit would guide His apostles to record His teaching for future generations of believers. When we read the New Testament, we do something far more amazing than a computer that understands human speech. We hear the very voice of Jesus directing our lives in the way of eternal life.

—C. B. Mc.

C. Strangers Are Rejected (v. 5)

5. And a stranger will they not follow, but will flee from him; for they know not the voice of strangers.

The sound of the voice that has accompanied care, security, and provision makes the difference between the sheep's following confidently and running away. The leader in the church

The good shepherd giveth his life for the sheep.

visual 8

needs to be around long enough to build confidence in a familiar, caring voice.

These first five verses clearly establish Jesus as the *shepherd*, in contrast to the false prophets, false messiahs, and heartless religious leaders (Matthew 23) who had taken advantage of the people.

II. Teaching Not Understood (John 10:6)

6. This parable spake Jesus unto them; but they understood not what things they were which he spake unto them.

Parable. The word John used indicates a comparison, analogy, or figure of speech, rather than the kind of story usually called a parable. The Pharisees did not see the point in what Jesus said. Thus they showed the dimness of their spiritual vision (John 9:39-41). How many times do any of us need to hear or read a Bible teaching before we really understand it and make it a part of ourselves? Jesus often felt the need to repeat and explain.

III. The Door and the Intruders (John 10:7-10)

From being the Shepherd of the flock, Jesus becomes the one through whom all others must come to establish their claims.

A. Wrong Entrance and Rejection (vv. 7, 8)

7. Then said Jesus unto them again, Verily, verily, I say unto you, I am the door of the sheep.

I am the door. The sheep would come through Him for protection and would go through Him to find pasture. Those who would claim the right to lead and feed their flocks must come through Him. Later He said plainly, "I am the way, the truth, and the life: no man cometh unto the Father, but by me" (John 14:6). That is echoed in the words of the apostle Peter, "There is none other name under heaven given among men, whereby we must be saved" (Acts 4:12).

8. All that ever came before me are thieves and robbers: but the sheep did not hear them.

Anyone else who claimed the authority Jesus did was claiming too much. The heroes of the Old Testament did not make such claims. But robbery was not foreign to some described in Jeremiah 23:1: "Woe be unto the pastors that destroy and scatter the sheep of my pasture! saith the Lord." Ezekiel 34:2-16 provides a fuller description of the same kind of rogues. The situation became even more serious with the end of the Old Testament prophetic period, when the

dominant teachers added their interpretations and adjustments as having authority sometimes supplanting Scripture. Jesus charged the teachers of His own time with making Scripture ineffective by their traditions (Matthew 15:3-9). And by their treatment of the recently healed blind man (John 9:22, 34), the Pharisees standing before Jesus at the moment demonstrated the truth of the charge He was making.

The sheep did not hear them. The common people were paying less and less attention to the clerical establishment—a fact that rendered that establishment intensely jealous of Jesus' popularity.

B. What Is the Purpose? (vv. 9, 10)

9. I am the door: by me if any man enter in, he shall be saved, and shall go in and out, and find pasture.

Entrance into the state of salvation is through Jesus Christ as Lord—trustful *faith* in Him, turning to Him and His way in *repentance, confession* of Him as Lord and Savior, burial with Him in *baptism*, and the *new life as His follower*.

The safety of the sheepfold is not enough. Christ is also the *door* through which one walks each day to feed one's spirit on Scripture and Christian fellowship, and to exercise oneself and grow in following Him as Shepherd.

I AM THE GATE

In 1846, the American explorer John Charles Fremont named the five-mile-long strait at the entrance to San Francisco Bay. He called it the Golden Gate. The famous Golden Gate Bridge spans that strait to connect San Francisco on the south with Marin County on the north. Begun in 1933, the bridge opened in 1937. Its center span is suspended from two towers 746 feet high. It reaches 4,200 feet across the strait, 220 feet above the water. It is one of America's most remarkable engineering feats and remains one of the longest suspension bridges in the world.

Jesus said He is the gate that spans the greatest gulf that ever existed: the eternal chasm between sinful men and a holy God. "Whoever enters through me will be saved" was His promise. He is the bridge, the entranceway into the kingdom, our golden gate into Heaven.

—C. B. Mc.

10. The thief cometh not, but for to steal, and to kill, and to destroy: I am come that they might have life, and that they might have it more abundantly.

The sheep-stealer would have no interest in the animal except to get what he could for its wool and its carcass. The false teachers' interest was to claim and count followers and to exercise control, thus depriving them of the life Jesus came to give. Such "leaders" have been known literally to murder persons unwilling to conform to their pattern. Jesus' enemies were even then plotting to kill Him.

The *abundance* of life to which the Lord Jesus provides access is notable first for its *extent*. It is everlasting (John 3:16). It abounds also in *quality*. Jesus is the source of all light and life. It abounds in *outreach*, encompassing fellowship with the family of God in all times and throughout all the earth. It abounds in *purpose and meaning,* extending to partnership with the Almighty in His work. Is there, in fact, any meaningful direction in which the Christian life does not extend beyond human limits? That is the reason, after all, for the apostle John's writing his Gospel: "These are written, that ye might believe that Jesus is the Christ, the Son of God; and that believing ye might have life through his name" (John 20:31).

IV. The Good Shepherd
(John 10:11-18)

A. Caring Shepherd, Cowardly Hireling
(vv. 11-13)

11. I am the good shepherd: the good shepherd giveth his life for the sheep.

The good shepherd. The one perfect and ideal Shepherd had been prefigured in Psalm 23, Ezekiel 34:23, and this from Isaiah 40:11: "He shall feed his flock like a shepherd: he shall gather the lambs with his arm, and carry them in his bosom, and shall gently lead those that are with young."

There are physical risks in protecting a flock from wild animals and vicious men (Genesis 31:39; 1 Samuel 17:34-36). Shepherds sometimes die in the attempt; and Jesus gave this "last full measure of devotion" to His ministry for mankind. This fact had been emphasized in Jesus' teaching, but it was not yet understood even by His closest friends. That would happen only after His death.

The *giving of life,* however, did not begin and end with physical death. The shepherd's life—his time, interests, and life-style—was given to his flock from the day he became a shepherd. It was even more so for Jesus, whose self-giving is spelled out in Philippians 2:5-8. Beginning with His surrender of heavenly glory for earthly limitations, it includes the acceptance of humble service in the path of obedience all the way to the cross. His was a lifetime of life-giving.

12, 13. But he that is a hireling, and not the shepherd, whose own the sheep are not, seeth the wolf coming, and leaveth the sheep, and fleeth; and the wolf catcheth them, and scattereth the sheep. The hireling fleeth, because he is a hireling, and careth not for the sheep.

Not every hired worker displays the *hireling* spirit that is interested only in his pay and his perks. Many hired shepherds care genuinely for the flock, just as many hired baby-sitters care for their charges and will protect them heroically in emergencies. What the Lord seeks among His people are servants who love and care for the folk who belong to the Lord.

There are, however, hireling spirits in the church, saying and doing what is popular for material gain, or looking around for a congregation where they can be most comfortable. The fault lies in putting their own advantage above the welfare of the Lord's flock.

The *wolf* is a major threat to the flock, killing some and scattering the rest to suffer all kinds of harm. Concerning God's human flock, Jesus warned against false prophets who "come to you in sheep's clothing, but inwardly they are ravening wolves" (Matthew 7:15); and Paul exhorted elders in the church to guard against the intrusion of "grievous wolves . . . not sparing the flock," and "speaking perverse things, to draw away disciples after them" (Acts 20:29, 30). It takes courage for any shepherd to stand up against well-disguised wolves.

B. Shepherd Knows and Is Known
(vv. 14, 15)

Here Jesus began to move from the Good Shepherd's relation with the sheep toward His relation with the heavenly Father.

14, 15. I am the good shepherd, and know my sheep, and am known of mine. As the Father knoweth me, even so know I the Father: and I lay down my life for the sheep.

There are three special qualifications that identify the Good Shepherd. First is His perfect *knowledge* of each member of His flock, answered by the sheep's recognition of Him as the shepherd. The knowledge in each instance includes awareness, recognition, and acquaintance, as one knows a friend so as to talk truthfully *about* him and to talk comfortably *with* him. Paul counted this knowledge of Christ as more valuable to him than anything or all things beside (Philippians 3:10).

Next among the Good Shepherd's qualifications was His perfect *intimacy with God* as His Father. That included Jesus' complete awareness of the Father's will and a total eagerness to perform it. So His every word or deed was accomplished with divine awareness, authority, and approval.

The third and crowning qualification was this: the Good Shepherd continually *lays down His life* for the sheep, in days of labor and nights of prayer, as well as in sacrificial death for them. "Greater love hath no man than this, that a man lay down his life for his friends" (John 15:13).

C. Welcomes the Larger Flock (v. 16)

16. And other sheep I have, which are not of this fold: them also I must bring, and they shall hear my voice; and there shall be one fold, and one shepherd.

The Good Shepherd could not limit His care to the sheep presently in one protective enclosure. That enclosure was obviously the Jewish people who would hear and follow Him. Non-Jews also would hear His invitation and come under His care. That had already started to happen in Samaria (John 4:39-42). It would go forward as the gospel was preached to Cornelius (Acts 10), then in Antioch (Acts 11:19-23), and then throughout the Roman Empire. Gentiles became part of the Lord's *one flock.* That oneness is made very clear in Acts 15 and Ephesians 2:13-18, and it is built entirely on their common loyalty to the one Good Shepherd, Jesus Christ.

D. Gives His Life for the Sheep
(vv. 17, 18)

17, 18. Therefore doth my Father love me, because I lay down my life, that I might take it again. No man taketh it from me, but I lay it down of myself. I have power to lay it down, and I have power to take it again. This commandment have I received of my Father.

God's love for His one and only Son was never conditional, but there were special occasions when God's pleasure was made known. Matthew 3:17 and 17:5 mention it in connection with

Jesus' baptism and His transfiguration. Philippians 2:9-11 emphasizes it in response to Jesus' willing obedience in going to the cross: "Wherefore God also hath highly exalted him, and given him a name which is above every name."

Matthew 26:53 emphasizes the voluntary self-sacrifice, noting that legions of angels were available to rescue Jesus from execution if He requested it. His was the *power*—the authority and the ability—to choose His course. That *commandment*—that commission, was bestowed by the Father. Our Shepherd is good beyond comparison, and beyond description, even in the words of His own choosing.

Conclusion
A. Who Follows Whom?

The teaching before us resulted in a division among the Pharisees who heard it, some being more than ever determined to follow their traditions in opposition to Jesus, whom they called insane and demon-possessed. Some, on the other hand, were drawn to follow Jesus, saying that a demon never could speak as Jesus spoke, nor produce such a miracle as healing a man born blind (John 10:19-21).

Our Good Shepherd does indeed create division when He comes as owner of the sheep and calls His own to follow Him. If He would limit himself to works of mercy and words of wisdom, all kinds of sheep would feed at His trough. But when He claims sole authority and asserts that none can come to the heavenly Father except by following Him, multitudes will choose to follow other leaders, more comfortably adjusted to the world around them. But the world around them is doomed to ultimate destruction.

John recalls another time when followers of Jesus decided that He demanded too much and turned away. Then Jesus asked the apostles if they would also go away, and Peter responded, "Lord, to whom shall we go? thou hast the words of eternal life" (John 6:66-69).

In choosing your leader, check his credentials and see where he is going. The Good Shepherd still offers the only lasting and abundant life.

B. Prayer of a Faulty Follower

Thank You, our eternal God, for sending Your Son to be our Good Shepherd, leading in the way of life by His willing death. Help us, we pray, to follow Him more faithfully in His way of life, abundant and eternal. Amen.

C. Thought to Remember

"The Lord is my shepherd; I shall not want" (Psalm 23:1).

Home Daily Bible Readings

Monday, Apr. 15—Sheep Without a Shepherd (Mark 6:30-34)
Tuesday, Apr. 16—Encourage One Another (Hebrews 10:19-25)
Wednesday, Apr. 17—God's Resurrecting Power (Hebrews 13:17-21)
Thursday, Apr. 18—Corrupt Leadership (Ezekiel 22:23-31)
Friday, Apr. 19—God Knows His Own (2 Timothy 2:14-19)
Saturday, Apr. 20—Genuine Security (John 10:23-30)
Sunday, Apr. 21—Authenticated by Works (John 10:31-42)

Learning by Doing

This page contains an alternate lesson plan emphasizing learning activities. Classes desiring such student involvement will find these suggestions helpful.

Learning Goals

As a result of participating in today's lesson, a student will be able to:

1. Identify the meaning of the various elements of the parable in John 10:1-18.

2. Explain the shepherd/sheep relationship we have with Jesus Christ.

3. Express the goodness of Jesus as our shepherd and the abundance of life we have in Him.

Into the Lesson

As far in advance as possible, ask someone to come to your class dressed as a first-century shepherd and talk for about five minutes about the role of the shepherd, the care of the sheep, and the practices associated with shepherding. The person will probably have to do some research for this information.

After this presentation, point out that the Bible writers used this as an analogy frequently. Today's lesson focuses on Jesus as our Good Shepherd.

Into the Word

Ask the class for volunteers to read John 10:1-18 two verses at a time. With everyone studying the passage, ask, "What does this passage tell us about the Shepherd?" (These questions are in the student book.) As students respond, write their answers in a column on a chalkboard or poster board. Possible answers: He enters by the gate; He leads; He knows the sheep by name; He is good; He is willing to die for the sheep; He has authority from the Father.

Ask a second question, "What does this passage tell us about the sheep?" Write the responses in another column on the chalkboard or poster board. Possible answers: They are in danger; they know the shepherd and listen to his voice; they follow him; they don't follow others.

Summarize this study by pointing out that we are like sheep spiritually, weak and in need of a shepherd who will feed, guide, and protect us.

Review what the Old Testament has to say about our role as sheep (this is in the student book). Refer the students to the following passages and seek insights into our spiritual lives: Psalm 23:1-4; Psalm 100:3; Isaiah 40:11; Isaiah 53:6, 7; Jeremiah 31:10; Ezekiel 34:1-16, 22-24; and Micah 2:12. Lead the class to see that God frequently has pictured himself as our Shepherd.

He leads, guides, and protects us. He meets our needs. We belong to the One who created us. His care is loving and gentle. Our sin has caused us to go astray; the Shepherd must save us. God will protect us from evil shepherds; Jesus is the Son of David who will be the Good Shepherd and bring all God's sheep together.

Into Life

In order to review these truths, play this game fashioned after the TV game show, *Jeopardy*. On large sheets of paper, print each of the following (the answer/question is also given for each):

1. He lays down his life for the sheep.
   (Who is the Good Shepherd?)
2. He kills and destroys the sheep.
   (Who is the thief?)
3. The place where the sheep stay overnight.
   (What is the sheepfold?)
4. The one from whom the sheep will run.
   (Who is the stranger?)
5. They know the shepherd's voice.
   (Who are his sheep?)
6. The type of life possessed by those who follow the Good Shepherd.
   (What is abundant life?)
7. He opens the gate for the shepherd.
   (Who is the porter or gatekeeper?)
8. He catches and scatters the sheep.
   (What is the wolf?)
9. As grass for sheep, it is our spiritual food.
   (What is the Bible?)
10. The promise to those who enter through the gate.
    (What is salvation?)

Divide the class into two or three teams, with each team selecting a leader to "buzz in." As you show and read each "answer" sheet, the leaders signal when they think their group has the correct "question" (or the groups could take turns answering). One point is given for each correct "question."

In Jesus we have a Good Shepherd and abundant life. After allowing a few moments for reflection, ask for volunteers to tell of the differences Jesus has made in their lives as the Good Shepherd who gives life more abundantly. Allow several minutes of sharing and then conclude with prayer.

Let's Talk It Over

The questions on this page are designed to encourage review of the lesson Scriptures and to promote discussion of the lesson by the class. The answers provided are only discussion starters. Let your class talk it over from there.

1. The Bible frequently compares us human beings with sheep. Since sheep are weak and foolish creatures, that may not seem a complimentary comparison. But in what ways is it accurate?

It is vital that we acknowledge our weaknesses. We are physically weak, prone to illness, accident, and aging. Even worse, we are morally weak, often making unwise choices that entangle us in sin and its damaging effects. That we are foolish is demonstrated in countless ways. Consider how we often wander away from God and the clear teachings of His Word. Remember how we let our physical appetites and such emotions as anger and pride control our behavior. Many human beings enjoy thinking of themselves as strong and self-sufficient. However, the truth is that we are all in need of a wise leader, a shepherd. And there is only one Shepherd wise enough and powerful enough to lead us to safety. With the psalmist we should gratefully confess, "We are his people, and the sheep of his pasture" (Psalm 100:3).

2. How is it helpful to think of Jesus as a door or gate?

To enter through a door or gate is generally a simple matter, and we can receive the salvation Jesus offers through simple faith and obedience. It is not always *easy* to enter a door. For example, we may have to force ourselves to enter a dentist's office or the home of someone to whom we owe an apology. It is not easy, though simple, to answer Jesus' call to a better life. Another noteworthy aspect of a door is that it may signify our entering a place of safety and calm. After a hectic workday, we may breathe a sigh of relief upon entering the door of home. One being pursued by an angry dog will find safety in closing the gate to his yard. In similar fashion we experience a sense of safety and calmness of soul when we enter through Jesus into His kingdom.

3. John 10:10 indicates that we should enjoy an abundant life in Christ. What does this involve, and how might this be misinterpreted?

We might think of abundance as only the eternal duration of our life in Christ. But Jesus surely meant more than that. Both now and in the heavenly existence to come our abundant life is to feature a growing knowledge of God the Father and Jesus Christ the Son. We shall come more and more "to know the love of Christ, which passeth knowledge" (Ephesians 3:19). We shall have an increasing appreciation of the riches of God's grace, of His unsearchable wisdom, and His inexhaustible power. Some Bible readers may look at John 10:10 and relate it to the popular idea that a Christian is promised material wealth and perfect health. But neither in this place nor elsewhere does the Bible support such a viewpoint.

4. Jesus the Good Shepherd lays down His life for His sheep. The lesson writer points out that this sacrifice of Jesus took in more than His death on Calvary. Like the shepherd with his sheep, Jesus spent His life in supplying the needs of His flock. Can you think of Scriptures that speak of His giving himself even today for His followers?

After delivering the Great Commission in Matthew 28:18-20, Jesus proclaimed the promise, "Lo, I am with you alway, even unto the end of the world." Jesus has committed himself to being with His church in its evangelism and teaching. Jesus' continuing service toward us is also described in Hebrews 7:25: "Wherefore he is able also to save them to the uttermost that come unto God by him, seeing he ever liveth to make intercession for them."

5. Jesus the Good Shepherd knows His sheep, and His sheep know Him. How is this a reassuring statement?

We are often made to feel like mere statistics. We are known by various numbers: our Social Security number, our employee number, our address and telephone number, etc. At times this world seems terribly impersonal. In Jesus' kingdom it is not so. He has a personal knowledge of each of us. He is personally interested in each one of His millions of followers living in various lands. And we also can know Him in a personal, intimate way. He is not distant, aloof, far removed from us. We can grow in our knowledge of Him through His Supper and His church, through our association with others who know Him and love Him, and through our personal devotion with the Word and prayer.

The True Vine

DEVOTIONAL READING: John 15:18-27.

LESSON SCRIPTURE: John 15:1-17.

PRINTED TEXT: John 15:1-17.

John 15:1-17

1 I am the true vine, and my Father is the husbandman.

2 Every branch in me that beareth not fruit he taketh away: and every branch that beareth fruit, he purgeth it, that it may bring forth more fruit.

3 Now ye are clean through the word which I have spoken unto you.

4 Abide in me, and I in you. As the branch cannot bear fruit of itself, except it abide in the vine; no more can ye, except ye abide in me.

5 I am the vine, ye are the branches. He that abideth in me, and I in him, the same bringeth forth much fruit: for without me ye can do nothing.

6 If a man abide not in me, he is cast forth as a branch, and is withered; and men gather them, and cast them into the fire, and they are burned.

7 If ye abide in me, and my words abide in you, ye shall ask what ye will, and it shall be done unto you.

8 Herein is my Father glorified, that ye bear much fruit; so shall ye be my disciples.

9 As the Father hath loved me, so have I loved you: continue ye in my love.

10 If ye keep my commandments, ye shall abide in my love; even as I have kept my Father's commandments, and abide in his love.

11 These things have I spoken unto you, that my joy might remain in you, and that your joy might be full.

12 This is my commandment, That ye love one another, as I have loved you.

13 Greater love hath no man than this, that a man lay down his life for his friends.

14 Ye are my friends, if ye do whatsoever I command you.

15 Henceforth I call you not servants; for the servant knoweth not what his lord doeth: but I have called you friends; for all things that I have heard of my Father I have made known unto you.

16 Ye have not chosen me, but I have chosen you, and ordained you, that ye should go and bring forth fruit, and that your fruit should remain; that whatsoever ye shall ask of the Father in my name, he may give it you.

17 These things I command you, that ye love one another.

GOLDEN TEXT: I am the vine, ye are the branches. He that abideth in me, and I in him, the same bringeth forth much fruit; for without me ye can do nothing.
—John 15:5.

Teachings of Jesus
Unit 2. Teachings About God
(Lessons 6-9)

Lesson Aims

This study should prepare the student to:

1. Identify several of the persons introduced or represented in the text before us.

2. Tell how the word *you* in Jesus' presentation applies especially to the apostles and how it applies to Christians generally.

3. Establish a pattern for increasing his or her own fruitfulness in Christ.

Lesson Outline

INTRODUCTION
    A. Who Pulled the Plug?
    B. Grapes of Provision and Judgment
    C. Lesson Background
I. THE VINE AND ITS CARETAKER (John 15:1-3)
    Leaves or Fruit?
II. THE VINE AND ITS BRANCHES (John 15:4-6)
    A. Connected and Fruitful (vv. 4, 5)
    Attached to the Vine
    B. Fate of the Unfruitful (v. 6)
III. VITAL CONNECTION (John 15:7-11)
    A. Reaching and Glorifying God (vv. 7, 8)
    Bearing Fruit
    B. Living in the Power of Love (vv. 9, 10)
    C. Equipped for Joy (v. 11)
IV. LOVE AS THE LINK (John 15:12-17)
    A. Command and Demonstration (vv. 12, 13)
    B. Friendship and Its Fruits (vv. 14-16)
    C. Establishing the Link (v. 17)
CONCLUSION
    A. "I Am With You"
    B. The Other Side of the Coin
    C. Prayer of a Needy Branch
    D. Thought to Remember

Visual 9 of the visuals packet illustrates the theme of today's lesson, bearing fruit by abiding in Christ. The visual is shown on page 301.

Introduction
A. Who Pulled the Plug?

"Come home, please! Now!"

The frantic tones of the wife's voice on the telephone brought a day's work at the office to a halt as the husband rushed to the rescue at home. Through the open door to the basement

came the smell of death—death of a winter's supply of roasts and steaks in the family's now-warm freezer chest. Removal and disposal of the mass decay was a long and memorable task. Meanwhile the family's playful puppy, at home in the basement, showed a continuing interest in the electric cord which he had apparently pulled free from its outlet several days previously.

Nothing works when it is deprived of its vital power! This fact is more familiar to many modern city dwellers than is the ageless principle of growing things. Nothing lives and grows unless it has a vital connection with sources of energy in light, moisture, and nutrition. In bushes, vines, and trees, life requires roots in the ground, bringing nutrients to standing trunks, which supply branches and leaves, flowers, and fruit. All must grow together.

The spiritual life of mankind is equally dependent on a vital connection with its source in God, through His Son, Jesus Christ our Lord. The Lord himself said so, in terms familiar to fruit growers everywhere.

B. Grapes of Provision and Judgment

In Scripture the grapevine became a symbol for Israel itself, as God's vine, transplanted from Egypt to a place prepared for it. The nation failed to produce the expected spiritual fruit, however; and God, in judgment, permitted it to be trampled down (Psalm 80:8-16; Isaiah 5:1-7; Jeremiah 2:21; Hosea 10:1, 2). Jesus also spoke judgment on men who withheld the proper return from God's well-prepared vineyard (Mark 12:1-12).

C. Lesson Background

Events of Jesus' final week moved swiftly. It was the Passover season, and the Lord made careful arrangements to observe the feast with His apostles. Near the end of the supper He used the ceremonial bread and fruit of the vine in establishing a memorial Communion to be observed by the church in time to come. Lingering at the table, Jesus spoke to the apostles about His departure to prepare a place for them in His Father's house. At last He said, "Let us go hence" (John 14:31).

The Lord's next recorded words provide the text for our study. Were the words spoken while the group was still in the upper room, seeing and smelling the "fruit of the vine"? Or was the group walking through the city toward Gethsemane, perhaps passing near the temple with its great ornamental golden vine, heavy with clusters, over the door? In either case, there was something nearby to illustrate what Jesus was talking about.

I. The Vine and Its Caretaker
(John 15:1-3)

1. I am the true vine, and my Father is the husbandman.

Jesus wove literal fact and symbolic comparison so skillfully that there is little need for explanation. He spoke literally of himself and His Father in Heaven. He spoke figuratively of the vine and the gardener who labored to make the vine productive.

Jesus had spoken of himself as *light* and *life* and *Good Shepherd* (John 9:5; 14:6; 10:14). Now He spoke of the *true vine* in contrast with Israel in its disappointing performance and in contrast with such material figures as were seen nearby.

The *vine* is, in fact, the entire growth—root, stalk, branches, and leaves. Christ's people are a part of himself, as members of His body, the church (1 Corinthians 12:12). Christ is all, and in all (Colossians 3:11).

2. Every branch in me that beareth not fruit he taketh away: and every branch that beareth fruit, he purgeth it, that it may bring forth more fruit.

In me describes the relationship of the believer to his Lord. In his epistles Paul uses the phrase, "in Christ," nearly one hundred times. Believers are baptized "into Jesus Christ" (Romans 6:3; Galatians 3:27). "If any man be in Christ, he is a new creature" (2 Corinthians 5:17).

Beareth fruit. Grapevines are cultivated to produce grapes. Grapes are produced, not on the stalk, but on the branches. The unfruitful branch is cut off and discarded (Matthew 7:16-20). The Lord's living branches are expected to produce "the fruits of righteousness, which are by Jesus Christ, unto the glory and praise of God" (Philippians 1:11).

God, the caretaker of His vine, does the pruning, first removing the unfruitful branches, and then clearing the fruitful branches of hindrances to their becoming even more fruitful.

So God allows to Christians the cleansing disciplines of sorrow, disappointment, and trial. He sometimes uses His pruning knife to remove excesses of luxury and pleasure that hinder the believer's spiritual development. So the most joyous and effective servants of the Lord may be those who have least of the world's "good life."

LEAVES OR FRUIT?

Matthew 21 records an unusual event in the last week of Jesus' earthly ministry. Walking from Bethany into Jerusalem, the Lord passed a fig tree. He examined it and found that it was full of leaves, but had no fruit. Jesus said it would never bear fruit, and it withered and died.

The tree wasn't exactly a lazy fig tree. It was full of leaves. It was busy. It was doing something. It had absorbed light from the sun. It had taken in carbon dioxide from the surrounding air. It had drawn up water and nutrients from the soil. And it had done something with all these resources. It had used them to build its own roots, stems, branches, and leaves. But it was missing the one thing God had created it to produce: figs! It was full of activity, but no fruit.

Churches and people also can be very busy and still produce no fruit. What happens as a result of the ministries carried on by your church? Do they result in changed lives, in the salvation of lost people, and in the making of disciples? Are you producing leaves or fruit?   —C. B. Mc.

3. Now ye are clean through the word which I have spoken unto you.

The sharp blade of Jesus' teaching had been at work on the apostles for about three years, cutting away at their worldly pride and ambition, convincing them to leave all else and follow Him. They still had much to learn, but they were on their way. The same cleansing word, conveyed through Scripture, is available to all who will hear, believe, and obey.

II. The Vine and Its Branches
(John 15:4-6)

A. Connected and Fruitful (vv. 4, 5)

4. Abide in me, and I in you. As the branch cannot bear fruit of itself, except it abide in the vine; no more can ye, except ye abide in me.

Abide translates a simple word with many applications—*remain, continue, dwell, live.* Jesus was asking the disciples to keep on living in Him even after His going back to be with His Father. This was said within the hour after Jesus had provided the most meaningful instrument for abiding in Him—the memorial bread and fruit of the vine, through which His people were to enjoy fellowship with Him until He comes again (1 Corinthians 11:26). Paul acknowledged the abiding as he wrote, "Christ liveth in me" (Galatians 2:20).

The branch cannot bear fruit on its own power; neither can it bear fruit that is foreign to its own vine. A grapevine does not bear figs (James 3:12), nor a Christian produce the works of the devil. "He that saith he abideth in him [Christ] ought himself also so to walk, even as he walked" (1 John 2:6).

5. I am the vine, ye are the branches. He that abideth in me, and I in him, the same bringeth forth much fruit; for without me ye can do nothing.

Jesus was talking directly to the apostles, but His statement applies also to "them also which shall believe on me through their word" (John 17:20). The reference is clearly to believers as individuals, related directly and intimately to Jesus as the vine.

The verse emphasizes, both positively and negatively, what has been said. The fruit-bearing capacity of the one living in Christ is amazingly great. For one who relies on his own power, there is no capacity at all.

ATTACHED TO THE VINE

Against their dad's orders, two brothers were playing football on the lawn next to their dad's tomato patch. "Go long," the quarterback called, as he rifled a pass just beyond the outstretched fingertips of his receiver. It was a beautiful diving catch, but the downfield brother landed on the tomato plants.

Frantically the boys retied the plants, but that still left the half dozen tomatoes they had broken off. To cover their crime, the pair worked a little magic with clear adhesive tape.

For close to a week their dad was none the wiser. But in time the atrophying tomatoes begged for a closer examination, which revealed that the dying fruit was not really attached to the vine. The ruse was up, and the two deceivers were brought to justice.

Jesus' analogy of the branches and the vine shows that unless we are connected to Him, we cannot bear fruit, and eventually we will die. Are you really connected to Him, or are you just taped up for show?   —C. B. Mc.

B. Fate of the Unfruitful (v. 6)

6. If a man abide not in me, he is cast forth as a branch, and is withered; and men gather them, and cast them into the fire, and they are burned.

When any person, for whatever reason, fails to live continually in vital relationship to Christ, that person is thrown away from God's fruitful vine and gradually loses even the appearance of spiritual life. This should serve as a solemn warning to anyone who supposes that he or she has no real need for such ongoing relationships as prayer, Bible reading, Communion at the Lord's table, and encouragement with the Lord's people (Hebrews 10:19-27). How else can a person sustain a meaningful life in Christ? The withering may be so gradual as to be for a time unnoticed, but it occurs with fatal certainty.

Men gather them. Matthew 13:41, 42 names angels as having the task of bringing together the scattered single branches and consigning them to the flames. They are worthless, even to be used as fuel.

Note the progressive fate of the branch that lacks a continuing vital attachment to the vine. It is *fruitless*; it is *cut off*; it *withers*; it is *bundled up* with others like itself; it is *cast into the fire and burned.* Can the process be halted and reversed? Only if the branch goes back to its beginning, with an eager strengthening of attachment to the True Vine!

Thus far the Lord's discourse has dealt with the True Vine in His relationships: with the Father, with believers, with moral values, and with those who reject Him. Now we turn to specific benefits of living in Him.

III. Vital Connection
(John 15:7-11)

A. Reaching and Glorifying God
(vv. 7, 8)

7. If ye abide in me, and my words abide in you, ye shall ask what ye will, and it shall be done unto you.

Here is a great promise based on a great condition, and leading to a great disappointment in the careless and inattentive: "Ye ask, and receive not, because ye ask amiss, that ye may consume it upon your lusts" (James 4:3).

Jesus' disciples must not only live in Christ; they must have Christ living in them. His teaching must come to life in the thoughts, words, and actions of the believer. The believer's prayer will be like Jesus' prayer in Gethsemane: "Not my will, but thine, be done" (Luke 22:42). The asking will be in harmony with the divine will expressed through Jesus, and God will respond to the prayer with His doing. The response may not follow the immediate plans of him who prays, but it will honor his loftier purpose. The Father will give what is asked in the name—the whole person—of Jesus (John 16:23).

8. Herein is my Father glorified, that ye bear much fruit; so shall ye be my disciples.

God the Father is glorified in what Jesus the Son says and does. God is also glorified in what the Son accomplishes through the disciples He has taught. Fruit-bearing does not make one a follower of Jesus, but it does reveal who is a follower. "By their fruits ye shall know them" (Matthew 7:20).

BEARING FRUIT

Hungry? Could I interest you in the ripened ovary of a seed-bearing plant, together with the edible fleshy accessory parts? What's that? Fruit. From insects to humans, fruits form an important part of the diet of many living things. We eat them raw. We cook them, dry them, can

visual 9

*I am the vine,
ye are the branches.
He that abideth in me,
and I in him, the same bringeth
forth much fruit;
for without me ye can do nothing.*

them, squeeze them into juice, and boil them into jellies and preserves.

Being food is only a secondary function of fruits. Their principal role is in reproduction. Fruit protects the developing seeds and aids in their distribution. Fruit is part of God's plan for ensuring that each kind of fruit-bearing plant will continue to exist. It is evidence that a plant is alive and will have a life in the future.

The New Testament often speaks of spiritual fruit. Righteousness, truth, and benevolence are all mentioned as fruit. In Galatians 5:22, 23 Paul names the fruit of the Spirit: love, joy, peace, patience, kindness, goodness, faithfulness, gentleness, and self-control. Spiritual fruit is evidence of Christ's life in us and a preview of the life He will lead us to live in eternity. —C. B. Mc.

B. Living in the Power of Love
(vv. 9, 10)

Love identifies the followers of Christ: "By this shall all men know that ye are my disciples, if ye have love one to another" (John 13:35).

9. As the Father hath loved me, so have I loved you: continue ye in my love.

God had publicly declared His pleasure in Jesus as His "beloved Son" (Matthew 3:17; 17:5). Jesus' life was a constant expression of self-forgetful love for all mankind, but He maintained a special affection for certain friends (John 11:5) and His closest companions (John 13:23). John 13:1 declares that Jesus, "having loved his own which were in the world, he loved them unto the end," or to the very limit.

Continue ye in my love. Here is the same word that is elsewhere translated *abide*. *Love* is the bonding agent for the union of vine and branch. As moisture must flow throughout a plant for it to live, so love must be continually received from Christ and returned to Christ for the believer to bear fruit.

10. If ye keep my commandments, ye shall abide in my love; even as I have kept my Father's commandments, and abide in his love.

Keep my commandments. The language indicates something more than a reluctant conformity. *Keep* suggests the work of a guard, protecting a treasure. The divine precepts are to be thus respected. First John 5:3 says it: "This is the love of God, that we keep his commandments: and his commandments are not grievous."

Obedience is surely a part of that protective regard for our Lord's commandments. If we love, we will obey; and when we obey, love is expressed and developed. Obedient love is the bond of "abiding," whether between the heavenly Father and the Son (John 14:31), or between the Son and His follower. It is not a sullen conformity!

C. Equipped for Joy (v. 11)

11. These things have I spoken unto you, that my joy might remain in you, and that your joy might be full.

How different this is from the popular idea that religion—especially a religion of obedience to divine commandments—is a killjoy operation! In fact, it is designed to provide *joy*, lasting and complete. How strange that Jesus should introduce it on the eve of His death! Yet joy provides a theme for the rest of the Lord's farewell discourse (John 16:20-24).

The proffered joy begins in Jesus himself, whose chief pleasure lay in doing His Father's will (Hebrews 12:2). He prayed that He might convey that joy in full measure to His disciples (John 17:13). Real joy comes out of real loving. Joy grows with loving obedience. The song says it well: "There is joy in serving Jesus."

IV. Love as the Link
(John 15:12-17)

A. Command and Demonstration
(vv. 12, 13)

12, 13. This is my commandment, That ye love one another, as I have loved you. Greater love hath no man than this, that a man lay down his life for his friends.

Jesus issued more than one commandment, but the love commandment was first in importance (Matthew 22:34-40), as covering the whole law, and as being newly taught by himself (John 13:34). Paul summarized it in Romans 13:8: "Owe no man any thing, but to love one another: for he that loveth another hath fulfilled the law."

Christians are to keep on loving, as they keep on living in Christ: "The Lord make you to increase and abound in love toward one another, and toward all men" (1 Thessalonians 3:12). Their example is Christ. The apostles were yet to see the ultimate demonstration in Jesus' laying down His life on the cross, not only for His friends, but also for His enemies. Yet they had seen Him lay down His hours and days, His rights and interests, in serving them and others.

B. Friendship and Its Fruits
(vv. 14-16)

14, 15. Ye are my friends, if ye do whatsoever I command you. Henceforth I call you not servants; for the servant knoweth not what his lord doeth: but I have called you friends; for all things that I have heard of my Father I have made known unto you.

Jesus has a right to regard any of His followers as servants—literally slaves, bought with the price of His life's blood (1 Corinthians 6:19, 20). Yet He laid out His plans before the apostles as a master does not do with slaves, but reserves for his friends. That gave them a higher motivation—grateful love—to serve Him well. We cannot lay claim to all the apostles' intimacies and privileges with Jesus, but we can go far beyond the slaves' compulsions, to serve Him with a friend's love and devotion.

16. Ye have not chosen me, but I have chosen you, and ordained you, that ye should go and bring forth fruit, and that your fruit should remain; that whatsoever ye shall ask of the Father in my name, he may give it you.

The apostles' friendship with Jesus was initiated by Him. He chose and called them, mostly one by one, but they accepted the invitation and followed.

Ordained is better translated *appointed*. The appointment is described in Luke 6:12-16. Mark 3:13-15 shows that the appointment was accompanied by special powers to be used in producing fruit that would last. The apostles were to prepare for the establishment of the church, lead it through its earliest years, and provide the Scriptures for its continuance through the ages. To that end they worked miraculous "signs, and wonders, and mighty deeds" (2 Corinthians 12:12) in response to special prayers for special purposes in the name of Christ.

C. Establishing the Link (v. 17)

17. These things I command you, that ye love one another.

The apostles' power in prayer was not to be used selfishly, but in continuing care for other members of the Lord's body—other branches in the True Vine. Every act of obedience to any other command must harmonize with the command to mutual love, patterned according to the love of Christ. Only this can sustain the living relationship of branches in the True Vine.

Conclusion
A. "I Am With You"

The Lord who taught that His followers must abide in Him promised also that He, through His Holy Spirit, would abide with them and in them forever. "Christ in you, the hope of glory" (Colossians 1:27) is the basis, and "I am with you alway, even unto the end of the world" (Matthew 28:20) is the pledge to the loving, obedient branch in God's vine.

B. The Other Side of the Coin

The positive aspects of life in Christ, bonded by love and committed to keeping His Word, become negative aspects in relation to God's enemies. Immediately after His command to "love one another" as those who live in Him, Jesus warned that the world will hate you if you do! (John 15:18—16:4) The world does not take kindly to having its sin revealed and rebuked. It hated and crucified Jesus when He claimed more than the world was willing to grant. It will hate also His people who press those claims in His name. Loving and living in Jesus is a matter of choice. That choice excludes while it includes. Its faith is spelled "Forsaking All I Take Him."

C. Prayer of a Needy Branch

Thank You, Father, for the love that ministers to us with a pruning knife when it is necessary to remove hindrances to our fruitfulness in You. May our praise be expressed in the fruits of righteousness and love that Jesus enables us to bear in His name. Amen.

D. Thought to Remember

Joy crowns the life that is built on, and in, Jesus as Lord.

Home Daily Bible Readings

Monday, Apr. 22—Preparing for the End (John 13:1-11)
Tuesday, Apr. 23—Telling What Would Happen (John 13:12-30)
Wednesday, Apr. 24—New Commandment (John 13:31-38)
Thursday, Apr. 25—No Separation (John 14:1-7)
Friday, Apr. 26—God Revealed Through Christ (John 14:8-14)
Saturday, Apr. 27—Continuing Guidance (John 14:15-20)
Sunday, Apr. 28—To Love Is to Obey (John 14:21-31)

Learning by Doing

This page contains an alternate lesson plan emphasizing learning activities. Classes desiring such student involvement will find these suggestions helpful.

Learning Goals

As a result of participating in today's lesson, a student will be able to:

1. Identify the truths Jesus relates in John 15:1-17.

2. Explain the role of the disciple in abiding, bearing fruit, and loving.

3. Express what is necessary for him or her to increase in obedience, love, and the bearing of fruit in Christ.

Into the Lesson

Prepare and bring to class one oversized glass of a soft drink, along with enough straws for the entire class. Pass out straws to all as they enter the classroom. As the lesson begins, bring out the large glass, invite the class members to have a drink, keep the glass to yourself and begin sipping the drink with your straw. As reactions begin to be expressed, pretend not to understand their problem. Slowly "catch on"—they cannot drink if their straws are not in the glass.

Putting the glass away, make the transition into the lesson. We must be firmly and continuously attached to our source of strength.

Into the Word

Read John 15:1-8 to the class. Ask them to isolate the points Jesus makes as you write them on a chalkboard or poster board. (This is in the student book.) Possible points:

• Jesus is the source of what we need to be fruitful and joyful.

• Branches that do not bear fruit are cut off.

• Productive branches are pruned by the gardener/God.

• Pruning produces greater fruitfulness.

• The Word prunes/cleans us.

• We cannot be productive apart from the Vine.

• Abiding branches bear much fruit and receive all they need.

• God is glorified when we bear much fruit.

• Fruit-bearing is a demonstration of being a disciple.

Divide the class into small groups of three to five persons. Assign each group one of the following questions: (1) How does God "prune" us to bear more fruit? (2) How do we abide or remain in Christ? (3) What does the branch/disciple receive from the vine/Jesus? (4) What fruit can we produce that will glorify God? After several minutes of group discussion, ask for a spokesperson from each group to summarize the group's answers for the entire class.

Now read John 15:9-17. Answer any specific questions regarding the meaning of this passage and proceed into the next exercise.

Into Life

With people still in their small groups, pass out a set of seven index cards to each group. The cards, prepared before class, should have the following phrases written on them, one phrase on each card:

• Loving God
• Obeying God
• Experiencing joy
• Loving others
• Being Jesus' friend
• Being chosen by Jesus
• Bearing fruit

Ask each group to work together to place the seven cards in the order in which the events happen in the Christian life. For example, a group may decide that "being chosen by Jesus" comes before "being Jesus' friend," or that several of the events come before "bearing fruit." Expect students to be puzzled, perhaps even frustrated; but hope that insightful discussions will help them realize that all these are interrelated and all are important. Move among the groups to encourage and make suggestions, but not to direct their conclusions.

After adequate time for discussion, ask each group to present its conclusions. If the conclusions are not alike, do not take time to argue about the differences. Point out that one Christian's experience may be different from another's, but emphasize that these experiences all continue together, and all are to be treasured.

Now ask class members to silently consider what each of them can do to experience a greater level of abiding, obeying, loving, fruitfulness, or joy. After several minutes (please don't rush this), ask for volunteers to share their thoughts. Finally, encourage each person to specify one thing he or she will do this week in order to abide in Christ and bear more fruit. Again, seek volunteers to share their specific commitments with the class.

Let's Talk It Over

The questions on this page are designed to encourage review of the lesson Scriptures and to promote discussion of the lesson by the class. The answers provided are only discussion starters. Let your class talk it over from there.

1. How do we obey Jesus' command to abide in Him?

The lesson writer speaks of the Lord's Supper as providing a means for abiding in Jesus. And since *abide* means *stay* or *remain*, applying it to the Lord's Supper reminds us of the need for faithful, Sunday-by-Sunday communing. How can the believer who carelessly misses many Sunday appointments at the Lord's table think he or she is abiding in Jesus Christ? The matter of personal devotions also comes to mind here. To abide in Him surely involves our having regular daily contact with Him through His Word and prayer. Certainly we also abide in Him when we serve others in His name.

2. "If ye abide in me, and my words abide in you, ye shall ask what ye will, and it shall be done unto you" (John 15:7). Does this promise reveal why many prayers fail? Explain.

Many who pray are not abiding in Jesus Christ. In connection with the previous question, we can say that many believers experience failure in prayer because they are not faithful in attendance at the Lord's table, because they neglect regular times of personal Bible study and general prayer, and because they are not active in service for Jesus' sake. The prayer promise above leaves no room for selfish, "my-will-be-done" prayers. It speaks of a prayer life centered in learning, embracing, and performing God's will. The context of this promise is Jesus' urging His disciples to bear spiritual fruit for the glory of the Father. The believer who makes such fruit-bearing a matter of first priority in his or her life will pray in accordance with that priority and will receive answers.

3. Jesus wanted His followers to experience fullness of joy. How can we have this joy?

During the same discourse from which we take our lesson text, Jesus described the sorrow His disciples would suffer when He was crucified. Then He promised them, "I will see you again, and your heart shall rejoice, and your joy no man taketh from you" (John 16:22). Like those first disciples, we know the joy of Jesus' victory over death. We can have an abiding sense of joy in the midst of the severest trials, because we know we also shall gain victory over death. But verse 11 of our text indicates that fullness of joy comes from loving, obeying, and serving Jesus. It is a joyous thing to know that Jesus loves us with an everlasting love and seeks our love in return. It is also joyous to realize that what we do for Jesus pleases Him now and will surely be remembered in eternity.

4. Our love for one another is to be of the same quality as Jesus' love for us. Do we come up to this standard in our church? If not, why not?

To put this question in terms of 1 John 3:16, do we "lay down our lives for the brethren"? Do we really make sacrifices of time and effort on behalf of one another, reflecting Jesus' loving sacrifice of His life? Perhaps we assume that we love one another because we exchange hugs and handshakes and verbal greetings on Sunday. These are legitimate expressions of love, but they are no substitute for a real sacrifice of time and effort. Are we available when a fellow believer needs a listening ear and an uplifting word? Are we willing to share our money and possessions to provide for another Christian who is in dire need? Our love for one another is to be something so special and unique that it draws the world's attention to the Christ we follow (John 13:34, 35).

5. We enjoy friendship with Jesus. What practical effects should result from this friendship?

A friend is someone with whom we can be ourselves. With Jesus we can practice openness and honesty, admitting our weaknesses and hurts. He is a friend who understands and wants to help. A friend is someone with whom we share something of importance. With Jesus we share a common interest in the building up of His church, in the winning of the lost, and in ministering to people in all kinds of need. A friend is someone we want to introduce to other friends. It should be our intense desire to introduce all of our earthly friends to our heavenly friend, Jesus Christ. In this effort we can follow the example of Levi, or Matthew, who became Jesus' friend and then prepared a banquet for the purpose of introducing his tax collector friends to his new Friend (Luke 5:27-32).

Teachings About Happiness

DEVOTIONAL READING: Psalm 1:1-6.

LESSON SCRIPTURE: Matthew 5:1-12.

PRINTED TEXT: Matthew 5:1-12.

Matthew 5:1-12

1 And seeing the multitudes, he went up into a mountain: and when he was set, his disciples came unto him:

2 And he opened his mouth, and taught them, saying,

3 Blessed are the poor in spirit: for theirs is the kingdom of heaven.

4 Blessed are they that mourn: for they shall be comforted.

5 Blessed are the meek: for they shall inherit the earth.

6 Blessed are they which do hunger and thirst after righteousness: for they shall be filled.

7 Blessed are the merciful: for they shall obtain mercy.

8 Blessed are the pure in heart: for they shall see God.

9 Blessed are the peacemakers: for they shall be called the children of God.

10 Blessed are they which are persecuted for righteousness' sake: for theirs is the kingdom of heaven.

11 Blessed are ye, when men shall revile you, and persecute you, and shall say all manner of evil against you falsely, for my sake.

12 Rejoice, and be exceeding glad: for great is your reward in heaven: for so persecuted they the prophets which were before you.

GOLDEN TEXT: Rejoice, and be exceeding glad: for great is your reward in heaven.
—Matthew 5:12.

Teachings of Jesus
Unit 3. Teachings About Living
(Lessons 10-13)

Lesson Aims

This lesson should help the student to:
1. Quote the Beatitudes in a chosen Bible version.
2. Contrast the world's ideas of happiness with Jesus' principles of highest joy.
3. Show how Jesus' life and ministry demonstrated the qualities He recommended.
4. Formulate a plan for developing his or her strength in the characteristics Jesus urged upon His disciples.

Lesson Outline

INTRODUCTION
   A. Pursuit of Happiness
   B. Lesson Background
  I. THE TEACHER AND HIS HEARERS (Matthew 5:1, 2)
  II. THE CHARACTER THAT BLESSES (Matthew 5:3-9)
   A. A Sense of Spiritual Need (v. 3)
     Poor in Spirit
   B. Godly Sorrow (v. 4)
   C. Gentle Strength (v. 5)
   D. An Appetite for Godliness (v. 6)
     How Hungry Are You?
   E. Patience in Practice (v. 7)
   F. Purity Within (v. 8)
   G. Campaigning for Peace (v. 9)
     Making Peace
  III. EXPERIENCE THAT BLESSES (Matthew 5:10-12)
   A. Enmity from God's Enemies (vv. 10, 11)
   B. Fellowship of God's Friends (v. 12)
CONCLUSION
   A. Down From the Mountain
   B. Prayer of a Hearer
   C. Thought to Remember

Visual 10 of the visuals packet is a photograph of a hill beside the Sea of Galilee. It is shown on page 308 and may be used to open today's lesson.

Introduction

A. Pursuit of Happiness

"Pursuit of Happiness" is named, along with "Life" and "Liberty," in the American *Declaration of Independence* among the "unalienable Rights" with which the Creator has endowed all men alike. None of us would deny that right to anyone, any more than we would deny to anyone the right to chase the end of a rainbow in search of gold. We would note, however, that the pursuit of what most folk regard as happiness in selfish indulgence is a primary source of misery rather than of well-being. The pursuit of happiness has led many to flit from one spouse to another; to cheat and steal in efforts to become rich; to ingest drugs in order to feel good, and so on and on, all because "I have a right to my happiness."

With Jesus, happiness was never a goal to be sought. It was, instead, a secondary result of seeking a right relationship with God. He said of himself, "I seek not mine own will, but the will of the Father which hath sent me" (John 5:30).

In that context, the Beatitudes (named from the Latin *beatus*, or blessed), may be considered a thesis on happiness. The Greek *makarios* has been translated "happy" as well as "blessed." In Matthew 5:3-12, however, most English language translations of the Bible render it "blessed."

Blessed implies a favorable judgment from Heaven. Psalm 1, for example, begins, "Blessed is the man that walketh not in the counsel of the ungodly . . . but his delight is in the law of the Lord," and concludes, "The Lord knoweth the way of the righteous: but the way of the ungodly shall perish." Scripture everywhere shows divine approval of the qualities described by Jesus. That approval bears fruit, moreover, in the utmost of well-being and eternal joy.

B. Lesson Background

Are Matthew's record of the "Sermon on the Mount" (Matthew 5—7) and Luke's account of the "Sermon on the Plain" (Luke 6:12-49) two reports of the same event? Many Bible scholars think so, and they wrestle with differences between the two. A respectable number of us, on the other hand, consider the two passages to be accounts of separate events, taking place several months apart. So now we shall consider Matthew's record.

Jesus had been preaching, teaching, and healing for about a year in Galilee and had become so famous that throngs of people were coming—many by several days' journey from all directions—to see, hear, and benefit from His ministry (Matthew 4:23-25). Among them were many who expected a politico-military Messiah to lead in rebellion against Roman rule in Palestine, and they wondered if their kind of Messiah had come. Some would even force Jesus to become their king (John 6:15). The time had come to spell out plainly—especially to His followers—that He was not that kind of king, and His was not that kind of kingdom. He would expect His disciples to be the kind of people He was—exactly the reverse of the cruel, power-hungry, and luxury-loving rulers so familiar in places of authority around them.

I. The Teacher and His Hearers (Matthew 5:1, 2)

1, 2. And seeing the multitudes, he went up into a mountain: and when he was set, his disciples came unto him: and he opened his mouth, and taught them, saying.

The traditional "Mount of the Beatitudes" (Horns of Hattin) is a low hill, perhaps lowered by centuries of erosion, several miles southwest of Capernaum. Jesus probably expected to be followed by the crowd, and He chose a place where He could be seen and heard.

The Lord seated himself in the manner of Eastern teachers. Thus His message had to be conveyed in words; lively dramatics were impossible. Yet His very presence provided a vivid demonstration of His message.

His committed followers, including the twelve who were to be called apostles, gathered around Him, probably also seated on the ground. At the outset Jesus talked straight to these men, no matter how many others may have come within the range of His voice as He continued. We are constantly amazed at the ability of any teacher under such circumstance to address large crowds without electronic help. The listeners must have given quiet attention!

The Sermon on the Mount has been called the constitution of the new covenant. At least it describes the citizens of Heaven's kingdom. The law of the old covenant had been given to Moses alone on a high and inaccessible mountain; this was given publicly on a mountain known only for the loftiness of its Teacher and His teaching. Jesus did not, and does not, expect strangers, not knowing or committed to Him, to adopt the lifestyle He described. Many would consider it foolishness. First they must know and be drawn to Him; then they could accept His direction.

II. The Character That Blesses (Matthew 5:3-9)

A. A Sense of Spiritual Need (v. 3)

3. Blessed are the poor in spirit: for theirs is the kingdom of heaven.

The heavenly kingdom belongs, Jesus says, to the one who comes as a beggar to its gate! *Poor* translates a word used of a destitute condition, hopeless in itself. In it we hear echoes of the tax collector in the temple, bowed and pleading,

"God be merciful to me a sinner," and going "down to his house justified" (Luke 18:13, 14). The blessed ones claim no spiritual assets; they acknowledge a spiritual need. Thus acknowledging, they are in a position to receive and accept Heaven's wealth. Paul caught this idea; he acknowledged that his standing as a law-abiding Pharisee was worthless in relation to his need for Christ and life eternal (Philippians 3:4-11).

After Jesus' introductory description of the most blessed of all persons, we are prepared to understand better the following items. Humility, purity, pity, etc., grow naturally in the soil of dependence on God for all we may become.

The acceptance of material poverty for the sake of spiritual values will also bring its blessing, as Jesus promised to the disciples who had surrendered homes and businesses to follow Him (Luke 18:29, 30); but that seems not to be the principal thrust of this Beatitude.

POOR IN SPIRIT

Imagine yourself applying for a credit card. A young account executive takes down the information to open your account.

"What is your income?" she asks.

"I don't have any income," you reply.

"No income?"

"That's right. No job, no salary, no income of any sort."

"Well then, what about your assets—stocks, bonds, real estate holdings?"

"I don't have any assets," you answer.

"No assets?"

"Right again. Nothing. Nothing in the bank, nothing stuffed in my mattress at home, and nothing in my pocket. I'm penniless."

"Let's see; what about your liabilities? Do you owe anything?"

"My debts? Oh, yes. I owe trillions of dollars," you respond.

"That's wonderful," she says. "Here's your card. You have unlimited credit, beginning immediately, and you will never see a bill. We've taken care of everything."

Far-fetched? Well, yes, if you're dealing with American Express. But not if you have come to Christ. Jesus said the *poor* in spirit enjoy the benefits of His kingdom. Membership is open by admitting that we own nothing that would make us worthy of salvation, that we have no way of earning God's favor, and that we owe a sin debt we cannot pay. Come to Jesus on those terms, and you're in. He's done for you what you could never do for yourself. To paraphrase the advertisement, "Don't leave home without Him."

—C. B. Mc.

visual 10

Seeing the multitudes,
he went up into a mountain
and he opened his mouth,
and taught them.
Matthew 5:1, 2

B. Godly Sorrow (v. 4)

4. Blessed are they that mourn: for they shall be comforted.

This, too, was addressed to Jesus' disciples, but can have limited application to other folk who, having suffered severe loss, learn not to place undue value on what is trivial and transient. Paul is helpful here: "Godly sorrow worketh repentance to salvation not to be repented of: but the sorrow of the world worketh death" (2 Corinthians 7:10). God's people know the kind of mourning for sin that caused Paul to acknowledge himself chief of sinners, while remembering that God still forgave and employed him (1 Timothy 1:15-17). Our mourning over the sins of others is a little like Jesus' lamenting over the sin and approaching destruction of Jerusalem (Luke 19:41-44). Our sorrowing in sympathy with suffering neighbors answers the admonition to rejoice with those who rejoice and weep with those who weep (Romans 12:15). God's people cannot take lightly the sin-damage that weighs so heavily on the heart of God.

The comfort promised after godly mourning calls to mind the Comforter promised to the apostles after Jesus' going to be with the Father (John 14:15-18). Just as the Spirit's coming awaited the death and resurrection of Jesus, so God's perfect comfort to His children comes only after they have known godly mourning.

C. Gentle Strength (v. 5)

5. Blessed are the meek: for they shall inherit the earth.

Meek—gentle or humble—describes a strength like that of a well-trained animal brought under control so as to serve purposes outside itself. It is the quality of the gentle giant, having no need to prove his power and having no wish to use it for himself. It is the quality of one who has bowed most humbly before God; hence has no terror for any man—Moses before Pharaoh, or John the Baptist before Herod, or Jesus before Pilate—King over all, but giving His all for others.

Psalm 37:11 says, "The meek shall inherit the earth." The entire psalm is their instruction

against being upset by the short-lived prosperity of the wicked, knowing that God will make His own final distribution of His assets. Even now the gentle ones can enjoy God's world as the arrogant and demanding ones can never do. They possess what never could be bought nor earned.

D. An Appetite for Godliness (v. 6)

6. Blessed are they which do hunger and thirst after righteousness: for they shall be filled.

Psalm 42:1, 2 describes this spiritual appetite: "As the hart panteth after the water brooks, so panteth my soul after thee, O God." So the longed-for *righteousness* is a positive relationship with the Almighty. The child of the King has no greater desire than to do his Father's will. "My food," said Jesus, "is to do the will of him who sent me and to finish his work" (John 4:34, *New International Version*.)

Here is an appetite that can be satisfied most fully in all who possess it. The opportunities are limitless. Isaiah 55:1, 2 expresses the Lord's invitation: "Ho, every one that thirsteth, come ye to the waters, and he that hath no money; come ye, buy, and eat . . . eat ye that which is good, and let your soul delight itself in fatness."

Keen physical hunger and thirst are not common among folk who seldom work hard or go long without refreshment. We deaden our appetites with too much indulgence. Spiritual appetite, also, increases with spiritual exercise and the avoidance of deadening self-indulgence.

HOW HUNGRY ARE YOU?

Exodus 33:18 is one of the most amazing verses in the Bible. Moses said, "Show me thy glory." Moses already had encountered God in the burning bush. He had seen God's power displayed in the ten plagues inflicted on Egypt. Here was a God who could humble entire nations. Moses had seen the power of God again when the Israelites miraculously crossed the Red Sea. At Mount Sinai Moses had spoken with God face to face. A thick cloud had covered the mountain that had burned with fire and lightning as God had descended upon it.

After all this, Moses still had the audacity to say, "Now show me Your glory." He just couldn't get enough. Do we have a similar hunger for righteousness?   —C. B. Mc.

E. Patience in Practice (v. 7)

7. Blessed are the merciful: for they shall obtain mercy.

Up to this point, the Lord's emphasis has been on attitudes toward God and qualities within the child of God. Now Jesus moves to a practical expression of those qualities in dealing with others. Jesus' compassion in feeding and healing the needy ones around Him provides the pattern for this Beatitude. It goes beyond Proverbs 14:21: "He that hath mercy on the poor, happy is he." It imitates the mercy of God in extending forgiveness when punishment is deserved, providing food for the thankless, and sustaining life in those who deny its source.

F. Purity Within (v. 8)

The Lord's test of character moves at this point from observable actions to the hidden wellsprings of thought and motive. These are known to God, and they become known to men as the thoughts grow into determination and doing.

8. Blessed are the pure in heart: for they shall see God.

"Keep thy heart with all diligence," urged the wise king, "for out of it are the issues of life" (Proverbs 4:23). And purity of heart is necessary for standing before God (Psalm 24:3, 4).

Pure translates a word that speaks of cleansing or purging. Jesus rebuked severely those whose passion for cleanness was limited to what could be seen by men. He spoke of such persons as whitewashed tombs, beautiful on the outside but filled inwardly with decay (Matthew 23:27). So He judged the thoughts and intents of the heart, linking hatred with murder, and lust with adultery (Matthew 5:21, 22, 27, 28).

Pure describes also that which is free from foreign substances. The pure heart does not include mixed motives or competing affections. When the pure heart speaks, the hearer does not have to wonder what is really meant. Thoughts, words, and deeds fall into one consistent pattern. Christians are urged to focus their attention on what is good and desirable (Philippians 4:8). It is a pattern not easily preserved in our society.

To see God, though, is worthy of the utmost attention. To recognize, understand, and perceive Him who is all-holy, all-just, all-wise, all-powerful, and eternal is reward enough for total effort. And it is impossible to one whose perceptions and senses of value are dominated or scrambled by the thought patterns of this present world. To see God with perfect clarity is not probable in this present world; but there will be plenty of opportunity to clear up the vision, face to face, after all hindrances are removed.

G. Campaigning for Peace (v. 9)

9. Blessed are the peacemakers: for they shall be called the children of God.

First Samuel 25 tells of a wise woman named Abigail who waged peace, preventing bloody conflict between David and her churlish husband, Nabal. Without surrendering any moral principle, but with timely use of her own resources, she achieved reconciliation.

So God's children are to exert themselves in word and deed to prevent and to heal misunderstandings and conflicts, even at the cost of great patience with personal wrong, but always with firmness for truth. "Peace in our time" must not be purchased through the surrender of moral principle, simply delaying more serious warfare. That is the folly of parents who shy away from the tensions of family discipline, and so condemn their sons and daughters to more serious conflict with society and with God.

Genuine *peacemakers* are acknowledged by God to be His children. They show the family resemblance to the "God of peace" in sharing "the peace of God" through Jesus Christ (Philippians 4:7-9). That is achieved through convincing persons to be reconciled—adjusted—to God (2 Corinthians 5:18-21). He cannot change in adjustment to sinful men; so He makes peace by forgiving the penitent ones and claiming them as His children.

MAKING PEACE

Back in 1990, Iraq sent 120,000 troops to take over little Kuwait. Months of negotiations and sanctions failed to dislodge them. Then the United Nations launched Operation Desert Storm. After 89,000 tons of explosives softened up the Iraqi army, ground troops drove it out in a mere one hundred hours; and peace returned.

Peace in the biblical sense is more than the absence of hostility. It is the general well-being that comes with righteousness. To bring lasting peace, sometimes we must confront the sin and evil that cause enmity and strife. Our weapons are not guns and bombs, but the Word of God (2 Corinthians 10:4).   —C. B. Mc.

III. Experience That Blesses (Matthew 5:10-12)

Children of God's kingdom are blessed not only in their character and relationships, but also in their response to what happens to them.

A. Enmity From God's Enemies (vv. 10, 11)

10. Blessed are they which are persecuted for righteousness' sake: for theirs is the kingdom of heaven.

God's peacemaking children are warred against by the forces that reject God. The God-hating world would *drive*, or *chase* (literal meaning of the word translated *persecute*) them out of its presence. That persecution had begun with Jesus and it would continue. First Peter 2:20-23 and 3:14 speak encouragement to those who endure patiently the unjust punishment that comes to them because of their allegiance to Christ. It identifies them as citizens of His kingdom and sharers in His glory. Having that, they have small use for the world's approval and favors.

11. Blessed are ye, when men shall revile you, and persecute you, and shall say all manner of evil against you falsely, for my sake.

This, too, is addressed specifically to faithful followers of Jesus. The *persecution* here described is mostly verbal. It is not true, however, that "words can never harm me." Insults and slander can destroy a career as surely as can violence, and the wounds are slow to heal.

Three qualifications attend the persecution that blesses. It is vicious, it is false, and it comes to the Christian because of Christ. It sounds like the kind of treatment accorded now to "bigoted, narrow-minded religious right-wingers" by folk who resist and resent any restriction or rebuke to their flagrant and destructive misbehavior. The experience is not new, nor without solace (1 Peter 4:14).

B. Fellowship of God's Friends (v. 12)

12. Rejoice, and be exceeding glad: for great is your reward in heaven: for so persecuted they the prophets which were before you.

Here the Lord recommends celebration of what the world would call misery. What a marvelous company was and is that of the prophets! Each in his own time was faithful in delivering God's message, in spite of rejection and mistreatment: "They mocked the messengers of God, and despised his words, and mis-

used his prophets" (2 Chronicles 36:16; compare Hebrews 11:32-40). Each generation seemed to revere the ancient prophets, while rejecting those who brought God's word to themselves (Matthew 23:29, 30; Acts 7:52).

The apostles learned from Jesus, however, and did not wait until after death to enjoy the approval of Heaven. When they experienced persecution—physical and verbal—for the sake of Christ, they went out "rejoicing that they were counted worthy to suffer shame for his name" (Acts 5:41; compare Philippians 3:10-14).

Conclusion

A. Down From the Mountain

The Sermon on the Mount, beginning with the Beatitudes, is indeed lofty teaching. It is so high, in fact, that many readers consider it wholly unrealistic. The principles here spoken go directly against the currents of both Jesus' time and ours, which measure the "good life" in terms of pride, power, pleasure, and possessions. But that "good life" has always ended in death and self-destruction.

Some would consider the spiritual view itself to be the way of life. Like the materialists, they would make happiness their goal, but they would seek it by a different route. They would grasp the teaching and forget the Teacher. That is to deny the ultimate reality behind the Sermon.

Happiness is not the goal, and to seek it as such is to lose it in utter frustration. God, in His Son Jesus, is the goal and the life. Joy is the experience of life in Him, found in obedient faith. And that means down-to-earth being and doing in His name. Before Jesus came down from the mountain after the Sermon, He warned against hearing and admiring without doing: "Not every one that saith unto me, Lord, Lord, shall enter into the kingdom of heaven; but he that doeth the will of my Father which is in heaven" (Matthew 7:21). Right there is the life-style of the kingdom where joy is unavoidable.

B. Prayer of a Hearer

We praise You, O God, for the depth of wisdom found in the words of Jesus. We praise You even more for the demonstration of that eternal wisdom in what He did. May our praise find expression in what we do as children of Your kingdom. In His name, amen.

C. Thought to Remember

"What good will it be for a man if he gains the whole world, yet forfeits his soul?" (Matthew 16:26, *New International Version*).

Home Daily Bible Readings

Monday, Apr. 29—Acceptable Sacrifice (Psalm 51:10-17)

Tuesday, Apr. 30—Comfort for the Distressed (Isaiah 61:1-7)

Wednesday, May 1—Support for the Meek (Psalm 37:8-13)

Thursday, May 2—Confident of God's Help (Isaiah 26:7-15)

Friday, May 3—God's Gracious Mercy (Psalm 103:6-14)

Saturday, May 4—Necessity of Peace (Hebrews 12:12-17)

Sunday, May 5—Prayer for Deliverance (Psalm 7:1-8)

Learning by Doing

This page contains an alternate lesson plan emphasizing learning activities. Classes desiring such student involvement will find these suggestions helpful.

Learning Goals

After today's lesson, a student will be able to:

1. Identify the contrast between the world's ideas of happiness and Jesus' principles of highest joy.

2. Explain the meaning of *blessed* and each of the Beatitudes in Matthew 5:1-12.

3. Determine to develop strength in the characteristics Jesus urged for His disciples.

Into the Lesson

Ask the class to brainstorm with you on the following: What is happiness, and how can it be found, according to people today? Write the answers on a chalkboard or poster board. Possible answers include: *Happiness is feeling good emotionally, being physically "in shape," or being in control of your own destiny. Happiness is found in exercise and diet plans, certain beverages, being accepted by others, or money.* Encourage people to reflect on TV and advertising, as well as conversations with others.

Make the transition to today's lesson by pointing out that in the Sermon on the Mount Jesus gave some very direct teachings about happiness (Matthew 5—7). This Sermon will be the source of this and three more lessons.

Into the Word

Divide the class into study groups of two to four persons each, and ask them to look up the following passages (write them on a chalkboard/poster board or on a handout; this exercise is also in the student book): Psalm 1:1; 32:1, 2; 94:12; Proverbs 3:13; Matthew 13:16; Luke 14:13, 14; Romans 14:22; Titus 2:13; James 1:12, 25; 1 Peter 3:14; 4:14; Revelation 19:9. If you prefer, each study group may look up a few of the passages and then report to the class. Ask each group to summarize their findings about being blessed and to develop a definition of what it means to be blessed. Tell the students they will find *happy* instead of *blessed* in some passages, but the Hebrew or Greek word is the one that is usually translated *blessed.*

After adequate time, ask a spokesperson from each group to share the group's findings. Guide the discussion to emphasize that being blessed is more dependent on our relationship with and obedience to God than on our circumstances. To be blessed is to have a happiness that comes

from God and has a sure future reward. Even while suffering, we are fortunate, content, and happy in God!

Before class, prepare several sets of index cards as follows: Write each of the eight character statements of Matthew 5:3-10 ("the poor in spirit," "they that mourn," etc.) on index cards, one per card. Do the same for each of the eight promises ("theirs is the kingdom of heaven," "they shall be comforted," etc.). Shuffle each set of sixteen cards, separate the class into the same number of groups as you have sets, and give each group one set. Ask students to close their Bibles and any other lesson-related materials they have. The assignment is for each group to correctly match each Beatitude with its promise and then put the pairs in their biblical order as found in Matthew 5.

After time for study, ask a group to identify the first pair and to explain what it means (for example, "poor in spirit" means realizing one's spiritual poverty and need; see the lesson materials for an explanation of each Beatitude). Then the next group identifies and explains the second pair, etc. Point out the meaningful progression of the Beatitudes: realization of poverty prompts sorrow for sin, which leads to humility and denial of self, which is followed by a search for righteousness, etc. The lesson material will help you to do this.

Into Life

Ask each class member to indicate how he sees himself in each characteristic. Use a scale from 1 ("This just isn't me") to 5 ("Yes, that's me"). Use the exercise in the student book or prepare a handout for each student with each characteristic and the numbers one to five; for instance:

"The poor in spirit"   1 2 3 4 5
"They that mourn"   1 2 3 4 5

Allow time for personal reflection and completion. Then ask, "What difference would it make in your life if you more fully developed each of these characteristics?" Encourage discussion, asking for specific examples (for example, how being peacemakers would affect family interaction). Ask for volunteers, each of whom will tell where he or she needs to focus for personal character development. Conclude with prayer.

Let's Talk It Over

The questions on this page are designed to encourage review of the lesson Scriptures and to promote discussion of the lesson by the class. The answers provided are only discussion starters. Let your class talk it over from there.

1. Perhaps we have heard someone say, "My religion is the Beatitudes," or "My religion is the Ten Commandments." How should we respond?

The Beatitudes do not specifically refer to the atoning death of Christ, to the grace of God, or to the ministry of the Holy Spirit. How can we master all their principles well enough to need no Savior? How can we appreciate the terribleness of sin so as to mourn over it, without recognizing that it required the death of God's Son to conquer it? How can we achieve purity of heart without the aid of the indwelling Holy Spirit? The Beatitudes and the Ten Commandments, rightly viewed, point us to our need for a Savior and for a divine helper like the Holy Spirit.

2. How do we feel about Jesus' requirement that we be "poor in spirit"? Why is this a spiritual principle that needs special emphasis today?

The idea of being "poor" in any sense of the term may trouble us. We live in a society in which the quality of people's lives is characteristically judged by the amount of money and possessions they have. Therefore, many find it unthinkable to be poor in material wealth. The desire for money and possessions ties in with the aim of being strong and self-sufficient and successful. Jesus' call to be "poor in spirit" stands in contrast to that. We are challenged to admit that we are weak, insecure, and, from a moral standpoint, prone to fail. Here at the very beginning the Beatitudes meet the prevailing humanistic philosophy head-on. We need God, His grace, His power, His wisdom, for without these we cannot find enduring success or happiness. All mankind must yield to the Creator.

3. Why is it vital that we learn to mourn over sin and the destruction it wreaks?

Our society takes sin very lightly. Either we laugh at it, or we blame it on our psychological make-up or the effects of our environment. Somehow we are able to overlook the fact that sin is the cause of many of our personal and social woes. Even Christians are guilty of trifling with sin and treating it as something less than the deadly reality it is. As a result many Christians live in moral and spiritual confusion, and

churches suffer because of the lack of holiness and commitment in their members. The blunt directives of James are an appropriate prescription for our time: "Cleanse your hands, ye sinners; and purify your hearts, ye double-minded. Be afflicted, and mourn, and weep: let your laughter be turned to mourning, and your joy to heaviness. Humble yourselves in the sight of the Lord, and he shall lift you up" (James 4:8-10).

4. Why do we have difficulty with Jesus' requirement that we be meek? What can we do to overcome this difficulty?

To be meek is to be weak—that is a common misconception. Perhaps it is because the words "meek" and "weak" rhyme, or perhaps it is because we have heard the word "meek" used too often to describe people who are weak. If meekness meant weakness in failing to stand up for moral principles, or excessive timidity in refusing to accept responsibility in the church, then it would be an undesirable trait. But consider the fact that Moses was described as "very meek, above all the men which were upon the face of the earth" (Numbers 12:3). Consider the fact that Jesus said, "I am meek and lowly in heart" (Matthew 11:29). Obviously, the meekness the Bible calls for is not a matter of weakness but of strength, the strength to resist striking back at those who offend us in any way.

5. How can we achieve purity of heart while living in a society where impurity abounds?

We still have a measure of control over what we see and hear. Job said, "I made a covenant with my eyes not to look lustfully at a girl" (Job 31:1, *New International Version*). It is possible for us to make a similar covenant regarding anything that could tempt us to impure thoughts. We can say, "Eyes, don't look at that immoral television program. Watch something wholesome and uplifting." "Ears, don't listen to that degrading music. Listen to music that is morally and spiritually edifying." A New Testament counterpart to Job 31:1 is Philippians 4:8, 9. It reminds us that purity is not merely a matter of saying no to what is vulgar and offensive. It is also a matter of saying yes to what is true, noble, right, pure, lovely, admirable, excellent, and praiseworthy (see *New International Version*).

Teachings About Loving Your Enemies

DEVOTIONAL READING: Luke 10:25-37.

LESSON SCRIPTURE: Matthew 5:38-48; Luke 10:25-37.

PRINTED TEXT: Matthew 5:38-48.

Matthew 5:38-48

38 Ye have heard that it hath been said, An eye for an eye, and a tooth for a tooth:

39 But I say unto you, That ye resist not evil: but whosoever shall smite thee on thy right cheek, turn to him the other also.

40 And if any man will sue thee at the law, and take away thy coat, let him have thy cloak also.

41 And whosoever shall compel thee to go a mile, go with him twain.

42 Give to him that asketh thee, and from him that would borrow of thee turn not thou away.

43 Ye have heard that it hath been said, Thou shalt love thy neighbor, and hate thine enemy.

44 But I say unto you, Love your enemies, bless them that curse you, do good to them that hate you, and pray for them which despitefully use you, and persecute you;

45 That ye may be the children of your Father which is in heaven: for he maketh his sun to rise on the evil and on the good, and sendeth rain on the just and on the unjust.

46 For if ye love them which love you, what reward have ye? do not even the publicans the same?

47 And if ye salute your brethren only, what do ye more than others? do not even the publicans so?

48 Be ye therefore perfect, even as your Father which is in heaven is perfect.

May 12

GOLDEN TEXT: I say unto you, Love your enemies, bless them that curse you, do good to them that hate you, and pray for them which despitefully use you, and persecute you.—Matthew 5:44.

Teachings of Jesus
Unit 3. Teachings About Living
(Lessons 10-13)

Lesson Aims

This study should enable the student to:

1. Summarize in his own words what Jesus told His followers not to do, and what to do, in response to the evil done to them personally.

2. Distinguish between the kind of love expressed in Mother's Day and the kind of love that Christians are to show to their enemies.

3. Establish a program of praying for someone who is particularly unfriendly to him.

Lesson Outline

INTRODUCTION
    A. Mother's Enemies
    B. No More Persecutors?
    C. Lesson Background
 I. ACCEPT ABUSE FOR JESUS' SAKE (Matthew 5:38-42)
    A. Accept Insult/Injury (vv. 38, 39)
    B. Accept Legal Intrusion (v. 40)
      So Sue Me!
    C. Accept Political Pressure (v. 41)
    D. Accept Material Burdens (v. 42)
II. LOVE AS GOD LOVES (Matthew 5:43-48)
    A. Return Good for Evil (vv. 43, 44)
      Kill Them With Kindness
    B. Imitating Our Father (v. 45)
    C. Be Different From the Ungodly (vv. 46, 47)
      Can We All Just Get Along?
    D. Growing Up to God (v. 48)
CONCLUSION
    A. "Be Good to My Grandchildren"
    B. Rejoicing to Run
    C. Prayer of a Growing Child
    D. Thought to Remember

Use visual 11 of the visuals packet as a way to illustrate the challenge to love our enemies. It is shown on page 317.

Introduction

A. Mother's Enemies

Mother's Day is properly a celebration of love. Mother love begins naturally as tender affection for the infant offspring. It becomes a bond with the child as a person, loving the mother; then a lifelong relationship, tested and changing as per-sonalities develop. Even after experience gives way to memory, Mother's Day never could be monotonous! Love is like that. But when a child is threatened, whoever poses the threat becomes the mother's enemy.

A Christian mother reveals a special quality, reaching out to other children in church, community, and beyond, with concern that all should know the blessings of a heavenly Father. Her enemies are those who threaten the wider family, especially in the realm of faith, morals, and character. So love and enmity are interwoven on Mother's Day, and so they are in Jesus' teaching on the subject.

B. No More Persecutors?

Last week we heard the Lord's blessing on those who, because they belong to Him, will be opposed, vilified, and excluded from positions of influence. They are to rejoice, Jesus said, in their fellowship with Him who endured greater persecution. Today's lesson may lead some to suggest that we may do away with enemies by making them our friends. Are we thus to forfeit the blessing we were so recently promised?

There is no danger of that, unless we surrender and join the enemy. And that would do away with all blessing forever. No, our Lord had enemies enough to kill Him, and He still has enemies enough to share with all His followers. That is true in spite of all our love and prayers. The blessing remains, along with the Lord's example and instruction about dealing with those who insist on opposing Him and His followers.

C. Lesson Background

The Sermon on the Mount presents a direct challenge to all that has gone before. The introductory "blesseds" upset the world's standard of values at every point on which they touch (Matthew 5:3-11). There was more to come, relating to the law of Moses and its application. Some would think that Jesus was attempting to destroy the law. Not so. He was defending the law from the deadening interpretations and shallow applications that had destroyed its force (vv. 17-20). In doing so, He spoke with an authority equal to that of the original presentation on that other mountain, Sinai. Six times He quoted popular interpretations of basic laws, and added, "But I say unto you —" (vv. 21-44).

Much that Jesus said was associated with purity in heart (Matthew 5:8). Deeds, good or evil, are begotten in thoughts and intentions known at first only to the thinker and to God (Proverbs 4:23; 1 Samuel 16:7). The way to avoid murder, Jesus said, is to avoid anger (Matthew 5:21-26). The way to avoid adultery is to avoid lustful thinking (vv. 27-30). The way to avoid endless conflict is to develop the attitude of Jesus in helpful love rather than prideful retaliation (vv. 38-48).

I. Accept Abuse for Jesus' Sake (Matthew 5:38-42)

A. Accept Insult/Injury (vv. 38, 39)

38. Ye have heard that it hath been said, An eye for an eye, and a tooth for a tooth.

The quoted law may be found in Exodus 21:24, 25; Leviticus 24:19, 20; and Deuteronomy 19:15-21. It prescribed punishments for crimes that had been confirmed by witnesses. Leviticus 19:17, 18 forbids private vengeance for personal offenses, and Proverbs 24:29 urges against it.

Two purposes were evident in the Old Testament law. One was to warn the potential offender that he could expect to be damaged as he damaged another. The second purpose was to limit retaliation and prevent escalating feuds. No person was to be killed for insulting his neighbor. Jesus would control personal retaliation with one tough principle.

39. But I say unto you, That ye resist not evil: but whosoever shall smite thee on thy right cheek, turn to him the other also.

Do not fight with the person who insults you. A right-handed blow to the right cheek would be made with the back of the hand. That kind of slap in the face would be a major insult, but not a major injury. And God's person, fully assured of his worth in the sight of the Almighty, is not overly concerned with his standing in the sight of men (compare John 13:3-5). He who loves does not keep books on personal slights and insults (1 Corinthians 13:4-7). Instead of "getting even" for the insult, the follower of Christ is to show his willingness to accept it in double measure! The offender will have failed in his effort to destroy the Christian's composure. Rather than being overcome with evil, the Christian will have overcome evil with good (Romans 12:21). He will have reflected the character of Christ, who "also suffered for us, leaving us an example, that ye should follow his steps . . . . who, when he was reviled, reviled not again; when he suffered, he threatened not; but committed himself to him that judgeth righteously" (1 Peter 2:21-23).

B. Accept Legal Intrusion (v. 40)

40. And if any man will sue thee at the law, and take away thy coat, let him have thy cloak also.

Jesus already had advised His followers to settle their differences out of court, even at loss to themselves. Lawsuits would cost much more (Matthew 5:25, 26). The basis for losing one's garments in a lawsuit is found in Exodus 22:26, 27 and Deuteronomy 24:10-13. The light *coat*, or tunic, and/or the heavier outer *cloak*, might be taken as security for a loan, but the creditor was not allowed to keep a poor man's cloak overnight, since it served also as his blanket. Jesus directed His disciples to yield twice as much as was required, giving up the blanket garment also to the claimant. The Christian is fully aware of his legal rights, but he will not press or demand them at the expense of another person.

SO SUE ME!

America is a litigious society. As a nation we file eighteen million new lawsuits every year. With only six percent of the world's population, the United States has seventy percent of all the world's lawyers. While much good is done by our legal system—defending the rights of the accused, prosecuting criminals, protecting the victims of negligence and injury—Americans are overrun with lawsuits.

In contrast with the litigious climate of our society, Jesus urged people to go out of their way to come to terms with their adversaries. The chief question for a Christian in conflict is not how do I get everything that's coming to me, but how can I restore this damaged relationship.

—C. B. Mc.

C. Accept Political Pressure (v. 41)

41. And whosoever shall compel thee to go a mile, go with him twain.

Cyrus king of Persia is said to have authorized his couriers to require citizens with horses to help them on their way with government business. Greek and Roman rulers copied the plan with variations. Roman officers in Palestine could demand help from residents for a distance of one *mile*. So Simon of Cyrene was pressed into service to carry the cross of Jesus to the place of execution (Luke 23:26). Such service was commonly rendered grudgingly. But Jesus again directed His followers to do twice as much as was required. The first mile was duty; the second was opportunity. The first was bondage; the second was freedom. It could be fun!

D. Accept Material Burdens (v. 42)

42. Give to him that asketh thee, and from him that would borrow of thee turn not thou away.

Proverbs 19:17 sounds a biblical theme: "He who is kind to the poor lends to the Lord, and he will reward him for what he has done" (*New International Version*). The question of motive remains. Does one give grudgingly, out of necessity? Second Corinthians 9:7 forbids it. Does he give mechanically, for an expected reward? That, too, is self-centered. Or does he give as he can, according to the real needs and eternal benefit—not necessarily the deserving character—of the recipient? When a lame man looked to Peter and John for money, they gave him healing instead (Acts 3:1-10). That was done in the name of Jesus Christ, who gave His all to us and for us. The Christian is directed to give *when* asked, but not necessarily *what* is asked. Jesus himself was known to give spiritual gifts rather than the material benefits requested (John 4:15).

Lending to the poor in his need is specifically commanded in Deuteronomy 15:7-11. The Jewish people were forbidden to charge interest on loans to one another. Jesus went a step farther: "If ye lend to them of whom ye hope to receive, what thank have ye? for sinners also lend to sinners, to receive as much again" (Luke 6:34). The serious follower of the Lord will be victimized occasionally in his refusal to protect his rights, but he would rather be mistreated many times than to mistreat another human being once. That is following and honoring Him who said, "Whatever you did for one of the least of these brothers of mine, you did for me" (Matthew 25:40, *New International Version*).

II. Love as God Loves (Matthew 5:43-48)

Jesus shows and prescribes the nature of God as the one way of real and lasting life.

A. Return Good for Evil (vv. 43, 44)

43. Ye have heard that it hath been said, Thou shalt love thy neighbor, and hate thine enemy.

The grand injunction to *love* one's *neighbor* shines out amid a cluster of laws on holy living, from Leviticus 19: "Thou shalt not avenge, nor bear any grudge against the children of thy people, but thou shalt love thy neighbor as thyself" (verse 18). Jesus called it the second greatest commandment of all, exceeded only by the command to love God wholly.

Scripture nowhere commands one to *hate* his *enemy*—especially his personal enemy. Yet the Israelites were forbidden to make peace with the Canaanites as enemies of God (Exodus 34:11-16), and Psalm 109 calls down judgment on the oppressors of the righteous. It would be easy to interpret such passages as approving, if not commanding, hatred of the enemy.

At best, those who were looking for the easy way could search the phrases, "thy neighbor,"

"thy brother," and "the children of thy people" for an interpretation that would excuse them from loving too many (see Luke 10:29).

Which of us, moreover, is not influenced somewhat by traditions implying that distaste for *them* is an important part of loving *us*? It had to be answered!

44. But I say unto you, Love your enemies, bless them that curse you, do good to them that hate you, and pray for them which despitefully use you, and persecute you.

The love here commanded and depicted is not an intense liking. It may, in fact, operate in the face of a strong dislike. The Greek *agape*, used here, is not basically emotional. It has been defined as "active and intelligent goodwill," an inclination to do good, rather than evil, to all persons, no matter how we may feel about them personally. Jesus' directive begins and ends with an appeal to God, who does good to all: *bless*—call down good on—those who call down evil on you; and pray that God will exercise His wisdom in dealing most helpfully with the offenders. Prayer is a benefit that can be bestowed on even the most reluctant recipient. Between blessing and petitioning, we are directed to do as we ask God to do—to work for the offender's best eternal welfare.

Those who have seriously tried the Lord's program have found that it becomes less difficult. They also find that the feelings of dislike for the enemy tend to fade, and their problem of enmity declines. If enmity continues, it is the other person's problem, not theirs.

Jesus was not alone in recommending the return of blessing for cursing and good deeds for evil. Exodus 23:4, 5 and Proverbs 25:21, 22 stipulate it, and Romans 12:14-21 extends and specifies concerning it. Judgment and vengeance belong to God, Paul says. He adds that judgment and punishment for civil crimes are to be carried out by the civil government (Romans 13:1-8).

Our Lord himself provided the perfect example of returning good for evil and blessing for cursing in that, "while we were yet sinners, Christ died for us" (Romans 5:6-8; compare 1 Peter 2:21-24). He prayed for His persecutors as He died (Luke 23:34).

KILL THEM WITH KINDNESS

In his book *Through the Valley of the Kwai*, Ernest Gordon writes about a group of American soldiers who encountered some wounded Japanese prisoners at a railway station in Burma. World War II was raging. Had these groups met on the battlefield, they would have tried to destroy each other; but now the prisoners were helpless, packed in railway cars, their uniforms incredibly filthy with mud and blood, their wounds uncared for. Quickly opening their packs, the Americans knelt by their enemies to give them food and water, to clean and bandage their wounds. The Japanese responded with grateful cries of "Arigato!" (Thank you).

Few things in the universe compare with the power that is unleashed when we love an enemy. Unexpected and undeserved kindnesses, gracious acts of mercy, soft answers in the face of wrath have the power to shatter walls of prejudice and enmity. According to Jesus, the best revenge we can exact upon our enemies is to kill them with kindness.   —C. B. Mc.

B. Imitating Our Father (v. 45)

45. That ye may be the children of your Father which is in heaven: for he maketh his sun to rise on the evil and on the good, and sendeth rain on the just and on the unjust.

Luke 6:35, 36 extends on the same idea: "Love ye your enemies, and do good, and lend, hoping for nothing again; and your reward shall be great, and ye shall be the children of the Highest: for he is kind unto the unthankful and to the evil. Be ye therefore merciful, as your Father also is merciful."

Are we something other than God's children if we fail to be like Him in these matters? Well, at least our lack of the family resemblance could raise questions about our spiritual paternity.

The basic evidences of God's love are offered alike to all mankind. His children also are to distribute their goodwill without quotas or special directives. Not all recipients, however, are equally benefited by the distribution. The same sunshine and rain that bring good crops to the prudent farmer will produce gullies and brambles for the sluggard. But God's favors and His children's love are still available to all.

C. Be Different From the Ungodly (vv. 46, 47)

46, 47. For if ye love them which love you, what reward have ye? do not even the publicans the same? And if ye salute your brethren only, what do ye more than others? do not even the publicans so?

Jesus turned for a moment from affirmative to negative motivation. Were His follower/hearers really content to be like "those people" to whom they felt most superior? For His comparison He chose *publicans*—Jewish tax collectors for the Roman government—who frequently became wealthy by lining their own pockets with unauthorized assessments. As betrayers, oppressors, and wealthy crooks, the publicans were generally despised. They would be most comfortable

visual 11

in the company of others like themselves—loving those who loved them. For a modern counterpart we think immediately of gangs and "families" who gain power and wealth by violence, while exercising the strongest of love and loyalty within their tight little circles. If we limit our love to our own families and social circles, how is our love more praiseworthy than theirs?

The same principle applies to *salute* or *greet*. The Greek text uses a word as warm as a smiling bow and as broad as the Hawaiian *aloha*. It could be used on any occasion, but always as an affectionate expression of good wishes.

So how do we conduct our greetings, in the place of worship, for example? Is it an occasion for meeting and visiting with our own family and friends? Do we have a limited hello and handshaking list? If so, how do we deserve more praise in this matter than do worldly folk who have words of encouragement for none beyond their own circles, and trade gifts with the same people on every holiday?

CAN WE ALL JUST GET ALONG?

In the spring of 1992, the nation watched in horror as South Central Los Angeles reacted to the acquittal of four police officers accused of beating Rodney King. Anarchy spread along the streets as gangs attacked, robbed, and left luckless drivers bleeding on the roadways. Wholesale looting went largely unchecked while more than 3,700 fires raged out of control. Fifty-five people died, and more than three thousand were injured before federal law officers were able to restore order to the riot-torn city.

In what *Time* magazine called the most emotional television moment of 1992, the man at the center of it all, Rodney King, stepped before the cameras and nervously asked, "Can we all just get along?"

It's a good question. One of the strong themes of the Bible is that of "getting along" with our fellowmen. Even when they aren't part of our family. Even when they aren't our neighbors. Even when they differ from us in race, nationality, or political perspective. Even when they are our enemies.   —C. B. Mc.

D. Growing Up to God (v. 48)

48. Be ye therefore perfect, even as your Father which is in heaven is perfect.
Perfect here translates a word depicting a goal or end that is achieved only after long striving. The admonition points to the grown-up status of God's children (v. 45). It is echoed in Ephesians 5:1, 2: "Be ye therefore followers [or imitators] of God, as dear children; and walk in love, as Christ also hath loved us, and hath given himself for us." Paul himself had followed (imitated) God in Christ for many years before he wrote confessing that he had not yet reached the goal of complete maturity, but he pressed "toward the mark for the prize of the high calling of God in Christ Jesus" (Philippians 3:12-14). God was not through with him yet.

God himself is the perfection, the goal toward which all growing is directed, just as He is the holiness toward which all dedication is aimed: "Ye shall be holy: for I the Lord your God am holy" (Leviticus 19:2). The Christian's maturity will follow the pattern of God's perfection, though it will not reach the same level. His saints are common believers who by His grace have become pure in heart and see God.

Conclusion

A. "Be Good to My Grandchildren"

A closing word for Mother's Day is still appropriate. After the day is past—communications have been made and tributes spoken, gifts have been received and flowers have served their mission—what does Mother most desire from her day? Would she not thoughtfully say, "If you really want to honor me, be good to my grandchildren"?

Home Daily Bible Readings

Monday, May 6—Love One Another (1 John 3:11-18)
Tuesday, May 7—The Christian's Assurance (1 John 3:19-24)
Wednesday, May 8—The Way to Greatness (Matthew 5:13-20)
Thursday, May 9—Practical Advice (Matthew 5:21-26)
Friday, May 10—Jesus' Attitude on Adultery and Divorce (Matthew 5:27-32)
Saturday, May 11—Reliable Words (Matthew 5:33-37)
Sunday, May 12—Loving Behavior (Luke 10:25-37)

Jesus our Lord did say, many times in many ways, "Love as I have loved you." Neither mother love nor Christian love, in any generation, is a minimum performance, limiting itself to those expressions that are required or necessary. Where love is lacking, the law can require a parent to provide decent housing and food for children; but mother love adds hugs and kisses, drying tears and sharing laughter, games and stories, favorite foods and pretty dresses, time for talking, listening, and praying together. Those build treasured memories.

B. Rejoicing to Run

Scripture frequently compares the Christian life to a footrace, to be run with disciplined preparation (1 Corinthians 9:24-27) and patience (Hebrews 12:1, 2) to the goal (2 Timothy 4:6-8).

Who, though, ever enters a footrace grudgingly, as a matter of necessity, dragging through it with the least possible effort? That's not the way it's done! Races are run with an eager enthusiasm noted in the words of Psalm 19:5, which says that the sun in its daily circuit "rejoiceth as a strong man to run a race." Otherwise it is no fun and no race.

Jesus was fully aware of the joyless drudgery with which many folk face their days, and He provided the answer for it, as we have just seen. We are encouraged to replace "Do I have to?" with "Let me at it!"

"You don't have to do that!"

"Of course I don't; but what fun is there in doing only what you have to do? That's a drag. The fun is in doing what you want to do, beyond the requirements."

So the joyous runner in life's race is strong enough to accept insults he doesn't have to, and accept legal adjustments he doesn't have to, and walk miles he doesn't have to, and give more generously than he has to, and pray for enemies he doesn't have to—all for the sake of the Lord who made all kinds of sacrifices He didn't have to, for our sakes, and for the joy that was set before Him (Hebrews 12:2). That is truly loving, and living!

C. Prayer of a Growing Child

We praise You, God our Father, for the wisdom that knows us, and even more for the love that saves us and persuades us to be continually more like You. Help us, we pray, to reflect Your love to those about us, whether or not they be friendly to us. In Jesus' name, amen.

D. Thought to Remember

To deal effectively with unfriendly folk, take them to the Lord in prayer.

Learning by Doing

This page contains an alternate lesson plan emphasizing learning activities. Classes desiring such student involvement will find these suggestions helpful.

Learning Goals

After this lesson, a student will be able to:

1. Summarize in his or her own words the teachings of Jesus regarding the response to evil done to the Christian personally.

2. Distinguish between the behavior and love of the world and the love that Christians are to show their enemies.

3. Begin to pray for someone who is particularly unfriendly to him or her.

Into the Lesson

Ask the class members to relate a specific memory of a mother's love in action. When did his or her mother show love in an unforgettable way? Lead the class in praising God for our mothers and those who have helped us become who we are, especially in Christ.

Into the Word

Jesus was aware of the fact that the world does not share our mothers' love for us as Christians. In Matthew 5:38-48, He instructs us to respond to evil and hate with self-control and love, in spite of our natural reactions and whatever we have been taught to the contrary.

Ask the students to separate into five groups with two or more people in each group. Give each group a card with one of these groups of Scripture references:

Matthew 5:38, 39; Exodus 21:24, 25; Romans 12:21

Matthew 5:40; Exodus 22:25-27; Philippians 2:3-7

Matthew 5:41; Luke 22:26; Ephesians 6:7, 8

Matthew 5:42; Deuteronomy 15:7-11; Matthew 6:2-4; Acts 20:35

Matthew 5:43, 44; Leviticus 19:18; Romans 5:8-10; 12:18-21

Ask each group to do three things: First, take a few minutes to study the Scriptures assigned. Second, tell the class what Jesus taught in the verse or verses from Matthew. Third, explain how the other Scripture passages are related to that teaching.

If a group seems to be stumped, you may want to help it with information from the lesson explanation in this book. When they give their reports, be ready to supplement them with your own comments or thoughts drawn from your advance study of the lesson.

These teachings are hard to understand and even more difficult to put into practice. Lead the class members in a brief discussion of why Jesus' teachings are so difficult to apply to our lives. Possible answers: *We tend to be selfish; our culture focuses on protecting one's rights; we do not want others to take advantage of us or take us for granted.*

Now read Matthew 5:45-48. We must be different from the world and more like our heavenly Father. Though we will never be perfectly loving and holy as He is, we should be growing toward that perfection. Ask someone to read Philippians 3:12-15. As we become more like Jesus, we love even our enemies. As we demonstrate love for *all* others, we become more like Jesus (Luke 23:34).

Into Life

Now divide the class into groups of three. People of each group are to think of a situation in which a Christian is insulted, slandered, or otherwise mistreated—a situation such as actually has happened or could happen in one of their own lives. They are to plan a short skit. Acting as the Christian, one will explain how he has been mistreated. The other two will act as the Christian's good self and his bad self. The bad self will stand beside him and suggest all sorts of mean and spiteful ways of getting even. The good self will stand on the other side of him, remind him of Jesus' teaching and suggest right ways of acting. Each skit should be played out to a conclusion, whether good or bad.

Give the groups time to plan their skits. Be ready to suggest possible situations: a husband carelessly slights his wife; a hateful fellow worker steals customers; an insolent teenager wants to borrow the car; a jealous rival slanders the new class president.

After each skit, lead the class in applause and appreciation. When all have been presented, lead a discussion of any insights gained from the presentations.

Ask each class member to think of a person who could be considered his or her enemy. Encourage prayer for that person as a first step in applying the teachings of Jesus. Keeping the groups of three, invite each group to pray together for their enemies and their ability to show love in the name of Jesus Christ.

Let's Talk It Over

The questions on this page are designed to encourage review of the lesson Scriptures and to promote discussion of the lesson by the class. The answers provided are only discussion starters. Let your class talk it over from there.

1. Jesus' command to turn the other cheek to the person who strikes us ranks high among His "hard sayings." What is involved in obeying this command?

Jesus often has been called "the man for others." In all His deeds and words He sought what would benefit other people. In following Jesus we should aim to be "a man for others" or "a woman for others." When we make it our goal to minister in some way to everyone we meet, we will find it easier to handle negative words or actions directed toward us. If a person should strike us either physically or verbally, the natural tendency would be to strike back. But we know that that only escalates a conflict. By responding with "a soft answer" (Proverbs 15:1) or an act of forbearance, we can defuse the situation and put ourselves into position for effective ministry toward that person.

2. Why do we need to combine discretion with generosity in giving to those in need?

We are well aware that there are unscrupulous people who think nothing of taking advantage of the generosity of Christians. Second Thessalonians 3:10 warns us not to support anyone who can and ought to support himself. If we give money to anyone who asks, we run the danger of supporting a person's drug habit or drinking problem. In this matter we need to be "wise as serpents, and harmless as doves" (Matthew 10:16). When we are asked to give to an organization that helps those in need, we must be certain it is a reputable, trustworthy organization. When an individual seeks help from us, it may be better to buy him or her food or gasoline, or to pay a rent or utility bill directly, instead of doling out cash.

3. Do we ever think it legitimate to hate an enemy? How can we overcome any tendency toward hatred of another human being?

Apparently some people who call themselves Christians have felt it legitimate to hate Madalyn Murray O'Hair. The famous atheist claimed that she received a great deal of hate mail from Christians. Perhaps we have bristled at the sight of Saddam Hussein on television. It could be that reading the militant statements of "pro-choice" or "gay-rights" activists stirs up strong

negative sentiments within us. However, we must not harbor hatred in our hearts toward these people. We can hate what they do or what they stand for, but we must love them. Jesus' "Father, forgive them; for they know not what they do" (Luke 23:34) applies. Some of the people mentioned above are blind, woefully ignorant, and spiritually lost. They are to be pitied more than hated; their misguided zeal should move us to compassion rather than anger.

4. Why is it essential that we learn to pray for those who have offended us?

Prayer is a positive response that we can make. Instead of merely trying to ignore the offense and to suppress the sense of anger and bitterness we feel, we can bring it all before God. It is a relief to admit to Him how upset we are about the matter and to confess our temptation to seek revenge. It is a joy to ask Him for a mighty victory over the entire situation. On behalf of the offender it is well that we ask forgiveness, even as Job prayed for his three misguided friends (Job 42:8-10). Prayer also can be a first step in resolving the matter. We can ask God for guidance in taking some positive steps toward overcoming any mutual ill-will and restoring an amiable relationship. Prayer is also a desirable response on such an occasion because it is consistent with the example of Jesus (Luke 23:34).

5. Jesus' call to perfection is in contrast to the excuse often heard for misbehavior: "Oh, well, nobody's perfect!" Why do we need to aim for perfection?

"If we say that we have no sin, we deceive ourselves, and the truth is not in us" (1 John 1:8). In this verse and in other places in the New Testament it is made clear that Christians are not immune to sin. While we are here on earth, moral perfection remains out of reach. But this fact does not give us license to indulge ourselves in any sin. Remember Paul's question in Romans 6:1: "Shall we continue in sin, that grace may abound?" and his decisive answer in the following verse: "God forbid. How shall we, that are dead to sin, live any longer therein?" We must aim for a completely pure and holy and righteous life. Then, even though we fall short, we will at least come closer to God's standard.

Teachings About Riches and Anxiety

DEVOTIONAL READING: Luke 12:13-21.

LESSON SCRIPTURE: Matthew 6:19-21, 24-34; Luke 12:13-21.

PRINTED TEXT: Matthew 6:19-21, 24-34.

Matthew 6:19-21, 24-34

19 Lay not up for yourselves treasures upon earth, where moth and rust doth corrupt, and where thieves break through and steal:

20 But lay up for yourselves treasures in heaven, where neither moth nor rust doth corrupt, and where thieves do not break through nor steal:

21 For where your treasure is, there will your heart be also.

. . . .

24 No man can serve two masters: for either he will hate the one, and love the other; or else he will hold to the one, and despise the other. Ye cannot serve God and mammon.

25 Therefore I say unto you, Take no thought for your life, what ye shall eat, or what ye shall drink; nor yet for your body, what ye shall put on. Is not the life more than meat, and the body than raiment?

26 Behold the fowls of the air: for they sow not, neither do they reap, nor gather into barns; yet your heavenly Father feedeth them. Are ye not much better than they?

27 Which of you by taking thought can add one cubit unto his stature?

28 And why take ye thought for raiment? Consider the lilies of the field, how they grow; they toil not, neither do they spin:

29 And yet I say unto you, That even Solomon in all his glory was not arrayed like one of these.

30 Wherefore, if God so clothe the grass of the field, which today is, and tomorrow is cast into the oven, shall he not much more clothe you, O ye of little faith?

31 Therefore take no thought, saying, What shall we eat? or, What shall we drink? or, Wherewithal shall we be clothed?

32 (For after all these things do the Gentiles seek:) for your heavenly Father knoweth that ye have need of all these things.

33 But seek ye first the kingdom of God, and his righteousness; and all these things shall be added unto you.

34 Take therefore no thought for the morrow: for the morrow shall take thought for the things of itself. Sufficient unto the day is the evil thereof.

May
19

GOLDEN TEXT: Seek ye first the kingdom of God, and his righteousness; and all these things shall be added unto you.—Matthew 6:33.

Teachings of Jesus
Unit 3. Teachings About Living
(Lessons 10-13)

Lesson Aims

This study should prepare the student to:

1. Explain the phrases, "Lay up treasure" and "Take thought," as used in today's text and as applying to our present experience.

2. Compare God's provision of food for birds and beauty for flowers with His provision of things necessary for the Christian.

3. Identify at least one point at which he or she will cease fruitless worrying in favor of fruitful service in God's kingdom.

Lesson Outline

INTRODUCTION
  A. Treasuring Treasures
  B. Lesson Background
 I. TREASURE IN HEAVEN (Matthew 6:19-21, 24)
  A. Material Investment (vv. 19-21)
    What's It Worth to You?
  B. Self-Investment (v. 24)
II. TRUST IN GOD (Matthew 6:25-32)
  A. Uncertainty About Necessities (v. 25)
    High Anxiety
  B. Birds and Basics (vv. 26, 27)
  C. Clothing and Flowers (vv. 28-30)
  D. Concerns of Unbelievers (vv. 31, 32)
    What's in It for Me?
III. PRIORITY OF HEAVEN (Matthew 6:33)
IV. TOMORROW'S INSURANCE (Matthew 6:34)
CONCLUSION
  A. Your Hobby Collection
  B. Prayer of an Investor
  C. Thought to Remember

Visual 12 of the visuals packet highlights how important proper priorities are. The visual is shown on page 326.

Introduction

A. Treasuring Treasures

Treasure Island! The very name of Stevenson's adventure story will quicken the pulse of one-time boys familiar with its account of conflict in search for hidden wealth. Long before Stevenson, however, Jesus caught the imagination of sober adults by comparing the kingdom of Heaven to buried treasure so great that the finder would sell all he possessed in order to claim it (Matthew 13:44).

Treasure! What a word! As a noun it speaks of riches, usually stored up or hoarded. It may speak of any precious items highly prized. *Treasure* is also a verb. It speaks of collecting and/or storing up things of value; also cherishing or holding on to what is most appreciated. One does treasure one's treasures.

Matthew 6:19-21 speaks literally of collecting, storing up, cherishing, and clinging to what one values most. In what are we most interested? On what do we spend time and money most freely? What do we collect, store, hide, or display, and protect most carefully? With Jesus it was and is the reign and the realm of God.

B. Lesson Background

In His Sermon on the Mount Jesus talked immediately about ultimate values, boldly challenging the ideas popularly accepted by His hearers, then and now. Pleasure, prosperity, and power are false gods, He showed. Thoughts and attitudes, He said, are basic to one's acceptance with God. And they are not the thoughts and attitudes popularly encouraged as leading to "success" in the "real world" (as though the changing styles among mortal men were more "real" than the unchanging character of the Creator).

Jesus spoke first of pure thoughts as the basis of moral behavior (Matthew 5). Then He considered three practices important in religious life—almsgiving (personal generosity to the poor), prayer, and fasting (Matthew 6:1-18). All such practices, He said, should be done without fanfare, as between the worshiper and God.

Then suddenly He turned to material considerations—money, buying groceries and clothing. The Sermon came down to earth with a thud that must have shocked some of His hearers as much as a church's passing the offering plates immediately after the Lord's Supper. The Lord insisted, though, that the Christian's *earth* maintains inseparable ties with *Heaven.*

I. Treasure in Heaven
(Matthew 6:19-21, 24)

A. Material Investment (vv. 19-21)

19. Lay not up for yourselves treasures upon earth, where moth and rust doth corrupt, and where thieves break through and steal.

Stop accumulating a stockpile of material goods in a place where nothing is ultimately secure. Jesus described that insecurity as it applied to His hearers' preferred investments—costly garments (see Joshua 7:21 and 2 Kings 5:22, 26) and metal objects such as coins. These could be eaten by moths or by corrosion so as to become worthless. Swifter destruction can come to present-day material investments through flood, fire, windstorm, or a stock market crash.

Thieves could dig through clay or rock walls of houses to get around barred doors, and so take anything of value. Modern security measures can hinder the process but can never prevent it. Solomon provides expert testimony about the fleeting nature of riches (Proverbs 23:4, 5). But Jesus warns more simply that the material world is no secure depository for wealth.

20. But lay up for yourselves treasures in heaven, where neither moth nor rust doth corrupt, and where thieves do not break through nor steal.

Start building up a treasury in Heaven, where there is real security. Luke 12:31-34 gives directions for turning material wealth into heavenly riches through gifts and activities honoring Christ. First Timothy 6:17-19 provides practical instruction for well-to-do Christians, to be rich in good works, generously sharing, "laying up in store for themselves a good foundation against the time to come" (v. 19). The Lord promised rewards, on earth and in Heaven, to those who left the security of homes and businesses in order to follow and serve Him (Luke 18:28-30).

Financial investment in eternity is clearly accessible, but not with the idea of buying one's way into Heaven. That purchase price has been paid in the only possible way by Jesus himself. But *treasures* suggests by definition an accumulation beyond what is necessary. Paul made investment in Heaven by forgoing his right to receive living expenses from the Corinthians and financing his work by making tents (Acts 18:1-4; 1 Corinthians 9:3-18). In this he has been joined by the nonpreaching elder who explains happily that his occupation is serving the Lord, but he operates a small business to finance it.

21. For where your treasure is, there will your heart be also.

God is not served with material things as though He were in need of them, since He is himself the source of all things material and otherwise (Acts 17:24, 25). He is, on the other hand, vitally concerned with the persons He has made in His own image, that they should love Him and seek Him with a whole heart. And that is not possible as long as their attention is fixed on things material and temporary.

WHAT'S IT WORTH TO YOU?

Psychology Today asked more than twenty thousand Americans what they would be willing to do for a million dollars. Twenty-three percent of the men and twenty-one percent of the women said they would marry someone they didn't love. Twenty-two percent of the men and ten percent of the women said they would tell a lie about a business associate. Twenty-one percent of the men and ten percent of the women said they would steal something. Eighteen percent of the men and ten percent of the women said they would bribe someone or take a bribe. Twelve percent of the men and ten percent of the women said they would divorce their spouses.

What would you do for a million dollars? Is there something more important than money in your value system? Jesus taught that some things are more permanent than money, and that a wise person will invest himself in something more lasting than earthly riches.

—C. B. Mc.

B. Self-Investment (v. 24)

Verses 22 and 23 provide an important link between treasure-building and self-commitment. Their theme is singleness of focus and purpose. The Lord warns against blurred double vision, conflicting interests, and uncertainty in one's course. "A double-minded man is unstable in all his ways" (James 1:8).

24. No man can serve two masters: for either he will hate the one, and love the other; or else he will hold to the one, and despise the other. Ye cannot serve God and mammon.

Serving two masters is described in language that indicates being slave to separate owners. No one is totally his own master: "To whom ye yield yourselves servants [slaves] to obey, his servants ye are to whom ye obey" (Romans 6:16). Obedience to competing masters is impossible, since the act of obedience to one is an act of disobedience to the other. The servant has to choose, on the basis of *feeling*—hating one and loving the other—or on the basis of *action*—following the command of one and disregarding the other.

Mammon, riches, is a tyrant opposed to God in direction and goal. It is not possible to keep *God* and *money* totally separate. A person can serve God *with* money, thus investing in heavenly treasure; or one may use the things of God in serving mammon, as the politician who attends church regularly for two months before each election, but not otherwise. Jesus sounds again and again the challenge issued by Joshua: "Choose you this day whom ye will serve" (Joshua 24:15); and by Elijah: "How long halt ye between two opinions? if the Lord be God, follow him: but if Baal, then follow him" (1 Kings 18:21).

Self-dedication in terms of time, energy, influence, and even one's personal rights is what gives meaning to any other investment in God's kingdom. In praising the generosity of Christians in Macedonia, Paul noted that they "first gave their own selves to the Lord" (2 Corinthians 8:5).

II. Trust in God
(Matthew 6:25-32)

The Christian has chosen to *serve* God rather than riches as his master, so he is to *depend on* God rather than money for his security.

A. Uncertainty About Necessities (v. 25)

25. Therefore I say unto you, Take no thought for your life, what ye shall eat, or what ye shall drink; nor yet for your body, what ye shall put on. Is not the life more than meat, and the body than raiment?

Take . . . thought. The verb here translated is the same one that is translated "be careful" in Philippians 4:6, urging Christians to avoid anxious concern, and to present their needs before God in thankful prayer. The word indicates a state of doubt or distraction, and may be translated "worry," "be anxious," or "be troubled with care."

The basic necessities of life are not to be matters for uncertainty. The life itself, which God gave in the first place, is infinitely more important than a well-stocked pantry to sustain it. God is not going to let you starve. So, too, the body that God made and caused to grow is vastly more important than the clothing that protects it. God will give what is necessary to sustain what He has already bestowed.

Much of our attention to food and clothing seems to deal, in fact, not with needs, but with likes and dislikes in taste and appearance.

In 1 Timothy 6:6-10 Paul echoes the Lord's warning against becoming entangled in the web of concern for wealth. He urges, "Having food and raiment, let us be therewith content."

HIGH ANXIETY

Upset stomach? Sweaty palms? Tense feeling? Pounding heart? You're not alone. America is a nation of worriers. Fears about health, finances, employment, children, career development, marriage, and other problems overwhelm many people. People with jobs worry about their work. People without jobs worry about not working. Mothers worry about illnesses or accidents involving their children.

To combat worry, people turn to prescription drugs, seminars, and self-help books. Some of the current advice is to set aside specific times

to worry, get more rest, exercise, or eat special diets. Then there is psychological counseling, behavior modification, and group therapy.

With so much to worry about and so many confusing options for treating it, how do we turn off the anxiety alarm? Jesus gave us the key by reminding us that the Creator who put us here is still in charge. In one sense, the common problems that worry us are not our problems. They are God's. He understands us and our needs better than we do. Try as you may, you cannot worry up a better answer to your needs than God can provide.   —C. B. Mc.

B. Birds and Basics (vv. 26, 27)

26. Behold the fowls of the air: for they sow not, neither do they reap, nor gather into barns; yet your heavenly Father feedeth them. Are ye not much better than they?

Birds may have been seen fluttering about as Jesus spoke. Clearly, these have no way of accumulating a season's supply of food ahead of time. Neither do they wait in their nests for food to be delivered to them. Instead, the birds live as God designed them to, finding, eating and/or carrying to their young what God's world makes available to them. Will God feed birds and neglect His own children? By no means! He provides for them also as they live according to the plan He has laid out for them.

Jesus' question, contrasting the worth of birds and of persons in God's sight, is central to His teaching. The biblical account of creation affirms that humankind, made in God's image, was given priority and dominion over the other creatures (Genesis 1:28). Many in our time, though, would dismiss the idea of God and creation, denying any clear distinction between mankind and "other animals," in worth or in moral responsibility. The result is to make men more bestial than the beasts (Romans 1:18-32), working destruction on themselves and all around them. Hear what Jesus says about creation!

27. Which of you by taking thought can add one cubit unto his stature?

A *cubit* is a unit of measure, originally from fingertip to elbow. *Stature* usually refers to physical height. But the words can apply as well to other measures of a person. Who, by worrying about it, can add even an hour to the measure of his life? Anxious concern is more likely, in fact, to shorten life than to lengthen it.

Perhaps Jesus was observing the inordinate concern of Greeks, Romans, and other pagans with physical development beyond any purposeful use. First Timothy 4:8 recommends exercise in godliness as infinitely more valuable.

C. Clothing and Flowers (vv. 28-30)

28, 29. And why take ye thought for raiment? Consider the lilies of the field, how they grow; they toil not, neither do they spin: and yet I say unto you, That even Solomon in all his glory was not arrayed like one of these.

Time, money, and concern may be overspent on clothing even more than on food.

Again, the Lord's illustrative item may have been visible as He spoke. Lilies, of the various kinds growing wild after the winter rains on Galilee's croplands and pastures, are known for their variety and beauty. Let the listeners learn well from observation! The flowers' adornment did not require the gathering of fiber to be spun into thread, woven into cloth, dyed for color, and fashioned into garments. Instead, it came naturally from God's creative provision.

The splendor of Solomon's court, including what he and his courtiers wore, was proverbial in his own day (1 Kings 10; 2 Chronicles 9:3-6) and continually through many Oriental traditions. The natural beauty of a small flower was still superior to the most lavish human provision.

30. Wherefore, if God so clothe the grass of the field, which today is, and tomorrow is cast into the oven, shall he not much more clothe you, O ye of little faith?

The leaves of lilies are like coarse grass, and in rainless months they dry up quickly. Then they become fuel badly needed in Palestine, since it has very few trees. Ovens—commonly of clay, were heated by burning dry grass and weed stalks in them. From flower to fuel was a brief journey for the lilies.

The contrast between these short-lived objects and God's faithful children was even sharper than that between birds and men. He who gave so much beauty to the grass would surely not abandon His own spiritual family. To doubt His care and provision, even for one anxious hour, would mark the followers of Jesus as "little faiths" or slight believers. That stands as Jesus' one spoken rebuke in a message of assurance. The disciples had seen enough of God's care surrounding them, and especially in Jesus himself, to support a faith much stronger than they were showing. The Lord's resurrection would go far to correct that deficiency.

D. Concerns of Unbelievers (vv. 31, 32)

31. Therefore take no thought, saying, What shall we eat? or, What shall we drink? or, Wherewithal shall we be clothed?

These are simple questions about basic necessities. A faith that will prevent anxious concern about these matters will surely be strong enough to prevent our being burdened with questions about the stock market, our television reception, or our standing in the community club.

32. (For after all these things do the Gentiles seek:) for your heavenly Father knoweth that ye have need of all these things.

Untaught Gentiles, having no hope beyond this present life, and no knowledge of a sustaining heavenly Father, had reason to be concerned about needs and treasures on earth—the only security they knew.

Christians, on the other hand, know an all-caring Father in Heaven, who is aware of their needs and able to supply them. They may cast all their care on Him who cares for them (1 Peter 5:7), and they may be free from anxiety as they bring their requests in thankful prayer. Thus assured, they can rest in the indescribable peace of God (Philippians 4:6, 7). Anxious worry on their part would be like heathen unbelief!

WHAT'S IN IT FOR ME?

A Florida minister told his congregation that "blessings, benefits, and rewards" would come to anyone who would give ten percent of his income to the church. One member promptly responded with a gift of eight hundred dollars.

Three years later, that member was unemployed. Claiming that he had received no blessings, benefits, or rewards, he sued the church. Before the case could come to trial, a Texas businessman read about it and sent the member a check for eight hundred dollars. The case was dropped.

Was this man wrong to think God refused to bless him? God often rewards faithful stewards with material things, but His blessings are not always counted in dollars and cents. Forgiveness,

Home Daily Bible Readings

Monday, May 13—Seeking God's Approval (Galatians 1:6-10)
Tuesday, May 14—Praising God for His Care (Psalm 147:1-11)
Wednesday, May 15—Hope in the Lord (Psalm 39)
Thursday, May 16—A Queen's Appraisal (1 Kings 10:1-7)
Friday, May 17—Confident of God's Watchcare (Psalm 23)
Saturday, May 18—Rewarded for Liberality (Psalm 37:21-26)
Sunday, May 19—Folly of Self-Centeredness (Luke 12:13-21)

God's peace and presence in our lives, adoption into the family of God, the promise of eternal life—these things have value far exceeding anything that can be bought with earthly currency.

—C. B. Mc.

III. Priority of Heaven (Matthew 6:33)

Christians' *seeking* as for hidden treasure, or *striving* as toward a fixed goal, will be quite different from the seeking of unbelievers.

33. But seek ye first the kingdom of God, and his righteousness; and all these things shall be added unto you.

There is something worthy of your total interest and devoted application. That goal is God's *realm* and *reign*. It includes your being accepted as a citizen there, approved of the King. Being right with Him—which is *righteousness*—is a part of that grand priority. God's kingdom is first in time, first in importance, first in the citizen's enthusiasm and affection. This is the order established in the model prayer of Matthew 6:9-13: God's glory and His reign, on earth as in Heaven, come first. Afterward is the expression of dependence for daily bread, forgiveness, and deliverance.

Seeking first the kingdom does not mean that the citizen does nothing but worship. He honors God by meeting his obligations to his family (1 Timothy 5:8), his community (Romans 13:1, 2), his neighbors (Luke 6:38), and his employer or employees (Ephesians 6:5-9), among other things. Life's necessities are met, then, as a matter of course. "In God we trust," inscribed on a nation's coinage, must stand as a solemn reminder that ultimate security is not to be found in money.

IV. Tomorrow's Insurance (Matthew 6:34)

34. Take therefore no thought for the morrow: for the morrow shall take thought for the things of itself. Sufficient unto the day is the evil thereof.

Today's focus on God's kingdom and our right relationship with Him is the one sure way to avoid the distractions of anxious thought about tomorrow. The laying up of treasure is always for tomorrow, either on earth or in Heaven. If on earth, there is reason for concern; it won't last. If in Heaven, it is secure and there is reason for contentment. So the right kind of thinking and doing *today* removes the basis for worry about *tomorrow*. Let each day's responsibilities be met that day. Don't load yourself with tomorrow's

burdens today, and don't load tomorrow with today's burdens that piled up while you were distracted with concern for tomorrow.

An old Christian song echoes the wisdom of faith: "Many things about tomorrow I don't seem to understand; but I know who holds tomorrow, and I know who holds my hand."

The wise will put off their worrying until the tomorrow that never comes.

Conclusion

A. Your Hobby Collection

What do you collect as a hobby? Stamps? Classic automobiles? China dolls? Family photos? Your collection may represent a sizable investment in time and money. You may have it insured, but you could not replace it. You could live without it, but you wouldn't enjoy life as much. You may enjoy it as long as you live. Will it then be equally valuable to someone else?

Can you imagine a perfect hobby collection—one without any drawbacks? It would offer keen pleasure in finding and acquiring, without anyone's suffering loss. It would be a joy to keep in order, to show and to share, with friends enjoying it as much as you do. It could not be lost, destroyed, or stolen; hence would need no insurance. It would persuade your best friends to enjoy the same hobby, without diminishing the value of your collection. Nothing to worry about —just enjoyment for you and others.

Well, how about the treasures and truths of God's kingdom, and the gathering of saints to enjoy them with you, forever?

B. Prayer of an Investor

Thank You, God, for the opportunity to invest ourselves and our resources in Your kingdom. Thank You especially for the gift of Your Son to make possible our citizenship with You. May our participation be the kind that leaves no room for doubt or anxiety. In Jesus' name, amen.

C. Thought to Remember

No one can serve God *and* money, but anyone can serve God *with* money.

visual 12

Learning by Doing

This page contains an alternate lesson plan emphasizing learning activities. Classes desiring such student involvement will find these suggestions helpful.

Learning Goals

Today students will be able to:

1. Identify the basic principles presented by Jesus in Matthew 6:19-21, 24-34.

2. Compare God's provision for birds and flowers with His care for the Christian.

3. Identify at least one thing for which he or she will cease fruitless worrying and will begin to trust God, seeking His righteousness.

Into the Lesson

Have several jokes and "one-liners" ready on the topic of money or finances. For example: "You know you can't take it with you. Have you ever seen a hearse with a trailer behind it?" "The difference between men and boys is the size of their toys." My favorite bumper sticker says, "I'm spending my children's inheritance."

Begin class by asking people to contribute such funny jokes and sayings, allowing a few minutes for levity.

Make the transition into the lesson by pointing out that the topic for today is money, finances, and the worry that too often comes with them.

Into the Word

Ask a class member to read Matthew 6:19-21, 24. Handing out sheets of paper (or using the exercise in the student book), ask class members to write a poem that summarizes the essence of what Jesus is saying. They can work alone or in small groups for several minutes. For example:

Treasures on earth are insecure,
Only what's saved in Heaven is sure.
Identify the treasure to locate the heart;
Serve God, not money, if you want to be smart.

Ask for volunteers to share their poems. Lead the class in applause after each. Point out any especially insightful or meaningful points that are made.

Ask if anyone has any questions about the meaning of this passage. Be ready to define terms (such as *mammon* in 6:24) and ideas (such as how to lay up treasures in Heaven). See the lesson material to prepare for this.

Ask a different class member to read Matthew 6:25-32. Guide a discussion by asking the following questions (also found in the student book):

• *What are the main concerns and worries that Jesus targets?* (Food, clothing, and physical appearance.)

• *Are these bad things? What is the problem?* (They are good, but a problem arises when we worry about them.)

• *Why does focusing on these things lead to worry?*

Lead the discussion to an understanding that we can never be satisfied when we focus on possessions. We allow our interest to move beyond need; we develop a desire to be superior to others. This leads to envy and anxiety. We are not comfortable with asking God to make us richer than our neighbors, so we begin to rely on ourselves rather than Him. What we have never seems to be enough; we worry about getting more. To those who worry, God says, "Trust me."

Now ask someone to read Matthew 6:33, 34. Have the class turn poetic once again, summarizing these two verses in rhyme. For example:

Seek to be right with God above,
Make sure it's He alone whom you love,
And all that you need you will receive;
Seek His kingdom and believe.

Again, let volunteers share their poems. Commend them, then make sure any questions about the meaning of this passage are answered.

Into Life

Ask each person to think of something he or she tends to worry about, such as wearing the right clothing, relating with a family member, finances, sickness, etc. (This exercise is also in the student book.) Without speaking, the class member should write down what he or she worries about most often (index cards would work nicely here).

Still silent, class members are to move about the classroom, showing their cards in order to form groups based on general topics of worry (for example, family, employment, health, etc.). Be ready to assist those with unique worries, perhaps including them with a related topic or grouping them together as a miscellaneous group. Each group discusses how individuals can change their focus from worrying to trusting God.

If time allows, ask a person from each group to share the group's ideas with the class. Write these on a chalkboard as they are reported.

To close, ask each group to spend several minutes in prayer, asking God to help them seek His kingdom and righteousness and cease worrying.

Let's Talk It Over

*The questions on this page are designed to encourage review of the lesson
Scriptures and to promote discussion of the lesson by the class. The answers
provided are only discussion starters. Let your class talk it over from there.*

1. What are some treasures we can lay up in Heaven?

We may anticipate receiving the "crown of righteousness" (2 Timothy 4:8) or the "crown of life" (Revelation 2:10). Whether or not literal crowns are involved, these terms speak of tremendous treasures. It will be a precious treasure simply to enjoy fellowship with our heavenly Father and with Jesus Christ. Beyond that, however, we will surely find additional joy in Heaven through beholding there persons whom we have influenced for Christ. The preacher, the teacher, the personal evangelist, the gospel musician, the Christian writer, and other laborers for the Lord will certainly gain immense satisfaction in seeing the results of their witness and work. We can lay up abundant treasures now through performing our service for the Lord diligently and lovingly.

2. How can we tell if we are allowing our money or our possessions, rather than Christ, to be our master?

Our giving to the Lord and His work is an excellent starting-point in order to test ourselves. Do we set aside as a matter of first priority a sacrificial portion of our income? If we give in haphazard fashion and only what it is convenient for us to give, it may be a sign that money is mastering us. Another test is simply to check on the general run of our thoughts. If we find that we are constantly thinking about how to make money, how to save it, and how to spend it, it may be our master. As far as our possessions are concerned, we can ask ourselves what our basic viewpoint is concerning them. Do we see them only as a means of ministering to our comfort, convenience, and pleasure, or do we regard them as belonging to the Lord, and as instruments we can use in accomplishing work for His greater glory?

3. Most of us have food and clothing enough. Why do we ever worry about these?

A great many of us have pantries and freezers well stocked with food, and wardrobes and dresser drawers stuffed with abundant clothing. And yet we have cause for worry. In the news as this is being written are accounts of families in Georgia who have lost homes and possessions as a result of severe flooding. Something like that could happen to us. We could lose our jobs—this is common in our time. Through accident or illness we could lose the ability to work, and even with insurance we sometimes worry over whether or not we could pay all our bills. All of us have good reason to look in trust to God to provide us with life's necessities.

4. In our industrialized, largely urban, society we often overlook the lessons we can gain from birds and other animals God has made. Why is it important that we heed Jesus' admonition to "behold the fowls of the air"?

Throughout the Bible, birds are used to illustrate spiritual truths. Eagles' wings can remind us of the strength God gives us to endure and prevail (Isaiah 40:31). Sparrows and swallows may call to mind the desirability of being in God's house (Psalm 84:3). We think of the dove as a symbol of peace, but the dove sent forth from the ark provided assurance that God was fulfilling His promise (Genesis 8:8-12). Mother birds covering their young with sheltering wings (Psalm 91:4; Matthew 23:37) illustrate God's protective care. We should be "spiritual birdwatchers," learning God's lessons through the habits of these small creatures.

5. Jesus indicated that lessons could be learned from observing the plant life around us. Why is it important that we heed Jesus' admonition to "consider the lilies of the field" and other plants?

In 1 Kings 4:33 we are told concerning the wise King Solomon that "he spake of trees, from the cedar tree that is in Lebanon even unto the hyssop that springeth out of the wall." It is wise for us also to learn from trees and flowers and other plants. Their beauty tells us much about the beautiful character of their Creator. Their ability to reproduce themselves through the marvelous power of seed (Genesis 1:11, 12) speaks of God's wisdom. The plant kingdom supplies much of our food, which testifies to our Father's gracious love for us. We can find an illustration regarding our own spiritual growth in the "tree planted by the rivers of water," with its verdant leaves and fruit-bearing branches (Psalm 1:3).

Teachings About Prayer

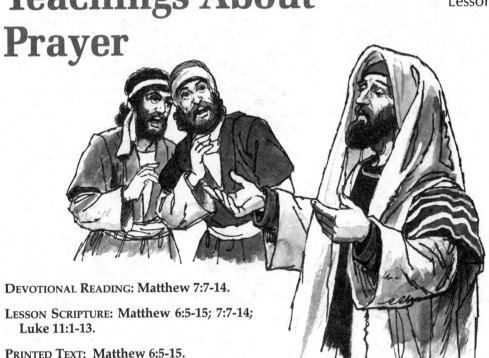

DEVOTIONAL READING: Matthew 7:7-14.

LESSON SCRIPTURE: Matthew 6:5-15; 7:7-14;
Luke 11:1-13.

PRINTED TEXT: Matthew 6:5-15.

Matthew 6:5-15

5 And when thou prayest, thou shalt not be as the hypocrites are: for they love to pray standing in the synagogues and in the corners of the streets, that they may be seen of men. Verily I say unto you, They have their reward.

6 But thou, when thou prayest, enter into thy closet, and when thou hast shut thy door, pray to thy Father which is in secret; and thy Father which seeth in secret shall reward thee openly.

7 But when ye pray, use not vain repetitions, as the heathen do: for they think that they shall be heard for their much speaking.

8 Be not ye therefore like unto them: for your Father knoweth what things ye have need of, before ye ask him.

9 After this manner therefore pray ye: Our Father which art in heaven, Hallowed be thy name.

10 Thy kingdom come. Thy will be done in earth, as it is in heaven.

11 Give us this day our daily bread.

12 And forgive us our debts, as we forgive our debtors.

13 And lead us not into temptation, but deliver us from evil: For thine is the kingdom, and the power, and the glory, for ever. Amen.

14 For if ye forgive men their trespasses, your heavenly Father will also forgive you:

15 But if ye forgive not men their trespasses, neither will your Father forgive your trespasses.

GOLDEN TEXT: When thou prayest, enter into thy closet, and when thou hast shut thy door, pray to thy Father which is in secret; and thy Father which seeth in secret shall reward thee openly.—Matthew 6:6.

Teachings of Jesus
Unit 3. Teachings About Living
(Lessons 10-13)

Lesson Aims

This study should equip the student to:

1. Show a distinction between praying alone and praying with other Christians.

2. Show how Jesus' own prayers exemplified His directions for praying.

3. Engage in personal prayer, seeking benefits for someone who has offended him or her.

Lesson Outline

INTRODUCTION

  A. Decoration and Memorial

  B. Needed Instruction

    He Who Taught Us to Pray Now Helps Us

  C. Lesson Background

 I. ON PRAYING ALONE (Matthew 6:5-8)

  A. Say It to God (vv. 5, 6)

  B. Say What You Mean (vv. 7, 8)

II. ON PRAYING TOGETHER (Matthew 6:9-13)

  A. Honor God First (vv. 9, 10)

    A Willing Father

  B. Ask for Necessities (v. 11)

  C. Find Forgiveness (v. 12)

  D. Seek Guidance and God's Glory (v. 13)

    Temptation

III. ADDED WARNING (Matthew 6:14, 15)

CONCLUSION

  A. Do It!

  B. A Learner's Prayer

  C. Thought to Remember

Display visual 13 of the visuals packet throughout today's lesson about the Lord's Prayer. It is shown on page 333.

Introduction

A. Decoration and Memorial

People in the United States will soon observe a two-sided memorial celebration. For some, it will have inspirational substance. For others it will be little more than a day off from work—much like Sunday. This holiday wears a double name, suggesting a double or divided emphasis. As *Memorial Day* it invites the observer to hold in cherished honor the dead, and to renew allegiance to the best of principles for which they lived and died. As *Decoration Day* it invites the placing of flowers on their graves in a visible expression of that honor and commitment.

The two forms of observance should be one, but they are not always so. Our Lord himself called attention to the tendency of some to decorate the graves of God's prophets, while continuing to follow in the ways of those who persecuted those same prophets while they lived (Matthew 23:29-32). Decoration can provide appearance without substance—and that always offends our Lord.

So it stands in Jesus' teaching and practice of prayer. Substance comes first with Him. If the substance happens to be seen by others, that is fine; but appearance must never be the goal in communicating with God, or in serving Him.

B. Needed Instruction

It has been reported from battlefields that there are "no atheists in foxholes," and a poet has written that "lips say, 'God be pitiful,' which ne'er said, 'God be praised!'" Desperate calls for divine help may be among the most genuine of prayers, but they do not indicate a lack of need for instruction in praying. They may, in fact, indicate just the opposite. They may reflect a false sense of security in a groundless appeal to an unknown God (see Acts 17:22-31). Multitudes may be persuaded that any and all appeals to any superhuman power are equally valid. So one may be prevented from seeking or accepting the very instruction he most greatly needs. Prayer, as described in the Bible, depends on knowing God as He is revealed in the Bible.

Even that, however, is not complete in itself. The people to whom Jesus came were well schooled in the Scriptures. Beyond emergencies they observed times for prayers morning, noon, and evening (Psalm 55:17). Yet when they saw and heard Jesus praying they sensed a lack and they asked for instruction (Luke 11:1). Observing the prayer habits of those around Him, Jesus recognized their need, and He taught them.

HE WHO TAUGHT US TO PRAY NOW HELPS US

During His earthly ministry, the Lord Jesus taught His disciples to pray. Romans 8 reveals that He continues to help us with our prayers. We have the aid of two divine prayer partners.

One prayer partner is the Holy Spirit. "We do not know what we ought to pray, but the Spirit himself intercedes for us with groans that words cannot express" (Romans 8:26, *New International Version*).

Another prayer partner is the Lord Jesus himself. Romans 8:34 declares that the Lord "is at the right hand of God and is also interceding for us" (*New International Version*).

As a Christian, you never pray alone. The Holy Spirit, who dwells in the heart of every believer, joins in your prayer. Then, as your prayer and the accompanying prayer of the Spirit reach the court of Heaven, the Lord Jesus turns to His Father and says, "One of our people is praying. Let me join in asking what he is asking."

Of course these partners never pray contrary to God's will (Romans 8:27). If we pray a selfish or wicked prayer, we have no help with that.

—C. B. Mc.

C. Lesson Background

Our lesson today grows from three backgrounds. First is its place in the Sermon on the Mount. Today's text was spoken before that of Lesson 12. Jesus began the Sermon with blessings of His followers because they exchanged the values of the world for the greater values of God's kingdom (Matthew 5:1-16). Then came the Lord's commentary on popular applications of the Old Testament law. Not outward actions for their own sake, but the wellsprings of action in one's thought and intentions are valuable to God, Jesus said (Matthew 5:17-48). Then He applied that principle to the religious practices of almsgiving, prayer, and fasting (Matthew 6:1-18). Of the three, prayer is the one most prominently exemplified and taught by Jesus and His apostles; so today we consider the Lord's teaching on prayer.

A second background will be found in Jesus' own praying, which becomes the basis of Luke's presentation of the pattern prayer (Luke 11:1-4). The Lord's disciples had observed Him at prayer on many occasions, some of which are recorded only in the gospel of Luke: at His baptism, for example (3:21). See also Luke 6:12; 9:18, 28, 29; 22:31, 32; and 23:34, 46. His disciples knew Jesus at prayer.

A background for application of today's lesson is provided by last week's teaching on riches and anxiety. Philippians 4:6 establishes the link with its warning against anxious care for anything. "In every thing by prayer and supplication with thanksgiving let your requests be made known unto God."

I. On Praying Alone
(Matthew 6:5-8)

Here the *King James Version* accurately represents the Greek text. The pronouns *thou* and *thy* are singular, indicating one person. This prepares us to accept verses 5 and 6 as teaching about private prayer in contrast to prayers spoken by and for groups of believers worshiping together.

A. Say It to God (vv. 5, 6)

5. And when thou prayest, thou shalt not be as the hypocrites are: for they love to pray standing in the synagogues and in the corners of the streets, that they may be seen of men. Verily I say unto you, They have their reward.

When thou prayest. The Lord assumed that His followers would continue in their practice of praying. But they were not to imitate the *hypocrites* (the word signified playactors), pretending to be something they were not. Jesus applied the term most often to the scribes—professional copyists and students of Scripture—and Pharisees, with their passion for outward conformity with the law and the traditions that had grown up around it (Matthew 23).

Standing for prayer (Mark 11:25) was customary at three prescribed hours each day. The worshiper would stand facing toward Jerusalem, with his head covered and his eyes cast down, and would recite a prayer of eighteen petitions. What Jesus objected to was the places where the hypocrites chose to be at the time for praying, making a public display of their private devotions. Their aim was to receive the admiration of observers. This would be fully accomplished in the performance. They should not expect anything additional from God.

6. But thou, when thou prayest, enter into thy closet, and when thou hast shut thy door, pray to thy Father which is in secret; and thy Father which seeth in secret shall reward thee openly.

The place for personal prayer is like the place for intimate family conversation. Privacy is most appropriate. You address your own personal prayers to *thy* Father. The address to *our* Father is proper when several are praying together.

Jesus found His own *closet* or "inner chamber" for prayer on the open hillsides before daybreak and after nightfall (Mark 1:35; Luke 6:12; John 6:15). His prayers were directed to "My Father" (Matthew 26:39) or simply "Father" (Matthew 11:25-27; John 11:41; 17:1).

God's being *in secret* is that He is simply not seen with the human eye; hence it is not appropriate to make a display of communication with Him. The openness of His response to our prayers is possible but not guaranteed. *Openly* does not appear in the older Greek manuscripts or the newer translations of this verse.

B. Say What You Mean (vv. 7, 8)

Here we see the plural pronouns *ye* and *your*. Jesus seems to have broadened His focus, no longer contrasting His individual disciples with other individual Jews, but contrasting His followers generally with pagan Greeks and Romans.

7. But when ye pray, use not vain repetitions, as the heathen do: for they think that they shall be heard for their much speaking.

The New English Bible provides a helpful commentary translation: "Do not go babbling on like the heathen, who imagine that the more they say the more likely they are to be heard." A notable example of such heathenism may be found in the priests of Baal who chanted for hours in a vain effort to bring fire to their altar on Mount Carmel (1 Kings 18:26).

Purposeful insistence, especially in private prayer, is not the same as vain repetition (Luke 18:1-8).

8. Be not ye therefore like unto them: for your Father knoweth what things ye have need of, before ye ask him.

Pagans may be expected to resort to all kinds of mechanisms to catch the attention and turn aside the anger of their insensitive deities. But those who know the living God revealed in Jesus Christ will pray as befits a child approaching the heavenly Father.

Thus we bring our expressions of love and our requests to Him, though He knows these matters better than we do. In trustful prayer we express our faith, not to make Him aware of us, but to develop our awareness of Him. So, too, we may discuss with Him the state of affairs in the world around us, not as informing Him, but to adjust our viewpoint to His will and His way.

II. On Praying Together
(Matthew 6:9-13)

The praying of Christians is not limited to private practice. As a family they pray together, and for that also they need instruction. Jesus' teaching pattern has been called the Lord's Prayer, but as a guide to praying by His followers it is appropriately called the Christian's prayer, or the church's prayer. In plan and purpose it is the model prayer.

A. Honor God First (vv. 9, 10)

9. After this manner therefore pray ye: Our Father which art in heaven, Hallowed be thy name.

This prayer offers an excellent guide for the kind of personal praying already recommended, but is more completely suited to the church's praying together. The instruction is, *After this manner therefore pray ye* (plural), not *pray thou* (singular).

Our Father. Those who join in this prayer acknowledge one another as brothers and sisters.

At least by suggestion the *our* includes the whole body of Christ in all places and all times.

Father recognizes the relationship noted in Romans 8:14-17, that Christians are adopted children of God, calling Him Father and enjoying the rights of inheritance along with Jesus. As our Father, God provides, loves, leads, and chastens His children. Identifying Him as *in heaven* indicates His deity as much as His home. He is also with His children on earth.

God's glory fills the first petition of the prayer. This, like the Ten Commandments, begins and is rooted in God. Later petitions and commandments are based on this and are not attainable without it. His *name*, like His person, is to be revered and held sacred. The child of God is to honor the family name by all he is and does. That name must never be profaned—made common or meaningless.

A WILLING FATHER

Jesus taught us to address God as our Father. Imagine yourself a father with young children at a drive-thru window. "Welcome to MacRocks. May I help you?" says the young man on the other end of the speaker.

"Yes, I would like three MacRock Funny Meals," you answer.

"Three MacRock Funny Meals. Do you want igneous, metamorphic, or sedimentary rocks?"

"Give me one of each," you say, "and give me some snakes for dessert."

"Do you want rattlesnakes, copperheads, or king cobras?"

"We'll have the rattlers."

An unlikely scene? Of course! No father in his right mind would order rocks and snakes when his children needed something to eat, and no restaurant would offer such a bizarre menu. Likewise our heavenly Father provides for our needs out of a willing heart that desires to give us His good gifts (Matthew 7:9-11). —C. B. Mc.

10. Thy kingdom come. Thy will be done in earth, as it is in heaven.

A *kingdom* is the realm and reign of a king—the nation over which he rules and his manner of ruling it. Jesus gave much of His ministry to teaching about God's kingdom. This much we know: it is where God is ruler and we are His subjects. The coming of the kingdom is the beginning and development of that realm. It exists in the world, especially since the birth of the church on the Day of Pentecost. It still needs to *come* to all those who are not yet identified with it. It needs to *come* more fully to immature Christians.

The prayer for God's *will* to *be done in earth* could not be demonstrated more fully than it was by Jesus in Gethsemane, pleading for release from suffering, but adding the overriding prayer for the Father's will, rather than His own, to be done (Mark 14:36). That is not weak resignation; it is earnest desire taking precedence over all other desires, giving oneself and all that one possesses to doing God's will.

B. Ask for Necessities (v. 11)

11. Give us this day our daily bread.

If *daily* needs were not met ultimately by God, who created the world to support its inhabitants, life would be impossible. So today we are dependent for everyday necessities, even though we may have supplies of a few things for a longer term. The acknowledgment relates us to the children of Israel in the wilderness, provided with manna for one day at a time (Exodus 16). We are not encouraged to hoard supplies on earth, where they are subject to mold and decay, but to prefer the bread of life eternal—Jesus Christ our Lord (John 6:48-58). The need in either case is personal, but everyone has the same need. This petition belongs to prayer together, *us* and *our*.

C. Find Forgiveness (v. 12)

12. And forgive us our debts, as we forgive our debtors.

Forgiveness is every person's need, as vital to spiritual life as food is for the body. *Forgive* translates a word that speaks of sending away. God is the only one who can so remove the guilt of our offenses against Him (Psalm 51:4). (See also Psalm 103:12.)

Offenses against God are identified by three different names. The most common word for *sin* is literally *missing the mark*—failing to meet God's rightful expectation. Another, translated "transgression" or "trespass," indicates a *false step* or *blunder* by which one violates another's rights. *Debt*, the word used here, speaks of an obligation legally due. In sinning we rob God of His rights and incur an obligation that must be paid by punishment or removed by forgiveness. In Jesus' teaching He compared sins to financial debts. Sins against God created massive debts, removed by His forgiveness. By comparison, human offenses against one another incurred small debts that also must be forgiven (Luke 7:36-50; Matthew 18:23-35).

The *Book of Common Prayer* for the Church of England uses *trespasses* in its rendering of this passage, and some churches follow that custom.

As we forgive. Here is a sobering reminder that the user of this prayer asks God to forgive him in the same way that he forgives others. A literal rendering, followed in the *New International Version*, is even more severe: "Forgive us . . . as we also have forgiven." Good intentions are not enough. Forgiveness of others belongs before the praying (Mark 11:25, 26). Yet Christians do not earn forgiveness by forgiving; they forgive because they have been forgiven.

D. Seek Guidance and God's Glory (v. 13)

13. And lead us not into temptation, but deliver us from evil: For thine is the kingdom, and the power, and the glory, for ever. Amen.

The prayer moves from dealing with past offenses to prevention of sins in the future. Two elements stand out: the concern that dreads the fall, and the confidence that in His own way God will prevent our falling.

Temptation (testing or trial) comes in two forms. First is the difficulty that develops strength and character as we overcome it. Christians are to welcome that, in spite of their human preference for ease (Romans 5:3-5; James 1:2-4). Second is enticement to sin. That, in any form, is Satan's weapon against mankind, and God never engages in it (James 1:13). Instead He promises that He will not allow us to be tempted beyond the means of overcoming it, but will in every temptation provide the way of escape (1 Corinthians 10:13).

Deliver us from evil is more specific in some versions. They read, "Deliver us from the evil one"—Satan, the author and agent of enticements to sin. The church, when it joins in prayer, may ask for deliverance from such evils as sickness, poverty, or oppressive tyranny; but it is fitting also to ask for deliverance from the one who lurks in all the areas of life, seeking whom he may devour.

TEMPTATION

Genesis 13 tells how Abraham and Lot parted when their pasture lands became too crowded. Abraham let Lot choose the lands he wanted. Genesis 13:10 says that Lot looked at the plain

where Sodom was, then verse 12 records that he pitched his tent toward Sodom.

When God's angels came to Sodom, they found Lot at the gate (19:1), the place where city leaders did their business. Lot also owned a house in Sodom (v. 2). He was slow to leave even when the angels told him the city was to be destroyed. The angels almost dragged him and his family out of town (v. 16).

Lot almost perished because he first looked at Sodom, then went near Sodom, then moved into Sodom. This is a model of how temptation and sin work. If you look at sin long enough, you don't mind being near it. Stay near it for a while, and you will get into it. Get into it, and you can't get out without divine help. It's better to stay at the other end of the valley. —C. B. Mc.

For thine is the kingdom, and the power, and the glory, for ever. Amen. This closing doxology is surely suitable to the use of the model prayer. David uttered similar words of praise (1 Chronicles 29:11), and Paul echoed them in his final writing (2 Timothy 4:18). These words do not appear in the oldest manuscripts of Matthew, and so are left out of some English translations.

III. Added Warning (Matthew 6:14, 15)

Because of the danger attending its possible misuse, one part of the prayer was flagged with comment and warning.

14, 15. For if ye forgive men their trespasses, your heavenly Father will also forgive you: but if ye forgive not men their trespasses, neither will your Father forgive your trespasses.

This admonition is repeated in Matthew 18:35, where the money debts described in the

Home Daily Bible Readings

Monday, May 20—God Understands Our Hearts (Jeremiah 17:5-11)
Tuesday, May 21—Restraint in Using Words (Ecclesiastes 5:1-7)
Wednesday, May 22—God Cares for His Children (Deuteronomy 32:4-8)
Thursday, May 23—God's Holiness (Isaiah 6:1-8)
Friday, May 24—Prayer for Others (Ephesians 3:14-21)
Saturday, May 25—Conditions for Answered Prayer (2 Chronicles 7:14-22)
Sunday, May 26—How to Pray (Luke 11:1-13)

foregoing parable were equated with trespasses. The same is repeated in Mark 11:25, 26. Calling the offenses sins, as in Luke 11:4, or debts, as in Matthew 6:12, or trespasses, as in the verse before us, makes no difference. He who would be forgiven must be forgiving. So every day becomes judgment day, in which we judge ourselves by the choices we make; and no choice is more important than the determined decision to forgive.

Conclusion

A. Do It!

Jesus, master teacher and storyteller, used one forceful conclusion, with variations, often and effectively: "This do!"

When a lawyer identified the greatest of the commandments, Jesus said, "This do." When the same man identified the helpful neighbor by what he did, Jesus said, "Go, and do thou likewise" (Luke 10:28, 37). He concluded the Sermon on the Mount by identifying the *doing* hearers of His teachings as wise builders and the *nondoing* hearers as foolish ones. He had no praise for those who called Him Lord, but did not *do* as He directed (Luke 6:46). So too He concluded His teaching on prayer. In case some hearer might miss the "do it" implications in verse 12 concerning forgiveness, He returned to the subject and said it plainly: Forgive, or you cannot be forgiven. Words were not enough. Forgiveness must be from the heart, or it was worthless (Matthew 18:35).

So it is with all of Jesus' "Do its!" Outward actions for the sake of appearance are worthless. The doing must come from inner purpose. Pray; don't pose as if praying. Pray; don't just say prayers. Revere God; don't just recite respectful words. Give life service, not just lip service, to God's will. Depend on God for what you need; don't just accept His bounties. Follow His guidance, not your own goals, to avoid Satan's snare. And pray earnestly, both for yourself and for your adversary, that forgiveness may be complete.

B. A Learner's Prayer

Lord, teach me to pray! Thank You, heavenly Father, for the open door to Your presence. May I have a mind open to Your instruction, a heart to understand, a spirit to will, and discipline to do as You direct. Through the name of Jesus Christ we pray. Amen.

C. Thought to Remember

Our Father in Heaven, hallowed be Your name.

Learning by Doing

This page contains an alternate lesson plan emphasizing learning activities. Classes desiring such student involvement will find these suggestions helpful.

Learning Goals

After this lesson, a student will be able to:

1. Identify the elements of prayer that is pleasing to God.

2. Explain how Jesus' own prayers exemplified His directions for praying.

3. Engage in personal prayer that follows Jesus' guidelines.

Into the Lesson

Begin by asking the students where they learned how to pray. Who taught them, and what are some of their earliest remembrances of praying? (These questions are also in the student book.) Some may tell of a parent or other relative who taught by example. Others may cite a minister or an elder who taught a meaningful lesson on prayer.

Make the transition to the lesson by saying that this final lesson from Jesus' Sermon on the Mount will help us focus on our prayers.

Into the Word

Divide the class into two teams, such as men versus women. Each team is to study today's text, Matthew 6:5-15, and write down words or phrases that describe the prayer Jesus commends. For example: *personal, private, to the point, praising, submissive, dependent, confessing, forgiving, desiring holiness, avoiding Satan.* (A related exercise is in the student book.) Ask each team to develop a list of six such words/phrases.

The game is played this way: Using a chalkboard or poster board, a person from Team One places spaces on the board, a space for each letter, to represent the first word or phrase on his team's list. Members of Team Two then guess letters. When they name one that fits in the word, it is written in its proper place. This continues till six letters are in place. Team Two then has fifteen seconds to identify the word or phrase. If they fail, leave the incomplete word/phrase on the board and go on with the game.

Team Two then places spaces on the board for their first word/phrase, which Team One gets to solve. The play rotates until all six words/phrases of both teams are used.

If some words/phrases are incomplete, go over the lists again. This time continue the guessing till all of them are complete.

As the master of ceremonies, keep the focus on how these words and phrases describe prayer as commended by Jesus.

On the board, write the following references. Ask class members to look up the passages and see what they can learn about Jesus' own praying. (This is also in the student book.)

• Luke 5:16
• Luke 6:12, 13
• Luke 11:1
• Luke 22:40-46

Ask for volunteers to point out how Jesus practiced what He taught about prayer, or how His praying is described by the words and phrases written earlier in the lesson.

Into Life

Giving each person a sheet of paper (or using the exercise in the student book), ask each class member to analyze his or her own prayer life on the basis of the words/phrases named in the game. For example: How *personal* are my prayers? How *to the point* are my prayers? How *confessing of sin* are my prayers?

Invite each person to write a paragraph of analysis, citing both strengths and weaknesses. When class members are done, ask each one to share as much (or as little) as he or she wishes with a person sitting nearby. Encourage openness, honesty, and confidentiality.

Spend a few minutes discussing what we can do to engage in prayer that truly pleases God. Highlight changes that could be made (such as spending more time in prayer, being more specific about needs and worries, being less dependent on memorized phrases and prayers). Think of practices that would be beneficial (such as keeping a prayer journal, always starting and ending with praise, being honest and specific with the confession of one's sin).

Close the lesson with "sentence prayers." Give careful instructions: Everyone is encouraged to contribute one sentence to a group prayer; one may add only one sentence at a time, though he may add another later; each one should try to pray with continuity, so the result will be one long prayer by the group. It is hoped that all will feel comfortable praying, but do not try to force anyone who is reluctant (especially a visitor). Begin the prayer with your own opening sentence expressing praise to God.

Let's Talk It Over

The questions on this page are designed to encourage review of the lesson Scriptures and to promote discussion of the lesson by the class. The answers provided are only discussion starters. Let your class talk it over from there.

1. Why do we need to be taught to pray? If we think of prayer as a child talking to his father, is it not something that comes naturally?

In order to communicate with an earthly father, a child must learn to speak, to approach his father with trust and respect, and to express clearly his concerns and wishes. It may be natural, but it still requires some learning. Romans 8:26 tells us that "we know not what we should pray for as we ought." We need instruction as to those things for which we should or should not pray. We also need to be taught what elements our prayers should contain: praise and thanksgiving, confession of our sins, intercession on behalf of others, and our own personal petitions. Jesus had much to say about persistence in prayer. We need to learn that, so that we will not become discouraged when answers seem slow in coming (see Luke 18:1-8).

2. Where are some places that may be our "closet" for private communication with our Father?

It is common for us today to think about kneeling by our bedside for prayer, but that may not work for everyone. A mother with small children or a young person with a roommate may need some other "closet." One of the marvelous aspects of prayer is that it may be offered anywhere. The Bible prescribes no single posture for prayer, nor does it require that we speak aloud. A "closet" can be under a tree in the backyard, beside the furnace in the basement, or amongst the lawn-care equipment in the garage. Some Christians take prayer walks, communicating silently with God as they move through woods, over meadows, or even along streets. Others have found that behind the wheel of their car they enjoy a relative privacy conducive to effective prayer.

3. Jesus' warning about using "vain repetitions" calls to mind the danger of adopting clichés or empty phrases from public prayers. Why do we need to be wary of this?

We can utter a cliché without really praying. If prayer involves a specific request made on behalf of someone else or ourselves, it is in line with biblical teaching. But what shall we say about generalizations such as "Bless all the mis-

sionaries," or "Help those who have lost loved ones"? If we are not thinking of anyone in particular, are we really praying? It must also be noted that even the Lord's Prayer can be repeated vainly. If we mouth the words without focusing our minds and hearts on their grand significance, then again we are not really praying.

4. If we are to pray, "Thy will be done in earth, as it is in heaven," then we must ask, "How is God's will done in Heaven?"

It is clear from biblical teaching that God's angels do His will completely. In offering the petition above we should envision for ourselves, our family, and our church an obedience to God that holds nothing back, but fulfills completely what God wants done. The angels surely accomplish God's will in a zealous manner. We should pray that God will never let us be content with service that is done out of mere necessity, but that He will stir us up to energetic, fervent, joyous labor. It is also obvious that angels do God's will humbly, not taking glory to themselves. Recognizing that we human beings are tempted to serve out of pride and self-exaltation, we must pray for strength to resist such temptation and focus on God's glory.

5. When we pray for deliverance from temptation and from the evil one, what kinds of changes in our behavior need to accompany that prayer?

In speaking of how to handle anger, Paul warned his hearers, "Do not give the devil a foothold" (Ephesians 4:26, 27, *New International Version*). While we pray for deliverance from the devil and his temptations, we need to search out any footholds he has within our attitudes and habits, and remove them. For example, when we pray for deliverance from the temptation to lust, we may need to cease viewing television shows that stimulate illicit desires. If we are praying to be delivered from the habit of lapsing into profane language, we may need to practice some forceful expressions that are not profane. If we pray for deliverance from an excessive desire for material things, then we may have to refrain from leafing through merchandise catalogs.

Summer Quarter, 1996

A Practical Religion
(James)

Special Features

God Is With Us
(Psalms)

Unit 1: Praising God

Unit 2: Responding to God

About these lessons

The letter of James stresses that Christians must put their faith into action. This is seen in the lessons based on James, as various issues of life are considered. The study in Psalms emphasizes God's presence in the world. The psalms praise God for His loving involvement in the lives of people, and call us to praise Him and to respond to His presence.

Jun 2
Jun 9
Jun 16
Jun 23
Jun 30
Jul 7
Jul 14
Jul 21
Jul 28
Aug 4
Aug 11
Aug 18
Aug 25

Quarterly Quiz

The questions on this page may be used in several ways: as a pretest at the beginning of the quarter; as a review at the end of the quarter; or as a review after each lesson. The questions are based on the Scripture text of each lesson (King James Version). ***The answers are on page 344.***

Lesson 1

1. What good results can come from being tempted? *James 1:2-4*
2. What is it in us that makes us give in to temptation? *James 1:14*
3. What two things does James mention as parts of pure religion? *James 1:27*

Lesson 2

1. Is respect of persons compatible with Christian faith? *James 2:1*
2. What commandment does James describe as "the royal law"? *James 2:8*
3. Who is best capable of judging the actions of Christians? *James 4:12*

Lesson 3

1. How does James describe faith that does not lead one to do good? *James 2:17*
2. We are justified by God's grace, by our faith, and by what else? *James 2:24*
3. What should a Christian do when he is afflicted? When he is merry? *James 5:13*

Lesson 4

1. How may one get wisdom? *James 1:5*
2. How should a wise man show his wisdom and knowledge? *James 3:13*
3. What fruit grows from the sowing of one who makes peace? *James 3:18*

Lesson 5

1. Where do our quarrels come from? *James 4:1*
2. What can we expect the devil to do if we resist him? *James 4:7*
3. What name does James give to our failure to do what we know we ought to do? *James 4:17*

Lesson 6

1. Where did the psalmist find God's riches displayed? *Psalm 104:24, 25*
2. Does God give food to His creation, or do they gather it for themselves? *Psalm 104:27, 28*
3. How long does the psalmist expect to praise God? *Psalm 104:33*

Lesson 7

1. According to Psalm 105, what should we make known among the people? *Psalm 105:1*
2. What should we remember? *Psalm 105:5*

3. What has God remembered? *Psalm 105:8*
4. When God brought His people out of Egypt, whose lands did He give them? *Psalm 105:44*

Lesson 8

1. According to Psalm 34, we are to join the psalmist in magnifying whom? *Psalm 34:3*
2. From what does God deliver or save the psalmist and others? *Psalm 34:4, 6, 19*
3. About what people does the angel of the Lord encamp? *Psalm 34:7*

Lesson 9

1. According to Psalm 139, who knew all about the psalm writer? *Psalm 139:1-4*
2. Where in the world can a person hide from God? *Psalm 139:7-12*
3. What did the psalmist ask God to look for in the psalmist himself? *Psalm 139:23, 24*

Lesson 10

1. From what kind of pit did the Lord rescue the psalmist? *Psalm 40:2*
2. What had the psalmist preached in the great congregation? *Psalm 40:9*
3. For whom did the psalmist ask joy and gladness? *Psalm 40:16*

Lesson 11

1. To what may a young man pay attention in order to make his way clean? *Psalm 119:9*
2. What did the psalmist hide in his heart to keep him from sinning? *Psalm 119:11*
3. What did the psalmist describe as a lamp to his feet? *Psalm 119:105*

Lesson 12

1. What did David want God to do with David's transgressions? *Psalm 51:1*
2. From what did David want God to hide His face? *Psalm 51:9*
3. After confessing his sin, what did David ask God to create in him? *Psalm 51:10*

Lesson 13

1. In Psalm 96, who is called to sing a new song to the Lord? *Psalm 96:1*
2. What are we to declare among the heathen and all people? *Psalm 96:3*
3. How will the Lord judge? *Psalm 96:13*

From James to Psalms

by John W. Wade

THE LESSONS FOR THIS QUARTER offer students a rather diverse menu. The first five lessons deal with the book of James, while the remaining eight lessons are taken from the book of Psalms. The central theme of James is the application of the Christian faith to the issues of everyday life. The study in Psalms, on the other hand, deals with such issues as the worship and praise of God, the forgiveness of sins, and commitment to the laws of God.

Someone has labeled this study in James "A Practical Religion." That is not to suggest that the lessons from Psalms will not be practical. To suggest that worshiping God or seeking the forgiveness of sins is somehow impractical would be to betray a serious misunderstanding of worship and sin. When we say James describes practical religion, of course we don't mean to say that any aspects of the Christian religion are impractical. What we are saying is that James deals plainly with some of the problems that Christians must face in their everyday work and in social contacts. This will be appreciated by students who are looking for help with these very problems.

James

While this study in James does not cover every verse, it does cover selections from each chapter. The central theme of the book may be summed up in the latter part of James 2:26—"Faith without works is dead." In the course of this study, we shall have an opportunity to view this theme from several different angles.

The first lesson, which covers most of the first chapter, deals with trials and temptations that come to everyone, Christians and worldlings alike. James provides encouragement and guidance for persons who are facing such problems. He informs us that sometimes the Lord allows us to be tempted in order to strengthen us and give us the wisdom to resist future temptations. When we successfully resist temptations, we are promised the "crown of life." However, the first chapter does not deal exclusively with resisting temptations. The chapter closes by presenting some ways in which Christians can live out their faith. They are urged to bridle their tongues, visit the orphans and widows, and keep themselves morally pure.

Lesson 2 deals with the problem of prejudice. James speaks specifically of favoritism toward the wealthy; but the principle he sets forth is that all kinds of biased prejudging are wrong. We live in a society where we face prejudices on every hand: race, religion, social status, and even physical appearance can win favor or disfavor before any other characteristics of a person are known. James sets forth the solution to all of these problems. He urges his readers to observe the "royal law," which requires persons to love their neighbors as themselves. You may use this lesson to challenge your class members to examine their own hearts and evaluate their behavior in the light of this teaching.

The third lesson, based on verses from chapters 2 and 5, presents ways in which a Christian can put his or her faith into practice. James draws on Hebrew history (the examples of Abraham and Rahab) to show how faith is justified by works. Christians are urged to pray for the sick and afflicted, since "the effectual fervent prayer of a righteous man availeth much."

Faith and wisdom receive attention in lesson 4. Wisdom is the ability to translate knowledge and information into good actions. Worldly wisdom leads to envy, strife, and confusion; but the wisdom James has in mind is "from above" and is pure, peaceable, and full of mercy. Teachers have great responsibilities to teach this wisdom, and so for this reason James warns against assuming this responsibility lightly. Not many ought to be masters or teachers. There is a great need for Christian teachers who will accept the responsibility, however. This lesson should not be used to discourage any who are gifted with the ability to teach.

In the final lesson from James, he warns against the "wars and fightings" that were dividing the congregation. The people were driven by a desire for things. The things they asked for they didn't receive because they asked with the wrong motives. Those who sought illicit sex were warned that "friendship of the world is enmity with God." You will certainly have no trouble relating this lesson to the problems of our society.

Psalms

You may find the final eight lessons of this quarter more difficult to teach. For one thing, most of your students are not likely to be familiar with many of the psalms chosen as the bases of these lessons. The very fact that the texts are from the Old Testament will be a "turnoff" to some students, who harbor the mistaken notion that the Old Testament has nothing to say to our generation. Help these students to see that some of the same sins that plague us today have been with the human race since the beginning.

Several of the lessons deal with the subject of worship, which for many people is not very exciting. Lead them to see that precisely because they are not very good at it they need to study it more. The typical American worshiper has become addicted to spectator sports. When he comes to a worship service, he expects to be entertained; and when he is disappointed, he blames everyone but himself. Help your students to understand that if they expect to get something out of worship, they must put something into it.

This study from Psalms is divided into two units. The first unit, "Praising God," includes lessons 6 through 9. The second unit, "Responding to God," is covered in lessons 10 through 13.

Lesson 6 urges students to praise God as Creator and Sustainer. This lesson is based on Psalm 104. The writer calls our attention to God's vast power as revealed in nature. When he contemplates what this means, he raises his voice in praise. You may want to use this lesson to urge your students to become more concerned about protecting the earth the Lord has entrusted to us; but do not let them become so concerned about the environment that they lose sight of the Creator or fail to regard Him with reverence and awe.

Lesson 7 continues the call to praise God because of His involvement in the world He has created. In this lesson the writer turns to God's acts in history, calling attention to the covenant He made with Abraham and continued through succeeding generations. It concludes with praise for bringing Israel out of Egypt and leading them into Canaan. The final verse exhorts them to observe God's laws. You may use this lesson to show how God has blessed us and how He expects us to obey His commandments.

Psalm 34 is the basis for lesson 8. The writer praises God for the deliverance that writer has received. His theme is "I sought the Lord, and he heard me, and delivered me." If your class is typical, some members will be hurting from the loss of a loved one, problems in the home, or disappointments in their careers. You can show them God's consolation that He offers to those who come to Him.

Lesson 9 will help a student realize that God is omniscient, that He knows everything about us—our motives, our thoughts, our actions. There is no place we can hide from His watchful eye. Help your students to see that this need not be frightening; in fact, it can bring us great comfort to realize that we are never outside the range of His love.

Lesson 10 introduces us to the second unit on Psalms. The psalmist relates how he waited patiently for God's deliverance; and when it finally came, he was able to sing the new song that God had put in His mouth. Use this lesson to strengthen the students' trust in God.

Students are likely to be more familiar with Psalm 119, the basis of lesson 11, than they are with most of the other psalms studied in this quarter. This psalm is unusual, not only because it is the longest psalm, but also because its structure is extraordinary. Psalm 119 exalts God's law and exhorts its readers to study it and obey it. This lesson gives you an opportunity to stress the importance of Bible study and memorizing Bible passages. ("Thy word have I hid in mine heart, that I might not sin against thee," Psalm 119:11).

Psalm 51, the text for lesson 12, is also familiar to many students. In it we find David calling out for forgiveness for his great sins against Bathsheba and Uriah. He comes before God humbly with a penitent heart, knowing that he deserves to be punished. But he also comes knowing that God will hear him because God will not despise a "broken and contrite" heart. Some members of your class may be carrying a heavy burden of guilt. They need this assurance that God will hear them if they repent.

The writer of Psalm 96, the basis for the final lesson of the quarter, urges us to "sing unto the Lord a new song." It is a joyous call to worship, but it is more than that. It is a call to share our joy with others who need it so desperately. Give an evangelistic thrust to your lesson. Urge your students to commit themselves to witness to one person in the coming week about the joy they know in Christ.

Conclusion

You will find it wise to consult the "Learning by Doing" and "Let's Talk It Over" sections of your teacher's manual. Perhaps you already use these sections; but if not, you will find that they have some excellent suggestions for different teaching methods. Using some new and different methods can inject a spark into your teaching that will make these lessons both lively and practical. You will also find the *Adult Visuals/ Learning Resources* packet very helpful.

Begin your lesson preparation early, and above all, surround your preparation with prayer that the Lord will use you to reach and move your students.

A Faith That Lives

by Roy S. Wheeler

I HAD ALWAYS THOUGHT OF MYSELF as a man of faith. After all, I had survived the ministry for forty-three years! Like any minister, I had experienced many ups and downs—good and bad days, good church members and bad church members. There were days when my faith was severely tested. Like some of the Old Testament prophets, I wanted to run off and hide! However, it was last November that I really received a lesson about a faith that lives. That lesson was taught not in "Christian" America but in "atheist" Belarus in the former Soviet Union.

I was on my second mission trip of the year to Minsk, Belarus, when I met Jacob Kaluchnic, Director of Ray of Hope Ministries. Ray of Hope works very much like a huge United Way. It is a Christian foundation assisting in humanitarian outreach to the needy people of Belarus, and helping also in spreading the gospel.

Jacob was born forty-five years ago. His father was a farmer on a corporate farm and pastor of an underground church. When Jacob was seven he accepted Christ as his Savior and desired to be baptized. He recalls that his family took him to a river very late at night for his baptism. When he made mention of this experience to his friends at school, he was immediately punished. He remembers many fights with other students because of his faith. His teachers made fun of him and increased his work load. They finally kicked him out of school, thus depriving him of an education. He married very young, and he and his wife went to work on a collective farm. They lived in a very small government-owned farmhouse with very few conveniences. Jacob, however, could not keep quiet about his faith. Because he believed in God, he was moved to an even smaller house with no heat or electricity. His wife almost died giving birth to their son under those frightful circumstances.

I had the opportunity to share tea with them while hearing him tell about the faith of his mother. It is a story rich in human courage.

During the late 1940s, women of the small village of Velikiye, just north of Minsk, stood united with his mother to stop the destruction of their church. It was the only one remaining. The others had been destroyed by the Communist rulers, who tried to convince the people, "There is no God! There is no Jesus Christ! We (USSR) will meet all your needs." When the military men and bulldozers arrived, they saw two rows of women standing with locked arms in a dual ring protecting their church from destruction. The commander of the demolition forces ordered the men to remove the women and proceed with the demolition of the church. The women stood firm, but many fell from the blows from the soldiers. Finally one of the soldiers said, "We are beating our mothers! We cannot do this!" The ranks of the women were reinforced from neighboring villages, and the two rows grew to four. Food and water were brought in. It was a fourteen-day standoff, twenty-four hours a day. On a final push by the military to destroy the line of women, the director of the local collective farm stood firm in the path of the advancing group and said, "You must not do this! If you do destroy this church, I'll tell you for certain that our fathers will restore it stone by stone." After much argument the military left. The women rejoiced, and the little church in Velikiye stands today as an early thorn in the side of an atheist government. It was a tremendous test of faith that won a victory.

When Mikhail Gorbachev came to power in 1985, Jacob seized the opportunity to start his own construction company. He used the money he made to establish Ray of Hope. Because he is a man of real faith he is a ray of hope for thousands of people. My faith has been strengthened by knowing him and working with him on our missions in Minsk.

My trips to Belarus, during which I have met Christians who have survived seventy years of Communism, make me wonder about our faith. How strong is it? Could it live under such testing? Let's look at "a faith that lives."

Faith That Lives Is a Saving Faith

Ephesians 2:8, 9 says, "For it is by grace you have been saved, through faith—and this not from yourselves, it is the gift of God—not by works, so that no one can boast."*

Three young boys were giving their definition of faith in a Bible school class. One said, "Faith is taking hold of God." The second one said, "Faith is holding on to God." The third one said, "Faith is never letting go of God." You know, all three boys were right. Let us look at some thoughts about saving faith:

Saving faith is faith in Christ as Savior. It is faith in Him as the one who came by the grace of God to redeem us with His blood. There is a great deal of difference between believing in someone and believing things about someone. For example, you may believe certain things about your doctor: he is a good man, a great surgeon, and so on. When you place your body in his hands, you show that you have faith in him. It is one thing to say, "I believe that Jesus lived, He was a good man, He performed miracles, He died and rose again"; but *saving* faith is turning our lives completely over to Him, trusting Him completely for our salvation, having no doubt that He and He alone can save us.

The fact that faith is an essential element in salvation cannot be denied. In Acts 16:30, 31 we read that a jailer asked, "What must I do to be saved?" Paul responded, "Believe in the Lord Jesus, and you will be saved—you and your household." Jesus said, "Whoever believes in Him is not condemned," and "To all who received Him, to those who believed in his name, he gave the right to become children of God" (John 3:18; 1:12). Other Scriptures confirm this. Faith is the channel through which God's grace is to be received. Faith is the hand that reaches out to receive the gifts of His love.

Saving faith is obedient faith. In the great Hall of Fame of the faithful (Hebrews 11), part of the record goes something like this: "By faith Abel offered . . . by faith Noah built an ark to save his family . . . by faith Abraham obeyed and went, even though he did not know where he was going . . . by faith Abraham was able to become a father." All of these were people who were saved by their faith that acted. James 2:22 says of Abraham, "You see that his faith and his actions were working together, and his faith was made complete by what he did."

Saving faith is acting faith. Repentance is faith changing a life. Confession is faith speaking out. Baptism is faith dying and being born again.

Faith That Lives Is Tested Faith

Make no doubt about it—our faith will be tested. Many times it will be put to the test, and we will cry out! We will echo Israel's cry: "My way is hidden from the Lord; my cause is disregarded by my God" (Isaiah 40:27).

I am reminded of another pastor I met in Belarus last summer. I was to speak to a group of pastors from several different denominational backgrounds on "Being a Pastor." I thought the session went well, and I was pleased with the response. Afterward, a distinguished gray-haired pastor came up to me and humbly thanked me and said that I had encouraged him. My interpreter later told me that this was Pastor Nikolai, who had spent seven years in a Russian prison

because he would not renounce his faith in God and Jesus Christ. Every day for seven years the authorities had visited him, urging him to deny his faith and be free to go back to his family. Every day for seven years he confessed his faith. Finally, the authorities gave up and let him go free. I thought after I heard this story that I had no business trying to teach such a man about faith! He did, however, teach me a lesson about the fact that living faith is tested faith.

Someone has written:

The clouds hang heavy around my way,
  I cannot see;
But through the darkness I believe
  God leadeth me;
'Tis sweet to keep my hand in His
  While all is dim,
To close my weary, aching eyes
  And follow Him;
Through many a thorny path
  He leads my tired feet,
Through many a vale of tears I go,
  But it is sweet
To know that He is close to me,
  My God and Guide;
He leadeth me, and so I walk
  Quite satisfied;
To my blind eyes He may reveal
  No light at all,
But while I lean on His strong arm,
  I cannot fall!

I have a plaque that I read each day. It says simply, "Peace is not the absence of trouble. Peace is the presence of God."

Faith That Lives Is Mountain-Moving Faith

Jesus said, "I tell you the truth, if you have faith and do not doubt, not only can you do what was done to the fig tree, but also you can say to this mountain, 'Go, throw yourself into the sea,' and it will be done" (Matthew 21:21).

We do not often find that we have real mountains of dirt and stone to be removed, but we have our mountain of difficulties each day. For Pastor Nicolai, his mountain was a prison door, and it took his faith seven years to remove it. For the women of Velikiye, the mountain was Soviet bulldozers and soldiers, and it took fourteen days and nights to remove it. Yet, because of their faith, those mountains were removed.

What is your mountain—that obstacle in your life that looms above you like a great peak, obstructing the way to your spiritual goals? Whatever it is, have faith in God. He specializes in moving mountains.

---

* Scripture quotations in this article are from the *New International Version*.

The Power of God's Presence

by David Roadcup

ONE OF THE MOST BEAUTIFUL PICTURES from the ministry of Jesus is recorded in Matthew 3:16, 17: "And after being baptized, Jesus went up immediately from the water; and behold, the heavens were opened, and he saw the Spirit of God descending as a dove, and coming upon Him, and behold, a voice out of the heavens, saying, 'This is My beloved Son, in whom I am well-pleased.'"* God's presence was clear. His blessing and favor were with His Son.

With God's presence comes His power. There is great power for ministry and living when the confirming presence of God is at work.

The opposite also is true, of course. When God's presence departs, so does His power. In the book of Judges, we are told the tragic story of Samson. Chuck Swindoll calls Samson "the he-man with a she-weakness." Samson judged Israel for years with God's blessing and presence. But after falling into disobedience, telling Delilah his secret, falling asleep and getting his hair cut, he heard Delilah tell him, "The Philistines are upon you, Samson!" One of the saddest pictures in Scripture emerges as we read, "But he did not know that the Lord had departed from him" (Judges 16:20).

Because of Samson's lustful sin and disobedience, the Lord's presence had departed, and His power with it.

Saul is another who experienced the Lord's presence and power, but lost them through disobedience. The Lord commanded him to destroy the Amalekites completely. Saul disobeyed by not destroying everything, and God was no longer with him (1 Samuel 15:1-12).

When we obey the Lord, we have His presence and His power. When we disobey, we are in danger of losing God's presence and power in our lives.

Through the Ages

God, His power, and His purposes have been at work through the course of history. We see the power of God unleashed in His dynamic acts of creation. By His word the heavens, earth, plants, animals, oceans, and mankind were formed and placed in order.

Disobedience entered the world through the sin of Adam and Eve. Then God's redemptive work was needed. Later He chose Abraham to father a nation through which the Redeemer would come.

Jesus came and brought redemption for mankind. Still unfolding His plan, God created the church to be the vehicle by which mankind could find God, grace, strength, fellowship, encouragement, and assistance in obeying God.

We are still waiting for God to bring the consummation of the age. Jesus our Lord will return to place the great period at the end of time and usher us to Heaven and our eternal life.

As history unfolds, we see the power of the presence of God. He is behind the plan. He is in control. His purposes are being accomplished according to His power and will.

At the Cross

The greatest act of God's redeeming power is seen at the cross. God broke the bonds of sin with the atoning sacrifice of His Son, Jesus. What once-and-for-all power! What overwhelming, accepting presence! God, keeping His promise, rescued man and restored him to sonship.

The word of the cross truly is the power of God! First Corinthians 1:18 says, "For the word of the cross is to those who are perishing foolishness, but to us who are being saved it is the power of God."

God certainly wanted His presence to be felt and understood by man through the cross. At Jesus' death, "the veil of the temple was torn in two from top to bottom" (Matthew 27:51). Through this act God was saying, "The wall that has divided us has now been torn down. Our fellowship is restored! The barrier is gone!"

When God visited us at Calvary, the power of His presence was awesome. His visit provided our recovery. What a wonderful God!

In Our Daily Lives

Not only has the power of God's presence been seen through His eternal plan, but each day that power is affirmed to us as we walk with Him.

The power of God's closeness comes to us when we accept Jesus Christ as our Lord and Savior. God's grace floods our spirits as we repent, confess Christ as Savior, and join Him in Christian baptism. In doing so, we establish a relationship with Christ, and so we really contact the power of God's presence.

It is wonderful to know that God desires to have fellowship with us. God not only loves us beyond our wildest imagination, but He also likes us and enjoys our fellowship!

There are several things we can do to continue to see the power of God's sustaining presence grow in our lives.

Reading, studying, meditating on, and memorizing the Word of God will feed our spirits and allow us to tap into the power of God. The presence of God is strong in the lives of those persons who spend time feeding themselves thus. Making Scripture a daily part of our devotional life will make God's power a reality in our sphere of service.

Prayer may truly be the greatest means of tapping into the power of God. Prayer ushers us directly into God's presence. You may be deeply concerned about teaching a Sunday school lesson, sharing the gospel with an unbeliever, giving special help to someone who is sick or in need, or service of some other kind. When you bathe your preparation in prayer, earnestly seeking the Lord's blessing on your effort, He responds by giving a heightened awareness of His presence, a firmer confidence in His help, and increased ability for the task before you.

When we attempt our ministry without prayer, we are working "in the flesh," not in the power of God's presence. Our efforts are likely to produce little or no fruit.

As a young minister I was invited to speak to a convention of young people. The size of the crowd made me extremely nervous. I remember vividly immersing that event and my message in prayer. I had a time of fasting. I prayed continually, not only for myself, but also for the people who were going to be present. I was spiritually prepared when the evening arrived. I delivered the message with everything I had, and the Lord gave it His special blessing. As a result, many people came forward at the invitation. Others later told me the Lord had used that message in a significant way in their lives.

Several months later, I received another invitation to speak at a youth gathering. I was extremely busy on the days before the event, and therefore took little time to pray or fast.

On the appointed evening, I preached the same message. I used the same words, same pauses, same vocal intonation; but the special blessing was not there.

At the end of the service, people left the church and said, "That was a nice talk." There were no decisions for Christ, and few changed lives, if any.

Driving home, I reflected on the difference in the two audience responses. That was when I learned about spiritual power in serving Christ. It is God's gift to His praying and trusting servants.

Prayer and the Word of God make a difference in our power and in our effectiveness as we work in our Lord's kingdom. Prayer brings the hand of God into tough situations and difficult times. God's presence truly moves in power when we have prayed.

Obedience also is a major key in seeing the power of the Lord's presence in one's life. This is illustrated in the lives of Samson and Saul, who have been mentioned above. When a life is obedient to the Lord, the Lord blesses that life with power and success. When disobedience is present, the Lord can and does remove His blessing and His presence; but the blessing of God is with an obedient man or woman who is serving the Lord from the purest of motives and the whole heart.

The blessing of God can also rest on a family, a business, a church, a group of church leaders, or a para-church organization. Scripture seems to indicate that cities and nations can also experience the blessing of God. The blessing seems always to depend on the obedience of a person or group of people.

The power of God's presence! If we know Christ and walk daily with Him, that power will always be with us. In the celebration of life, in facing death, in great joy, in severe problems or difficulty, the power of God's presence is ours as promised. Hallelujah!

---

* Scripture quotations are from the *New American Standard Bible.*

Answers to Quarterly Quiz
on page 338

Lesson 1—1. patience, maturity. 2. lust. 3. Care for the needy, unspotted character. **Lesson 2**—1. no. 2. Thou shalt love thy neighbor as thyself. 3. God, the lawgiver. **Lesson 3**—1. dead. 2. works. 3. pray; sing psalms. **Lesson 4**—1. Ask of God. 2. meekly, by a good way of life. 3. righteousness. **Lesson 5**—1. our lusts. 2. flee. 3. sin. **Lesson 6**—1. in earth and sea. 2. both. 3. all his life. **Lesson 7**—1. God's deeds. 2. God's marvelous works. 3. His covenant. 4. the heathen's. **Lesson 8**—1. the Lord. 2. fears, troubles, afflictions. 3. those who fear the Lord. **Lesson 9**—1. the Lord. 2. nowhere. 3. any wicked way. **Lesson 10**—1. horrible. 2. righteousness. 3. those who seek the Lord. **Lesson 11**—1. God's Word. 2. God's Word. 3. God's Word. **Lesson 12**—1. blot them out. 2. David's sins. 3. a clean heart. **Lesson 13**—1. all the earth. 2. God's glory and wonders. 3. with righteousness.

Faith and Faithfulness

June 2
Lesson 1

DEVOTIONAL READING: Romans 6:5-14.

LESSON SCRIPTURE: James 1.

PRINTED TEXT: James 1:2-4, 12-15, 19-27.

James 1:2-4, 12-15, 19-27

2 My brethren, count it all joy when ye fall into divers temptations;

3 Knowing this, that the trying of your faith worketh patience.

4 But let patience have her perfect work, that ye may be perfect and entire, wanting nothing.

. . . .

12 Blessed is the man that endureth temptation: for when he is tried, he shall receive the crown of life, which the Lord hath promised to them that love him.

13 Let no man say when he is tempted, I am tempted of God: for God cannot be tempted with evil, neither tempteth he any man:

14 But every man is tempted, when he is drawn away of his own lust, and enticed.

15 Then when lust hath conceived, it bringeth forth sin; and sin, when it is finished, bringeth forth death.

. . . .

19 Wherefore, my beloved brethren, let every man be swift to hear, slow to speak, slow to wrath:

20 For the wrath of man worketh not the righteousness of God.

21 Wherefore lay apart all filthiness and superfluity of naughtiness, and receive with meekness the engrafted word, which is able to save your souls.

22 But be ye doers of the word, and not hearers only, deceiving your own selves.

23 For if any be a hearer of the word, and not a doer, he is like unto a man beholding his natural face in a glass:

24 For he beholdeth himself, and goeth his way, and straightway forgetteth what manner of man he was.

25 But whoso looketh into the perfect law of liberty, and continueth therein, he being not a forgetful hearer, but a doer of the work, this man shall be blessed in his deed.

26 If any man among you seem to be religious, and bridleth not his tongue, but deceiveth his own heart, this man's religion is vain.

27 Pure religion and undefiled before God and the Father is this, To visit the fatherless and widows in their affliction, and to keep himself unspotted from the world.

GOLDEN TEXT: The trying of your faith worketh patience. But let patience
have her perfect work, that ye may be perfect and entire,
wanting nothing.—James 1:3, 4.

A Practical Religion
(James)
(Lessons 1-5)

Lesson Aims

As a result of studying this lesson, each student should:

1. Gain a growing appreciation for the importance of being faithful to God.

2. Be able to mention an experience in his or her life that demonstrates how one becomes stronger by overcoming temptations.

Lesson Outline

Visual 1 of the visuals packet is a photograph depicting the thought found in James 1:23, 24. The visual is shown on page 348.

Introduction

A. Hammer and Anvil

Near the house where I grew up stood a little shop where the town blacksmith worked. Many mornings at the crack of dawn we were awakened by the ringing sound of his hammer. My brother and I enjoyed stopping by his shop to watch him work. Sometimes he made horse-shoes. Starting with a bar of iron, he would heat it white hot in his forge and then begin beating it into the right size and shape for the horse he was shoeing. Once he had the horseshoe finished, he placed it in the forge and heated it again. Removing it from the forge, he would plunge it into a vat of water or of oil. Sometimes he would repeat this process. When we asked him why he did this, he replied, "Boys, it takes a lot of heating and beating to make a horseshoe, and it takes a lot of heating and quenching to make it tough enough to stand the hard treatment the horse will give it."

James had something like this in mind when he wrote about facing and surviving temptations. One who has never faced temptations has not developed the moral stamina to resist them when they come. Only when we have been heated, beaten, and quenched are we strong enough to handle more severe temptations.

B. Lesson Background

The writer of this letter identifies himself as "James, a servant of God and of the Lord Jesus Christ" (James 1:1). Most Bible scholars agree that this is the brother of Jesus (Galatians 1:19), a son of Joseph and Mary (Matthew 13:55). He was a leader in the church at Jerusalem (Acts 15:13-21).

Some students suspect a disagreement between Paul and James because Paul speaks of salvation by grace and faith, not by works (Ephesians 2:8, 9), while James calls us to be doers of the word (James 1:22). But there is no contradiction. James emphasizes the kind of life one lives when he is saved by faith, and so does Paul (Romans 12).

I. Joy Through Temptation
(James 1:2-4)

A. Rejoicing in Temptation (v. 2)

2. My brethren, count it all joy when ye fall into divers temptations.

James opens his letter with a paradox, a statement that seems to fly in the face of all our experience. First of all, it will help if we recognize that the word here translated *temptations* is translated "trials" in the *New International Version*. The word can mean trials or testings, or it can mean temptations to do wrong, as in James 1:12-14. The difficulties and troubles that try our patience and test our endurance are also temptations. They tempt us to evade our duty, to find an easier way, even to do wrong to avoid what is hard or painful.

How can trials or testings be a source of joy? Perhaps we can better understand what James is writing about if we understand the difference between pleasure and joy.

Pleasure is passing; joy is lasting. An athlete who trains strenuously for a contest must suffer much pain. He can hardly find pleasure in those long hours when every muscle in his body is aching and he is consumed with fatigue. But even then he can know joy as he looks forward to the contest with the hope of victory.

So it is with temptations. As they come upon us, they often bring suffering and strife. Yet at the same time we can find joy in them because we know that overcoming them will make us spiritually stronger and better able to resist future temptations. We can also find comfort in the knowledge that no matter how threatening a temptation may be, the Lord will not allow us to be tempted beyond that which we can bear. With every temptation God will provide us a way of escape (1 Corinthians 10:13).

The Many Colors of Temptation

James speaks of "divers temptations," or as the *New International Version* renders it, "trials of many kinds." The Greek word translated "divers" or "many kinds" is a word that sometimes means "many colored." Indeed, there are temptations or trials of many colors in our experience.

Confronting our circumstances, sometimes we look at a blank white page. We must make some mark on that austere whiteness; but we hesitate, reluctant to mar it. As we enter a new school year or a marriage or a career, we are timid and uncertain. Faith and fortitude are needed.

Often we face rose-tinted prospects. They encourage us to feel we can do no wrong. This color of life may make us try to do more than we can, or to be more than we are, or to depend on good luck more than on a good God.

Often we look at a future that seems to be uniformly black. No lights relieve the darkness; no "gleams of glory" are to be seen. The death of one we love, or the closing door of opportunity, leaves us gazing into blackness. We need to hold on, hold up, and hold out with faith.

There are also periods when the colors of life are golden and glowing. When we see energetic,

reliable grandchildren, when we find some success has crowned years of effort, when God's grace has lifted burdens and opened closed doors, we rejoice and are thankful. Then we need to guard against pride, self-satisfaction, and arrogance. Truly, trials and temptations have many colors.   —J. G. V. B.

B. Testing Develops Patience (v. 3)

3. Knowing this, that the trying of your faith worketh patience.

One is not born with patience; it is a virtue that must be acquired, and its acquisition does not come easily. Every Christian will have his or her faith tested. Sometimes this testing comes in the form of physical persecution. At other times it comes in the form of alluring temptations. But more often than not, it comes in the form of subtle pressures, not to surrender our convictions, but to compromise them.

In withstanding these temptations we learn patience, the patience that will allow us to recognize and resist new temptations. Just as a refiner's fire burns the dross from gold, leaving it pure, so suffering and surviving temptations is morally purifying.

C. Patience Brings Growth (v. 4)

4. But let patience have her perfect work, that ye may be perfect and entire, wanting nothing.

We often think of patience as the passive acceptance of whatever may befall us. But it is much more than this. As infants we have very little patience. Only as we grow and mature are we able to develop this wonderful virtue. We sometimes become impatient even as we try to develop patience. We are like the man who prayed, "Lord, give me patience, and give it to me right now." Patience is essential if we are to become perfect. The term *perfect* here does not mean that a person is morally faultless; it means mature or full grown.

The Perfect Work of Patience

James encourages his readers to "let patience have her perfect work." The development of Christian character is not a "sudden thing." We cannot develop joy, trustworthiness, goodness, and self-control overnight. More than eight years ago we noticed two small oak trees newly planted on a lawn. They looked frail and vulnerable. Months went by with very little change. Finally they grew taller, but an ice storm bent one of them over. The lawnkeeper placed a pole by the leaning one and tied it up.

Now, after more than eight years, the trees are over forty feet tall. The trunks are thick and sturdy; the leaves flourish, wide extended and beautiful. It takes time, care, and persistence to grow an oak tree.

So it is with our growth in Christ. The writer of Hebrews says, "We have come to share in Christ if we hold firmly till the end the confidence we had at first" (3:14, *New International Version*). Jesus stated, "He who stands firm to the end will be saved" (Matthew 24:13, *New International Version*). The psalmist said of the person who finds delight in God's law, "He is like a tree planted by streams of water" (Psalm 1:3, *New International Version*).

Let us send down roots of study, meditation, and godly living so that our tree of life may stand amid storms and be beautiful in life's sunlight.   —J. G. V. B.

II. Enduring Temptation
(James 1:12-15)

A. Endurance Brings the Crown (v. 12)

12. Blessed is the man that endureth temptation: for when he is tried, he shall receive the crown of life, which the Lord hath promised to them that love him.

To the Beatitudes that Jesus mentioned in the Sermon on the Mount (Matthew 5:1-12), James adds another. The blessings that Jesus promised are enjoyed by those who have reached a high level of spiritual maturity. In the same way, the blessing that James offers is for the spiritually mature, for those who endure to the end. The winner in a race most often is the one who has trained the hardest and disciplined himself the best (1 Corinthians 9:24).

In 2 Timothy 4:7, 8, Paul uses similar language to stress the importance of faithfulness to the end: "I have fought a good fight, I have finished my course, I have kept the faith: henceforth there is laid up for me a crown of righteousness, which the Lord, the righteous judge, shall give me at that day: and not to me only, but unto all them also that love his appearing." Being a Christian is not some light commitment that may be kept for a time and then laid aside when it becomes heavy or inconvenient. One does not enlist in the Lord's army for six months or a year, but for the duration of one's life or until the Lord returns.

B. The Source of Temptation (vv. 13, 14)

13. Let no man say when he is tempted, I am tempted of God: for God cannot be tempted with evil, neither tempteth he any man.

Facing up to one's own responsibility for one's sins has never been easy. Evasion started with Adam. He blamed Eve, who in turn blamed the serpent. We have been trying to "pass the buck" ever since. Certain schools of modern psychology make it easy to blame our infancy or early childhood or our genes for all the problems we create for ourselves by our own misdeeds. But this is a "cop out," and it just won't wash with God.

God may allow us to pass through trials, and He may even allow us to be tempted, but He never deliberately tries to entice us to sin.

14. But every man is tempted, when he is drawn away of his own lust, and enticed.

A popular television character of a few years ago attempted to excuse his foibles by saying, "The devil made me do it." There is a bit of truth in this statement, for temptations do come from Satan. But he can intrude into our lives only when we leave the door open. He may come in through the door of physical desire or he may enter through the door of pride. But in either case, we are responsible for keeping the door closed to his intrusion.

Jesus gave us an example of how to handle temptations. Each time Satan made Him an offer, our Lord answered it with Scripture. The psalmist had it right when he said, "Thy word have I hid in mine heart, that I might not sin against thee" (Psalm 119:11). The best defense against the evil one is to say no and back it with Scripture.

C. The Result of Untamed Lust (v. 15)

15. Then when lust hath conceived, it bringeth forth sin; and sin, when it is finished, bringeth forth death.

James compares the origin of sin with conception and childbirth. The life of a child begins at conception, not at birth. In the same way, sin begins when it is first considered, not when it finally is seen in the act. Satan tempts us through our physical appetites and our egos. But usually we do not succumb to his wiles the first time he makes an offer. Only as we allow the idea to take root and grow does it become a visible sin. Jesus made the very important point that a sin conceived in one's heart is just as serious as an overtly sinful act (Matthew 5:21, 22, 27, 28).

visual 1

The result of allowing a sin to grow and emerge in an overt deed is certain—death!

In some cases sin might lead to physical death, but James here has in mind spiritual death. As Paul observes in Romans 6:23, "The wages of sin is death." Only by God's gracious forgiveness can that result be avoided.

III. Hearers and Doers (James 1:19-27)

A. Importance of Hearing (vv. 19-24)

19, 20. Wherefore, my beloved brethren, let every man be swift to hear, slow to speak, slow to wrath: for the wrath of man worketh not the righteousness of God.

In verse 18 James states that God has begotten Christians through the word. Since that is the case, verse 19 stresses the importance of every person being *swift to hear* the word. One cannot respond to the word unless one hears it. Many things keep us from really hearing the word—our prejudices, our involvement in things of the world, our unwillingness to make the kind of commitment that God requires of us.

Slow to speak. We usually learn more when we are listening than when we are talking. Some of us become enamored with the sound of our own voices, and as a result we utter a lot of nonsense. Our tongue is off and running before our mind gets in gear. In chapter 3 James has much more to say about the tongue.

Slow to wrath. One who speaks quickly is often quick to become angry. Some excuse their quick tempers by acting as if this quality were inborn and uncontrollable. A big part of the problem is that these people have not learned patience, a problem that James has already addressed in the early verses of this chapter.

On every hand we see evidence that anger produces wickedness and violence. A quick loss of temper may cause a person to do physical harm to another person. A slow, simmering anger may lead to a desire for revenge. Our violence-prone society needs to listen to what James is saying here.

21. Wherefore lay apart all filthiness and superfluity of naughtiness, and receive with meekness the engrafted word, which is able to save your souls.

James urges his readers to lay aside their moral filth like a dirty garment. Unless they are willing to do this, they cannot receive the word of God that He desires to engraft or implant in their hearts. The word is the good news that offers salvation, but it is also the moral teachings that a saved person must live up to.

22. But be ye doers of the word, and not hearers only, deceiving your own selves.

Simply listening passively to the word just won't do. A hearer of the word must translate it into his or her life. The church is crippled today by a great number of members who never make this translation.

23, 24. For if any be a hearer of the word, and not a doer, he is like unto a man beholding his natural face in a glass: for he beholdeth himself, and goeth his way, and straightway forgetteth what manner of man he was.

Looking in a mirror, a man sees a smudge on his face; but then he forgets what he has seen instead of removing the smudge. He is like the man who hears God's word, but does not do what it says to do.

HEARING AND DOING

James urged his readers to be "doers of the word, and not hearers only." His emphasis is on possession and expression, not mere profession. An actor may play the part of a king, a regal possessor of sovereign authority; but he is only a make-believe king, lacking any genuine power. James was concerned lest Christians make a confession of faith without any outcome in works of love, helpfulness, and compassion.

James always insists that word and way must be united. Hanna More (1745-1833) wrote of *Faith and Works:*

> If faith produce no works, I see
> That faith is not a living tree.
> Thus faith and works together grow;
> No separate life they e'er can know:
> They're soul and body, hand and heart:
> What God hath joined, let no man part.

Let us not divide words and works in our lives. While at times we may deceive others, we end up deceiving our own selves! Such deception is like making a life jacket of straw and wearing it in a storm at sea.
—J. G. V. B.

B. Blessings for the Doer (v. 25)

25. But whoso looketh into the perfect law of liberty, and continueth therein, he being not a forgetful hearer, but a doer of the work, this man shall be blessed in his deed.

The perfect law of liberty is not the Mosaic law. It is the engrafted word of verse 21. It is the new covenant written in the hearts of God's people (Jeremiah 31:31-34). It sets one free from slavery to sin; but only if one not only *looketh into* the word, but also *continueth therein*, keeps on doing what the word says to do. If the word reveals a smudge on his character or way of life, he gets rid of that smudge—and God blesses his doing.

C. Dangers of an Unbridled Tongue
(v. 26)

26. If any man among you seem to be religious, and bridleth not his tongue, but deceiveth his own heart, this man's religion is vain.

We think of a doer as one who is busily involved in some activity. But here the doer of the word appears as one who is not using his tongue —at least, not using it recklessly or harmfully. A person who misuses his tongue may deceive himself and others into thinking he is religious because he never misses a church service, but he is fooling himself, and his religion is vain.

D. Pure Religion (v. 27)

27. Pure religion and undefiled before God and the Father is this, To visit the fatherless and widows in their affliction, and to keep himself unspotted from the world.

What one believes is important, and James is not denying that. What we believe will in a large measure determine what we do. But James's emphasis is on practical matters, not on theology. James mentions two aspects of pure religion: helping orphans and widows, and keeping oneself morally pure. In the first of these two aspects, he echoes what Jesus said in Matthew 25:31-46. One standard for the final judgment will be how one ministers to the poor and helpless. But helping others does not atone for foul talk or immoral acts. One must not compromise God's standards of holiness.

Conclusion
A. Learning Patience

A pious old farmer had a cow that was a kicker. She could hardly get through a milking without either kicking him or kicking over the milk bucket. More than once he considered selling her to the butcher. He kept praying to God to give him patience to deal with her, but his prayers seemingly did no good.

Finally he went to his minister with the problem. "Preacher," he said, "I've been praying for months for patience to deal with this critter, but God hasn't answered me."

"Oh," replied his minister, "I think God is answering your prayer all right. He is testing you, and you just haven't passed the exam yet; so He keeps testing you."

B. Pure and Undefiled

In his description of pure and undefiled religion, James does not mention the importance of sound doctrine. Rather, he emphasizes service to others (visiting the orphans and the widows in their afflictions) and moral purity (keeping oneself unspotted from the world). This should not lead us to suppose that sound doctrine is unimportant. We need to recognize, rather, that these practical aspects of religion result from receiving God's Word and doing what it tells us to do (vv. 21, 22).

We need to emphasize Christian action today. There is no shortage of places to serve the hurting and the hungry, the angry and the anguished. Yet too many of us have made our Christianity into a spectator sport. We sit on the sidelines and politely cheer others without ever really becoming involved. Many are willing to give of their money without ever giving of their time or of themselves.

We need sermons and we need theology; but we also need examples of what Christian love means. A Mother Theresa ministering to the poor speaks more loudly to the unbelieving multitudes than do a thousand sermons on love.

Even as we serve, we must give attention to our own lives. As we venture out into an unbelieving and morally decaying world, we must take care that unbelief does not erode our faith or that moral corruption does not cause us to become cynical or to compromise our commitment to our Lord.

C. Let Us Pray

Dear Father, we know that we must be tested in order to grow spiritually. We pray that You will give us the strength and the patience to rejoice when testing comes. In Jesus' name we pray. Amen.

D. Thought to Remember

God will not allow us to be tempted beyond what we can bear.

Home Daily Bible Readings

Monday, May 27—The Supremacy of God's Wisdom (Job 28:12-23)
Tuesday, May 28—Confident of Being Heard (1 John 5:13-21)
Wednesday, May 29—God's Eternity, Man's Transience (Psalm 90:1-6)
Thursday, May 30—The Lord's Discipline (Hebrews 12:3-11)
Friday, May 31—Sharing God's Good News (1 Timothy 1:3-11)
Saturday, June 1—Wholehearted Trust (Proverbs 3:5-12)
Sunday, June 2—Alive in Christ (Romans 6:5-14)

Learning by Doing

This page contains an alternate lesson plan emphasizing learning activities. Classes desiring such student involvement will find these suggestions helpful.

Learning Goals

After this lesson students will be able to do the following:

1. Cite practical benefits that come to a Christian life through enduring trials.

2. Understand James's view of the basic nature of temptation.

3. Identify specific ways in which God's Word can bring needed change to personal lives.

Into the Lesson

Begin by having the class respond to this imagined complaint: "I don't find the Bible very practical. What I need is something that tells me how to get through the day."

Allow the response, and then state, "While the Bible holds many complex truths, it is also filled with intensely practical advice. And in no book of the New Testament (other than the Gospels) do 'right ideas' find more practical application toward 'right living' than in the epistle of James."

Lead into today's study by noting that James begins by discussing *the benefits of enduring trials;* a few verses later, he examines *the nature of temptation;* and he closes Chapter 1 by saying that God's Word needs to have *practical impact upon our everyday lives.*

Into the Word

Step One: Have someone read James 1:2-4, 12. Then ask the class, "Have you ever heard the saying, 'When life hands you a lemon, make lemonade'?" Personal experience shows that it's often easier to smile at this statement than actually to practice it.

Step Two: Have another student read 1:13-15. Then share how our tendency is often to blame sin on everyone but ourselves (*see lesson commentary*). Some even point a finger at God.

Step Three: Ask a third student to read 1:19-27. Ask students if they can tell one thing they have done in the past week because of something they have read in the Bible.

Step Four: Now it's time to dig further. Divide your class into groups of no more than four to six, and give each group a card on which you have copied one of the following activities. (*These projects are also in the student book. Group B will need a marker and paper or newsprint.*)

GROUP A: JAMES 1:1-4, 12
Read the above text and then discuss:

1. How is it possible to "count it all joy" when troubles come your way? Isn't "joy" an unnatural response? J. B. Phillips translates James 1:2, "When all kinds of trials and temptations crowd into your lives . . . don't resent them as intruders, but welcome them as friends!" How do these words strike you?

2. James indicates at least two benefits of enduring trials: the development of patience and the promise of future reward. Is patience something "learned"? What does "faith" gain in the process? How does a promise of future glory ease the consequence of present difficulties? Compare 2 Corinthians 4:16-18.

3. Share personal ways in which troubles have brought joy and growth into your lives.

GROUP B: JAMES 1:13-15

1. Take a piece of paper, draw a horizontal line, and then mark and label at various points what the above verses describe as the progressive stages of temptation and sin. Discuss how each step leads toward the final end.

2. Looking at your chart, consider practical ways in which the deadly flow might be interrupted to avoid the final consequences.

GROUP C: JAMES 1:19-27

1. Using the above text, create a short sketch, or series of sketches (which you can later act out for the class), to illustrate practically the teaching of these verses.

2. As an *option*, discuss the struggles that group members have in allowing God's Word to make changes in their lives. Consider practical ways in which you might increase the personal impact of Bible study in your lives this week.

Step Five: After allowing about twelve to fifteen minutes for work, call time and ask each group to share its project.

Into Life

Hand out index cards and ask class members to make a "To Do" list for the coming week of personal life changes that today's lesson leads them to consider making. Encourage each one to put the card in a Bible so that as they "look into the Word" during the week they will also see how they might better "practice" it as well. Close with prayer asking for help in being "doers" as well as "hearers" of God's Word.

Let's Talk It Over

The questions on this page are designed to encourage review of the lesson Scriptures and to promote discussion of the lesson by the class. The answers provided are only discussion starters. Let your class talk it over from there.

1. What is the joy in suffering temptation? Why is it more beneficial to suffer "divers" temptations rather than the same temptation over and over?

Temptations are a proving of our faith under pressure. As we succeed in resisting the temptations, we build patient endurance and increase our ability to resist. If the temptations are varied, this positive effect is increased. If we continue to suffer the same temptation, it is probably an indication that our resistance is weak in that area, and that our faith needs to be strengthened at that point.

2. Name some sins that spring from impatience.

Lies are often told because of impatience with what is, and in an effort to pretend better circumstances. Covetousness and theft may result from a lack of patience to work hard and save for some desired item. Swearing may be used by an impatient person to indicate sincerity or strength of emotion.

3. Does enduring temptation (v. 12) mean never having any moral failure? If we ever succumb to temptation, do we forfeit the crown of life?

If one sin disqualified us from the crown of life, then no one would ever receive it. In 1 John 1:8 we read, "If we claim to be without sin, we deceive ourselves and the truth is not in us" (*New International Version*). That statement was addressed to Christians, and the very next verse confirms that forgiveness is available to penitent believers. Enduring temptation, then, must mean learning to resist successfully, and having our faith proven and purified through the experience. We may have to ask forgiveness many times before we learn to overcome rather than being overcome.

4. At what point have we lost the battle with temptation? If we conceive the sin in our mind, is it any worse to do it? Why, or why not?

The life of a sin begins with conception in our mind, fathered by our own lust or desire. If we compare what Jesus said about hatred in relation to murder, or sexual lust in relation to adultery, we conclude that simply mulling over an immoral act in the mind is sin already. Even so, it is still better to extinguish the thought rather than to compound our sin by committing the deed. It is easy to demonstrate the practical difference between a sin conceived and a sin committed. If you hate me, you have sinned; but I would still prefer that to being murdered by you. Every sin makes us guilty, but not all sins have the same practical consequence.

5. How would you argue for the value of being "slow to wrath" with someone who claims he must vent his anger in order to dispel it and feel better?

To let yourself scream, curse, or otherwise "fly off the handle" increases the likelihood that you will respond similarly the next time you are frustrated or irritated. If expression of anger relieves one person, it usually leaves others stunned, hurt, or angry. Being slow to speak means we give ourselves time to carefully evaluate a matter, giving full consideration to every point of view, so we can respond rationally rather than in the heat of emotion.

6. What methods help you become more of a doer of the word? How could your church be more helpful in this matter?

There is a vast difference between only hearing the word of God and both hearing and practicing it. Jesus compared it to the difference between building a house on sand or on a rock foundation (Matthew 7:24-27). Many churches have put a high value on hearing the word at worship, at Sunday school, at Bible studies, and in personal devotion. Application of the word is often neglected, however, since it is more difficult and requires much more personal discipline. You may find it helpful to establish goals for yourself based upon what you study. You can give greater strength to your commitments by confiding in a trusted friend and asking that person to hold you accountable. Churches are helping people apply the Bible by establishing such accountability relationships in classes, in support groups and nurture groups, or between prayer partners. Churches can also help by providing organization and support for practical ministries, such as visitation to the fatherless and widows (v. 27).

Faith and Relationships

DEVOTIONAL READING: Romans 14:1-12.

LESSON SCRIPTURE: James 2:1-13; 4:11, 12.

PRINTED TEXT: James 2:1-13; 4:11, 12.

James 2:1-13

1 My brethren, have not the faith of our Lord Jesus Christ, the Lord of glory, with respect of persons.

2 For if there come unto your assembly a man with a gold ring, in goodly apparel, and there come in also a poor man in vile raiment;

3 And ye have respect to him that weareth the gay clothing, and say unto him, Sit thou here in a good place; and say to the poor, Stand thou there, or sit here under my footstool:

4 Are ye not then partial in yourselves, and are become judges of evil thoughts?

5 Hearken, my beloved brethren, Hath not God chosen the poor of this world rich in faith, and heirs of the kingdom which he hath promised to them that love him?

6 But ye have despised the poor. Do not rich men oppress you, and draw you before the judgment seats?

7 Do not they blaspheme that worthy name by the which ye are called?

8 If ye fulfil the royal law according to the Scripture, Thou shalt love thy neighbor as thyself, ye do well:

9 But if ye have respect to persons, ye commit sin, and are convinced of the law as transgressors.

10 For whosoever shall keep the whole law, and yet offend in one point, he is guilty of all.

11 For he that said, Do not commit adultery, said also, Do not kill. Now if thou commit no adultery, yet if thou kill, thou art become a transgressor of the law.

12 So speak ye, and so do, as they that shall be judged by the law of liberty.

13 For he shall have judgment without mercy, that hath showed no mercy; and mercy rejoiceth against judgment.

James 4:11, 12

11 Speak not evil one of another, brethren. He that speaketh evil of his brother, and judgeth his brother, speaketh evil of the law, and judgeth the law: but if thou judge the law, thou art not a doer of the law, but a judge.

12 There is one lawgiver, who is able to save and to destroy: who art thou that judgest another?

GOLDEN TEXT: If ye fulfil the royal law according to the Scripture, Thou shalt love thy neighbor as thyself, ye do well.—James 2:8.

A Practical Religion
(James)
(Lessons 1-5)

Lesson Aims

After this lesson, each student should:

1. Understand that favoritism is not consistent with Christian faith and love.

2. Understand that we will be judged without mercy if we show no mercy to others.

3. Have a concern for others who are different in race, language, or socioeconomic status.

4. Invite a person of another race, language, or socioeconomic status to Sunday school.

Lesson Outline

INTRODUCTION
    A. A Son of a Carpenter
    B. Lesson Background
  I. ACTING IN RESPECT OF PERSONS (James 2:1-7)
    A. The Sin Condemned (v. 1)
      Consciousness of Caste and Class
    B. An Example of the Sin (vv. 2-4)
    C. The Basis for Condemnation (vv. 5-7)
      God's Concern for the Poor
  II. OBSERVING THE ROYAL LAW (James 2:8-13)
    A. Commendation for Obeying (v. 8)
    B. Condemnation for Disobeying (v. 9)
    C. Obeying the Whole Law (vv. 10, 11)
    D. The Law and Judgment (vv. 12, 13)
      Mercy and Justice
 III. EVIL SPEAKING AND JUDGING (James 4:11, 12)
    A. Evil Speaking (v. 11)
    B. Evil Judging (v. 12)
CONCLUSION
    A. Actions Speak Loudly
    B. Why We Are Partial
    C. God's Laws
    D. Let Us Pray
    E. Thought to Remember

The evil of favoritism is the theme of visual 2 of the visuals packet. The visual is shown on page 355.

Introduction

A. A Son of a Carpenter

Some years ago an assembly of Anglican bishops was discussing the appointment of a man to an important post in the church. The man was quite adequately qualified for the position, but there seemed to be some hesitancy about giving him the appointment. Finally one of the bishops spoke up: "I recognize that the man has the qualifications; but, after all, he is only the son of a carpenter."

Another bishop then replied, "This morning in my devotions I was reading about a man who was only the son of a carpenter." There was a moment of embarrassing silence, and then the bishops voted unanimously for the candidate.

B. Lesson Background

James, the brother of the Lord, was the author of the epistle that is called by his name. James had become a leader in the church in Jerusalem. As a leader, he had to guide new Christians as they tried to apply their faith to their daily lives. Since the church had several thousand members, James and the other leaders had to deal with a multitude of problems.

But James was writing for more than the church at Jerusalem. His letter is addressed to "the twelve tribes which are scattered abroad," and its inspired advice applies to many beyond the literal twelve tribes of Israel. It has application and value to all Christians in every age.

Today's lesson deals with the problem of favoritism. In our modern society, showing partiality takes many forms. We sometimes are guilty of showing favoritism to a person because of his or her social or economic status, race, or language. We may also show prejudice against a person for one of those same reasons. In either case, such action is wrong.

I. Acting in Respect of Persons (James 2:1-7)

A. The Sin Condemned (v. 1)

1. My brethren, have not the faith of our Lord Jesus Christ, the Lord of glory, with respect of persons.

The Phillips translation puts this verse in contemporary language: "Don't ever attempt, my brothers, to combine snobbery with faith in our glorious Lord Jesus Christ!"

Respect of persons. This term requires a little study. It is not wrong to have a special concern for members of one's family (1 Timothy 5:8), or for members of God's family (Galatians 6:10). It is not wrong to give respect to one who has earned it by his character and action. As the phrase is used in our text, *respect of persons* means respect given for reasons of a very different kind. Some of those reasons will appear as our study goes on.

Faith in God and unfair partiality toward other persons do not go together. If we love and respect God, then we must love and respect those whom He has created. When we reject people simply because they are different from us in some way, then we are, in effect, rejecting the God who made them.

CONSCIOUSNESS OF CASTE AND CLASS

After a church service in India, an American couple was talking with a young Indian Christian about the faith in Jesus that all His followers hold in common. The young man said receiving Communion was difficult for him. He was of a higher caste than some in the congregation. Outside of the church, it was considered wrong for one of his caste to receive food from "untouchables." When one of that caste served the Communion, the young man found it hard to forget what he had been taught.

Verse 1 of our text says we are not to hold our faith "with respect of persons." Like our Indian brethren, we must not let differences of education, social status, wealth, or occupation cause us to draw back from, ignore, or slight our fellow believers. May the ideal expressed in the great hymn by John Oxenham be true of us.

> In Christ now meet both East and West;
> In Him meet South and North;
> All Christly souls are one in Him
> Throughout the whole wide earth.
>
> —J. G. V. B.

B. An Example of the Sin (vv. 2-4)

2-4. For if there come unto your assembly a man with a gold ring, in goodly apparel, and there come in also a poor man in vile raiment; and ye have respect to him that weareth the gay clothing, and say unto him, Sit thou here in a good place; and say to the poor, Stand thou there, or sit here under my footstool: are ye not then partial in yourselves, and are become judges of evil thoughts?

The favoritism that James condemns here is based on a person's economic status. A rich man and a poor man, perhaps both strangers to the congregation, arrive for worship. The rich man, readily identified by his gold ring and fine clothing, is given a choice seat, probably in the front of the auditorium. That might be done even now, though we ourselves seem to prefer the rear pews. The poor man had to stand, or sit on the floor at the feet of other worshipers.

A century or so ago, some churches used to charge rent for pews. The rich and the powerful rented the prominent pews. The less affluent had pews in the rear, while the poor had to stand or sit on the floor. Few churches follow this practice today, but favoritism is shown in numerous other ways. The rich and the

visual 2

prominent often wield undue influence in making decisions in the church, not because their decisions are wiser or more spiritual, but because of who they are. The values of our secular world all too easily become the values we follow in the church.

C. The Basis for Condemnation (vv. 5-7)

5. Hearken, my beloved brethren, Hath not God chosen the poor of this world rich in faith, and heirs of the kingdom which he hath promised to them that love him?

Wealth and position should not merit special privileges within the church. The people told to sit on the floor may be the very persons God honors. God does not measure persons by the cut of their clothes, the size of their bank accounts, or the opulence of their dwellings. Rather, God measures people by their faith. In the past He has often used the poor and the weak to accomplish His purposes (1 Corinthians 1:26-29).

This is not to say that God despises the rich just because they are rich, or that He chooses the poor just because they are poor. God's concern is not with what a person has, but with what a person is. A rich person can be just as poor in spirit as an impoverished person; a poor man can be just as devilish as a rich man. What one has in his heart is more important than the clothes that cover his chest.

6. But ye have despised the poor. Do not rich men oppress you, and draw you before the judgment seats?

James next points out that the rich, whom they were honoring, were the very ones who oppressed them outside the church. Of course, he is not suggesting that all rich people are oppressors. Some are quite humble and generous. But some rich people cruelly mistreat others, and so we should not honor anyone just because he or she is rich.

Draw you before the judgment seats. This refers to the practice of bringing people into court to collect debts. The poor could not afford a lawyer; and besides, the judges were often bought off by the rich. In those days persons could be thrown into jail or even sold into slavery for failing to pay their debts.

7. Do not they blaspheme that worthy name by which ye are called?

James's next charge is even more serious. The rich and the powerful who abuse the poor also misuse the name of Christ. They speak it with ridicule or contempt. Not all rich people do this, but as long as some do, it is a mistake to honor anyone just because that person possesses wealth.

GOD'S CONCERN FOR THE POOR

In eighteenth-century England, a series of "Enclosure Acts" passed by Parliament resulted in the fencing and redistribution of land. Many peasants lost their land entirely or had to accept poorer plots. Many small villages were deserted.

In a moving poem, *The Deserted Village,* Oliver Goldsmith indicated his sympathy with the poor victims. He pictured the deserted land and expressed his concern:

Sunk are thy bowers, in shapeless ruin all,
And the long grass o'ertops the moldering wall;
And, trembling, shrinking from the spoiler's hand,
Far, far away, thy children leave the land.
Ill fares the land, to hastening ills a prey,
Where wealth accumulates, and men decay.
. . . .

Along the lawn, where scattered hamlets rose,
Unwieldy wealth and cumbrous pomp repose;
And every want to opulence allied,
And every pang that folly pays to pride.

In our printed text, verses 5-7 indicate James's concern with the way many of the poor people were oppressed in his era. This is a sample of the way biblical writers deplore and condemn any exploitation of the less fortunate people by greedy persons of wealth.

—J. G. V. B.

II. Observing the Royal Law (James 2:8-13)

A. Commendation for Obeying (v. 8)

8. If ye fulfil the royal law according to the Scripture, Thou shalt love thy neighbor as thyself, ye do well.

The *royal law* is so called because it is sovereign over all other laws. This law quoted from Leviticus 19:18 is one of the two commandments upon which the whole law depends (Matthew 22:37-40). Love of God always comes first, but unless it is followed by the love of one's neighbors, a person has not lived up to God's law. It makes no difference whether the neighbor is rich or poor.

B. Condemnation for Disobeying (v. 9)

9. But if ye have respect to persons, ye commit sin, and are convinced of the law as transgressors.

Convinced means convicted. One might profess that he loved his neighbor as himself, but if he gave preferential treatment to some and not to others, he was violating the law. To some this might seem like a trivial sin, but not in the eyes of God. Are not all of us, in one way or another, guilty of this transgression? We may openly, even blatantly, show favoritism to some and not to others. Sometimes our favoritism may be subtle, or even unconscious. We need constantly to work at sensitizing ourselves so that we are not guilty of this transgression. No matter how we may regard it, God considers it a sin.

C. Obeying the Whole Law (vv. 10, 11)

10, 11. For whosoever shall keep the whole law, and yet offend in one point, he is guilty of all. For he that said, Do not commit adultery, said also, Do not kill. Now if thou commit no adultery, yet if thou kill, thou art become a transgressor of the law.

God is a God of absolute righteousness who demands conformity with His will at every point. God's law is a unit; and since the wages of sin is death, even one sin is fatal. We make all kinds of clever distinctions between sins, considering some much more serious than others. We are inclined to minimize our own sins and consider other people's sins much worse. But that is not the way God views the matter. James is making the point that treating people with unjust partiality is a transgression just as surely as adultery or murder is.

D. The Law and Judgment (vv. 12, 13)

12, 13. So speak ye, and so do, as they that shall be judged by the law of liberty. For he shall have judgment without mercy, that hath showed no mercy; and mercy rejoiceth against judgment.

James urges his readers to recognize that they will be judged both by their words and by their actions. This is another example of his emphasis upon acting as well as hearing and believing. We should live our lives with the knowledge that every act and thought will be a part of the basis for our judgment.

The law of liberty. Compare this with "the perfect law of liberty" in last week's lesson (James 1:25). We shall be judged by God's truth, by His New Covenant that we know through Christian teaching. We should live every moment with that judgment in mind. Even so our living will not be faultless, but our faults can be forgiven by God's mercy—but we cannot expect God's mercy unless we are merciful in our dealings with others.

MERCY AND JUSTICE

Shakespeare's drama, *The Merchant of Venice,* tells of a desperate borrower who pledged to forfeit a pound of his flesh if he failed to repay his loan. He did fail, and the lender went to court to demand his pound.

The debtor could not deny his pledge, but his lawyer urged the creditor not to take the pound of flesh. Eloquently she described the virtue of mercy:

> It is enthroned in the hearts of kings,
> It is an attribute of God himself;
> And earthly power doth then show likest God's
> When mercy seasons justice.

Rejecting the lawyer's plea for mercy, the heartless creditor continued his demand for justice. The lawyer then turned on him. According to law, this creditor was a criminal because he threatened the life of the debtor. So the one who demanded justice found himself justly condemned.

All of us share that condemnation if we refuse to forgive others. "He shall have judgment without mercy, that hath showed no mercy."

—J. G. V. B.

III. Evil Speaking and Judging (James 4:11, 12)

A. Evil Speaking (v. 11)

11. Speak not evil one of another, brethren. He that speaketh evil of his brother, and judgeth his brother, speaketh evil of the law, and judgeth the law: but if thou judge the law, thou art not a doer of the law, but a judge.

This verse may refer to the one preceding it: "Humble yourselves in the sight of the Lord, and he shall lift you up." Some people betray a lack of humility by running down others. By making others look inferior, they exalt themselves.

On the other hand, James may have been thinking of a larger context in which he was spelling out a number of failings among the brethren: faith without works (1:22), respect of persons (2:1), loose talk (3:2), conflicts (4:1). These sins were upsetting the church, threatening to divide it. For example, one conflict was the controversy over letting Gentiles become Christians without becoming Jews. In that dispute people were speaking evil of their brethren in order to run them down and gain an advantage in the argument. When this dispute finally

came to a head, James played a leading role in working out a reconciliation (Acts 15).

In speaking against one another, the people were sitting in judgment upon others. We are reminded of Jesus' admonition: "Judge not, that ye be not judged" (Matthew 7:1, 2). What they didn't realize was that in judging others they were also judging the law. Apparently this means "the law of liberty" that has been discussed earlier in this lesson. When one violated that law by slandering others, he was rejecting the law.

B. Evil Judging (v. 12)

12. There is one lawgiver, who is able to save and to destroy: who art thou that judgest another?

When one sets himself up as a judge, he usurps the position that rightfully belongs to God. The *one lawgiver* is God. His judgment is always right, and He is able to forgive or to punish. It is highly presumptuous for anyone to take His place. We may dismiss speaking evil as a minor infraction of the law, but assuming the authority of God is far from minor.

Conclusion

A. Actions Speak Loudly

I have a friend who has a wonderful ministry of helping people who are in wheelchairs. With a special van he takes them shopping, to the doctor's office, or on other errands. On Sunday he brings several of them to church. When he first began this ministry, he sought a church that was accessible to people in wheelchairs. In many churches built several years ago, entrance steps presented formidable barriers. He brought his people to a church where the chairs had to be lifted up several steps in order to enter the sanctuary. When he arrived, no one offered to give him a helping hand in getting the chairs up the steps. He concluded that the people in that church did not want people in wheelchairs worshiping with them, and so the next Sunday he visited another church. There he received the same reception.

Finally, he found a church that had only one or two steps. Further, he found many helping hands to move his friends into the building. At the conclusion of the service, he explained his ministry to some of the leaders. They gave him a warm invitation to return. When he returned the following Sunday, he found that a ramp had been installed, allowing easy entrance to the building. In the sanctuary he discovered that a pew had been removed so he had room for the wheelchairs.

Perhaps the congregations that my friend first visited did not intentionally discriminate against people in wheelchairs, but in their actions they seemed to be saying that they really didn't want to be bothered with them.

B. Why We Are Partial

We have various motives for being partial toward others. Sometimes our partiality grows from our prejudice for or against a person or group. If we are clear-sighted and honest, all of us have to admit that we harbor some prejudices. Such biases, either positive or negative, may stem from experiences, either happy or unhappy, that we have had with other persons or groups. Sometimes we form an opinion about a group when we have had contact with only one or two persons from that group. We project upon an entire group the attributes we observed in only a few members of it. Sociologists speak of this as "stereotyping." Stereotyping simplifies the process of making decisions about others. It's much easier to say, "All _____ are _____" (you fill in the blanks), than it is to carefully evaluate every person. By taking this action, we become respecters of persons, a stance that God labels sinful.

We may have other motives for practicing favoritism. We may give a person the "red carpet treatment" in order to curry favors with him. We may go out of our way to oblige him, or may make complimentary remarks about him (in his presence, of course. What we say behind his back may be another matter.) We do this out of selfish motives, to gain favor in one way or another. We do this to get a job or to hold a job. We do this to gain the favor of the rich and those we consider powerful. "Buttering up" the boss is a time-honored behavioral pattern. Such

actions also stand condemned by God, and rightly so.

We stand appalled at the suffering and strife caused in our world today by racial and ethnic hatreds. We have trouble understanding how people can hate one another so intensely. We need to recognize that these hatreds are instilled in the hearts of children from the moment they are born. As parents and grandparents, as teachers and leaders, we need to recognize our responsibility to teach our children in such a way that these hatreds can never take root. If we are to know a "kinder, gentler" world, we must find ways to prevent bitter prejudices from developing. And in lives where they have taken root, we must do all we can to eradicate them.

C. God's Laws

A basic law of the physical world is that for every action there is an equal and opposite reaction. That reaction immediately follows the action. While we cannot break the laws of nature, we can break ourselves upon them. If we should jump from the top of a ten-story building, we would immediately demonstrate the validity of this law (and probably kill ourselves in the process.) We would not break the law; we would break ourselves upon it.

The moral law operates in a similar fashion— with one notable exception. When we break a law, the consequences do not follow immediately. God in His infinite mercies spares us and gives us another chance, and another, and another. If, however, we repeat this process long enough, we will have to pay the price.

God has reserved the power of judgment to himself. Only He is wise enough to mete out final judgment. But we are tempted at times to assume the prerogatives of God and engage in that activity. When we do, we place ourselves under His judgment. That is neither a safe nor a pleasant place to be.

D. Let Us Pray

Dear God, we come before You confessing that we have sinned in that we have sometimes been respecters of persons in our relations with others. Teach us to overcome our prejudices, both those that are obvious and those that we conceal even from ourselves. May we learn to sing again the song we sang as children: "Jesus loves the little children, All the children of the world; Red and yellow, black and white, They are precious in His sight." In Jesus' name we pray. Amen.

E. Thought to Remember

God does not respect persons, and neither should we.

Home Daily Bible Readings

Monday, June 3—No Room for Boasting (1 Corinthians 1:26-31)

Tuesday, June 4—Just Treatment (Leviticus 19:15-19)

Wednesday, June 5—Divine Disapproval (Deuteronomy 27:15-26)

Thursday, June 6—Moral Qualities (Psalm 15)

Friday, June 7—Abuse Not Your Liberty (Galatians 5:13-25)

Saturday, June 8—Following Christ's Attitude (Philippians 2:1-11)

Sunday, June 9—Proper Restraint (Romans 14:10-23)

Learning by Doing

This page contains an alternate lesson plan emphasizing learning activities. Classes desiring such student involvement will find these suggestions helpful.

Learning Goals

As a result of this lesson students will:

1. Understand that favoritism and prejudice are attitudes inconsistent with genuine Christian character, and that love is the sovereign law of God's kingdom.

2. Realize that all people stand under God's judgment if they do not practice mercy.

3. Develop practical steps to change attitudes inconsistent with the above principles.

Into the Lesson

Begin class by saying, "A few years ago, a noted Christian leader was asked what he thought was the greatest problem facing the church. Without hesitation he said, 'It's not liberalism or debate over the Bible. The most serious problem facing today's church is *materialism*.' Do you agree or disagree?" Allow three minutes for discussion.

Continue to probe, saying, "A contemporary observer of our society argues that the most segregated hour in America is eleven o'clock on Sunday morning; and the most segregated site is the church. How does this assessment strike you?" Ask class members to share their thoughts with those nearby. After two or three minutes take another agree/disagree poll.

Tell students that today's lesson strikes at the heart of several sensitive issues that are faced in life and in the church: favoritism and prejudice, poverty and wealth, judgment and mercy. Though old problems, these continue to have impact and pose eternal consequences.

Into the Word

Part One. Now have three people, previously selected, read aloud these verses from James 2— verses 1-4, verses 5-7, and verses 8-11.

Lecture. Present a short lecture (ten minutes) using the lesson commentary to examine the background and meaning of the above verses.

Role-Play. After the lecture, ask for four volunteers to play different roles for a class discussion. Signs—previously prepared and designed, by attached strings, to hang over the head— should read: (1) "Ethnic American," (2) "Homeless Vagrant," (3) "Disabled Person," and (4) "Fortune 500 Executive."

Have the role-players escorted through the class to stand up front. (If a wheelchair is available, seat the "Disabled.") Then have class members discuss how each person might be treated if he or she were an actual visitor to your class or worship service. Allow three or four minutes for comments on each person, and then ask the role-players themselves to express feelings from their imagined frames of reference.

Analysis. Have students analyze the makeup of your class and congregation, considering whether issues of partiality or prejudice have had impact. Consider how observing "the royal law" (2:8) could bring change, and how disregard invites God's judgment (see 2:9-11).

Part Two. Read 2:12, 13; 4:11, 12, and then write on the board the following:

Attitude/Spirit

Judgmental	Merciful
Slanderous	Gracious
Arrogant	Humble

Discuss with the class how these perspectives are contrasted in the text. Then ask, "How does attitude influence relationships?" and, "How do selfishness and pride impact our opinion and judgment of others?" After five or six minutes of discussion read this humorous yet thought-provoking poem by C. R. Hemree:

I dreamed death came the other night;
And heaven's gates swung wide.
With kindly grace an angel
Ushered me inside.
And there, to my astonishment,
Stood folks I'd known on earth.
Some I'd judged and labeled
Unfit or of little worth.
Indignant words rose to my lips,
But never were set free;
For every face showed stunned surprise . . .
No one expected me!

Into Life

Class Project. Have the class brainstorm ways in which acceptance, graciousness, and love can be demonstrated toward *all* types of persons. *Be specific!* Focus, particularly, on practical steps your class can take to bring about change.

Closing. Form prayer circles of four or five each, joining hands with all but one, who is left to stand outside the circle. Then have groups pray that hearts will be moved to love and include *everyone* within the fellowship of God's family.

Let's Talk It Over

The questions on this page are designed to encourage review of the lesson Scriptures and to promote discussion of the lesson by the class. The answers provided are only discussion starters. Let your class talk it over from there.

1. Who are the people you believe would receive the warmest reception at your church, and who would receive the coldest reception? Why?

Partiality can be based on many issues. As in our text, it may have to do with money. Some people favor the rich; others resent the rich and favor the middle-class or the poor. With some, education is the issue; with others, it is race or place of birth or cultural background. Be brave enough to admit it, if there is partiality displayed in yourself, or by others in your church. Would a stranger be welcomed as quickly as the relative of a member? Would a wealthy professional be treated any differently from an hourly laborer or someone currently unemployed? Would a skeptical but inquiring sinner be as warmly received as a long-term believer?

2. We may agree that favoritism is morally repugnant, but how is it also counterproductive to our mission as Christians?

As Christians we have been commanded to make disciples of all people groups (Matthew 28:19, 20). When we show favoritism we send a false message that some people are valued more highly than others in God's kingdom. Those favored may get an exalted view of themselves and be filled with pride. Those neglected may react with disappointment or bitterness, and may have an even more difficult time accepting the message of God's love and forgiveness. The truth is that God loves every individual, and the gospel is good news for everyone who will believe. Can we make our treatment of others convey that truth?

3. The law of love demands more than tolerance. Genuine love will be evidenced in deeds. What evidence can you give of your love, or your church's love, for people unlike yourself?

Churches and individual Christians are learning to show love through several means. These include traditional benevolence ministries like providing food or clothing, but also more innovative helps like after-school activities for latchkey kids, child care programs, support groups for parents, single parents, the newly divorced, the grieving, singles ministries, English language classes, reading classes, and other efforts.

4. If favoritism is wrong, do we sin if we have special friends with whom we spend more time than we do with others?

If developing special friendships were a sin, then Jesus would be guilty. It seems that He spent more time with Peter, James, and John than He did with the other disciples. We may choose to invest time and interest in some special friendships, but we can also take care not to disregard others. The blessings of a few close friendships must not be a rationalization for ignoring others or treating them with haste or indifference.

5. Why is it so easy for Christians to fall into a judgmental attitude? What are the reasons why a Christian should be merciful toward others?

After investing great effort in learning and accepting Jesus' standards, one may find it easy to be harshly critical of the self-indulgent, permissive life-style of some unbelievers. Maintaining a merciful attitude requires that we remember (1) that we too are sinners dependent upon forgiveness, and (2) that the one who fails to show mercy will receive no mercy. Jesus said it very explicitly: "If you do not forgive men their sins, your Father will not forgive your sins" (Matthew 6:15, *New International Version*).

6. What do you believe constitutes speaking evil of another? Why is that so objectionable?

We would all agree that slander or malicious gossip is covered by the prohibition of verse 11. One of the Ten Commandments is "Thou shalt not bear false witness." To make an accusation based on suspicion or hearsay, or to pass along an unfounded rumor, is unfair and un-Christian. As we study our text further, however, we find that truth is not the only issue. The issue is how we speak of our fellow believers. Even though they may be guilty of something, it is not up to us to "try, convict, and sentence" them in our conversations with others. The New Testament contains clear teaching on proper ways of confronting a believer who sins (Matthew 18:15-17; 1 Corinthians 5; Galatians 6:1-5). Our conversation should be "good to the use of edifying, that it may minister grace unto the hearers" (Ephesians 4:29-32).

Faith and Action

Devotional Reading: Genesis 22:1-8.

Lesson Scripture: James 2:14-26; 5:7-20.

Printed Text: James 2:14-26; 5:13-16.

James 2:14-26

14 What doth it profit, my brethren, though a man say he hath faith, and have not works? can faith save him?

15 If a brother or sister be naked, and destitute of daily food,

16 And one of you say unto them, Depart in peace, be ye warmed and filled; notwithstanding ye give them not those things which are needful to the body; what doth it profit?

17 Even so faith, if it hath not works, is dead, being alone.

18 Yea, a man may say, Thou hast faith, and I have works: show me thy faith without thy works, and I will show thee my faith by my works.

19 Thou believest that there is one God; thou doest well: the devils also believe, and tremble.

20 But wilt thou know, O vain man, that faith without works is dead?

21 Was not Abraham our father justified by works, when he had offered Isaac his son upon the altar?

22 Seest thou how faith wrought with his works, and by works was faith made perfect?

23 And the Scripture was fulfilled which saith, Abraham believed God, and it was imputed unto him for righteousness: and he was called the Friend of God.

24 Ye see then how that by works a man is justified, and not by faith only.

25 Likewise also was not Rahab the harlot justified by works, when she had received the messengers, and had sent them out another way?

26 For as the body without the spirit is dead, so faith without works is dead also.

James 5:13-16

13 Is any among you afflicted? let him pray. Is any merry? let him sing psalms.

14 Is any sick among you? let him call for the elders of the church; and let them pray over him, anointing him with oil in the name of the Lord:

15 And the prayer of faith shall save the sick, and the Lord shall raise him up; and if he have committed sins, they shall be forgiven him.

16 Confess your faults one to another, and pray one for another, that ye may be healed. The effectual fervent prayer of a righteous man availeth much.

Golden Text: For as the body without the spirit is dead, so faith without works is dead also.—James 2:26.

A Practical Religion
(James)
(Lessons 1-5)

Lesson Aims

This lesson should allow students to:

1. Have a growing understanding that faith in Christ must be demonstrated by good works.

2. Come to a deeper appreciation of the importance of showing our faith by our service to others.

3. Be able to mention at least one act of service for Christ that he or she can perform.

Lesson Outline

INTRODUCTION
    A. Faith Without Works
    B. Lesson Background
 I. WORKS THE TEST OF FAITH (James 2:14-19)
    A. A Barren Faith Is Useless (v. 14)
    B. Faith Demonstrated (vv. 15-18)
       A Reality Check
    C. Even the Devils Believe (v. 19)
 II. FAITH AND WORKS TOGETHER (James 2:20-26)
    A. The Example of Abraham (vv. 20-23)
       No Chart but Faith
    B. Faith With Works (v. 24)
    C. The Example of Rahab (vv. 25, 26)
III. PRACTICAL APPLICATION (James 5:13-16)
    A. Prayer and Praise (v. 13)
    B. Caring for the Sick (vv. 14, 15)
       Oil, Faith, and Healing
    C. Confession and Prayer (v. 16)
CONCLUSION
    A. Faith Versus Works
    B. Let Us Pray
    C. Thought to Remember

The possession of faith requires more than mere profession of faith. This is the message of visual 3 of the visuals packet shown on page 364.

Introduction

A. Faith Without Works

When Hudson Taylor, founder of the China Inland Mission, made his first trip to China, he went on a sailing ship. The voyage brought him and his shipmates close to an island in the East Indies where a notorious tribe of cannibals lived. As they neared the island, the wind ceased to blow, and the ship lay motionless in the waters. Then the currents caused it to drift toward the island. As they drew closer, they could see the islanders watching them and anticipating a meal.

Knowing that Taylor was a missionary, the captain of the ship asked him to pray that God would send a breeze to carry them away from the island. "Certainly I will pray that God will send a breeze," responded Taylor, "but first you must set the sails to catch the wind." At first the captain was unwilling to change the sails until the wind started to blow, but as the ship continued to drift toward the island, he finally complied with the missionary's request. Almost as soon as the sails were unfurled, a favorable wind began to blow, and the ship moved to safe waters.

Taylor was a man of great faith, but he realized that prayer is meaningless unless one is willing to work also. His later ministry in China gave a powerful demonstration that he understood what James meant when he said, "Faith without works is dead."

B. Lesson Background

In today's lesson, as in the two previous lessons, James deals with a practical problem that the church in the first century faced. Faith in God is absolutely essential, but a faith that is completely intellectual without any commitment to service is useless. As James puts it, "Faith without works is dead."

In the first few months of its existence, the church in Jerusalem certainly understood this. When it became obvious that many of the members were in need, "all that believed were together, and had all things common; and sold their possessions and goods, and parted them to all men, as every man had need" (Acts 2:44, 45). Faith and works combined to see a problem and to solve it.

Apparently things changed in the years that followed. If the people had continued to demonstrate their faith by their works, James would not have had to write the admonition that we find in today's lesson. We don't know why this change came about, but we can offer some possible reasons. Very often new converts have a zeal and enthusiasm for their faith that older members lack. As time passes, so does the zeal. Perhaps the change came because many of the most zealous members of the Jerusalem church had been imprisoned or had fled from Jerusalem to escape persecution. In any event, James thought it necessary to remind his readers, whether in Jerusalem or among the "twelve tribes which are scattered abroad" (James 1:1), that faith cannot be separated from works.

I. Works the Test of Faith
(James 2:14-19)

A. A Barren Faith Is Useless (v. 14)

14. What doth it profit, my brethren, though a man say he hath faith, and have not works? can faith save him?

In this verse James returns to the subject he has dealt with in 1:22-27. Again he emphasizes the importance of practical Christian service. Some may have interpreted the doctrine of justification by faith to mean that Christian service is not required; or perhaps some had just become apathetic in doing what they knew to be right. In either case, it was important that such an error be pointed out and condemned, lest later generations accept it as right. *Can faith save him?* James raises a rhetorical question, the answer to which obviously is no. A faith that does not lead to good works is clearly not a saving faith.

B. Faith Demonstrated (vv. 15-18)

15, 16. If a brother or sister be naked, and destitute of daily food, and one of you say unto them, Depart in peace, be ye warmed and filled; notwithstanding ye give them not those things which are needful to the body; what doth it profit?

To make sure that no one misunderstands the point he is making, James gives his readers an example. To make the example more obvious, he mentions a brother or a sister, not a stranger, who is in need. Of course helping a stranger is no less proper than helping a brother or a sister. Instead of supplying what a person needs, a would-be benefactor may supply only words—pious words, of course: "Go in peace; may your needs be met. Praise the Lord!" One can almost hear the sarcasm dripping from James's words as he writes. It would be hard for anyone to miss the point.

There may be occasions when all we can offer or all that are needed are kind words. But James does not have this kind of a situation in mind. He is speaking to a situation in which a person has the means to give substantial help and gives only words instead.

17, 18. Even so faith, if it hath not works, is dead, being alone. Yea, a man may say, Thou hast faith, and I have works: show me thy faith without thy works, and I will show thee my faith by my works.

A good Christian does not have either faith without works or works without faith. James is saying that the best way for a person to show his faith in Christ is by doing the kinds of things Christ teaches His people to do. That proposition

seems fair enough. We can test our own faith by it, but we must exercise care in evaluating other people's ministry by what we see them doing. One person's ministry may be in a public arena that everyone can see. Another may be called to serve quietly in some obscure spot. Only God knows which one is demonstrating the greater faith.

A REALITY CHECK

For some time a television news program used part of its time for what was called a "reality check." Various claims, assumptions, and emphases made by political or business leaders were examined to see if things they asserted were actually true. There can be rosy promises or optimistic rhetoric about all an orphanage is doing for neglected, abandoned, or abused children. However, what does an open-eyed inspection of the actual living conditions and treatment of the residents of the institution reveal?

We find James saying that it is one thing to tell people, "Be ye warmed and filled," but if we don't really provide heat and nourishment for them, we are offering only words—not deeds. We are devising fantasies instead of realities. I think it was Phoebe Cary (1824-71), now almost a forgotten poet, who wrote:

> When a man can live apart
> From works, on theologic trust,
> I know the blood about his heart
> Is dry as dust.

Our faith in Jesus should lead us to bring to men good news about how sin can be forgiven, new life in God begun, and noble and uplifting character formed.
—J. G. V. B.

C. Even the Devils Believe (v. 19)

19. Thou believest that there is one God; thou doest well: the devils also believe, and tremble.

The position that James seeks to make clear is that the issue being discussed is not the content of one's faith; it is whether one translates his or her faith into action. To illustrate this point, James uses the touchstone of the Jewish faith—the belief in one God: "Hear, O Israel: The Lord our God is one Lord" (Deuteronomy 6:4). *The devils* ("demons" in most modern translations) are allies of Satan, opposed to everything Christ stands for. They certainly believe in God, whom they consider the archenemy; but just as certainly they are not going to obey Him. For this reason their belief in God leads only to fear and trembling. James challenges his readers to move beyond this level of faith to a faith that produces useful fruit.

II. Faith and Works Together
(James 2:20-26)

A. The Example of Abraham (vv. 20-23)

20, 21. But wilt thou know, O vain man, that faith without works is dead? Was not Abraham our father justified by works, when he had offered Isaac his son upon the altar?

Abraham's whole life was a picture of trust in God. The writer of the epistle to the Hebrews extols his faith in some detail (Hebrews 11:8-12). The one incident in the life of Abraham that James chooses to emphasize is God's order for him to sacrifice his son Isaac. It is difficult for us to imagine a greater test of faith than this. Not only was human sacrifice repugnant to Abraham, but God was asking him to sacrifice his only son who could lead to the fulfillment of the covenant; or at least, that is the way Abraham must have looked at it. No matter how difficult this test was, Abraham obeyed God and passed it with flying colors.

22, 23. Seest thou how faith wrought with his works, and by works was faith made perfect? And the Scripture was fulfilled which saith, Abraham believed God, and it was imputed unto him for righteousness: and he was called the Friend of God.

Faith and works are not in opposition to one another: they complement one another. Works, in order to be acceptable to God, must be based on faith in Him. Faith, if it is to be saving faith, must result in a life committed to works for the glory of God.

The Scripture that James quotes is Genesis 15:6. The previous verse records that God sends Abraham out to look at the starry heavens and asks him to count the stars. He then assures him that his seed will be as numerous as the stars. At that time Abraham saw no way the promise could be fulfilled, for he had no children. In spite of this, Abraham believed.

Imputed means reckoned or counted. This does not mean that Abraham's obedience atoned for earlier sins. Rather, God, in His infinite wisdom and mercy, chose to count him righteous

because he believed God and obeyed Him. As Christians we share in God's mercy, for the blood of Christ brings us this same imputation of righteousness if our faith issues in obedience as did the faith of Abraham.

Because Abraham believed God and obeyed Him, Abraham *was called the Friend of God* (Isaiah 41:8). We can enjoy a similar friendship if we also trust and obey. To His disciples Jesus said, "Ye are my friends, if ye do whatsoever I command you" (John 15:14).

NO CHART BUT FAITH

Columbus found a world, and had no chart,
Save one that faith deciphered in the skies.
                    —George Santayana

It is true there was no chart to guide Columbus on his heroic western voyage. There was a conviction that land lay out there beyond the miles and miles of tossing water. Neither he nor any of his crew knew absolutely that this was true until the land finally came into view.

It was the "work" of sailing that made "perfect" the "faith" in the reality of the western land. The *New International Version* translates verse 22, "You see that his faith and his actions were working together, and his faith was made complete by what he did."

In our lives we must act upon faith in the biblical testimony to Jesus' life, death, and resurrection. We believe in the God "whom no man hath seen, nor can see" (1 Timothy 6:16). We walk and work by faith and not by sight. However, as we obey Jesus and do what He tells us we become increasingly assured about His salvation. As Jesus asserted, "If anyone chooses to do God's will, he will find out whether my teaching comes from God or whether I speak on my own" (John 7:17, *New International Version*). Obedience validates faith.   —J. G. V. B.

B. Faith With Works (v. 24)

24. Ye see then how that by works a man is justified, and not by faith only.

James concludes by affirming once again his basic position that a person is not justified by faith alone. We need to understand, however, that he is not saying one can be saved by works alone. His emphasis is that one cannot be saved by a dead, lifeless, intellectual faith that does not issue in a holy life, given to benevolence.

C. The Example of Rahab (vv. 25, 26)

25, 26. Likewise also was not Rahab the harlot justified by works, when she had received the messengers, and had sent them out another way? For as the body without the spirit is dead, so faith without works is dead also.

As the body without the spirit is dead, so faith without works is dead also.
James 2:26

visual 3

James might very well have concluded his argument with verse 24, but he chose instead to strengthen his position by citing another example in which a person was saved by faith and works. The example he chose may at first thought seem inappropriate. Rahab was a prostitute in the city of Jericho. She saved the lives of the Israelite spies who slipped into the city (Joshua 2). James does not hold up her earlier life as a model to be followed by others, but her faith changed her way of life. The point that James makes is that she believed in the God of the Israelites enough to risk her life to save them. From this example a person may draw the conclusion that salvation by faith and works is not limited only to the Israelite people, and that conclusion is verified by Jesus' commission to His disciples (Matthew 28:19, 20).

III. Practical Application (James 5:13-16)

A. Prayer and Praise (v. 13)

13. Is any among you afflicted? let him pray. Is any merry? let him sing psalms.

James closes his epistle very much as he began it, by dealing with trials and suffering. *Afflicted.* This term is broad enough to cover any problem or disaster. It certainly includes those who were suffering because of their faith, but it can also include those suffering from illness, poverty, or business loss.

For those who were suffering difficult times, his solution was not to grumble or engage in an extended pity party. Instead, James suggested that they *pray.* Such a prayer might be that the cause of the suffering be removed, or it might be that one would bear the suffering with strength and grace.

Serving the Lord is not always a painful experience. Sometimes it brings joy. Such happy occasions should give rise to singing, either as a part of congregational worship or in personal songs as one goes about his or her work. Christianity, more than any other religion, is a singing religion. Some of the world's greatest music has arisen as persons have sought to express their love of God through music.

B. Caring for the Sick (vv. 14, 15)

14. Is any sick among you? let him call for the elders of the church; and let them pray over him, anointing him with oil in the name of the Lord.

Today we probably offer more prayers for the sick than for persons suffering any other affliction. In many congregations it is considered a duty of the elders as well as the minister to visit the sick. *Let him call for the elders.* Sometimes elders and ministers are criticized because they do not always carry out this ministry, but they may fail because they are not aware of all the illnesses in the congregation. The ill person has a responsibility to inform the leaders of his or her need. Anyone who has experienced an illness knows how encouraging and helpful visits and prayers can be. Jesus encouraged such visits when He said, "I was sick, and ye visited me" (Matthew 25:36).

Anointing him with oil. These words have stirred no little controversy. Some have held that the anointing carries almost miraculous powers of healing. Others see it as a medical treatment. The skin of one who has been ill, especially one who has suffered a high fever, may be dry and cracked. The oil is a soothing balm to hasten healing.

15. And the prayer of faith shall save the sick, and the Lord shall raise him up; and if he have committed sins, they shall be forgiven him.

Prayer can open us to receive the power of God. We must not understand this verse in the absolute sense—that God will restore to health every person over whom we pray. Every prayer that we utter must come within the framework of God's will. Jesus in His ministry did not heal every sick person in Palestine. Apparently it was not God's will that all be healed. Even though we don't understand this, yet if we pray with faith we will accept it.

Like the healing, the forgiveness of sins is conditional. Forgiveness requires repentance on the part of the sinner. Serious illness can bring a person face to face with his own mortality. Under these conditions, one is likely to repent and turn to God. Many times, however, those who repent under these conditions soon fall back into their sinful ways. We may be able to prevent this by continuing our encouragement and prayers.

OIL, FAITH, AND HEALING

C. T. Studd was a remarkable British athlete and deeply committed Christian who did missionary work in China, India, Africa, and the United States. In 1885 he was on an extended trip into interior China, walking more than twenty miles a day. One of his feet became infected. In his account Studd wrote, "Though I rested it, it would not heal, but got very puffy and discharged a good deal. So I asked Hogg [one of his companions] if he would anoint me with oil in the name of the Lord. . . . He hesitated at first, but we read James 5 together and prayed about it, and then he said he could see no reason against it, and did so. Since then my foot has got most rapidly better."

Many diverse views are taken of this "anointing" passage in James 5:14. It is true that oil often was used as a medicinal agent in biblical times, as it is today. Christians often combine medical treatment with prayer. Many times God honors the "prayer of faith" to "save the sick." However, it is still true that "it is appointed unto men once to die" (Hebrews 9:27). As did our Lord, we submit ourselves to the will of our heavenly Father.   —J. G. V. B.

C. Confession and Prayer (v. 16)

16. Confess your faults one to another, and pray one for another, that ye may be healed. The effectual fervent prayer of a righteous man availeth much.

Much suffering does come as a direct result of a sinful life-style, yet we must recognize that the innocent often have to suffer through no fault of their own. We know that many illnesses are due in part to the wrong kinds of mental attitudes. When one has cleansed one's soul by the confession of sins, that person's body is given a better chance to regain its strength. The latter part of this verse is more clearly translated by the *New International Version:* "The prayer of a righteous man is powerful and effective."

Conclusion

A. Faith Versus Works

The argument about whether we are saved by faith or by good works has gone on for centuries. Jesus had to face this in His ministry. Many of the Jewish leaders, especially the Pharisees, taught that one is saved by observing the law, including the countless regulations they had added to the law of Moses. Often their concern for the law was a cover to hide their greed, a cloak that Jesus on several occasions pulled aside.

Later in the early church when Gentiles became Christians, some of the Jewish Christians began to object. These Judaizers, as they were called, insisted that Gentiles had to conform to the Mosaic law besides being Christians. It was in this context that Paul insisted that salvation is by faith, not works of the law. This issue was discussed at the Jerusalem conference about A.D. 50. At that meeting Paul's view prevailed (Acts 15:1-29).

This did not end the matter with Paul. In his Roman epistle, Paul set forth very emphatically that salvation is by grace through faith. "Where sin abounded, grace did much more abound"

(Romans 5:20). Some seized upon this as permission to sin freely "that grace may abound" (Romans 6:1). Paul disposed of this idea just as emphatically, insisting that a faith that did not result in a new life was not a saving faith at all (Romans 6:2-4).

Several centuries later, some church officials restated the idea of salvation by works. They said a person could have his sins removed by paying money, going on a pilgrimage, or doing some other act of penance. To this error Martin Luther found the answer in Romans 1:17: "The just shall live by faith." Luther was so devoted to this truth that he had trouble with the book of James. For a time it seemed that James was contradicting Paul. But a close study shows that there is no contradiction; the two men were simply emphasizing different parts of the truth that both of them believed: We are justified by faith (Romans 5:1), but faith cannot live without works (James 2:17). So one is justified by works as well as faith, and not by faith alone (James 2:24).

B. Let Us Pray

We thank You, O Father, for showing us the way of salvation, a way that requires us to believe in You and to trust in You so that we can walk the path of holiness that You have set before us. May our faith in You never become just an intellectual thing, inactive and dead. Show us instead the ways by which we can serve You by serving our fellowmen. Teach us to sing, "O Master, let me walk with Thee in lowly paths of service free." In the name of our Master, who came as a lowly servant, amen.

C. Thought to Remember

Creed without deed leaves a person in need.

Home Daily Bible Readings

Monday, June 10—Faith Tested (Genesis 22:9-14)

Tuesday, June 11—The Least of These (Matthew 25:31-46)

Wednesday, June 12—Blessed by Faith (Galatians 3:6-14)

Thursday, June 13—A Hero of Faith (Joshua 2:1-14)

Friday, June 14—Sustained by Faith (Hebrews 11:29-39)

Saturday, June 15—Futility of Legal Works (Galatians 5:2-12)

Sunday, June 16—Faith and Authority (Mark 6:7-13)

Learning by Doing

This page contains an alternate lesson plan emphasizing learning activities. Classes desiring such student involvement will find these suggestions helpful.

Learning Goals

Through the study of this lesson you will help your students:

1. Understand the teachings of James and Paul regarding faith, works, and salvation.

2. Appreciate the vital link between faith (belief) and works (deeds) in Christian life.

3. Cite past and current examples of how genuine faith is translated into practical deeds.

Into the Lesson

Put the following Scripture references on the board or on a poster. Do not include the words that follow the references, but leave blank spaces. Ask students to study the Scriptures and make a list of persons and things by which we are saved or justified.

Who or What Saves Us?

Romans 8:33 God	Romans 3:24 grace
Matthew 1:21 Jesus	Romans 5:1 faith
Romans 5:9 blood	Romans 8:24 hope
1 Corinthians 15:1, 2 gospel	Acts 2:40 selves

If you want this to be done more quickly, assign each reference to one person or pair or group so all the Scripture references can be found at the same time. Students may write the answers on the board as they find them, or call them out and let you write them.

If questions arise about the words *saved* and *justified*, you can point out that these are two features of the same event. When God forgives us, our sins are taken away and we are justified: that is, we are made just or righteous. By the same forgiveness we are saved from sin and Satan and Hell. Everyone who is justified is saved, and everyone who is saved is justified.

Explain that our salvation is accomplished by God and Jesus. The grace that saves us is their grace, their favor that we do not deserve. The blood that saves us is Jesus' blood, shed when He accepted the punishment for our sins so we can be forgiven. God and Jesus provide the gospel, the good news that salvation is available.

Still Peter could say, "Save yourselves." We will not be saved unless we ourselves believe in Jesus. The faith that saves us is our faith; the hope that saves us is our hope. In this lesson we shall see more about our part in our own salvation.

Into the Word

Step One: Divide the class into groups of four to six. Ask each group to pick one of the following activities. Copy directions on a card for each group, and be sure each option is done by at least one group. Supply paper and markers as needed, and allow fifteen minutes for the work.

Option 1

Read James 2:14-26 and compare it with Paul's statement in Ephesians 2:8, 9. Discuss these questions: (1) Do you see why some people think James's teaching contradicts Paul's statement? (2) Does saying you have faith prove that you really do have it? If not, how do you prove that your faith is real? (3) How do good works give life to faith? (4) Can you show that the teachings of Paul and James are in harmony? Choose one of your group to explain this to the class, and help that person prepare his or her explanation.

Option 2

Read James 2:14-26 and then write a modern short story illustrating verses 14-16. Appoint someone as scribe, but brainstorm plot and action together. Have an artist or two sketch illustrations for your story. If you prefer, put it in the form of a drama that you can act out for the class.

Option 3

Read James 2:14-26 and then work together to write a short poem about Abraham's action-filled faith, and another poem about Rahab's. For more about Rahab, see Joshua 2:1-21; 6:15-25; Hebrews 11:31. For Abraham, see Genesis 22:1-18; Hebrews 11:17-19.

Step Two: Give three-minute and one-minute warnings for groups to finish their activities. Then let those who chose options 2 and 3 present their projects. Follow with the explanations from groups with option 1.

Step Three: Read James 5:13-16 and briefly discuss how prayer, praise, caring, and confession are practical expressions of faith.

Into Life

Read James 2:24 and add one more item to your list of things by which we are saved: *James 2:24 Good Works.* Ask the students to work together to build a list of practical ways in which their faith may be complemented by good works this week. Close with prayer.

Let's Talk It Over

The questions on this page are designed to encourage review of the lesson Scriptures and to promote discussion of the lesson by the class. The answers provided are only discussion starters. Let your class talk it over from there.

1. Give examples of occasions when you or your church responded to help a fellow believer. How was that a demonstration of faith?

Most churches have some plan for meeting material needs among the members. Some typical means are maintaining a food pantry or giving vouchers to a grocery store, maintaining a benevolence fund for distribution as needs arise, establishing an information network for those seeking employment, collecting and refurbishing used furniture for those who need it, and announcing a special offering when a crisis occurs. Hopefully you can recount the joy of participating in one or more of these efforts to meet a genuine need. To be generous in the face of need is in keeping with the example and teaching of Jesus, but it is contrary to human selfishness. Unselfish service, then, provides testimony of the sincerity of our faith in Jesus and our desire to follow Him.

2. Why is it reasonable to expect people of faith to behave differently from the rest of the world? What is reasonable to expect?

The foundation of Christianity is personal faith in Jesus as the Christ, the Son of God, the promised Savior. If we believe that Jesus is the divine Son of God, and if we are trusting in Him for forgiveness and eternal life, then it seems reasonable to apply seriously His teachings and commands. He said, "If ye love me, keep my commandments" (John 14:15). The behavior we expect of believers is increasing conformity to the teaching and example of Jesus.

3. What level of belief in God do devils possess? Why is that less than saving faith?

The devils, or demons, know God exists; but they have chosen to seek their own will, and have set themselves in opposition to God. People who say they believe, but who disregard God's will, have a faith similar to that of devils.

4. Abraham showed his faith when he obeyed God and offered Isaac. What demonstrations of faith does God desire in our lives?

When the disciples preached the gospel publicly, there were many who believed the message. They came under a strong conviction of their sin and their need for forgiveness. Peter told them to repent and be baptized in the name of Jesus (Acts 2:38). We understand this as an authoritative word for every generation. Repentance and submission to baptism are evidence of saving faith. Repentance literally means a change of mind. Practically it means learning to seek and apply the will of God at every turn instead of following personal whim or natural inclination. Repentance involves some change that can be noticed. Instead of offering another, as Abraham did, we present ourselves as a living sacrifice to God (Romans 12:1). Our baptism is symbolic of burial and resurrection: burial of the old person, resurrection of the new creation in Christ (Romans 6:3, 4; 2 Corinthians 5:17). Beyond our baptism, every act of obedience is added evidence of our faith.

5. If good works are an evidence of faith, so is prayer. What kind of prayer life testifies to a strong faith? What results can we expect from our prayers?

If we believe in God as the Almighty, able to intervene in the course of events, able to restore health, and able to preserve life, then it is logical that we should address Him when circumstances trouble us. Part of our prayer, however, should be "Thy will be done." The best outcome of a situation may not be what we first guess. Our preference may not coincide with the will of God. Still, we should never give up praying. The promise is that the fervent prayer of a righteous person will accomplish much.

6. Why is confessing our faults to one another mentioned with prayer and healing? Is there any practical advantage to this?

As Christians we take great comfort in the fact that Jesus is our high priest and intercessor. We can confess our sins directly and receive forgiveness (Hebrews 4:14-16; 1 John 1:8, 9). We do not believe that every illness is God's punishment for sin, but that much suffering does result from sinful habits, and a guilty conscience from concealed sin will inhibit healing. To confide in a trusted Christian friend and ask him or her to pray for you does have a practical advantage. Confession relieves anxiety, and having a partner in prayer gives increased power and an added motive for resisting temptation.

Faith and Wisdom

DEVOTIONAL READING: Job 28:12-18, 23-28.

LESSON SCRIPTURE: James 1:5-8; 3:1-5a, 13-18.

PRINTED TEXT: James 1:5-8; 3:1-5a, 13-18.

James 1:5-8

5 If any of you lack wisdom, let him ask of God, that giveth to all men liberally, and upbraideth not; and it shall be given him.

6 But let him ask in faith, nothing wavering: for he that wavereth is like a wave of the sea driven with the wind and tossed.

7 For let not that man think that he shall receive any thing of the Lord.

8 A double-minded man is unstable in all his ways.

James 3:1-5a

1 My brethren, be not many masters, knowing that we shall receive the greater condemnation.

2 For in many things we offend all. If any man offend not in word, the same is a perfect man, and able also to bridle the whole body.

3 Behold, we put bits in the horses' mouths, that they may obey us; and we turn about their whole body.

4 Behold also the ships, which though they be so great, and are driven of fierce winds, yet are they turned about with a very small helm, whithersoever the governor listeth.

5a Even so the tongue is a little member, and boasteth great things.

. . . .

13 Who is a wise man and endued with knowledge among you? let him show out of a good conversation his works with meekness of wisdom.

14 But if ye have bitter envying and strife in your hearts, glory not, and lie not against the truth.

15 This wisdom descendeth not from above, but is earthly, sensual, devilish.

16 For where envying and strife is, there is confusion and every evil work.

17 But the wisdom that is from above is first pure, then peaceable, gentle, and easy to be entreated, full of mercy and good fruits, without partiality, and without hypocrisy.

18 And the fruit of righteousness is sown in peace of them that make peace.

GOLDEN TEXT: Who is a wise man and endued with knowledge among you? let him show out of a good conversation his works with meekness of wisdom.
—James 3:13.

A Practical Religion
(James)
(Lessons 1-5)

Lesson Aims

After this lesson, each student should:

1. Have a better understanding of the importance of wisdom in our relationship both with God and with those about us.

2. Have a growing appreciation for the part wisdom can play in making this a better world.

3. Appreciate the fact that true wisdom comes from the study of God's Word.

Lesson Outline

INTRODUCTION
   A. Wisdom Can Be Lost
   B. Lesson Background
 I. WISDOM FOR THOSE WHO ASK (James 1:5-8)
   A. God Is the Source of Wisdom (v. 5)
     Our Instruction Manual
   B. One Must Ask in Faith (vv. 6-8)
II. THE POWER OF THE TONGUE (James 3:1-5a)
   A. Caution to Teachers (v. 1)
   B. Complete Maturity (v. 2)
   C. Example of Horses (v. 3)
   D. Example of Ships (v. 4)
   E. The Tongue, Small but Mighty (v. 5a)
     Timely Truths About the Tongue
III. THE FRUITS OF WISDOM (James 3:13-18)
   A. Wisdom Shown in a Good Life (v. 13)
   B. Strife Shows Lack of Wisdom (v. 14)
   C. Results of False Wisdom (vv. 15, 16)
   D. Marks of True Wisdom (vv. 17, 18)
     Two Kinds of Wisdom
CONCLUSION
   A. Too Many Teachers
   B. Whose Wisdom?
   C. Let Us Pray
   D. Thought to Remember

Not all "wisdom" is truly wise; only the wisdom that originates in God qualifies. That is the theme of visual 4 shown on page 373.

Introduction

A. Wisdom Can Be Lost

When Solomon came to the throne of Israel, he was young and inexperienced. In Gibeon, God appeared to him in a dream and offered him whatever blessing he might choose. Solomon might have asked for long life or riches. He asked instead for wisdom to rule his people well. This choice pleased God, who granted him both wisdom and riches, plus long life if he would walk in God's ways.

Solomon demonstrated his wisdom in many ways, and soon his reputation as a wise ruler spread to neighboring lands. The queen of Sheba heard these reports and came to visit. As a result she said, "The half was not told me: thy wisdom and prosperity exceedeth the fame which I heard" (1 Kings 10:7).

Unfortunately, wisdom is not a once for all gift. It can be lost, and that's exactly what happened to Solomon. As he grew older, many things began to distract him—his building activities, his growing wealth and business enterprises, and his many wives and their pagan religions. Solomon's experience was not unique. Most of us have known persons who lived prudently for most of their lives, and then seemed to abandon wisdom in their later years. We have a saying for it: "No fool like an old fool."

Wisdom is a precious gift, valuable to those who possess it and to all those about them. Solomon's example should warn us, however, that such a gift must be guarded and nurtured lest we lose it.

B. Lesson Background

In last week's lesson the apostle James dealt with faith and works. He said faith that does not lead to good works is not saving faith. From the emphasis he gives this issue, it seems apparent that this was a problem in the early church. Throughout the centuries the church has had to deal with this problem, and still must cope with it. Thus the admonitions of James are quite relevant.

In this week's lesson James deals with another problem. Too many persons wanted to be teachers. Most churches today don't have this problem. Our problem is just the opposite: we have trouble finding enough teachers! One reason for the difference is that in the early church teachers were given considerable respect. No doubt some were attracted to the office because of the prestige attached to it. At times teaching became a lucrative profession, especially if a teacher could attract a large following.

Whatever may have been James's concern about teachers, the standards he set for them are certainly applicable today as well. A teacher, above all, should be well-grounded in the faith. He or she should lead a life that is a model for students and for others. A teacher's life should exemplify wisdom, wisdom that is based on the Word of God.

I. Wisdom for Those Who Ask
(James 1:5-8)

A. God Is the Source of Wisdom (v. 5)

5. If any of you lack wisdom, let him ask of God, that giveth to all men liberally, and upbraideth not; and it shall be given him.

In this chapter, James talks quite a bit about trials and temptations. Thus it is reasonable to suppose that the wisdom he has in mind deals with how Christians may find joy in the midst of trials. Most of us would rather complain about our suffering than rejoice in it. After all, how can one gain much sympathy from others while he is rejoicing in his hardships?

Rejoicing over suffering does not come easy. Indeed, we need to have wisdom from God, if we are to rise to that level of Christian maturity. We also need a great deal of wisdom to accept the fact that often we bring suffering upon ourselves by our sins or our foolishness. Such wisdom comes from God through the Scriptures. It is available to those who prayerfully seek it.

OUR INSTRUCTION MANUAL

An Instruction Manual comes with each new automobile. The vehicle represents the abilities of engineers to plan and to produce an outstanding machine. We look at it from tires to rooftop, from bumper to bumper—the product of the combined knowledge of the people who produced it.

However, the wisdom to use this complex mechanism is detailed in the Instruction Manual. How do we turn the lights on and off? Where is the hand brake? Where is the control for the turn signals? All these and scores of other instructions are in the Instruction Manual. With them we are able to start and stop, to steer and back up.

James says we need to ask of God to receive wisdom. We have God's Instruction Manual in the Bible. God's creative ability has given us the whole fabric of humanity: the body, the human associations, the ability to know, love, move, rest, and express our intelligence and affections. God has also told us how to use all this so it will operate with effectiveness. The Instruction Manual is the place we look for the wisdom God gives so liberally and clearly.   —J. G. V. B.

B. One Must Ask in Faith (vv. 6-8)

6. But let him ask in faith, nothing wavering: for he that wavereth is like a wave of the sea driven with the wind and tossed.

Anyone who comes to God asking a favor must come in faith. "He that cometh to God must believe that he is, and that he is a rewarder of them that diligently seek him" (Hebrews 11:6). Throughout this epistle James uses graphic figures to make his points. Such is the case here. A person who doubts is like *a wave of the sea*. Like a wave, the unstable person is driven this way and that, first on a high and then wallowing in the trough of despair.

7, 8. For let not that man think that he shall receive any thing of the Lord. A double-minded man is unstable in all his ways.

One who doubts stands in danger of losing his blessings from the Lord. There are honest doubters like Thomas (John 20:24-29). He was willing to believe, but he needed evidence. God provided it to Thomas, and in His Word He provides it to us.

Some doubters, however, are cynical and even arrogant in their unbelief. The Pharisees, Jesus' most aggressive enemies during His ministry, displayed this kind of doubt. Many of them had witnessed His miracles, but this only entrenched them in their unbelief. Their minds were so closed that no amount of evidence would change them.

Then there are some who just can't make up their minds. *Double-minded* means unstable or wavering. It described some who were wavering in the face of persecution, but it also describes any person whose faith is not stable regardless of the circumstances.

II. The Power of the Tongue
(James 3:1-5a)

A. Caution to Teachers (v. 1)

1. My brethren, be not many masters, knowing that we shall receive the greater condemnation.

Masters here means teachers. Teachers were held in high esteem among Jews. To be called a rabbi was to receive a title of honor and respect. It was an honor that was not conferred lightly. For one thing, a teacher had to spend many years in preparation, years that involved hard study and discipline.

It is not surprising that many would seek such an honorable office. From James's warning, we gather that some had sought it who were not worthy of it or who were not prepared to fill it in a responsible fashion. Some desired to become teachers for selfish reasons. In the first century many teachers traveled about, using their skills to take advantage of the people, little caring that their false teaching might lead people astray. James warned them: *knowing that we shall receive the greater condemnation.* Teachers must bear the responsibility for what they teach and the impact their teaching has on their students. One who teaches false doctrine that leads souls astray will be accountable when he or she stands before the judgment seat of God.

B. Complete Maturity (v. 2)

2. For in many things we offend all. If any man offend not in word, the same is a perfect man, and able also to bridle the whole body.

The word here translated *offend* may mean to sin, or it may mean to stumble or to make a mistake. Mistakes, even honest ones, can lead to unhappy consequences as serious as those of malicious sins. In the immediate context, James has reference to those who would become teachers. Those who make no mistakes in what they say are *perfect,* which means mature or complete. A mark of maturity is that one is in control of oneself. If a person is mature enough to make no mistakes in what he or she says, that person is not likely to make mistakes in what he or she does either.

C. Example of Horses (v. 3)

3. Behold, we put bits in the horses' mouths, that they may obey us; and we turn about their whole body.

To illustrate his point further, James uses an example that everyone would understand. A horse weighing several hundred pounds can be controlled by a bit that weighs only a few ounces. In the same way, the tongue can control the whole person. We understand, of course, that the rider actually controls the horse by using the bit. In the same way, the mind is behind the tongue, directing what it says.

D. Example of Ships (v. 4)

4. Behold also the ships, which though they be so great, and are driven of fierce winds, yet are they turned about with a very small helm, whithersoever the governor listeth.

Compared to the size of a ship, a rudder is very small. Yet it gives direction to the ship even in violent winds. The *governor* or helmsman can control a ship weighing hundreds or even thousands of tons.

E. The Tongue, Small but Mighty (v. 5a)

5a. Even so the tongue is a little member, and boasteth great things.

James now applies the two illustrations. The bit and the rudder are both small compared to the size of what they control. In the same way, the tiny tongue has tremendous power over the entire person. One who speaks hastily or carelessly or angrily may find oneself committed to doing things he or she should not do.

TIMELY TRUTHS ABOUT THE TONGUE

James just mentions the importance of the tongue in verse 5 and develops the theme in verses 6-13. Though this latter material is not in our printed text, this reference to the tongue may be enough to lead us to a survey of several wise statements about this "little member" of our bodies.

"Keep thy tongue from evil, and thy lips from speaking guile" (Psalm 34:13).

"A fool's tongue is always long enough to cut his own throat" (English proverb, 1732).

"Keep your tongue a prisoner and your body will go free" (Scottish proverb).

> "But far more numerous was the herd of such,
> Who think too little and who talk too much"
>   (Dryden, 1682).

"The tongue is but three inches long, but it can kill a man six feet high" (Japanese proverb).

"Think all you speak, but speak not all you think" (Patrick Delany, died 1768).

> "If wisdom's ways you widely seek,
>   Five things observe with care,
> *Of* whom you speak, *to* whom you speak,
>   And *how,* and *when,* and *where*"
>   (Anonymous)

"By examining the tongue, physicians find out the diseases of the body, and philosophers the diseases of the mind and heart" (Justin, c.100-105).

"It has been said ten commandments have been given as the foundations for moral and religious life. Of these, two concern the tongue: 'You shall not take the name of the Lord your God in vain' and 'You shall not bear false witness against your neighbor'" (ascribed to Bishop Leighton, 1811-84).   —J. G. V. B.

III. The Fruits of Wisdom (James 3:13-18)

A. Wisdom Shown in a Good Life (v. 13)

13. Who is a wise man and endued with knowledge among you? let him show out of a good conversation his works with meekness of wisdom.

James may have reference to teachers mentioned in verse 1, but certainly the verse has a more general application. The evidence of wisdom is seen in how one lives. *Conversation* includes more than one's speech. In King James English it refers to every aspect of a person's life. A humble life is clear evidence of wisdom. One who has a great deal of knowledge is tempted to become proud, but true wisdom is not compatible with an arrogant, know-it-all attitude.

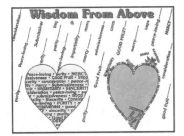

visual 4

B. Strife Shows Lack of Wisdom (v. 14)

14. But if ye have bitter envying and strife in your hearts, glory not, and lie not against the truth.

A teacher who is arrogant is likely to have *envying and strife* in his heart. His attitude creates a party spirit among his students. Some copy his arrogance; some rebel against it. It is likely that James had seen some of this in the church.

This problem does not belong exclusively to those who propagate false doctrine. It is quite possible for one who tells the truth to display a narrow, factious spirit that leads to strife. Paul urges us to speak "the truth in love" (Ephesians 4:15). When we confront those who are in error, we must do so with gentleness and humility, always showing love toward the person who is in error. All too often in religious disputes we are more concerned about winning a victory than about advancing the cause of truth.

C. Results of False Wisdom (vv. 15, 16)

15, 16. This wisdom descendeth not from above, but is earthly, sensual, devilish. For where envying and strife is, there is confusion and every evil work.

God is not the source of the kind of wisdom that makes one arrogant and contentious. Such wisdom is *earthly* in its origins, arising from selfish desires. These desires are demonic in that they lead to envy, strife, and discord, not to the peace and harmony God desires. Satan has no more effective weapon to hinder the work of God's kingdom than strife among Christians. It leads to *every evil work.*

Over the past two thousand years of its existence, the church has been hampered by discord and division. In some situations it has been necessary for believers to separate themselves from faithless leaders or churches; but all too often strife has been caused by pride and jealousy. No wonder that Jesus prayed for the unity of His followers (John 17:20, 21). The world desperately needs the message of salvation that Christ offers, but it will not be able to hear that message very well as long as we are fighting among ourselves.

D. Marks of True Wisdom

(vv. 17, 18)

17, 18. But the wisdom that is from above is first pure, then peaceable, gentle, and easy to be entreated, full of mercy and good fruits, without partiality, and without hypocrisy. And the fruit of righteousness is sown in peace of them that make peace.

After listing some of the marks of worldly wisdom, James now turns to *wisdom that is from above.* This wisdom is first of all *pure,* that is, it is free from worldly contamination. Since it is free from personal ambition that characterizes worldly wisdom, it is *peaceable,* free from the strife that so often accompanies the wrong kind of ambition. It is *gentle,* willing to go the second mile to avoid conflict. *Easy to be entreated* does not describe one who is driven to and fro by every wind of doctrine, but one who is willing to listen to others and weigh the evidence. Such a person does not hesitate to change his or her mind in the face of compelling evidence. A person who has heavenly wisdom is able to make decisions *without partiality.* This harks back to what James has written in chapter 2, forbidding Christians to show favoritism.

Seed that is sown produces fruit after its own kind. Those who make peace are sowing the kind of seed that produces righteousness. It is difficult for righteousness to flourish in the midst of strife. But when peace is made without giving up truth or right, there is a climate where righteousness can come to full fruition.

TWO KINDS OF WISDOM

John Oxenham wrote these perceptive lines:

> But to every man there openeth
> A high way and a low,
> And every man decideth
> The way his soul shall go.

Presented in Psalm 1 is the contrast between the man who walks in "the counsel of the ungodly" and the one whose "delight is in the law of the Lord." Jesus spoke of the decision that had to be made between the broad road "that leads to destruction" and the narrow road that "leads to life" (Matthew 7:13, 14, *New International Version*).

James presents the distinction between the wisdom that is "earthly, sensual, devilish" and the wisdom that is "from above." This wisdom is pure, peaceful, gentle. The one wisdom engenders confusion and every evil work, while the other results in mercy, good fruits, and peace.

It takes intelligence to develop a bomb—a knowledge of explosives and wiring and trigger mechanisms. This work of intelligent organization is meant to destroy, to harm, to maim, and to kill. Its detonation is a victory for hatred, bitterness, and vindictiveness.

On the other hand, it requires wisdom to learn ways of bringing enlightenment to minds yearning for truth, to bring healing to sickly bodies, or to bring harmony where there has been discord. Let us choose and use the wisdom that is "from above."   —J. G. V. B.

Conclusion

A. Too Many Teachers

From James's remarks we conclude that the church had an unusual problem. It had too many teachers! At least it had too many people who wanted to be teachers. Most churches today wish they had such a problem. We seem always to be in need of more teachers, and we spend a good deal of time and energy recruiting and training teachers for the various teaching ministries of the church.

The problem in James's day was that many desired to become teachers for the wrong motives. He warned that teachers bear a heavy responsibility. That responsibility applies to their words, what they teach. They must teach sound doctrine, and they must teach it persuasively and with love. But beyond that, they must be a living embodiment of what they teach. Actions speak more loudly than words. A teacher's job is not finished when he or she pronounces a benediction at the end of the lesson. The teaching responsibility—and opportunity—go on seven days a week.

B. Whose Wisdom?

We live in an age when knowledge is exploding at an incredible rate. The horizons of information are expanding so far and so fast that no individual can begin to comprehend all that is known. The result is that we are becoming a society of specialists. We know more and more about less and less. This fact alone should not frighten us. After all, God created our vast universe, and any truth that man discovers is God's truth. He endowed us with intellectual powers, and He intends us to use those powers to unlock the secrets of His universe for the benefit of mankind.

The problem is that in this frantic search for knowledge we have almost abandoned our search for wisdom. We have at our fingertips vastly more information than our parents or grandparents possessed, and yet we seem to lack wisdom about how to use this information in matters that are really important. Scientists can tell us how to split the atom, but science does not give scientists the wisdom to know when and under what conditions to unleash the tremendous power of the atom. Genetic engineers hold out the promise of developing better crops and eliminating some of the diseases that have plagued the human race for untold centuries. Yet that science does not provide the wisdom we need to draw up moral guidelines for how and when this knowledge should be used.

Where, then, shall we find this wisdom? Do we need more and larger government research grants to probe the far reaches of our universe? Do we need more scientists directing their skills to unlocking creation's secrets? James gives us the answer. True wisdom comes down from Heaven! It does not come in the form of flashing lights or divinely powered supercomputers. We find heavenly wisdom revealed to us through the Scriptures. It provides the moral standards that allow us to know right from wrong in a society that tries to ignore or obliterate such standards. God's Word tells us what kind of people we ought to be—kind, humble, loving, serving. It also shows us what such a life should be by giving us the divine model—God's only begotten Son, Jesus Christ.

C. Let Us Pray

Most gracious God and Father, Creator of all true wisdom, may we come before You humbly and hungrily seeking heavenly wisdom, that we may show in our lives that we truly are Your children. In our Master's name we pray. Amen.

D. Thought to Remember

"The fear of the Lord is the beginning of wisdom: a good understanding have all they that do his commandments" (Psalm 111:10).

Home Daily Bible Readings

Monday, June 17—Wisdom Granted by God (Job 28:12-22, 28)
Tuesday, June 18—Messiah's Spirit of Wisdom (Isaiah 11:1-5)
Wednesday, June 19—Surprised by His Wisdom (Matthew 13:53-58)
Thursday, June 20—Wisdom Of Obedience (Matthew 7:21-28)
Friday, June 21—Superior Wisdom in Committed Lives (Daniel 1:17-21)
Saturday, June 22—Faith Begets Wisdom From Above (1 Corinthians 2:1-8)
Sunday, June 23—Folly of Worldly Wisdom (1 Corinthians 3:16-23)

Learning by Doing

This page contains an alternate lesson plan emphasizing learning activities. Classes desiring such student involvement will find these suggestions helpful.

Learning Goals

After the completion of this study students should:

1. Understand that the source of genuine wisdom is God.

2. Discover that wisdom can be received from God by those who ask for it in faith.

3. Appreciate that those who teach (dispense wisdom) assume added accountability.

4. Recognize that genuine wisdom is shown by a righteous life.

Into the Lesson

Open today's lesson by posing this question: "If you could ask for any one thing in life, what would it be?" Before students answer, suggest such possibilities as money, success, popularity, and good health. After hearing other answers, relate how young King Solomon was asked this very same question by God (1 Kings 3:5-15). Then brainstorm for two or three minutes why Solomon's choice—a plea for wisdom—brought such pleasure to God.

Move toward the lesson text by asking the class to define and contrast knowledge and wisdom. Then suggest that knowledge centers on the accumulation of information and facts, while wisdom has more to do with the practical application of what is learned.

Into the Word

Step One: Read James 1:5-8, alternating verses responsively with the class. Then ask, "Where is the true source of wisdom?" James points us to God. Have students help you make a list of other places where people typically turn as a source of wisdom (for example, universities, gurus, libraries, philosophers).

Step Two: Give a three- to five-minute lecture focusing on the nature of God as *teacher* and our approach to Him as *students*. Illustrate your comments on the board or on newsprint by the following outline:

Teacher (God)
　　Generous: "giveth to all liberally"
　　Gentle: "upbraideth not"
Student (Me)
　　Believing: "ask in faith"
　　Focused: not wavering, not double-minded.

Emphasize that God takes delight in teaching generously, and that His sensitive Spirit doesn't treat anyone as a "dummy" in the classroom. As students we need to have absolute confidence in Him.

Step Three: Divide the class into groups of four to six, and ask each group to do one of the following projects. Copy instructions on cards, provide pens and poster paper, and allow ten to twelve minutes:

Option 1

James 3:1-5a speaks of the special accountability of teachers (translated as *masters* in the *King James Version*). Pretend that your group is asked to prepare a visual aid for a Bible school teachers' meeting using this text as a theme. Create a poster and slogan that illustrate the potential of a teacher's words for good or for bad.

Option 2

Wisdom is much more than just something of the head. It is shown by practical activity. Read James 3:13-18, then write the following captions on a poster:

　　earthly wisdom　　*wisdom from above*

Below each caption list the characteristics of that wisdom. Discuss the contrasts.

After calling time, ask each group to summarize its discussion and display its work. Allow ten or twelve minutes for this.

Into Life

Move toward closing with this story: Before the days of modern navigational aids, a traveler made an Atlantic crossing in a boat equipped with two compasses. One was fixed to the deck, where the man at the wheel could see. The other was fastened high on the mast where a sailor would climb for frequent reading. The curious passenger asked the captain, "Why do you have two compasses?" The captain replied, "Because this is an iron vessel, and the compass on the deck is sometimes affected by its surroundings. This is not the case with the compass high on the mast. It is above the influence of the ship." Then he added, "We steer by the higher compass."

James tells us that genuine wisdom comes from above; and that if we really want to be wise, we need to ask. Have the class form prayer groups of two or three and spend the closing minutes asking God to give the gift of being wise.

Let's Talk It Over

The questions on this page are designed to encourage review of the lesson Scriptures and to promote discussion of the lesson by the class. The answers provided are only discussion starters. Let your class talk it over from there.

1. If God gives wisdom to those who ask, what is the point of supporting schools and colleges?

This question points up the distinction that must be made between knowledge and wisdom. Knowledge is the product of education, formal or informal. It has to do with the assimilation of information, and an awareness of systems and relationships between objects, forces, and people. God gives us the capacities to learn and the curiosity to inquire, but He does not give any shortcuts to knowledge. If we want to know proper English grammar, or the properties of electricity, or the names of the twelve apostles, we must try to learn. Wisdom has more to do with discernment and good judgment, the ability to recognize truth and to make good choices. The promise in our text is that God will give wisdom, but He gives it especially to those who look for it in His Word.

2. How can we develop an unwavering confidence that God will answer our prayers?

First of all, remember that our confidence is in God, not in our faith. Our faith may always be imperfect, but God is perfect. We can build confidence by reviewing the testimony of others for whom God has answered prayer: testimony from the pages of the Bible, and testimony from believers today. We become more confident when we see our circumstances in light of some of the huge obstacles God has overcome at times to complete His will. We increase our confidence as we gain understanding of the will of God, and as we make our requests conform to what we are sure He desires.

3. Why should teachers of spiritual things be held to a higher standard? In what sense are we all teachers?

The role of teacher is not just a position of status; it creates a relationship. Is there a teacher if there is no student? The teacher-to-student relationship is one of influence. If the teacher is wrong about something, that error is compounded by the number of his or her students. Teachers must be very careful about what they teach and what they model by behavior. To the degree that we have a sphere of influence, we are teachers.

4. Is James arguing that right character results in right speech, or that right speech results in right character? Explain.

Jesus said, "Out of the overflow of the heart the mouth speaks" (Matthew 12:34, *New International Version*). His point seems to be that our speech reveals our heart or our character. Our text's illustrations of the power of the tongue, like the horse's bit and the ship's rudder, seem to make a different point. As the bit dictates direction for the horse and the rudder for a ship, so our tongue (speech) will establish the direction for the entire person (character).

Who is right, Jesus or James? Both are right. Our speech reveals what is in us; but if we let it reveal only good, then what is bad will fade away.

5. James speaks of the "meekness of wisdom." Why should we expect true wisdom to be accompanied by meekness?

Meekness should not be thought of as timidity. More accurately, it has to do with gentleness, with restrained behavior and controlled emotions. Think of the opposite—brash, impetuous behavior and emotional outbursts. Which kind of behavior would you be inclined to associate with wisdom? By observation or experience it does not take long to conclude that explosive emotions or lack of restraint will produce undesirable consequences in most cases. If wisdom includes the ability to assess value, to forecast outcomes, and to make prudent choices, then wisdom and meekness will be found together, one the complement of the other.

6. Can you name examples of people thought to be wise who were disgraced or discredited because of envy and strife? How are moral behavior and wisdom related?

Saul was selected by God to be the first king of Israel, but his envy and subsequent strife with David consumed him to the point that he was not effective as a king. God's moral laws are not arbitrary, but are designed to be life-giving and life-protecting. True wisdom must always choose that which is morally right. Wisdom that is "earthly, sensual, devilish," may more properly be called cunning or shrewdness. In the end it will prove to be shallow or hollow, and will do much damage.

Faith and Righteousness

DEVOTIONAL READING: 1 Corinthians 3:10-15.

LESSON SCRIPTURE: James 4:1-10, 13-17.

PRINTED TEXT: James 4:1-10, 13-17.

James 4:1-10, 13-17

1 From whence come wars and fightings among you? come they not hence, even of your lusts that war in your members?

2 Ye lust, and have not: ye kill, and desire to have, and cannot obtain: ye fight and war, yet ye have not, because ye ask not.

3 Ye ask, and receive not, because ye ask amiss, that ye may consume it upon your lusts.

4 Ye adulterers and adulteresses, know ye not that the friendship of the world is enmity with God? whosoever therefore will be a friend of the world is the enemy of God.

5 Do ye think that the Scripture saith in vain, The spirit that dwelleth in us lusteth to envy?

6 But he giveth more grace. Wherefore he saith, God resisteth the proud, but giveth grace unto the humble.

7 Submit yourselves therefore to God. Resist the devil, and he will flee from you.

8 Draw nigh to God, and he will draw nigh to you. Cleanse your hands, ye sinners; and purify your hearts, ye double-minded.

9 Be afflicted, and mourn, and weep: let your laughter be turned to mourning, and your joy to heaviness.

10 Humble yourselves in the sight of the Lord, and he shall lift you up.

· · · · · · · · · · · ·

13 Go to now, ye that say, Today or tomorrow we will go into such a city, and continue there a year, and buy and sell, and get gain:

14 Whereas ye know not what shall be on the morrow. For what is your life? It is even a vapor, that appeareth for a little time, and then vanisheth away.

15 For that ye ought to say, If the Lord will, we shall live, and do this, or that.

16 But now ye rejoice in your boastings: all such rejoicing is evil.

17 Therefore to him that knoweth to do good, and doeth it not, to him it is sin.

GOLDEN TEXT: Therefore to him that knoweth to do good, and doeth it not, to him it is sin.—James 4:17.

A Practical Religion
(James)
(Lessons 1-5)

Lesson Aims

As a result of completing the study of this lesson text from James 4, each student should be able to:

1. Understand that much of the strife in the world is the result of our desiring wealth and power.

2. Have a growing appreciation of the importance of humility before God.

3. Appreciate the fact that a person is not the final master of his or her destiny, for destiny rests in the hands of God.

4. Be able to mention one way by which he or she can show recognition of God's control in his or her life.

Lesson Outline

INTRODUCTION
    A. Sunk by Greed
    B. Lesson Background
  I. THE CAUSE OF CONFLICT (James 4:1-3)
    A. Strife Begins in Lust (v. 1)
    B. Lust Causes Violence (v. 2)
      Not Asking
    C. Improper Asking Fails (v. 3)
 II. ALIENATION FROM GOD (James 4:4-6)
    A. Worldliness Alienates (vv. 4, 5)
    B. God Offers Grace (v. 6)
III. SUBMISSION TO GOD (James 4:7-10)
    A. Resist the Devil (v. 7)
      Not Resisting
    B. Turn to God (v. 8)
    C. Humble Yourselves (vv. 9, 10)
IV. GOD CONTROLS OUR DESTINY (James 4:13-17)
    A. Man Excludes God (vv. 13, 14)
    B. Accepting God's Will (vv. 15, 16)
    C. The Sin of Omission (v. 17)
      Not Doing
CONCLUSION
    A. Wars and Rumors of Wars
    B. Let Us Pray
    C. Thought to Remember

Sin may be found in what a person doesn't do, as well as in what a person does. This is the message brought to us from James 4:17 and visual 5 of the visuals packet. The visual is shown on page 381.

Introduction
A. Sunk by Greed

A ship laden with treasure was making its way from a colony to the mother country. In the middle of the Atlantic, the ship sprang a leak. The sailors worked desperately to stop it, but in vain. An order was given to abandon ship.

One of the sailors seized this opportunity to enrich himself with as many gold bars as he could hide in his clothing. Encumbered by the weight as he stepped into a lifeboat, he lost his balance and plunged into the sea. The heavy gold took him swiftly to the bottom. His greed was his undoing.

For their own safety James spoke out against those who selfishly sought things and more things. They sought wealth for the wrong reason, that they might satisfy their lusts.

How timely this warning is now! An observer of our society could not draw a more accurate picture of its problems than James gives us. Daily we are bombarded by advertisements that entice us to buy things. We sacrifice our good name for material possessions, we sacrifice our children for them, and we sacrifice our peace of mind for them. Tragically, we sometimes even sacrifice our lives.

B. Lesson Background

In the third chapter, James gave his attention to teachers. He urged them to control their tongues and thereby show wisdom. Those who gained this divine wisdom enjoyed rich blessings, including the blessing of peace.

Chapter 4, in stark contrast, begins not with peace but with war and strife. James depicts a situation in which people seem caught up in the scramble for material things and in the pursuit of worldly pleasures. These people may wear the name of Christian, but they certainly are not allowing the Lord to direct their lives.

I. The Cause of Conflict
(James 4:1-3)
A. Strife Begins in Lust (v. 1)

1. From whence come wars and fightings among you? come they not hence, even of your lusts that war in your members?

Wars and fightings. It is probably best to understand these in a figurative rather than a literal sense. It is impossible to imagine that Christians were actually engaging in bloody warfare. The Roman government would not have tolerated that. James is referring to the kinds of strife that arise among members of a Christian community.

It is not possible for Christians always to avoid strife. When we stand firm in the faith, we can be certain that Satan will find some way to disturb our peace. But James is not talking about this kind of fighting. He is concerned about the strife that is rooted in lust. The Greek word here translated *lusts* may more accurately be translated *pleasures*. The English word *hedonism*, meaning devotion to worldly pleasures, comes from this word. Paul speaks of a civil war that rages within the heart of each one of us between fleshly lusts and our higher spiritual being (Romans 7:15-20). This spills over into conflict with others.

History bears ample testimony to the truth of James's statement. Across the centuries tribes and nations have fought bloody wars for plunder, for power, or for revenge. Historians would be hard pressed to find a war that did not have its roots in these baser motives. On a smaller scale these motives have led individuals to commit acts of violence. We may accumulate vast armaments to deter aggressors and we may pass laws to protect us from violent persons; but unless we can change the hearts of men and women, we will never see an end to violence.

B. Lust Causes Violence (v. 2)

2. Ye lust, and have not: ye kill, and desire to have, and cannot obtain: ye fight and war, yet ye have not, because ye ask not.

The word here translated *lust* is a different word from the one used in verse 1. This word means strong desire, which in certain situations may be proper. But in this context, clearly it is wrong. Moved by social pressures and lured by clever advertising, we seek this world's baubles. Heightened expectations are hard to satisfy, and when they go unfulfilled we are likely to become frustrated and turn violent. We want these things and we want them *now!* When we don't get them, we *kill . . . fight and war.*

We fail to gain these because we resort to violence to get them. Violence breeds violence, and in the ensuing struggles what we desire escapes us. Our culture tells us that "to the victor belong the spoils." We hold up aggressive people as models for our young people and then wonder why children resort to violence and even murder. Jesus' words, "Blessed are the meek: for they shall inherit the earth" (Matthew 5:5), get lost in the din of the struggle.

NOT ASKING

An old story tells of a church in search of a new minister. The officers were using a method that is unwise, generally speaking. A succession of ministers gave "trial sermons," after which a vote was taken to determine which one would be employed. Finally a selection was made. A friend of one of the members asked how this particular choice came about. The reply was, "It wasn't so much how his trial sermon came out. No, our decision came because of how he prayed in public. He asked the Lord for blessings and benefits none of those other fellows knew the Lord had!"

How true those seven words in James 4:2 are! "Ye have not, because ye ask not." These words apply to many things besides prayer. We do not understand or do not enjoy numerous things because we really do not care enough to investigate or explore—in other words, to "ask." What really *is* a symphony concert? What is the difference between various coniferous trees—the identifying characteristics of pine, spruce, balsam, hemlock, fir?

God was present in the burning bush, but He did not speak to Moses until Moses turned aside to see why the bush burned and was not consumed (Exodus 3:1-4). In many ways God speaks to us only when we "ask."   —J. G. V. B.

C. Improper Asking Fails (v. 3)

3. Ye ask, and receive not, because ye ask amiss, that ye may consume it upon your lusts.

Some do not receive what they want because they do not ask (v. 2). Some, however, ask and do not receive because they *ask amiss* (literally, badly: that is, with evil intent). Because they pray selfishly, God does not give them what they pray for. People whose only concern is to satisfy their own lusts are not likely to pray unselfish prayers. Of course, God hears and answers every prayer, but a selfish prayer He usually answers with a resounding no!

II. Alienation From God
(James 4:4-6)
A. Worldliness Alienates (vv. 4, 5)

4. Ye adulterers and adulteresses, know ye not that the friendship of the world is enmity with God? whosoever therefore will be a friend of the world is the enemy of God.

In the oldest manuscripts only the female *adulteresses* is found. Even if this was the original reading, we should not understand James to suggest that men are not included. He is using a familiar Old Testament figure. God often described His relationship with His people as a marriage, and their unfaithfulness as adultery. God is a jealous God, who does not take lightly the dalliance of His people with other gods.

The *world* here is not the physical world, but the sensual, sinful aspects of the world. Some

Christians live in hermitages or monasteries, cut off from that world; but we cannot think this verse suggests that. To withdraw from the world is to reject the Great Commission that commands us to go into all the world. We must live in the world, but live as friends of God.

Many Christians would like to serve God and at the same time dabble in the alluring fruit that Satan offers. James makes it very clear that this arrangement will not work. *Friendship of the world is enmity with God.* We have no trouble understanding this principle. The difficulty arises when we try to apply it. Satan often tempts us, not to completely reject our Christian standards, but to compromise them. In the process he tries to convince us that God is unfair and even cruel because He demands our absolute loyalty. But we have to choose. "No man can serve two masters" (Matthew 6:24).

5. Do ye think that the Scripture saith in vain, The spirit that dwelleth in us lusteth to envy?

This verse poses a problem. In the *King James Version* it leaves the impression that the latter part of the verse is a quotation from the Old Testament, but it is not. Students have found various ways of solving the problem. For example, the *American Standard Version* divides this verse into two questions. The first asks, "Or think ye that the scripture speaketh in vain?" That may refer to many passages that show the world in opposition to God, as indicated in verse 4. Obviously, the answer is no! The Scripture never speaks in vain. The second question then follows: "Doth the spirit which he made to dwell in us long unto envying?" Again the answer is an emphatic no! In no way can we blame our lust and envy on the Holy Spirit who dwells in us.

Home Daily Bible Readings

Monday, June 24—Assured of Innocence (Job 27:1-11)
Tuesday, June 25—Worthy Resolves (Psalm 66:13-20)
Wednesday, June 26—A True Relationship (1 John 2:12-17)
Thursday, June 27—An Expression of Faith (Psalm 138)
Friday, June 28—Blessings of the Righteous (Proverbs 3:27-35)
Saturday, June 29—Trust in God's Grace (Isaiah 55:6-11)
Sunday, June 30—Qualified to Enter God's Presence (Psalm 24:1-6)

B. God Offers Grace (v. 6)

6. But he giveth more grace. Wherefore he saith, God resisteth the proud, but giveth grace unto the humble.

Instead of producing lust and envy (v. 5) the Holy Spirit in us *giveth more grace,* more divine favor. This is verified by a quotation from Proverbs 3:34 in the Septuagint, a Greek version of the Old Testament. His Jewish readers would be familiar with these words, and many, especially the Jews of the dispersion, would be able to read it in the Greek.

Pride is one of the great barriers to receiving God's grace. Many people who intellectually believe in God and in their hearts accept Him still remain alienated from Him because of pride. Those who humbly submit to Him God will receive, but He is unyielding to those who arrogantly resist Him. "The sacrifices of God are a broken spirit: a broken and a contrite heart, O God, thou wilt not despise" (Psalm 51:17).

From time to time Christian scholars have drawn up a list of what they consider the most serious sins, the "seven deadly sins." Pride often heads this list, and for good reason. Interestingly, pride, which causes persons to elevate themselves and their desires even above God, is the root of most other sins. Satan used Eve's pride as a weapon against her in the garden, and he is eager to use mine against me. Pride causes one to become a law unto oneself, unmindful of either man's law or God's law.

III. Submission to God (James 4:7-10)

A. Resist the Devil (v. 7)

7. Submit yourselves therefore to God. Resist the devil, and he will flee from you.

In the ancient world (as in ours) submission to anyone was looked upon as weakness. Yet those who submit to God gain strength, strength to resist the devil. With the power of God we can face the evil one, and he will beat a hasty retreat. Peter describes Satan as a roaring lion, but faced by God's power he becomes a paper lion.

In resisting the devil we ought to follow Jesus' example. He used Scripture as His chief weapon. We may be tempted to argue with Satan, but that is a mistake because he is a master of clever argument. When he tried to use his clever arguments against Jesus, our Lord quoted Scripture. That soon put the devil to flight. Of course, to use Scripture we must know it, which is a good reason for stressing the importance of Sunday school and other situations in which we study the Bible.

visual 5

NOT RESISTING

One of the most enduring of relatively modern legends is that of Faust, the German scholar-magician. This is the story of a man who sold his soul to the devil for twenty-four years of power, knowledge, and pleasure.

This is exactly the opposite of the advice James gives us in verse 7 of our printed text. He says we are to *resist* the devil, not to enter into an agreement with him. Neglecting our Christian resources, forgetting to pray, forsaking Bible reading, being absent from public worship—all these are ways we diminish our strength to resist the evil one.

The story of Faust first came to general view in England about 1600 with the publication of the drama entitled *Dr. Faustus,* by Christopher Marlowe. In that play the agent of Satan, Mephistopheles, tells Faust how it is that evil spirits come to tempt and assault men:

For when we hear one rack the name of God,
Abjure the Scriptures and his Saviour Christ,
We fly, in hope to get his glorious soul;
Nor will we come, unless he use such means
Whereby he is in danger to be damned.

If we are going to be able to resist Satan, we need to eliminate wicked attitudes and actions and encourage those qualities that God's Spirit seeks to instill in us. Instead of hatred, let us seek love; instead of pessimism and gloom, joy; in place of unrest and agitation, peace. Thus we resist the devil, who will indeed flee from us.

—J. G. V. B.

B. Turn to God (v. 8)

8. Draw nigh to God, and he will draw nigh to you. Cleanse your hands, ye sinners; and purify your hearts, ye double-minded.

We must remain close to God if we are to resist the devil successfully. In the parable of the prodigal son, Jesus depicted God as a loving Father who waited for his wayward son and greeted him with love and forgiveness when he returned. This parable gives us assurance that in the same way God waits for us when we return to Him from our wandering.

When we do return to God, two things are required of us. We must come with clean hands; our actions must show that we have turned away from sin. We must also come with pure hearts to provide the motivation for our actions.

C. Humble Yourselves (vv. 9, 10)

9. Be afflicted, and mourn, and weep: let your laughter be turned to mourning, and your joy to heaviness.

Be afflicted. Some have interpreted this to mean that one must endure suffering, even to the point of self-torture, to be pleasing to God; but it is hard to believe that God desires the mutilation of one's body. On the other hand, the giving up of luxuries or pleasures in order to serve the Lord better is certainly quite appropriate. A missionary would certainly be approved of God.

In this verse, James seems to be addressing Christians who had become careless in their lives and who were devoting too much time and too many of their resources to the pleasures of this world, even sinful pleasures. They should weep over their wickedness and abandon it.

This is not to suggest that a Christian's life should be totally devoid of joy. Quite the contrary. A Christian who gives wholeheartedly to the service of the Lord will know joy and satisfaction that this world cannot match.

10. Humble yourselves in the sight of the Lord, and he shall lift you up.

James sums up his previous admonitions by returning once again to the theme of humility. The emphasis he gives to this matter leads us to believe that the lack of humility was a serious problem among the churches of his day. Pride has been a besetting sin in every age. The rich and the powerful seem to be especially tempted at this point, but even the poor are not exempt.

IV. God Controls Our Destiny
(James 4:13-17)

A. Man Excludes God (vv. 13, 14)

13. Go to now, ye that say, Today or tomorrow we will go into such a city, and continue there a year, and buy and sell, and get gain.

In a few words James sums up the attitude of successful business leaders, people who have control of their lives and make their own decisions. Such a person is likely to receive a laudatory write-up in the *Wall Street Journal* or make the cover of *Time.* The executive suites of major corporations are filled with people like this. James is not censuring their ambition, their planning, or their hard work. What he censures is that they order their lives as if they were in complete control—as if God had no place in their plans.

14. Whereas ye know not what shall be on the morrow. For what is your life? It is even a vapor, that appeareth for a little time, and then vanisheth away.

James puts his finger squarely on the problem—life's uncertainty. None of us knows for sure what tomorrow will bring, let alone a year. We sometimes hear this verse read at funerals. It is certainly appropriate there, but we ought to be reminded of it daily.

B. Accepting God's Will (vv. 15, 16)

15, 16. For that ye ought to say, If the Lord will, we shall live, and do this, or that. But now ye rejoice in your boastings: all such rejoicing is evil.

A person who plans his or her life without taking God into consideration is, for all practical purposes, an atheist. Such a person may speak eloquently of serving God, but one's actions reveal his true loyalties. The rejoicing and boastings of a self-sufficient person are sinful in the eyes of God.

James is not suggesting that we live aimless lives, driven hither and yon by the tides of life. His point is that when we do our planning, God should be considered at every step of the way.

C. The Sin of Omission (v. 17)

17. Therefore to him that knoweth to do good, and doeth it not, to him it is sin.

This verse applies specifically to those who ought to include God in their planning, but do not. But it also has broader application. We are quick to condemn the overt sins such as murder, lying, stealing, and adultery, especially if they are not our sins. Many times, however, we fail to note the sins of omission—the good deed we didn't do, the kind word we didn't speak. James doesn't make any special allowance for these sins.

NOT DOING

One of the most impressive passages in all of Scripture is the dramatic depiction of the judgment scene in Matthew 25:31-46. As the *New International Version* has it, the Son of man is seen as having come "in his glory, and all the angels with him." For the judgment of "all the nations" He is seated "on his throne in heavenly glory." We are familiar with the sentences of judgment coming from this awesome and ultimate Judge. Those who are sentenced to final doom are those who did not give the Lord food when He was hungry, nor give Him drink when He was thirsty, nor visit Him when He was imprisoned. When they say they cannot remember these failures, the reply comes: "Whatever you did not do for one of the least of these, you did not do for me."

Here the conduct is not evaluated by the wrong things done which should not have been done. Rather, the condemnation is based on the right deeds *not* done that *should* have been performed. This agrees with James's words found in 4:17 of our lesson today: "To him that knoweth to do good, and doeth it not, to him it is sin."

Have we been silent when we should have spoken, stingy when we should have been generous, self-regarding when we should have been self-giving? When Jesus' disciples criticized a woman who had poured expensive perfume over Him, He defended her action by saying, "Why trouble ye her? . . . She hath done what she could" (Mark 14:6). Our question to ourselves must be, "Have we done what we could?"

—J. G. V. B.

Conclusion
A. Wars and Rumors of Wars

If James had been taking his cue from this morning's newspaper, he could not have more accurately described the present world situation. When the twentieth century began, many optimistically believed the day of world peace had arrived; but, tragically, ours has been the bloodiest, most violent century in all of human history.

Many factors have been blamed for this, among them racism, nationalism, advanced technology, Communism, and religion. Certainly these factors were involved, but James gets to the root of the problem: lust. We lust for things and we lust for power. Until we can find a way to control lust, any thought of peace in our world is a hopeless dream.

The problem is that man in his own strength cannot eliminate lust from his life. Only by yielding to Christ can we hope to overcome the power of greed and desire. That is why it is so essential that our efforts be turned to winning people to Jesus.

B. Let Us Pray

Dear Father, we come to You as prodigal children, acknowledging our sins and our inability to save ourselves. Cleanse our hearts and make us receptive to Your Word, that we may walk in paths of peace. In Jesus' name we pray. Amen.

C. Thought to Remember

"All men desire peace, but very few desire those things that make for peace."

—Thomas à Kempis

Learning by Doing

This page contains an alternate lesson plan emphasizing learning activities. Classes desiring such student involvement will find these suggestions helpful.

Learning Goals

Through the study of this lesson students will:

1. Learn that conflict springs from selfish desires.

2. Discover that a person cannot pledge allegiance to both a sinful world and a holy God.

3. See that humble submission to God is the key to ultimate harmony in life.

4. Work to begin trusting their lives to God's will and not their own.

Into the Lesson

Before the lesson, secure some large pictures, check out a video or set of slides, or get a sound-effects recording to capture the sights and sounds of war. (A public library or video store would be a ready source.) As the class session begins, use one or more resources to set the stage for study. As students look and listen, encourage them to consider the harsh realities of war. Then have them supply one-word descriptions of what conflict brings about.

Next, in rhetorical fashion, ask, What causes wars and fightings? Tell the class that this question occupied the mind of the New Testament writer James, too, and that he helps us consider both conflict's cause and its cure.

Into the Word

Step One: Introduce the text by commenting that James's words, even if figurative, describe harsh circumstances. Further, the "battle" is not remote, but is evidently being waged right in the Christian community.

Invite two class members to come to the front, face each other in close proximity, and read (in alternating fashion) James 4:1-4. Encourage them to capture the fierceness and heaviness of the words as they speak.

After the reading, write on the board in bold letters: THE BATTLE WITHIN. Then comment, "Before conflict ever goes public, it begins in the privacy of the heart. The seeds of destruction are sown within the fertile soil of a troubled spirit."

Beneath THE BATTLE WITHIN heading list two causes of conflict cited by James: Selfish Desires (vv. 1-3) and Misplaced Allegiance (vv. 4, 5). Use thoughts from the lesson commentary to build a four- to six-minute lecture.

Step Two: Lead the class on from the cause to the cure for conflict. Divide the class into groups and supply copies of the following instructions:

ON A MISSION OF PEACE

You are members of a team charged with the task of bringing peace to a troubled hotspot. The conflict has been fierce and deadly; and, unfortunately, those "at war" are believers. Your peacemaking skills will be honed by a careful reading of James 4:6-10. Key points for you to make to combatants are the need for:

• Humble submission before God (vv. 6, 7a, 10)

• Active resistance to the devil (v. 7b)

• Cleansing from sin (v. 8)

Appoint a leader to help guide your team in a brief study of how the above concepts can bring hope to the battlefield. Try to move beyond abstract concepts to concrete ways in which the peace principles can be applied.

Allow 15 minutes for work, then have team leaders give brief summaries of discussions.

Step Three: Conclude study of today's text by commenting that genuine surrender means trusting our lives to God's will and giving up prideful confidence in ourselves. Read 4:13-17 and offer three or four minutes of commentary.

You might illustrate with this story: Some church folk, in earlier generations, when writing letters that spoke of future plans or appointments would often add the initials "D. V." The letters stood for the Latin, *Deo volente,* which means "God willing." Perhaps it is a practice that could be revived today—living and planning always with an eye toward God; yielding the future, not to our choice, but His.

Into Life

Have class members share experiences of how some of their best-made plans have been dramatically changed by circumstances, and what they have learned from such experiences.

In C. S. Lewis's classic work, *Mere Christianity,* he refers to pride as "The Great Sin." Share this quote: "A proud man is always looking down on things and people; and, of course, as long as you're looking down, you can't see something that's above you."

Ask students to pray a closing prayer with you. Have them look up and picture their eyes placed upon God—seeking *His* will, longing for *His* desires, experiencing *His* peace.

Let's Talk It Over

The questions on this page are designed to encourage review of the lesson Scriptures and to promote discussion of the lesson by the class. The answers provided are only discussion starters. Let your class talk it over from there.

1. How does our text (4:1, 2) explain the increase of violence and crime in our society? Do you agree or disagree? Explain.

James sees wars, fighting, and murder as directly related to lust and desire to obtain. Our society seems to prove the point, on the personal level as well as the national. We have experienced consistent increases in violent crime over the last three decades or more. During those same years our desire for material things has been fueled by invention, by accelerating technological changes, accompanied by multiple fashion revolutions, and by a barrage of new advertising methods. Physical lusts have been ignited by more explicit talk of sex and portrayal of sex in the media, and by the overthrow of most standards of modesty. In a society where lust, envy, covetousness, greed, and selfishness are promoted, is it any surprise that there is an increase in violence and crime?

2. In order to receive a blessing from God, what motive should underlie our prayers? How does that change what we ask?

Prayer should not be considered a time to address God with our wish list of preferred private blessings. If we are only asking God to meet our selfish desires, as though He were a celestial candy-man, James contends that we will not receive because we "ask amiss." Our highest desire should be the will of God. Jesus taught us to pray, "Thy will be done." Faith means trusting God, trusting that He is wiser than we are and that He is able to direct our lives toward higher and nobler aims. If we have that trust, we will test all our requests against what we know of God's will. When we are not sure, we will ask for greater discernment, but always defer to His wisdom.

3. How would you define the "friendship with the world" that is "enmity with God"?

This is a very sobering thought for people who enjoy many of the comforts of this world. Is an easy life necessarily sinful? Some of us have also had the opportunity to travel and have enjoyed the great beauty in much of this world. Is that bad? And what about ecology? Are Christians not supposed to be good caretakers of earth?

James does not have in view the planet, but the value system of this world and the pursuits of this world that compete with our loyalty to God. He refers to friends of this godless world as adulterers and adulteresses: that is, they have forsaken the love of God for the love of this world.

Is it your highest aim to glorify God in your life, or has love for this world's rewards consumed your attention? Remember, even good things can become the enemy of the best.

4. In practical terms, how do we submit to God and resist Satan?

Our text holds some clues to submitting to God. We are to draw near to Him, and we are to be cleansed and purified. A good illustration of this process is the experience of Isaiah the prophet, as recorded in Isaiah 6:1-8. It was in the context of worship (drawing near) that Isaiah had a vision of being in God's presence. Immediately he was moved to confess his own sinfulness in contrast to the holiness of God. He received cleansing, and then he heard the call to service, "Whom shall I send, and who will go for us?" He responded, "Here am I; send me." These elements of worship, confession, forgiveness, and surrender to service may be seen as standards for submitting to God.

Resisting Satan means identifying temptations to sin and finding ways of countering their attraction. To focus on God and obey Him is an excellent way to resist Satan.

5. When does faith become presumption in regard to future plans? Why is that unacceptable in believers?

We all make some plans for tomorrow. In order to make those plans we must have certain expectations about what conditions may be tomorrow. Previous experience gives us confidence to believe that day will follow night and that certain opportunities will probably be available for us. As long as we factor in the element of uncertainty, we are kept from presumption. We must humbly admit that we cannot control all circumstances. Only God has power over all the contingencies that will determine whether our plans come to pass or not. We expect our plans to succeed if that is what He wants.

Praising God as Creator and Sustainer

DEVOTIONAL READING: Isaiah 40: 25-31.

LESSON SCRIPTURE: Psalm 104.

PRINTED TEXT: Psalm 104:24-34.

Psalm 104:24-34

24 O LORD, how manifold are thy works! In wisdom hast thou made them all: the earth is full of thy riches.

25 So is this great and wide sea, wherein are things creeping innumerable, both small and great beasts.

26 There go the ships: there is that leviathan, whom thou hast made to play therein.

27 These wait all upon thee; that thou mayest give them their meat in due season.

28 That thou givest them they gather: thou openest thine hand, they are filled with good.

29 Thou hidest thy face, they are troubled: thou takest away their breath, they die, and return to their dust.

30 Thou sendest forth thy spirit, they are created: and thou renewest the face of the earth.

31 The glory of the LORD shall endure for ever: the LORD shall rejoice in his works.

32 He looketh on the earth, and it trembleth: he toucheth the hills, and they smoke.

33 I will sing unto the LORD as long as I live: I will sing praise to my God while I have my being.

34 My meditation of him shall be sweet: I will be glad in the LORD.

GOLDEN TEXT: O LORD, how manifold are thy works! In wisdom hast thou made them all: the earth is full of thy riches.—Psalm 104:24.

> ### God Is With Us
> ### (Psalms)
> #### Unit 1: Praising God
> #### (Lessons 6-9)

Lesson Aims

After this lesson, each student should:

1. Have a better understanding of nature's dependence on God.

2. Have a growing appreciation for the provisions God has made to give us food, shelter, and clothing.

3. Have a greater appreciation for the interdependence of the earth's ecosystems.

4. Be able to mention one specific way he or she can help protect our environment.

Lesson Outline

INTRODUCTION

    A. No Hawks, No Harvest

    B. Lesson Background

  I. GOD'S WISDOM IN CREATION (Psalm 104:24-26)

    A. His Boundless Works (v. 24)

    B. The Wonders of the Sea (vv. 25, 26)

      This Great Sea

  II. GOD PROVIDES (Psalm 104:27-30)

    A. He Gives Food (vv. 27, 28)

    B. He Gives and Takes Life (v. 29)

    C. He Gives Renewal (v. 30)

      The Creator Spirit

  III. MAN'S RESPONSE (Psalm 104:31-34)

    A. He Praises God's Glory (v. 31)

    B. He Sees God's Power (v. 32)

    C. He Sings Praises (v. 33)

    D. He Rejoices in God (v. 34)

      A Medieval Canticle of Praise

CONCLUSION

    A. Man's Response

    B. Let Us Pray

    C. Thought to Remember

God provides all things necessary to nurture and sustain His manifold creation. So says visual 6 of the visuals packet shown on page 389.

Introduction

A. No Hawks, No Harvest

In a certain area in the Midwest, farmers grow clover for seed. One year the crop looked especially good. The plants grew luxuriantly, bloomed prolifically, and had few problems from disease or parasites. But when harvest time came, the farmers were disappointed. Their crops produced few seeds.

An expert was brought in to try to find out what caused the failure. This particular variety of clover could not be pollinated by honeybees, but required bumblebees. He soon discovered that there were almost no bumblebees in the entire area. He did find, however, that the fields were overrun with field mice. Many of the farmers also raised chickens in open lots. The baby chickens were easy prey for chicken hawks, and so two or three years earlier the farmers had declared open season on the hawks, practically exterminating them in the entire area.

The pieces of the puzzle were beginning to fall into place. When the hawks were eliminated, the mice population, with no natural enemies, exploded. Mice, it was found, destroyed bumblebee nests, and so there were no bumblebees to pollinate the clover, and thus no seed.

This incident indicates how delicately balanced the forces of nature are. When we change one small item in the system, we run a risk of upsetting that balance. Often we do this quite ignorantly, because we are just beginning to learn a few of the wonderful things God has provided in His creation. As Christians we should treat the world about us with awe and respect, learning all we can about it so that we can treat it more wisely.

B. Lesson Background

The author of this psalm is unknown, nor is there any agreement about when it was written. There is little in the psalm that even gives us hints about its authorship or date. Some feel that it was designed to be sung by an individual in the worship in the temple. Certainly the psalm would lend itself to that purpose, because the pronouns *my* and *I* appear at the beginning and near the end.

The psalm opens with words of praise to God, who created the physical universe. In language that is both rich and colorful, the writer mentions many aspects of God's creation—the sky, the sea, the mountains, the vegetation, the animals. But, to the psalmist, God is more than a Creator; He also sustains the world He has created. God established the earth and then placed limits on the seas (vv. 5-9). He made the springs that feed the streams that quench the thirst of the wild animals, and He sends the rain that waters the mountains (vv. 10-13). Verses 14-18 tell that He makes grass grow for the cattle and provides food for man, while the mountains and forests give habitat for the animals and birds. The sun and moon mark daylight during which man works, and darkness in which beasts prowl (vv. 19-23).

The writer sees a God who is both powerful and loving. As a result he is filled with both awe and joy. This is his mood as he raises his voice in honor and praise to God. As we study this psalm in detail, we should share his worshipful attitude.

I. God's Wisdom in Creation
(Psalm 104:24-26)

A. His Boundless Works (v. 24)

24. O LORD, how manifold are thy works! In wisdom hast thou made them all: the earth is full of thy riches.

The psalmist sees all of nature as a revelation of God's power and majesty. On occasions God reveals himself to man directly, but these occasions are relatively rare. On the other hand, at every tick of a watch God's works speak of His power. Only one who is spiritually blind would fail to see this. We gaze into the heavens and with the naked eye see thousands of stars, but with the telescope we can detect countless millions. The microscope unlocks miniature worlds that increase our awe of the Creator.

In wisdom hast thou made them all. The ancient psalmist lacked the technology that we have to probe the secrets of the universe; but in the intricate workings of what he could see, he marveled at God's wisdom. How much greater our reverence should be! With our tools we see a universe far more complicated than he could even dream of.

B. The Wonders of the Sea (vv. 25, 26)

25, 26. So is this great and wide sea, wherein are things creeping innumerable, both small and great beasts. There go the ships: there is that leviathan, whom thou hast made to play therein.

Things creeping innumerable. The psalmist's knowledge of the vast oceans and the life they contain was slight compared to what scientists know today. Yet even he knew that the number of sea animals was beyond counting. If his limited knowledge caused him to raise his praises to God, how much more should we today praise Him! The more we understand about the oceans, the more we marvel at the bounty of God's creation. He made the whales, the most massive creatures on land or sea, and He made the tiny plankton upon which the whales feed.

On the surface of the seas sail the fleets of the nations, carrying men and their various products great distances. Ships of today are more and bigger and swifter than those seen by the

psalmist, but God made the oceans big enough for all of them.

Leviathan may be a name for any big creature that plays in the water. Some students think the one described in Job 41 is a crocodile, but it seems more probable that our text speaks of a dolphin or a whale.

THIS GREAT SEA

The psalmist is awed by God's greatness as seen in the wisdom of His creation. The many evidences on land are called to mind, but he also contemplates the vast and mystic sea. Here is an awesome testimony to the might and majesty of the Creator.

Lord Byron's long poem, "Childe Harold's Pilgrimage," contains some of the most beautiful and vivid thoughts ever expressed about "this great and wide sea."

Roll on, thou deep and dark blue Ocean—roll!
Ten thousand fleets sweep over thee in vain;
Man marks the earth with ruin—his control
 Stops with the shore;—upon the watery plain
 The wrecks are all thy deed, nor doth remain
A shadow of man's ravage, save his own,
 When, for a moment, like a drop of rain,
 He sinks into thy depths, with bubbling groan—
Without a grave—unknelled, uncoffined, and
 unknown.

This awareness of man's frailty and finiteness compared with the expanse and power of the sea is followed shortly by a magnificent passage explaining and extolling the ocean as an unequaled and unparalleled expression of the wondrous wisdom of God.

Thou glorious mirror, where the Almighty's form
Glasses itself in tempests; in all time,
Calm or convulsed—in breeze, or gale, or storm—
 Icing the Pole, or in the torrid clime
 Dark-heaving—boundless, endless, and sublime—
The image of Eternity.
—J. G. V. B.

II. God Provides
(Psalm 104:27-30)

A. He Gives Food (vv. 27, 28)

27, 28. These wait all upon thee; that thou mayest give them their meat in due season. That thou givest them they gather: thou openest thine hand, they are filled with good.

Some believe in a Creator God, who, once He had made the physical universe, retired from it, leaving it to run on its own. These deists believe that God no longer intervenes in the world, either to care for His creation or to answer prayers. This is certainly not the view of the psalmist. He sees God on every hand sustaining

His creation. All living creatures depend upon God for their sustenance. As we learn more about our environment, we have growing appreciation for the intricate balance necessary to sustain life. We have also learned some of the devastating results when man upsets this balance.

We also learn how God has built into nature recuperative power that allows life to be revived when disaster strikes. Few things are more disheartening than to see a once majestic forest that has been ravaged by fire. All life has been destroyed, and it seems that years must elapse before life once again can be restored. But the very next spring, green shoots begin to appear. Some seeds are brought in by wind or birds or animals, a method of replanting planned by God. However, some seeds have been there all along, waiting for a fire. They may lie for several years without germinating. Then after the fire that is so devastating, they spring into life. All across nature we see similar examples of God's provision. How can anyone doubt His existence and His love?

B. He Gives and Takes Life (v. 29)

29. Thou hidest thy face, they are troubled: thou takest away their breath, they die, and return to their dust.

When God turns away from His creation, trouble comes to all His creatures. Drought or flood or fire may destroy habitat and food supply. God does not reject His creation whimsically, but rather when His holy will has been violated. Human sinfulness contributes to the suffering of nature. "For we know that the whole creation groaneth and travaileth in pain together until now" as we wait for our redemption (Romans 8:22, 23).

Home Daily Bible Readings

Monday, July 1—The Lord as Creator (Psalm 33:1-9)
Tuesday, July 2—Creation by God's Word (Genesis 1:1-8)
Wednesday, July 3—Separation of Land and Water (Genesis 1:9-13)
Thursday, July 4—Celestial Bodies Provide Light (Genesis 1:14-19)
Friday, July 5—Animals Created by God (Genesis 1:20-25)
Saturday, July 6—People to Dominate the Earth (Genesis 1:26-31)
Sunday, July 7—Made to Need Each Other (Genesis 2:18-24)

When God created Adam, He breathed into him the breath of life and he became a living soul (Genesis 2:7). When that breath is withdrawn, man ceases to live and returns to the dust whence he came. "Then shall the dust return to the earth as it was: and the spirit shall return unto God who gave it" (Ecclesiastes 12:7).

C. He Gives Renewal (v. 30)

30. Thou sendest forth thy spirit, they are created: and thou renewest the face of the earth.

The creation of new life is an ongoing process. Even as some die and return to dust, others are being called into existence and given the breath of life. God's initial creative acts were completed in six days, but His renewal of life never ceases. *Thou renewest the face of the earth.* We see this happening every springtime; we see it happening after a disastrous fire or flood; we see it happening as animals and people die and are replaced by new generations.

THE CREATOR SPIRIT

In verse 30 of our text, "Thou sendest forth thy spirit" could be translated, "Thou sendest forth thy breath." Either translation tells us God is personally active in the continuing creation of living things. The complex process by which the face of the earth is renewed is no mindless, mechanical process. It is due to the creating power of God flowing through the natural order. Wordsworth may have felt that when he wrote:

And I have felt
A presence that disturbs me with the joy
Of elevated thoughts; a sense sublime,
Of something far more deeply interfused,
. . . .
A motion and a spirit, that impels
All thinking things, all objects of all thought,
and rolls through all things.

—J. G. V. B.

III. Man's Response
(Psalm 104:31-34)
A. He Praises God's Glory (v. 31)

31. The glory of the LORD shall endure for ever: the LORD shall rejoice in his works.

The *New International Version* translates this "May the glory of the Lord endure forever; may the Lord rejoice in his works." This is not only a prayer to God in Heaven; it is also a reminder to people on earth. May they use their voices to give glory and honor and praise to the Creator, and may they live their lives in a way that will make Him happy.

B. He Sees God's Power (v. 32)

32. He looketh on the earth, and it trembleth: he toucheth the hills, and they smoke.

In recent years hurricanes, earthquakes, floods, and volcanic eruptions remind us of God's power latent in the earth He has created. These displays of power also remind us of how puny we are in contrast. We now have a better understanding of the laws that work to unleash the vast powers of nature, but we are still powerless to do anything about them.

C. He Sings Praises (v. 33)

33. I will sing unto the LORD as long as I live: I will sing praise to my God while I have my being.

Of all of God's creatures, only man uses his voice to praise Him in songs like the one we are reading. God gave us voices to communicate with our fellowmen, but He intended that we also lift them up to Him in songs of praise and thanksgiving. As the psalmist contemplates God's power in nature and His renewal of life, he uses his voice to break out in exultant praise of Jehovah.

Christianity has produced a larger, more varied body of hymns and songs to praise God than has any other religion. Christian music varies from culture to culture, and even between generations in a culture. Today the younger generation prefers praise songs and Christian rock, while the older generation prefers traditional hymns. Yet any music that is offered to God in sincere worship and praise is acceptable. This very psalm was probably used in public worship in the temple.

D. He Rejoices in God (v. 34)

34. My meditation of him shall be sweet: I will be glad in the LORD.

We worship God in our songs, but we also worship Him in our meditations and prayers. In the busy world in which we live, most of us do not spend enough time in meditation. Our world is so intrusive that it is difficult to find even a few minutes when the noise and clatter about us does not break into our thoughts. We may wish for a slower, simpler life-style, but few of us have that option. We try to set aside a bit of time each day for devotions, but outside a monastery such a routine is difficult to maintain. Still, there are those occasional moments when we are able to enter into this special relationship with God. It may happen when we stand on a mountaintop and see His majesty stretched out before us, or when a golden sun sends its rays across the radiant garb of autumn trees, or when

visual 6

winter casts a blanket of pristine snow and glistening ice across the landscape. Perhaps it is when in the middle of a sleepless night we find ourselves drawn closer to God.

A MEDIEVAL CANTICLE OF PRAISE

One of the greatest men in the Middle Ages was Francis of Assisi. Somewhere around A.D. 1225 he issued his "Canticle to the Sun," which really is a lyric of praise to God. This is the sort of thing our text suggests when it speaks of singing praise to God and of being glad in the Lord.

O Most High, Almighty, Good Lord God, to Thee belong praise, glory, honor, and all blessing.

Praised be my Lord God, with all His creatures, and especially our brother the Sun, who brings us the day and who brings us the light: fair is he, and he shines with a very great splendor.

O Lord, he signifies us to thee!

Praised be my Lord for our sister the Moon, and for the stars, the which He has set clear and lovely in the heaven.

Praised be my Lord for our brother the wind, and for air and clouds, calms and all weather, by which Thou upholdest life and all creatures.

Praised be my Lord for our sister water, who is very serviceable to us, and humble and precious and clean.

Praised be my Lord for our brother fire, through whom thou givest us light in the darkness; and he is bright and pleasant and very mighty and strong.

What a great thing to be *glad* in the Lord! Some are much too often *sad* in the Lord, while others are *mad* about something or other. Our faith should not lead us to some *fad* or to do something *bad*. Let's really be *glad* in Him!

—J. G. V. B.

Conclusion

A. Man's Response

When man is confronted by the great power and magnitude of God's handiwork in creation, how should he respond? Some are totally oblivious to everything about them. They not only fail to notice God's world of nature, they are equally unconcerned about the technological wonders that make their lives easy and comfortable. They are so concerned about their own little world that they never give even a nod to the larger world that surrounds them. They are, as Browning says, "finished and finite clods, untroubled by a spark."

Others live their lives openly or covertly in rebellion against God. They ignore the evidence of God about them, because to acknowledge this evidence would require them to acknowledge His power and His authority. To acknowledge this would require them to acknowledge that He has authority over their lives. This they are unwilling to do.

Others see God, not only in nature, but in science and technology. They see God in the vast expanse of space revealed by the instruments of science, a universe far greater than a person with the unaided eye could even dream of. They watch in reverent amazement as men unlock the secrets of electronics, genetics, and the subatomic realm, secrets that God in His wisdom put there. Persons who are so endowed and so blessed respond in several ways.

Awe. As we come to understand the complexity of the world that we are living in, we are driven to our knees in awe. The human body, for example, must maintain a delicate chemical balance if it is to function properly. Even the presence or absence of a few milligrams of this chemical or that can make the difference between health and sickness. Stop for a moment and consider human vision. The light rays emitted from some distant star can strike the eye and create an image that is transmuted into electrical energy that carries a message to the brain. One would have to be a clod indeed if he did not stand in awe of the Creator of such a marvelous process.

Humility. We live in an age that prizes its independence. We go to great lengths to create our own little worlds in which we are self-sufficient. Such a world is an illusion; it doesn't exist. In the very act of breathing, we recognize our dependence upon our Creator. After all, He created the air, and He gave us the ability to breathe it. Should not we with every breath humbly accept our dependence?

However, this humility need not be that of a slave of a tyrannical despot. We are slaves indeed, but we are much more. We are children of a loving heavenly Father. The rich bounty He heaps upon us every day ought to instill within us a sense of dependent humility.

Worship. A person who humbly acknowledges God as the source of every good and perfect gift (James 1:17) will naturally want to praise Him. Those who refuse to trust God will still worship, but they will turn to false worship. "Because that, when they knew God, they glorified him not as God, neither were thankful; but became vain in their imaginations, and their foolish heart was darkened. Professing themselves to be wise, they became fools, and changed the glory of the uncorruptible God into an image made like to corruptible man, and to birds, and four-footed beasts, and creeping things" (Romans 1:21-23).

Of course, few people in our culture would bow down before animals or idols of wood or stone. They turn to more sophisticated idols— money, power, pleasure, things. The principle is the same, however. Whether persons are primitive barbarians or sophisticated moderns, they worship those things they have put first in their lives.

Service. Christians usually unite their hearts to worship together. We find strength and encouragement in that. Our worship is not complete, however, when the final benediction is said. Worship finds its fulfillment beyond the walls of the church building. A vital worship service not only will encourage its participants to seek areas where they may serve, it also will provide some help and direction in how they may serve. A worship service that lifts us to an emotional high and makes us feel good falls short if it does not send us forth with directions about how and where we may serve.

The same is true of a Sunday school class meeting or small group meeting. It would be quite appropriate at this point to ask the students to discuss the different ways in which they are currently serving the Lord. Then have them go beyond this to mention other possible ways to serve. Encourage them to be as specific as possible in their suggestions.

B. Let Us Pray

O mighty Creator and loving Father, we humbly come before You recognizing Your great power and great wisdom in creation. Please give us a better understanding of the wonderful and beautiful world You have created and placed us in, and teach us how to protect and use it for Your glory. Open before us paths of service. In Jesus' name we pray. Amen.

C. Thought to Remember

This is my Father's world,
I rest me in the thought
Of rocks and trees, of skies and seas—
His hand the wonders wrought.
—Maltbie D. Babcock

Learning by Doing

This page contains an alternate lesson plan emphasizing learning activities. Classes desiring such student involvement will find these suggestions helpful.

Learning Goals

As a result of participating in this class session, a learner should:

1. Notice and appreciate the beauty of God's creation that is on display all around him.

2. List characteristics of God that are revealed through nature.

3. Choose one attitude or action that is the result of God's creation and put it into practice.

Into the Lesson

Before class write the following instructions on the board: *Describe places you have visited that display God's creation.* Begin the lesson by asking your learners to describe places they have visited that display the beauty of God's creation. You may want to write the names of the places mentioned on the board under your instructions. Your list will most likely include several well-known places, such as the Grand Canyon. Be prepared to mention a common place yourself to encourage more people to participate. Not everyone has gone to far-off places, but all have been to a forest or local park.

After you have allowed time for people to describe the visible beauty of our invisible Creator, write the word *revelation* on the board above the list of places your people have visited. Explain that not all of God's revelation is in the Bible. We learn much about a skilled craftsman by scrutinizing his work, and we learn much about God through His creation (Romans 1:20). If time permits, you may want to read the story *No Hawks, No Harvest,* found in the introduction of the lesson on page 386.

Into the Word

After your learners have taken time to reflect on God's wonderful works that are on display all around us, divide them into smaller study groups. To promote cooperative learning, your study groups should have from five to seven members. You can divide them into groups or ask them to form small groups on their own. Each group will need a reader, a recorder, and a reporter. The reader's task will be to read Psalm 104 aloud to the group. Another option would be to assign each group a portion of Psalm 104 instead of the entire chapter. This would allow time for fuller discussion. The recorder will take notes on what the group discovers. The reporter

will summarize the group's findings to the whole class when the group is asked to report.

Your prompts for the group should include the following two questions:

1. *What did the psalmist learn about God from nature?* Responses would include: God is the Creator; He sustains the world He has created; He provides for His creatures; He gives renewal; He is powerful; He is loving; and He is wise. Use material from the Lesson Background and sections I and II to help you here.

2. *What have you learned about God from nature?* One response would be that He is a God of order and detail. The class should have no trouble adding to this list.

Start a new list on the board under the heading, *What nature teaches us about God.* When you call for the group reports you may need to think about time. If necessary, ask the groups to delete from their reports any responses that have already been given. This will give each group an opportunity to report to the class.

Into Life

One of the ways God reveals himself to us is through nature. Concentrate upon specific ways the learners can respond to what they learn about God through nature. Use material from the conclusion of the lesson to guide your class discussion. Don't limit your responses to the four given by the lesson writer—awe, humility, worship, and service. Encourage each learner to choose one specific attitude or act and then commit himself or herself to putting this into practice in the week ahead. On an index card have each one write a characteristic of God and a planned response. An example would be, *Because God created and cares for nature, I will pay more attention to recycling around my home, starting this week.* The pattern for the learner to follow is first to state the characteristic of God (*Because God*—) and then to add his or her planned response (*I will*—starting this week). Be ready to share your response with the class. Invite others to read their cards aloud as time permits. Encourage each learner to put the card in a visible place as a reminder of his or her commitment.

Conclude with a silent prayer time as each learner humbly enters God's presence and praises Him for His wonderful works.

Let's Talk It Over

The questions on this page are designed to encourage review of the lesson Scriptures and to promote discussion of the lesson by the class. The answers provided are only discussion starters. Let your class talk it over from there.

1. How is the complexity and the variety in the natural world a testimony to God?

Any explanation of what exists requires some faith. Some people choose to believe in the eternal existence of matter, in a big bang that began the universe, in evolution, or in some other theory that does not include a conscious, all-wise, all powerful, personal Creator. Other people look at what is and agree that a marvelous designer has been at work. That is the most plausible explanation of the order, beauty, and balance in the world. The apostle Paul contends that the testimony of creation alone leaves no excuse for not believing in God (Romans 1:19, 20).

2. How is salvation in Christ related to God's glory and His desire to rejoice in His works?

God created us capable of being tempted and capable of sin, so that the obedience we give is a true sign of faith and devotion. We have all sinned (Romans 3:23), and the justice of God demands that sinners be condemned. "The wages of sin is death" (Romans 6:23), but God takes no delight in seeing His created beings condemned. That God chooses to love sinners adds to His glory, and out of His love He has provided a means of escape from condemnation (Romans 5:8-11). The sacrifice of Jesus on our behalf satisfies the claim of justice, and allows God to extend forgiveness and eternal life to believers. Clearly, God takes joy in this work of salvation, since He is the one who initiated it (John 3:16). We glorify God for creating us and for recreating us in Christ.

3. The power within God's creation is awesome. How can we explain the destruction that sometimes occurs through natural events (earthquakes, floods, etc.)?

If we believe that God is all-knowing, all-powerful, and full of love, how can we explain natural disasters? There is no easy answer, but there are thoughts that help our understanding. The sin of man has altered the entire created order. This world is no longer the perfect estate that existed prior to the fall (Romans 8:22). We know that God's perfect will is not always done in this world, and is a matter for prayer (Matthew 6:10). Satan was responsible for the storm that destroyed Job's family (Job 1:6-22).

Being subject to the tribulations and the imperfect justice of this world should make us yearn for the perfect estate of Heaven (John 16:33). The calamities and suffering we endure prove to us the grace of God under trial, and they develop our character (Romans 5:1-5).

We know also that God sometimes uses natural disasters to punish sinners (Deuteronomy 11: 16, 17). Disaster in our nation is a call to consider our nation's sins. Do they demand punishment? At least we are reminded that there are forces beyond our control. It is wise to live in harmony with the will of the Creator who can control them all.

4. When we worship, how is it important to God? How is it important to us?

Did you ever wonder if your worship of God was more for His sake or for your sake? According to Jesus, God seeks or desires our worship when we worship in spirit and truth (John 4:23, 24). It is reassuring to think that God is blessed when we give heartfelt worship that is grounded in the truth that He has revealed about himself and His will.

Worship is essential also to our Christian walk. "Let the redeemed of the Lord say so" (Psalm 107:2). Jesus warned that those who deny Him should expect to be denied by Him (Matthew 10:33). The alternative is to acknowledge Jesus, and certainly our attention to worship is a way of acknowledging Him. Worship also helps us regain our perspective as we exalt God and recount His wonderful deeds.

5. Give some ideas for increasing our practice of private worship.

Traditionally, many Christians have set aside quiet time in the morning or evening for Bible reading, meditation, and prayer. Using a Bible study guide or devotional guide may help stimulate your thinking and your interest. In our hurried world people are trying creative ways of combining activities. That may mean listening to worship tapes or the Bible on tape while commuting to work or while working at home. Meditating and praying while exercising can bring a double blessing. We need to be in constant touch with God, thanking Him for every joy and asking help in every difficulty.

Praising God for Mighty Acts

DEVOTIONAL READING: Psalm 106:1-12.

LESSON SCRIPTURE: Psalm 105.

PRINTED TEXT: Psalm 105:1-11, 43-45.

Jul
14

Psalm 105:1-11, 43-45

1 O give thanks unto the LORD; call upon his name: make known his deeds among the people.

2 Sing unto him, sing psalms unto him: talk ye of all his wondrous works.

3 Glory ye in his holy name: let the heart of them rejoice that seek the LORD.

4 Seek the LORD, and his strength: seek his face evermore.

5 Remember his marvelous works that he hath done; his wonders, and the judgments of his mouth;

6 O ye seed of Abraham his servant, ye children of Jacob his chosen.

7 He is the LORD our God: his judgments are in all the earth.

8 He hath remembered his covenant for ever, the word which he commanded to a thousand generations.

9 Which covenant he made with Abraham, and his oath unto Isaac;

10 And confirmed the same unto Jacob for a law, and to Israel for an everlasting covenant:

11 Saying, Unto thee will I give the land of Canaan, the lot of your inheritance.

. . . .

43 And he brought forth his people with joy, and his chosen with gladness:

44 And gave them the lands of the heathen: and they inherited the labor of the people;

45 That they might observe his statutes, and keep his laws. Praise ye the LORD.

GOLDEN TEXT: O give thanks unto the LORD; call upon his name: make known his deeds among the people.—Psalm 105:1.

God Is With Us
(Psalms)
Unit 1: Praising God
(Lessons 6-9)

Lesson Aims

As a result of studying this lesson each student should:

1. Understand that God's goodness is ongoing.

2. Appreciate the fact that God keeps the covenants He makes with man.

3. Be able to mention some specific ways in which God has shown His goodness throughout his or her life.

Lesson Outline

INTRODUCTION
   A. "History Is Bunk"
   B. Lesson Background
 I. A CALL TO PRAISE (Psalm 105:1-6)
   A. Give Thanks and Praise (vv. 1-3)
   B. Seek the Lord (v. 4)
     The Search for Strength
   C. Remember His Works (vv. 5, 6)
     The Declaration of Deeds
II. GROUNDS FOR PRAISE (Psalm 105:7-11)
   A. The Lord Is God (v. 7)
   B. God Remembers His Covenant (v. 8)
   C. A Covenant With All Israel (vv. 9, 10)
     One God, Different Men
   D. The Covenant Fulfilled (v. 11)
III. A CLOSING EXHORTATION (Psalm 105:43-45)
   A. Basis for the Exhortation (vv. 43, 44)
   B. Israel's Responsibility (v. 45)
CONCLUSION
   A. When the Singing Stops
   B. Where Have You Been?
   C. Let Us Pray
   D. Thought to Remember

"Praise be to God for all the wonderful things He has done" is the theme of visual 7 shown on page 397.

Introduction

A. "History Is Bunk"

"History is bunk," Henry Ford is reported to have said on one occasion. And many people would agree with him. After all, history is nothing more than a bunch of names, dates, places, and events that happened a long time ago. Besides that, history is usually taught by dull lecturers who obviously would rather be somewhere else doing something else. And the students would rather be somewhere else doing something else. A more serious complaint is that writers of history don't know all the facts and sometimes misinterpret facts they do know.

History may be bunk to some people, but not to the ancient Israelites. Wise men among them never forgot their roots, where they were and how they got there. They knew they were a special people. They knew God had intervened in history on their behalf. Their teachers talked about their roots. Their prophets called them to repentance on the basis of their roots. They even sang about their roots when they came to the temple to worship. Psalm 105 is an example of such a song. History might be bunk to some people, but not to the Israelites. From history of the past they learned what they ought to do in the present and the future. And their history was written by inspired men who made no mistakes.

B. Lesson Background

Many believe that this psalm was designed to be used in public worship. Verses 1-15 appear in 1 Chronicles 16:8-22 as part of the song David gave to the musicians when the ark of the covenant was brought to Jerusalem. This was undoubtedly a joyous occasion calling for praise and thanksgiving. It was also a time for renewing the covenant and for exhorting the people to live according to God's commandments.

The people had come through some difficult times during the reign of Saul and during the early years of David's reign. Now things were looking up, and so they could rejoice. But it was also a time for taking stock of what had happened to them and why it had happened. It was a time to renew their commitment to God. The psalmist helped them do this by singing about their history.

I. A Call to Praise
(Psalm 105:1-6)

A. Give Thanks and Praise (vv. 1-3)

1. O give thanks unto the LORD; call upon his name: make known his deeds among the people.

The first six verses of this psalm serve as an introduction, setting the tone for the rest of the song. This verse is a call for thanksgiving, always an appropriate way to address our Lord, the giver of all our benefits. Worshipers are to call upon His name—Jehovah or Yahweh, the special name that belongs only to the real God.

A major reason for thanksgiving was the way Jehovah had blessed His people, calling them out of Egypt, keeping them during their wandering in the desert, and then leading them into the promised land. The people were not to keep these blessings a secret among themselves. They were to *make known his deeds among the people*. The word is really plural, *peoples*. The Israelites were to tell the facts of their history to the tribes around them.

2. Sing unto him, sing psalms unto him: talk ye of all his wondrous works.

It was quite natural for their gratitude to break forth in song. God's people are singing people. Those who have alienated themselves from God have less to sing about. "Let those refuse to sing who never knew our God." The singing is to be *unto him,* not to please an audience; but *his wondrous works* in Israel's history were to be told, not only in Israel, but to other peoples (v. 1).

3. Glory ye in his holy name: let the heart of them rejoice that seek the LORD.

People of the world glory in their wealth or their power, but the people of God find glory in His name. The word *Lord* is used to translate the Hebrew word *Jehovah* or *Yahweh*. This is the unique name of God, who is the God of the covenant, the God of Abraham, Isaac, and Jacob. The Third Commandment warns about using this name lightly or taking it in vain (Exodus 20:7). To avoid the danger of violating this commandment, the Jews eventually considered this name so holy that they would not pronounce it, even when they were reading Scripture. As a result, later generations forgot how to pronounce the word. It has come into English as *Jehovah,* but many scholars today prefer *Yahweh.*

It is widely believed that the followers of God are a rather solemn bunch, rarely finding joy in life. Nothing could be farther from the truth, as the writer here indicates. While it is true that God first of all requires His people to be holy (1 Peter 1:16), yet He also wants them to be happy. Holiness and happiness are not mutually exclusive. The truth is that the happiest people in the world are those who have surrendered their lives to God. They may not experience the worldly pleasures that others crave, but they have a hope in eternity that assures them of everlasting joy.

B. Seek the Lord (v. 4)

4. Seek the LORD, and his strength: seek his face evermore.

God's search for man is a theme that runs through the entire Bible. Even as God searches for man, however, man must also seek God, actively and diligently. To *seek the Lord* is to desire His presence and His favor. As we seek His presence, we also seek *his strength.* We can be certain that Satan does all he can to discourage us in this search for God, but God gives us strength to continue our search.

THE SEARCH FOR STRENGTH

After a protracted illness, a special diet supplement may be taken to speed recovery. Some liquid preparations are full of minerals and vitamins that "recharge" us physically.

At times there is also a weakening of our spiritual and ethical resources. A constant attrition is caused by our contacts with much that is bitter, cruel, cynical, and superficial. Our efforts to comfort and cheer others may subtract from our own store of inner vitality.

In the Twenty-third Psalm, David says of the Lord, "He restoreth my soul." Isaiah 40:31 says, "They that wait upon the Lord shall renew their strength." Paul writes in Philippians 4:13, "I can do everything through him who gives me strength" (*New International Version*). Psalm 138:3 gives beautiful testimony to the resources we have in our heavenly Father: "In the day when I cried thou answeredst me, and strengthenedst me with strength in my soul."

Verse 4 of our text urges us, "Seek the Lord, and his strength." He is indeed the Sun of our soul who gives us warmth, light, energy, and all we need for guidance, growth, goodness, and, finally, glory. Let us seek Him!   —J. G. V. B.

C. Remember His Works (vv. 5, 6)

5, 6. Remember his marvelous works that he hath done; his wonders, and the judgments of his mouth; O ye seed of Abraham his servant, ye children of Jacob his chosen.

Psalm 104, which was the subject of last week's lesson, praised God for His wonderful works in nature. Psalm 105 encourages the people to remember *his marvelous works* in history: those occasions when God actively directed His people, or saved them from disaster, or gave some other special help. We are often prone to forget all the good things He has done for us and remember only the times He didn't give us exactly what we wanted. We need to have our memories jogged so that we won't forget, but also so that we may pass these memories on to our children and our grandchildren.

His wonders means the miracles He wrought. The miraculous delivery from Egypt loomed large in Hebrew history. *The judgments* were punishments inflicted on Israel or others. God's people were to remember the happy occasions when God rescued them or blessed them, but they were also to remember the times His holy wrath had fallen upon them.

The Israelites were reminded that they were children of Abraham, inheritors of the promise made to him. They would remember that in his life Abraham saw both God's marvelous works and His judgment. For example, Abraham from a distance watched the destruction of Sodom and Gomorrah (Genesis 19:27, 28). As he watched the smoke arise from those doomed cities, he knew this was God's judgment upon them for their wickedness. Jacob also had an opportunity to see God's marvelous works. When a famine descended upon his family and the surrounding tribes, God already had made provision for them in Egypt through Joseph.

THE DECLARATION OF DEEDS

The high honor given to George Washington is due not so much to what he *said* as to what he *did*. He left a peaceful estate in Virginia to cast his lot with uncertain forces seeking to form an independent nation. His presence in struggles around Boston, his sharing with his troops in the bitter winter at Valley Forge, his crossing the icy Delaware River to lead an attack on the Hessians at Trenton—all were evidences of his sacrificial dedication to the cause of independence.

After the war he rejected suggestions that he become a king, but served eight years as president. He tried to bring calm, constructive order to the political life of the new nation. Then he gave up power and retired to Mount Vernon. What he did marked him as "first in war, first in peace, and first in the hearts of his countrymen."

Verses 1, 2, 5 of Psalm 105 speak of God's deeds, works, and wonders as evidence of His power and His care for His people. In what He did His care and His character were made known. Redemption from Egypt, deliverance from perils, and blessings in the lives of biblical characters all testify to His concern and evoke our gratitude and praise.

Have we not known God's blessing in our own lives? We have been rescued, sustained, and enlightened as we have walked in His way and trusted in His love. Praise Him for His wondrous works!   —J. G. V. B.

II. Grounds for Praise
(Psalm 105:7-11)

A. The Lord Is God (v. 7)

7. He is the LORD our God: his judgments are in all the earth.

The writer hails the Lord, that is, Yahweh, as the God of the Israelites. He called them out, entered into a covenant with them, and richly blessed them. But Yahweh was not the God of the Israelites only. *His judgments are in all the earth.* The tribal gods of the pagan peoples around the Israelites were not real gods. Yahweh is real. In His covenant with Abraham He promised to bless Abraham, but He also promised to bless "all families of the earth" through him (Genesis 12:3). That blessing, of course, came through God's Son, Jesus Christ. But as God's blessings extend to the whole earth, so also do His judgments.

B. God Remembers His Covenant (v. 8)

8. He hath remembered his covenant for ever, the word which he commanded to a thousand generations.

God had kept His part of the covenant. That was the reason for the strong exhortation in verse 5, urging the people to remember their part. *To a thousand generations.* Century after century God kept His end of the bargain, but again and again the people failed to live up to their commitment. As a result, God promised to establish a new covenant with His people: "Behold, the days come, saith the Lord, that I will make a new covenant with the house of Israel, and with the house of Judah" (Jeremiah 31:31). This new covenant or new testament was established by Christ (Matthew 26:28).

C. A Covenant With All Israel
(vv. 9, 10)

9, 10. Which covenant he made with Abraham, and his oath unto Isaac; and confirmed the same unto Jacob for a law, and to Israel for an everlasting covenant.

God's covenant with Abraham is first recorded in Genesis 12:1-3 and then in Genesis 17:1-18. It was later affirmed to Isaac (Genesis 26:3, 4) and then Jacob (Genesis 28:10-15). After Jacob wrestled with an angel, he was given the new name of Israel (Genesis 32:24-28). Later this name was applied to the whole nation of his descendants. That seems to be the meaning of *Israel* in this verse.

ONE GOD, DIFFERENT MEN

In verses 9 and 10 we read of God's covenant made with Abraham, then with Isaac, and later with Jacob and Israel as a nation. It was a promise to give them the land of Canaan, a promise conditioned on their obedience to the Lord. There was and is but one continuing God, but He deals in promises and pledges with generations of men as they come, live their lives, and go into eternity.

There is a beautiful chapter in the apocryphal book of *Ecclesiasticus* that begins,

Let us now praise famous men,
And our fathers in their generations.

The chapter is a recital of the dedication and deeds of many worthies of Israel, beginning with Enoch.

Now we have accepted God's new covenant sealed by the blood of Jesus. Our responsibility is to be faithful in our generation.   —J. G. V. B.

D. The Covenant Fulfilled (v. 11)

11. Saying, Unto thee will I give the land of Canaan, the lot of your inheritance.

Centuries earlier the land had been promised to Abraham (Genesis 17:8). He had lived there as a wandering shepherd. After centuries in Egypt, God led Abraham's people back to that land. *The lot of your inheritance* is literally *the cord of your inheritance,* suggesting that Canaan had been measured out with a cord. A brief description of how the land was portioned out among the tribes of Israel is recorded in Numbers 34.

III. A Closing Exhortation (Psalm 105:43-45)

A. Basis for the Exhortation (vv. 43, 44)

43. And he brought forth his people with joy, and his chosen with gladness.

God brought the Israelites out of Egypt with a tremendous display of His power. The ten plagues, along with the miraculous crossing of the Red Sea, convinced even the most skeptical that God was leading the people (Exodus 14:31). Once the people were safely out of the reach of Pharaoh, Moses led them in a great song of rejoicing. We are told that Miriam, Moses' sister, led the women with music, singing, and dancing (Exodus 15). Praising God with songs was certainly a normal response after such a great deliverance.

44. And gave them the lands of the heathen: and they inherited the labor of the people.

After reminding the people how the Israelites praised God following their escape from the Egyptians, the psalmist reminds them that they have much more for which to be thankful. The land that God led them into was already a developed land. The Canaanites, whom the Israelites replaced, had spent centuries building houses, walling cities, digging wells, clearing fields, and planting vineyards. The hard work had been done; all the Israelites had to do was to move in.

In some respects we are like these ancient Israelites. Our generation has inherited a land that has been richly developed by the hard work of those who have gone before us. We are the heirs

of a government that grants us religious freedom, a blessing still denied in many places around the world. We live in a country that has become the envy of the rest of the world, and yet we often fail to appreciate it. In spite of our blessings we never seem satisfied, always wanting more. It is perhaps not entirely coincidental that "Count Your Blessings," which we used to sing regularly, is now missing in many of our song books: "Count your many blessings, name them one by one, and it will surprise you what the Lord hath done."

B. Israel's Responsibility (v. 45)

45. That they might observe his statutes, and keep his laws. Praise ye the LORD.

God fulfilled every promise He made to His people. With these blessings, however, came responsibilities. The tragedy of the Israelites was their short memory. When they accepted God's covenant, they undoubtedly intended to keep their end of the bargain. After a time, however, they became involved in enjoying their blessings and they forgot to observe God's statutes. They failed to pass along to all their children the faith that had brought them to the promised land. They turned to the idols of Canaan and brought disgrace upon themselves.

This script sounds all too familiar, and certainly it should, for we are seeing the same process unfold in our own land. We have forgotten the blessings we have received and have turned to the idols of possessions and pleasures.

Conclusion

A. When the Singing Stops

Our culture has a frightening way of intruding into our Christian faith and bringing changes. Some of them are good, but some of them are bad. Those who oppose innovations are right in keeping out worldly elements that may erode the faith, but in defending present patterns they may reject elements that are good.

O give thanks unto the LORD;
call upon his name;
Make known his deeds
among the people.
Sing unto him, sing psalms unto him;
talk ye of all his wondrous works.
Glory ye in his holy name:
let the heart of them rejoice
that seek the Lord.
Seek the Lord, and his strength;
seek his face evermore.

visual 7

The New Testament gives us very little specific information about how Christians worshiped in the first century. Early Christians put more emphasis on people's attitudes when they worshiped and on how they lived after the worship service ended.

Many Christians are disturbed by some of the changes they see being instituted in worship. They don't know the praise choruses that are replacing the gospel songs and the old familiar hymns. They are shocked by clapping and the raising of hands. It is right to be concerned, for every generation must evaluate changes in worship patterns lest we become enthralled with practices and values that reflect the world rather than the Scriptures. However, change in Christian worship has been a continuing process over the past two thousand years, and change will continue for another two thousand years, if the Lord delays His coming. Change is not necessarily bad. We need to examine each change to see what it is and what it does.

More important than worship styles is this question: What happens when the singing ends? God accepts any worship if it is in keeping with His laws and if it comes from grateful, joyous hearts. If a worship service is followed by changes that make people more loving, more generous, more responsible, more faithful in their commitment to the Lord, then we ought to rejoice; but if our worship fails to remind us of God's nature and His will, then we, like the ancient Israelites, are worshiping in vain. What happens in your church after the singing stops?

B. Where Have You Been?

Most of us have had the experience of traveling down a highway and not paying too much attention to where we were. By remembering the exits that we had passed, however, we could orient ourselves on the map and locate where we were. In other words, we knew where we were by remembering where we had been.

That is what Psalm 105 is all about. The Israelites throughout their history were surrounded by enemies who wished nothing more than to do them in. This psalm recounts their history as a means of giving them assurance. It tells how God called Abraham and made a covenant with him. That covenant was renewed with the descendants of Abraham. God watched over and protected His people. An outstanding example of that protection was their deliverance from Egypt.

As they sang this psalm or listened to it, they knew where they were in history. Even more important, they knew Whose they were. In the trying times they faced, that knowledge gave them great assurance.

We share many things with the ancient Israelites. We worship the same God—Jehovah. The Israelites were His chosen people under the Old Covenant. Christians are His chosen people under the New Covenant. The Israelites were often led to pursue false gods, and in the process they lost their way. They needed to be reminded of where they had been in order to know where they were. We too have often been led astray, enticed by the world. We have lost our way; and to find our way back, we need to know where we have been. For that reason we need to study the Old Testament to learn what God has done for His people under the Old Covenant, and we need to study the New Testament to understand where He wants us to go today. We also need to study the history of the church in order to see some of the mistakes others have made and the results of those mistakes. We need to learn of the faith and courage of some of the saints who worked and suffered so that we may enjoy the blessings God has in store for His own. Let the Bible be our road map to let us see where the church has been, where we are now, and where we ought to be headed.

C. Let Us Pray

Dear Father, let our hearts sing our praises to You. Let our voices exalt You. Kindle in our hearts the memories of all that You have done for us. Help us to understand Your statutes. Give us the strength to keep Your laws. Above all, teach us to trust in You as the hope of our salvation. In Jesus' name we pray. Amen.

D. Thought to Remember

"It is only as men begin to worship that they begin to grow."   —Calvin Coolidge

Home Daily Bible Readings

Monday, July 8—Covenant Initiated by God (Genesis 17:1-8)
Tuesday, July 9—A Helper Provided (Exodus 4:10-17)
Wednesday, July 10—Dependent on God's Mercies (Deuteronomy 8:1-10)
Thursday, July 11—Praise, Prayer, and Confession (Psalm 106:1-12)
Friday, July 12—Confident of God's Help (Isaiah 26:7-15)
Saturday, July 13—God's Discipline (Jeremiah 32:17-25)
Sunday, July 14—God's Provisions for Humankind (Luke 1:67-79)

Learning by Doing

This page contains an alternate lesson plan emphasizing learning activities. Classes desiring such student involvement will find these suggestions helpful.

Learning Goals

After this class, students should:

1. Appreciate the good from each family.

2. Discover how God's saving acts from the past influence how people live now and in the future.

3. Reflect on God's intervention in the lives of His people, knowing that He is always present.

Into the Lesson

Before class draw two columns on the board using the following headings: "Joyful Times" and "Difficult Times."

Begin the lesson by pointing out that life is not all joyful nor all difficult, but rather a combination of the two. We all desire more joyful times, but both have their places in our family life. Ask each learner to take a few moments to think back over his or her family's history and write down a brief description of joyful and difficult times that come to mind. Encourage all to emphasize the joyful times, but not to ignore the difficult times. Give each a sheet of paper that is divided as the board is. People will need time to think, so allow several minutes for this writing.

Ask for volunteers who are willing to share some of the joyful times from their family's past. Repeat the same type of sharing for difficult times. If your learners like to share, you may have to limit each to one response from each category. Be ready to share from your family history as well.

Into the Word

Do you remember the suggestion from last week's lesson on dividing your class into smaller study groups? This time divide your class into three study groups. Again, each group will need a reader, a recorder, and a reporter. One of the assignments below should be given to each study group to get the thinking started. To save time you can write out the Scripture reference and assignment for each group on a separate index card before class. Then distribute the cards to your groups when you divide the class.

Assignments

1. Psalm 105:1-6   List the ten imperatives
2. Psalm 105:7-11, 42-45 Describe the covenant
3. Psalm 105:12-41   Summarize God's helpful acts

Write the following phrase on the board before the groups start: "How God's intervention influences our future." Ask the groups to keep this thought uppermost in mind as they complete their assignments. Use the following information to clarify the assignments.

Group 1: As you list the ten imperatives, consider how these would be influenced by a past relationship between God and His people.

Group 2: While describing the covenant between God and the Israelites, consider how a past promise influenced the future relationship.

Group 3: In summarizing God's helpful acts, be thinking about how these past actions influenced God's people in the future.

To ensure that every group gets a chance to make a report, set a time limit. Before the first group reports tell them that each group has four minutes to summarize their study. Suggest that a member of the reporting group watch the clock and say "time" when four minutes are up. Use the lesson material in sections I, II, and III to prepare you for any questions the class members may ask concerning what they read in Psalm 105.

Into Life

Write the following statement on the board: "History is bunk," then ask the class if they agree or disagree. Use the material in the Introduction section of the lesson to guide you in this discussion. Explain that history may be bunk to some people, but not to the Israelites. They got in trouble whenever they forgot their roots, where they were, and how they got there. They were a special people, and God had intervened in history on their behalf. We also need to recognize that God intervenes in our lives as well. He is present in the joyous times and the difficult times. We know this because He promised to be with us always (see Matthew 28:20).

Have the learners look over the sheets where they listed joyous and difficult times in the history of their families. Ask them to consider how God may have intervened in these circumstances. Ask for several of the class members to describe how they see God's hand in the events they have listed.

Close the class session with sentence prayers thanking God for His presence in our past, present, and future.

Let's Talk It Over

*The questions on this page are designed to encourage review of the lesson
Scriptures and to promote discussion of the lesson by the class. The answers
provided are only discussion starters. Let your class talk it over from there.*

1. As you think about worship at your church, which of God's deeds are celebrated in thanksgiving, and how is that done?

While worship styles vary from place to place, certain elements of Christian worship are fairly constant. There is nearly always singing, and often the singing not only praises and exalts God for His character, but also recounts His deeds as subject for thanksgiving. Prayers may explicitly give thanks to God for all kinds of blessings. The giving of offerings is an act of faith and of thanksgiving for the way God provides our needs. In observing Communion we recall God's greatest deed, the giving of His Son, Jesus. Certainly it is with thanksgiving that we remember what was accomplished for our sakes in the death of our Savior.

2. What are some practical reasons that those who seek the Lord may rejoice?

Unbelievers may think that seeking God will result in heavy obligation and unwelcome constraints. Jesus explicitly stated, however, "Come unto me, all ye that labor and are heavy laden . . . and ye shall find rest unto your souls. For my yoke is easy, and my burden is light" (Matthew 11:28-30). Those who love God discover that His commands are designed to give life, and are therefore not distasteful (1 John 5:3). Seeking God leads to forgiveness of sin, a transformed character, a compelling purpose in life, and the promise of a blessed eternity. These are all good reasons for rejoicing.

3. How long a memory do we need in order to acknowledge God's works? What "marvelous works" does He do today?

Often the focus of our worship is on the mighty deeds of God recorded in the Bible. Certainly they are reason enough to praise God, but it may give new vitality to our worship if we can also recount contemporary evidence of God at work. In some worship meetings opportunity is given for Christians to "testify," recounting how God has intervened to work a great blessing. Each day God continues to answer prayers and to reclaim lives given to Him, and He should receive glory and thanksgiving for those works as well as His mighty works in history.

4. How are God's judgments evident among those who ignore Him today?

The law of sowing and reaping is always in effect. "Whatsoever a man soweth, that shall he also reap. For he that soweth to his flesh shall of the flesh reap corruption; but he that soweth to the Spirit shall of the Spirit reap life everlasting" (Galatians 6:7, 8). All of us can name people whose sins have made shipwreck of their career, their marriage, or their health. Our entire society suffers because of failure to acknowledge certain immutable precepts of God. The judgments Paul describes in Romans 1:21-32 have been fulfilled many times over. When people refuse to acknowledge God, their reasoning is affected and the moral results are devastating.

5. What caused God to favor the descendants of Abraham? How can we participate in God's new covenant and share in His blessings?

God made a covenant with Abraham because of Abraham's faith. The terms of the covenant were that Abraham's descendants would be blessed as the people of God, but their part was to remain faithful: to trust God and obey Him. God has established a new covenant in Jesus that is available to all who will believe in Him. The terms are that God will forgive, will adopt us into His spiritual family, and will give us the benefit of His indwelling Holy Spirit to equip us for service and prepare us for eternity with Him. Our part in this covenant is faith, faith that is both belief and trust. True faith will compel us to repentance and obedience.

6. How does obedience relate to worship?

Worship that is not accompanied by obedience, or at least a sincere effort to follow God's will, is contemptible hypocrisy. God complained that His people honored Him with their mouths, but their hearts were far from Him (Isaiah 29:13). Jesus rebuked those whose worship was a vain show not matched by a godly character (Matthew 23:23-28). The apostle Paul maintains that a consecrated life is our "reasonable service" (Romans 12:1), or, as translated in the *New International Version,* our "spiritual act of worship." John adds, "If we say that we have fellowship with him, and walk in darkness, we lie, and do not the truth" (1 John 1:6).

Praising God for Deliverance

DEVOTIONAL READING: Psalm 121:1-8.

LESSON SCRIPTURE: Psalm 34.

PRINTED TEXT: Psalm 34:2-10, 18-22.

Psalm 34:2-10, 18-22

2 My soul shall make her boast in the LORD: the humble shall hear thereof, and be glad.

3 O magnify the LORD with me, and let us exalt his name together.

4 I sought the LORD, and he heard me, and delivered me from all my fears.

5 They looked unto him, and were lightened: and their faces were not ashamed.

6 This poor man cried, and the LORD heard him, and saved him out of all his troubles.

7 The angel of the LORD encampeth round about them that fear him, and delivereth them.

8 O taste and see that the LORD is good: blessed is the man that trusteth in him.

9 O fear the LORD, ye his saints: for there is no want to them that fear him.

10 The young lions do lack, and suffer hunger: but they that seek the LORD shall not want any good thing.

. . . .

18 The LORD is nigh unto them that are of a broken heart; and saveth such as be of a contrite spirit.

19 Many are the afflictions of the righteous: but the LORD delivereth him out of them all.

20 He keepeth all his bones: not one of them is broken.

21 Evil shall slay the wicked: and they that hate the righteous shall be desolate.

22 The LORD redeemeth the soul of his servants: and none of them that trust in him shall be desolate.

**Jul
21**

GOLDEN TEXT: The LORD is nigh unto them that are of a broken heart; and saveth such as be of a contrite spirit. —Psalm 34:18.

God Is With Us
(Psalms)
Unit 1: Praising God
(Lessons 6-9)

Lesson Aims

As a result of studying this lesson, each student should:

1. Understand that God is a sure help in time of trouble.

2. Appreciate the consolation that God provides through the psalms.

3. Be better able to provide encouragement to those who sorrow.

Lesson Outline

INTRODUCTION
  A. In Protecting Hands
  B. Lesson Background
I. A SONG OF PRAISE (Psalm 34:2-7)
  A. Freely Given (vv. 2, 3)
  B. A Cry for Help (vv. 4, 5)
    The Glow of Glory
  C. The Cry Answered (vv. 6, 7)
II. KNOWING GOD (Psalm 34:8-10)
  A. Through Experience (v. 8)
    Take a Taste
  B. Through His Care (vv. 9, 10)
III. GOD AND HIS PEOPLE (Psalm 34:18-22)
  A. God Is Near (v. 18)
    The Touch of Tenderness
  B. God Delivers His Own (vv. 19, 20)
  C. The Wicked Shall Perish (v. 21)
  D. The Lord Redeems (v. 22)
CONCLUSION
  A. The Only Way You Can Look Is Up
  B. Dialing the Divine 911
  C. Let Us Pray
  D. Thought to Remember

God hears and delivers those who in humility cry out to Him. See visual 8 of the visuals packet shown on page 406.

Introduction

A. In Protecting Hands

In the early months of the Protestant Reformation, the pope sent a representative to try to persuade Martin Luther to abandon his activities. The representative, a skilled theologian, did his best to show him the error of his ways; but Luther was also a theologian and a student of the Bible. He was able to answer every challenge thrust at him.

Finally the papal envoy realized that Luther would not be changed by argument, and so he turned to threats. "Dr. Luther," he said, "the pope has more power in his little finger than all these German princes put together. If he unleashes that power, where will you be then?"

Unmoved by the threats, Luther calmly replied, "I'll be right where I am now—in the protecting hands of the Almighty." In his faith Luther was reflecting the faith shown by the writer of Psalm 34: "The angel of the Lord encampeth round about them that fear him."

B. Lesson Background

The structure of this psalm is unusual. Each verse starts with a different letter in the Hebrew alphabet. Verse 1 begins with the first letter, *aleph*. Verse 2 begins with the second letter, *beth*, and so on through the alphabet. We don't know why the author used this acrostic literary form. Perhaps it was to make the psalm easier for singers to memorize. Perhaps it was a popular form at that particular period in history. Several other psalms are similar in style. For whatever reason, the writer used this form as a framework upon which to build his poem, much as English writers for many years have used limericks or various sonnet forms for their work.

The title of Psalm 34 ascribes it to David during the time when he was fleeing from King Saul. David found refuge in Gath, a Philistine city (1 Samuel 21:10-15). There he met Abimelech, the king (also known as Achish). When Achish was told that this was the general who had defeated the Philistines in battle, David became fearful for his life. To escape he pretended to be insane. Displeased with such a demented person, the king sent him away. David then took refuge in the cave of Adullam, southwest of Jerusalem. There he was surrounded by friends, and for a while was relatively safe from Saul.

I. A Song of Praise
(Psalm 34:2-7)

A. Freely Given (vv. 2, 3)

2, 3. My soul shall make her boast in the LORD: the humble shall hear thereof, and be glad. O magnify the LORD with me, and let us exalt his name together.

In verse 1 the psalmist affirmed that he would bless the Lord at all times. Certainly this included the good times, but it also included the bad times. David was in a life-and-death struggle. His effort to find a safe refuge with Abimelech had come to naught, and now he had to endure the life of a fugitive. His safety was uncertain even when he was hiding in a remote cave among friends. Still he declared he would praise the Lord.

This vow to praise the Lord regardless of circumstances finds fulfillment in verses 2 and 3. We read in 1 Samuel 22:2 that when David was at Adullam "every one that was in distress, and every one that was in debt, and every one that was discontented, gathered themselves unto him; and he became a captain over them: and there were with him about four hundred men." Such a motley crew of down-and-outers, placed a heavy responsibility upon David; and this psalm may have been written to reassure them and direct them to God as the source of power.

Boasting is not ordinarily considered a virtue, but David had no intention of boasting in his own strength. Rather, his boasting would be *in the Lord*. The *humble* (the *New International Version* has "afflicted") would respond gladly to the Lord when they understood that He was the source of their power. Certainly the group that was attracted to David would be considered humble and afflicted. In verse 3 David encourages them to join with him in glorifying the Lord. There are times when it is most appropriate for an individual to pour out his heart in praise to God. There are other occasions when corporate praise is proper, and this was one of those times. This group of outcasts lifting their voices would praise God, but their song would also lift their spirits and bring encouragement.

B. A Cry for Help (vv. 4, 5)

4, 5. I sought the LORD, and he heard me, and delivered me from all my fears. They looked unto him, and were lightened: and their faces were not ashamed.

David's flight to the Philistines had proved to be unwise. He had sought safety with them instead of trusting wholly in the Lord. He had come to recognize his folly and had come to God. When he humbly sought the Lord, the Lord heard him: that is, answered his prayer for protection. God not only delivered him from physical danger, but also delivered him from fear. In many situations fear is a more dangerous enemy than physical danger. Physical danger often arises suddenly and just as suddenly passes, but fear can linger to gnaw at our very vitals. Medical science now recognizes that anxiety can cause heart and circulatory problems and lead to ulcers and many other ills. Fear weakens us physically and erodes our resolve. Freed of this fear, David had every reason to praise God.

Jesus on occasion also spoke to this problem. "Let not your heart be troubled," He said, and

How to Say It

ABIMELECH. Uh-*bim*-eh-lek.
ACHISH. *A*-kish.
ADULLAM. A-*dull*-lum.
ALEPH (Hebrew). *ah*-leff.
BETH (Hebrew). bayth or bait.

lifted the eyes of His disciples to the hope of Heaven for reassurance (John 14:1-3). John dealt with the same subject: "There is no fear in love; but perfect love casteth out fear: because fear hath torment. He that feareth is not made perfect in love" (1 John 4:18).

The men with David likewise trusted in God and had fear lifted from their hearts. They *were lightened*. The *New International Version* has "are radiant." There was a glow in their countenances and a joy in their lives.

THE GLOW OF GLORY

Our faces have a way of revealing the emotional state we are experiencing. We often see a friend with a gloomy or downcast look, so much so that we ask, "What's wrong?" Sometimes there is a happy aura about one's expression, and we say, "Aren't you a cheerful cherub today!"

In verse 5 of today's text we are told that those trusting in God and looking to Him were "lightened" so that it showed in their faces. The *New International Version* translates this, "Those who look to him are radiant."

When Moses came down from Mount Sinai after receiving the Ten Commandments, he "wist not that the skin of his face shone" (Exodus 34:29). That radiance passed away, but as Christians we are changed "from glory to glory" as we look to God in Christ (2 Corinthians 3:7-18). What a great promise and reassurance this is! As we look to the Lord Jesus our faces express the glow with which our trust in Him fills our lives.   —J. G. V. B.

C. The Cry Answered (vv. 6, 7)

6, 7. This poor man cried, and the LORD heard him, and saved him out of all his troubles. The angel of the LORD encampeth round about them that fear him, and delivereth them.

This repeats the sentiments found in verse 4. Now David writes in the third person, but he is still speaking about himself. *This poor man* is David. He was poor indeed. His life was in jeopardy, and he had no powerful friends to whom he could turn. In his extremity he turned to God, who heard his prayer. The eternal King does not play favorites. High or low, rich or poor, every person has access to the heavenly throne. David was still sought by the troops of Saul, but his fear was swept away when the Lord heard his prayer.

The *angel of the Lord* appears in Scripture as God's special agent in dealing with man. Sometimes He is the agent of judgment and destruction (2 Samuel 24:16; 2 Kings 19:35). In other situations He protects and delivers (Exodus 14:19, 20). That is obviously His role in the passage we are studying. Like a mighty army, the angel of the Lord surrounds those who fear Him, giving them protection and deliverance.

II. Knowing God
(Psalm 34:8-10)

A. Through Experience (v. 8)

8. O taste and see that the LORD is good: blessed is the man that trusteth in him.

Persons who have walked with God most of their lives know from experience that He has protected them and delivered them. They have "tasted" His blessings. There are others whose faith may be completely intellectual. In their own lives they have never felt God's strong presence. David invites such people to open their hearts so they can experience Him. Intellectual faith is important, of course, but it is never complete in itself. It needs the support of knowing firsthand God's blessings. Since David had just gone through a harrowing experience, he was in an excellent position to invite others to share in the same joy.

TAKE A TASTE

Scientists say there are only four tastes: sweet, sour, bitter, and salt. But different combinations of these, plus odor and texture, give us a tremendous number of different sensations. One cannot always tell how something tastes by how it looks, or describe to another the special delight of a certain taste. So we say, "Just taste it and see!"

Peanut butter is an example. It certainly does not look as attractive as a crimson apple or a golden orange. However, as I have expressed it in a poem, it is

> A sticky and a tawny treasure,
> A nutrient, yet a source of pleasure.

It is not by looking at peanut butter but by tasting it that one discovers the mouth-watering gusto it can create.

The psalmist is concerned that people may not realize how good and gracious God is. He knows they will not find out by standing at a

distance, arguing about God, or speculating about what "religious experience" is. God is best known by taking Him into one's life—by "tasting" of His nature, by "trying Him out."

—J. G. V. B.

B. Through His Care (vv. 9, 10)

9. O fear the LORD, ye his saints: for there is no want to them that fear him.

To fear God is to give Him humble reverence that leads to a faithful observance of His laws. Anyone who claims to be a follower of God must demonstrate that fact by leading a life of obedience. The *saints* in the Old Testament period were people devoted to God. In the New Testament all Christians are called saints. This does not so much describe the level of their moral attainment as it describes their status before God. Every saint is one who has been set apart or dedicated to God.

The saints enjoy the knowledge that they will suffer *no want*. They learn to distinguish their desires from their needs. Most of us are still trying to do this. Only a few have been in situations where we had nothing but the bare essentials needed to sustain life. Those who have had that experience have come to realize how little it takes to survive. Further, we should understand God's promise in an eternal sense. In the past, many saints have refused to give up their faith and have perished because they lacked food, shelter, and clothing. To them the Lord says, "Great is your reward in heaven" (Matthew 5:11, 12).

10. The young lions do lack, and suffer hunger: but they that seek the LORD shall not want any good thing.

The lion, frequently referred to as king of the beasts, is feared by other animals. But at times even powerful young lions do not find prey, and as a result go hungry. The point the psalmist is making is that strength and cunning are not always enough to keep one from experiencing want. By contrast, *they that seek the Lord* will find that their needs are met. The world does not readily comprehend this paradox. Jesus expressed a similar idea when He affirmed that the meek "shall inherit the earth" (Matthew 5:5).

III. God and His People
(Psalm 34:18-22)

A. God Is Near (v. 18)

18. The LORD is nigh unto them that are of a broken heart; and saveth such as be of a contrite spirit.

The Lord is everywhere, and so He is near everyone. And yet in a sense He is especially

Home Daily Bible Readings

Monday, July 15—Victory in Battle (Psalm 18:6-19)
Tuesday, July 16—Delivered From Enemies (2 Samuel 22:1-7)
Wednesday, July 17—Delivered From Burning (Daniel 3:24-30)
Thursday, July 18—Delivered From Prison (Acts 12:6-11)
Friday, July 19—Delivered From Shipwreck (Acts 27:39-44)
Saturday, July 20—Delivered From Temptation (1 Corinthians 10:6-13)
Sunday, July 21—Delivered to Heavenly Kingdom (2 Timothy 4:9-18)

close to those who have *a broken heart*. The brokenhearted here are not those so crushed that they give up their faith, neither are they those who meet trouble with stubborn rebellion. They are the humble and contrite, those who yield themselves to God's will. They are the ones who will be blessed. The world often honors those who are bold and aggressive, even arrogant. But in both the Old and New Testaments we find God honoring those who are humble and submissive before Him. For example, in Micah 6:8 we read, "He hath showed thee, O man, what is good; and what doth the Lord require of thee, but to do justly, and to love mercy, and to walk humbly with thy God?" In the Sermon on the Mount Jesus expressed the same idea in these words: "Blessed are the poor in spirit: for theirs is the kingdom of heaven" (Matthew 5:3).

God offers salvation to those of a contrite spirit. This is not to say they will escape all danger and all suffering. God does not assure us that life will be a bed of roses if we submit to Him. But we do have the assurance that when suffering and sorrows come, He will provide the strength to triumph over them.

THE TOUCH OF TENDERNESS

Many of us know what it is to be "brokenhearted." Some have trusted in another's faithfulness and have been betrayed. Some have lost loving life partners through death. Some have met failure in some great endeavor. The psalmist is not singing of such tragedies so much as of the condition of the heart—a heart neither rebelling nor giving up hope, but humbly submitting to God.

What an assurance we have in the statement that our heavenly Father is near us! Jesus reminds us in Luke 12:6, "Are not five sparrows

sold for two farthings, and not one of them is forgotten before God?" As a stanza from Civilla D. Martin's hymn says so vividly:

"Let not your heart be troubled,"
His tender word I hear,
And resting on His goodness,
I lose my doubts and fears;
Tho' by the path He leadeth
But one step I may see:
His eye is on the sparrow,
And I know He watches me.
—J. G. V. B.

B. God Delivers His Own (vv. 19, 20)

19, 20. Many are the afflictions of the righteous: but the LORD delivereth him out of them all. He keepeth all his bones: not one of them is broken.

Many are the afflictions of the righteous. The saints have ample evidence of the truth of this statement. Some suffer because they are righteous. The pages of the history of the church are stained with the blood of martyrs who suffered because they refused to compromise their faith. Sometimes, however, the righteous suffer because they have sinned. The righteous, like everyone else, may succumb to temptation; and when this happens they suffer the consequences just like any other sinner. In some situations people suffer, not because they are sinners, but because they are foolish or ignorant. A child who plays with matches and is burned is not a sinner. He or she is simply ignorant.

From recent events in his own life, David recognized that the life of the faithful is not always healthy and wealthy. When a righteous man falls into sin and suffers as a result, God uses chastening to cleanse and purge him from that sin. This idea is expressed in Hebrews 12:6: "For whom the Lord loveth he chasteneth, and scourgeth every son whom he receiveth."

All his bones is to be understood as the whole body. While this refers to protection from physical harm, its meaning can be extended to the spiritual realm, where God has promised protection for His own.

C. The Wicked Shall Perish (v. 21)

21. Evil shall slay the wicked: and they that hate the righteous shall be desolate.

Justice is not perfect in this life; the righteous often suffer and the wicked seem to prosper. And yet justice is often meted out. One who sets out upon a life of violence comes to a violent end: a person who is motivated by hatred becomes the object of hatred.

The psalmist may have had more in mind than justice in this life. He may have been looking to the ultimate judgment with God as the supreme judge. In that day all of us will stand guilty before Him. Our only hope is that we have "an advocate with the Father, Jesus Christ the righteous" (1 John 2:1). We escape the penalty we deserve because Jesus bore it for us.

D. The Lord Redeems (v. 22)

22. The LORD redeemeth the soul of his servants: and none of them that trust in him shall be desolate.

God takes care of His own. No Bible truth is more certain than this. We doubt that David had more than a faint glimpse of the salvation God has in store for the faithful. Yet he seems to envision more than just physical redemption. We have a much fuller understanding of God's plans for the righteous because He sent His Son to reveal those plans to us. Should we not then lift our hearts in more joyous song because we have so much more for which to be thankful?

Conclusion

A. The Only Way You Can Look Is Up

"When you're at the bottom of a well, the only way you can look is up," my grandmother used to say. This statement summarized her outlook on life. And it was a most appropriate philosophy, for she knew little but hard times and sickness. Yet in spite of all of this, she was a happy person, always singing or humming a hymn as she went about her daily work. As a young girl she had committed her life to the Lord, and through the years that commitment grew and deepened. She knew that no matter how bad things might seem, she could always look up to the Lord and pray. And she never doubted for a moment that God would answer her prayer, not always in the way she had asked, but always in His way and in His time.

My grandmother lived and died in obscurity. And yet she left behind a living memorial. More than a half dozen of her grandchildren and

great-grandchildren are today ministers, ministers' wives, or missionaries, and most of the others are active in the Lord's work.

In her own quiet way Grandmother was able to pass along to her descendants that serene faith that sustained her through all kinds of difficulties. But she had no exclusive claim on that faith. Any one of us can lay hold of it. It was the kind of faith that sustained David during his many trials. We are not told how he acquired his faith, but we can be sure he learned it from his parents and his friends and from God's Word. Just as important was his growth in that faith. As life battered and bruised him, he did not spend much time feeling sorry for himself or becoming bitter. Instead he looked increasingly to God, not only for help, but to praise Him.

B. Dialing the Divine 911

When we moved into our present home, our county was considered a rural area. But the city soon began to encroach upon our rustic environment, bringing with it many of the amenities and the problems of a big city. The fire department was practically nonexistent, and so a volunteer fire department was organized. The sheriff's department was enlarged. Then came water lines with fire hydrants so the fire department could effectively fight fires. Our telephone system was enhanced so that we could dial 911 for help in an emergency.

In spite of all the money and efforts expended to make our county safer, most of the residents here don't feel as safe as we did twenty years ago. Even though we can dial 911 in an emergency and expect to get help much quicker than we used to, yet that doesn't seem enough.

As our concern for our safety grows, we who are Christians need to be reminded that we have a divine 911 that we can call and expect an immediate response. We can call out to God for help at any time. He never leaves His post, never becomes unconcerned, and never sleeps. "Behold, he that keepeth Israel shall neither slumber nor sleep" (Psalm 121:4). If our call is to be effectual, however, we must keep the lines open by regular prayer, Bible study, and meditation.

C. Let Us Pray

Dear Father, we realize that we are often burdened by problems because we don't call upon You. Teach us to "come boldly unto the throne of grace, that we may obtain mercy, and find grace to help in time of need." In Jesus' name we pray. Amen.

D. Thought to Remember

Prayer is the golden key that opens Heaven.

The Lord is close to the brokenhearted and saves those who are crushed in spirit.

visual 8

Learning by Doing

This page contains an alternate lesson plan emphasizing learning activities. Classes desiring such student involvement will find these suggestions helpful.

Learning Goals

This lesson will enable students to:

1. List evidences of God's care and provision for the afflicted and brokenhearted.

2. Sense God's presence as they experience life's difficulties.

3. Pray daily one week for a Christian who is brokenhearted or facing affliction.

Into the Lesson

Begin by displaying a poster with the following question written in large letters: "When should Christians praise God?" Brainstorm and list situations when people should praise God. Acknowledge all answers listed. Then tell the class, "Today we hear the psalmist call us to praise God with him. It is easy to praise God for His blessings in good times. But the psalmist also models praising God as we ask His help in some of the difficulties of life."

Ask class members to tell of Bible characters who praised God while or after they experienced troubles or difficulties in their lives (for example, Miriam's singing and dancing, Exodus 15:20, 21; Paul and Silas in prison, Acts 16:19-25). Today's lesson is David's praise for God's deliverance from a very difficult situation and a reminder of God's presence when we face life's difficulties.

Into the Word

Early in the week make assignments to two students. One is to prepare a three- to five-minute lesson background for Psalm 34, focusing on the story of David in 1 Samuel 21:10-15. Give the student a copy of the second paragraph of the Lesson Background section.

The other student is to prepare a three- to five-minute report on the work of the angel of the Lord (v. 7). Give this student a copy of the comments under verse 7.

Lend the students a Bible dictionary in which they can find additional material. The first student can read about the Philistines and Achish, their king; the second can read about angels.

Begin this portion of the study with the student's presentation on the background of Psalm 34. Then display a poster with the heading "Word Pictures of God's Care and Deliverance." Ask students to watch for word pictures in the text that illustrate God's care for us.

Read today's Scripture aloud. Allow students to share the word pictures or illustrations they find. These may include "delivered me from all my fears" (v. 4), "the angel of the Lord encampeth round about" (v. 7), "they that seek the Lord shall not want" (v. 10), "The Lord is nigh" (v. 18), and others.

As the students list their findings on the poster, discuss the significance of each, using thoughts from the comments on the text in this book. When the angel of the Lord is mentioned, have the student who did the research on that topic share his or her findings.

Into Life

This psalm is a grand assurance of God's care. Point to the poster, which lists the assurances David gave. Be sure the following are included: God is near (v. 18); God delivers His servants (vv. 19, 20); the wicked shall perish (v. 21); the Lord redeems His servants (v. 22).

Discuss this question: "When God promises such care to His people, why do some Christians have trouble, poverty, sickness, and suffering of other kinds?" The Bible has more than one answer to the question of why good people suffer: suffering is discipline (Proverbs 3:11, 12; Hebrews 12:4-11); suffering is a test (Job 1:8-12; 2:3-10); suffering is a means to maturity (James 1:2-4; Romans 5:3, 4); faithfulness in spite of suffering brings glory to God (1 Peter 4:16); faithful endurance is rewarded in Heaven (Matthew 5:11, 12). God does not promise we will not suffer, but He does assure us of His presence and care.

David's experience of affliction and God's care is a wonderful testimony to us. One of the great things Christians learn as we experience suffering or difficulty is that God is near.

Ask class members, "What can we who are Christians do to foster David's attitude of confidence in our daily lives? How can we be aware of God's presence day by day and hour by hour? Is there some special thought or exercise we can foster to help us remember God's presence?" Let the class discuss answers that are given.

Ask them to think of a Christian who is suffering, brokenhearted, or facing affliction. Ask each class member to make a commitment to pray daily for seven days for the person he or she has selected. Close with prayer.

Let's Talk It Over

The questions on this page are designed to encourage review of the lesson Scriptures and to promote discussion of the lesson by the class. The answers provided are only discussion starters. Let your class talk it over from there.

1. How is your life a tribute to God? How may those who are around you recognize that you acknowledge God as the source of every good thing?

Like the psalmist, we may "boast in the Lord," or "magnify the Lord." We do that in our times of worship. We directly magnify the Lord through our praise and thanksgiving, and our neighbors recognize that when they see us leave home at the same time each Sunday morning to go to church. Our entire life becomes a tribute to God as we try to conform to His will and serve Him. When co-workers understand that your ethical and moral standards are due to reverence for God, it is a tribute to Him. When your family learns that your budget is arranged with tithes and offerings as the first disbursement, it is a tribute to God. When your friends learn not to call you on Wednesday evening because you will be at church for Bible study, choir practice, or coaching a teen Bible Bowl team, it is a tribute to God. These are all ways of letting our lights shine in order to bring glory to God (Matthew 5:16).

2. Can you name a time when God delivered you from a fear? Explain. What took the place of the fear?

God is able to relieve our fears even before circumstances change. Fear is an internal reaction, an attitude, based upon perceptions that may be accurate or inaccurate, and upon anticipated events that may or may not occur. A related word that we hear often is anxiety. Anxieties or fears may have caused you to seek the Lord at times, and hopefully you can testify that He met your need. In Philippians 4:6, 7 we are promised that if we address our anxieties and fears to God in prayer, we can exchange them for the peace that passes understanding. Learning to trust God relieves our fears.

3. Have you ever prayed for God's angels to protect you (Psalm 34:7)? What are some circumstances when this promise is especially comforting?

Safety is a big issue. We want cars that are safe. We want homes and appliances that are safe. We add security in our communities by adequate police and fire protection. We purchase insurance to provide for us if we become ill or disabled, to replace possessions that are destroyed or stolen, and to protect us from liability in case of an accident. In spite of all our efforts, however, we are still vulnerable. Parents become acutely aware of this when their children leave the nest. The promise of protecting angels is one parents especially cling to, but it is a precious promise for any of us.

4. How were you first convinced that God is good? What has added to your confidence since then? What would you recommend for those who are not sure?

Most believers have a personal story of how God became real to them and how they came to love God. It is good for us to share those stories and be encouraged by God's blessing in different lives. God invites us to a dynamic personal relationship. As in any good relationship, the more we invest, the more we receive. The longer we walk with God, the more His goodness is confirmed to us. That should lead us to encourage others to "taste and see."

5. How are those who "seek the Lord" better off than "young lions"?

The young lion depends on strength, agility, speed, and endurance to capture its prey. These are enviable assets, but they do not guarantee that the lion will not go hungry. No matter what our personal resources, our greatest reason for confidence is the presence of the Lord. He is still able to provide.

6. Why does God favor the humble and contrite, but resist the proud and arrogant?

A relationship with God begins with acknowledging who He is and what we are. He is God, and we are not. He is the potter, and we are the clay (Isaiah 45:9). Proverbs 6:16-19 lists seven things that God hates, and the first one is a proud look. Jesus testifies that the poor in spirit will inherit the kingdom of Heaven. God is full of love and willing to bless, but those who would make Him their servant are in for a surprise. We must acknowledge our desperate need for God. "Every one that exalteth himself shall be abased; and he that humbleth himself shall be exalted" (Luke 18:14).

Praising God Who Knows and Cares

DEVOTIONAL READING: **1 Peter 5:6-11.**

LESSON SCRIPTURE: **Psalm 139.**

PRINTED TEXT: **Psalm 139:1-14, 23, 24.**

Psalm 139:1-14, 23, 24

1 O LORD, thou hast searched me, and known me.

2 Thou knowest my downsitting and mine uprising; thou understandest my thought afar off.

3 Thou compassest my path and my lying down, and art acquainted with all my ways.

4 For there is not a word in my tongue, but, lo, O LORD, thou knowest it altogether.

5 Thou hast beset me behind and before, and laid thine hand upon me.

6 Such knowledge is too wonderful for me; it is high, I cannot attain unto it.

7 Whither shall I go from thy Spirit? Or whither shall I flee from thy presence?

8 If I ascend up into heaven, thou art there: if I make my bed in hell, behold, thou art there.

9 If I take the wings of the morning, and dwell in the uttermost parts of the sea;

10 Even there shall thy hand lead me, and thy right hand shall hold me.

11 If I say, Surely the darkness shall cover me; even the night shall be light about me.

12 Yea, the darkness hideth not from thee; but the night shineth as the day: the darkness and the light are both alike to thee.

13 For thou hast possessed my reins: thou hast covered me in my mother's womb.

14 I will praise thee; for I am fearfully and wonderfully made: marvelous are thy works; and that my soul knoweth right well.

· · · · · · · · · · · · ·

23 Search me, O God, and know my heart: try me, and know my thoughts:

24 And see if there be any wicked way in me, and lead me in the way everlasting.

Jul 28

GOLDEN TEXT: Search me, O God, and know my heart: try me, and know my thoughts.
—Psalm 139:23.

God Is With Us
(Psalms)
Unit 1: Praising God
(Lessons 6-9)

Lesson Aims

As a result of studying this lesson, each student should:

1. Realize more fully that God is everywhere, watching us.

2. Find comfort in the realization that God watches over us no matter where we go.

3. Be able to face life more confidently, knowing that with God watching over us we are never alone.

4. Be able to share this confidence.

Lesson Outline

INTRODUCTION
    A. Looking in All Directions
    B. Lesson Background
I. GOD'S KNOWLEDGE OF US (Psalm 139:1-6)
    A. He Observes All Our Ways (vv. 1-3)
    B. He Knows Our Words (vv. 4-6)
II. GOD'S VAST DOMAIN (Psalm 139:7-14)
    A. Includes Heaven and Hell (vv. 7, 8)
    B. Extends Across the Sea (vv. 9, 10)
    C. Includes the Night (vv. 11, 12)
      The Inescapable God
    D. Precedes Birth (v. 13)
    E. Leads to Praise (v. 14)
      What Our Bodies Tell Us
III. GOD'S SEARCHING (Psalm 139:23, 24)
    A. God's Searching Needed (v. 23)
    B. The Purpose of God's Search (v. 24)
      God Searching Us
CONCLUSION
    A. "You Cannot Hide From God"
    B. Never Alone
    C. Let Us Pray
    D. Thought to Remember

Visual 9 of the visuals packet represents the psalmist's desire for God to know him through and through. The visual is shown on page 413.

Introduction

A. Looking in All Directions

A father involved his son in a scheme to steal some apples from a neighbor. As they approached the orchard, the father told the boy to look to the north and east to see if anyone was watching. The father looked to the south and west. "Do you see anyone, Son?" asked the father.

"No, nobody in my direction," he replied.

"I don't see anyone in my direction, so let's sneak in."

"But, Dad, you didn't look in every direction," protested the lad.

"Sure we did," came the father's response. "You looked to the north and east and I looked to the south and west."

"But, Dad, you forgot to look up."

The father stood silent for a moment, and finally replied, "You're right, Son. Let's go home." The son remembered what we all at times may forget. We may be clever enough to hide our deeds from our fellowmen, but we cannot hide from God.

B. Lesson Background

The heading of Psalm 139 carries these words: "A Psalm of David," but it is generally agreed that this is not a part of the original writing. Some scholars think the language of the psalm indicates a later date and another author. But the content of the psalm seems worthy of David, and there is no proof that he is not the author.

I. God's Knowledge of Us
(Psalm 139:1-6)

A. He Observes All Our Ways (vv. 1-3)

1-3. O LORD, thou hast searched me, and known me. Thou knowest my downsitting and mine uprising; thou understandest my thought afar off. Thou compassest my path and my lying down, and art acquainted with all my ways.

The writer says his life is an open book before Jehovah; there are no secrets. In recent years we have read about public officials who have recorded their thoughts and deeds in diaries or on tape. When questioned about these records, they have often shown great reluctance to make them public. In some cases it has taken subpoenas or other legal action to open up these records. God doesn't have any such problems. He knows us inside and out.

God knows our activities. He knows when we sit down for a meal or a rest, and when we rise up to engage in some other activity. He knows our thoughts even before we think them. After all, He created our brains and designed the way our minds function.

He watches over us when we travel, and no path is too obscure for Him to find. If we follow the path of righteousness, He certainly knows that; but just as certainly He knows when we choose paths of wickedness. The psalmist sums it up by saying, *Thou . . . art acquainted with all my ways.*

B. He Knows Our Words (vv. 4-6)

4. For there is not a word in my tongue, but, lo, O LORD, thou knowest it altogether.

God's omniscience, His power to know everything, is illustrated in another way. He knows every word the psalmist speaks. It is as if God has a vast cosmic recorder. No conversation, no matter how private, escapes His notice. He hears persons plotting crimes or other misdeeds. He hears the offhanded remarks that often more accurately reveal our real character than do our guarded statements. He even hears us when we talk to ourselves.

But there is a positive side to this. God also hears the kind things we say or the words of encouragement we give to others. He hears us when we share the gospel with those who so desperately need it. He knows when we lift our voices in praise to Him.

5. Thou hast beset me behind and before, and laid thine hand upon me.

God is not some far-off king who only occasionally looks in on His subjects. Jehovah is involved in every aspect of human behavior. God does not play favorites: every human being receives His attention regardless of rank. He is actively involved in giving direction to our lives. In times past He has directly revealed himself to men, as when He called Moses to lead the Israelites out of Egypt (Exodus 3), or when He called Isaiah to become a prophet to his people (Isaiah 6). In most situations, however, God leads us providentially. Often we are not even aware of His leading until long after the event. But even a delayed knowledge of His presence is reassuring.

6. Such knowledge is too wonderful for me; it is high, I cannot attain unto it.

As the writer of the psalm contemplates God's knowledge and power, he is brought to his knees in humility. How could it be otherwise? Pity the poor atheist who arrogantly asserts that there is no God. To be able to make such an assertion, he would have to be as omniscient as God. He would have to know everything, for the one thing unknown might be that there is a God.

The psalmist's words remind us of Job's experience. When Job had talked glibly about himself, God asked him a series of questions that exposed his ignorance. Humbled by this, Job cried out, "I know that thou canst do every thing, and that no thought can be withholden

from thee. Who is he that hideth counsel without knowledge? Therefore have I uttered that I understood not; things too wonderful for me, which I knew not." Then he concluded, "I abhor myself, and repent in dust and ashes" (Job 42:2, 3, 6).

The apostle Paul expressed the same idea this way: "Where is the wise? where is the scribe? where is the disputer of this world? hath not God made foolish the wisdom of this world? . . . Because the foolishness of God is wiser than men; and the weakness of God is stronger than men" (1 Corinthians 1:20, 25).

II. God's Vast Domain (Psalm 139:7-14)

A. Includes Heaven and Hell (vv. 7, 8)

7, 8. Whither shall I go from thy Spirit? Or whither shall I flee from thy presence? If I ascend up into heaven, thou art there: if I make my bed in hell, behold, thou art there.

Verse 7 poses two rhetorical questions that are expanded in the verses that follow. In this verse we see a transition from God's omniscience to His omnipresence: that is, the fact that God is everywhere. Suppose one sought to escape from God. Where could one flee to avoid Him? From the answers that the psalmist gives, it is clear that God is not limited to one spot at any given time. That fact is frightening to those who seek to avoid God; on the other hand it is a wonderful source of assurance to those who trust in Him.

If I ascend up into heaven. This is purely hypothetical, for man under his own power could never enter Heaven. In fact, Heaven would be the last place one would want to go if one wanted to avoid God. The writer searches for every hiding place. Thus he starts with the least likely spot to hide—Heaven—and then turns to the place where one would least expect to find God—Hell.

Hell. The Hebrew word used here, *sheol*, means the place of the dead. It sometimes is translated "grave"; but here, since it is used in contrast to Heaven, it means the eternal dwelling place of the dead. The Hebrew concept of Hell was not as well developed as the concept we see in the New Testament, but clearly the writer understood that it was as far from Heaven as he could imagine. The mention of Hell as a refuge from the presence of God is logical enough. If there were one place in the whole vast universe where God would not be, then it would be Hell. But even Hell could not provide a hiding place from God.

B. Extends Across the Sea (vv. 9, 10)

9, 10. If I take the wings of the morning, and dwell in the uttermost parts of the sea; even there shall thy hand lead me, and thy right hand shall hold me.

Since neither Heaven nor Hell could offer a hiding place from God, the writer now turns to other possibilities. Morning light sweeps swiftly westward over land and sea. If he could go like that to the remotest part of the ocean, still God would be with him.

There shall thy hand lead me. There is no place so remote that God would not be there to guide him. *Thy right hand shall hold me.* This may mean that God's hand would be there to restrain him, or that God's hand would be there to sustain him. In either case, his point is clear: God would be there.

C. Includes the Night (vv. 11, 12)

11, 12. If I say, Surely the darkness shall cover me; even the night shall be light about me. Yea, the darkness hideth not from thee; but the night shineth as the day: the darkness and the light are both alike to thee.

Since distance cannot separate the writer from God, can darkness surround him with a robe that even God's vision cannot penetrate? With electric lights both in our homes and in our streets, we can scarcely imagine how dark a moonless night can be without these conveniences. The psalmist echoes a statement we find in Job 34:22: "There is no darkness, nor shadow of death, where the workers of iniquity may hide themselves."

Even the most intense darkness we can imagine cannot shield us from God's scrutiny. As far as God is concerned, *the night shineth as the day.* Since God is not a physical being, His vision is not limited to that which can be seen by physical eyes. The psalmist has explored just about all the possibilities of a person who would limit God's omniscience and omnipresence. A god who could not be everywhere is not the almighty God the psalmist worships. Nor could he be the almighty God if one's activities could be shielded from him by a blanket of night.

THE INESCAPABLE GOD

In verse 7 of Psalm 139 the questions are asked, "Whither shall I go from thy Spirit? Or whither shall I flee from thy presence?"

The British poet, Francis Thompson, dealt at length with this matter in "The Hound of Heaven." He pictured God pursuing him as a criminal is tracked down by authorities using bloodhounds. The poem is quite autobiographi-

cal, for Thompson had made many mistakes in his life. He had dropped out of medical college and had left his home and gone to London. He became a drug addict, lost touch with all his family, and became destitute. He wrote of his long "running away" from his heavenly Father:

I fled him down the nights and down the days;
I fled Him down the arches of the years;
I fled Him down the labyrinthine ways
Of my own mind; and in the mist of tears
I hid from Him and under running laughter.

But all this flight was in vain. At point after point in the poem, a section concludes with a statement by God about how inescapable He is:

All things betray thee, who betrayest Me.
Naught shelters Thee, who wilt not shelter Me.
Lo, naught contents thee, who content'st not Me.
Lo, all things fly thee, for thou flyest Me!

At last Thompson gives up and surrenders to God and hears His tender words,

Ah, fondest, blindest, weakest,
I am He Whom thou seekest!
Thou dravest love from thee, who dravest Me.

We can't escape from God. But why should we want to? He pursues us so He can save us, bless us, and pour out His love upon us.

—J. G. V. B.

D. Precedes Birth (v. 13)

13. For thou hast possessed my reins: thou hast covered me in my mother's womb.

The *New International Version* puts it this way: "For you created my inmost being; you knit me together in my mother's womb." Jehovah God, who created the heavens and the earth, who made the vast seas and the majestic mountains, is just as much concerned about the individual, even the unborn infant. We know much more about the process of conception, gestation, and birth than did the ancients. Still, when we contemplate the process that culminates in birth, we cannot help being filled with awe and wonder. The writer shared that wonder and awe, and readily recognized that God was involved in it. God was as much concerned about him when he was an unborn fetus as when he became a mature adult. Persons who are ready to terminate an unwanted pregnancy by abortion will do well to give some thought to this verse.

E. Leads to Praise (v. 14)

14. I will praise thee; for I am fearfully and wonderfully made: marvelous are thy works; and that my soul knoweth right well.

After contemplating the vast universe that God had made, the psalmist was compelled to raise his voice in praise of the Creator. We are indeed *fearfully and wonderfully made.* Even the psalmist's meager understanding of the body's functions led him to praise God. Modern science is probing ever deeper into the mysteries of the human body. Even though we know vastly more than we did a generation ago, we still have not unlocked all the secrets of its functions. What we do know should certainly cause us to fall on our faces and praise our Maker. Yet all too often we casually ignore all of this and forget Him who designed us and made us.

WHAT OUR BODIES TELL US

When we want to emphasize the reality of the work of God in the world, we don't have to look farther than our own bodies. Think of all the evidences of design and planning they reveal!

First is our *skin.* This is a marvelous covering over our entire bodies, from the soles of our feet to the tops of our heads. It tucks everything in and keeps us from oozing out all over. Further, it has thousands of pores through which perspiration can flow to cool us.

How interesting is our *digestive system!* We eat food, aided by saliva excreted in our mouths. It passes into our stomachs, where chemical agents process it into nutrients that blood carries to cells throughout our whole body. The waste is also processed for disposal through channels prepared for this purpose.

There are all the *special function organs* of our bodies—the heart, lungs, liver, kidneys, and others. There are the *eyes* with all their intricacy, the *ears,* and the *nostrils* with their delicate power of smelling.

There is the *brain* with its power of conceptualizing and problem solving. How marvelous are its abilities to control body movements, and also to dream dreams and envision possibilities and design futures!

Truly does the psalmist say, "I am fearfully and wonderfully made." —J. G. V. B.

III. God's Searching (Psalm 139:23, 24)

A. God's Searching Needed (v. 23)

23. Search me, O God, and know my heart: try me, and know my thoughts.

In verses 19-22 the writer speaks out against the wicked. He expresses his hatred for those who hate God. He is certain that God will slay the wicked. Clearly, he is distancing himself from the wicked and aligning himself with God.

The psalmist has no doubt about whose side he is on. He understands that God knows every thought and motive of his heart, and he is willing

visual 9

Search me, O God, and know my heart: try me, and know my thoughts: and see if there be any wicked way in me, and lead me in the way everlasting.

to let God search for any improper thoughts or feelings that might be harbored there. The writer may seem a bit too sure of himself, even to the point of arrogance, supposing that his life can stand the close scrutiny of God's penetrating eye. But see the next verse.

B. The Purpose of God's Search (v. 24)

24. And see if there be any wicked way in me, and lead me in the way everlasting.

This call for God to search his heart was not really an exercise in spiritual arrogance. The psalmist had a purpose in this search. If God found anything undesirable there, he wanted Him to cleanse his heart and set his feet upon the path that leads to everlasting life. In this he showed an openness to God's leading, a willingness to remove whatever was wrong. We are like the psalmist in that we too must constantly search for anything in our hearts that may be foreign to God's holiness. But we enjoy one very important advantage over him. We have Christ as our example and the New Testament as a direct guide. We will not be held guiltless if we neglect either of these.

GOD SEARCHING US

We are accustomed to searches today. We misplace our glasses, or a favorite pen, and spend a long time trying to find the missing article. There is a sense in which we may urge God to help us find some quality of life we seem to have lost—such as joy, sympathy, hopefulness, or compassion.

This is not the sense in which our psalmist speaks of God's search of our lives. He is thinking of the presence of some unlovely quality, some evil propensity we may be harboring. God's search is like that of a law officer who obtains a search warrant so he can go through a house and examine all the nooks and crannies, the drawers and closets, to see if some illegal drug or dangerous agent may be hidden there. The psalmist is eager for God to conduct a search of his personality. He does not want some "wicked way" to deter him from walking in the "way everlasting." A character in Tennyson's "Maud" says,

> And ah for a man to arise in me,
> That the man I am may cease to be!

There may be things in us that should "cease to be." May the light of divine discernment shine into all the hidden recesses of our hearts, so that all that is ugly, crass, or misshapen may be revealed and rectified.   —J. G. V. B.

Conclusion

A. "You Cannot Hide From God"

Years ago we used to sing a song in church, "You Cannot Hide From God." As one reads the words of the song, one cannot avoid the conclusion that the writer was familiar with Psalm 139. Part of the chorus went like this:

> You cannot hide from God.
> Wherever you go,
> Whatever you do,
> You cannot hide from God;
> His eye is fixed on you.

I was always a bit apprehensive when I sang this song. I had ways of avoiding the surveillance of my parents, but I wasn't sure I could escape God's constant scrutiny. Mentally I kept looking over my shoulder to see if He really was there with His eye fixed on me.

I haven't heard the song in years. Of course the music is a bit old-fashioned, and the lyrics are simplistic. But perhaps a more important reason we don't sing it is that the whole idea of a God constantly watching us goes against the contemporary emphasis on individual autonomy. We really don't want to have anything to do with a God who is something of a cosmic "Big Brother." After all, we have a right to privacy.

But in insisting upon our privacy even from God, we may be paying a rather high price. If we reject the idea of a God who watches us, we also lose the idea of a God who watches *over* us. The closing stanza of the song turns to this very theme:

> If you would save your sinful soul,
> If you would be made pure and whole,
> If you would reach the highest goal,
> Your soul must hide in God.

Exactly! An all-seeing, all-knowing God may be a threat to us if we are determined to go our own way rather than His. But if we are willing to surrender ourselves *to* Him, we will no longer have to hide *from* Him. We will be able to rejoice in the comfort and protection we have when we hide *in* Him.

B. Never Alone

In the 1950s *The Lonely Crowd* was a widely read sociological study. One of the points made by the book was that as our society becomes more urbanized, we are brought into contact with more and more people every day. Yet the paradox is that the more people we meet each day the lonelier we become. The reason is not hard to find. The more people we contact each day the less time we have to develop a trusting, intimate relationship with any one person. In the four decades since the book was published the situation has not improved; indeed, it has become much worse.

Amidst the growing crowd, people are lonelier than ever. As a result, they enter into all kinds of relationships, many of which prove disappointing or disastrous, leaving them lonelier than ever. But we can have a fellowship with God that supports and sustains. And the church, through its members, can help bring people into that fellowship. More than at any other time in history, Christians need to be reaching out to the lonely crowd to show people that they never need to be alone.

C. Let Us Pray

All-knowing, all-seeing God, our heavenly Father, we come to You with thanks that we have a God who is concerned about us as individuals. Search our hearts, O Lord, and cleanse us from any wicked thought or deed, and lead us in the way everlasting. In the name of Your Son Jesus we pray. Amen.

D. Thought to Remember

We cannot get away from God, though we can ignore Him.

Home Daily Bible Readings

Monday, July 22—God Is Mindful of Us (Psalm 115:3-15)

Tuesday, July 23—God Is Aware (Luke 12:1-9)

Wednesday, July 24—God Cares (1 Peter 5:6-11)

Thursday, July 25—God Strengthens (Isaiah 41:8-13)

Friday, July 26—God Perseveres (Isaiah 46:3-11)

Saturday, July 27—God Sees All (Hebrews 4:1-13)

Sunday, July 28—God Is Our Confidence (Romans 8:26-35)

Learning by Doing

This page contains an alternate lesson plan emphasizing learning activities. Classes desiring such student involvement will find these suggestions helpful.

Learning Goals

This lesson should enable students to:

1. Identify and list illustrations or evidences of God's omniscience and omnipresence.

2. Find comfort in God's presence and His knowledge of our personal lives.

3. State appreciation and praise for God's intimate relationship with His people.

Into the Lesson

Begin by breaking the class into pairs (not immediate family members). Ask each student to share with his partner any information he will about himself (biographical data, interests, little-known facts, etc.) for two minutes. The other partner is to jot notes. Then reverse roles.

After the sharing exercise, ask for volunteers, each of whom will share with the class one interesting fact about his partner that he did not know before.

Then tell the class, "Probably the information that you shared with your partner was information you are willing for everyone to know. But what you *did not* share may also be significant. There are parts of our lives that we will not share with just anyone. There may be hurts that are too deep, activities of which we are not proud, or personal problems that we just don't care to share with everyone. We need a close friend with whom we can share the more intimate portions of our lives. And we treasure a friend who knows and understands us intimately. God can be that friend."

Today's psalm is written by one who treasured the intimate knowledge and presence of God. The psalmist invites God thus: "Search me, O God, and know my heart: try me, and know my thoughts" (139:23). This is a wonderful devotional psalm that not only teaches us something about the character of God, but also invites a closer and deeper relationship with Him. Do we really want God to know all about us? Are we willing to tell Him everything we do, everything we think, all our most secret feelings?

Into the Word

Give each student a piece of paper with two headings over two columns. Printed over the top of column one should be the words *Evidences or Illustrations of God's Omniscience.* Printed over column two should be the words

Evidences or Illustrations of God's Omnipresence. Ask students to define "omniscience" and "omnipresence." (The prefix *omni* means "all.") Omniscience is knowledge of all things. Omnipresence is presence in all places at all times. Omniscience and omnipresence are two of the things that make God superior to us. Another is omnipotence, which means all power. After discussing those words, read the Scripture aloud clearly and slowly while students listen and jot evidences in the appropriate columns.

An interesting alternative would be to play a dramatic recording of Psalm 139 while students listen and make notes.

After the reading, have students share their notes while one student makes a master list on two pieces of poster board.

Ask these discussion questions:

1. Contrast verses 1 and 23, 24. Verse 1 tells us God has already searched the heart of the psalmist. Verses 23 and 24 invite God to continue the searching of his heart. Why do you think the psalmist would offer that invitation to God? Why does he ask God to search his thoughts and know his heart?

2. What do verses 23 and 24 imply about the character and values of the psalmist?

Into Life

Continue with the discussion questions to bring the Scripture into life.

1. Some adults may be frightened by the idea that a higher power than themselves sees and knows their every thought and action. Others would find that comforting. Why would some be frightened and why would some find this comforting?

2. Should Christians find God's knowledge and presence intimidating and frightening, or find His knowledge and presence comforting, or both? Why? How do you think God uses His knowledge of us?

3. Ask class members to share any new or reinforced perceptions of God they have gained from Psalm 139. Ask, "If you were to lead a prayer right now, what appreciation or understanding of God would you express to Him?"

Share the "Never Alone" section from the lesson commentary. It is point B of the Conclusion section. Study it so well that you can tell it, not read it, to the class.

Let's Talk It Over

The questions on this page are designed to encourage review of the lesson Scriptures and to promote discussion of the lesson by the class. The answers provided are only discussion starters. Let your class talk it over from there.

1. What support in addition to Psalm 139 can we find in the Bible for the assurance that God is acquainted with the intimate details of our lives?

The psalmist is not alone in asserting that God knows all about us. For example, when Samuel was sent to the house of Jesse to anoint the next king for Israel, he first thought that surely Eliab, the eldest, would be God's choice. But God chose the eighth son, David. He said, "Man looketh on the outward appearance, but the Lord looketh on the heart" (1 Samuel 16:7). Jesus said God knows even the number of hairs on our head (Matthew 10:30); and in Hebrews 4:13 we read, "All things are naked and opened unto the eyes of him with whom we have to do."

2. Is the fact that God knows so much about you threatening or reassuring? Explain.

Most of us make an effort to put our best foot forward, to cast ourselves in the best light. We are afraid people would think less of us if they knew everything about us. We may suspect the same about God. If we are trying to hide a sinful habit, that definitely will cause us to feel threatened. The wonderful fact is that, even though God knows all about us, He loves us. As one song puts it, "He who knows us best loves us most." God's love for us does not rest on our righteousness. In Romans 5:8 we read, "God commendeth his love toward us, in that, while we were yet sinners, Christ died for us." We can rejoice in the fact that God knows us and loves us anyway.

3. What is the practical difference between believing that God is everywhere and believing that God is in everything?

The fact that God is present everywhere means that we cannot hide from Him, but it also means that He is available to us in any place. We do not have to visit a temple, a shrine, or even a church building in order to pray or worship. There are real advantages to gathering with other Christians for worship, but any place can become the door to God's throne of grace when we begin to pray. That is not the same as believing that God is in everything. Some believe that God is in all nature, and therefore everything is of equal value. God is the Creator, but He is not a part of His creation. It is a sign of

depravity to worship the creatures and ignore the transcendent Creator (Romans 1:25). Man has been given dominion over the rest of the creatures (Genesis 1:26) to be a thoughtful and wise caretaker, but not to revere them.

4. What are the implications of this psalm for missionaries and missionary work?

God is equally available in all places. When missionaries pack to travel to distant shores, they need not worry about transporting God. He is already present, but needs ambassadors who will introduce Him to the inhabitants of the land. We must look to other parts of Scripture to learn the missionary motive of God toward all the peoples of the earth, but it is reassuring to know we cannot outdistance Him.

5. How does the design of the human body bring praise to God?

Most of us are self-conscious about parts of our bodies that we feel are too long or too short, too round or too flat. We may consider that we are far from the ideal, but we must agree with the psalmist that we are "fearfully and wonderfully made." Our advanced knowledge of the human body gives us all the more reason to come to that conclusion. For instance, the ancients knew that blood was essential to life, but modern biochemistry has taught us amazing things about the blood's work and how it is cleansed and replenished in our bodies. Each new marvel we find is a tribute to our Creator.

6. Why is it a good idea to invite God to make a close inspection of our lives?

This psalm acknowledges that God knows all about us and that there is no way to hide from Him. Finally, the psalmist invites God to search his heart. We may wonder why, since God knows our heart whether we want Him to or not. The psalmist, however, is not just conceding to the inevitable. He has a practical motive in mind. He is eager for God to examine his heart (affections) and his thoughts and to disclose any wickedness found there. We are capable of rationalizing our sin or otherwise ignoring it until we fail to recognize it. We may need God to expose our sin until we are repentant, seek forgiveness, and return to a more righteous way.

Trust in God

DEVOTIONAL READING: Psalm 36:5-12.

LESSON SCRIPTURE: Psalm 40.

PRINTED TEXT: Psalm 40:1-5, 9-11, 16, 17.

Psalm 40:1-5, 9-11, 16, 17

1 I waited patiently for the LORD; and he inclined unto me, and heard my cry.

2 He brought me up also out of a horrible pit, out of the miry clay, and set my feet upon a rock, and established my goings.

3 And he hath put a new song in my mouth, even praise unto our God: many shall see it, and fear, and shall trust in the LORD.

4 Blessed is that man that maketh the LORD his trust, and respecteth not the proud, nor such as turn aside to lies.

5 Many, O LORD my God, are thy wonderful works which thou hast done, and thy thoughts which are to usward: they cannot be reckoned up in order unto thee: if I would declare and speak of them, they are more than can be numbered.

. . . .

9 I have preached righteousness in the great congregation: lo, I have not refrained my lips, O LORD, thou knowest.

10 I have not hid thy righteousness within my heart; I have declared thy faithfulness and thy salvation: I have not concealed thy loving-kindness and thy truth from the great congregation.

11 Withhold not thou thy tender mercies from me, O LORD: let thy loving-kindness and thy truth continually preserve me.

. . . .

16 Let all those that seek thee rejoice and be glad in thee: let such as love thy salvation say continually, The LORD be magnified.

17 But I am poor and needy; yet the Lord thinketh upon me: thou art my help and my deliverer; make no tarrying, O my God.

Aug
4

GOLDEN TEXT: Blessed is that man that maketh the LORD his trust.—Psalm 40:4.

Lesson Aims

After this lesson, each student should:
1. Learn the importance of patience.
2. Learn that God can give deliverance from threats even when the situation seems hopeless.
3. Rejoice in the Lord when good things happen.

Lesson Outline

INTRODUCTION
   A. Latchstring on the Outside
   B. Lesson Background
  I. THE PSALMIST'S DELIVERANCE (Psalm 40:1-5)
   A. He Waited Patiently (v. 1)
   B. His Deliverance Came (v. 2)
   C. He Has a New Song (v. 3)
     A New Song
   D. Blessed Is the Man Who Trusts the Lord (v. 4)
   E. God's Works Are Wonderful (v. 5)
 II. THE PSALMIST'S RESPONSE TO GOD'S DELIVERANCE (Psalm 40:9-11)
   A. He Preached Righteousness (vv. 9, 10)
     Unhidden, Unconcealed
   B. He Looked to the Lord to Preserve Him (v. 11)
III. THE PSALMIST'S PRAYER (Psalm 40:16, 17)
   A. Let the Lord Be Magnified (v. 16)
     Gladness in God
   B. God Is His Deliverer (v. 17)
CONCLUSION
   A. Songs of Praise
   B. Salvation
   C. Let Us Pray
   D. Thought to Remember

The truly happy person is the one who trusts in the Lord. Visual 10 of the visuals packet shown on page 422 carries this message.

Introduction

A. Latchstring on the Outside

A Quaker family who lived on the frontier of the newly settled Pennsylvania colony was having family devotions. They chose for their Bible study that evening a passage from one of the psalms that spoke of God's deliverance of His people. As they prepared to retire, the father pulled the latchstring inside so the door could not be opened from the outside.

"Father, why did you place the latchstring inside?" asked one of the children. "If we trusted in God like the man who wrote the psalm, we wouldn't have to be afraid of anyone." Moved by the child's faith, the father placed the latchstring on the outside of the door.

In the middle of the night, they heard the door open and heard men whispering. Then the door was closed again and all was quiet. When the family arose in the morning, they discovered that every other house in the village had been burned and the people massacred. Amid their sorrowing over their neighbors, they paused to give thanks for their own deliverance. Years later an old Indian told them how he had led a raiding party to the village, intending to destroy it and kill everyone in it. When he saw the latchstring on the outside of the door, however, he knew that the people in the house were Quakers and trusted in God. He also knew that the Quakers had treated the Indians fairly, and so their lives were spared.

B. Lesson Background

The superscription, which is not a part of the original psalm, assigns Psalm 40 to David. Other authors have been suggested, but the situation that seems to provide background for the psalm fits the life of David. In fact, the psalm could very well describe either of two different crises in his life. One occurred during the reign of Saul, when David was forced to flee for his life and live for some time as a fugitive from the king who sought to kill him. He lived in the desert for years (1 Samuel 18:6—30:31). The other situation came later in David's career, when his son Absalom sought to seize the throne and threatened his life. This brought death to Absalom and terrible grief to David. The record of it is found in 2 Samuel 15—18.

I. The Psalmist's Deliverance (Psalm 40:1-5)

A. He Waited Patiently (v. 1)

1. I waited patiently for the LORD; and he inclined unto me, and heard my cry.

The psalmist waited patiently under trying circumstances. Verse 2, if it is taken literally, indicates that he had been thrust into a muddy cistern or some similar pit. (See Jeremiah 38:1-13 for that prophet's experience in a miry dungeon.) On the other hand, verse 2 may be figurative, meaning a political or military crisis that brought considerable agony. In any event, the psalmist suffered through this experience with patience. We today would do well to look to his example.

He inclined unto me. This depicts God as leaning forward to give His attention. The sufferer waited patiently; God heard his cry and attended to it.

B. His Deliverance Came (v. 2)

2. He brought me up also out of a horrible pit, out of the miry clay, and set my feet upon a rock, and established my goings.

The pit was a terrible place to be. If it was literally a cistern, the soft mud in the bottom, accumulated over years, might be a foot or more deep. This made it very difficult to move one's feet. Further, there might be considerable water in the cistern, adding to the difficulty and danger. If the mud is figurative, it represents some confining and dangerous situation.

Whatever the situation was, God rescued the psalmist from the crisis, set his feet firmly upon a rock, perhaps even saved his life. God established his goings, or, as the *Revised Standard Version* has it, made his "steps secure." Being free on solid ground, he could move in the direction he believed the Lord was calling him.

C. He Has a New Song (v. 3)

3. And he hath put a new song in my mouth, even praise unto our God: many shall see it, and fear, and shall trust in the LORD.

Praising God through song is a natural response for people who have known His deliverance. We are not told what the new song was, but it was given by God and it involved praise of God. We are reminded of the song of rejoicing raised by the Israelites after their deliverance from the Egyptians at the Red Sea (Exodus 15:1-18). The deliverance that God had provided would be witnessed by many. It would produce reverent fear among them, and they would *trust in the Lord.* God's mighty works usually produce one of two responses. Some people become angry and rebellious, and their opposition to God is intensified. The pharaoh of Egypt and many religious leaders in Jesus' day are good examples of persons who responded in this fashion. The other response is to come to trust in God or to become an even stronger believer in Him. Many who witnessed Jesus' miracles belong in this category.

A NEW SONG

It is a human characteristic to sing. Of course there are many songs to be sung. We give voice in our love songs to our need for human affection, for tenderness of touch, for interconnectedness of life. Sentiments of familiarity and love of our natural surroundings lead to songs of patriotism and celebration of our heritage.

The psalmist tells us he can sing a *new* song. He does not just call upon God for help, but *praises* Him for what He already has done.

The redeemed express their joy in God's saving love in Jesus, the Lamb of God. They sing a *new* song—no longer one of despair, or gloom, or hopeless longing. "Worthy art Thou . . . for Thou wast slain, and didst purchase for God with Thy blood men from every tribe and tongue and people and nation" (Revelation 5:9, *New American Standard Bible*).

Across the years we give voice to lyrics of love, patriotism, and college "alma maters." But the most important song is the new one that tells of sin and death escaped, and righteousness and life achieved through Him who loves us, Jesus our Lord.   —J. G. V. B.

D. Blessed Is the Man Who Trusts the Lord (v. 4)

4. Blessed is that man that maketh the LORD his trust, and respecteth not the proud, nor such as turn aside to lies.

Those who put their trust in the Lord will enjoy greater blessings than those who put their trust in men or money. *Respecteth not the proud.* Some people attempt to curry favor with men proud of their wealth or power, even if the wealth or power has been won by dishonesty. Some commentators take this to refer to those who followed Absalom in his rebellion against David. Proudly they advanced their cause by lies and treason (2 Samuel 15—18).

E. God's Works Are Wonderful (v. 5)

5. Many, O LORD my God, are thy wonderful works which thou hast done, and thy thoughts which are to us-ward: they cannot be reckoned up in order unto thee: if I would declare and speak of them, they are more than can be numbered.

Not only was the writer thankful for God's deliverance; he also expressed appreciation for God's other *wonderful works.* The ancient Israelites lived closer to nature than most of us do, and so they were more aware of God's works in nature. Their pastoral lives allowed them to observe the starry heavens, the growing plants, the animals. This made them more respectful of nature and more reverent toward the God who had created it.

Most of us today live in cities or are caught up in the busy rush of urban life. The bright lights of the city cause the stars to pale into insignificance, and buildings and paved streets have eliminated most of the flora and fauna that were an important part of ancient pastoral life. As a result, we rarely stand in awe of the vast celestial canopy or watch with interest the plant and animal life about us. Thus we miss the sense of awe and reverent fear of God that the ancients knew.

Thy thoughts which are to us-ward. Jehovah God is much more than just a mighty Creator of the physical world. He never ceases to show His concern for His creation. The human race, the crown of His creation, is especially the center of His attention. The psalmist readily recognizes that he can't begin to number the ways that God is involved in human affairs.

II. The Psalmist's Response to God's Deliverance (Psalm 40:9-11)

In verse 6 the writer says, "Sacrifice and offering thou didst not desire." Of course he is not opposing the sacrifices required by God's law. He is saying God wants something more. Many were going through the motions of worship by offering the appropriate sacrifices, but this was just an empty exercise that left their hearts unchanged.

The psalmist's criticism of vain sacrifices was not unique. Samuel said to King Saul, "Behold, to obey is better than sacrifice, and to hearken than the fat of rams" (1 Samuel 15:22). God expressed the same idea through Amos: "Though ye offer me burnt offerings and your meat offerings, I will not accept them; neither will I regard the peace offerings of your fat beasts" (Amos 5:22). The offering of sacrifices should not be stopped, but reverence and obedience should be added.

A. He Preached Righteousness (vv. 9, 10)

9. I have preached righteousness in the great congregation: lo, I have not refrained my lips, O LORD, thou knowest.

Sermons are not the only way of preaching. The writer was a musician; perhaps he often proclaimed righteousness in his singing. Large parts of the prophetic books of the Bible are poetic. The prophets may have sung them to throngs of listeners. Some modern songs also preach righteousness, if we listen to the words we are singing. "Yield Not to Temptation" is an example. Of course there is much prose preaching too. See Moses' long address in Deuteronomy, or read Christian sermons in the book of Acts.

The *great congregation* means a major assembly, perhaps for worship. Three times a year all

Israel gathered for a great religious festival. Acts 2 records Peter's sermon to such an assembly. There were other great assemblies too. Joshua assembled many of the people at Shechem to hear his farewell address (Joshua 24:1). Ezra and others read the law to a great congregation the first day of the seventh month (Nehemiah 8:2, 3).

I have not refrained my lips. Probably the message of righteousness was not welcomed by everyone, and it took some courage for the psalmist to speak up as he did. But he was quite willing to risk disfavor with his opponents in order to remain faithful to the truth. That situation has not changed greatly. A person who contends for righteousness today may be ostracized or even attacked for the stand he or she takes.

10. I have not hid thy righteousness within my heart; I have declared thy faithfulness and thy salvation: I have not concealed thy loving-kindness and thy truth from the great congregation.

The psalmist had not hid God's righteousness in his heart in some kind of secret piety. He had proclaimed it every chance he had, and with it he had proclaimed God's *faithfulness*, His *salvation*, His *loving-kindness*, and His *truth*. No doubt he understood that it was not enough just to say the right things; he needed every day to demonstrate righteousness in his activities. Our faith too ought to produce lives that illustrate that faith. Many today have grown cynical about preaching and reject it, but a Christian life will silence these critics as words cannot.

UNHIDDEN, UNCONCEALED

There is an irrepressible quality about our inner feelings and convictions that makes them come to expression in our lives. We cannot detest something and never speak about it or

Home Daily Bible Readings

Monday, July 29—Wait Patiently (Psalm 37:1-7)
Tuesday, July 30—Take Refuge (Psalm 118:1-9)
Wednesday, July 31—Trust God Forever (Isaiah 26:1-6)
Thursday, Aug. 1—Taught by God (Isaiah 50:4-11)
Friday, Aug. 2—Hampered by Fear (Proverbs 29:22-27)
Saturday, Aug. 3—Protected by God (Psalm 31:11-24)
Sunday, Aug. 4—Surrounded by Love (Psalm 32:6-11)

indicate the utter distaste the very thought of it brings to us. Likewise, matters about which we are enthusiastic and thrilled are bound to come out.

So it is with our faith in God and our gratitude for His goodness and mercy. The psalmist says, "I have not hid thy righteousness within my heart . . . I have not concealed thy loving-kindness and thy truth." There has to be a declaration, even to the "great congregation," of those deep convictions and elements of devotion that lie within.

In the New Testament account of Jesus' death and resurrection we are told of what Joseph of Arimathea did for Him. He gave Him the use of his new tomb. The account in John tells us something else about this man. "After this Joseph of Arimathea, who was a disciple of Jesus, but secretly, for fear of the Jews, asked Pilate that he might take away the body of Jesus" (John 19:38, *Revised Standard Version*). The time came when Joseph could no longer conceal his devotion to Jesus. There is no way real discipleship can be hidden. How terrible it would be if we were not proud and honored to be His disciples!

> Ashamed of Jesus! that dear Friend
> On whom my hopes of heaven depend!
> No; when I blush, be this my shame,
> That I no more revere His name.
> —Joseph Grigg

Well does the psalmist insist, "I have not hid thy righteousness within my heart."
—J. G. V. B.

B. He Looked to the Lord to Preserve Him (v. 11)

11. Withhold not thou thy tender mercies from me, O LORD: let thy loving-kindness and thy truth continually preserve me.

In the previous verses the writer set forth his faithfulness to God. He has faithfully proclaimed God's righteousness. He has not withheld God's truth from the people. Now he asks God not to withhold His *tender mercies*.

Faithfulness to God does not guarantee freedom from trouble. Job, for example, though he was faithful to God, did not escape painful trials. Yet those who are faithful have one definite advantage. They know how to call upon God in prayer for His blessings. God intends for us to lay our problems before Him, to pray with the anticipation that He will hear us and deal with us according to His purposes.

In spite of his rejoicing in the Lord, the psalmist still faced serious problems. He tells some of them in verses 12-15. His troubles had

surrounded him. It is not surprising that he had become faint of heart. Further, he recognized that his own iniquities had "taken hold upon" him. Although he doesn't specifically say so, it is quite possible that his sins had contributed to some of his troubles. Even when we have been faithful to the Lord, the problems that we face are sometimes the result of our own shortcomings.

The psalmist asks to be delivered from his trials. At the same time, he asks God to overcome those who have brought these trials upon him. He asks that they be "ashamed and confounded," "driven backward and put to shame," and made "desolate." This may seem to fall short of Jesus' teaching to love our enemies and pray for them. We must note, however, that the psalmist prayed for the defeat of their evil purposes rather than for injury or death to the persons themselves.

III. The Psalmist's Prayer (Psalm 40:16, 17)

A. Let the Lord Be Magnified (v. 16)

16. Let all those that seek thee rejoice and be glad in thee: let such as love thy salvation say continually, The LORD be magnified.

In verses 12-15 the writer unburdened himself before the Lord. For a little while he thought of himself and all of his problems. Now his thoughts turn again to God. His self-pity turns to rejoicing, and he calls for others to join him in that rejoicing. Those who have known the Lord's salvation ought to magnify Him. We can certainly agree with the psalmist at this point. At times our problems may seem overwhelming, but when we stop to count our blessings, the problems melt into insignificance.

GLADNESS IN GOD

One of the qualities of the religious faith of the Hebrew people was their joy in their Lord. The psalms are full of the praise of God, and a constant note in worship is the expression of gladness in God's service. The people of many other nations believed in deities who were easily offended and under whose wrath the worshipers cowered in abject fear. Some of these religions required their devotees even to sacrifice their own babies as offerings. It is difficult to see how such worship of Moloch or other gods could be anything but a source of grief and despair.

A characteristic note of New Testament worship is that of gladness and exultation. The beginning of a fine hymn by Henry Van Dyke expresses the genuine quality of Christian praise:

Joyful, joyful, we adore Thee,
God of glory, Lord of love.

Not long after this we come to these joyous lines:

Thou art giving and forgiving,
Ever blessing, ever blest,
Well-spring of the joy of living,
Ocean-depth of happy rest!

The Christian views life as related to the "blesseds" of the Beatitudes rather than to a series of "curseds." The essential message of the church is "the gospel" which, of course, means "the good news." The message is not what bad things God might do to us, but rather the marvelous good things He has done for us in the sending of Jesus and in His redemptive love.

—J. G. V. B.

B. God Is His Deliverer (v. 17)

17. But I am poor and needy; yet the Lord thinketh upon me: thou art my help and my deliverer; make no tarrying, O my God.

When the writer contemplates how blessed he is, he sinks to his knees in humility. With all his blessings he is still *poor and needy*. There is no way that he can defeat his enemies through his own strength. He is forced to rely upon God to deliver him. *Make no tarrying.* Even in his humility he shows a trace of impatience: "Hurry up, God; deliver me now!" Doesn't that sound like us?

Conclusion

A. Songs of Praise

The writers of the psalms lived thousands of years ago in a culture that seems almost primitive to us. Yet the songs of praise they lifted up to God rival or surpass anything we produce today. There are reasons for this. For one thing, most of the psalmists were farmers and shepherds who spent much of their time outdoors. Their extensive contact with nature made them appreciate its wonders. It was only natural for them to revere the God who had created the physical world.

Another reason they so readily praised God was that they knew they had to depend on Him for their livelihood. He supplied the rain and sunshine needed for their crops; He protected their fields from plagues of locusts. Today we are less inclined to turn to God than we are to resort to science and technology for our help. We feel more comfortable with this arrangement because we have a better chance of controlling science than we have of controlling God.

So when we sing our songs, let us sing them with understanding. Let us note that many of our songs use themes that were familiar to the psalmists. Realizing this may help us recapture the simple but dynamic faith that characterized their lives.

B. Salvation

The writer of this psalm rejoiced as he looked to God for salvation. Probably he had in mind salvation from his enemies who surrounded him. The faith that God could provide him salvation under such distressing circumstances seemed reason enough for him to offer up praise and thanksgiving to his divine benefactor.

The writer did not know about the salvation that God offers us through His Son, Jesus Christ. We too have the assurance that God watches over us, helps us through our day-to-day problems, and guides us through our major crises. Besides that, we have the promise of eternal salvation. Our praise ought to be far greater than that of the psalmist.

Courageously he stood before the congregation and proclaimed God's righteousness. At times he faced opposition from his enemies, but that did not keep him from being a bearer of good news. With such an example before us, shall we not be bearing witness to all the good things our Lord has done for us and has promised to everyone who will accept him?

C. Let Us Pray

Dear Father in Heaven, we come before You, poor and needy as we are, seeking Your wisdom to guide us and Your strength to uphold us. Put a song of praise and thanksgiving in our hearts, and put it on our lips that all may know of the salvation You offer. In the name of Your Son Jesus we pray. Amen.

D. Thought to Remember

Gratitude is born in hearts that pause to count past blessings.

Happy is the person
who trusts in the Lord.

visual 10

Learning by Doing

This page contains an alternate lesson plan emphasizing learning activities. Classes desiring such student involvement will find these suggestions helpful.

Learning Goals

A good preface for this lesson is to learn about the great amount of suffering and pain in your part of the world. Call your city or county planning commission to obtain the number of homeless in your community. Visit a facility for the physically and mentally impaired, or visit some of the shut-ins of your congregation.

In this lesson we find David hurting, distressed, and crying out to God for relief. The exact experience of his life is not pinpointed, but the pain is very real.

Suffering drives us to seek relief. Futile searching causes despair. This lesson from God's Word tells us that trusting in God is an effective way of dealing with pain and suffering. From this week's study, students of this lesson should be able to:

1. Describe several types of human suffering.

2. List several typical and ineffective ways of addressing suffering.

3. Explain how trusting in God is the best approach to suffering.

Into the Lesson

At the beginning of class, or as your students come in, pass out sheets with these questions:

1. What kind of people need to cry to the Lord for help?

2. What circumstances in life can cause us such pain we will cry to the Lord for help?

3. Describe a time when it seemed plain that the Lord answered a cry for help.

4. Can you remember an incident in your life when God put a new song in your mouth?

Ask students to think of possible answers and to write them down.

Lead your class in a brief discussion as they share their answers to the above questions. Write their answers on the left half of your chalkboard or on an overhead transparency.

You can supplement this part of your lesson with newspaper or magazine clippings illustrating situations in which people need to cry out to God as well as have a new song put in their mouth. Some things to look for would be: a story of a crime victim, a person arrested for a crime, an unemployed person having trouble finding a job, a stillborn child, the death of a spouse or loved one, or the discovery of a serious illness.

Into the Word

Today we focus on the presence of God in the midst of suffering. The specific issue is trusting Him during these times. Job's wife advised, "Tell God off and die." When we are tempted to follow that advice, we need to focus on trusting our real source of security and help.

The Lesson Background section suggests that Psalm 40 may have arisen from David's crisis during Saul's kingship (1 Samuel 18:6—30:31) or from another crisis when his son Absalom rebelled against him (2 Samuel 15-18). List these two possibilities on the right side of your chalkboard or overhead transparency opposite your list of student answers to questions given out before the lesson started.

Have one of your students read the printed text aloud. Lead your class in a discussion of how the things listed on the chalkboard fit into the thought of the psalm. Be sure the discussion includes the following thoughts. Ideas from the lesson commentary in this book will help in discussing them.

1. The psalmist waited patiently.

2. His deliverance did come.

3. That deliverance gave him a new song.

4. Blessings come to one who trusts the Lord.

5. The psalmist responded by preaching righteousness, looking to God for preservation, and by joyous prayer.

Into Life

The student book suggests a chart that you may want to use. On your chalkboard make three columns with the headings "Problem," "Worldly Answer," and "Better Answer." Let students suggest problems and answers. For example, if the problem is "unwanted pregnancy" the worldly answer may be "abortion" and the better answer may be "help from a crisis pregnancy center."

On the bottom of the sheet given out at the first of the lesson, let each student write:

1. A past situation in which God has provided deliverance.

2. A present situation in which he or she needs the deliverance of God.

Close with a challenge for each student to pray often, both thanking God for past deliverances and seeking His help in present difficulties or problems to come.

Let's Talk It Over

The questions on this page are designed to encourage review of the lesson Scriptures and to promote discussion of the lesson by the class. The answers provided are only discussion starters. Let your class talk it over from there.

1. The psalmist waited patiently for the Lord. What would it mean to wait impatiently, or not to wait at all? What are the dangers in that?

Many of us are familiar with waiting impatiently. When stress becomes distress, we want our prayers to be answered immediately. Instead of feeling the quiet confidence that comes from trusting God, we become worried and upset. Our anxiety may make us physically ill, or it may move us to some drastic action fueled more by emotion than reason. Waiting patiently on the Lord is not an excuse for inaction. It means that we have done everything we can, and now we are trusting God to intervene for an outcome that is according to His will.

2. Have you ever been trapped in a set of circumstances, or in a habit, or in a relationship that felt like being mired in a clay pit? Explain. How did you find deliverance?

This picture of mire and rock has been applied as a metaphor of salvation. Sin is the miry clay that has us trapped, and the rock is Jesus Christ. There are many different types of addictions or compulsive behaviors that can entrap people. Recovery groups can be very helpful, but the most effective deliverance is that which comes from God. To free us from destructive, sinful habits, God gives the deliverance of salvation, and the loving encouragement of mutual ministry between Christians.

3. Since God's wonderful works are so varied and numerous, is there any point in naming them? What benefit may we derive from such an exercise?

The highest motive for enumerating the wonderful works of God is to glorify and exalt Him, but there are other benefits. There is an old song that admonishes us, "Count your many blessings, name them one by one." That can help us overcome discouragement, overcome envy, and overcome doubt. As we name God's works we realize anew how great God is and how blessed we are. Our faith is enlarged, love and devotion are renewed, and our hope is restored.

4. The psalmist defended a righteous standard. Where is such defense needed today? What risks are involved?

Our society is coming unraveled for the want of moral values. Standards of right and wrong have been so compromised and rewritten in the name of fairness, freedom, and personal rights that what God considers sin is now protected, and appealing for righteousness is considered bigoted. We need people of moral courage who will live by a righteous standard themselves, and promote that standard to others at home, in the workplace, in the schools, and in government. It is risky because "every one that doeth evil hateth the light" (John 3:20). The attacks upon those who stand for righteousness have become more vicious in recent years, but evil will certainly prevail when good people are silent. That is not a happy prospect.

5. Verse 10 of our text sounds a lot like what we call testifying. What do you think this psalmist would say to someone who objects that testimonies are undignified and draw too much attention to self?

The psalmist obviously felt that God deserved to be praised publicly and explicitly for His works. He directed praise and glory to God. To fail in that would appear ungrateful or proud, as though a man alone were responsible for his well-being. The psalmist might also contend that failure to testify would risk having God withdraw His blessing, since they were met with indifference or ingratitude.

6. Do Christians today love God's salvation? What would cause them to love it more?

It is dangerous to generalize, but it does appear that there are many Christians who are not very passionate about the salvation God has given. It may be that they have little understanding of what they have been saved from and what they have been saved to. If we consider that we were always pretty good folk who simply needed a little moral boost to be worthy of Heaven, we will be lukewarm in our enthusiasm over such a salvation. When we understand that without Christ we were hopeless, condemned sinners, and that in Him alone we now have forgiveness, new life, and an eternal hope, that is a salvation we can love. That will get us motivated to magnify the Lord and proclaim His goodness.

Obey God's Laws

DEVOTIONAL READING: Matthew 7:21-28.

LESSON SCRIPTURE: Psalm 119:1-16, 45, 105, 129, 130.

PRINTED TEXT: Psalm 119:1-16, 45, 105, 129, 130.

Psalm 119:1-16, 45, 105, 129, 130

1 Blessed are the undefiled in the way, who walk in the law of the LORD.

2 Blessed are they that keep his testimonies, and that seek him with the whole heart.

3 They also do no iniquity: they walk in his ways.

4 Thou hast commanded us to keep thy precepts diligently.

5 O that my ways were directed to keep thy statutes!

6 Then shall I not be ashamed, when I have respect unto all thy commandments.

7 I will praise thee with uprightness of heart, when I shall have learned thy righteous judgments.

8 I will keep thy statutes: O forsake me not utterly.

9 Wherewithal shall a young man cleanse his way? By taking heed thereto according to thy word.

10 With my whole heart have I sought thee: O let me not wander from thy commandments.

11 Thy word have I hid in mine heart, that I might not sin against thee.

12 Blessed art thou, O LORD: teach me thy statutes.

13 With my lips have I declared all the judgments of thy mouth.

14 I have rejoiced in the way of thy testimonies, as much as in all riches.

15 I will meditate in thy precepts, and have respect unto thy ways.

16 I will delight myself in thy statutes: I will not forget thy word.

. . . .

45 And I will walk at liberty: for I seek thy precepts.

. . . .

105 Thy word is a lamp unto my feet, and a light unto my path.

. . . .

129 Thy testimonies are wonderful: therefore doth my soul keep them.

130 The entrance of thy words giveth light; it giveth understanding unto the simple.

Aug 11

GOLDEN TEXT: Thy word is a lamp unto my feet, and a light unto my path.
—Psalm 119:105.

God Is With Us
(Psalms)
Unit 2: Responding to God
(Lessons 10-13)

Lesson Aims

After this lesson, each student should:

1. Have a stronger desire to live by God's laws.

2. Understand that applying God's laws to everyday living is not always easy.

3. Feel a responsibility to study God's laws.

4. Be better able to apply God's laws to his or her life.

Lesson Outline

INTRODUCTION

  A. God's Road Map

  B. Lesson Background

  I. BLESSEDNESS OF OBEDIENCE (Psalm 119:1-8)

    A. Integrity of Heart (vv. 1-3)

    B. Consistency in Conduct (vv. 4, 5)

    C. Avoidance of Shame (v. 6)

    D. Resulting Praise (vv. 7, 8)

  II. HOLY ADVICE (Psalm 119:9-16)

    A. Heed the Word (vv. 9, 10)

      Cleansing and Correction

    B. Insurance Against Sin (vv. 11, 12)

    C. Proclaim the Word (vv. 13, 14)

    D. Meditate on the Word (vv. 15, 16)

  III. A WALK IN THE WORD (PSALM 119:45, 105, 129, 130)

    A. It Brings Freedom (v. 45)

    B. It Brings Light (v. 105)

      Lighted Steps

    C. It Brings Understanding (vv. 129, 130)

      The Great Psalm

CONCLUSION

  A. Let's Relight the Lamp

  B. Let Us Pray

  C. Thought to Remember

The guiding light for our lives is the focus of visual 11 of the visuals packet. The visual is shown on page 429.

Introduction

A. God's Road Map

Traveling in an unfamiliar part of the country, I missed a turn. After a few miles, I realized that I was lost. I pulled over to the side of the road and searched in my glove compartment for a map. I found a map of the area, but I still had a problem. The map was not detailed enough to help me find my way on the back road where I was. Then I found a more detailed map. Following it, I was soon back on a marked highway and feeling greatly relieved. Then suddenly I came to a dead end. The map I was following was an old one. A new highway had been built, and the old highway ended at a stream over which there was no bridge.

There was nothing to do but to find some help. Finally I came to a service station where I bought an up-to-date map. Following it, I was able to reach my destination.

Life itself can be like my experience. Often we try to negotiate the highway of life guided only by our own sense of direction. This is a sure way to get lost. Then we turn to other plans. Some are not detailed enough; others are out-of-date. This lesson offers a map for traveling life's highway from birth to our heavenly reward. God's law, God's Word, is that map. Following it will insure us a safe journey.

B. Lesson Background

Psalm 119, containing 176 verses, is the longest psalm. Its structure is unusual. It is divided into twenty-two stanzas, one for each letter of the Hebrew alphabet. This makes it one of the most unusual of the alphabetic psalms. All eight verses of the first stanza begin with the letter *aleph,* the first letter in the Hebrew alphabet. All the verses in the second stanza begin with *beth,* the second letter, and so on through the entire psalm.

Through all twenty-two stanzas, the writer emphasizes knowing and obeying God's law. To provide variety, he uses several synonyms for "law." Among these are "testimonies," "judgments," "statutes," "word" or "words," "precepts," "commandments," and "promises."

I. Blessedness of Obedience
(Psalm 119:1-8)

A. Integrity of Heart (vv. 1-3)

1-3. Blessed are the undefiled in the way, who walk in the law of the LORD. Blessed are they that keep his testimonies, and that seek him with the whole heart. They also do no iniquity: they walk in his ways.

Blessed does not come from the Hebrew word meaning "to bless," but from a word that means "happy." *Blessed* is an appropriate translation, however; for if one is truly happy, it is because he is blessed of God. *Undefiled in the way* describes one who follows God's leading completely, one who keeps himself "unspotted from the world" (James 1:27). *The law of the Lord.* Sometimes this expression refers specifically to the law of Moses, but in this case it seems to include all of God's Word.

Testimonies comes from a word that means "to witness" or "to testify." God's commandments testify to His divine nature and to man's duty. *Seek him with the whole heart.* This was at the center of the Old Testament law: "Thou shalt love the Lord thy God with all thine heart, and with all thy soul, and with all thy might" (Deuteronomy 6:5). Jesus reaffirmed this (Matthew 22:37, 38).

Iniquity is derived from a word that means "to turn" or "to twist." The blessed man neither turns from God's way nor twists His commandments.

B. Consistency in Conduct (vv. 4, 5)

4, 5. Thou hast commanded us to keep thy precepts diligently. O that my ways were directed to keep thy statutes!

To be pleasing to God we must be consistent in walking in His way. He has laid out for us a definite course of conduct, and He expects us to follow it. To wander hither and yon wherever our whims may take us cannot be pleasing to God, and it can be disastrous to us. To pursue a consistent course is not easy. Even the apostle Paul struggled with temptations that could have led his feet astray (Romans 7:21-23). Psalm 1 indicates how a person may stray. First, one walks in "the counsel of the ungodly," then stands "in the way of sinners," and finally sits "in the seat of the scornful."

C. Avoidance of Shame (v. 6)

6. Then shall I not be ashamed, when I have respect unto all thy commandments.

When one turns from the ways of God, he or she may suffer physically; but often a more intense suffering comes from the shame that wicked deeds bring. A good name that has become soiled by sin never can be restored to its original purity, nor can one ever completely regain the trust of others when sin has destroyed that trust.

D. Resulting Praise (vv. 7, 8)

7, 8. I will praise thee with uprightness of heart, when I shall have learned thy righteous judgments. I will keep thy statutes: O forsake me not utterly.

Praise toward God came naturally to the psalmist, not just from his lips but from his heart. This praise was not just the gushing forth of strong emotions; it was based on knowledge of God and His Word.

How to Say It

ALEPH (Hebrew). *ah*-leff.
AMNON. *Am*-nun.
BETH (Hebrew). bayth or bait.
REHOBOAM. Re-ho-*bo*-um.
TAMAR. *Tay*-mer.

We are not born with a knowledge of God. We acquire that knowledge through experience. Some of that experience is unplanned; it just happens. We view the vast expanse of the heavens or we see a majestic mountain raising its snowy head above its surroundings, and deep down we sense the existence of a power greater than ourselves. However, recognizing God's power in nature does not necessarily lead us to see His love and concern for us. For that we need special revelation through the Scriptures. We do not come to understand the Scriptures effortlessly through some magical process of osmosis. Rather, we must devote long, arduous hours to study if we are to understand God's will for us. That is why Sunday school and every other educational activity within the church are so important.

Studying the Scriptures as simply an intellectual pursuit is not what the writer had in mind. His studies led him to keep God's statutes. Any study of God's Word that does not lead to a change in attitudes and actions is less than Christian education.

O forsake me not utterly. These words suggest that there may have been some crisis in the psalmist's life, some suffering or some threat that turned him to God for help. Possibly he had turned from God's way and needed to be forgiven. His need was so pressing that he feared that God was forsaking him. Most of us can identify with the writer, for we have passed through times of fear and despair, times when we have pleaded for God to be with us.

II. Holy Advice
(Psalm 119:9-16)

A. Heed the Word (vv. 9, 10)

9, 10. Wherewithal shall a young man cleanse his way? By taking heed thereto according to thy word. With my whole heart have I sought thee: O let me not wander from thy commandments.

Verse 9 introduces the second stanza in this psalm. It is labeled *beth*, the second letter in the Hebrew alphabet, and each verse in the stanza begins with this letter.

The stanza begins with a question that every young person ought to face. The writer may be an older man giving advice to a younger one. Every generation in one way or another passes along certain values to the next generation. The teaching of values may be done carefully and systematically, with constant reinforcement from the lives of the teachers. On the other hand, it may be done haphazardly by parents and church leaders, or what is worse, by outside forces that contradict what parents teach.

Young people are bombarded by media crosswinds that blow in every direction. Is it any wonder that some young people are like rudderless ships, turning hither and yon with each wind change? The tragedy is that some are blown upon reefs that destroy them morally and physically. Will God hold guiltless the older generation that stands by and allows this to happen?

Unlike some leaders, who seem to have lost their sense of direction, the psalmist knew how a young man can make his way clear: *By taking heed thereto according to thy word.* The writer had sought God with all his heart, and now he was trying to teach others the truths he had learned. He knew the value of example, for he prayed that God would not let him wander from His commandments.

CLEANSING AND CORRECTION

Many problems arise in a young person's way. There is a temptation to think one is especially girded with strength. There is an awareness that one is better looking than are older people. There is an adroitness in doing physical acts that older people may be less competent to perform. One is keenly aware of what one's peers are wearing, saying, and doing; one feels a pressure to conform. Sexual impulses may be extremely urgent in youth, and one may act rashly.

Rehoboam, Solomon's son, was strong, vain, arrogant, and impulsive. He acted as his young companions advised: proudly, thoughtlessly, and boastfully. As a result, he caused the Hebrew kingdom to split apart, and brought about years of bloodshed. He did not take heed to his way according to God's Word (1 Kings 12:1-20).

One of David's sons, Amnon, became enamored of his half-sister, Tamar. His desire for her led to deception and rape. Tamar's brother then killed Amnon and fled (2 Samuel 13). So David's family was disrupted because young Amnon did not take heed to his way and cleanse it.

It can be said that *awareness* is the first thing a young person needs, awareness of God's Word by which his or her life can be cleansed. The Word of the Lord is what can purify, perfect, and protect a young person.   —J. G. V. B.

B. Insurance Against Sin (vv. 11, 12)

11, 12. Thy word have I hid in mine heart, that I might not sin against thee. Blessed art thou, O LORD: teach me thy statutes.

It is the word in our hearts, not a book in the house, that keeps us from doing wrong. That word cannot be implanted in our hearts by some surgical process, nor is there a pill that can put it there. It finds a home in our hearts by a process of diligent study. This is a strong argument for encouraging people, especially young people, to memorize Scripture.

C. Proclaim the Word (vv. 13, 14)

13, 14. With my lips have I declared all the judgments of thy mouth. I have rejoiced in the way of thy testimonies, as much as in all riches.

We have an obligation to share our knowledge of God with others. As we do this, we share in the joy it brings to those who learn. We realize another blessing too. As we teach others, our own knowledge and understanding grow.

Many things can cause people to rejoice: wealth, power, family, service to God. What brings joy to a person depends on that person's values. If one searches for joy only in wealth, power, or even family, he or she may be terribly disappointed. All of these may turn sour, and certainly they all will pass. Faithful service to God lasts into eternity. That is why the psalmist found joy in God's testimonies *as much as in all riches.*

D. Meditate on the Word (vv. 15, 16)

15, 16. I will meditate in thy precepts, and have respect unto thy ways. I will delight myself in thy statutes: I will not forget thy word.

Much can be said in favor of memorizing portions of God's Word. Thus we hide His precepts in our hearts and minds (v. 11). We need to go beyond knowing the words, however. We must ponder them, meditate over them, discuss them so that we know how to apply them to specific situations.

In our increasingly complicated world, there are no easy answers to many situations. Where, for example, does one find proof texts to deal with the ethical issues being raised by the science of genetic engineering? What Scriptures does one quote to cope with all of the complex problems that arise when the government increasingly becomes involved in our lives? For this reason we must study the Scriptures and meditate over them to find the general principles that God has established to meet any problem that life may dump on us.

Meditation is important for another reason. It causes one to examine the inner recesses of one's own heart and to measure its contents by God's standards. Christians have an obligation to relate their faith to the world; but in order to do this effectively, their own hearts must be right. In our busy schedules we struggle to find time for this kind of meditation; and worse, when we have a little extra time, we hardly know what to do with it.

Many of us deal with Bible study as if it were a business responsibility: a serious responsibility, to be sure, but still a responsibility. The psalm writer, on the other hand, found delight in God's statutes. He approached Bible study as we approach a hobby—something we look forward to with delight, something we enjoy while we are engaged in it.

III. A Walk in the Word
(Psalm 119:45, 105, 129, 130)

A. It Brings Freedom (v. 45)

45. And I will walk at liberty: for I seek thy precepts.

We hear much today about political freedom. People have suffered, even died for it. We understand people's willingness to sacrifice for political freedom, even though such freedom brings its own burdens and responsibilities. The psalmist's concern was for spiritual freedom, a far more important kind. Persons who know and follow God's law enjoy important blessings. However, those who follow God's commandments in a legalistic way are still under bondage. Such were the Pharisees in Jesus' day. One goal should be to grow in understanding until we follow God's law, not because we have to, but because we love God so much that we want to. One who attains this level of discipleship enjoys real freedom that no one can take from him or her.

B. It Brings Light (v. 105)

105. Thy word is a lamp unto my feet, and a light unto my path.

Stumbling around in a dark room is a disturbing experience. How much more threatening it is to try to find one's way in a darkened moral situation without any spiritual light! The consequences can be painful, even disastrous. Our society seems to be in that kind of a situation. We stagger from one crisis to another, only to be confronted with a still more serious problem—all because we have no light. To be more precise, we have an available light, the Bible; but many people prefer humanistic theories that only compound the darkness.

LIGHTED STEPS

The psalmist tells us God's Word is a lamp that lights his pathway. The picture here is not a long road brightly illuminated with electric lights. Rather, it is a scene of gloom with no gleam of light in the surrounding blackness. Only a few steps ahead are lit by a lamp.

The great British spiritual leader, John H. Newman, caught this idea and expressed it in the first stanza of his famous hymn:

> Lead, kindly Light, amid th' encircling gloom,
>   Lead Thou me on!
> The night is dark, and I am far from home;
>   Lead Thou me on!
> Keep Thou my feet; I do not ask to see
> The distant scene; one step enough for me.

This is an experience we have many times in our Christian walk. We may be going through a trying time. Someone close to us may be very ill, loved ones on whom we have depended in crises may seem indifferent to or unaware of our needs. Our duties may press upon us. We may be unable to see how we can comfort and cheer and challenge others who need our help. We need to let God's truth help us to see just one step at a time. We can't do it all at once—and can't do it *at all* unless we let the light lead us little by little.   —J. G. V. B.

C. It Brings Understanding
(vv. 129, 130)

129, 130. Thy testimonies are wonderful: therefore doth my soul keep them. The entrance of thy words giveth light; it giveth understanding unto the simple.

God's *testimonies are wonderful* in that they reveal to us His power and majesty, His love and mercy. There is no way that we can understand all these things apart from His revelation. That revelation culminated in His Son, Jesus Christ. In Him we are able to understand why we are here and where we are going. This understanding is not confined to just a handful of scholars hidden away in some ivory tower. The way of salvation has been made simple enough that all may find it.

visual 11

THE GREAT PSALM

If ever a literary production deserved to be called "great," Psalm 119 certainly qualifies. It is great in *length*. Its 176 verses make it the longest of the psalms. It is great in *literary finesse* and intricacy. It goes through the Hebrew alphabet and gives each letter a section of eight verses, each one of which starts with that letter. The psalm is great *in its theme*, which is the Word of God, the commandments, precepts, testimonies, and statutes of the Lord. All of these many verses say something uplifting, challenging, or comforting about God's truth in relationship to human life.

It is difficult to include these and other truths about this psalm in one poem, but I have tried to do so in a sonnet, "The 119th Psalm."

> O Psalm of long and linked loveliness,
> Successively the Hebrew alphabet
> Quite through, with simple and yet seemly stress,
> You pass, and ne'er the Word of God forget.
> For, in each verse, the law or the command
> Of the Almighty you do bring to view,
> A rock whereon our questing feet may stand,
> And yet a spring for our refreshment, too.
> We learn how the young man may cleanse his way,
> How, through the truth, we may have liberty,
> How light will guide us back though we may stray,
> And how we may our hearts from sinning free.
> O, open now our eyes to God's great law,
> And we'll behold with gladness and with awe.

However, while this psalm is a vivid example of literary artistry, its aim is not to amaze us with the virtuosity of the writer. Rather, its aim is to help us see the wonder of God's Word and to see how it relates to our guidance, challenge, comfort, and renewal.   —J. G. V. B.

Conclusion

A. Let's Relight the Lamp

It is a well-documented fact that the majority of Americans know little about the Bible. There was a time when editorials and speeches abounded in Bible quotations and allusions. No more! Most people would not understand these biblical references now.

How did this sorry state of affairs come about? We can point to the growing secularization of our society, for one thing. We have become so obsessed with things of this world that things eternal are ignored. We may also point to the growing pluralism of our society. In our efforts to provide freedom of religion for every sect under the sun, we have accomplished freedom *from* religion for many. Our courts have interpreted the constitution in ways the founding

fathers never dreamed of. As a result, the study of the Bible and even its distribution are severely restricted in our public schools. The practical result is that the one book that has had the greatest impact on our civilization is hidden from our children.

What can we do about the situation? We have several options. One, we can stand around and complain, wringing our hands in impotency. Two, we can work through legal process to get court decisions changed. Three, we can use the opportunities we have right at hand to teach people the Bible. Parents can teach it to their children in their homes. We can encourage greater participation in the educational programs offered in our churches. And we can develop new and creative educational programs to meet the changing circumstances in our society.

Suppose we are stumbling down a rough pathway in the dark. Suppose we have a lantern, oil, and matches, and yet we refuse to use them to provide light for our path. Such reluctance to use what we have would be called foolish. We have the means to provide light, God's Word, to sweep away the moral darkness that surrounds us. Are we any less foolish if we don't find ways to use it?

B. Let Us Pray

Amid the darkness that surrounds us, Father, we pray for light. Show us how to use the light You have given us through the Scriptures to guide our footsteps. Show us how to share this light with others. In the name of Jesus, the light of the world, we pray. Amen.

C. Thought to Remember

"Thy word is a lamp unto my feet, and a light unto my path" (Psalm 119:105).

Home Daily Bible Readings

Monday, Aug. 5—Keep God's Laws (Deuteronomy 26:15-19)

Tuesday, Aug. 6—Be Strong and of Good Courage (Joshua 1:1-9)

Wednesday, Aug. 7—To Obey Is Better Than Sacrifice (1 Samuel 15:22-29)

Thursday, Aug. 8—Ready for Rain (Genesis 6:11-22)

Friday, Aug. 9—Nothing Left Undone (Joshua 11:10-15)

Saturday, Aug. 10—Holding Fast to the Lord (2 Kings 18:1-8)

Sunday, Aug. 11—Learned Obedience (Hebrews 5:1-10)

Learning by Doing

This page contains an alternate lesson plan emphasizing learning activities. Classes desiring such student involvement will find these suggestions helpful.

Learning Goals

Some people in our society view obedience to authority as a necessary evil. This may be due to childhood experiences, to the misuse of power by political figures, or to our constant approval of liberty from tyranny. The reality is that true freedom is found in a life that coincides with our design as humans and with the basic needs of group living. One of these is the need for order and regulation. Ask students to tell what life would be like in our town if no one were in authority.

Help your class members to understand that obeying God is in their own best interest. Sin is a great liar. It says we can be free by rejecting the authority of law, of police, of God himself. We can do as we please. But the freedom sin promises leads to slavery and disappointment. True freedom is found in the bosom of our heavenly Father.

As a result of this lesson students should be able to:

1. Explain the inner conflict between obedience and disobedience (right and wrong) in each of us.

2. Describe several cultural developments that encourage disobedience to authority.

3. Describe several cultural developments that encourage obedience to authority.

4. List several of the blessings and advantages of obeying God.

Into the Lesson

Ask a member of your class (preferably a few days in advance) to prepare to read 1 Samuel 15:1-9, 13-16, 22 at the beginning of the lesson. This is the record of King Saul's near-obedience. God told him to destroy the Amalekites completely—all the people and all the property. Saul obeyed this command—almost. He saved the king of the Amalekites alive, and he let the soldiers bring back some very fine cattle and sheep. Samuel confronted Saul about his disobedience. The sound of sheep and cattle made it plain that not all of them had been destroyed. Saul explained that his soldiers had brought some of the best livestock for a sacrifice to the Lord. Samuel answered that obedience is better than sacrifice. Explain that Saul was doing his own thing. He should have been doing what the Lord told him to do.

Have the class suggest examples of people doing their own thing. Write them down. Some examples may be spraying graffiti on public or private buildings, being unfaithful to a spouse, becoming sexually active before marriage, disobeying parents.

Into the Word

Divide your class into three groups and give each group its instructions written on a card.

All groups: Choose a group leader/reporter.

All groups: Study Psalm 119:1-16, 45, 129, 130.

Group 1: List blessings of obeying God.

Group 2: List ways of promoting obedience in ourselves.

Group 3: List responses to obedience.

You can refer the students to the student book for help. Allow them ten minutes to finish, then have each group report its findings. Compare what they report with the following:

Possible blessings in the text:
1. Heart of integrity (vv. 1-3)
2. Avoidance of shame (v. 6)
3. Pure life (v. 9)
4. Personal freedom (v. 45)
5. Light for our way (vv. 105, 130)

Ways to promote obedience:
1. Studying and learning God's laws (v. 7)
2. Hiding God's word in your heart (v. 11)
3. Meditating on God's laws (v. 15)
4. Seeking God (v. 10)

Our response to obedience:
1. Appreciation of God's laws (v. 129)
2. Delight in God's law (vv. 14, 16)
3. Praise and worship of God (vv. 7, 12)

Into Life

Ask your students to think of the law, principle, or teaching of God that is easiest to obey. Attending worship and studying the Bible in Sunday school may be two of the responses.

Next ask students to tell what law, principle, or teaching of God is most difficult to obey. Some responses may be forgiving, loving an enemy, bringing up children in the Lord, daily Bible study and prayer, managing one's temper.

After a short discussion, challenge your students to keep on obeying the easier commands, but also to pick out a difficult one and obey it this week.

Let's Talk It Over

The questions on this page are designed to encourage review of the lesson Scriptures and to promote discussion of the lesson by the class. The answers provided are only discussion starters. Let your class talk it over from there.

1. What would help you be more whole-hearted and diligent in following God's ways?

To be obedient to God and follow His will, like most worthwhile objectives, takes initiative and discipline. Most believers agree that they should obey diligently; but they also agree that they should exercise regularly, but seldom do. When we get serious about giving wholehearted obedience, there are measures that may help keep us motivated. For example, you could begin a file of illustrations of the practical consequences of sin. You could agree with your Bible school class or other study group on application goals from your study, and then hold one another accountable for reaching those goals. You could reward yourself somehow for practicing some obedience over a period of time, and let every misbehavior trigger a self-imposed punishment.

2. Is shame ever constructive? Explain. What happens when someone feels no shame?

Authority figures are cautioned against using shame as a motivation because it is damaging to the self-esteem of a person. Encouragement, positive reinforcement of desired behavior, and other forms of discipline are preferred. There is a shame, however, that is completely internal. It comes from an accusing conscience when we know we have done something wrong. That shame is uncomfortable, but can be constructive if it averts wrong behavior or produces right action. Someone who feels no shame either never does anything wrong, or else has an underdeveloped conscience that excuses his or her mean, immoral, or otherwise sinful behavior.

3. God's commandments in the Bible are ancient. What would be wrong with modifying them to fit today's culture?

In a 1994 survey, sixty-nine percent of respondents agreed that the accepted rules about religion and morality are too restrictive, and that each individual should choose his or her own religious beliefs and moral code. It is frightening that so many people think they can improve God's rules. The commands of God are the Creator's instructions, revealing how mankind is designed to act. His moral commands are not bound to a particular time or culture. Who are we to think we know a better way?

4. How does memorizing Scripture protect against sin?

Unless we have a good grasp of God's Word, we may not recognize sin when we are tempted to it. In the temptations of Jesus recorded in Matthew 4, He countered the words of the devil with the words of Scripture. The Word of God is the sword of the Spirit, the one offensive weapon in the armor of God described in Ephesians 6:10-18. Memorizing Scripture insures that it will be available to us in the face of temptation, reminding us what we must do and what we must not do, prompting us to action.

5. Are there meditation techniques that you have found helpful? Describe them. What are the benefits of meditation over memorization?

Meditation may involve memorization, but it lingers long over an idea or a text. You may restate a thought many times, each time emphasizing a different word, looking for additional understanding. You may restate a verse, injecting your name and making it very personal. You may try praying the verse or thought back to God, letting it be the focus of your prayer. Try setting the verse to music, or find and sing a song that incorporates the same idea.

6. If the Bible is so valuable, why do so many Christians know so little about it? What could be done in your church to encourage Bible knowledge?

Perhaps laziness and procrastination can explain much ignorance of the Bible among well-meaning and good-hearted people. There are helpful measures that we can take. The entire Bible is available on tape at moderate cost, and that is helpful for some who have difficulty reading. Churches can report the number of Bibles carried to church, and give opportunity for people to use their Bibles while at church. The minister can preach a series of messages on a Bible book, giving people time to find the text and follow along. You may challenge classes, individuals, or youth groups to memorization projects. Cooperate with a Christian bookstore to create a display of Bibles and study helps. Insert Bible knowledge quizzes in the bulletin occasionally, and give recognition or awards to those who complete them.

Repent and Confess

DEVOTIONAL READING: Ezekiel 18:25-32.

LESSON SCRIPTURE: Psalm 51.

PRINTED TEXT: Psalm 51:1-13, 17.

Psalm 51:1-13, 17

1 Have mercy upon me, O God, according to thy loving-kindness: according unto the multitude of thy tender mercies blot out my transgressions.

2 Wash me thoroughly from mine iniquity, and cleanse me from my sin.

3 For I acknowledge my transgressions: and my sin is ever before me.

4 Against thee, thee only, have I sinned, and done this evil in thy sight: that thou mightest be justified when thou speakest, and be clear when thou judgest.

5 Behold, I was shapen in iniquity; and in sin did my mother conceive me.

6 Behold, thou desirest truth in the inward parts: and in the hidden part thou shalt make me to know wisdom.

7 Purge me with hyssop, and I shall be clean: wash me, and I shall be whiter than snow.

8 Make me to hear joy and gladness; that the bones which thou hast broken may rejoice.

9 Hide thy face from my sins, and blot out all mine iniquities.

10 Create in me a clean heart, O God; and renew a right spirit within me.

11 Cast me not away from thy presence; and take not thy Holy Spirit from me.

12 Restore unto me the joy of thy salvation; and uphold me with thy free Spirit.

13 Then will I teach transgressors thy ways; and sinners shall be converted unto thee.

. . . .

17 The sacrifices of God are a broken spirit: a broken and a contrite heart, O God, thou wilt not despise.

GOLDEN TEXT: Create in me a clean heart, O God; and renew a right spirit within me.
—Psalm 51:10.

God Is With Us
(Psalms)
Unit 2: Responding to God
(Lessons 10-13)

Lesson Aims

As a result of studying this lesson, each student should:

1. Understand that God is willing to forgive penitent sinners.

2. Come to know the relief that results when one's sins are forgiven.

3. Be able to share this understanding of God's grace with others.

Lesson Outline

INTRODUCTION
    A. Repenting and Doing Penance
    B. Lesson Background
  I. A PLEA FOR FORGIVENESS (Psalm 51:1-4)
    A. A Cry for Mercy (v. 1)
    B. A Plea for Cleansing (v. 2)
      The Call for Cleansing
    C. An Acknowledgment of Sin (vv. 3, 4)
 II. A CONFESSION OF SIN (Psalm 51:5-9)
    A. An Admission of Guilt (vv. 5, 6)
      Truth Within
    B. A Further Plea for Cleansing (v. 7)
    C. A Plea for Joy (vv. 8, 9)
III. A PLEA FOR RESTORATION (Psalm 51:10-13, 17)
    A. A Prayer for a Clean Heart (v. 10)
    B. A Plea for Acceptance (v. 11)
    C. A Plea for Salvation (v. 12)
      Salvation's Joy
    D. A Commitment to Service (v. 13)
    E. The Right Sacrifice (v. 17)
CONCLUSION
    A. Awareness of Sin
    B. The Perfect Sacrifice
    C. Let Us Pray
    D. Thought to Remember

The renewal that comes from God's cleansing the human heart is graphically represented by visual 12 of the visuals packet, shown on page 436.

Introduction

A. Repenting and Doing Penance

A minister was conducting a Bible study class for several of the young people in the church. He invited them to bring in as many different versions of the New Testament as they could find. In one passage most of the versions had the word "repent," but one version had "do penance." One of the girls illustrated the difference between them: "Both Judas and Peter sinned against Jesus. Judas did penance when he went out and hanged himself. But Peter repented and went out and wept bitterly."

The writer of the Fifty-first Psalm does not actually say he wept; but as we read it, we cannot escape the feeling that tears were streaming down his cheeks as he wrote. Not every penitent sinner displays his or her emotions by weeping; but when one stands before almighty God as a sinner, strong emotions are certain. These emotions move over a wide range. They may begin with agonizing fear as a sinner has to face a holy God. There is a growing sense of pain with the awareness that one has violated this holiness. The irony of this is that the greatest saint is likely to feel that he or she is the greatest sinner, because such a one is most aware of God's holiness. Then comes a sense of forgiveness, followed by joy at the realization that the stain of sin has been wiped away. With all these is a resolve to do better from now on, to commit oneself to service to the Lord. We find all of this in Psalm 51. Though it was written three thousand years ago, it has never lost its relevance.

B. Lesson Background

The superscription credits this psalm to David, and indicates that it was written at one of the most painful crises of his life. The background for the psalm is the prophet Nathan's confrontation with David after he had committed adultery with Bathsheba and had conspired to have her husband, Uriah, murdered (2 Samuel 11, 12). David might have responded to Nathan with anger and threats, but the prophet's words, "Thou art the man," melted David's heart and he voiced his repentance.

I. A Plea for Forgiveness
(Psalm 51:1-4)

A. A Cry for Mercy (v. 1)

1. Have mercy upon me, O God, according to thy loving-kindness: according unto the multitude of thy tender mercies blot out my transgressions.

It is interesting that throughout this psalm David never addresses God as Jehovah. Perhaps he felt himself so unworthy that he dared not use the name that was so closely associated with the special covenant between Jehovah and Israel. David knew he had violated this covenant, and perhaps he felt that he could address God only as *Elohim,* the Creator God.

David asked first of all for mercy. He knew very well that he deserved punishment. Only by God's mercy could he hope to escape it. David stood where every one of us must stand—before a righteous God, a God of justice. If He were not also a God of mercy, our pleas for forgiveness would be futile. David asked that God in mercy would *blot out* his transgressions. He thought of his sins being inscribed in a divine record book. He wanted the bookkeeper to cross them out, eradicate them.

B. A Plea for Cleansing (v. 2)

2. Wash me thoroughly from mine iniquity, and cleanse me from my sin.

David now changed his figure from bookkeeping to laundering. Not content with a clearing of the divine record, he sought personal cleansing that would purge him of the sins that defiled him. His act of adultery was not the whole problem. That would not have happened if his heart had been clean. He sought to be thoroughly cleansed so that future temptations would not find him vulnerable.

Jesus later pointed out this great truth. Sin is not the outward act alone, but the condition of the heart that allows temptation to take root and grow until it results in overt action (Mark 7:21-23). If we are to live moral lives, we must ask God to purge our hearts of those things that defile us.

THE CALL FOR CLEANSING

Shakespeare's *Macbeth* provides a dramatic statement of how one feels when one's soul is stained with sin. Macbeth has taken part in a bloody murder. Now his hands are stained with blood. As he looks at them, the enormity of his guilt becomes increasingly clear to him.

Will all great Neptune's ocean wash this blood
Clean from my hand? No, this my hand will rather
The multitudinous seas incarnadine,
Making the green one red.

David likewise was aware of the terrible deeds he had done. He had committed adultery, and had added to that the sin of murder. He had used others in his sordid plot to bring about the death of brave, faithful, and earnest Uriah. It is startling to think that the same David who could compose the Twenty-third Psalm could fall into this complex of sins.

"Wash me thoroughly from mine iniquity," he cried. That shows how keenly he was aware of the slime and muck of sin that lay upon him. As Christians we find there are times when in word or deed or in cowardly silence we besmirch ourselves with the clinging filth of sin. What a

---

> ### How to Say It
> ELOHIM (Hebrew). El-o-*heem*.

consolation it is to be aware that "the blood of Jesus Christ . . . cleanseth us from all sin"! "If we confess our sins, he is faithful and just to forgive us our sins, and to cleanse us from all unrighteousness" (1 John 1:7, 9).   —J. G. V. B.

C. An Acknowledgment of Sin (vv. 3, 4)

3, 4. For I acknowledge my transgressions: and my sin is ever before me. Against thee, thee only, have I sinned, and done this evil in thy sight: that thou mightest be justified when thou speakest, and be clear when thou judgest.

In our courts today, we see accused people denying their guilt or blaming others for their problems. Without making any reservations or blaming someone else for his problems, David admitted his guilt; nor did he attempt to plea-bargain to get a lighter sentence. *My sin is ever before me.* David may have concealed his sins from most of the world, but he could not hide from his own conscience. It kept his sins ever before him. Nathan's accusation reminded him that he was not hidden from God either. He could find no peace until he had unburdened his soul before the Lord.

Against thee, thee only, have I sinned. In committing adultery and murder, David had sinned against others, but this paled into insignificance when compared to his sin against God. He recognized this when Nathan confronted him: "I have sinned against the Lord" (2 Samuel 12:13). One may sin against God without sinning against other persons, but one cannot sin against one's fellowmen without sinning against God.

That thou mightest be justified. In confessing his sin, David acknowledged that God would be perfectly just in condemning him. This raises a profound theological issue. How can God, who is just and holy, overlook human sin? Of course He cannot, except—and this is a crucial exception—by His grace extended through His Son, Jesus Christ (Romans 3:23-26).

II. A Confession of Sin (Psalm 51:5-9)

A. An Admission of Guilt (vv. 5, 6)

5. Behold, I was shapen in iniquity; and in sin did my mother conceive me.

Some theologians see this verse as proof of man's inherent depravity; others take it as a hyperbole confessing David's own complete sinfulness. We shall leave that argument to the theologians. David may be saying he was born into a sin-filled world, but he is not using that to excuse his own sins, as do some today when they blame all their problems on society. Quite the contrary, David is taking the responsibility for his own sinfulness, not trying to blame others for it.

6. Behold, thou desirest truth in the inward parts: and in the hidden part thou shalt make me to know wisdom.

God is not satisfied with an external appearance of righteousness, which one might attain through careful attention to the ritualistic provisions of the law. Rather, God requires *truth in the inward parts*. He makes us to know such truth when we study and meditate on the Scriptures. (See the comments on Psalm 119:15 in last week's lesson.)

TRUTH WITHIN

We senior citizens remember a physician we observed in our youth. He came to our home when anyone in our family was sick, and he carried a black bag with a stethoscope and many bottles of pills. The physician looked the patient over, decided what most likely was wrong, and doled out a supply of pills.

Today's physician can look deeper with X-ray and ultrasound machines. A look within often tells more about a patient's condition than does a look at the outside.

David was aware that God wanted "truth in the inward parts." He appeared as a king, in royal splendor and public acceptance; but within he had lacked integrity, honesty, purity, sympathy, constancy. Instead there had been selfishness, lust, callousness, faithlessness.

The *appearance* of righteousness, the mouthing of platitudes, and the assuming of a religious attitude are not enough for us. No, our heavenly Father desires "truth in the inward parts." May we not have to learn this as David did through moral collapse, rebuke, tragedy, sorrow, and remorse. "Blessed are the pure in heart: for they shall see God" (Matthew 5:8).

—J. G. V. B.

B. A Further Plea for Cleansing (v. 7)

7. Purge me with hyssop, and I shall be clean: wash me, and I shall be whiter than snow.

Hyssop is a small shrub. Under the Old Testament law it was used in certain ceremonial activities for cleansing, such as the cleansing of lepers or persons who had touched a dead body (Leviticus 14:1-7; Numbers 19:14-19). David

visual 12

here uses the term figuratively as another way of expressing his desire to be cleansed of sin.

Whiter than snow. Snow falls occasionally in Palestine, and it was the whitest thing the psalmist could think of. Nothing is whiter than a blanket of fresh-fallen snow. In Isaiah 1:18 we read a similar expression.

C. A Plea for Joy (vv. 8, 9)

8, 9. Make me to hear joy and gladness; that the bones which thou hast broken may rejoice. Hide thy face from my sins, and blot out all mine iniquities.

Pardon brings peace of heart and mind, but the psalmist seems to be asking for more. He wants again to experience *joy and gladness*. Following his confrontation with Nathan, David had gone through a period of dark despair while his child lay dying (2 Samuel 12:13-18). Only comfort from the Lord could restore joy after those dark hours.

The bones which thou hast broken. We take this to be figurative. The emotional pain David suffered was like the pain one would suffer from broken bones. Even as he pleads for God to send him joy, he once again asks that God will blot out all his sins.

III. A Plea for Restoration (Psalm 51:10-13, 17)

A. A Prayer for a Clean Heart (v. 10)

10. Create in me a clean heart, O God; and renew a right spirit within me.

David prayed for cleansing from past sins, but he wanted more than that. He wanted a clean heart so he would not succumb to temptation and sin again. Interestingly, he asked for a new clean heart, not a cleansing of his old heart. The kind of spiritual change that David wanted was a radical change. This was the kind of change Jesus demanded when He told Nicodemus that he must be born again (John 3:3). Paul expressed a similar idea: "If any man be in Christ, he is a new creature" (2 Corinthians 5:17).

As Christians we need to be concerned about efforts to solve some of the pressing problems of our society. We ought to work for and support laws that will improve these conditions. But we need to realize that the passing of laws can have little effect on these problems unless people's hearts are changed. Christians have the message that can change people's hearts. That's why we must give top priority to evangelism and Christian nurture.

B. A Plea for Acceptance (v. 11)

11. Cast me not away from thy presence; and take not thy Holy Spirit from me.

When we come to realize the magnitude of our own sinfulness, we realize that a great chasm exists between ourselves and God. We also realize that it is humanly impossible to bridge that chasm. We know that we deserve to be cast out. No wonder there is a note of desperation in David's plea.

David was afraid he might lose the Holy Spirit. The Spirit of the Lord came upon him when he was anointed to become king (1 Samuel 16:13). He knew that he could lose the Spirit of the Lord, for he certainly was aware that the Spirit had departed from King Saul because of his disobedience (1 Samuel 16:14). Christians who have received the Holy Spirit at their baptism (Acts 2:38) need to understand that they also can lose the Spirit.

C. A Plea for Salvation (v. 12)

12. Restore unto me the joy of thy salvation; and uphold me with thy free Spirit.

Earlier, David had faithfully followed God. God had saved him from many perils, and David had known joy. Sin had taken away that joy, and now he wanted it back again. Many persons who have fallen into sin know the soul-sickness that overwhelms them and brings agony to their hearts. They know sleepless nights. In Psalm 6:6 David mentions his own agonies: "I am weary with my groaning; all the night make I my bed to swim; I water my couch with my tears."

Uphold me with thy free Spirit. The words *with thy* are not in the Hebrew text, but were supplied by the *King James* translators. The *New International Version* renders it this way: "Grant me a willing spirit, to sustain me." This translation indicates that David wanted a spirit that would be willing to obey God. When a person is truly repentant, he or she wants to learn God's will and then obey that will.

SALVATION'S JOY

One reason David fell into sin was that he had lost the joy of God's salvation. It had become a happier thing to please himself than it was to please God.

To be saved from sin, Satan, and death is always a cause for rejoicing. We have reason to be "rejoicing in hope" (Romans 12:12). Paul admonished Christians to "rejoice in the Lord" (Philippians 3:1).

It is remarkable that the early pilgrims who settled New England held a thanksgiving observance when they did. Far from England, on the edge of a vast unknown wilderness, with few material blessings, they still rejoiced in their survival. They were grateful for so little, while we sometimes are gloomy with so much.

We need to retain or to regain our joy in God's salvation. David's religious life must have become routine. His sense of God's presence and glory, which shines in many of his psalms, had become dull. He prayed for a restoration of joy.

—J. G. V. B.

D. A Commitment to Service (v. 13)

13. Then will I teach transgressors thy ways; and sinners shall be converted unto thee.

When one has surrendered oneself to God, that person looks for ways to serve Him. One of the most obvious ways a believer can serve God is to share with others the faith that brought release from bondage to sin and restored joy to life. That's exactly what David promised to do: *Then will I teach transgressors thy ways.* In many situations the best witness to God's grace is a person who was submerged in sin and then rescued. The alcoholic who has thrown off the chains of addiction is likely to be a better witness to a drinking alcoholic than one who has never tasted strong drink. As a grievous sinner, David could speak understandingly to another sinner.

When the great prophet Isaiah was confronted by a vision of the Lord, he felt himself undone because he knew that he was a man of unclean lips dwelling among a people of unclean lips. The Lord first cleansed him and then challenged him to a special ministry. Isaiah's response was unhesitating: "Here am I; send me" (Isaiah 6:1-8). Even as he made the commitment, the prophet must have realized that the task would be difficult if not futile (Isaiah 6:9, 10). Those who have been cleansed by God do not volunteer with reservations, however; they volunteer and place their complete trust in God.

E. The Right Sacrifice (v. 17)

17. The sacrifices of God are a broken spirit: a broken and a contrite heart, O God, thou wilt not despise.

In the Mosaic law, God instituted an elaborate system of sacrifices and offerings. The priests observed detailed rituals in making these offerings. These rituals were designed to make people conscious of their sins and to cause them to repent. In many cases they produced this result. On the other hand, many people carefully observed the rituals without ever experiencing a change in heart. The psalmist in this verse expresses what God really wants: *a broken and a contrite heart*. God did not ask that the rituals be suspended; He asked that they lead to the desired end. We would be quite wrong to interpret this verse to mean that God wants us to abandon all rituals in our worship. Our concern should be that our rituals produce contrite hearts.

Conclusion

A. Awareness of Sin

Satan has a way of blinding us to our sins until events force us to confront them. That was David's experience when Nathan finally faced him. We need to understand, however, that something more than this confrontation was involved. The prophet's message would have been so many words in the wind, if David had not been taught God's standards for human conduct. The Scriptures do not tell us how David came to a knowledge of God, but we can make a reasonable guess. The Old Testament placed upon the father the responsibility for the religious training of his children (Deuteronomy 6:4-9). It is apparent that Jesse, David's father, lived up to this obligation. Then David's long, lonely hours as a shepherd opened his heart to the truths about God that nature reveals. After David became king, he had frequent contact with priests and prophets, whose teachings deepened his understanding of God and sensitized his conscience to God's will. Therefore Nathan's words quickly brought him to his knees in repentance. Had David been a barbarous savage,

he might have had Nathan executed on the spot. Had he been a highly educated and sophisticated modern pagan, he likely would have sneered or laughed at Nathan and continued on his sinful way.

Our society is showing signs that it is plunging toward moral collapse. Many of our prominent leaders display an utter disregard for God's commandments against lying, stealing, and adultery. Thousands of young people roam the streets armed to the teeth, ready to snuff out a human life at the bat of an eye. How did we get in such a tragic situation? Many reasons may be cited, but the fundamental problem is that we have failed to teach our children and our grandchildren the important truths about God. We have allowed ourselves to become so busy making money, or building a career, or seeking pleasure, that we have neglected God's mandate to us as parents. If we thought about it at all, we thought that somehow our children would grow up knowing the Bible just as earlier generations did. How wrong we were!

What can we do about the situation? First of all, like David we need to repent of our sins, whether of omission or commission, and pray that God will extend forgiveness to us. Then, like David, we must teach transgressors God's ways. Some of us need to become involved in formal teaching in Sunday school, Vacation Bible School, or Christian camps. All of us can teach in family situations or in informal one-to-one situations.

B. The Perfect Sacrifice

In certain Old Testament rituals, the perfect sacrifice was a lamb without spot or blemish. Under the New Covenant, the perfect sacrifice is Jesus, "the Lamb of God, which taketh away the sin of the world." But from us God still wants "a broken and a contrite heart." In our worship we need to lay aside the distractions of the world and enter into our songs, our prayers, our meditations, and the Lord's Supper with such a heart. If we do, we have the assurance that God will not despise our worship.

C. Let Us Pray

We pray earnestly, O Lord, for forgiveness for succumbing to the sins of the flesh, for allowing pride to harden our hearts and make us arrogant. Teach us to submit humbly to Your will and serve wherever You may call us. In the name of Jesus Christ, we pray. Amen.

D. Thought to Remember

"A broken and a contrite heart, O God, thou wilt not despise" (Psalm 51:17).

Home Daily Bible Readings

Monday, Aug. 12—Repentance the Only Hope (Ezekiel 18:25-32)

Tuesday, Aug. 13—Rend Hearts, Not Garments (Joel 2:10-14)

Wednesday, Aug. 14—No Exemptions (Luke 13:1-5)

Thursday, Aug. 15—All May Be Saved (Romans 10:5-13)

Friday, Aug. 16—Sin Acknowledged (Psalm 32:1-5)

Saturday, Aug. 17—Renewal of Israel (Ezekiel 36:22-28)

Sunday, Aug. 18—Transgressions Swept Away (Isaiah 44:18-23)

Learning by Doing

This page contains an alternate lesson plan emphasizing learning activities. Classes desiring such student involvement will find these suggestions helpful.

Learning Goals

This lesson should enable students to:

1. Explain God's nature and His teachings as the ultimate measure of right and wrong.

2. Describe David's experience of sin, guilt, and restoration.

3. Describe how many people deny sin.

4. Develop an awareness of their own tendency to deny their wrongdoing instead of confessing it and seeking forgiveness.

Into the Lesson

This lesson provides an opportunity to consider the denial of guilt and sin in our society. As the teacher, you can help your students hear, feel, and understand this denial. The following story will help establish a background for this.

Several years ago a drama portrayed a war veteran turned businessman. When he was robbed of his briefcase, he gave chase and caught the thief. A struggle ensued, and almost subconsciously the businessman called upon his military training and killed the man with his bare hands. It was all over in a matter of seconds.

Thus the businessman regained his briefcase, but he was arrested and charged with manslaughter. During the ensuing trial, the judge and jury were about to acquit the killer of any wrongdoing. Military experts testified of his training, and character witnesses supported his integrity. When the accused took the stand, however, he said, "Look, I appreciate what has been said, but the bottom line is that I killed a man who did not deserve to be killed. He deserved punishment, but not death. I have a responsibility to this would-be thief's family and to myself. I ought to pay for what I did."

I don't recall how the drama ended, but I remember that the judge, jury, and people in the courtroom were deeply moved by the man's feeling of guilt and his determination to be responsible for his actions.

How unlike the customary attitude today! We blame our parents for not rearing us properly. For every criminal act we blame the criminal's environment, or poverty, or society, or the system. So the wrongdoer is exonerated of any responsibility or guilt. How unlike the attitude of David!

Ask students to tell of television shows, books, stories, movies, or their own experiences in which guilt or wrongdoing has been denied.

Into the Word

Compare God's measure of right and wrong with humanity's.

God's measure. Ask your class how God determines what is right and what is wrong. The answer can be that He has made human beings so they will be happy and prosperous together if they act in unselfish and mutually helpful ways. He has made this plain in His Word. Obeying the commands leads to joy and life. Disobeying them leads to pain and judgment.

Humanity's measure. Ask your class how most people determine what is right and what is wrong. One answer is found in Judges 17:6: each person did what he or she felt was right. Our society is much the same. However, we make laws because we know people cannot be trusted to choose their own ways without limit. Too many would choose profit or pleasure rather than right.

Then focus on God's way of dealing with sin and humanity's ways.

God's way. Ask your class how God led David to deal with his sin. See verses 1-4 and 10-12. We see that God confronted David through the prophet Nathan: "Thou art the man" (2 Samuel 12:1-7). David followed God's wishes. He confessed, repented, sought God's forgiveness, and as a result found restoration.

Humanity's ways. Ask your class how humans deal with sin. Several answers are possible. (1) Denial: "I didn't do anything wrong." (2) Reinterpretation: "I made a mistake. I didn't know it was wrong." (3) Repression: Guilt is pushed into the back of the mind and seems to be forgotten, but it can come out as anxiety or depression. (4) Rationalization: "Everyone is doing it. It isn't so bad."

Into Life

Pass out slips of paper and ask each learner to write down a situation in which someone has committed a sin and has reaped a great deal of pain for himself or herself and others.

After a few minutes ask each one to write down a situation in which a person has confessed and repented of a sin, and has found forgiveness and freedom.

If no one's privacy is invaded or any confidences broken, some of the incidents may be shared. Be very careful!

Close with silent prayer over these situations.

Let's Talk It Over

The questions on this page are designed to encourage review of the lesson Scriptures and to promote discussion of the lesson by the class. The answers provided are only discussion starters. Let your class talk it over from there.

1. Name some ways that people deal with guilt. What is the most constructive way?

Guilt is the source of a lot of anguish and can lead to physical illness or mental illness or both. Denial is a common but very unhealthy way of repressing guilt. Some people try to rationalize their behavior, inventing good features of bad actions. Another response is to blame others or to blame circumstances. Some people spend many hours and large amounts of money for the help of trained counselors. None of these methods is as effective as humbly admitting one's fault, expressing sincere regret, and seeking forgiveness.

2. David considered his greatest offense was his sin against God. Why is our sin always an offense to God?

We owe our very existence to God. Certainly He has a right to draw the boundaries of acceptable behavior. For all that He has done He deserves our complete devotion and obedience. When we transgress His boundaries, others may be hurt by our actions; but God also is offended. We cannot sin without disregarding His claim on us and, like selfish children, pursuing what we want. By our sin we are saying, "Stand aside, God. I don't care what You say is right or best; I am going to do my thing."

3. Is it really necessary for us to be so self-deprecating to be forgiven by God? It seems so humiliating.

"God resisteth the proud, but giveth grace unto the humble" (James 4:6). Pride makes us want to minimize our offenses. Until we acknowledge our guilt, we do not seek forgiveness. The Corinthian Christians were saddened by Paul's criticism. He responded with rejoicing, because "godly sorrow worketh repentance to salvation" (2 Corinthians 7:8-10). There is no virtue in false humility or in being overly self-deprecating, but we must have an honest understanding of our sin and of how desperately we need God's forgiveness.

4. How much forgiveness is enough? What do we long for when we are aware of our sin?

Partial forgiveness would not be good news. When we are under conviction, like David we want God to blot out *all* our iniquities and make us white as snow. We do not want to come out dingy gray, still tainted with some guilt of our sin. When we are truly under conviction we long to be restored, as if the sin had never been committed. The knowledge that God is willing to forgive like that is very appealing.

5. Why is it important in facing future temptations that we have a clean heart and a right spirit?

Unforgiven sin lowers our resistance to temptation. It lowers our estimation of ourselves. Our reasoning is affected with thoughts such as "I'm already guilty; what difference will this make?" If we have repented of past sins and been forgiven, however, we are operating from a position of restored purity, a position we are not likely to surrender easily.

6. Why are joy and a clear conscience so closely associated? How does a clear conscience contribute to joy?

A guilty conscience is a constant accuser, a persistent nag. When it is accusing, we find it hard to summon joy. We cannot believe that we deserve to be fully happy about anything. Unhappiness is a self-imposed punishment that can result in full-blown depression. When we have confessed our faults, made restitution if possible, and sought forgiveness from those offended, beginning with God, we gain a great sense of peace. When our conscience is no longer accusing us, we can achieve an honest self-acceptance and give ourselves permission to enjoy life.

7. "Christians are not perfect, but forgiven." Why is that such a hopeful thought?

All thinking persons must admit that they are not perfect morally. If acceptance with God were based upon perfect performance, we would be without hope. Suppose the Bible had glossed over the faults of all the heroes and told only of their faith and obedience. How discouraging that would be! I could not relate. However, to know that God loves and forgives, to know that very devout people sometimes have severe moral lapses but can be restored and given a clean record—that is wonderful news.

Worship and Witness

DEVOTIONAL READING: Psalm 98:1-9.

LESSON SCRIPTURE: Psalm 96.

PRINTED TEXT: Psalm 96.

Psalm 96

1 O sing unto the LORD a new song: sing unto the LORD, all the earth.

2 Sing unto the LORD, bless his name; show forth his salvation from day to day.

3 Declare his glory among the heathen, his wonders among all people.

4 For the LORD is great, and greatly to be praised: he is to be feared above all gods.

5 For all the gods of the nations are idols: but the LORD made the heavens.

6 Honor and majesty are before him: strength and beauty are in his sanctuary.

7 Give unto the LORD, O ye kindreds of the people, give unto the LORD glory and strength.

8 Give unto the LORD the glory due unto his name: bring an offering, and come into his courts.

9 O worship the LORD in the beauty of holiness: fear before him, all the earth.

10 Say among the heathen that the LORD reigneth: the world also shall be established that it shall not be moved: he shall judge the people righteously.

11 Let the heavens rejoice, and let the earth be glad; let the sea roar, and the fulness thereof.

12 Let the field be joyful, and all that is therein: then shall all the trees of the wood rejoice

13 Before the LORD: for he cometh, for he cometh to judge the earth: he shall judge the world with righteousness, and the people with his truth.

GOLDEN TEXT: Sing unto the LORD, bless his name; show forth his salvation from day to day.—Psalm 96:2.

Lesson Aims

After this lesson students should:

1. Become more aware of the hand of God in the world about us.

2. Recognize that God stands in judgment over the world.

3. Find new reasons to rejoice in worship.

4. Be better able to share their joy with others.

Lesson Outline

Visual 13 of the visuals packet is a call to worship Jehovah, the God of creation and our salvation. The visual is shown on page 446.

Introduction

A. Giving the Best

In Yucatan, Mexico, stand the remains of an ancient temple and altar. On this altar a young maiden would be placed; then a priest with a stone knife would rip her heart from her body and hold it aloft, still throbbing with life, as a sacrifice to the Mayan god.

Archaeologists excavating the ancient city of Carthage in North Africa uncovered hundreds of small urns near a temple to one of the gods. When the excavators opened these urns, they found charred bones of tiny babies. It is quite evident that this was the final resting place for the remains of babies sacrificed in the temple.

We shudder as we realize how brutal many of the ancient religions were. Yet we are forced to give grudging respect to the devotion of these ancient peoples who were willing to sacrifice their most precious possession, a child, to their gods. Are we equally devoted to Jehovah God? We are not for a moment suggesting that we engage in human sacrifice, but we are insisting that we ought to worship with the same wholehearted devotion that these ancient pagans did.

The truth is that many of us enter worship rather casually. We go through certain ceremonies in a perfunctory way, or we fail to concentrate on what we are doing. Psalm 96 can be a healthy antidote to some of these weaknesses in our worship.

B. Lesson Background

Psalm 96 is a joyous song of praise and worship of Jehovah. It has none of the soul-wrenching agony of Psalm 51 or the systematic tribute to the law found in Psalm 119. It is a happy song, the type of song one would sing in a worship service. It is longer and more detailed than a contemporary "praise chorus," but is similar in some respects. It has no superscription to tell of its author or its date.

I. A Song
(Psalm 96:1-3)

A. A New Song (v. 1)

1. O sing unto the LORD a new song: sing unto the LORD, all the earth.

When we put our trust in Jehovah and devote our lives to doing God's will, we feel a new joy, a new confidence, a new strength. These break out in such singing as we have not done before. The psalmist calls *all the earth* to sing thus.

B. A Song of Salvation (v. 2)

2. Sing unto the LORD, bless his name; show forth his salvation from day to day.

Singing praises to Jehovah and blessing His name are vital to our worship, but they have a definite purpose beyond worship. This purpose is to *show forth his salvation.* In the Old Testament, salvation often means protection or rescue from national or personal enemies, but sometimes it means deliverance from sin. See Psalm 51:14 in last week's lesson, for example. The New Testament concentrates on this latter meaning, for it tells us of God's Son who came to save us from our sins.

One can *show forth* God's salvation not only by telling about it, but by living a joyous, victorious life that exemplifies God's moral standards.

This demonstration is to be *from day to day*. It is not limited to special days or special situations. This verse should be heeded by Christians who attend church on Sunday and then live the rest of the week pretty much as the pagans about them do.

SING TO THE LORD

One peculiar human quality is the gift of song. While birds "sing" their songs, most of them are stereotyped melodies that are seemingly encoded into their makeup.

Human beings have many songs to express the various pleasures, pains, yearnings, and forebodings of life. So we have songs of love, patriotism, battle, and nostalgia, plus rollicking songs of fun and exuberance. Of all our songs, however, the most wonderful and evocative are our songs of devotion, our lyrics of aspiration toward God, and our exalted praise to our Creator and the Guarantor of our well-being.

One of the characteristics of the psalms is their expression of praise for God's creative work. Even more deep are the phrasings of awareness of God's desire and ability to save humanity from sin and sorrow and death. This becomes even more prominent in our songs of relationship with Jesus, the Messiah, our Savior and Lord.

Compare the minor tonality and monotonous chants of Buddhist and Hindu devotion. There is seemingly no bright delight in a loving and saving God. How marvelous is the cry, "O sing unto the Lord. . . . Sing unto the Lord, bless his name; show forth his salvation from day to day"!
—J. G. V. B.

C. A Missionary Song (v. 3)

3. Declare his glory among the heathen, his wonders among all people.

It is not enough just to sing among ourselves about God's dominion over all the peoples of the world. His glory must be declared *among the heathen*. When God called Abraham, He promised to bless him and then through him to bless all the nations of the world (Genesis 12:3). Scattered here and there through the Old Testament are clear indications that God never changed His concern for the whole world. Unfortunately, these points of light were largely

obscured by the Israelites' concern for themselves. Christians have received a much firmer and clearer mandate to go into all the world, yet among most Christians this mandate does not take high priority. Dare we criticize the ancient Israelites for their narrow parochialism, when ours is even worse?

II. Reasons for the Song (Psalm 96:4-6)

A. God's Greatness (v. 4)

4. For the LORD is great, and greatly to be praised: he is to be feared above all gods.

Greatness, whether it be in a person, a place, or a thing, normally elicits praise. How much more, then, should we praise Jehovah God, whose greatness is unique, one of a kind, far surpassing the greatness of everything else! We know God is greater than anything else, because He made everything else.

He is to be feared above all gods. The writer is not saying that other gods really exist, but he recognizes that many people think they exist. This was true among Israel's neighbors, who worshiped such imaginary gods as Baal, Chemosh, Dagon, Asherah, and others. In the long history of Israel many of her people were enticed by such false gods and began to worship them. The writer, rather than trying to prove that these gods really didn't exist, chose instead to urge the people to serve Jehovah because He is greater than all the so-called gods.

B. God the Creator (vv. 5, 6)

5. For all the gods of the nations are idols: but the LORD made the heavens.

Idols. This Hebrew word primarily means *empty* or *nothing*. It is a fitting name for the gods invented by men. Many of the people worshiped images of wood, stone, or metal; but their worship was in vain because there was nothing behind those images. The apostle Paul echoed this sentiment when he wrote, "We know that an idol is nothing in the world" (1 Corinthians 8:4). The pagan idols were nothing and therefore could do nothing, but Jehovah God could and did create the heavens. The writers of the psalms pointed frequently to the starry heavens as evidence of God's greatness and majesty. This

---

How to Say It

CHEMOSH. *Kee*-mosh.
DAGON. *Day*-gon.
ASHERAH. Uh-*she*-ruh.

was an impressive argument for people who spent much time out in the open where they could view the stars in all their splendor. Living in or near large cities whose bright lights obscure the stars, we miss this blessing.

6. Honor and majesty are before him: strength and beauty are in his sanctuary.

Jehovah God is himself more glorious than anything else, but His surroundings are glorious too. This certainly is true in Heaven (Revelation 4). The word *sanctuary*, however, usually means the Holy of Holies in the tabernacle or temple. There Jehovah communed with His people from His place between the golden cherubim on the ark of the covenant (Exodus 25:22). The cherubim and the ark therefore were as majestic and beautiful as human hands could make them.

STRENGTH AND BEAUTY

It is not too often that we find strength and beauty combined. Often beautiful things are fragile and evanescent, like spiderwebs or rainbows. Beauty frequently is related to the delicate, the intricate, and the dainty. Strength is associated with bigness, such things as bulging biceps and huge earth-moving machines.

One of the most striking combinations of strength, utility, and loveliness is found in the great suspension bridges of our land—such as the George Washington Bridge, the Golden Gate Bridge, and the Mackinac Bridge.

Someone has called these beautiful suspension bridges "symphonies in steel." Viewed from a distance they are wonderful by day and fairy-like when illuminated by thousands of sparkling lights by night. Yet they are fortresses of great strength, too.

Just as these mighty bridges combine the beauty of symmetry and proportion with the strength of steel and concrete, so God's power in our lives is a combination of strength and beauty. His love is strong and true, His Word a fortress of power and promise. Yet the quality of life He seeks to inspire in us involves kindness and gentleness, humility and helpfulness, compassion and tenderness. Truly, strength and beauty are in His sanctuary.   —J. G. V. B.

III. The Worship of Jehovah (Psalm 96:7-9)

A. Give Glory to Him (v. 7)

7. Give unto the LORD, O ye kindreds of the people, give unto the LORD glory and strength.

Kindreds of the people. The *New International Version* translates this "families of nations." This more accurately represents the idea here, for this call to worship was not directed

exclusively to the Israelites but to all the nations of the world. This reinforces the idea introduced earlier in this psalm that Jehovah God is not a tribal deity who confines His activities to one small group of people. To give God *glory and strength* is to honor Him because of His divine glory and unsurpassed strength.

B. Bring Gifts to Him (v. 8)

8. Give unto the LORD the glory due unto his name: bring an offering, and come into his courts.

Every human being has an obligation to glorify the Lord's name. That we have often failed to do this only increases our debt to Him. The praise and glory offered God here foreshadow the praise and glory that are His in Heaven. For example, the four beasts "rest not day and night, saying, Holy, holy, holy, Lord God Almighty." The twenty-four elders fall down before God, saying, "Thou art worthy, O Lord, to receive glory and honor and power" (Revelation 4:8, 10, 11).

Worshipers were instructed to *bring an offering* to the place of worship. Similar instructions are given in 1 Chronicles 16:29. This is good advice for God's people today.

C. Worship in Holiness (v. 9)

9. O worship the LORD in the beauty of holiness: fear before him, all the earth.

God demands that all who come before Him to worship must come *in the beauty of holiness.* The *New International Version* has "splendor of his holiness," while the *Revised Standard Version* renders it "in holy array." In spite of these differences, holiness is at the very heart of the worship of Jehovah. If the holiness mentioned here is Jehovah's rather than ours, we remember that He said, "Ye shall be holy; for I am holy" (Leviticus 11:44).

The worship of Jehovah stands in stark contrast to the worship of pagan gods, in which holiness played no part. Pagan gods were often depicted as powerful and awe-inspiring, but not as holy. Indeed, their supposed behavior was often anything but holy, and so was the behavior of their worshipers.

Worship acceptable to God has several requirements. First, its intent and activities must be in keeping with His will. Human sacrifice or sexual orgies, often practiced by devotees of pagan gods, would be totally unacceptable to Jehovah. Worship of Jehovah must be pure. The Jewish priests donned clean linen when they brought offerings before God. The clean garments represented the moral cleanliness that God requires of His worshipers. This same emphasis is made in Psalm 24:3, 4: "Who shall ascend into the hill of the Lord? Or who shall stand in his holy place? He that hath clean hands, and a pure heart; who hath not lifted up his soul unto vanity, nor sworn deceitfully."

Worship must be sincere if it is to be acceptable. It is only a meaningless routine unless the heart is in it. Many of us at times have been guilty of entering into worship while our thoughts were a thousand miles away.

Finally, our worship must be joyous. If there is one thing we should gather from our study of the psalms, it is that we should come before God with thankful, joyous hearts.

IV. The Universal Worship (Psalm 96:10-13)

A. Among the Heathen (v. 10)

10. Say among the heathen that the LORD reigneth: the world also shall be established that it shall not be moved: he shall judge the people righteously.

The psalmist has been encouraging his people to enter into a joyous worship of Jehovah. Now he turns his attention to the *heathen,* or *nations,* as it is in many modern translations. They too have an obligation to worship God because He is their king also, even if they have not recognized Him. In their ignorance the nations have not given Jehovah, the universal King, the recognition due Him. As a result, their lives have been lived in darkness. They "changed the truth of God into a lie, and worshipped and served the creature more than the Creator" (Romans 1:25).

The psalmist now lays upon his own people the task of enlightening those living in darkness. The heathen need to hear this message because the time is coming when God will *judge the people righteously.* Most of the Israelites never really got this message. As time went on they became more and more exclusive. Yet throughout the Old Testament are clear messages like this one that God's love and concern include all nations.

B. In Nature (vv. 11, 12)

11, 12. Let the heavens rejoice, and let the earth be glad; let the sea roar, and the fulness thereof. Let the field be joyful, and all that is therein: then shall all the trees of the wood rejoice.

The psalmist personifies the forces of nature and has them join in the praise of God. Hebrew poets frequently used this device. They had the heavens declaring God's glory, floods and trees clapping their hands, and mountains skipping like rams. There is a sense in which nature is involved in God's plan for the universe. Nature

has suffered because of man's sinfulness. Paul tells us that "the whole creation groaneth and travaileth in pain together until now" as a result of this sin (Romans 8:22).

C. Because of Judgment (v. 13)

13. Before the LORD: for he cometh, for he cometh to judge the earth: he shall judge the world with righteousness, and the people with his truth.

This psalm deals with Jehovah as King. In ancient Israel the king often served as a judge over his subjects. Solomon, for example, established a great reputation as a judge (1 Kings 3:16-28). The general tenor of this psalm is joyous and optimistic, but if God judges the *world with righteousness,* then the outcome will not be happy for everyone. In fact, none of us wants justice when we stand before the great Judge; we want grace and mercy instead.

Some commentators see this as a messianic psalm. They see the coming judge as Christ returning to claim the church as His own and to mete out justice to the wicked. Such an interpretation certainly would not be foreign to the book of Psalms.

JUDGING RIGHTEOUSLY WITH TRUTH

Man Child in the Promised Land is an autobiographical book written several decades ago. It tells of a boy who grew up in a very depressed area of an American city. He came from a home with dedicated parents; but he fell in with bad associates, became a criminal, and eventually went to prison. Later he became an able and successful attorney. He said his parents counseled him to "be good," but among his friends being good meant being good at stealing without getting caught!

Home Daily Bible Readings

Monday, Aug. 19—In Spirit, the Only Way (John 4:19-26)

Tuesday, Aug. 20—A Warm Invitation (Psalm 95:1-7)

Wednesday, Aug. 21—Preparation Required (Psalm 96:1-9)

Thursday, Aug. 22—Heaven's Command (Revelation 14:1-7)

Friday, Aug. 23—All People to Be Told (Isaiah 43:8-13)

Saturday, Aug. 24—Appointed to Witness (Acts 22:6-16)

Sunday, Aug. 25—Make Disciples of All Nations (Matthew 28:16-20)

There can be judgment that is entirely wrong because those judging are wicked, and there is no real understanding about what is true. Socially approved truth in reality may be false, and normal standards may be abnormally twisted or perverted. Jesus was judged to be worthy of death, but there was no righteousness or truth in the decision that convicted Him.

The psalmist tells us that God is evaluating men's conduct and that He will judge the people righteously. His righteousness is absolutely valid and unwavering. God's ethical standards are found in the Old Testament law where He is revealed as holy, with integrity that is absolute. Further, He shall judge the world with *His* truth. This will not be the truth as men may bend and distort it, but as the Holy God reveals and enforces it.

The question is unavoidable—where do we stand? We and our fellows make judgments now, but the day arrives when *He* comes. Then "he shall judge the world with righteousness, and the people with his truth."   —J. G. V. B.

Conclusion

A. Right After the Benediction

Many years ago a man was visiting in a small town in eastern Pennsylvania. When Sunday came, he wanted to attend church. The only church in town was that of the Quakers, so he went there.

In the old-fashioned Quaker meeting everyone sat quietly until someone was "moved by the Spirit" to speak. The visitor entered the building and sat quietly with the others. After fifteen or twenty minutes no one had spoken. The visitor turned to a man sitting beside him and asked, "When does the service begin?"

"Right after the benediction, friend," came the reply. "Right after the benediction."

Exactly! Service in the name of God ought to follow worship. If worship does not result in Christian service, then something is lacking in the worship. Psalm 96 envisions a joyous time of worship when the name of God is exalted, but the psalmist is also concerned about what

Sing unto the Lord, bless his name: show forth his salvation from day to day.

visual 13

happens when the worship ends. Worshipers are told to "declare his glory among the heathen" (v. 3), "bring an offering" (v. 8), and "say among the heathen that the Lord reigneth" (v. 10).

The mandate for Christian service is not limited to the professional clergy. Each one of us has an obligation to use his or her talents, time, and resources to glorify the Lord. Most of us will not be called to serve as missionaries on some distant shore, nor to proclaim the message from the pulpit. However, one may teach a Sunday school class, serve as a nursery attendant, or direct traffic in the church parking lot. We may visit the sick, counsel the discouraged, or share our faith with non-Christians. Most of us can witness in the school, work place, or even at home.

B. Singing a New Song

Occasionally we hear people complain about the new music being used in our worship services. They are upset that the old familiar hymns and gospel songs are being replaced by "praise choruses" with new tunes and new lyrics. Are these the "new songs" mentioned by the psalmist?

Not necessarily. The new song of Psalm 96 is much like an older song we read in 1 Chronicles 16:23-33. It was new, however, to people who had not been singing it. It was new to people who had not been worshiping in the beauty of holiness. It was new to people who never had thought of telling the heathen about the Lord. To all such people it came with new enthusiasm, new optimism, new joy. Some modern songs may likewise tell the old, old story with new vigor and challenge.

Our concern for singing a new song ought to go beyond new tunes and new lyrics. It ought to lead us to worship with renewed enthusiasm. It should cause us to come before the Lord "in the beauty of holiness" by purging our hearts of those things that stand between us and Him. It ought to cause us to cast aside the idols of power, pride, and possessions. Then we will indeed be singing a new song.

C. Let Us Pray

Dear Lord, teach us to sing a new song, not just with our lips but with our hearts as well. Help us to know the joy that comes to those who worship You in the "beauty of holiness." Show us how and where we may serve when we leave the place of worship. In Jesus' name, amen.

D. Thought to Remember

"It is only when men begin to worship that they begin to grow."

—Calvin Coolidge

Learning by Doing

This page contains an alternate lesson plan emphasizing learning activities. Classes desiring such student involvement will find these suggestions helpful.

Learning Goals

As a result of this lesson your students should be able to:

1. List five biblical themes relating to worship: (a) praise and celebration; (b) reciting and remembering the mighty acts of God; (c) confession and repentance; (d) commitment; (e) preparation for judgment.

2. Experience worship with a fuller understanding of what God expects.

3. Appreciate the several dimensions of worship.

Into the Lesson

We can name at least five biblical themes (see learning goals) relating to worship. Pass out hymnals to your class members. Write the five worship themes across the top of the chalkboard or an overhead transparency. Ask your class members to find hymns expressing each of these themes. For example, the hymn entitled "Holy, Holy, Holy" signifies praise and celebration. Have several of your class members share the hymn titles they have selected.

Into the Word

Lead your class in a discussion of these five biblical themes, using the following helps.

1. Praise and celebration

a. Lead your class in a discussion of Psalm 96:1-3, using the comments on the text that you find in this book.

b. In view of recent changes in congregational worship, ask your class how God is praised in the old and new worship styles.

c. How is the praise element of worship connected with missions in verses 2 and 3?

2. Reciting and remembering the mighty acts of God

For this section refer to the devotional reading of this lesson—Psalm 98—especially verses 1-3.

a. What marvelous things has God done? (Let students give examples. A great number of wonderful things may be named. Be sure to include God's acts of creation, rescuing His people from Egypt, sending His only begotten Son to be our Redeemer, raising Christ from the dead, and promising a new heaven and earth.)

b. What part of the worship service is designed for remembering one of God's great acts? (The Communion service).

3. Confession and repentance

Some congregations use these as the main part of their worship service, intending to lead the flock of God to His throne with broken and contrite hearts. Confession of sins, cleansing, renewal, and strength for service are stressed. The worship of a congregation is incomplete, however, if it does not include the other elements we are considering.

Ask your class to consult Isaiah 6:1-7. Verses 5-7 of that section emphasize confession and cleansing. Ask your class:

a. During worship do you feel led to the throne of God with a broken and contrite heart?

b. How can this aspect of worship be strengthened in our congregational services?

4. Commitment

In verse 8 of the text an offering is urged. This is one way commitment may be expressed. Worshiping God with material blessings was a strong part of the Old Testament system, and it is stressed in the New Testament also.

Verse 9 focuses on holiness. In 1 Peter 1:16 we are encouraged to be holy as God is holy. This is a second way we can express commitment: by living a holy life. Direct your class to do the following:

a. Name several practices that one should give up or exclude from a holy life.

b. Name several practices that are needed in a holy life.

5. Preparation for judgment

Have your class note verse 13. Regular worship should keep us face to face with God and stimulate our daily consciousness of Him. Being constantly aware of Him will help us live holy lives and keep us in a good relationship, thus preparing us for judgment. Ask your class:

a. How are worship and preparation for judgment connected? Refer to the previous paragraph for the answer.

b. Are you regularly reminded of God's coming judgment in your worship experiences?

Into Life

Worship is coming to God with our sins and our victories. He cleanses us through the blood of Christ, and we can then celebrate His great victory over sin in our lives. It is like a berry vine bringing forth fruit and at the same time finding water and nourishment to renew itself.

Let's Talk It Over

The questions on this page are designed to encourage review of the lesson Scriptures and to promote discussion of the lesson by the class. The answers provided are only discussion starters. Let your class talk it over from there.

1. We are told to declare God's glory among the heathen (v. 3). How well do we do that to unbelievers who visit us in our meeting? What could we do to convey a clearer message to a newcomer just investigating the Christian faith?

Our worship together is meant to exalt the Lord, to praise Him for who He is and what He has done. We want the visitor to understand that as well as we do. Communion may require explanation so one not acquainted with Christianity can understand its significance. So does baptism if it is done in the meeting for worship. It is helpful to the outsider if the Scripture is read in modern English, and if the songs do not contain obscure references. The line, "Here I raise my Ebenezer," for example, means nothing to one not acquainted with its biblical background. Prayers can be worded in conversational language and tone, and can be focused on matters readily understood. Preaching is most helpful when it is personal and practical in its application, without assuming a high degree of Bible knowledge on the part of the hearers.

2. We see no idols of wood and stone today. What are the competing gods in our culture? How is our Lord superior to them?

People today are caught up in worshiping material things, entertainment icons, sports heroes, pleasure, fame, personal achievement, and nature, among other things. It is only our God who created us and is in control of the universe. It is only our God who has revealed a perfect moral law for governing our lives. It is only our God who loves us so much that He gave His only Son that we might be saved from condemnation and receive eternal life. It is only our God who has promised that one day His justice will prevail, that the wicked will be punished and that the believing will experience eternal joy in Heaven.

3. What is the message communicated by those who come to worship without bringing an offering?

A message is conveyed by those who give an offering at worship, and a different message is conveyed by those who do not. When we know a Christian consistently fails to give an offering, we may infer one of several messages, all of

them negative: (1) "What I have worked for is mine, and I am not going to give it away." This is the message of pride. (2) "God has not given me enough so I can give. When He gets more generous with me, I will give." The message is ingratitude. (3) "I do not have enough in savings for tomorrow. When I have saved more, then I will give." The message is lack of trust in God. (4) "There are plenty of people better off than I am. Let them be the ones who give." The message is envy.

4. What does worship "in the beauty of holiness" mean practically? What is included and what is excluded?

The vain, vulgar, or immoral excesses of pagan worship have no place in Christian gatherings. Anything insincere is out of order—anything done for show without any real commitment of the heart. Jesus taught that God desires the worship of those who worship in spirit and truth (John 4:23). The apostle Paul objected to the disorderly way the Corinthian Christians were worshiping, and to the fact that they had turned the observance of Communion into a drunken party. He appealed to them to "let all things be done decently and in order" (1 Corinthians 14:40).

5. Why is impending judgment a reason to worship and rejoice today?

God knows us very well. He knows about our tendency to procrastinate, and perhaps that is one reason why He has not revealed when Judgment Day will fall. If we knew it would not be for another year, or twenty years, or one hundred years, we would be tempted to postpone obedience and postpone worship. Not knowing means that we must behave as though this could be the day. We have reason to rejoice because there will be a day when God sets all things right according to His righteousness. We also give attention to worship and rejoicing because when the Lord comes for judgment we want to be current on our accounts with Him. We want to be among the people of faith who are welcomed into eternity. Whether we think of the judgment or not, however, we worship with joy because we are grateful for what God is doing for us day by day.